THE SAGE and the SEEKERS

THE SAGE and the SEEKERS

The Search for Truth
on God, Religion, and Life's Meaning

by

Michael William Posner

TALL
PRAIRIE
PRESS

Tulsa, Oklahoma

ISBN 978-0-9820264-0-3

Library of Congress Control Number: 2009902363

Library of Congress subject headings:

   Religion
   Philosophy and Religion
   Faith and Reason
   Psychology, Religious
   Spiritual life
   Self-actualization
   Secular humanism

The paper used in this publication is acid free and meets all standards for archival quality paper as specified by the American National Standard for Information Sciences—Permanence of Paper for Printed Library Materials, ANSI Z39.48-1992

Published in the United States of America, by Tall Prairie Press, Tulsa, Oklahoma: www.TallPrairiePress.com

V1.2

ACKNOWLEDGEMENTS

The song that I came to sing remains unsung to this day;
I have spent my days in stringing and in unstringing my instrument.

Those haunting words are Rabindranath Tagore's, in *Gitanjali*. With the completion of this book, while my entire song is, I trust, not yet sung, I have—after much stringing and unstringing—at least strummed the first bar of its melody, and escaped the fate of eternal silence. And I wish to thank the many who—though not necessarily agreeing with its contents—have provided help, of one kind or another, in the book's formulation, refinement, and production.

The Crossroads Writers Group in Tulsa—its leader Steve Amos, as well as Cisco Cividanes, Carol Johnson, Carolyn Steele, Gale Whittington, and others—provided a year's worth of Monday evening critiques, challenges, and friendly feedback. Roxanne Eesley, a friend and fellow writer, has been especially gracious in reviewing the manuscript at several stages, and Adina Cucicov was exceedingly patient in preparing the cover for printing. Thanks, too, to Jamie Saloff for her advice on book production. My uncle and aunt, Arnold and Sue Korman, reviewed portions of the manuscript, offered good ideas, and were consistently supportive over the years of its development. Daniel Holeman, a good friend, reviewed portions of the manuscript, too, provided substantive suggestions, moral support, and reminders on the virtues of bringing the project to a close.

Those whose teachings informed or nurtured me toward intellectual independence on matters of the spirit are many. Listing renowned philosophers would be redundant, and mentioning every writer and scholar whose works I have read and in some ways learned from would be impracticable and of little relevance. (Indeed, our greatest influences come from those whose work in earlier generations was so successful, that their lessons and innovations have faded into common knowledge—and so are nearly impossible to identify.) But perhaps it would be worthwhile to name a few lesser-known philosophical thinkers, or those who are better-known for other contributions, the likes of Thomas Paine, Robert Ingersoll, Sigmund Freud, Eric Hoffer, and, most of all, Walter A. Kaufmann, whose *Faith of a Heretic* and *Critique of Religion and Philosophy* were, for me—in the early stages of my existential wanderings—water from a rock and manna in the wilderness, and a guiding pillar of fire and cloud.

All errors of form or content in this work, and all its opinions deemed by some to be offensive, are my responsibility alone—and, again, many who have helped do not share my views. Yet to the above-mentioned, and to some whose names are not mentioned, I say: Thank you for making a difference in a project I hold so dear. Thank you for helping me to begin my music.

For in much wisdom is much vexation: and he that increaseth knowledge increaseth sorrow. ECCLESIASTES

Question with boldness even the existence of a God; because, if there be one, he must more approve of the homage of reason, than that of blindfolded fear. THOMAS JEFFERSON

In general, there is a degree of doubt and caution and modesty which in all kinds of scrutiny and decision ought for ever to accompany a just reasoner. DAVID HUME

Nothing hath an uglier look than reason when it is not on our side. MARQUESS OF HALIFAX

We run fastest and farthest when we run from ourselves. ERIC HOFFER

The voice of the intellect is a soft one, but it does not rest till it has gained a hearing. FREUD

The critic who attacks idolatry does the most serious thing of which a man is capable. WALTER A. KAUFMANN

A soft answer turneth away wrath: but grievous words stir up anger. PROVERBS

The pursuit of truth will set you free; even if you never catch up with it. CLARENCE DARROW

I would not give a fig for the simplicity this side of complexity, but I would give my life for the simplicity on the other side of complexity. OLIVER WENDELL HOLMES

Love truth, and pardon error. VOLTAIRE

CONTENTS

CONTENTS

III. THE PERSISTENCE OF RELIGION

CONTENTS

IV. EXAMINING CLAIMS FOR GOD AND RELIGION

CONTENTS

CONTENTS

xi

CONTENTS

CONTENTS

V. SHALL WE RELY ON FAITH?

CONTENTS

CONTENTS

VI. ON THE BIBLE

CONTENTS

CONTENTS

CONTENTS

VII. DANGERS AND DISADVANTAGES OF RELIGION

VIII. AGAINST THE SAGE

CONTENTS

IX. RIGHT AND WRONG WITHOUT SUPERNATURAL RELIGION

X. MEANING AND PURPOSE

CONTENTS

XI. TO PREVENT MISUNDERSTANDING:
WHAT THE SAGE IS *NOT* SAYING

XII. CONCLUSIONS

XIII. PROPHECIES AND FAREWELL

Preface

This is the book I did not have when I was young—and agonizing over questions I was afraid and ashamed to ask others, questions it took awhile even to ask myself: What can I responsibly believe about God, religion, and life's meaning? Are my people's traditions, my sacred beliefs, accurate? Can I be sure? Why do so many, of all allegiances, remain closed-minded on these issues, or avoid studying them with care? Where can I find a deeply honest, intelligent yet comprehensible, and respectful, even warmhearted, discussion on the search for truth? And can different people legitimately hold different truths, or must there be only one standard?

If you have entertained such questions, too—whether aloud, or in the inner chambers of your heart—this book is for you. If you have not, I wonder if you might consider doing so. Night falls early. Our existence is tenuous, vulnerable to illness, accident, and violence; and notwithstanding the admonitions of priests, poets, and philosophers through the ages, we repeatedly forget that even the longest life slips away so soon. "Ask thy father and he will tell thee, thy elders, and they will say unto thee,"[1] that before we learn to value our early energies, youth races on by; before we integrate the lessons of adulthood, our bodies degenerate into brittle age; and before we glean the slow harvest of wisdom, death renders all wisdom moot.

In the face of inevitable and impending obliteration, why not, then—for these few moments we live—choose authenticity and honor, and wrestle with the profound? Why not examine with vigor our deepest beliefs, those about God, religion, and life's meaning? Rather than avoiding the most essential matters while busying ourselves with the trivial—or devoting ourselves to conclusions on ultimate issues, based on insufficient premises—how noble it would be to confront, bold and unblinking, the ambiguous spectacle of existence, without trembling at uncertainty or running from mortality; to ask untrammeled questions and pursue investigations to whatever tragedies or magnificence they unveil. How dignified, to explore these ultimate issues with courage, honesty, and intellectual independence; to employ reason, not as a bridled packhorse on well-worn trails, loaded down with the dead weight of dogma, and being led, con-

---

[1] This phrase, its modified echo, "parallelism," typical of one common form of biblical poetic expression, is found in Deuteronomy 32:7—though in the service of a different point than the one being made here, and of a far different point than the one made by this book, overall.

strained by bit and blinder, to a predetermined destination. Rather, as a wild stallion on the open range, free to roam where he will, to run with power on unmarked turf, with no burdens on his back, and no preconceived notion of a trail's end.

And reverential and idealistic as we may wish to be, it will not do to pretend that religion speaks only about the spiritual realm, that her teachings are only poetic, metaphoric, and inspirational, and do not overlap, and so cannot contradict, factual reality. The faiths with which we are most familiar, in their large and significant denominations, make claims not only about transcendent realms but about that which intersects with our real physical lives—they state that God is this; that God said that; that this historical figure performed that miracle in our real world; that this sacred scroll we hold in our real hands contains the inspired word of God; and, most important, that God wishes of us such and such—in today's real, tangible world—and that this path of conduct or belief leads to happiness or salvation in, what they say, is the very real afterlife. These claims are either reliably true or not; either responsible to believe, or not. And each of us—if we value our integrity—must, on such matters, pursue clarity.

Toward that end, if I may speak the familiar language of nature's simple metaphors, permit me to show you a number of select trees with their dark roots in the angst of restless nights and in the achings of solitary seasons, but with their vivid blooms and succulent fruit in the warm light of happier years. And allow me to share with you understandings that at first seemed to me pits of disorientation and despair, but ultimately showed themselves to be wellsprings of freedom and healing. And though each of us must go forth to explore upon his own legs and only establish his house on that truth acknowledged by his own spirit and his own best thinking, perhaps you might take shelter for a while under these trees and beside these wells, and sate your hunger and take the edge off your thirst, and I might point out a few paths to investigate, and a few snares to avoid, and why. Perhaps after I whisper in your ear about what I have seen, you might resume your own journey, and find it more illuminated and less alone.

I was not always eager, however, to publicize such things. "Not all thoughts should be spoken; not all that is spoken should be written; and not all that is written should be published." This maxim I heard long ago while attending theological seminary in Jerusalem, and perhaps its admonition, reverberating within me for years, helped delay the writing of this book. I have been loath to trespass on the fragile, though tenacious, flower of religion, to which so many cling so desperately for some sense of comfort and meaning. I ultimately concluded, however, that greater wisdom, even greater compassion, is served by speaking softly on these issues rather than by remaining silent. Still, I do not minimize the suffering often incurred by calling into question foundational beliefs. Having been raised in a faith-filled home, having lived into adulthood within a religiously insular community, and having spent years studying and training for the clergy, I endured intense distress of just this kind while challenging, and ultimately leaving behind, my own inherited beliefs.

Yet the sometimes-terrible pain of greater awareness is the disorienting birth-shock of emerging into larger life; and the sometimes-debilitating despair is but a temporary hobbling, healthy growing pains in the legs of a spirit soon to stride easy and strong. Beyond the anguish of lost religion, and the mourning that must follow, lies the peace of mind, the existential poise of deep understanding and authentic engagement with life. And as I would not recommend that a child remain in the womb, though birth may have its traumas; and as I would not attempt to shield a youth from maturing, though remaining childlike might avert some of adulthood's wounds; and as I would not forever withhold from a man the news of his father's death, though such ignorance might forestall the bitter tears of grief; so, too, I do not stay my hand from writing that which may afford growth, even if those who choose the path of growth will unavoidably be required to endure some pain.

And a choice it is; for any book's audience is self-selecting. If one reads this book and feels its sting—if one should conclude that I am right, and suffer deeply because of it—such resolute attention is the clearest sign of a spirit strong enough to absorb whatever sorrows the reading may bring. The vigilant unconscious mind protects us well from becoming aware of those losses it suspects we cannot bear. And so it is that no matter how accurate or distressing the material of this volume, those who cannot endure the reconsidering of their deepest beliefs will generally not be wounded. They will tend not even to begin reading this book; and those who do begin will likely put it aside quickly—their conscious experience being boredom, distraction, confusion, indignation, the call of remembered responsibilities, or any of the ten thousand other tools at the disposal of the unconscious mind, as it shields us from seeing what it fears will be too painful for our tender eyes.

But beyond the matter of whether one can bear to think freely on these issues, a reader needs motivation to invest time and energy in the printed page. Some thoughts, then, on motivations: Although as humans we have much in common, different temperaments are often driven by different priorities in general, and therefore, too, when considering issues of religion and truth. Here, then, are a few thoughts that might pique the interest of each major temperament.

To the meaning-centered idealists I offer this book as a gentle invitation to the garden of authenticity, along whose paths can be found the blossoms of profundity and meaning; some will recognize the grounds at once, and need no further urgings. Others, deeply committed to religion, may wish to flee these heresies or assail them zealously with the intensity and devotion of which only true believers are capable. I remind them with all empathy and compassion that even the most profound connection to religion or her God has real value only if her claims are accurate, and her God real; that authenticity and meaning do not diminish, but grow, if mistaken beliefs are identified and abandoned; and that heroism of the soul consists not in clinging at all cost to what some have said is sacred and true, but in risking all forms of comfort in the cause of determining what, indeed, may be *justly* considered sacred and true.

To the rational and competitive knowledge-seekers I offer this book as a respectful but vigorous challenge, that they may test the validity of some of their most important ideas. I remind them that although one may gain confidence and pride if one is knowledgeable with religion's knowledge, competent and honorable expertise consists not merely in holding information, but in holding accurate information—and that one who knows the limits of his knowledge is far superior to one who pretends to know what he does not, in fact, know. And I say what they must surely recognize, that debating with cleverness and will does not equate to honesty or seeking truth. And I ask them to remember that pragmatism is far from the only standard; that insisting upon a foundation of accuracy and reason on existential issues is the honorable and noble course, even though enticing arguments can be made in favor of useful lies. I remind them, too, that true autonomy consists in deciding for oneself what is to be most deeply valued, and why—and certainly what, if anything, is to be worshiped, and why.

To the stabilizers and traditionalists of the world, I offer this book as a practical set of tools that will help them examine whether the tradition they uphold is truly responsible, and whether the legacy they leave their children is, in fact, reliable and secure. I ask them to consider that belonging is too expensive if it comes at the price of truth. And I remind them that although change can be painful and disorienting, and although tradition can sometimes seem intrinsically correct, one does greater service to oneself, one's family, one's community, and posterity, by correcting even long-standing, familiar errors, and establishing upon more reliable foundations, new, more stable traditions. And I remind them, too, that nearly all the social and political values they hold dear—and do not wish to see changed—can be argued for as well, or better, without appealing to dubious supernatural premises.

And to the pragmatic excitement-seekers of the world I offer this book as a set of adventures. I ask them: What greater boldness is there than to reexamine deepest beliefs? What greater way to make an impact upon oneself and others than by exercising radical honesty on such intimidating topics? What greater freedom than to be liberated from false and confining rules that would unnecessarily control behavior and belief? And what greater virtuosity than demonstrating one's skill on these, the most formidable of issues? And I say to them, too, "Would it not be a boon if what you knew in your bones all along was true—that the time to live is now, neither overly weighed down by the authority of dead ages past, nor overly impressed by rumors of what awaits us beyond the grave?"

A word of moderation and balance: Although in this work I argue primarily against religion, I mean to imply neither that religion is without benefit nor that atheism, or even agnosticism, is beyond all error or threat of danger. Much less do I see all forms of godlessness as a panacea for every ill, whether individual or communal, or every manifestation of religion as equally harmful. Religion, along with her essential errors and unpardonable sins, has ever brought to humanity myriad forms of civility and wisdom, of comfort and succor. In addition to her obvious gifts of hope, felt meaning, ethics, and community, and her less noticed, and admittedly less consistent, contributions to the development and preservation of art and learning,[1] I cite a small, personal, and ironic example: Much of the material for this book was nurtured—toward the end of its decade-long formative process—for a year of Monday evenings by a writers' group meeting in an Oklahoma Methodist church. And some governments, Stalin's Soviet Union being one infamous example,[2] have, under the flags of atheistic philosophies not only made a mockery of honesty and a crime of free thought, but also engaged in extensive campaigns of cruelty, oppression, and mass murder.[3] Disparate hands, then—some hoisting crimson-stained banners in religious crusade, others extending frenzied arm in salute to secular hate—have spilled the lifeblood of their brother, after making him a wanderer and a refugee, selling him into naked bondage, and stealing from him his truest birthright: compassionate reason.

---

[1] Religion has, of course, been responsible for stifling and destroying a good deal of art and learning, too.

[2] Though, as others have argued, working with a populace predisposed to submitting to tyranny, conditioned as it was by centuries of serfdom under the mortal terrors of the throne and the immortal terrors of the church.

[3] "Precisely," say some atheists, "bad people will do bad things under any banner—but only religion can get good people to do bad things." But those who remember the legions of idealists who sincerely believed in the mission of communism, those who recall how good people who thought they were ushering in the brotherhood of man stooped to depravity and inhumanity in pursuit of this high-minded vision, shake their heads and say, "No, it is not religion alone that perverts the good: The good can be perverted by many forms of unjustified certainty and their readiness to impose upon others the painful consequences of their arbitrary convictions—whether such convictions presume to speak for God or for the best interests of man."

PREFACE

This work is no trumpet call to join the ranks of dogmatic atheism[1]—for she commits the same error as religion, unwarranted certainty, only in the opposite direction. Religion reaches too far one way when she claims to know there is a God, and what He wishes of us; dogmatic atheism reaches too far the other way in claiming to know there is *not* a God, and therefore, among other things, that He wishes nothing of us. Why, then, does this book focus primarily on religion? Because belief systems making unjustified claims of supernatural significance most usurp our urge toward meaning, and most degrade the dignity and spirit of mankind. Moreover, one cannot launch every conceivable battle against even one enemy; much less can one take up arms against all enemies. Having been reared in the bosom of religion, having studied her texts and been ordained to lead her flocks, and then having painfully wrested myself from her hundred-handed grasp, I see it as my responsibility to speak on religion and supernatural belief first. Perhaps in future works I shall attempt to address other forms of dishonesty and error.

It is also worth noting that calling religion's confident claims into question—even rejecting them definitively—is not to be equated with embracing or rejecting any pre-packaged set of values or political opinions on matters that often evince societal passion and discord. It is not true that one who rejects religion must adopt permissive views on all issues about which religionists have tended to be conservative. Good arguments can be made for or against several sides of controversial social, economic, and moral issues, from abortion rights to gun rights to taxes to capital punishment to war, and so on, even if nobody claimed to know of the existence or will of God. Policy on such matters can and should be argued based on what one thinks will be best—manifesting the noblest values, most productive results, and the best balance between the rights of the individual and the welfare of the group, and attempting to take into account unintended consequences, too—for the inhabitants of humble earth, irrespective of the unseen, unknown, possible deities in other realms. Going along with the fashions of political opinion and loyalties of one's irreligious group is not more admirable than going along with the fashions of religious opinion and loyalties in one's faith-based group. Our best societies will emerge when people think for themselves issue by issue on matters political and social, instead of parroting the common arguments and insults of any ideological group, on an entire "package deal" of issues. And intellectual honesty, or its ignoble alternatives, has never shown itself be the exclusive property of the political Left, Right, or any style of Center.

---

[1] For more thoughts on the definition and use of the word "atheism" see *Glossary of Terms* in the back matter of this book.

PREFACE

On originality and value: Every thoughtful writer is confronted with the question,[1] "Am I truly adding a helpful or desirable volume to mankind's already crowded library?" In considering this question it occurred to me that, paradoxically, this book may well be the object of criticism for opposite and incompatible reasons. Those among the scholarly who are already familiar with, and persuaded by, the major arguments against religion—and, in general, those who conceive of the learning process as comprising nothing more than the gathering and classifying of new information—may argue that what is here presented offers little original substance, is unimportant, and will be insignificant in its effect. Conversely, those who still hold religion dear and see how many even today orient themselves and their children by its ancient teachings, and understand the bonds of blood and tears by which people are wedded to tradition,[2] may warn that this book constitutes an outrage, and is likely to bring harm and distress to many lives.[3]

To the concern that these materials may disrupt the lives of religious readers, I have spoken above. In short, I believe both that spiritual disruption for authentic cause is existentially preferable to misinformed serenity, and also that those truly unable to cope with a book's message generally do not read it seriously, or are unconsciously well-defended against it, and thus remain unharmed.

---

[1] This question was warranted many years ago when, upon abandoning religion, I began formulating the material for this book and much of this preface was written; the question is ever more warranted now, in the wake of several widely read anti-religion books, and by the many further such works undoubtedly being rushed to press.

[2] The bold predictions of some independent thinkers concerning just how quickly mankind would shake off religion's dogmas have not been borne out by centuries of ensuing history. Thomas Paine confidently ends his anti-religious book *The Age of Reason*, written in 1794-1796, by saying, "…and I leave the ideas that are suggested in the conclusion of the work, to rest on the mind of the reader; certain as I am that when opinions are free, either in matters of government or religion, truth will finally and powerfully prevail." And Thomas Jefferson, only a few decades later said, "I trust that there is not a young man now living in the United States who will not die a Unitarian." Their rational and autonomous temperaments may have obscured from them how heady the masses find the old wine of religion, and how orienting her collars and chains. In our moments of optimism we may hope that these men, though not realizing how far ahead of their day they were, were not essentially wrong in their predictions, only premature.

[3] These different reactions to arguments against religion are reminiscent of the second and third stages in Schopenhauer's well-known aphorism: "All truth passes through three stages. First, it is ridiculed. Second, it is violently opposed. Third, it is accepted as being self-evident."

PREFACE

As for originality, I trust that the vast majority of readers will find within these pages unfamiliar—and inspiring, consoling, educational, or at least entertaining—thoughts, sentiments, and applications. But it is not the primary aim of this book to present entirely novel, heretofore-unrevealed wisdom—this work is intended not as a feat of innovation but as an attempt at communication. A symphony comprises many instruments, a choir many voices, and the song of reason needs many to play their parts. And though I hope to sing a few small solos, or at least suggest some unique arrangements, I remember, too, that not only are harmonies created by compatible yet different notes, even those sounding the same notes in unison add richness and depth in contributing to the music their different instruments and voices.

Indeed, the most helpful wisdom is rarely surprising or novel. Instead, it is often that which we have heard before but have avoided or forgotten, or that from which we have allowed ourselves to be seduced or distracted in the chaotic chase-dance of everyday living. If repeated reminders, presented by different teachers varying in their approaches, are necessary on matters of health, finance, and other practical arenas of life, how much more are they needed on the foundational and complex matters of religion and philosophy—matters which most find so terrifying to examine that they successfully wall off from their consciousness any awareness of the danger reason poses to their creed. And because examining these issues can be so painful, gentle and engaging reminders are more helpful in bringing people back to the search for truth than are the most brilliant teachings or the most original insights.

Moreover, for many of us, how well we absorb knowledge depends more on the manner of its presentation than on the specifics of its content. Each mind learns best when material is offered in ways most natural to that mind. And because there are different learning styles, varying teaching styles are needed. Here the attempt is to speak the language of some whose minds have not comfortably related to other texts and approaches on these important matters.

In addition, a great number of arguments against religion have, after careful deliberation, been left out of this text. Unfortunately, some writers seem so intent on discrediting religion that they present—among their points—unconvincing, even unfair or inaccurate arguments. Such philosophical partisanship is merely one more form of the intellectual dishonesty or negligence for which they so vigorously assail religion. In writing this book I have repeatedly reviewed the manuscript, removing arguments I thought possibly unfair, or less than compelling, because the aim of this book is to encourage honest reflection and evaluation—not to win a debate by any and all means.

Also, books criticizing religion are often written with such harshness, attacking and ridiculing scriptures, teachings, and traditions—even mocking clergy and flock—that many among the faithful cannot see beyond such hostility to notice whether any legitimate arguments are being offered.[1]

Many believers find it painful enough to consider other points of view on religion and life's meaning even when such matters are discussed in gentleness and kindness; they can find it nearly impossible when these alternative views are presented antagonistically. By contrast, I hope that the soft, respectful tone of this book will engage the heart, or at least not offend it, thus allowing the mind to wrestle honestly with intellectual content that may prove profoundly troubling.

And while I recognize the value of polemics, and know that some will hear, even respect, the ringing challenge over the gentle invitation, I recognize, too, that an entire swathe of humanity can never be reached except by softer means. And, in this book at least, I have chosen that voice.

On authority: The reader will notice that in this text I do not attempt to prove or even support points by appealing to famous or authoritative sources (though I do provide selected footnotes, and suggestions for further reading and at times quote a passage directly—not for the approbation of authority, but

---

[1] In the interests of harmony and civility, I point only to generations past. The writings of Thomas Paine in *The Age of Reason*, Robert Ingersoll in *Some Mistakes of Moses*, and Bertrand Russell in *Why I Am Not A Christian*, although reflecting the great courage of these men—and manifesting as these writers did, respectively, independence, eloquence, and great learnedness—constitute three examples. While they advance many good arguments against religion, they include, too, scathing, sarcastic, and exaggerated attacks on the Bible and clergy. My heart turns away at some of their assaults—and I imagine that the hearts of many religious people turn away more so, and more quickly. Thus it seems to me that their aforementioned works suffer—on moral, aesthetic, and pragmatic grounds—not only because they allowed their nobility and reason to become alloyed with ungenerous passions, but because they lost the ears of so many who might have listened.

Still, I am grateful for their contributions, and I do not pass judgment against them as people, for I bear in mind their other great and compassionate words and deeds, and I also do not know to what degree they felt persecuted and maligned by religious doctrines, communities, and clergy of the intolerant eras during which they lived. Indeed, the danger posed by religion was far greater in these lands in days past, and a more aggressive approach may have seemed to them necessary—and more an act of necessary battle than unwarranted hostility. I concede, too, that some hardy souls are more influenced by frontal attack and polemics than by kind discourse, and will find my own writings too gentle and bland—and, indeed, that others will think my writings too harsh.

And though in the case of warm-hearted Ingersoll in particular one winces when a bellicose shout or a sneering sarcasm drowns out the song of his lyrical compassion—that an eagle who regularly flirted with the clouds in flights of poignant, majestic oration felt compelled to dive to the dust and peck about in the foul dung-piles of caricature and derision—still, he *was* a grand man, and oh for more eagles in the struggle for mankind's soul, and fewer parrots and pigeons.

simply to broaden the conversation, to share a particularly well-worded or well-weathered piece, and to give credit to the many worthy writers and thinkers of the past). This is not because such references are unavailable: there is no shortage of well-known and accomplished skeptics—statesman, philosophers, scientists and others—who have written or spoken on these issues through the centuries. But it is a key premise of this book that truth must stand on reason or experience tested by reason, not on reputation or authority. A compelling argument should be taken seriously no matter how humble its source, and a faulty argument abandoned no matter how stately its history or how storied its origins.

On comprehensiveness: This book is not intended as a scholarly treatise, nor offered as a painstakingly documented set of arguments in the academic tradition. This is for two reasons: First, to cover in such a manner the range of topics with which this text deals would require not one modest book but an extensive series of imposing tomes, whose prospects for either creation or wide utility would be dubious. Second, and more to the point, my intention is not to provide ironclad, ponderous conclusions, but to stimulate honest and lively thinking. This book is primarily a plea to reconsider sacred, or even anti-sacred, certainties, not a demand to submit to a prescriptive set of new doctrines—and positively not an attempt to be the final word. In such a context, proof and comprehensive documentation are less relevant than a creative, wide-ranging, clear-thinking exploration that raises intelligent, even disturbing, questions on matters most meaningful. The presentation of important issues and arguments enables sincere seekers to reexamine the premises of their convictions, and provides direction for further study and contemplation. A list of suggested reading at the end of the book as well as selected footnotes sprinkled throughout the text offer starting points for such ongoing learning.

On scope and intended audience: No book on any complex subject can speak to all people on all the things about which they wish to hear, and on only those things. Invariably, while some readers will consider my selection and treatment of topics close to ideal, others will find that I address much of what they already know, and still others will be disturbed that I assume a level of knowledge they do not yet possess. Some readers, for example, may never have encountered a responsible list of biblical contradictions; to others, such a list is old news—but they might find it interesting to read discussions on theology or numerology, or on the many possible sources of religion, or on whether society needs religion. Still others may value the material not for what they might learn, but for what they might be reminded of, or for the way in which it is written—or for the footnotes with their roundtable of notables and varied quotations and expanded, sometimes entertaining, commentary. Balance, moderation, and variety, then, in the range of topics and the depth and detail in which they are covered, seemed to me wisest in such a work—and I hope that, as when coming upon a well-varied buffet, most will find something of interest or delight in which they can partake.

And when addressing religion, this book deals primarily with Christianity and Judaism; less, and often indirectly, with Islam; and still less, with Hinduism, Buddhism, and others. But many of the arguments, and the book's main themes, can—with a little imagination—be applied to any religious, spiritual, or even secular belief system claiming to know what it does not, in fact, responsibly know.

On how this book is meant to be read: In short, this book is meant to be read in its entirety. This is not so much because what is said in one section cannot be understood well without reading the other sections—though at times that is surely the case—but because so much that I think relevant to the content and process of seeking truth, even to any specific topic, is not included in one section, yet is addressed in the book overall. And to have included in every section all the material even indirectly relevant to that section would have resulted in much redundancy, and in a book the thickness of which might have discouraged a good percentage of even the open-minded, intrepid, and patient seekers willing to examine this more moderately sized volume.

On my motivations: Although some believers will be tempted to dismiss, as the product of bitterness or malice, any work critical of traditional faith, this book is not the result of resentment or ill will. True, not all my experiences within religion were delightful, but many were rich with sweetness and savor, and many were tender and inspiring—and I continue to feel warmly toward a good number of her teachings and a great many of her believers. Having extensive religious experience and education; recognizing that religion has bequeathed gifts to mankind, and not only burdens and chains; and with a sympathetic awareness of the many kind, intelligent, well-intentioned, even heroic people who hold religion dear, I do not see religion, overall, as an enemy fortress manned by horrid barbarians and deserving of any and all forms of attack. Rather, I see religion, especially moderate or peaceful religion, as a comforting home—though, I believe, resting upon insecure and dangerous foundations—peopled by human beings, many of them good and well meaning, people with whom I wish to converse honestly and kindly, and with great respect.

And though the most cynical of agnostics and atheists might think this naïve, I believe that, the many exceptions aside, religion, even if in error has generally been pious and sincere—and not a conspiracy of ambition and greed. And I believe this holds true not only for the majority of believers, the many salt-of-the-earth, well-meaning religious followers the world over—but for most religious leaders, too. True, religionists tend not to go to great lengths to challenge their beliefs, and if they do challenge them it is nearly always with a pre-determined conclusion that all challenges will be met with self-satisfying apologetics—and, at times this may constitute culpable negligence—but such avoidance of the emotionally painful is far from intentional fraud.

Throughout the millennia, people of faith have, in the main, sought to lead virtuous lives, according to what they believed God wished and their families and communities required. It is the same today. I was raised by devotees of religion, and know from long experience that most of them mean well; and having been, for a long while, awed by religion's power and seduced by her charms, I do not wonder at her enduring hold on the human spirit. When I address people of faith, therefore, I do so not only with respect, but also with the sympathy of one who knows their path and has walked for miles its ancient, winding ways.

On form: A wise man addressing disciples or the gathered throngs is no original literary scheme, but a familiar, perhaps archetypal, model. Back through the ages, this theme of an extraordinary individual teaching a group has been lived by all peoples with their wise men and elders, and all tribes with their shamans and chiefs—indeed, it has deep echoes in the bones of every one of us sent as a youngster to school, and perhaps deeper echoes, still, in the universal childhood experience of a wise and knowing parent addressing the children of the home. It has also been echoed in storytelling, literature, and sacred writings. Examples abound in the Bible—most prominently, Moses and Jesus—and also in the accounts of the Buddha, and in many other hallowed traditions and secular tales. In recent centuries, too, writings of varying degrees of influence have employed this model.[1]

---

[1] Nietzsche's *Thus Spoke Zarathustra* and Gibran's *The Prophet* are two of the better-known examples (and both these characters, some have noted, are apparently built upon the New Testament's portrayal of Jesus: Zarathustra overthrowing the message but emulating the messenger's sometimes imperious, obscure bitterness; and the Prophet selectively emphasizing his softer wisdom and compassion). The style I use in this book is somewhat influenced by these writers—though in counterpoint more than imitation. I admire much in the works of Nietzsche and Gibran—the fierce autonomy and brilliant iconoclasm of the one, and the radical gentleness and lyrical insight of the other. But if the writing of so great a personage as Emerson has been famously characterized as "islands of brilliance in a sea of obscurity," perhaps I might be forgiven for saying of Nietzsche and Gibran—with regard to their above-mentioned works—that the former kindled penetrating lanterns, but in a bitter landscape of mocking twilight; and the latter scattered stars of gentle wisdom, but across idealism's vague and velvety skies. By contrast—and I say this not claiming to rival those men in many respects—in this text I have endeavored to present powerful protests without sarcasm or bitterness; intelligent arguments without undue obscurity; some gentle idealism without retreating from

That this theme resonates with us and recurs in our literature is no mystery. Do we not all yearn for wise, compassionate guidance—strain our inner ears for the faintest echoes of sure and sacred counsel from the ideal fathers and mothers we never had? And does not every community long for the leader who combines an incisive mind with a generous and tender heart? Yet are we not, most often, constrained to trudge onward without such faultless direction? Moreover, do not many of us, in our most inflated hubris, fancy ourselves possessing the remarkable discernment of a sage, but as of yet remaining unrecognized, unappreciated by the masses?

And so the form is not new. Yet surface similarities must never be mistaken for agreement on content. Whether a sage is the hero of the narrative is far less important than what the hero says—and whether it is accurate and honest.

On key words and phrases: Any discussion of a topic as complex and ancient as religion is bound to use terms—like soul, spirit, and faith, even the word religion itself—that mean different things to different people. For purposes of transparency, then—to explain just how such words are intended in this book—I have included a Glossary of Terms.

On footnotes: In many books, notes are printed not on the pages to which they refer, but gathered at the end of each chapter, or even at the end of the book. When notes are primarily long lists of authors, text titles and page numbers—or where most readers are not expected to research those references while reading the book—banishing the notes to the rear seems warranted. But where notes include substantive or even merely entertaining comments intended for all readers, I have always appreciated seeing each one printed on the page to which it relates—so the eye is greeted immediately with what it wants to see. And I have extended that courtesy to readers of this book.

On tone, concision, and style: The poetic, sometimes biblical feel to portions of the text may strike some as stilted, affected, pretentious, or encumbered; and the more lush and lyrical passages may be seen by some as indulgent, unsophisticated, even cloyingly romantic and "purple." But my instinct whispers to me that matters of ultimate meaning are best raised above the mundane style

---

pragmatic realities; and some metaphor and lyricism without avoiding all complexity or necessary detail.

Yet while I trust that some readers will share my sensibilities and appreciate the tone and content of this work, matters of voice and style are, of course, subject to the varieties of temperament and the vagaries of taste; and the enduring popularity of the aforementioned works illustrates that what seems caustic or nebulous to some, will seem vigorous or graceful to others. In short: It is well that there are many voices, for there are twice as many ears.

of unadorned prose, and presented in writing softer and more elaborate than the metallic efficiency of spare precision. This is no time to eschew stately and evocative language for fear of seeming either stuffy or unrefined.

To the contrary, when the context calls for it, such formal tones and emotional and aesthetic intensity are especially fitting. The verbal pageantry of all ages bears compelling witness to the apt resonance of evocative words in momentous times and on weighty issues. Heartfelt prayers; fervent love poems; urgent or majestic prophecies; statesmen's rousing calls to arms or earnest pleadings for peace; the ancient and memorable aphorisms of the wise; the epic account or the saga recorded by a historian with an ear for the ages; and the haunting eulogy—that final kiss of graceful words upon the mortal brow—these do not content themselves with the grays of mere utilitarian communication. Instead, they paint freely with a broad, even extravagant verbal palette and vivify their words with the affecting colors of the passionate and poignant.[1]

Indeed, it is the categorical avoidance of grand and tender expression that sometimes falls short of maturity and betrays a lack of confidence or courage: the unwillingness to allow oneself or others to encounter the vulnerability of one's sentiments and the depth of one's commitments. For yes, there is the legitimately narrow emotional range native to some pragmatic and analytical temperaments; but there is also the unhealthy emotional constriction, the calcified cynicism of the craven, the wounded, and the jaded who have long ago built walls against the more intimate voices of their souls—and there is also the studied, neurotic blandness of those attempting to appear poised and sophisticated in the eyes of these intimidating legions.

Of course, on serious matters, style should never take the place of substance. But colorful, warm expression does not preclude precision of thought—nor does

---

[1] Valéry was right in cautioning us on the tendency to mistake "paradox for discovery, metaphor for proof, a flood of verbiage for a wellspring of essential truths, and oneself for an oracle." Packaging should not be mistaken for content, nor hubris for mission. But, of course, this does not mean that in cases of legitimate content and mission one should eschew creativity, imagery, elaboration, and embellishment. For much as some distrust or dislike it, elevated and beautiful language—not unlike a well-dressed beauty seducing with singing and dance—has more often moved the hearts of men than has unadorned, plodding plainness, notwithstanding the possibly equal fertility of that which lies beneath the two presentations.

Less obvious is that beauty exerts its influence not only upon the audience: Many who are gifted with great capacities for fecundity can best activate their creative energies by the inspirations of the muse. Thus, not only is it a grave error to mistake the accurate conveying of information for the limits of effective communication, it is also mistaken to insist that thinking unalloyed with aesthetics and passion necessarily leads one to widest, clearest knowledge, much less to deepest wisdom.

gray, soulless expression guarantee such precision.[1] And while those of dry disposition may legitimately protest that many who speak the language of the heart often give too much weight to the subjective and the emotional, it might also be remembered that those inclined to think and speak in an impersonal style are often somewhat blind to the subjective and the emotional, and therefore give these little to no weight. In some fields of study, such as mathematics and the physical sciences, that impersonal approach may be appropriate.[2] But when studying the varied phenomena of culture-bound, tear-streaked, and all-too-often blood-soaked, religion, what is necessary is not merely memorizing or refuting the rules of ecclesiastics and the constructs of theologians, but attempting to understand the fervent worship and daily sacrifice and celebration of believers—not only the myriads of today's faithful, but the long procession of generations peopled by our religious forebears. In such an arena, sensitivity to the warm nuances of psychology is as important as a predilection to the cold strictures of logic.

And because it seems to me that matters getting to the core of this sad-sweet existence call to be expressed in a manner befitting their noble and evocative content, part of me wanted to compose this entire manuscript in epic and lyrical poetry. But even had I hopes of succeeding at that ambitious venture, such writing, though it may have been beautiful, would have been considerably less clear. And for a book attempting to speak lucidly on the deeply significant, poetry's ambiguity and density would constitute grievous flaws.[3]

---

[1] Walter Kaufmann's writing spoke this message, and often exemplified it. For the former, see the prologue to his wise and incisive work, *The Faith of a Heretic*; for the latter, read that entire book.

[2] But even in mathematics and the physical sciences we must not conflate researchers' pursuit and analysis of knowledge with the successful communication of such knowledge. Mathematics and science often suffer from their teachers' inability to reach the many whose minds relate but poorly to an approach devoid of story and song, of warm-worded welcome or tear-moistened eyes.

[3] Just as some tend to lust after possessions they cannot acquire, and yearn after the lover whose heart remains cool to their affections—while appreciating far less what property and hearts are within easy reach—so, too, do many venerate a teacher only if his teachings are inaccessible or obscure. Presumably, what is difficult to understand is judged to be deep and necessarily complex, and the one who conveys such information is seen, cognitively, as possessing a brilliant mind and message; and is associated, emotionally, with parents or teachers who, when we were children, were in positions of power and respect—and due to their greater intelligence, knowledge, and wisdom, knew and said things which we found difficult to grasp.

I call your attention to the prologue of another of Kaufmann's works—his translation of Martin Buber's *I and Thou*—in which Kaufmann takes Buber to task for the obscurity of the writing, and states that although a book that endures is generally seen as being of

Deviating from clarity of message on such matters, then, would be ill advised. Still, a little obliqueness, engaging the imagination while allowing for some psychological space, often helps us see better—helps us become more *willing* to see. Children learn from animal tales what they might not as easily accept or remember if taught directly and without story. Even Aesop populated his fables with characters at least a species removed—the wolf, the hare, the stork, the mouse, the fox, the lion, and so on—and only afterward, if at all, provided the human moral. And in the Bible,[1] when the prophet Nathan came to chastise King David for sinning with Bathsheba, he did not begin by directing criticism at David. Instead, he told a story—about a rich man who stole a poor man's beloved lamb. Only when David grew angry, and cried out, "As God lives, the man who did this deserves death!" did Nathan say: "You are that man."

In this book, a sage of ambiguous epoch, speaking in a sometimes archaic style, and given to lyrical metaphor, addresses the beliefs and arguments of people in a fictional crowd—in a setting perhaps across the seas and of an age bygone. These several forms of engagement and distance, when combined with the sage's mild manner, will, I hope, reduce—though on such controversial matters one cannot expect to eliminate—the religious reader's discomfort.

On concision and redundancy: I have deliberately sacrificed brevity on the altar of clarity. The frugal eye will notice that the text is, at times, wordy—the

---

high quality, its longevity is often due, at least in part, to its shortcomings, an almost indispensable one for such purposes being a lack of clarity.

And, the trouble is, of course, that while obscure writing may be accorded honor and may be read for perpetuity, what is being read is not really the author's message—but whatever projections and interpretations and half-understandings each unnecessarily impressed and insufficiently honest reader, student, and professor bring to such a text. One even suspects that as a mother finds her own baby most delightful, a reader finds that text most profoundly satisfying which is so obscure as to allow him to conceive of it as reflecting his own image.

And the fascination with the unclear extends beyond books and learning, to the very topic this book addresses. Jean Meslier, a Catholic priest in France, apparently left behind at his death toward the beginning of the 18th century one of the early European anti-religious works, in which he wrote: "If religion was clear, it would have fewer attractions for the ignorant. They need obscurity, mysteries, fables, miracles, incredible things, which keep their brains perpetually at work."

Yet short-lived though accessible works may prove to be, the alternative of sacrificing authenticity and honest communication in the hopes of varied forms of veneration and pragmatic gain should be, especially when writing on such matters, unthinkable—for it would constitute some of the very crimes against the spirit this book criticizes in religion. And we may hope, too, that other things can at times compensate, in the judgment and affections of history, perhaps even of academia, for a dearth of obscurity.

[1] II Samuel, Chapter 12

first example being this unusually long preface. If ever I thought an extra word, phrase, sentence or paragraph reduced the likelihood of confusion or misunderstanding, I gladly spent the words—and I ask the reader's indulgence in these expenditures. Also, each section—though informed and supplemented by the rest of the book, which, as mentioned, is meant to be read in its entirety—is intended to stand alone to some degree as argument and response; thus, points in one section are often intentionally restated in another. Moreover, deeply held beliefs and allegiances are so difficult to dislodge, that if one hopes for any reasonable chance at influence, one must speak of the same ideas in various ways. And I have also, at times, employed what may seem to be superfluous words in order to improve the text's rhythm and to cushion its potentially painful impact. To be compassionate, to write in a soft and comforting style, has seemed to me a critical ingredient in addressing such sensitive matters.

And the writing style varies. At times, when dealing with the detailed or the analytical, including the careful examination of biblical texts, the epic and lyrical are unwieldy and ineffective: Specific verses must be quoted and direct points must be delineated. At other times, when writing on matters of the heart and spirit, or history and destiny, the subject matter lends itself to more expansive, evocative prose. Ironically, the Bible shows similar variation: the emotionally intimate stories of Joseph and his brothers; the eloquent, sometimes sweeping, poetry of Jacob, Balaam, and Isaiah; the grand awe and spectacle of the Ten Commandments at Sinai, and the pronouncements of blessings and curses on Mounts Gerizim and Ebal; the melancholy, philosophical musings of Ecclesiastes; the image-rich, symbolic, sometimes opaque Revelations; and the demanding, metaphor-leavened saintliness of the Sermon On The Mount—all these contrast sharply with the dry detail in parts of Exodus, Leviticus and Numbers describing, to name a few, the requirements of priestly sacrifices and ritual cleanliness, the dimensions of the tabernacle, and a census of the ancient Israelites.

Influenced by that rich and varied model and others, this book does not aim for one narrow style, but adapts itself, in addition to the vagaries of the writer's muse, to the material under discussion. Indeed, the discerning reader, familiar with the Bible's many faces—her words, moods, patterns and cadences—will notice how often I speak in her tongue.[1] (Does not the memory of a lover's scent haunt one long after she is discovered faithless?)

And in writing on the search for truth, there is no end to the degree of refining that can be attempted both to a manuscript's form and content. And it is but a poor artist, and a poorer philosopher, who does not see the imperfections in

---

[1] Yet I try to avoid emulating her moments of wrath and intolerance—which, it must be noted, glare out from her texts with immortal ferocity, too.

his own work. But it is poorer art and philosophy still, to hesitate and refine indefinitely, to tempt capricious time and fate, to so lust after the great that one spurns the earnest overtures of the good. And life in its many other duties and delights continues to call, and time inexorable seems, with the author's passing years, to run ever faster[1]—so one must make an arbitrary end to such a project, even if one were not "slow of speech, and of a slow tongue," but rather possessed of such potential eloquence and genius that, upon putting down one's pen, Art and Philosophy themselves were to sigh and shake their heads at what might have been.

On my own views and conclusions: On such controversial matters as those with which this book deals, emotions run high, and vigilance and longing make people see enemies and friends where they do not exist. If a writer on such topics does not spell out clearly what are his views, and sometimes even when he does, he is likely—in addition to being seen by many as hedging or hiding or being wholly unclear—to be inaccurately accused by some of holding views they deem offensive, and inaccurately lauded by others for holding views akin to their own. And it is my wish that if I be held in contempt or in high esteem that it be only for what I truly stand for, and for who I really am. It is tempting, therefore, here in the preface, to spell out in detail my conclusions.

Yet doing so would take from the reader the adventure and independent thinking gained by following the arguments as they unfold, without knowing exactly where they lead. So although I have already implied that I cannot number myself either among those who claim to know about God and His wishes or among those who claim to know that there is no God—it is only toward the end of the book that my more specific conclusions, placed in the mouth of the sage, are directly stated.

Here, then, is the book I did not have when I was young. It attempts to pursue truth with some measure of gentleness and beauty, while yet maintaining clarity and reason. But since truth has rarely cast eyes upon unanimity; and since people differ in their needs for gentleness; and since what is beautiful to one is unappealing to another, this work—in both style and content—will unavoidably displease some. But I trust it will prove a welcome discovery for others, shining new light upon their spiritual landscapes, and offering glimpses of authenticity's simple peace and of her profound, even if bittersweet, consolations.

---

[1] Longfellow, in a familiar echo of ancient Hippocrates, writes in *A Psalm of Life:*
Art is long and time is fleeting,
And our hearts, though stout and brave,
Still, like muffled drums, are beating
Funeral marches to the grave.

DEDICATIONS

To my mother, who believed in me early. A deeply religious and ethical woman who took ultimate matters seriously and sacrificed much for her beliefs, had she lived to see this book I trust that in perceiving its sincerity she would have shed a few tears of pride among the likely tears of sadness, for a son who in one sense strayed so far from her values, and in another yet cleaves to them so closely.

To my father—a man loyal to religious tradition, and whose views are not reflected in the message of this book—for awakening me in childhood to the urgency and beauty of words, by treating my siblings and me to dramatic readings at bedtime; and for modeling the appreciation of books, and the practice of setting down one's thoughts in writing.

To one who played a later parenting role, who celebrated my voice and calling, and served as a catalyst in nurturing them to fruition. I have never known anyone with such a generous spirit. J., this book, and I, would have been far less without your encouragement and help. Thank you forever.

To Walter Arnold Kaufmann, the first philosopher whose voice resonated with me, a man of courage and independent thinking, and fiercely dedicated to intellectual honesty—a man I wish were still alive when I discovered his writings. In graduate school, wandering the library stacks between classes, I came upon his Faith of a Heretic, *and finally found a teacher. One early morning some weeks later, having read through the night, I finished his* Critique of Religion and Philosophy, *closed the volume and brought it slowly to my lips. Professor Kaufmann, I kissed your book then, and I kiss your memory now.*

1. The coming of the sage

Always it is too early to speak, and always too late. Ever there is further wisdom to distill, before the sacred chalice of truth is full, and ready to pour forth her sad-sweet nectar. Yet how many souls have already shriveled from bewilderment and despair, for want of a few drops! And always night falls early, before even the wisest might fill up the measure, or even the strongest might bear it home.

The gentle sage, thinking these thoughts and walking a quiet path, turned to behold the blazing trees of autumn. Moses, he reflected, saw fire in the foliage, and heard the voice of God; I, however, see the color but not the flame, have studied the prophecies and chanted the prayers—but from God I have heard not even a whisper.

Yet profound silence is as shattering a Call as any, and his soul had long been stirred to listen well to what had *not* been said. He inhaled the sharp, decay-perfumed air, smiled softly, and continued down the path. Cool gusts of wind blew against his face, early messengers of winter's approach, as all about him the trees swayed in red, gold, and purple splendor—softly rustling the haunting lullaby of eternal change. The sun, he saw, was climbing the eastern sky, and would soon begin her descent toward the sobering horizon. Yes, he knew—though he would never be wholly prepared, and was already too late for some; and though he had no divine revelation to share, but only the humble words of man—now was the only time to speak.

And as he walked toward the people, he thought with sadness and compassion of those who could not hear, knowing they were far more numerous than those who did not wish to hear. He remembered how long his own soul remained closed, and how it still yielded but slowly to what it found troubling. And words seemed so inadequate to the task of opening hearts and engaging minds—of getting beyond the iron walls of tribe, dread, custom, conceit, and all manner of gain—that he did not think of himself as a man of words, and wished there were something more. He knew that few ears would hear him, and fewer hearts. But his eyes swept across the tapestry of intense leaves, each summoning the last of her passions for one exhaustive offering, though constituting no more than an ephemeral speck in a vast landscape, and his quickening steps carried him closer to the people.

And many gathered to the sage: some seeking knowledge, others yearning for wisdom; some agitating for challenge and debate, others aching for comfort and inspiration; some determined to defend their traditions, others merely curious, eager for spectacle.

And the sage spoke to the people, saying: Blessed are you, my brothers and sisters, who expose your naked souls to the threatening skies of truth. Perhaps you have heard her distant rumblings and wish to quickly quiet the storm, or perhaps you have already endured her fury and seek to build anew. And even you who know not her shattering power, nor yet dream of the profound calm in her tempest's wake, might soon behold darkened heavens gathering ominous and gray on your unsuspecting horizons. May you remember the sun behind the clouds, and the deep peace beyond the battering winds.

I come not to preach fierce certainty, with enchanting promise of paradisiacal bliss or thunderous warning of fiery hell. Rather, I speak of greater things: the noble dignity of unchained reason, the sovereign peace of uncoerced convictions, and the unparalleled contentment of today's joy chosen—neither surrendered to yesterday's dogmas nor postponed till dubious eternity. Again I say, I bring not the comforting confidence of ancient answers, but the authentic innocence of today's questions. For in the music hall of truth, answers are but cymbals crashing at song's end, while questions are flowing, soaring melodies—the sweetest expressions of the human soul.

And though questions may awaken sorrow and are, at times, the saddest of songs, they cultivate within us an enduring power, a paradoxical poise, and a keen, unblinking gaze. For in the depths of our souls we are weak in proportion to what we have not battled, ashamed in proportion to what we have not confessed, and blind in proportion to what we have not seen. And when our spirits seek a rhythm of authenticity, the shackles of repressed truth weigh heavy upon our steps, creating a slow-footed shuffle or a posturing march, where life might be walked at a dignified stride, even celebrated in inimitable dance.

Brothers and sisters, I do not come to you as an all-knowing prophet. The treasure vault of truth is immense; none can know all her sparkling contents, even estimate her fathomless dimensions. And, brothers and sisters, the farther one sails from the bay of innocence,[1] ever wider stretches the shoreless sea; therefore the voyage of my learning has always just begun. Still, I dare not withhold today what perspectives I have seen, for I know not when my time, or yours, comes to lie down in the earth. Therefore I speak to you today—and not because all truth is mine.

And much of what I will say, your ears have already heard and your minds have once known. But such is the armor protecting the heart, that we must repeat disturbing truth lest it be walled off from awareness. I come today not to perform signs and wonders nor to proclaim astonishing things, but to encourage you to hear and honor the questions that lie forgotten in the corners of your own

---

[1] Here meant in the sense of ignorance and naiveté.

souls—to walk on with holy inquiry though you feel awkward and unsure of your steps, and to resist the impulse to sit down content with comforting, convenient, or merely confident, answers. Come, let us reason together. Let us have gentle dialogue, that knowledge of the head may begin the slow journey down to the heart and belly.

I speak the words of a thousand teachers, and tens of thousands I never knew. Even the best of my lessons were not born of my thoughts alone, nor wholly fashioned in my own isolated heart. They draw heavily on the legacy of the wise, noble, and brave come before, who often spoke their burning words into the bared fangs of hostile power and into the blind stampede of the terrified mob.[1] I, in contrast, have been blessed to study in peace and reflect in freedom, persecuted by little save my own imaginings. Yet though I have learned much from these bold teachers of the ages, I alone remain accountable if I should speak any errors—and not only errors of my original thought—for I have chosen which arguments and conclusions of others to accept.

Lastly, if any among you think me mistaken, I ask that you give voice to your challenges, and see if I have a persuasive response; for if you remain silent, how will you know if I am truly in error? And, even if you are confident that I am mistaken on one point or several, do not disregard all my words. Honesty teaches that every idea must stand or fall on its own merits, not upon a general impression gathered of its speaker.

Now, my brothers and sisters, those of you with questions, ask of me what you would know, and those without questions, share with me the reasons for your certainty.

---

[1] Robert Ingersoll, in *Individuality*, wrote with his characteristic passionate eloquence: "Who at the present day can imagine the courage, the devotion to principle, the intellectual and moral grandeur it once required to be an infidel, to brave the church, her racks, her fagots, her dungeons, her tongues of fire, to defy and scorn her heaven and her hell, her devil and her God? They were the noblest sons of earth. They were the real saviors of our race, the destroyers of superstition and the creators of Science. They were the real Titans who bared their grand foreheads to all the thunderbolts of all the gods."

I. TRUTH: WHAT IS IT AND WHY IS IT IMPORTANT?

2. On seeking truth

And a community elder called out and said: We have gathered to hear your thoughts on the search for truth. Speak first, then, on the importance of seeking truth.

And the sage said: Brothers and sisters, is it worthwhile to seek truth—to closely examine what we believe holy, though we may stagger, disoriented, upon discovering the foundations of our worship houses unsound, and the pillars of our temples buckling? And what if by questioning we risk the public wrath of family and friends, and the private shame of long-held error? And can we bear the pangs of guilt and despair as entire edifices of memory and meaning, and ancestral libraries of kin and tribe, are lapped at by the flames of doubt, even consumed by the fires of truth? The price may be terrible, indeed.

Yet if truth is not of supreme value, declare what is. For even the seeker's sackcloth of truth-smitten sorrow protects far better than the emperor's imaginary clothes of contentment—spun from deception on the wheel of custom, and woven tightly at conformity's loom. And does not the lone coin in hand buy far more at market than do imaginary treasure houses overflowing with gold? And would not a solitary moment of communion with truth yield more integrity than lifetimes of kneeling before mute idols, devout fantasies, and desperate illusions?

When at the market, would one buy clothing without checking for holes—wine without tasting for vinegar, or bread without searching for mold? Would one pay the price of expensive wares, without examining them closely, and checking well the seller's claims? And would not a wise man hold his money tight where thieves and swindlers roam—and where conjurers ply their trade, and a cacophonous variety of merchants hawk mysterious elixirs, all of which are said to heal every ailment and woe? Yet how easily we squander our greatest wealth at the bustling and clamorous bazaar of faith! Our dignity, our life's energies, our deepest values, our sense of purpose, our legacy for all eternity, and the very authenticity of our souls, we quickly throw at the nearest vendor.

Open the ears of your heart and hear that all too soon we lie down in the earth with our fathers and mothers, dust or ashes, buried forever or scattered to oblivion, utterly silenced and soon forgotten. Weep, then, for the certainty and indignity of death—but salt, with your tears, life's daily bread. For when we know well how soon we go, our days may glow with passion, and our nights with loving urgency.

Knowing we shall die, then, what meaning will we give to our brief quickening? Shall we accept the first, second, or third bundle of beliefs we encounter—thrust upon us by others, or grasped at by our own weary or impatient hearts—beliefs that seem comforting or imposing, yet which we cannot responsibly know to be true? Or will we, on the shores of eternity, search fearlessly for the real?

And if we cannot for the sake of our own souls find the motive and courage to pursue truth, perhaps we can find these when we consider that each of us, in choosing what and how we shall believe, strikes a blow either for the dignity and nobility of mankind, or for its spiritual perversity and shame. If we choose to savage our own innocence, and neglect our own authentic callings, shall we be so unkind to visit the same upon our children, and upon our neighbors and friends? Can we studiously avoid thinking and speaking truth on what we say are life's most important matters, and be surprised at society's rampant dishonesty and corruption on a thousand lesser things—of civic function, of business and commerce, of governance and statecraft—or at the innumerable means of inebriation and escape employed by the millions to run from intimacy with themselves and others?[1]

Profound honesty on ultimate issues is difficult and rare, far more easily subscribed to than fulfilled—and even those who teach that "the unexamined life is

---

[1] William Kingdon Clifford, a 19th century mathematician and philosopher, addressed the issue of civic responsibility on matters of belief. In his *Ethics of Belief* he wrote: "I cannot help doing this great wrong towards Man, that I make myself credulous. The danger to society is not merely that it should believe wrong things, though that is great enough; but that it should become credulous, and lose the habit of testing things and inquiring into them; for then it must sink back into savagery. The harm which is done by credulity in a man is not confined to the fostering of a credulous character in others, and consequent support of false beliefs. Habitual want of care about what I believe leads to habitual want of care in others about the truth of what is told to me. Men speak the truth to one another when each reveres the truth in his own mind and in the other's mind; but how shall my friend revere the truth in my mind when I myself am careless about it, when I believe things because I want to believe them, and because they are comforting and pleasant? Will he not learn to cry, 'Peace,' to me, when there is no peace? By such a course I shall surround myself with a thick atmosphere of falsehood and fraud, and in that I must live. It may matter little to me, in my cloud-castle of sweet illusions and darling lies; but it matters much to Man that I have made my neighbours ready to deceive. The credulous man is father to the liar and the cheat…it is wrong always, everywhere, and for anyone, to believe anything upon insufficient evidence…If a man, holding a belief which he was taught in childhood or persuaded of afterwards, keeps down and pushes away any doubts which arise about it in his mind, purposely avoids the reading of books and the company of men that call in question or discuss it, and regards as impious those questions which cannot easily be asked without disturbing it—the life of that man is one long sin against mankind."

not worth living," often live and die with beliefs they do not seem to have expended great courage or energy in examining.[1] Yet how sweet it is to live up to

---

[1] In Plato's *Apology*, the same work which tells us about Socrates teaching that "an unexamined life is not worth living," we learn that Socrates believed that throughout his life he received communication from an oracle, warning him away from that which would be damaging to him, and also that God's will for his life was made clear to him by means not only of oracles, but of visions, and more—and that the fact that the oracle did not warn him away from making his last unrepentant speech to those who could, and ultimately did, sentence him to death, indicated that death is not a bad thing. And Socrates having left us no surviving writings, the great bulk of what we know of him we take from the accounts of his disciple Plato. (And if one argues that perhaps Socrates was, in real life, different from Plato's portrayal of him, such an argument opens up the possibility that he was in fact inferior to Plato's version, and such an argument is also no different from religious people defending Jesus by saying that he was misquoted in the Gospels. In the cases of both Jesus and Socrates, we know of their teachings and actions primarily through the aforementioned sources; speculation beyond these sources, to defend the reputation of one's hero, and suggesting that these sources are inaccurate— these very sources without which one would probably never have heard of one's hero—is both groundless and pointless.) Here are several passages from Plato's *Apology*, all featuring Socrates speaking at the trial ending in his sentence of death:

"You have heard me speak at sundry times and in divers places of an oracle or sign which comes to me, and is the divinity which Meletus ridicules in the indictment. This sign, which is a kind of voice, first began to come to me when I was a child; it always forbids but never commands me to do anything which I am going to do..." and "...Now this duty of cross-examining other men has been imposed upon me by God; and has been signified to me by oracles, visions, and in every way in which the will of divine power was ever intimated to any one..." and "Hitherto the divine faculty of which the internal oracle is the source has constantly been in the habit of opposing me even about trifles, if I was going to make a slip or error in any matter; and now as you see there has come upon me that which may be thought, and is generally believed to be, the last and worst evil. But the oracle made no sign of opposition, either when I was leaving my house in the morning, or when I was on my way to the court, or while I was speaking, at anything which I was going to say; and yet I have often been stopped in the middle of a speech, but now in nothing I either said or did touching the matter in hand has the oracle opposed me. What do I take to be the explanation of this silence? I will tell you. It is an intimation that what has happened to me is a good, and that those of us who think that death is an evil are in error. For the customary sign would surely have opposed me had I been going to evil and not to good..." and finally, "But I see clearly that the time had arrived when it was better for me to die and be released from trouble; wherefore the oracle gave no sign."

So while we justly gaze upon the figure of Socrates with gratitude and admiration for urging us to think more carefully and live more meaningfully, and for gifting us with a model of calm and courage in the face of death, even this man who not only spent his life challenging others' beliefs, but also was killed for doing so, seems to have held some

such a lofty standard. For can we aspire to any greater peace than meeting with pride our own children's eyes, yea, even boldly meeting the gaze of the Universe, through the unforgiving looking-glass of conscience, knowing that the deepest caverns of our souls conceal neither hollow commitments nor sacred lies?

3. What is meant by "truth"?

And a scholar raised his voice and said: How can we discuss searching for truth, when we have not clarified what we mean by the word "truth"?

And the sage said: Indeed, my brother, the good ship of meaningful discourse may be unable to leave harbor if her sailors do not understand each other's speech. Worse yet, is the ship that departs for the heaving ocean, her crew believing they speak the same tongue, only to discover later, in the raging winds and storm-tossed seas, that each uses the same words but intends different meanings.

My brother: Truth, as I use the word, is that which is consistent with the facts of reality, as best we can determine them through experience and reason. In other words: that which we can responsibly accept as being so.[1] This does not

---

supernatural beliefs of his own on evidence we would today easily dismiss, or even take as sign of mental illness.

And it bears noting, too—in that it says something about the corrupting influence on honesty of group norms and ideological bias even among those who claim to speak for reason freed from the shackles of dogma—that many who fancy themselves secularly enlightened hold up Socrates as a shining example of intellectual honesty, in ignorance of or in spite of his stated supernatural beliefs and claims, yet are quick to mock those among the religious or superstitious—whether contemporaries or those from the past, even those featured in the Bible—who have believed virtually the same thing: that they received messages from a supernatural source.

[1] This, of course, is along the lines of the correspondence theory of truth. And I will be so bold to suggest that notwithstanding stacks of treatises and debates over just what constitutes truth (indeed, over whether the word "true" adds any meaning to a proposition) every mentally well adult can distinguish the concept of the real from that of the imaginary, and understands in his bones—even if he is unable to articulate as much to the satisfaction of certain formula-bound academics—not only the distinction between accuracy and inaccuracy, but the significance of that distinction, too.

It may also be worth pointing out that the second half of the definition used here—"as best we can determine them through experience and reason"—makes it immune to the ancient objection to the correspondence notion of truth (an objection attributed by Kant to the Greek skeptics' critique of the logicians, and which Kant approves of by saying: "The charge was certainly well founded." See his *Introduction to Logic*, section VII). The ancient objection is that in attempting to determine if a proposition held in our mind corresponds to external reality, and is therefore "true," we can only evaluate evidence

mean that we must conceive of, or arrive at, all truth strictly by experience or reason—for surely ideas come to us by intuition, dreams, unbidden epiphanies, and various processes not strictly logical or empirical—but it does mean that we should not consider something truth until it passes the test of experience or reason,[1] and both when possible. And today we will not speak of minor truths, such as the facts that birds often fly and fish often swim. Instead, we will pursue truth as it relates to some of life's most important matters—our beliefs about God, religion, and life's meaning.

4. Argument that truth varies from person to person

Then a poet said: You presume to teach one truth to all; but there are many truths, a different truth for each soul. And so there is no way to persuade others of truth. Such deeply personal and intuitive issues are not easy to explain, and impossible to truly share. Each of us is our own beautiful flower, and our own island. We all have our own truths, and they should be respected.

And the sage said: My sister, I commend you for your kindness and your generosity of spirit. Indeed, each of us perceives the world somewhat differently—and deeply personal issues are often difficult to speak of, both because it can be challenging to find words and reason for what may have been arrived at

---

through our mind, and thus any claim to having determined truth would involve a circular, self-supporting process.

But while we may concede that humans cannot achieve knowledge unmediated by the human organism itself, and therefore our knowledge cannot be seen as perfectly objective, it is important to remember the critical differences both in degree of accuracy and in degree of responsibility, between those who expend their best efforts in thinking and living more honestly, and those who dismiss such attempts merely because they cannot achieve legitimate absolute certainty. For though sincerity is no substitute for accuracy, hardly any aspect of life is an all-or-nothing proposition, and neither is epistemological legitimacy. Even if ideal knowledge is beyond our reach, we have ample evidence that our minds are generally able to ever more accurately discern reality, to the degree we exert our best efforts to understand, and adjust our beliefs to the expanding evidence of experience and the refining arguments of reason.

In short, I ask of myself and others not epistemological certainty, but moral integrity; not the wizardry of perfect knowledge, but the heroism of an ongoing effort at deep honesty; not the transcendent power of superhuman perception, but the will and stamina to persist in our humble yet *best attempts* at discerning what is accurate and real.

[1] Bertrand Russell, in his essay *Mysticism and Logic*, writes: "…insight, untested and unsupported, is an insufficient guarantee of truth, in spite of the fact that much of the most important truth is first suggested by its means. It is common to speak of an opposition between instinct and reason...But in fact the opposition of instinct and reason is mainly illusory. Instinct, intuition, or insight is what first leads to the beliefs which subsequent reason confirms or confutes…"

by neither, and because none of us wishes to risk being seen, even by oneself, as mistaken on important matters. I ask you to consider, though, that an honest and loving dialogue on religion and truth can benefit us all, and there is no escaping such effort if we value our integrity.

Indeed, it is precisely those deeply personal, intuitive, and emotionally-laden thoughts that are most prone to being distorted by our deepest fears and desires. Our convictions can only be seen clearly—and their accuracy only judged fairly—in the new and searching light of others' perspectives and reason.

Gentle soul, is it not true that yonder tree's leaves are golden-colored today? Is it not true that my hands have five fingers each, and flying birds two wings each? Do we have different truths on these? And have you not raised your voice and spoken to us and, in speaking, expected us to understand what you said, not in ways vastly different from your intent? Furthermore, my sister, this very language in which you argue that we cannot learn from each other—how have you learned this language if not from others?

My sister, some loving souls so value the dignity and unique perspective of the individual, that they cannot bear the thought of anyone losing their cherished views in the telling glare of open discourse. But the flower of deepest authenticity blooms best not when hiding from the light of day; rather, only when opening its petals, absorbing the light, and welcoming the buzzing visitors of cross-pollination, does it thrive in beauty and send forth its seeds.

And though each of us may be an island, and may experience the world in unique ways, we must find or build bridges across which we can walk, and ships upon which we can sail, to engage in the blessed commerce of truth and learning. Yes, each of us must be allowed the sacred freedom to follow the call she hears, and none should be forced to renounce her uniqueness and conform to a rigid, uniform mold. Yet our freedom, indeed our duty, to maintain individuality applies only to those areas wherein there exists a range of justifiable choices.

On matters of taste, of emotion, of aesthetics, of vocation, of speculation, and of many other forms of inclination, individual choice and opinion can and should vary. Even on matters where the preponderance of experts coalesce around a particular position or theory or interpretation or suggested remedy, dissent may not only be acceptable, it may end up being more accurate than its more popular rival, convention. On complex matters—of political thought and social policy and economic theory and interpretation of fact, and on prediction based upon fact—though many hold passionate views, and may quickly grow impatient with those they think deeply mistaken, such matters are not bald facts, but rather a variable mix of objective fact and subjective theory, value judgment, and inclination rooted in many unseen places—in short, positions on such things cannot honestly be characterized as definitive knowledge, and differing viewpoints should not be dismissed as rejecting truth.[1] And allowing the voice of dissent to speak is for the good of all; for often we have learned from the one what the many did not see.

On matters of truly objective fact, however, there is no room for individuality to flout reality. Gentle sister: The belief that we are each entitled to our own truth, regardless of whether our opinions agree with reality, is well-intentioned, but mistaken. If a man insists that two added to two amounts to nine—and he intends to truly disagree, and does not merely use different terms to refer to the same mathematical facts[2]—he is simply incorrect. It is neither kindness nor wisdom for us to declare that it is *his* truth that two and two make nine. It is not his truth, but his error. And we, if we do not help him see this, deprive him of

---

[1] In every generation, debates arise on various issues of the day, and passionate partisans characterize each other's views as divorced from reality. And, in some cases and in some arguments this may be a fair charge. But in many cases, the accuser has mistaken his subjective certainty for objective reality—and it has repeatedly been observed that the shrillness and intolerance to dissent of the advocates of a position tend to increase in inverse proportion to the legitimate evidence for the truth of their position.

And so it is that in this era, on matters such as capitalism vs. socialism, abortion, military intervention, capital punishment, what to do about climate change, what policies to adopt in reaction to an economic recession…on these issues and many more, strongly held views are the norm, yet conclusive facts and arguments that would settle such issues for every reasonable person are hard to come by. Therefore, as frustrating as one may find opposing views, dissent should not be dismissed—because as much as we are convinced of our positions, if we are to be honest we must admit that our positions are not constituted of fact alone, but of a subjective amalgamation of fact and interpretation and values and more. Where disagreement is over facts and not values, when the time comes that further discoveries have indeed provided sufficient data to settle the issue conclusively, at that point dissent loses its credibility—though even then it should not lose its voice. But it is tempting to too quickly insist that sufficient facts have been amassed for one's own side of the argument, and that the matter should be considered settled. Honesty is as important on social and political matters as it is on religious matters—and often as difficult and as rare.

[2] It would be beside the point, therefore, to argue that in number systems other than base 10 the equation "$2 + 2 =$" would end in a sum other than 4. Because in such cases people do not hold different "truths" about mathematics, they merely use terms and symbols differently—and it would not be an argument over fact, but a misunderstanding based on semantics. Indeed, the number 2 itself is referred to as "two" in English, as "dos" in Spanish, and as "deux" in French. Surely one would not say that these languages disagree with each other on mathematical truth. Instead, they simply use different terms to refer to a perception of reality about which they agree. It is the same with different base number systems in mathematics. By contrast, in the example in our text I refer to someone who truly disagrees with the reality of a mathematical sum.

the knowledge he needs to effectively operate in the real world, in which two and two amount to four, and never to nine. Worse, we disparage the foundations of all reality, and scorn the dignity of the human mind when, through a sympathetic but misguided attempt at maintaining a non-judgmental stance, we equate error with reason and fantasy with fact.

It is more loving to sometimes disagree with some, than to always agree with all. Disregarding the lessons of reason may bring short-term harmony and comfort, but comeuppance cannot be far behind; for the laws of the universe recognize only what is, and cannot reward even the best-intentioned of errors. Let us rather, with courage and good cheer, gently but honestly help ourselves and others think more clearly about matters most vital.

My sister, the deepest parts of our souls know whether we have strenuously sought truth, and we respect ourselves accordingly—indeed, we know ourselves accordingly. For when we glimpse our reflection in the great mirror of the universe, our eyesight is blurred by unconscious repressions, and our image distorted by clever rationalizations. Only when we liberate the vision of our souls, and with intrepid humility refrain from twisting what we see, can we behold ourselves as we truly are.

Ironically, my sister, the deepest respect we can give another is not to shelter her in the shifting shadows of intellectual twilight, within which all things seem like other things dimly perceived—but rather to encounter her under the warm, bright sun of unabashed reason where our eyes are able to see her as she really is. For the true self is found nowhere else, and all other representations are but frightened imposters—for whom every glance carries the risk of discovery, and every embrace deepens secret shame.

5. Intuition as truth

And a musician objected, saying: The best knowing is the knowing of the heart. A person must follow his intuition. It is a mistake to reason logically about such matters as truth and meaning.

And the sage replied: My brother, indeed there is a time for consulting the heart; not all issues are best decided with the logical mind. Thus, when choosing between different reasonable paths of preference and fulfillment, it is wise to consult the heart—for reason can teach but little of mission and poetry, of vision and song. Moreover, intuition can suggest brilliant possibilities and delightful ideas, often gifting us with sudden bounty unattainable by logic alone.

But for these possibilities and ideas, these offerings of the intuition, to be accepted as truth they must be subjected to the rigors of reason and the test of studied experience. When attempting to separate the true from the merely inspiring, the accurate from the merely impressive, and the valid from the merely familiar, it is the mind and its most rigorous reason that must be consulted—and the heart and its most darling intuitions that must be scrutinized, though we do so with loving care.

For is it not common that intuition and personal conviction lead our beliefs astray? Intuition may whisper that your wife is pregnant with a girl, but reality may prove this wrong by delivering a boy. A young woman may be racked by the fearful conviction that her husband has perished in battle, yet may be proven blessedly mistaken when he walks again through their front door. Or if she knows in her heart that he is alive, but his cold remains are carried through that same door—does not crushing grief take the place of what was so recently intuition's complacency? And does not a gambler throwing dice, with the desperate confidence that wealth is mere heartbeats away, most often meet with harsh disappointment when the dice fall still?

My brother, in the arena of religion, too, the lights of reason, knowledge, and experience can prove our deep convictions wrong. In ages past our forebears worshiped the sun and moon, and prayed to them for assistance and salvation. Today, even those who say we each have our own truth believe that the devotees of sun and moon were mistaken—for stars and stones and such cannot answer prayers. Science has illuminated the benighted heavens, and reason has persuaded us of our fathers' follies. But were not worshipers of the sun and moon as intuitively committed to their religions as we are to ours? And yet their beliefs were erroneous. Are we so arrogant, then, to insist that our intuition is inherently more valid than that of our forebears? Remember: Not in intuition do we outshine our ancestors, but in the accumulated fruits—in the arts, industry, and sciences; in academic and, perhaps, moral development—of many generations' craftsmanship, experience, critical thought, and well-tested imaginings.

My brother, though it may sorely try our spirits, we can and must speak with each other on truth. Authentic dialogue is one of the richest gifts we offer each other, and begins to allay the deepest poverty of our own souls, too. And without such dialogue how are we to trust what we see and hear? For only by exposing our dearest convictions to our neighbors' reason can we adjust for the tears and lusting in our own eyes, and for the too-loud beating of our own hearts.

6. What of artistic "truth" and the "truth" of beauty?

Then an artist spoke, saying: The deepest truth is beauty. A rose is true, a poem is true, a sunset and a melody are true, as are the mysterious yearnings of your heart and mine. Of what use is it, then, to argue about truth? It is a matter of feeling, and cannot be settled by arguments.

And the sage said: My gentle brother, for dialogue to be fruitful, both speaker and listener must intend the same meaning for the key words used. In this discussion, then, it is our duty not to become entangled in mere labels, the surface of words, but rather to focus upon content and ideas.

Let us note, then, that you and I are using the word "truth" differently. The meaning I intend when I use the word is this: that which is consistent with the facts of reality, as best we can determine them through experience and reason.[1] Mind you, I do not say that all truth originates in experience or reason, only that it must be verified by these in order to legitimately be called true, as I mean the word. A scientist, for example, may awaken with a complete theory formulated in his sleep by some unknown process of the unconscious mind, but he would be irresponsible to call his theory true until it is confirmed by reason or experience—and contradicted by neither.

By contrast, you, my brother, in saying that a melody or a rose is true, are using the word "true" to denote a different meaning and to discuss a different topic than the one of which I speak. Perhaps you intend to say that melodies and roses evoke emotion, induce inspiration, or provide aesthetically intense experiences. It might, therefore, be best to simply state that these things are emotionally, inspirationally, or aesthetically significant—instead of calling them true.[2]

Yet it is not my aim to instruct others on how to use words—even if I disapprove of their choices.[3] A word may have several widely accepted meanings,

---

[1] See footnote in section 3 which compares this to the correspondence theory of truth.

[2] See Walter Kaufmann's *Critique of Religion and Philosophy*, section 24, "Truth and correctness," where he makes essentially the same point, but takes a stronger stand. He argues vigorously against using the word "truth" to denote anything other than accuracy, and especially against the position that what is merely accurate is not "true." He says of this that it is nothing more than romantic, though it sounds profound, and he speaks of the "…false prophets of truth, who disparage correctness…" His point is well taken, that stretching the meaning of the word "truth" can make people less sensitive to the importance of accuracy. And I, too, would far prefer such a venerable and crucial word as "truth" not be prostituted to less noble, even if more seductive, uses. How I wish that more of us—layman, yes, but philosophers and academics, too—shared Kaufmann's "passionate impatience with…incorrectness." Nevertheless, I did not wish our discussion of ultimate issues to founder in the rocky shoals of a debate on just how the word "truth" must be used. If the word is at times used by some—artists, relativists, but even some serious philosophers, too—to denote aesthetic or emotional qualities, or all manner of other concepts, we shall be unable to prevent this. We can, however, at least urge everyone to exercise care when using the word "truth" in any substantive discussion, and to clarify just what meaning of the word they intend.

[3] As suggested above, even clear and profound thinkers do not always reserve the word and concept of "truth" exclusively for that which is consistent with fact. Santayana, for example, in his *Reason in Religion*, speaking of mythology, writes: "But truth, in a myth, means a sterling quality and standard excellence, not a literal or logical truth." And later, "The religion of Apollo is therefore a true religion, as religions may be true: the mythol-

and any word can be appropriately used to mean anything, provided that such a usage gains sufficient acceptance—as has often been said, "Language is convention." It is beside the point, then, for us to argue over the meaning of the word truth—because what is important is not which word is used, but rather which idea the word is trying to communicate in any particular instance.

Thus, it is more profitable to simply understand the idea or meaning intended when a specific person uses the word in a specific case. Once more, then: When I speak of truth, I mean that which is consistent with the facts of reality. And just which claims are consistent with the facts of reality is not up to each of us to select by mere impulse or intuition. Instead, we must finally determine truth by employing the most reliable of arbiters: experience and reason.

And because we may help each other better understand truth, better understand what is consistent with the facts of reality, as best we can determine them through experience and reason—therefore we gather today.

---

ogy which created the god rested on a deep, observant sense for moral values, and drew a vivid, if partial, picture of the ideal…" Yet note: Even while using the term "truth" for things other than literal truth, Santayana is careful to qualify this use of the word by phrases such as "in a myth" and "not a logical and literal truth," and "as religions may be true." Indeed, here Santayana does what I hope we can all do—and what I urge and model in the text—when using the word truth, be clear as to what meaning we intend.

But from this flexible but reality-respecting use of the word and concept of truth, let us turn to an example that takes things much further, and equates truth with aesthetics. I sympathize with those whose bile rises at Keats's "'Beauty is truth, truth beauty'—that is all/Ye know on earth, and all ye need to know," and I heartily approve of a better-tutored successor, attributed to Nadine Gordimer: "Truth isn't always beauty, but the hunger for it is," so long as there we (whatever her intent) take the word "truth" to mean accuracy, not merely some aesthetic or emotional, self-referenced quality.

Indeed, the aforementioned Santayana, in his *Life of Reason,* in Chapter 6 of *Reason in Art,* has strong words for poets, on the matter of truth. He writes: "Lying is a privilege of poets because they have not yet reached the level on which truth and error are discernible. Veracity and exactness are not ideals for a primitive mind; we learn to value them as we learn to live, when we discover that the spirit cannot be wholly free and solipsistic. To have to distinguish fact from fancy is so great a violence to the inner man that not only poets, but theologians and philosophers, still protest against such a distinction."

Had Keats ripened to his mature wisdom, he might have—though of course we cannot know—agreed to the important distinction between the subjective and aesthetic nature of the beautiful, on the one hand, and, on the other, the objective and verifiable nature of the true. But he never saw his 26th birthday. And though beauty is not truth, it *is* often delightful, and a great gift to the family of earth—and for this we owe the artists and poets, Keats among them, high praise. And though he lived but a few short years, how many among us will look back—even from advanced old age—and see creative achievements as many and appreciated as his?

14

7. Argument that traditional religions mean something different by "truth" than does science, and therefore we cannot hold them to the same standard

And a scholar said: You make an elementary error. You attempt to apply to religion your meaning of the word truth—that it must be defensible by reason and experience—but traditional religions like Judaism and Christianity and Islam do not use the word truth that way.[1] To them, truth means that which is consistent with their scriptures and sacred traditions.

And the sage said: My brother, indeed, traditional religions have generally neither sought their truth in, nor tested their beliefs against, the best guidance of experience and reason. But the question to ask is not what have religions done, but rather what is legitimate for us, and indeed for religions, to do?

And as I have said, we are not now discussing how the word truth should be used. I cannot prevent others from using the word truth to refer to all manner of things other than accuracy—distasteful though I may find such other uses of the word. The question before us is rather: How much care should we all take—including religion—to determine whether our deepest beliefs are, indeed, accurate, and consistent with the facts of reality as best they can be determined?

And religion does not say she is discussing a make-believe world, in which case she might be justified in claiming whatever she wishes for that world. Religion makes claims about actual events and factual reality in our real lives. Religion teaches that specific miracles occurred in the real world, at actual times and places, and were witnessed by real people. And she claims that in this real world today, a supernatural being—or beings—wishes us to take specific actions and forbids us to take specific other actions, or requires us to believe, in this actual existence, certain specific propositions about God, life's purpose, and what follows death. All these are her claims and demands about the real world in which we live—and about this real world, religion does not have the legitimate privilege of choosing how she wants to go about determining what is true.

More to the point, my brother: What about us? If we conduct a careful examination, and try our best to discover what we can honestly know to be accurate about such matters, do religion's claims withstand such inquiry? And if they do not, can we consider her claims any more credible merely because she has not disciplined herself to look at them more carefully, and has contented herself for lo these many centuries with the self-supporting system of confirming

---

[1] A somewhat similar argument is addressed in the context of a discussion of faith. See section 84: "Argument that faith is a different form of knowledge than scientific reason…"

15

her own beliefs by citing her own scriptures and appealing to the authority of her own traditions?

8. Argument that truth and reality are relative, that modern thinkers have explained that no point of view can be considered definitive, and it is therefore pointless to try to arrive at objective truth, or to insist on employing facts or reason

And a man said: You make an obvious and outdated error. Writers of the postmodernist[1] approach have shown that rationalism and claims of objective truth are unsophisticated, and the poststructuralists have shown that meaning is fluid and cannot be objectively identified. In short, there are no facts: We create our own truth, and all this serious talk about finding *the* truth, and improving the world through rationalism, is silly and misinformed.

And the sage said: My brother, those who live in the world of abstractions sometimes become so enamored of the ways in which words and ideas can be shaped that they lose sight of obvious reality.

While no reasonable person would deny that some things are open to varying points of view—and that some thinkers in every age have been too quick to insist that they had arrived at definitive truth on complex, even subjective matters—still, taking this to an extreme and denigrating the entire idea of objective reality is not a sign of greater maturity, but reflects, rather, the regrettable error of "all-or-nothing thinking."

If, upon observing that a horse can be ridden regardless of its color, that there are different effective ways of riding the horse, and alternative routes by which one can ride it into town, one should then say, "Aha! Since there is no one truth on the matter of horses and riding and towns, it is all the same whether I ride a horse or a flea; that a town is a tomato if I wish it to be so; and that instead of riding a horse to town, we should ride the town to the horse," I hope I need not persuade you that the one saying such things is not more sophisticated; neither does he demonstrate more accurate thinking.

---

[1] The term "postmodernism," like various other terms such as "existentialism," or even "religion," has, by many over time, been applied to denote a range of meanings; and much has been written by the proponents and opponents of these somewhat differing concepts of postmodernism. This brief section is, of course, not intended to address these matters comprehensively, but rather to offer a limited but vigorous critique of some commonly understood pillars of (skeptical) postmodernism—the claims that reason is optional or unreliable, and that the search for any form of objective truth is misguided, even impossible. Indeed, some have gone so far as to say that reality is "nothing more than a linguistic convention." Views such as these are insults, it seems to me, not only to human nature but to the universe, overall.

And, my brother, I notice that you yourself take certain aspects of objective reality rather seriously, and do not in your actions reflect the belief that all reality and truth are simply subjective or arbitrary. Will you agree to stop breathing now, and for the rest of the day, and demonstrate that the human need for breathing is not based on objective reality? Will you eat stones from now on, and demonstrate that there are no facts, that the needs and limits of the human digestive system are merely arbitrary, and that we can create our own truth? Will you leap unprotected off a mountain and demonstrate to us that it is mere subjective conclusion that your body will fall, and upon landing hard will be injured or killed? I notice that you do not do these things.

Moreover, I notice that you speak to me and to others and in so doing affirm the underlying assumptions that the sound of your words will carry through the air, that our ears will detect those sounds, and that our minds will translate those sounds into a meaning that is largely consistent with the meaning you intended. Is it not remarkable that you rely on so much objective reality? Is it possible that even you concede—in behavior, even if not in debate—that some aspects of objective reality *can* be identified, and that some things *can* be said to be objectively true?

My brother, must it really be pointed out that the laces holding together your shoes, and the threads holding together your clothes, are not some subjective construction of truth—but objectively exist?

If religion teaches that a supernatural Creator exists; that He wishes us to live in specific ways as taught by Bible or tradition; and that a real heaven and hell await mortals to reward or punish us after death; these claims are either accurate or not. Beyond the fog of strange and imposing words in some academic nomenclatures, and beneath the slippery ice of complex and self-referencing concepts, patiently sits the firm soil of fact—which is either what one claims it to be, or it is not.

My brother, not every idea espoused by every theorist need be seen as helpful, much less as the final word. Simply because some professors advocate a point of view does not make that point of view authoritative. Indeed, the notions you mention are opposed by many other intelligent and equally qualified academics who find these claims grievously misguided. Even those among us, then, with neither the time nor the inclination to delve into these matters for ourselves, cannot responsibly rely on the claim that modern scholarship, overall, sees all truth as relative, and rationalism as outdated. It does not.[1]

---

[1] In a hoax well-known within the scientific and academic community, Alan Sokal, a professor of physics at New York University, published in 1996 an article in the American cultural studies journal *Social Text* (#46/47, pp. 217-252, spring/summer 1996)

And as I have earlier explained,[1] some things are so, and no amount of long words or evasive condescension will do anything to change these. If I visit my father in his house, that is what I have done; no linguist torturing the definitions of "visit" or "father" or "house" will change the bare fact of what occurred; nor will debates on the legitimacy of private property or the validity of the word "his;" nor existential homilies on the concept of "I." Of course, the felt importance of the visit, the interpretations and intentions of the people involved, these and other subjective elements can and often do vary greatly from person to person. But the fact that I visited my father at the house in which he lives—that proposition understood in the common sense of its words—is true.

To return to matters at hand: Traditional religions such as Judaism, Christianity, and Islam claim that a Creator exists, that He has worked miracles in the days of our forefathers and demands of us specific behavior today. These claims are either reliably true or not; and we owe it to ourselves and to our children to investigate such matters as best we can. And if after long and open-minded inquiry, welcoming and truly reflecting upon the best points of religion's advo-

---

titled: *Transgressing the Boundaries: Towards a Transformative Hermeneutics of Quantum Gravity*. The article accurately quoted many prominent intellectuals making, as it turns out, false or nonsensical mathematical and scientific claims often cloaked in sophisticated terminology. Predictably, when the hoax was revealed a furor ensued with energetic defenders and detractors of all sides' arguments and motives.

Calling attention to the hoax, its author, Alan Sokal, wrote an article, too, in *Lingua Franca* (May/June 1996) explaining the hoax's point and purpose. In the article, titled *A Physicist Experiments With Cultural Studies*, Sokal explains that the experiment was conducted to see if a respected journal would publish utter scientific nonsense so long as it sounded sophisticated and flattered the subjectivist worldview of that journal. The answer, he concludes, was yes. And against that subjectivism he writes: "There *is* a real world; its properties are *not* merely social constructions; facts and evidence *do* matter. What sane person would contend otherwise?"

So simple and obvious, and yet how many proponents of sophisticated sophistry and confusion have sprung forth, not only from their expected sources in the steepled cloisters of theology and dogma, but over the past few generations—and, maddeningly, often with more rigid certitude and self-righteous condescension—from the ivied halls of secular academia!

(Incidentally, Sokal's hoax is not a case of conservative-liberal antipathy. He self-identifies as a leftist, and explains that he is angered at a sector of academic leftists who, according to him, have turned the traditional Left's respect for reason and science on its head. Indeed, in a more recent book, he attacks what he sees as abuses of science and reason by the political and religious Right.)

For more on Sokal's critique of postmodernism, see the book, *Fashionable Nonsense: Postmodern Intellectuals' Abuse of Science* (previously published under the title, *Intellectual Impostures*) by Alan Sokal and Jean Bricmont.

[1] See section 4, and other sections nearby.

cates as well as her detractors, we discover that no religion has compelling argument or evidence for its supernatural claims, this is a conclusion that we not only have the right to consider better than merely equal to all other subjective conclusions—we have a duty to ourselves, to our families, to our communities, and to the great host of mankind, to so consider it.

9. Argument that the word "truth" is meaningless

Then a university man said: The problem with searching for truth is that the word truth is meaningless. The deflationary theories of truth have shown that nothing is added to the meaning of a sentence by adding the word "true." For a simple example, if I say "The sky is blue," nothing is added by saying, "It is true that the sky is blue." So truth is an empty word, and we should not waste our energy arguing over empty words.

And the sage said: My brother, if reality were limited to linguistic analysis, or making sentences ever more efficient, perhaps the deflationary theories of truth would be relevant to the quest for truth of which I speak.

My brother, it is not the word "truth" that I hold in such high esteem, or that I urge you to pursue—it is what the word, to me, denotes: the real, the accurate, that which is. In sincere discourse on matters profound, words are primarily vehicles to transmit meaning; they are not an end, but a means. Yes, words are important, and one must be clear about one's definitions of key terms, or most discussion and much thought is muddled. But if one focuses so much on the analysis of individual words that one misses the plain meaning of the overall message, one has lost sight of the task by obsessing over the tools.

The quest for spiritual and existential truth—the yearning to know what we can honestly believe to be so, about some of the most meaningful aspects of life—such a sacred and pressing enterprise, beating hard in the chest and catching urgent in the throat, is rightfully not much concerned if the academic, in the narrow confines of his sentence parsing, considers the word "truth" redundant or even meaningless.

What can I believe? How shall I lead my life? What shall I teach my children? Answers to these questions can only be pursued honestly by investigating, among other things, what is more likely to be true and less likely to be true on such matters as God, religion, and life's meaning. Pursuing knowledge of reality as it relates to religious and spiritual claims is, of course, not sufficient for shaping a full and noble life—but it is necessary.

Thus we ask: Is there a supernatural, conscious being who created the universe? And, if so, did He reveal Himself to humans and teach us to live by certain laws or beliefs? And if He did, did He send later revelations or true prophecies to add to His original teachings? In short, do we have responsible reason to believe that we know what, if anything, a possible Creator wants of us? These are some of the basic questions a spiritual seeker asks; and if one comprehends their straightforward sense and avoids unnecessary linguistic play, both their meaning and their relevance are clear.

My brother, if a clever science student argued that there are no clear boundaries between physical entities, that at the microscopic and smaller levels there is much interaction between an entity and its environment or between what appear to be two separate entities, and therefore no exact boundaries can be definitively drawn, and that it is, therefore, meaningless to speak of separate and distinct entities—should this persuade the police detective to stop investigating how many people were involved in a particular murder? No, because however the fine points of definition are resolved, we know that in the real world of daily and compelling experience separate individuals do exist, and that it is, for the detective, not only a practical but a moral responsibility to identify how many individuals—yes, separate entities—were involved in the murder. So, too, my brother: The finer points of linguistic analysis let us leave to those who do such work; but let us not shirk our existential duty to ask the straightforward questions about what we can know to be true on deeply important matters such as God, religion, and life's meaning.

And let us not pretend, my brother, that any sane one of us dispenses with the notions of truth and reality. You have survived long enough to raise your objection here today, only because you have respected the facts of reality in numerous ways, every day. You are careful to avoid being hurt by things much larger and heavier than you, because you respect the reality that they can crush you. You avoid touching fire to your drapes or wood furniture, because in your bones you acknowledge the reality that fire can damage, even consume your home. You sit on a chair, but not on a needle; you put on a coat before going into the bitter cold; and you eat food fit for humans when you wish to sate your hunger. All these things you do based on an ongoing understanding of reality, of what expectations and propositions are true or likely to be true.

My brother, not only does your daily life for all your years testify to how you depend on an understanding of what is real and true and what is not, but even your very statement to us today was based on your understanding that some things are likely to be real and true—among them, that when you attempt to speak, words will come out of your mouth; and that if you speak well, we will comprehend the general sense of your words; and, most ironically, that your words about the meaninglessness of the word truth—are true.

My brother, as brilliant as some theorists may be, and as much as their advances may contribute to certain areas of study, they may not be of much help to the seeker. Let us, in our search for how to conduct a deeply honest life, focus on what truly relates to the search, and resist the barrenness of clever but pointless debates. For if we hope to walk our mortal way with integrity's confident gait and with authenticity's eager step, we must commit our hearts and minds to grappling with real and profound matters, and not demean ourselves by toying with word puzzles on matters most sacred. My brother: Even without turning aside to contend with such things, is it not difficult enough to gain our existential bearings among all the shouts and shadows of our hurried and distracted days?

10. Argument that relying on reason makes the world worse—full of inhuman technology, and devoid of community, hope, and enchantment.

And a woman said: All this talk of truth and reason, all this idolizing of the intellect, has resulted in a world driven by inhuman technology, and has robbed us of what religion used to allow—hope, community, and abundant enchantment. And in the world you envision, a world that banished faith, things would become even more inhuman and machine-like.

And the sage said: My sister, I sympathize with your inclination toward human warmth, and with your distaste for the cold and the impersonal. I remind you, however, that we can be honest with ourselves and our children about what we know and what we do not know on God, religion, and life's meaning, and still be tender and warm. Indeed, profound honesty on these most important matters can help cultivate authenticity and emotional intimacy to a degree otherwise impossible.

And if you have seen among those who denigrate religion many who seem impersonal and merely analytical, I wince at this, too—but I remind you that many of such temperament have ever existed within the monasteries, the cathedrals, and the study halls of religion, too. And some of the warmest, most humane people subscribe to no religion.

I remind you, too, that technology need not be inhuman any more than other tools or means. How we apply technology is, of course, the determining factor. And truth and reason in no way dictate that you cannot apply technology to deliver a lover a poem, to cure a neighbor of her illness, to transmit to a grandmother images of her infant grandson, or to console a friend across the world on the death of his father.

Overall, my sister, technology is neutral: it can be brought to bear with compassion or indifference, with tenderness or cruelty. And need I remind you that religion has a long history of less than warm and inspiring behavior in its many days of resisting the advance of human knowledge and solidarity—and that it did these things without the benefit of modern technology?

Among the innumerable religious persecutions of the ages, let us consider two notorious examples: The Spanish Inquisition tortured and burned to death those it accused of religious crimes, and used for such purposes the relatively non-technological means of iron, wood, rope, and fire; and the biblical Israelites, according to the Bible's account, employed similarly non-technological means in carrying out the genocides of some nations they vanquished, using nothing more advanced than "the edge of the sword." And today, so many lifesaving surgeries and visits to distant loved ones, so many inspiring films and photographs that recall warm memories to a shivering heart, so many recorded songs that invigorate our days and bring comfort to our nights—to name but a few examples—are achieved by advanced technology. To argue that truth and reason must result in inhuman technology, or to imply that religion prevents inhumanity, is simply at odds with the facts.

And remember, too, that the same technology which may seem to you today to be impersonal and cold, can be made to be more comfortable for those seeking greater warmth. Machines and buildings need not be gray, sharp edged, and steel. Vibrant colors, curved contours, and friendlier surface materials are well within our capacity to fashion. Indeed, the softest cushions on your couch are likely weaved not by human hands, but by the plastic and steel of machines. Let us not confuse technology with the stark presentation it is often given. And let us remember, too, that what seems cold and inhuman to one, may seem admirably efficient to another. Those of tender and sentimental disposition have no monopoly on the definition or proper standard of what it means to be human.

And on community, my sister: I agree that community is a great good, and I would wish for us all, close and healing bonds with neighbors and friends, and a spirit of unity throughout our cities and towns. I should like communities to continue gathering in solidarity and song, in teaching and learning, in gratitude and inspiration. Only let such activities and events be honest, based on the humility of holding no pretensions to supernatural knowledge, and on the joy of giving and receiving human aid and delight—instead of on the hubris and superstition of pretending to know God's identity and will, and the arrogance and self-satisfaction of claiming to be His chosen flock.

And if you believe that community can only be built through lying to ourselves and to our children about the most important matters, I not only disagree, I think that if such were community's price, the price would be too high.

And on enchantment, my sister, it would depend on how you mean the word. If by enchantment you mean being dishonest with ourselves and our children about that which gives meaning to our existence, so long as such beliefs tingle our skin and stimulate feelings of grandeur and awe, then I agree, and proudly so, that truth and reason are against this. But if by enchantment you mean the honest feelings of grandeur and awe at the wonder of life, and at the

22

wonder of the universe, overall; at the ineffable beauty of music and poem, and the wild but honest adventures of theatre and fiction; at the gazing into the eyes of a beloved, and then turning to behold the racing clouds in an autumn sky; and at the ever-renewing curiosity that expands our knowledge of nature, and enables us to fashion objects of usefulness and delight; if by enchantment you mean such things and the unfathomed further potential of natural enthusiasms, then not only are truth and reason not against these, truth and reason celebrate such honest forms of enchantment as the only legitimate kind. Indeed, one may argue that truth and reason have shined far more light, and enabled and discovered and created far more enlightened wonder and enchantment, than ever did the whole tangle of religions and superstitions, in all their millennia of dark ascendancy.

11. Argument that all may be a dream, thus discussion on truth is pointless

And a young philosophy student protested, saying: We cannot prove that anything is real or true. Perhaps this is all a dream. For in the midst of a dream, it too seems real.[1] Or perhaps everything that seems real to me is only a production of my own mind. Perhaps there is really nothing outside of my own mind. Therefore, all this talk of truth is a waste of time.

And the sage said: Indeed, my son, legitimate, absolute certainty is unattainable. The notion that all we think and do is merely a dream, or merely an illusion created by our own minds, is one that may not be open to conclusive disproof. Nevertheless, it would be a mistake to treat it as a certainty, or even a strong likelihood. For we have no persuasive evidence even to *suggest* that all is a dream or illusion, much less any legitimate basis upon which to draw such a conclusion. Instead, to the best of our ability to discern—through our senses and reason—it seems that our conscious lives and choices take place in reality, and are neither visions nor dreams.[2] Our deepest beliefs, therefore, deserve to be taken as significant and worthy of reflection.

---

[1] Many—including philosophers—have pondered the disturbing possibility that they may not be able to distinguish between wakefulness and dream. Descartes, for one, grapples with this matter in his *Meditations on First Philosophy*, toward the beginning of Meditation I.

[2] Kahlil Gibran, in the introductory section of his most popular work, *The Prophet*, has the main character cry out to the sailors in his arriving ship, "How often have you sailed in my dreams. And now you come in my awakening, which is my deeper dream." If taken at face value, this too-convenient paradox blurs the line between reality and fantasy, between responsible wakefulness and passive unconsciousness. And, though many before him have spoken of life as a dream—and, given the vanities and inevitable vanishing of each life, the metaphor is not without some legitimate resonance—one is tempted to say that in much of the aforementioned lush and gentle work, Gibran seems to prefer

And my son, is it not so that neglecting the pursuit of truth on the small chance that nothing is real constitutes recklessness, the likes of which we neither risk nor encourage in other arenas? In no aspect of our lives do we demand absolute certainty; rather, we think and act according to our best information and instincts. When hungry, we eat—though it is not impossible that the hunger is merely a dream, or the food an illusion. We do not cast away our money and best clothing, though it is not impossible that they, too, are mere chimeras, experienced within a dream or within the insubstantial confines of our own imaginations. We avoid the tiger in the tall grasslands, and the snake in the jungle brush; we build sheltering homes and weave protective coverings to shield us from sun and snow; and we construct prisons for protection against the thieving and cruel. All this vigilance we labor, though it is not impossible that all is illusion or dream, and all dangers, therefore, harmless. And you, my son, spoke your views on the assumption that I and all these people truly exist. In short, we live according to what seems real—for what else is reasonable and responsible? So, too, we must pursue truth in this existence that appears to be real.[1]

And, if all really is only a dream or production of one's own mind, what will have been lost by thinking carefully within the dream or illusion? But if all is rather the waking vigor of our very existence, do we not do justice and honor to the universe and to our souls by reasoning carefully on how we should live?[2]

My son, if we wish to face the universe with dignity and innocence, it is not asked of us that we know what we cannot know, or that we avoid all error in

---

lyricism of expression over precision of thought, and paradox and hyperbole over careful accuracy. Yet *The Prophet*, though dismissed as a mere pastiche, by some whose judgment I respect, does contain helpful wisdom, and is presented in memorable fashion. Also, to many, it speaks a soothing beauty; thus, aside from any teachings it might offer, Gibran's gift is a song of comforting—and one does not overanalyze a lullaby.

[1] This should not be confused with the argument some make for faith—that nobody can be absolutely certain of anything, and yet we "have faith" in many things; thus, they say, we should have faith in God, too. See section 79 where this argument is addressed.

[2] Pascal's Wager may come to mind—in which he argues that we have nothing to lose and everything to gain by adopting religious belief. But, for at least three reasons, this should not be seen as similar to Pascal's Wager. First, to assume life is real is not so much a wager as it is accepting as true what our senses confirm every moment, and what reason does not in any significant way dispute. Second, there is no noble principle embedded in resisting the assumption that life is real—yet there is a noble principle, namely honesty, in not pretending we know God and His will. Third, if we were to treat life as a dream, there is no intelligent argument that this would please any God there may be—unlike the case against Pascal's Wager, wherein a God valuing intellectual honesty may heartily approve of us resisting religion's call to unwarranted certainty and likely elitism. See section 51 where Pascal's wager is addressed directly.

thought and deed; rather, we need only learn, on matters most meaningful, what we *can* know, and to deliberate and act in a manner consistent with our knowledge. If later events prove us mistaken, we need not be ashamed, nor fear the wrath of any fair God—for we have pondered with a pure heart, and built with honest hands.

12. Argument that truth is not so important, and denial is valuable, even necessary

And a kind physician said: Must we always look at the hard, ugly truth? Is it not the case that each of us will die, and likely suffer in many ways, too, before our end comes? I have seen too many of the aging and the ill; they were not seeking more truth and reality, but more comfort, even if it meant denial. Why this obsession with truth? Denial is valuable; in fact, it is necessary. If our religions are mistaken, so be it. But they bring us comfort, they help us deny our mortality, they help us feel important as we spin along, tiny and adrift in this terrifying universe. They encourage us to keep on fighting this mortal battle. So let us continue to rationalize, and deny, and change the subject, and look away, and do whatever we can to preserve our religions. Truth and reality are not nearly so wonderful as you think.

And the sage said: My brother, you make a passionate and pragmatic case for pushing truth down a few notches on the hierarchy of life's values. And our discussion today on seeking a philosophy of life is, indeed, about which values should be upheld over which other values. And I do not claim by the authority of divine revelation or incontrovertible empirical fact that truth must always be upheld over all other values. Indeed, there are many cases in which I, like you, would not counsel truth and reality over other considerations.

If, for example, a dying man should tell me that he looks forward to heaven and to basking in God's light, I should not dream of challenging him on his beliefs. Neither should I tell another man's small child emerging from church singing a hymn that the teachings upon which that song is based are unlikely to be true. Instead, in both those cases, I would place the value of human kindness to such vulnerable minds above the value of factual truth.

Moreover, on a thousand small matters of everyday living I would not either press the case for strict accuracy: If my neighbor shows me her baby and says, "She is the cutest little girl ever," I should not find it necessary to point out how unlikely that is to be true, or that such a judgment is subjective and that many would disagree. Nor, if invited to my friend's home for dinner would I consider it either my duty or my place to suggest that next time a little less salt be added to the rice. But, my brother, let us not confuse diplomacy and discretion on small matters, with misleading oneself and others on life's most important matters.

And we are not all on our deathbeds, and we are not all small religious children, that we are to be deemed incapable of dealing with truth on life's fundamental issues. Indeed, to me it seems condescending and undignified to treat healthy adults as the infirm dying or the fragile young.

Our lives, small and mortal though they are, stand upon what is real. Yes, we all need escape to some degree—but healthy and effective living knows the difference between diversion and denial, between diplomacy and delusion. Each of us knows in our bones that a glass or two of wine, or an hour or two of absorption in watching a show or in reading a fanciful tale, can be pleasant and good, and part of a well-lived life. But each of us also knows in our bones that drinking all through the day every day and remaining in an ongoing state of intoxication, or continuing to believe one is living the fictional life depicted in the theatre show or the storybook, is unhealthy, and both reflects and portends serious life difficulties, and that aside from any pragmatic price, such flight from our real world and rejection of our real selves constitutes self-betrayal, and betrayal of human life, overall.

True, at times we can do nothing but live poorly. If we were to see someone in unbearable agony, and the only remedy available were strong whiskey, many good and reasonable men would hasten to offer their whiskey to help alleviate such suffering. But these same men would rightly be indignant at the suggestion that healthy people be numbed with whiskey all the time.

My brother, I ask you to be more honest with yourself about how much you value truth on significant issues. If you married a woman who was truthful with you about most things of a practical day to day nature, but was untruthful about the foundational issues of the marriage—such as the inconvenient fact that she is still married to another man, or that her name is really nothing like the one you heard proclaimed at the wedding ceremony and the one by which you have always called her; that she has been spending great sums of your money at gambling while crying to you of poverty and pressing you to work harder, or that she indulges in primal embraces with other men when you are away from home and that the children you believe yours were really fathered by someone else— would you be at peace with such untruths? Yet was it not you who argued that truth is not so important?

And would you be anything but deeply disturbed if your son said he was going to school but instead went to a friend's house and indulged in wild drinking? Or what if he told you that your silverware was stolen by a burglar, but in truth he himself sold it for the convenience of a bit of money? Would you not become incensed at such dishonesty—at such infidelity to truth on important matters? Or perhaps you are a gentle father, not given to expressions of anger; would you still not sit your son down for an earnest discussion on just how critical is sobriety,

26

not running from reality, and just how important is truth between parents and children?

Yet here you argue that it is fine to lie to yourself, to your wife, and to your children about eternity, about the bases of human dignity, and about the foundational meaning of your life and theirs. Again, my brother, I ask you to be honest with yourself about what you think of honesty, and truthful with yourself about what you think of truth.

And the highest forms of love, of courage, of meaning, of wisdom, and of many other noble ideals—chief among them, authenticity—are achieved not by shielding ourselves from the truths, even the searing truths, of existence, but by encountering them with compassion. And of course this does not mean that we must contemplate them without interruption or rest; instead, to live well we must not only think of heavy and somber things, but also engage in delightful and joyous things, some of which partake in various means and measures of diversion and escape. But if we wish to be real, and to deeply respect ourselves and each other, we must periodically return to contemplate important unpleasant truths, and even during our days and moments of more pleasant preoccupation, we must never deny reality, as best we can determine it through the tests of experience and reason.

And, my brother, as with any steep path, the lazy will not wish to walk it, and the lame may be unable to walk it. But the vigor of the climb, and the view at the heights, is unparalleled. I say, let us urge the indolent up the mountain, and let us be willing to carry the lame—but let us not suggest that everyone remain in the dark valley.

II. THE GIFTS OF RELIGION

13.   "Has not religion brought us many blessings?"

And a priest said: Has not religion brought us many blessings, and is she not the cause of much good in our troubled world? You complain about religion, and are quick to speak of her faults. Why not, instead, speak of all her many points of excellence, and the manifold benefits she has, throughout the ages, brought to mankind?

And the sage replied: My brother, religion is a mystery-clad guest who does, indeed, come bearing gifts. It is not from ignorance of what she gives that I urge you to scrutinize her teachings, but from knowledge of what she takes—and not from blindness to her blessings do I ask you think again, but from clear vision of her often unintended curses. Indeed, we are wise to learn from her, to appreciate and retain the much she has brought that is sound and beneficial—yet still to honor her best intentions, and our best selves, by improving upon her legacy.

And I thank you for speaking of religion's gifts—for they do merit recognition. Of religion's many gifts to society, let us celebrate ten of the best.

13.1   Kindness

Though we live only by her bounty, nature is no ever-nurturing mother, but often a ruthless mistress who cuts down the weak and the wounded, and discards the unlucky and the unprepared. The sun takes no pity upon the parched-mouthed traveler staggering in the baking sands; neither do winter's sleet and winds give any thought to the shivering woman in the wet and cold. When famine bites at empty bellies, when grief tears at a broken heart, when illness and age dim one's powers, our most ready help comes not from nature, but from the compassion of fellow humans. Yet left to uneducated development, humans are not always merciful. Thus it is a gift of religion that she has often taught charity, kindness, and love.[1]

---

[1] I neither mean to suggest that humans cannot be compassionate without religion, nor that religion has consistently taught compassion. Many of us have it in our blood and bones to feel the pain of others and to relieve their suffering, and even those who need to be taught to care, can be taught this without claiming to know the existence or will of a supernatural being; and religion has not always taught charity, kindness, and love—especially regarding the treatment of heretics, or those of other faiths. As with all the gifts of religion mentioned in this section, the above virtues have been far from consistent. But there will be time and pages enough to make the case against religion; for the

Many are the hungry fed by houses of worship, and many more are the famished given sustenance by those to whom religion has taught benevolence. And many are the wounded and afflicted of body who have been cared for by hospitals founded by religious charity. And for ages, now, those acting with piety learned of religion have, as individuals, clothed the naked, comforted the bereft, healed the sick, given aid to the needy—and sheltered the homeless and downtrodden from harsh elements and harsher hate. And many a quarrel between a man and his fellow has been quelled by religion's humble wisdom and by the noble forgiveness born of her word.

13.2 Direction

Little dampens the spirit of man more than squinting out at life through the fog of confusion and the mists of indecision—and little galvanizes his energies more than clear and confident vision. Religion, in many of its forms, offers a sense of conviction, an unambiguous compass of right and wrong, on life's many complexities.[1] Thus, individuals can be more directed, and feel more oriented and competent in their daily lives. And communities benefit too; they unite, feeling convinced that they know the proper way to live. Both for its practical benefits and for the emotional comfort it provides, then, many owe much of their equilibrium to the direction offered by religion.

13.3 Community

The long shadows of separation can set even the strongest of spirits shivering. We need each other's company, and it is not good that we be too alone. And few things are more noble and pleasant than coming together in unity and fellowship with other members of the human family. Thus it is a fine gift that religion offers when she gives us a way to join in cooperative kinship with others. By gathering in congregation, joining hands or hearts in group ceremony, taking part in faith-sponsored events, and thus becoming known to others, many have basked in the warmth of welcoming community, who otherwise might have huddled in forlorn isolation. Indeed, even when satisfying human contact is unavailable, a person need not feel alone; for religion has provided a God with whom one can, always and anywhere, commune.

---

moment, we celebrate what have been, at least at some times and in some cases, her positive points.

[1] Though, of course, such conviction is often purchased at the price of honesty and dignity. Voltaire is credited with saying, "Doubt is not a pleasant condition, but certainty is an absurd one."

13.4 Encouragement in times of suffering

It is a rare man who escapes deep suffering, or never needs encouragement. For yes, there are years of plenty and seasons of joy, when the earth seems to serenade our blessings with birdsong, and decorate our moments with fragrant and colorful flowers; when the sun seems to light our days golden, and to sparkle her rays upon our path to cheer our steps along. But darker things come: years of rage, agony, and terror; seasons of pain and persecution; times when the earth seems to taunt us and mock all our efforts; mornings when the rising sun awakens us only to another turn beneath the overseer's whip; evenings when we stagger home, bent and weary from bearing ruinous burdens; and nights when even the moon and stars seem but to conspire against us in all their frosty distance. Yet for such times, too, religion brings a gift. Our suffering forebears through the ages endured their afflictions by crying out to God, by believing that He does things for the best, and by trusting that their lives, though painful, played some small role in His great cosmic plan. And this allowed their arms the stamina to hold aloft life's singeing torch one more day. Even in desperate moments, with all earthly hope extinguished, a different kind of optimism was kindled: the belief that a transcendent God might intervene in the matters of men and orchestrate glorious salvation, sudden and supernatural.

13.5 Hope for an afterlife and ultimate justice

When we touch the terrible finality of death in the form of a lifeless loved one, whose eyes will never again see us, whose ears will never again hear us, whose arms will never again hold us and—the most brutal and undignified blow—whose once dear flesh will putrefy and decompose into fodder for maggots; or else be reduced to lifeless ash, while we are forced to stand by, passive and impotent; or when, after all our frantic efforts to build a life worth living we glimpse in a terrifying moment of clarity our own similar and inevitable end—at such times we are gripped by unspeakable sorrow and are shaken by a profound sense of futility. But as we reel beneath the anguish or specter of unthinkable loss, religion[1] beckons with an offer of ready hope and consolation. She speaks of a God who cares for the souls of our loved ones whom, she says, have gone to a better place. And she assures us that we, too, shall live on in heaven after our days on earth have ended and we are gathered unto our fathers and mothers, though our bones lie buried in the earth or burned to ashes and scattered to the winds. Thus religion not only allows believers to hope they will endure beyond the grave, it also helps the bereaved to more easily bear overpow-

---

[1] Not all religions, of course, but many, including Christianity, Islam, and the traditional rabbinic Judaism of the past two millennia.

ering grief, bury their dead in greater peace, and more confidently rejoin the family of the living.

And the promise of an afterlife also allows one to hope for justice. The dying and the defeated, the despairing and the downtrodden, know with a bitter clarity that earthly fate does not dispense fair recompense for all the good and evil done under the sun. Yet religion offers comfort for such distress by assuring us that God will wreak divine vengeance upon our tormentors and disburse handsome rewards for the virtuous and righteous—in a forthcoming, spiritual realm.[1]

13.6 Beauty

The dull rounds of daily routine, often devoid of beauty and uplifting sentiment, leave the spirits of many discouraged and deadened; and the challenge of wringing sustenance from the soil of our lives is, for many, achieved only by the sweat of our furrowed brows and the tears of our lined and weathered faces; and a thousand painful and menial tasks make burdensome the bringing forth and raising up of our children. So we long for something more, we ache for a taste of the garden, tantalized by dim memories of delight long ago lost—the exquisiteness of early being, ever beyond recapture.

And here, too, religion offers a gift. Her rituals and worship services, her heroic fables and ambitious ideals, her chanting, poetry, ceremony and song, especially when performed in a grand and imposing house of God, confer a measure of grace and beauty upon a life that may otherwise seem colorless and mundane. And her visions of an afterlife, abundant with bliss and radiant with splendor, round out the promise of delights and enchantments not known since last man and woman walked naked and unashamed, eastward in Eden.

13.7 Stability

Many in the family of earth[2] feel the need for predictability and routine; they are more oriented and confident when their days follow consistent patterns. For such people religion offers the gift of her rites and ceremonies, her holidays and feasts, even her days of penance and mourning. And these help set the sacred rhythm for the march-dance of life, in its days and in its weeks, in its months and in its seasons.

---

[1] And though one may justly question the honesty and dignity of such assurances, and point to some of the dangers they pose, one cannot deny that they bring to many a great comfort. And for the moment we speak of religion's gifts.

[2] For this warm phrase I am indebted to Wayne Muller, whom I have seen use it both orally and in print. See his compassionate, evocative, and wise—yet somewhat religiously oriented—book, *How, Then, Shall We Live?*

13.8 A sense of profound purpose

For many among us, daily life without weighty objectives would seem tedious, wearisome, even meaningless. Religion inspires such people[1] and enables them to believe they live for a great cause, and that their actions yield significant implications, echoing on in the vast mansions of heaven and through the endless eons of eternity.

13.9 Transcendent and expansive experience

Man can conceive of grand visions and extraordinary spectacles, and ever whispering to his inner ears and flitting before his inner eyes are hints of glory and unimagined superlatives; but his body languishes, imprisoned in a cell among whose unyielding bars are time, space, flesh, society, and mortality. The proud spirit, held captive in such undignified straits, yearns for escape, for a taste of boundlessness and infinity. And religion offers this in prayer, ritual, meditation, religious study, even mystical ecstasy—and, ultimately, in the promise of meeting with God beyond the grave. Through these, it seems to believers, one can be liberated from the frustrating ignominy of earth-bound limitations; forget the degradations of smallness and frailty; and, even if only briefly and episodically, here on earth touch the God-face of blinding light.

13.10 Scholarship and education

Humans transmit knowledge to each other to a degree far surpassing other species. The spider crawls into life possessing the skills to spin her web; the frog emerges into watery existence apparently knowing by instinct how to swim and what to eat. But these creatures do not teach each succeeding generation much new. Even the more social species—the elephants, the monkeys, the wolves and others—do not significantly increase their knowledge down through the centuries. Man, by contrast, lives mostly through skills he was taught by others, and by an ever increasing legacy of knowledge bequeathed to him by the combined ingenuity and experience of all preceding ages. He is not born with knowledge of reading and writing, of building houses or playing music, or of a thousand other human innovations he will use to navigate and bring richness to his existence. Human learning has been slowly wrested from the strong arms and silent lips of nature, and these hard-won gains have been passed on to later generations who did not labor for them.

Religions have often played an important role in creating or preserving such knowledge. In many eras, the clergy were far more educated than the general

---

[1] Though, as I argue consistently throughout the book, this religious inspiration pays insufficient attention to deep honesty.

populace, and thus learned and transmitted knowledge that may otherwise have been lost. Moreover, religions' scribes and scholars, mystics and monks, often dedicated long years to writing and copying various forms of wisdom and understanding. And religions have founded many of our schools of both basic and higher learning. Thus, the wizardry of our words and numbers, and the magical machines and skills they have conjured, owe some of their latter-day valor to their early incubation and care in the cradle of faith.[1]

14. If religion has given humanity so many gifts, why question religion?

And the priest said: If you know this, if you know how many gifts religion has given the human race, why would you challenge her, and ask people to rethink their sacred convictions? Should you not, instead, encourage us to express to her our gratitude, and to reinforce our religious commitments?

And the sage replied: My brother, all the gifts I have mentioned, and more, has religion bestowed upon mankind during her eventful stay. And as each of us is the master of our spirit's abode, it is well that we express our gratitude for these offerings. The wise master of the house, however, considers not only how many gifts the guest brings, but also whether these outweigh the damage she wreaks upon his house and upon the souls of its inhabitants—even if the harm is unintended. And religion has done such great harm that even her most excellent gifts come at too high a price.

For if religion has encouraged kindness and fostered compassion, she has also commanded hatred and incited violence, and taught the terrible libel and debasing lesson against human nature that we treat each other well only because commanded by a god; if religion has given direction, such direction has been dishonest and degrading, for she claimed to know what she did not know on life's most important matters—and stole our ancestors' dignity and their earnest tears; if religion has facilitated community for some, she has also made outcasts of others, and pitted community against community in fervent discord, even in catastrophic wars of annihilation; if religion has encouraged many in times of suffering, she has also taught that many will go to eternal suffering, she has persecuted, even tortured those who would not submit to her teachings, and has,

---

[1] Again, I do not mean to exonerate religion for the many ways in which she has discouraged, prohibited, even persecuted the free exercise of inquiry and learning, and crushed the natural curiosity that finds its flower in science. Yet religions have varied—through the ages and across the climes—in their attitudes toward, and their treatment of, various forms of knowledge and learning. And for this brief moment, at least, we speak of the good religion has sometimes wrought. A little graciousness to a worthy opponent has ever been a mark of noble engagement.

even in less violent days, often tormented all her followers with the soiling agony of indelible guilt; if religion has given hope of an afterlife, she has also invented the horrors of hell, and burdened untold believers with fears of eternal, unspeakable pain; if religion has brought us beauty, she has also forbidden many forms of beauty, replaced the carefree smile of innocence and the dancing eyes of joy with the drawn face of anxiety and the downcast gaze of shame, hidden the delightful form of the human body behind dark clothes and barriers, and darker threats, and cast a shadow upon the very sun itself by disparaging all forms of earthly beauty; if religion has helped maintain stability, her powerful grip on society and on individuals' daily lives has also postponed for centuries all manner of freedom, progress, and earthly hope; if religion has brought a sense of profound purpose, it was but illusory purpose, built upon error or worse; if religion has brought transcendent and expansive experience, she has brought limiting and impoverishing experience, too, by discouraging or forbidding various forms of learning and practice, science and exploration; and, thus, if religion has brought scholarship and education, it has been only a chained and blinkered learning—where truth was neither sought nor welcomed, save where it agreed with her doctrines and traditions.[1]

More important, my brother, even if the benefits of religion's gifts far outweighed their costs, this would tell us nothing about the accuracy of her claims; it would merely tell us that she was, on balance, useful. And what is useful is quite a different matter from what is true. My brother, if it were proven that should I believe myself the emperor of Rome—and don purple robes and set upon my head a diadem and fiercely believe that in far-off lands centurions and their men swear to me their allegiance—I would be far happier than if I acknowledged

---

[1] William Kingdon Clifford, in his essay *The Ethics of Religion,* cites some claims that religion has done good for mankind, and argues vigorously against them. He writes: "…Somewhere and at some time mankind had derived benefits from a priesthood…I have never been able to get any evidence for that statement… 'In the Middle Ages the priests and monks were the sole depositaries of learning.' Quite so; a man burns your house to the ground, builds a wretched hovel on the ruins, and then takes credit for whatever shelter there is about the place…. 'Then again, the bishops have sometimes acted as tribunes of the people, to protect them against the tyranny of kings.' No doubt, when Pope and Caesar fall out, honest men may come by their own. If two men rob you in a dark lane, and then quarrel over the plunder, so that you get a chance to escape with your life, you will of course be very grateful to each of them for having prevented the other from killing you; but you would be much more grateful to a policeman who locked them both up. Two powers have sought to enslave the people, and have quarrelled with each other; certainly we are very much obliged to them for quarrelling, but a condition of still greater happiness would be the non-existence of both."

myself to be without crown or kingdom, would you not counsel me to live by truth anyway, to not demean my spirit by reaching for an imaginary scepter, donning fictitious finery, and commanding phantom legions—royal and useful though such indulgences may be?

Thus, my brother, just as we pick through the possessions of a departed loved one, deciding what is of value to keep, and what must be discarded with an aching heart, so must we pick through the legacy of religion, retaining her many treasures that can be used to build a new framework of values, community, and transcendence—and summoning the courage to part with anything inconsistent with profound honesty.

For on matters that touch our tender souls, shape our deepest loyalties and hopes, and speak to the very essence of who we are, we dare not merely ask what is comforting, what is convenient, or what is crudely advantageous. My brother, in so sacred a landscape, we must abandon all other charms and ever seek naught but the fierce beauty of truth.

III. THE PERSISTENCE OF RELIGION

15. Why the search for truth is avoided and religions endure

And a young man spoke, saying: If truth is so important, why do not more people question their beliefs, especially when doubts and difficulties are brought to their attention? Why do they not spend their days and nights pursuing such a meaningful quest? Why do they instead seem eager to avoid looking at these matters too closely? And why does religion live on?

And the sage replied: My son, the diverse temperaments of men, and their endlessly varying societies and circumstances, result not in one, but in numerous motives and reasons for avoiding truth and perpetuating religion. And most of these are unconscious, hidden from ordinary awareness, and thus terribly difficult to detect, much less overcome.

Moreover, wise men have shown that the reasons for a thing's beginning—whether an object, a behavior, a movement, a force, and idea or a belief—are not always the reasons driving its perpetuation. The grown bull eats grass, and does not suckle for his sustenance as once he did while a calf; nor does even the day-old calf gain nourishment in the way he once did while developing in his mother's belly. The flitting butterfly is not limited to the diet of the caterpillar; and the eagle and the vulture beat their wings furiously to gain the heights, but once there may soar and glide on wind currents unknown nearer the ground. So, too, my brother: The reasons people avoid questioning religion, the reasons they perpetuate its beliefs and practices, are not limited to those reasons stimulating religions' birth[1]—though, clearly, some are the same.

As for just how many reasons conspire against spiritual authenticity, know this my son: Truth's jailors are numberless and insidious, and the more of them we seek, the more we find. Today we shall recount some of the foremost obstacles to existential honesty on the matter of religion—thirty-one forbidding sentries in the Bastille of the soul.

15.1 Fear of disorientation and loss of stability and meaning

One of our more powerful human needs is to feel oriented, to believe that we understand our environment and our life. Therefore, we are deeply afraid of losing foundational values, those that seem to give us direction, stability, and fundamental meaning, and we cling desperately to familiar traditions and

---

[1] For a discussion on the causes of religion's birth, see section 67.

beliefs—and avoid thinking carefully about whether they are true. This is, perhaps, the most common reason we avoid the quest for truth.

And those of us gripped by this profound aversion to losing the familiar and to risking profound change generally do not know it. Instead, our subjective experience is usually one of being confident in our beliefs, or too busy and distracted to look into such matters. The unconscious mind labors to prevent us from becoming aware of that which it fears will be too difficult for us to bear.

15.2 Need to belong: the fear of isolation and social costs

Humans are social beings, and need to belong. Our hearts are pained if we find ourselves isolated or rejected or even faced with the danger of losing a friend, for one of our strongest needs is to be accepted by family and tribe. And in order that we do not risk angering the group, our unconscious minds often prevent us from even entertaining thoughts that challenge premises important to the group. In the deep regions of the mind, those of high social status fear losing their status, while those of moderate or low social status fear losing more basic acceptance or belonging—thus the inclination to avoid opposing, even questioning, the religious beliefs or practices important to our people.

Indeed, aside from the pain of actual isolation and rejection, there is the fear of being too alone in one's beliefs and opinions. And this, too, leads one to avoid heretical thoughts even in the mute solitude of private rumination.[1]

15.3 Resistance based in emotional experiences and allegiances

Notwithstanding theologians' concepts and apologists' arguments, reason is often the least important cause of religious commitment. Powerful emotional allegiances and connections to one's religion develop early and deep—and these intense bonds combine to offer great resistance to anything that would challenge native belief. Religion insinuates herself into the hearts of children with holidays' gifts, foods, and celebrations, and with the thorned roses of prohibition and taboo. And from infancy through advanced old age, religious prayers and ceremonies mark the most intense of life's passages—milestones of growth and maturity, matrimony, childbirth, serious illness, and the death of loved ones— and thus continue to bind the emotions, throughout the lifecycle, to religion.

Emotional bonds can be passed on indirectly, too. A child sees his mother's tears as she whispers a prayer, and observes his father paying homage to God in

---

[1] Santayana said: "Man is a gregarious animal, and much more so in his mind than in his body. He may like to go alone for a walk, but he hates to stand alone in his opinions." And as with most valid generalizations, though we can point to striking exceptions, it remains generally true.

sober worship. Close in the child's heart is born the loyalty to what moves his parents and others so deeply.

Jeopardizing those deep emotional connections to symbols, beliefs, and practices, then, by questioning one's religion can be deeply disorienting, and can bring down upon oneself the fierce and amorphous swarm of stinging loss and grief. Most are driven by powerful instinct to avoid such risk and pain.

My son, our hearts are drawn to our native faiths and our minds rarely rebel, for in the house of heritage wafts the aroma of grandmother's soup, and echo the plaintive notes of mother's hushed lullaby; and outside—outside lurk dangers unknown, and loneliness and guilt, and the dark and the cold.

15.4 Fear of punishment, on earth or in hell

My son, religions often threaten horrific divine punishment, including hell, for those who dare cast off the blindfold of belief. Many have been told from childhood of the pain that lies in wait for the unbeliever—especially he who was once committed to religion but later goes astray. And this early-learned fear cows the faithful, and they avoid examining the bases of their beliefs; they turn away from seeking the light, for they were taught it is nothing but a terrible heat.

15.5 Habit

There is also a simple functional matter to consider: We are creatures of habit. Most of what we do on most of our days is done not out of original thought, but out of routine. The brain conserves energy by noticing patterns of thought and behavior and directing us to automatically repeat those patterns, thus reducing the need for new, high-energy, thinking—and leaving our awareness available to whatever new may arise. And so it is that thoughts about God, truth, and religious behavior are early formed into habits that continue of their own momentum, absent some cause leading us to think anew. And for most, the cause must be compelling, for deep forces—hopes, loyalties, flatterings, fears—hold the religious mind securely under the sway of pious behavior and thought.

My son, habit flees truth on its own powerful legs, but when its speed is hastened by the wings of terror and the shouts of tribe, how fast and far it escapes from any glimpse of discomfiting truth! And one need not reckon with what one does not see.

15.6 Difficulty of mental exertion and conceptual thinking

Philosophical exploration is not easy. In order to understand well the issues relating to religion and truth, one must engage in long and often complex learning. Most of us are not eager to confront such a difficult task and are, therefore, motivated to avoid realizing that any search for truth is necessary.

Moreover, my son, in order to adequately comprehend the large and sweeping issues related to the search for truth, and to see how various fields—including psychology, philosophy, sociology, anthropology, history, the hard sciences, and comparative religion, among others—have lessons to teach about the search for truth, it helps to have a natural bent for conceptual thinking. Many do not possess the easy ability to think in this way, but are, instead, more oriented to action, detail, and matters practical.[1] Since one must grapple with many large issues in the extensive search for truth, those not endowed with well-developed conceptual thinking are likely to give up quickly, or entirely avoid the subject—and hold on to beliefs less well examined.

A related point: Most of us are not sufficiently knowledgeable and intelligent to comfortably wrestle with the complexities of philosophy and religion—but are too prideful to admit this, even to ourselves. We therefore turn away from such an endeavor, for it would force us to confront our intellectual limitations. Thus, indolence and pride conspire in most to persuade us that we are in possession of sufficient understanding to be confident in our religious commitments, and have no need for further seeking.

15.7 Insufficient patience
My son, the search for truth frustrates those who demand instant results. The process is grueling and time consuming—for intellectual, emotional, and other reasons. Patience asks of us not to give up while the inner mind struggles with terrifying questions for which the outer mind has no quick answers. And such stoic forbearance is exceedingly uncommon.

15.8 Difficulty tolerating uncertainty and not knowing
Many have the inclination to feel convinced and assured, to arrive at firm conclusions. Such people find it difficult to tolerate a lack of certainty, at times

---

[1] A practical and detail-oriented mind has its strengths, too, in the search for truth—one of them being that it is less seduced into theoretical models, and is sometimes refreshingly unwilling to be talked out of what it sees, or doesn't see, with its own eyes. But when it comes to a broad-ranging, big-picture investigation into what we can know about religion and existential truth, the concrete thinking, detail-oriented mind is often at something of a disadvantage, because it is less able to quickly grasp and assess conceptual points. Yet I am in no way implying that conceptual thinkers are likely to seek truth. The conscious functioning of the intellect does not often escape the vise-grip of the unconscious mind as it keeps us from awareness of that which it fears we would find too deeply troubling. And, as with other kinds of ability, conceptual thinking can easily be misused—in this case, to create apologetics, theory-laden special pleading, and creative, perhaps impressive, but less than honest "answers."

even on mundane matters, but especially on deeply important ones. Not knowing can leave them feeling vulnerable, disoriented, irritated, even despairing and lost.

But in searching for truth, the urge toward conviction can be unhelpful. As the young cat sees a mouse's tail in every moving string, the man with a need for absolute assurance sees confident conclusions in every wisp of evidence that can be construed as friendly to his cause. My son, certainty is ever to be suspected on the path of truth, where the seeker's best friends are wayfaring, persistent questions, not settled, self-satisfied answers.

15.9 Fear of loneliness, of losing relationship with God

Many experience what they believe to be a relationship with God, from which they draw guidance, nurturing, and inner peace. Those among the religious who are anxious, sad, lonely, or have a history of troubled or unsatisfying relations with humans,[1] are, perhaps, especially likely to depend upon this sense of connection with the Divine, and to invest therein their keenest emotions—for it is the most reliably loving relationship many believe they will ever know.

And we all long to be loved, to be truly known and accepted, and to never be abandoned; we can all, then, feel drawn to formulate a relationship with God. Indeed, many of us were raised from infancy to do so, and have often turned, especially in moments of friendlessness, confusion, and pain, to this felt bond with the supernatural. And so, to scrutinize our religious beliefs risks a terrible loneliness; for it places our assumed relationship with God in fundamental jeopardy, and leaves us naked again to face the winds of abandonment. Should we wonder, then, that such scrutiny is so often avoided?

15.10 Practical considerations

And, my son, for some there are more obvious reasons to avoid challenging their beliefs. Many—and not only clergy—depend for a good part of their status and livelihood on fellow-religionists who approve of their lifestyle and professed

---

[1] This turning to God for connection, by those who find it difficult to maintain deeply satisfying relationships with humans, is somewhat similar to another strategy for satisfying a significant portion of one's instinct for connection, while avoiding the too-similar human with his too-seeing eyes and his too-sharp tongue: adopting a pet animal. The two strategies each have their benefits and drawbacks. The God option allows the believer to experience relationship with a Being of unlimited power, wisdom, and love, and also confers upon one a sense of virtue and superiority over non-believers; the pet animal option, for its part, allows one not only the sensory reassurance of a tangible companion and the emotional resonance of a fellow sentient creature, but also the high compliment of being needed, even obeyed or worshiped. And because these two strategies, while in some ways overlapping, provide different benefits, it should come as no surprise that many invest in both.

creed. For these people, the search for truth might put at risk social position and financial security. Moreover, many have invested some of their best years and energies in raising a religious family. While some in this situation may consciously choose to be dishonest about what they believe, most are simply guided by their unconscious minds to avoid thoughts that challenge their religious commitments and thus threaten their practical welfare—their family stability, their social connections, and their financial wellbeing.[1]

15.11 Naïve trust, and the yearning to follow leaders

My son, many trust their religious leaders deeply, and do not consider it a matter of personal responsibility to verify the truth of what these leaders teach. For some, this stems from the instinct for hierarchy, an instinct we may assume to be present in many members of any organized, social species. And such an instinct is often reinforced by parents who raise children to obey them and other authority figures, without resistance and without delay. Others feel an urgency to follow because the responsibility to make life's decisions weighs heavy upon them, and they are eager for somebody to relieve them of this burden. And the inclination to submit to authority can obscure for many the inconsistencies and mistakes of leaders' teachings. It can also blind them to the reasons it is unwise, even illogical, to rely on leaders for guidance on truth about religion. People do not often enough consider that different religious authorities teach very different lessons on the same matters; that each tradition advances arguments as to why it is superior to the others; and that if all people were to rely on their leaders, the vast majority would be wrong—by any religion's account.

15.12 Instinct for hierarchy extended to supernatural leadership

Some take the instinct for hierarchy and for following leadership even further. In their bones they so expect ever greater levels of hierarchy and leadership, that they naturally conceive of human leaders being led, in turn, by a supernatural force, in charge of the entire universe. This deep predisposition, based upon hierarchical instinct, toward belief in God constitutes an important unconscious reason some avoid challenging their religious traditions—for to give up this comforting belief that God is in charge, would leave them feeling disoriented and unsafe, ultimately leaderless in a vast and unpredictable universe.

And so strong in some is the longing to be led, that just as children are sometimes more frightened of being abandoned than of being abused, so do many religionists prefer even a harsh and demanding God to no God at all.

---

[1] As Upton Sinclair is credited with saying, "It is difficult to get a man to understand something when his salary depends upon his not understanding it."

15.13 Instinct for loyalty

Many find it difficult even to consider challenging inherited religious beliefs, because their very bones urge them toward loyalty to their family and people. When one hears one's native culture and commitments being attacked, one often feels the powerful instinct to rise up and defend them; and when the attack comes from within, the most effective defense is not even to notice it. And this is, perhaps, the favorite strategy of the unconscious mind. Thus, most people who are more than intelligent enough to see difficulties with their religious beliefs, seem not to be aware of such difficulties. For in the heart's calculus, problems never considered need not be solved; and where no solutions are wanting, one does not begin to dream of abandoning one's people.

15.14 Needing a reason for suffering

My son, many have endured long suffering, or have grieved and shuddered from early youth at the stories of martyrs and victims among their kin and tribe, and have consoled themselves by believing religion's claim that God has profound reasons why such suffering was necessary. If they entertain the possibility that religion is mistaken, they would be putting at risk the desperate consolation that all this suffering had transcendental meaning. Many cannot bear such a risk.

15.15 Expecting a heavenly reward

The devoutly religious have expended great efforts and resources over many years in obeying religious rules, attending worship services, contributing to religious charities, performing religious rituals, denying themselves forbidden pleasures, and bearing with grace various burdens and deprivations. After such extensive investment of the mind, the heart, the body, and the purse, one desperately hopes—no, one insists one *knows*—that religion is accurate in its teaching that God rewards the good deed, the noble sacrifice, the pious restraint, and sacred study and prayer—if not here, then in a life hereafter. And to challenge one's religious beliefs would force one to consider the possibility that no divine reward awaits—and, for some, this is a prospect too painful to ponder.

15.16 Demanding divine justice

My son, life has brought for many great indignity, injustice, and persecution. Such people are often desperate to believe religion's teaching that, soon or late, evil will be subjected to divine justice—and accounts will be squared.[1] Some

---

[1] The Bible, in both Old and New Testaments, gives voice to the age-old hope of the powerless and pious—that their agonies and humiliations will be supernaturally avenged. Deuteronomy 32:43, "...for he will avenge the blood of his servants...and will be

endured their suffering—and witnessed the mistreatment, the humiliation, the ravishing, even the torture and murder of loved ones—and did not have their spirits crushed, because they assured themselves that God would punish their persecutors, if not in this world, then in the next. To question religion is, among other things, to surrender this confidence in a final reckoning and retribution. For some, this is a price too terrible to consider.

15.17 Need to feel universally important

Religion assures us that we are important, that our lives count for something in the grand enterprise of the universe. And many religions teach, in one way or another, that humans are the princes of creation. Questioning religion means entertaining the possibility that we humans, as individuals and as a species, are not uniquely important to a Creator—indeed, that there may not be any Creator. Once raised with the belief of one's cosmic significance, putting such a belief at risk requires more courage and humility than most are willing to exert.

15.18 Fear of obliteration at death

The prospect of death is so disorienting, so painful and humiliating, that although it is inevitable, our minds work to prevent us from remaining aware of this shattering truth for long. But now and then, thoughts of death break through, and nighttime the head rests uneasy on the pillow, and daytime the hands fall weak in all their cunning labors, and we grow desperate for some elixir to relieve this terrible aching of the soul. And many religions offer just such a remedy—the promise of an afterlife in which one lives on after physical death. Those who have accustomed themselves to this expectation can find it too painful to consider the possibility that their religion is mistaken, and that upon death their consciousness may be utterly obliterated.[1]

---

merciful unto his land, and to his people." And Romans 12:19, refers to another passage of the Old Testament, and says, "Dearly beloved, avenge not yourselves, but rather give place unto wrath: for it is written, Vengeance is mine; I will repay, saith the Lord."

[1] This fear of death, though presumably universal to some degree, is greater in some individuals than in others, and in some cultures than in others—for any number of reasons. (It has been observed that while some religions were for centuries comforting their flocks with reassurances that the righteous will ultimately be revived to resume earthly life, other religions were laboring to teach their flocks how to avoid reincarnation and escape the wheel of life.) And although it is wise to recognize the human fear of death—and our remarkable tendency to repeatedly forget our inevitable demise—and worthwhile to reflect upon how such fear may influence various aspects of life, it strikes me as excessive, overly self-referenced, and insufficiently appreciating the vigor of the life instinct and its many manifestations, to see—as Ernest Becker did in his Pulitzer-Prize-winning book *The Denial of Death*—all of humanity as pervasively driven by such fears in

15.19 Desire to be reunited with dead loved ones

For many, when life's wares are weighed in the balance, no possessions or delights hold for them as much value as the people they have loved. But death has taken some of these, and will ultimately take them all, and this is one of man's deepest agonies. But many religions come to the rescue, it seems, in claiming that a heaven exists where one can be reunited with loved ones who have died. Those who have lost innocent children to death, or long-loved spouses, or dear parents, are often desperate to believe religion's teachings about such a heaven. For them, therefore, questioning religion can be almost unthinkable.

15.20 Fear of being wrong or feeling foolish

My son, people do not easily admit to being wrong, even on trivial matters. How much less likely they are to exert the profound humility and courage necessary to consider that they may be mistaken on the most important of matters—especially intelligent and accomplished people who have lived religiously all their lives! Most cannot bear this risk of existential humiliation, and studiously shy away from challenging their religious beliefs.

15.21 Need for mission, transcendence or inspiration

My son, more than merely the urge to feel important or to be oriented toward a worthwhile goal, some feel an emotional need to be inspired by a transcendently significant mission. These people are gripped by a desperate yearning to rise above the utilitarian ends and mundane tasks of practical living. Religions offer their followers such magnified meaning, and many of the most loving and sincere among the faithful rely heavily upon this for their emotional equilibrium. Daily life without the conviction of transcendent significance would be, for them, a terrible letdown, and many, therefore, strenuously avoid questioning the source of their glorious inspirations.

15.22 Need for reassurance and direction on the overwhelming and the unknown

My son, religion offers a ready answer, or at least a ready set of prescribed behaviors, for those moments and events when many feel puzzled or overwhelmed. Marriage, childbirth, illness, suffering, the onset of poverty or wealth,

---

daily life, and all human heroism as "first and foremost a reflex of the terror of death." For surely a quick glance at the ambitious projects and selfless sacrifices of members of other species—species who cannot foresee, and therefore cannot fear, their own death—teaches that the terror of death is far from the only animator of heroism. And surely one does not go about curing the denial of death by instead denying the urge toward life.

the unknown future, the meaning of life, war, the death of loved ones, the afterlife, and so many other challenging or confusing issues and passages, are readily handled by religion—through prayer, blessing, ritual, ceremony, obligation, reassurance, theology, and more—so that man need not be dashed naked against the unpadded granite of tragedy and deprivation, nor must he behold without intermediary the often forbidding countenance of unembroidered reality. Most are terrified of giving up sacred cushionings and embellishments, and will not think any thoughts that call their religious beliefs into question.

15.23 Need to worship the powerful: a social instinct

My son, in all social species, including our own, some have the instinct to dominate, but many have the instinct to submit and worship the powerful. This instinct results in more efficient group behavior, as leadership is usually followed. It is also of survival value to individuals, because the submissive are less likely than the assertive to be hurt, banished or killed by the leader; instead, they might hope for his protection and favor. Thus we observe social species as diverse as wolves, baboons, and bees displaying dutiful or worshipful submission to their leaders or betters. The human species seems to share this instinct, and—we may speculate—many individuals channel it to the worship of God.[1]

---

[1] Thomas Carlyle in his *Heroes and Hero Worship* speaks to this issue when he says: "No nobler feeling than this of admiration for one higher than himself dwells in the breast of man. It is to this hour, and at all hours, the vivifying influence in man's life. Religion I find stands upon it; not Paganism only, but far higher and truer religions—all religion hitherto known. Hero-worship, heartfelt prostrate admiration, submission, burning, boundless, for a noblest godlike Form of Man—is not that the germ of Christianity itself? The greatest of all Heroes is One—whom we do not name here! Let sacred silence meditate on that sacred matter; you will find it the ultimate perfection of a principle extant throughout man's whole history on earth. Or coming into lower, less unspeakable provinces, is not all Loyalty akin to religious Faith also? Faith is loyalty to some inspired Teacher, some spiritual Hero. And what therefore is loyalty proper, the life-breath of all society, but an effluence of Hero-worship, submissive admiration for the truly great? Society is founded on Hero-worship. All dignities of rank, on which human association rests, are what we may call a Hero-archy (Government of Heroes)—or a Hierarchy, for it is 'sacred' enough withal! The Duke means Dux, Leader; King is Kon-ning, Kan-ning, Man that knows or cans. Society everywhere is some representation, not insupportably inaccurate, of a graduated Worship of Heroes—reverence and obedience done to men really great and wise."

And though Carlyle's views and actions were in some cases offensively wedded to the notion of superior and inferior groups of humans, this only speaks more strongly to the inclination in the hearts of many men—and, we may presume, among them some who originated or perpetuated religions—to see or conjure, in earth and heaven, notions of

Indeed, in human beings, the social instinct toward submission finds a particularly convenient expression in worshiping the supernatural, for two reasons. First, surrendering to a transcendent force provides a more intense experience of feeling overpowered, and thus increases the sense of instinctual satisfaction and safety in submitting to and worshiping power. Second, it can even help prevent the loss of status and face, the price usually associated with social beings submitting to and worshiping superiors—for in worshiping God we are not humbling ourselves to other humans.[1] Thus, my son, for many, questioning belief in God would put at risk an arrangement that has long been satisfying their deep, though likely unconscious, social need for submission.[2]

15.24 Desire for good news: Somebody is making it all work out well

Many among the religious reassure themselves that regardless of how confusing or worrisome—even agonizing—are their circumstances, God is arranging all things for the best. This belief can impart feelings of safety, confidence and well-

---

inferior and superior, and to heap scorn upon the former and fall prostrate before the latter.

[1] Yet, ironically, this worship inclination which may have its roots in social instinct, at times comes full circle when submission to God is turned into submission to man—when religious or political leaders have persuaded men and women to give over their labors, their fortunes, even their bodies and lives, to the service of a king or a pope or a prophet or a sage said to be favored of God—or even said to *be* a god.

[2] Though perhaps scandalous to those whose education or imagination on these matters is limited, the instinct toward submission—or its counterpart, dominance—manifests for some in another intense realm: sexuality. Most who feel these urges are, perhaps, too timid or propriety-bound to enact such dramas, but in their fantasies they may thrill to encounters with power—whether in the role of conqueror or conquered.

Perhaps not surprisingly, some early religions combined these two intense realms—the religious and the sexual, and enacted rites of sexual service to gods—or to priests and shamans, their often eager representatives. And in this early expectation of congress between "the sons of God" and "the daughters of men" we find the likely roots for not only that unusual passage in Genesis 6, but also for many lands' legends and mythologies peopled with heroes, monsters, and saviors, the products of such unions. And we might presume, too, that the many rulers whose subjects considered them gods had legions of fawning worshippers eager to provide them primal satisfaction, and that this commerce was not as one-sided as it may seem, for it has long been noted that the largest sex organ is the brain—so the felt experience of mating with, and bringing pleasure to, a deity is likely to have been a highlight of many a mortal's life. And some approximation of such intensity may be seen in how eagerly some "worship" a new love—or fawn over celebrity actors and musicians, and fall over themselves, frantically offering their bodies in the desperate wish to bond with the charming or the elect—though these latter-day objects of amorous worship, being unambiguously mortal, may never quite equal the intensity of gratification some ancients may have felt when giving themselves to their gods.

being—or at least of consolation and hope. Thus, many are strongly averse to challenging their religion, the source of this happy reassurance.[1]

15.25 Experience of religious ecstasy

My son, some, through religion, taste moments not only of joyous worship, but of mystical union and ecstasy. While perhaps not felt by most of the religious, such experiences are not rare. Our minds can create a sense of ecstasy when contemplating God, or when involved in intense ritual. And some believers of every religion, and of many cults, have felt this natural, mind-born intensity and bliss.[2] Those who have been visited by such powerful states, and have interpreted them to confirm their religious beliefs, are strongly motivated to maintain these beliefs—not only because they seem to have been proved accurate in such dramatic and intense fashion, but also that they may be spared the shame and disappointment of reassessing the meaning of their ecstasies— likely the most compelling experiences of their lives.

15.26 Distraction, spectacle, and a break from the mundane

At times, all of us yearn for diversion and escape, in one or more of its variations. Crude and direct forms of such excursions of the mind are found in wine and whiskey and all manner of substances smoked or swallowed or otherwise introduced to the body. But circuses and performances, shows and theatre, storytellers and imaginative books—and many other avenues of fascination and

---

[1] This finding solace in the conviction of a Good Shepherd is the theme of the Bible's well-loved 23rd Psalm, and has calmed and encouraged countless among the faithful through the millennia. For another example, this one only a few centuries old, Joseph Addison, in his essay *Household Superstitions*, criticizes those who are gripped by fears, and then says: "I know but one way of fortifying my soul against these gloomy presages and terrors of mind; and that is, by securing to myself the friendship and protection of that Being who disposes of events and governs futurity. He sees, at one view, the whole thread of my existence, not only that part of it which I have already passed through, but that which runs forward into all the depths of eternity. When I lay me down to sleep, I recommend myself to His care; when I awake, I give myself up to His direction. Amidst all the evils that threaten me, I will look up to Him for help, and question not but He will either avert them, or turn them to my advantage. Though I know neither the time nor the manner of the death I am to die, I am not at all solicitous about it; because I am sure that he knows them both, and that He will not fail to comfort and support me under them."

We may easily see that such all-serving confidence, which cannot be procured among earthly vendors at any price, would be far too dear for many to consider sacrificing for what they may see as so meager a virtue as intellectual honesty.

[2] William James in his classic *Varieties of Religious Experience* provides interesting examples of such states.

interest—have excited the fancy of the human mind, and served well the purpose of entertaining and diverting it from the burdens and sufferings, or at least the boring familiarity, of life's daily routines.[1]

And religion has been one of the more successful forms of diversion and pageantry. From its miracle-laden, mystery-filled scriptures, to its soulful choirs and sacred chants; from its grand houses of worship to the passionate oratory of its clergy; from its holidays with special foods and rituals to worship services where all go decorated in best attire; from its call to ideals to its promises and warnings of ecstasies and agonies in eternal life hereafter; from its prayers calling upon a transcendent God to its many community roles and titles and ceremonies enabling the individual to escape his solitary, mundane self; from its Sabbaths and holy days fixed to the calendar of every week and season to its role in intensifying life's passages of wedding and war and all else between birth and death, religion has, in these ways and others, constituted a most pervasive and effective avenue for shaking off the dust of common drudgery, and participating for an interval in exciting, ennobling, or at least distracting, spectacle.[2]

15.27 The urge to feel superior

Religions often teach that their believers are the elite—more deserving, more favored, or more blessed than other humans—the infidels, the benighted, the unbelievers, the unchosen. And this feeling of superiority has helped many weather the inevitable difficulties and indignities life throws in every mortal's path. This conceit, then, is difficult to part with, or even to put at risk, by critically examining one's religious beliefs.

---

[1] Marx famously wrote in his essay, *A Criticism of the Hegelian Philosophy of Right*, "Religion is the moan of the oppressed creature, the sentiment of a heartless world, as it is the spirit of spiritless conditions. It is the opium of the people." And on a related theme, though focusing more on entertainment and spectacle than on comfort and anesthesia, Emerson said in his essay and lecture, *New England Reformers*: "A man of good sense but of little faith, whose compassion seemed to lead him to church as often as he went there, said to me that he liked 'to have concerts, and fairs, and churches, and other public amusements go on.'" "I am afraid," continued Emerson, "the remark is too honest, and comes from the same origin as the maxim of the tyrant, 'If you would rule the world quietly, you must keep it amused.'"

[2] Indeed, one may wonder whether the decline of religion in the modern age is related in part to the growing variety of easily accessible secular amusements and spectacles: books and magazines, recorded music, radio, television, movies and films, electronic games and technology's many other contrivances, have filled our eyes and ears and hearts with such glare and noise and intrigue that we no longer hunger, in the same numbers and to the same degree, for the stimulation traditionally offered by church and creed. And, conversely, no longer haunted and amazed by gods, we bring forth alternatives.

15.28 Lack of original thinking

Man, being a social creature, is greatly influenced in his thinking by the thoughts of his contemporaries—loved ones, friends, neighbors and peers.[1] And since so few around him think deeply and courageously about religion and philosophy,[2] he does not get the message from his social environment that thinking into these matters is important or desirable. Indeed, he gets the opposite message: that such investigation is to be avoided. And not only is intellectual independence rare, thus unlikely to be learned from one's social environment, it is to some degree antithetical to society—for conformity is a necessary tendency for most within any herd species, including our own, and the bones hold forth with such unified counsel and their terrible voices drown out all else.

15.29 Orientation toward immediate gratification

Much of what many do on most days involves acting for immediate gratification—pursuing benefit or pleasure, or avoiding loss or pain. For most, philosophically challenging one's religious beliefs neither offers much short-term pleasure, nor prevents much short-term pain. To the contrary, such inquiry is

---

[1] Though when taking our own measure we prefer to see ourselves as exceptions, when we reflect upon our species overall, most can see how rare is truly independent thinking. Oscar Wilde said in *De Profundis*: "It is tragic how few people ever 'possess their souls' before they die…Most people are other people. Their thoughts are someone else's opinions, their lives a mimicry, their passions a quotation."

Yet ironically, Wilde, in that very paragraph, was in the midst of a pages-long, wildly partisan idealizing of the Christian Savior—attributing many distinctions and perfections to the figure of Jesus, who, he said, eclipsed by far anybody and anything before or since—with the very next sentence after the passage quoted above saying, "Christ was not merely the supreme Individualist, but he was the first in History," and later, "out of the carpenter's shop at Nazareth had come a personality infinitely greater than any made by myth or legend…" After several more pages of finding various forms of incomparable uniqueness in Jesus, he even uses the following crude argument to dismiss inconvenient evidence of great men who lived earlier than Jesus: He writes, "Of course, just as there are false dawns before the dawn itself…so there were Christians before Christ."

Do we see individuality of thought in such unbalanced assessments, or do we not rather see a man who, though he ostentatiously rebelled against some of its norms, was deeply influenced by his culture and some of its obvious biases, a man who if raised in an Islamic culture would likely have held forth with a similarly immoderate eulogy of the Prophet Mohammad, or if raised in the Far East might have done the same for the Buddha or Confucius—and do we not see a man who, at least in this important case (though, to be fair, he was writing this from prison, and in a state of suffering; and it may not be representative of his more settled thinking) does not "possess his soul," a man whose "thoughts are someone else's opinions" and whose "passions [are] a quotation"?

[2] For a variety of reasons, including the many listed in this section.

likely to *cause* short-term pain. It is only the unusual person who is driven by a need for authenticity stronger than his aversion to humiliation and disorientation, and truly feels the urge to clarify and investigate deepest beliefs.

15.30 Feeling unworthy of challenging tradition and society

To many it does not even occur to seriously question their tradition because they do not feel sufficiently wise, worthy, or authoritative to think for themselves on such ancient and imposing beliefs. Unconsciously, they think: Who am I to have an independent opinion on such issues? Surely the scholars of my religion have dealt with these questions, and in their wisdom have provided satisfactory answers. Thus, insufficient self-regard can be an obstacle to intellectual honesty.

15.31 Having deeply invested in religion.

My son, many of the religious have paid so high a price for their beliefs—in pleasures denied, efforts expended, independence foregone, and anguish endured—that this costly allegiance settles, over the decades, deep in the bones, atop the already formidable memories of parents and elders, legends of holy men and ancestors, and tales of miracle and revelation foundational to sacred tradition. As parents value a child increasingly the more they labor for its welfare, so the very extent of the sacrifice and investment in religion leads some to value it almost beyond the possibility of surrender. Therefore, questions do not occur to them and, if they do, are quickly put to rest by means or arguments they would never consider persuasive if advanced in the cause of another religion. Well has it been said: "The value of a thing sometimes lies not in what one attains with it, but in what one pays for it—what it *costs* us."[1]

*****

And so, my son, we have spoken of more than a score and ten ways in which we are dissuaded from honest thinking on matters of ultimate truth. But even such a list of blindnesses and evasions is only a beginning. Seek with open eyes, and you shall discover many more; for the thoughts of man are complex and varied, his hungers and fears numerous, his imagination is unbounded, and his heart ever longing for comfort. Who, then, shall number his means or fathom his motives—who shall seek out the caves in which he takes shelter or follow the shadows into which he retreats—in fleeing the unflattering light of truth?

---

[1] Nietzsche, in *Twilight of the Idols*, said this in a different context—in a discussion of freedom—and with a somewhat different intention.

IV. EXAMINING CLAIMS FOR GOD AND RELIGION

16. What do we mean by the word "God"?

Then a lawyer said: If we are to speak about God we must first clarify our terms. What do you mean when you use the word God? Do you mean the Christian conception of God, the Islamic or the Jewish conception of God—and, if one of those, the God concept of which of their denominations or sects? Or maybe you mean one of the concepts held by those innumerable peoples who have worshiped, or today worship, many gods—or one of the numerous different concepts of God held by the mixed multitude of metaphysicians and theologians. Which of all these do you mean?

And the sage replied: My brother, you ask well. It is easy to mistakenly assume that we all refer to the same meaning when we say "God." But humans have used the word God, or gods, to denote many different beings—among others—carved statues,[1] powerful human-like creatures, invisible spirits, deceased ancestors, animals, groves of trees, Zeus, Yahweh, Jesus, and the omnipotent and omniscient Creator of the universe. And notions of the divine have differed in many other ways, too; all manner of gods and goddesses, of varying powers and personalities, have peopled the lore of diverse nations, and animated their worship rites and festivals. And some have bowed to a myriad of gods while others have not only limited their worship to one God, but believed that God can be but One.

So that our words may be relevant to the broad range of religious beliefs in the human experience, yet also reflect what is of greatest interest to most gathered here today, we will not restrict ourselves to any one understanding of God in our discussions, but we shall—when using the term "God" in the singular form—generally be referring to the biblical Creator-God, worshiped by Christianity, Judaism, and Islam. And unless I specify otherwise, or the context makes it clear, my brother, when I use the terms God or gods I refer to one or

---

[1] Consistent with some biblical claims—and contrary to some who wished to conform ancient people's practices to modern rational sensibilities—evidence points to the conclusion that some, even if not all, societies that used carved figures, idols, in their worship rites, did indeed consider these objects to be gods. See James Kugel's interesting and accessible book, *The God of Old*, where in the context of discussing ancient Israelite biblical conceptions of God, he speaks of surrounding cultures' beliefs, too. See chapter 4, and especially note 77 with the heading, "these images were not described or treated as mere representations of the gods; they were actually said to be the gods" where he elaborates and provides references.

more supernatural beings with awareness, who may have created, or may have supernatural influence over, part or all of our universe. And as we deal with various questions and arguments relating to God, we may take a closer look at precisely what sort of God is being discussed in a particular case.

17. Argument that the term "God" is too vague to mean anything, and the phrase "God exists" makes no sense, so it is pointless to discuss God

And a young atheist said: The first question to ask is whether God exists. But not only is the term "God" too vague and elastic to be useful in discussion, how are we going to speak about whether a deity exists? In what conceivable way could the term "exist" apply to a non-physical being, which is what religion claims God to be? It could not apply, so the whole discussion is pointless.

And the sage said: My son, you present a vigorous and interesting challenge. Yet let us examine the matter carefully, and I will offer a different perspective.

I remind you, my son, that arguments from ignorance, or from poverty of imagination, are no valid arguments.[1] Indeed, much of what we now employ daily was once inconceivable. If you lived a thousand years ago, and overheard someone say, "Perhaps it is possible for a person to speak and the sound of his voice be heard on the other side of the world," or "Perhaps it is possible for a wagon-car to travel, even uphill and for hours at a time, without being pulled by any human or beast," might not an impatient empiricist also have objected by saying, "That makes no sense: In what conceivable way could a voice possibly travel so far, and in what conceivable way could a wagon-car move on its own?" Thus, one might have said it was pointless to even consider those possibilities. Yet today, millions of voices travel around the world daily, and millions of vehicles travel without being pulled by humans or horses or oxen or mules.[2]

---

[1] By the same token, arguments from ignorance, or poverty of imagination, are no more valid when used by religionists—who often insist they know there is a God because they cannot imagine how else the universe with all its complexity would have come to be. Such intuitions and general impressions may be just cause for keeping one's mind open to the possibility of a Creator, and continuing to educate oneself further on the arguments and evidence of all sides to such debates—but incredulity by itself is no argument, especially on matters that lie beyond the easy reach of the human mind, everything from issues relating to the vast expanses of space (can we easily conceive of the distance involved in one light year, much less billions of light years?) to theories on the possible beginnings of the universe and the development of life.

[2] This argument is not to be confused with someone arguing for belief in religion's miracles on the rationalization that "after all, they may be true." I agree that nearly anything "may" be true, but belief that far-fetched propositions such as biblical supernatural miracles *are* true is quite a different, and unwarranted, conclusion. The question of whether there is a Creator God, represents, to my mind, a more balanced question than

Moreover, if while sitting in a house one night we were to behold a bright glow through the window, and a profusion of colors and shapes, would you consider me unreasonable if I asked, "Do you think someone caused all that beauty and light?" And here we sit in the perpetual night of our creature-bound limitations, and glimpse through mortality's dark glass all manner of colorful mysteries and tantalizing lights—is it, then, unreasonable to ask whether some great power caused all that we see, and the many things we surely do not see?

And, as mentioned, my son, when we speak about God, we need not limit our discussion to any one meaning of the word, so long as we clarify which meaning of the word God we have in mind, in cases where not doing so would lead to confusion. And unless I specify otherwise, or the context makes it clear, when I use the terms God and gods I refer to one or more supernatural beings with awareness, who may have created, or may have supernatural influence over, part or all of our universe. And we need not have a very specific conception of just what a possible God would be, or even how He could be, in order for us to wonder if some such great power or powers have some type of existence, some kind of awareness, and some form of influence over humans. For such a being or beings would necessarily be far more powerful and complex than we are and, being supernatural, would not be limited by our conceptions, which are bound by nature's laws. Thus, it is no proof of atheism that we struggle to name or describe the possible Creator about which we wonder. The humble question is neither surprised nor ashamed that it is not an answer.

My son, two wild dogs that had never seen a human came upon an abandoned city. They sniffed cautiously at great buildings and at mounds of unfamiliar rubbish, and trotted about old walkways, and waded through decorative ponds. Finally, they came upon a pile of clothing and for the first time caught a strong whiff of the human scent. One said, "Ruff, ruff, ggrrrrrugchh," and the other said, "Grghhh, ghruff!" And they wagged their tales and said nothing more.

My son, simply because their vocabulary is limited—as are their conceptions—must we conclude that what they have no precise terms to express does

---

whether supernatural miracles occurred during the course of human history. After all, whether the complex universe we know came about through the agency of a Creator or without any supernatural aid, it is a process well beyond the range of human ken. We have no experiential frame of reference within which to judge whether any hypothesis for the universe's origin, or lack thereof, is likely to be true—for we have not witnessed entire universes coming into being. But on the matter of miracles within human history—of the kind taught by the Bible—our daily experience, and the shared human history of hundreds of years of scientifically aware generations debunking the superstitious beliefs of their forebears, and of their contemporary primitives, should legitimately lead us to consider it doubtful that supernatural miracles ever occurred in any human age.

not exist? Do not humans wield written language, build grand and subtle structures, invent astonishingly complex machines, and discern the conceptual laws of science and mathematics, the very pillars upholding the universe? And if the dogs sense that there exist creatures of great and varied powers, but, being dogs, can only bark and grunt and whine, and cannot fully conceive, much less express, just what may be the nature of such beings and such powers, must they assume their curiosity and wonderment at humans are but foolish illusions?

No, although the dog is constitutionally incapable of understanding much of what a human does, and is—consider, for example, the notions, inconceivable to the mind of a dog, of flying across an ocean on a motorized airship, or of writing a poem, or advancing a theory and achieving influence on future generations by means other than biological reproduction—the intelligent dog is entitled to wonder, so to speak, at humans, and not precipitously conclude that nothing is relevant, indeed, nothing can exist, beyond his own canine conceptions.

My son: Our universe is not perfectly analogous to the abandoned city of which I spoke, for the abandoned city we know—though the dogs do not know—to have been built by humans, while the precise origin of our universe remains, to the honest, a mystery. Yet even though when we wonder about a Creator and attempt to think clearly about such matters we have great difficulty imagining, and even greater difficulty expressing in coherent words, just what the term God would mean, and just what mode or form or kind or nature of existence would be His, this not only does not prove there to be no Creator God, it need not even make it more difficult to believe that this possible God may have communicated with humans, or may be able to understand us when we attempt to communicate with Him.

To be clear: I do not condone religious people claiming to know who God is, and what God wants—or even that a God exists—for none of the religions of which we know have responsible evidence to support such conclusions. And along with dogs who insist that no being can do anything, or be anything, beyond canine conceptions, dogs who insist without responsible evidence that their canine brains know the nature and will of those responsible for all the mysterious sights and smells in the discovered city—especially if they have never seen nor interacted with any such beings and cannot honestly know any other dog to have seen or interacted with such beings—these are misguided, too.

In short, my son: That religion's answers on these matters have usually been too much confident and too little honest does not make her questions pointless. We can indeed with good sense wonder, and with honest humility refrain from hasty conclusions, about whether there exists a God.

18. Argument that the design of nature proves a compassionate God

Then a gentle nurse spoke, saying: Does not the Lord's mercy overwhelm you, when you see how many are cured of illness, or saved from calamity? And look around you at the world, and see how it is designed with kindness and love. Trees give us fruit, and the earth our daily bread. See how the rain quenches our thirst, and helps our food to grow. See how delightful are the flowers of spring, and how beautiful the leaves of autumn. Surely all this could only have been created by a compassionate and loving God!

And the sage replied: My dear sister, blessed are those who share your life— for eyes that see but kindness often seek ways to love. Gentle soul, would that the entire universe were as nurturing as you, healing without savaging, and bequeathing but benevolence. Instead, when we look about us, a landscape of kindness and beauty is far from all we see. For the jaws of privation ever nip at the heels of repose, and death's many claws slash repeatedly at life's tender throat.

If the world has been designed, can we honestly say the designer was concerned with preventing suffering and pain? As unpleasant as it may be to observe, do not many species eat only by chasing and killing, or otherwise bringing pain and discomfort to, other living beings? And although it offers various pleasures and sundry delights, is life not designed in such a manner that misery is not uncommon, and agony not rare? What of the mother zebra who watches her baby slaughtered and devoured by lions, or the mother bird flapping about in distressed frenzy, unable to save her eggs from the canopy's climbing marauders? What of the wildebeest calf, his mother killed by hyenas, wandering about gnawed by hunger and chased by terror, rejected by the herd to a fate of slow starvation on the baking savanna, or savage butchery in a predator's jaws? And what of the mother monkey who sees her baby fall from a high branch to the jungle floor, and for days desperately attempts to awaken his dead body?

My sister, pray tell who it was that created the lion, the tiger, the jaguar, the leopard, the cheetah, the hyena, the wolf, the fox, the eagle, the owl, the hawk, the alligator, the cobra, the mamba, the crocodile, the shark, the barracuda, the piranha, the fire ant armies, the predatory and parasitic wasps, the spiders, the scorpions, the mosquito swarms, the lice, the ticks, the fleas, the parasitic worms, and the ten thousand other agents of poison, fang, claw, and beak—of all sizes and habitats—whose hungry bellies can only be sated by killing, or bringing suffering upon, other living beings?[1] Could not even you and I, severely limited

---

[1] A whimsical expression of the many layers of life eating off of life is credited to the 19th century British mathematician Augustus De Morgan. He wrote:

mortals, conceive of a more compassionate way to maintain a balance of species—without all the chasing and killing and infecting, without all the terror and pain?[1]

And what of the multitudes of humans and other creatures savaged by all manner of other natural forces—by fire, by frost, by earthquake, by hurricane, by tidal wave, by disease, by drowning and by drought? Yes, there are rains that nourish, but also floods that obliterate; gentle sunshine calls forth life, but cruel suns come, too, beating down and searing all into parched death. The sea provides travel and expansive view, but numberless souls are early extinguished by her colossal waves and unforgiving reefs. The earth provides the solid ground upon which we build our homes, and the fertile soil from which we draw our food; but when the earth shakes and houses fall, shall we forget how many innocents are crushed? And majestic mountains rise high and raise our spirits too, yet who has counted the number of men overtaken and roasted by the molten fire of mountains' fury? And how many multitudes, even blameless babes, have suffered and perished from nature's many diabolical diseases, where the only mercy shown was the final stroke of death? No, my sister, whatever justifications the devout may attempt, one thing is certain: The design of nature does not reflect pure compassion and love, in any normal sense of these words. Yes, it allows for much good—but it insists upon much evil, too.[2]

Great fleas have little fleas
Upon their backs to bite 'em
And these again have lesser fleas,
And so—ad infinitum.

[1] "I don't know if God exists," said Jules Renard, "but it would be better for His reputation if He didn't." But Woody Allen had a more forgiving, though not more religious, attitude when he said, "God is not evil. He's just an underachiever."

[2] In every age many have seen nature as encompassing good and bad. Pliny the Elder, the ancient Roman, is credited with saying, "It is far from easy to determine whether Nature has proved to man a kind parent or a merciless stepmother." Still, over the centuries and millennia there have also been some—poets, romantics, idealists, and the like—who saw nature as essentially good, beautiful, and kind. Yet theirs is an assessment seemingly at odds with unfiltered observation.

John Burroughs, the American naturalist, writing in Chapter II of his early-20th-century work, *Accepting The Universe*, addressed the issue and said: "When Wordsworth declared himself a worshiper of Nature, was he thinking of Nature as a whole, or only of an abridged and expurgated Nature—Nature in her milder and more beneficent aspects? Was it not the Westmoreland nature of which he was a worshiper?—a sweet rural Nature, with grassy fells and murmuring streams and bird-haunted solitudes? What would have been his emotion in the desert, in the arctic snows, or in the pestilential forests and jungles of the tropics? Very likely, just what the emotion of most of us would be…The Nature that to Wordsworth never betrays us, and to Milton was 'wise and frugal,' is a

And why is it that we consider a man a monster if he plans the destruction of several thousand civilians—but we do not hold similarly accountable a God who designed a system resulting in the deaths of a hundred and fifty thousand innocents in one violent incursion of the massive sea? Or when a hundred thousand perish when the earth shakes; or when millions of children's lives are taken in one year alone by famine and disease?

And the survivors, the lucky ones—those who haven't fallen early prey or victim to all the perils and evils of life's gauntlet—what awaits them after all, but decline and death, the loss of all for which they have toiled, all for which they have endured. Well has it been said:[1] "Kill one man, and you are a murderer; kill millions of men, and you are a conqueror; kill everyone, and you are God."

My tender sister, I do not wish to seem ungrateful for all the bounty and beauty life offers. But in seeking truth we must be willing to see—and, at times, speak[2]—all we can of what is, and not only what our kind inclinations wish there

---

humanized, man-made Nature. The nature we know and wrest our living from, and try to drive sharp bargains with, is of quite a different order."

(Incidentally, Burroughs then goes on to explain the view of nature as God's art, and that an artist thinks not of good and bad but of lights and shadows, etc. But this seems to be just another arbitrary, anthropomorphic conceptualization, in the style of the apologists, theologians, and poets whom he criticized. And for purposes of our discussion, surely traditional religion—which Burroughs was not there defending—or its earnest advocates like the gentle nurse in our text, would not find it satisfying to explain away nature's indifference to suffering as a reflection of its Creator being more focused on art, and light and shadow, then on the agonies of those with whom He makes "art.")

[1] Attributed to Jean Rostand.

[2] In his heroic and evocative *Atalanta in Calydon*, Algernon Charles Swinburne has the chorus deal with such matters and say (beginning at line 1158, and in a version I have abridged):

> Yea, with thine hate, O God, thou hast covered us...
> Thou hast kissed us, and hast smitten; thou hast laid
> Upon us with thy left hand life...
> And with thy right hand laid upon us death...
> Thou hast made sweet springs for all the pleasant streams,
>   In the end thou hast made them bitter with the sea.
> Thou hast fed one rose with dust of many men;
>   Thou hast marred one face with fire of many tears;
> Thou hast taken love, and given us sorrow again;
>   With pain thou hast filled us full to the eyes and ears.
> Therefore because thou art strong, our father, and we
>   Feeble; and thou art against us, and thine hand
> Constrains us in the shallows of the sea
>   And breaks us at the limits of the land...
> Because thou art over all who are over us;

were. Nature is far from an always friendly garden. Although she is, at times, good and satisfying, and offers us pleasure and beauty, too—she is also often agonizing, and exceedingly ugly. Even when the sun, the seas, the winds, the rains, the earth, the cold, the heat, the fires, the diseases, the predators, and the parasites are not doing violence, Mother Nature is far from all-loving with her children. She weakens, shrivels, and degrades them with the ravages of age—and in the end kills every last one.[1]

19. Sub-argument that what seems evil to our limited minds is actually good; therefore God is good.

But the gentle nurse persisted and said: All this seeming evil and pain is truly good, only our minds are not able to perceive it accurately because of our human limitations. If our minds were but capable, we would understand it all to be good. Sometimes from the darkest abyss comes forth the brightest light, and from the deepest wound the most profound healing. Therefore, even though to our eyes the universe does not seem compassionate, it actually is. And God its creator is perfectly compassionate.[2]

> Because thy name is life and our name death;
> Because thou art cruel and men are piteous,
>   And our hands labour and thine hand scattereth;
> Lo, with hearts rent and knees made tremulous,
>   Lo, with ephemeral lips and casual breath,
>   At least we witness of thee ere we die
> That these things are not otherwise, but thus...
>   That each man in his heart sigheth, and saith,
>   That all men even as I
> All we are against thee, against thee, O God most high.

And even if we choose conciliation or decorum over angry grieving, and do not go so far as Swinburne's text either in saying that (a possible) God hates us, or in accosting this Creator with enmity and desperate defiance, we may still give an honest accounting of life and the universe as we know it—that it is at best a bittersweet affair of tragedy and joy, and much in-between, and not any vision of paradise nor any reflection of perfect love.

[1] Goethe says: "Nature! Surrounded by her and locked in her clasp, we are powerless to pull away, and powerless to draw near. Without asking, without warning, she snatches us up into the whirl of her dance and hurries us along—until weary, we fall from her arms."

[2] This inclination to see the substance or seed of strength in weakness, victory in defeat, love in persecution, even life in death, is found throughout history and across cultures. It peeks out as a consistent theme from the Old Testament, at least indirectly, in that the younger and weaker, from a state of danger and despair, often reverse the natural course and outdo the senior and more powerful—Isaac is barely spared from the binding,

And the sage said: My dear sister, there are indeed times when paradox is king—when circumstances birth their opposites, when plenty is the son of famine, and joy the daughter of sorrow; when the race goes not to the swift, nor the battle to the strong. But exceptions do not disprove general rules. And on the matter of which we speak, the general rule remains that suffering is bad, does not necessarily lead to anything better, and that a world with a great amount of suffering does not reflect the handiwork of a perfectly compassionate Creator.

Moreover, my sister, have you not abandoned your original claim? You no longer ask us to observe with our own eyes the evidence of a compassionate God. Rather, you now concede that our eyes see in nature not only beauty and nurturing, but what appears to be ugliness and cruelty, too—only you would have us distrust our own perceptions.

Furthermore, could one not make the opposite argument? If we cannot trust our own eyes and ears when they perceive nature to be inflicting upon us

---

and then chosen over Ishmael; Jacob is in grave danger from Esau, but is spared and chosen over him; Joseph is raised to the position of viceroy from the straits of slavery and prison, and ultimately lords over his older brothers and rescues them from famine; the Israelites are raised up from the slavery and persecution of Egypt into being God's holy nation of grand destiny, and chosen over the great civilization and long-established culture that was Egypt, and then over the Canaanites, whose land they are given; and David is chosen over his older, taller brothers, and eventually over King Saul who had sought to kill him. And, much later, too, Israel's defeats were interpreted by its prophets as signs of God's involvement with them—and, therefore, of their greatness as a people even when vanquished and humiliated.

But in Christianity we have the notion of victory in defeat elevated to an even more prominent position—death on the cross like a common criminal being transformed, as believers see it, into the culmination of supernatural compassion, the high point of history, and the salvation of all mankind. Though the New Testament has Jesus himself complaining, "My God, my God, why hast thou forsaken me?" this notion of one's greatest flowering coming with one's apparent destruction—of the seemingly bad being the best of the good—has been driven deep into the Christian psyche, and can be found in innumerable manifestations not only in religious teaching but in literature and art, too. Let us snatch a quick example from *Amiel's Journal*, where, presumably after great suffering, in his October 27, 1853 entry he writes: "I thank Thee, my God, for the hour that I have just passed in Thy presence. Thy will was clear to me; I measured my faults, counted my griefs, and felt Thy goodness toward me. I realized my own nothingness, Thou gavest me Thy peace. In bitterness there is sweetness; in affliction, joy; in submission, strength; in the God who punishes, the God who loves. To lose one's life that one may gain it, to offer it that one may receive it, to possess nothing that one may conquer all, to renounce self that God may give Himself to us, how impossible a problem, and how sublime a reality! No one truly knows happiness who has not suffered, and the redeemed are happier than the elect."

deprivation and evil, why should we trust ourselves when it seems that nature bestows upon us beneficence and good? Could not one, arguing for an evil creator—or for a malevolent universe with no creator at all—as easily claim that whatever seems good or compassionate in nature is merely an illusion, and that if our minds were but capable we would understand it all to be evil? My sister, I do not believe nature is, on the whole, malevolent and evil, but is not such an argument as persuasive as the argument that nature—and, therefore, its possible Creator—is entirely compassionate and good?

In short, the world comprises much beauty and offers much pleasure; yet involves much pain, much horror, and much gruesomeness, too—and, in the end, death for all. Thus, from the design of nature one might postulate a creator more concerned with establishing a complex balance of species than with preventing the suffering, or ensuring the safety and wellbeing, of individuals.

And the sage continued in a gentle voice, saying: My dear sister I, too, have yearned for an all-merciful God. For long watches in the existential night I scoured the dark, sudden-twisting paths of the soul, searching for Him, frantic-ally. And when reason's disturbing light finally dawned, and I beheld but an empty landscape, I fell sobbing and grieving for a God gone missing. And now, unable to bask in the warm embrace of infinite mercy, unable to tremble in the transcendent intimacy of divine communion—unable, even, to rely upon theology's cerebral comforts—I savor the bittersweet flavors of authenticity and seek, at least, the bracing dignity of truth.

20. Sub-argument that suffering creates wisdom and also helps us appreciate the good; therefore, although God causes suffering, it is good

And a theologian said: If we try, we can see the kindness and mercy in all of God's works. Yes, God causes suffering; but suffering stimulates our greatest gifts, such as wisdom and compassion, and art; and helps us savor moments of pleasure, too. And, yes, mortality is tragic, but it helps us appreciate life. Thus, even in causing pain and death, God does great kindness and shows great mercy.

And the sage said: My brother, though suffering in some instances helps our greatest gifts to blossom, and poets and sages have spoken of such things,[1] in many other instances it crushes those gifts in the bud. Moreover, many of the worst forms of suffering are followed in short order by death, the victims never

---

[1] For three examples of many: Shakespeare, in Act III of *Romeo and Juliet,* writes, "…Adversity's sweet milk, philosophy, to comfort thee, though thou art banished…" and Samuel Butler wrote, "And poets by their sufferings grow/As if there were no more to do/To make a poet excellent/But only want and discontent," and Shelley wrote, "Most wretched men/Are cradled into poetry by wrong/They learn in suffering what they teach in song."

to recover and create anything of value from the agonies they endured. Indeed, how many infants suffered and died, who never learned to walk or speak—and shall never create gifts to redeem their suffering! And if we could see but a bit below the sod, we would behold the bones of innumerable children lying wrapped in blankets beneath their measure of earth, perhaps with a rattle or toy placed tenderly beside them by the shaking hands of a sobbing mother. For these reasons, and more, one cannot ascribe perfect compassion to a possible Creator—and explain away suffering as essentially a good and valuable thing.

My brother, if causing suffering and death is kind, our judges should praise thieves and highwaymen, and our priests and elders should exalt murderers. For do not these criminals, too, provide us with suffering, which, as you say, stimulates wisdom and compassion—and with death, which helps us appreciate life?

By your lights, a man whose house has been set aflame can be said to have been done a great good, for the loss of his home awakens him from his dreary life of deadened routine, and invigorates his days with the intensity that only crisis knows. Moreover, the man will better appreciate his next dwelling, when he reflects on the despair he felt upon encountering the smoldering ruins of his earlier one. Indeed, according to this logic, should not the homeless victim reward the one who torched his home, in appreciation for the increased vitality of outdoor living, and for the wisdom and gratitude born of fire?

And do not bandits constitute a great good, too? Though when they take from a man his dearest possessions they are generally seen as evil, perhaps—would argue the disciples of this form of theology—they should be celebrated, instead, as benefactors. After all, do not many religions teach that earthly riches distract us from spiritual living? And does not a man live intensely when hungry for bread, and forced by circumstance to marshal his energies in the service of survival? To be reduced to poverty, then, might be of the greatest gifts we can be given, and should call forth gratitude—or so would argue corrupt ingenuity.

And a murderer of children can be seen—by the same misguided thinking—as a compassionate hero. For do not many religions teach that though adults are guilty sinners, children are yet innocent? Dying while still blameless, then, children are prevented from living sinful lives, and thus spared the eternal fires of religion's hell. And is any kindness greater than rescuing another from endless torture? Moreover, will not these dead children's parents—and other parents who learn of the horror—now better appreciate the children who yet remain?

Furthermore, have not many poets and mystics pined for the hereafter, when the soul could finally break free from what they saw as the heavy chains of cursed earth—to soar what they were confident were the ecstatic expanses of blessed heaven? Should we, then, laud loudest the man who murders most, for mercifully liberating the greatest number of captive souls?

Yet religions agree that murder and theft, and the infliction of pain upon others—at least others among the "faithful," and when not by authority of the courts or mandate of God or His spokesmen—are evil acts. If these are to be seen as merciful when engaged in by a deity, why are they forbidden as evil and cruel—and punished severely—when engaged in by humans? And do not answer that God owns us all and therefore can do what He pleases, even if it causes suffering—for this abandons your argument that suffering is good. If it is good, all of us should be morally and legally permitted to cause others suffering, too.

Moreover, if God is both omnipotent and loving, as a number of major religions have taught, why did He not create our universe in such a way that we could achieve wisdom and experience compassion and pleasure without the need to suffer for these—indeed, why did He create a universe with so much suffering not even leading to these?

For again, have not multitudes of children died agonizing deaths with no opportunity to turn such horror into wisdom and compassion, or to cultivate from their knowledge of pain a greater appreciation of pleasure?

My brother: Let us not minimize the heartrending afflictions of our ancestors through the ages, and of our fellow humans even today. Though at times some good may result from such torments, let us not debase ourselves and them by saying that agony is essentially good.

Suffering can, at times, stimulate wisdom and compassion and help us better appreciate life's fine and pleasant aspects. And when we are inevitably buffeted by life's blows, it would be well for us to remember this, and to squeeze from those bitter moments what drops of sweetness we can. But surely this does not make suffering primarily a good thing, nor does it make compassionate those who intentionally cause suffering—or those able to prevent it who choose not to.

With but a little cleverness and a profound deafness to the quiet voices of conscience and candor, there is no evil that cannot be hailed as high virtue, and no goodness beyond being labeled the devil's most despicable vice. Yet if we wish to respect ourselves in the quiet moments of deep solitude, we must—even in the clamorous fray of spirited debate—keep our distance from duplicity. Though the mouth rushes forth with glib apologetics, the heart in her inmost chamber is never deceived; and she cringes in disgrace at the spectacle of an indolent and craven mind—wriggling free of the burdens of truth and fleeing in terror the lessons of honest sight.[1]

---

[1] If I may leaven the heavy bread of suffering a bit…On the matter of creatively avoiding painful truth by insisting upon an overly generous interpretation, the joke is told of a man celebrating at his wedding with family and friends, all making merry with wine and song. At one point, wishing to speak to his bride but not seeing her, he looks in the next room, and there, on a couch, are his friend and his bride engaged in an act of primal

My brother, when searching for the true and real in treacherous existential terrain, obscured by long shadows and startling illusions and all manner of conflicting signs and desperate urgings, let us be merciful unto our souls by selecting the true over the clever, and by ever submitting with humble dignity to the supreme law of impartial reason.

21. Argument that all religions are equally valid paths to the Divine

Then a generous man said: Why bicker about details, or wonder and worry about how to know God, and what He wants? All religions are but different paths to the same destination. Let us hold hands and remember that he who follows any religion worships the same God.

And the sage said: My dear brother, your spirit is a blessing to the family of earth, which too often endures tragedy and brutality over distinctions of dogma and diversities of worship. So it might be well if your words were true. Would that the soft brush of kindness could blend away the sharp lines of indelible disparity, and bring into pleasing harmony the clashing hues of conflicting beliefs. But the magical arts yet elude the sons and daughters of man, so paint precisely we must on the sacred canvas of our mortal days.

My brother, your warm heart is admirable, but these thoughts of yours are mistaken. For while on some teachings religions concur, they differ strongly on many others. When a crowd of religions dispute what God said, and to whom—and when they contradict each other not only on historical accounts of miracles and revelations, but on laws, morality, and essential beliefs, too—they cannot all be correct.

Some religions instruct the worship of many gods and the use of statues in spiritual ritual, while others teach that such forms of worship are the greatest abomination to the only true God. Some teach that God requires adherence to an original biblical law code, while others believe these laws were nullified by a new covenant and a New Testament. Some claim salvation can be attained only by believing God had a son whose death can forgive all sin, while others insist such teaching is mistaken, even blasphemous. Some teach that God's greatest prophet lived long after the days of the Bible, in the desert regions of Arabia, and there revealed God's most sacred words and had them recorded for posterity as the holy Koran. Still other faiths believe neither in the prophet nor his book. Some have taught perpetual and universal peace in the name of God, while

---

betrayal. After a moment of confusion he begins laughing uproariously. Hearing the commotion, others gather around and, taking in the scene, ask him why he's laughing. Pointing to the couch and stifling another laugh he says: "Look at Klaus. He's so drunk, he thinks he's me!"

others have spoken of God's desire for bloody war and eternal vengeance; some have worshiped deities with rites of lusty pleasure, while others have prohibited such practice as an outrage to a chaste and holy God; some have taught of an afterlife with rewards and punishments, while others have taught only of terrestrial rewards and earthly recompense for all the good and evil men have wrought under the sun.

These contrasts between religions, my brother, are no mere differences of detail; they are, instead, fundamental disagreements. Consider, then, can all these be accurate accounts of the will of the same God? Would God contradict Himself so often in instructing us on who He is; on which humans speak in His name; and on which laws, beliefs, and teachings He would have us live by?

And, my brother, a religion seeing other religions as wrong and unacceptable is not an aberration or the excess of misguided clergy veering off the pure path of original faith. The Bible itself commands intolerance for the Canaanite peoples' religions—and commands the destruction of their altars, images, and sacred groves—lest they influence the Israelites to worship in a manner different from the teachings of Yahweh, as conveyed to Moses. Exodus 34:11-16 states:

> Observe thou that which I command thee this day: behold, I drive out before thee the Amorite, and the Canaanite, and the Hittite, and the Perizzite, and the Hivite, and the Jebusite. Take heed to thyself, lest thou make a covenant with the inhabitants of the land whither thou goest, lest it be for a snare in the midst of thee: But ye shall destroy their altars, break their images, and cut down their groves: For thou shalt worship no other god: for the Lord, whose name is Jealous, is a jealous God: Lest thou make a covenant with the inhabitants of the land, and they go a whoring after their gods, and do sacrifice unto their gods, and one call thee, and thou eat of his sacrifice; And thou take of their daughters unto thy sons, and their daughters go a whoring after their gods, and make thy sons go a whoring after their gods.

And Deuteronomy states in 12:2-3 and 12:29-31:

> Ye shall utterly destroy all the places, wherein the nations which ye shall possess served their gods, upon the high mountains, and upon the hills, and under every green tree: And ye shall overthrow their altars, and break their pillars, and burn their groves with fire; and ye shall hew down the graven images of their gods, and destroy the names of them out of that place…When the Lord thy God shall cut off the nations from before thee, whither thou goest to possess them, and thou succeedest them, and dwellest in their land; Take heed to thyself that thou be not snared by following them, after that they be destroyed from before

thee; and that thou enquire not after their gods, saying, How did these nations serve their gods? even so will I do likewise. Thou shalt not do so unto the Lord thy God...

The Bible, so far from seeing all religions as equally valid paths to the Divine, even punishes with death one who promotes the worship of other religions. Deuteronomy 13:6-10 states:

If thy brother, the son of thy mother, or thy son, or thy daughter, or the wife of thy bosom, or thy friend, which is as thine own soul, entice thee secretly, saying, Let us go and serve other gods, which thou hast not known, thou, nor thy fathers; Namely, of the gods of the people which are round about you, nigh unto thee, or far off from thee, from the one end of the earth even unto the other end of the earth; Thou shalt not consent unto him, nor hearken unto him; neither shall thine eye pity him, neither shalt thou spare, neither shalt thou conceal him: But thou shalt surely kill him; thine hand shall be first upon him to put him to death, and afterwards the hand of all the people. And thou shalt stone him with stones, that he die; because he hath sought to thrust thee away from the Lord thy God...

And neither does the New Testament teach that all religions are equally good paths to the same God. John 3:14-18, and 35-36 states:

And as Moses lifted up the serpent in the wilderness, even so must the Son of man be lifted up: That whosoever believeth in him should not perish, but have eternal life. For God so loved the world, that he gave his only begotten Son, that whosoever believeth in him should not perish, but have everlasting life. For God sent not his Son into the world to condemn the world; but that the world through him might be saved. He that believeth on him is not condemned: but he that believeth not is condemned already, because he hath not believed in the name of the only begotten Son of God...The Father loveth the Son, and hath given all things into his hand. He that believeth on the Son hath everlasting life: and he that believeth not the Son shall not see life; but the wrath of God abideth on him.

And the scriptures of various other faiths similarly teach that only their religions are correct; and their churches and clerics—in the ages and lands in which they wielded power—often supported the violent suppression of other religions. Indeed, numerous wars were fought because religions taught their people to banish or kill practitioners of other faiths, in order to uphold the "true" word of

God. Could all the men on all sides possibly have been following God's will in doing the killing, if all the warring faiths were rightful paths to the same God?

In short, my brother, since religions teach that other religions are misguided, how can they all be true? For if they are true, their teachings about other religions being mistaken are true, too.

My brother, at times the greatest kindness is not to agree with another's error, but to respectfully point it out, and patiently speak of a better way. The kiss of gentleness is admirable, and blessed are the hugs and clasps of harmony; but these must not be allowed to smother honesty—especially on matters of signal importance. It is simply not true that all religions worship the same God. The scriptures of these varied religions say as much with sacred vehemence, and their armies and mobs have written these wretched verses on the sad and cursed soil of every continent, with their sisters' tears and their brothers' blood, in every tragic age.

Let us have the good courage to acknowledge this, even if we shall then be unable to reconcile all dogmas or nod our assent to every faith and creed. For the noble maiden Truth does not respond eagerly to all who would court her, and of necessity cannot acquiesce to all her suitors. Yet is not her selective embrace of greater value than the ever-ready consent of the harlot, and her immediate, undistinguishing welcome?

22. Argument that we can know God through intuition

Then a poet said: All these arguments mean little to me. In my heart I know that God exists, and I know what He wants me to do. I feel it intuitively.[1]

And the sage said: My brother, would that our hearts always provided reliable counsel. Yet on matters of strong emotion they are vulnerable to earnest ignorance and sincere error—not rarely, but consistently.

When a child is delayed in his return from school, does not his mother know in her heart—with the terrible confidence of fast-falling despair—that some unthinkable evil has overtaken him? And does not the murderer's grandmother know in her heart that her grandson is innocent, that he could never have committed the act of which he stands accused? And do not young lovers know in their hearts that their bliss will endure forever? Yet how often events prove such convictions mistaken!

My brother, intuition, this knowing of the heart, is neither sacred nor infallible; it is, rather, the unconscious mind's hasty supposition based upon disparate thoughts and impulses, lessons early imbibed, and an amalgam of primitive instinct and varied experience and knowledge. Yet all these elements, and the

---

[1] A similar, but not identical, issue is discussed in section 5.

conclusions at which they arrive, may be significantly misguided. When traversing the territory of religion, then, fields on which deep loyalties march and passionate convictions ever contend, intuition predictably raises the shield of discomfort to ward off all ideas or claims threatening her cherished beliefs. Her rousing calls for defense, then, are not appeals to which we should rally without due reflection and exceeding caution.

Indeed, intuition reflects not the accuracy of truth, but the readiness of the heart and mind to commit or remain committed to a particular standpoint. On the matter of God and His will, our intuition, like any adviser, must not be ignored. But, also like any adviser, it must not be followed blindly—especially in the face of contrary evidence and evident bias.

My brother, intuition does have its place—but there are places it does not belong, at least not in the lead position. The clamor and frenzy of a surprise battle is best led by a man of action and tactical instinct, but when time allows for deliberations on whether and how to wage a prolonged war, these are best conducted by a council of wise strategists. So, too, on matters of the spirit: When we are called upon to make sudden decisions, intuition may be the only guide to which we can turn, but when careful reflection is possible, it is nothing less than reckless to rely solely upon intuition—for it is vulnerable to partiality and error no less than the unrelenting urges of our hungry flesh, the headstrong demands of our ambitious minds, and the insistent whispers of our ever-yearning hearts.

23. Argument that "There are no atheists in a foxhole"

Then a physician said: You speak of battle. At the battlefront I have seen strong men, proud men, clever men, all tremble at death's approach and desperately call out to God. All soldiers bargain with God, offering their virtuous devotion if He will but spare their lives. One need only observe men at war to know there is a God—as the saying goes: There are no atheists in a foxhole.

And the sage said: My brother, though on the killing fields many succumb, there are undoubtedly courageous warriors who do not surrender their dignity to desperate hope or doubtful worship even in the face of implacable doom, but instead remain honorable as eternity nears—honest about their lack of true knowledge of God, and about their ignorance of what follows death.

But surprised by the sudden menace of the tomb, when terror's icy fingers encircle the throat, most of us do indeed reach frantically for God. With life now tenuous, we long for something more, something to give meaning to years already lived, something beyond the terrestrial to spare us from utter obliteration, and someone to treat us mercifully in our terrifying helplessness. At such a time, belief in God is intensely seductive, for it offers the prospect of transcendent significance to our fragile, fleeting existence; the magical aspiration that super-

67

natural providence might yet prolong our lives; and—should death insist—the tantalizing promise of idyllic life beyond the grave.

Yet do we not all know that powerful emotions draw the mind away from sound judgment? In the heated chase of a beautiful woman, cannot even brilliant men abandon their poise, squander their resources, and lose all sense of dignity? And cannot a woman in love seem sadly deluded to her friends, as she sees naught but enchanting qualities in her chosen one? Has not the wisdom of ages warned us away from the seductive sway of ruinous lust, the false friendship of flattery's fixed smile, the intoxicated folly of hatred and rage, the blinding glare of gilded greed, and the craven submission to fear and dread—temptations and fevers that fog our minds and corrupt our souls?

And is there any stronger lust than the yearning for life—or any stronger flattery than whispers assuring us of eternal significance? Is there any greater anger than our fury at death, or any greater greed than our hope for immortal bliss, or any greater fear than that of encountering the void? Is it any wonder, then, that when death threatens, most yield to these onslaughts of passion and terror, and in primal stampede rush headlong to kneel before possible salvation?

In short, my brother, that people turn to God in the face of death does not prove God's existence. Illustrated only is man's propensity for being surprised at, and unprepared for, his demise—and his tendency to employ any and all measures on that terrible day.

And the many frenzied psalms sung to God in the dark shadow of the valley of death, tell not of a Great Being who hears such desperate music of the soul; rather they tell of our own mortal longings for a Good Shepherd to shield and succor us in the presence of terrifying foes, to guide us from imminent doom to soothing sanctuary, and to cause goodness and mercy to follow us all of the days of our lives.[1]

24. Argument that we cannot trust our own judgment, but must rely on religious authorities

And a devout man said: These matters are too important to decide by our own judgment. We must rely on the proper authorities, our religious leaders.

And the sage said: My brother, your inclination to rely upon authorities is, in part, well founded. For caution is advised when leaning upon our own under-

---

[1] And these universal hungers for guidance and support—for the rod and the staff—and for the idyllic nurturing of green pastures and quiet waters, and for safe passage through the valley of the shadow of death, and for a table of provision and protection in the face of want and oppression, and for reassurance of a bright and enduring future dwelling in the house of the Lord—these are what make Psalm 23 one of the more famously beloved chapters in all of Scripture.

standing, as we may have neither adequate knowledge nor sufficient wisdom to discern truth—and we may also be seduced by our own fears, yearnings, and ambitions, and thereby arrive at mistaken judgments.

Yet, my brother, there is cause, too, for us to be wary of authority. Though we long for perfect leaders—those who will give wise, just, truthful, and all-knowing direction—no leader is ideal. And any fair reading of the record of mankind tells as much of religious leaders' errors and abuses as of their excellent guidance. For although they accumulate much knowledge, such knowledge is often limited in scope, and unbalanced in verdict. The authorities of any faith study far less of others' sacred scriptures and commentaries than those of their own tradition; they scrutinize the former with a critical eye seeking the many damnable or tragic errors they are certain lurk therein, but study the latter with an adoring gaze, seeking, instead, the unlimited wisdom they are certain is hidden therein; and they rarely deign to respectfully consider the intelligent writings that argue against all religion. In short, passionate allegiance to a particular creed makes honest scholarship and deliberation exceedingly difficult, in weighing the relative merits of arguments for different religions or for no religion at all.

So although in the dim rays of first light it may seem that religious leaders—because they are better informed—can engage in a superior analysis on these ultimate issues of truth, and most effectively judge the many conflicting points of view, often it is these very leaders for whom honesty on such matters is most challenging and least likely. For when a man's vocation, social standing, relations with family and friends—indeed, his very identity—rests upon the familiar foundation of a particular people and faith, to break free of the crushing bias toward his own community's beliefs becomes nearly impossible. Thus, though we are constrained by shortcomings in knowledge and hindered by all manner of emotions and needs, so too is the religious leader limited by deficiencies in knowledge, and besieged, too, by various—often all but impregnable—emotional and existential barriers to fair thinking on the matter of God and His will. My brother, we must abandon the fantasy of the all-wise, all-seeing, all-truthful leader who might do our most important thinking in our stead. To assume that such leadership exists is irresponsible; how much more so to flatter ourselves that it happens to be ours.

Indeed, even if following religious leaders were legitimate, I ask you: Which religious leaders? Each tradition's authorities disagree, on foundational issues, with the authorities of other religions—and sometimes with each other. Understand well, then, that if we choose to follow our own leaders, it is not leadership that we follow, but rather the pride or comfort of the familiar—for the authorities of other religions are leaders too, yet we choose not to follow them.

Consider, too, that on matters we value deeply or desperately, we tend not to rely solely upon others' expertise—especially when the supposedly well-informed contradict each other. Instead, though we do, indeed, seek counsel, we think for ourselves, too. Observe how many mothers gather knowledge from disparate sources and develop expertise on diseases that plague their children.

So, too, my brother, do not be tempted to rely upon me. I ask you neither to follow me by authority nor to revere me for virtue—not only because I make no claims to either, but because when seeking truth, authority and virtue are irrelevant. Accuracy is the only standard, and reason and experience the only reliable arbiters.

Yet you may ask: If I do not wish you to rely upon me, why do I speak to you today? To that I answer, my brother, that I speak to offer for your consideration ideas and arguments, my fashionings and weavings of reason, with which one may equip and attire oneself in dignity and authenticity—but it is you who must finally decide what to make of these thoughts, it is you who will determine what you will acquire and what you will wear.

My brother, I would not have you trust me; I would have you become worthy of trusting yourself. I would not have you seat me on the throne from which you will have chased he who claims to be a prince of God; I would, instead, have you fashion for yourself a judge's chair, and have you sit upon it in humility, and ask yourself with deep honesty—on one issue at a time—whether my arguments are valid; if not, why not; and, if yes, what that means for how you live, and for what you tell yourself and your children on matters most meaningful.

In sum, my brother, on our most important beliefs we are, indeed, wise to consider the guidance of the learned and the direction of those in authority—but it is each of us who must weigh the alternatives and choose our own path. For in the end, when called upon to answer to the Universe, we shall not find shelter beneath the titles of our leaders, nor absolution behind the robes of our priests; neither shall we be rescued by the fiery chariots of the prophets of old, nor held immune by their fierce proclamations—even the kindest sage cannot make right the errors of wayward years. On matters of spiritual belief, my brother, only our own earnest efforts at grappling with the Mystery, enduring the stinging shame of our people's long-held errors, and walking in humility the path of honest not-knowing—only these can deliver us innocent to the sacred bosom of eternity.

25. Argument that those with a personal relationship with God know He exists

And a man said: I may not know fancy philosophical arguments, but I know in my heart that God is real, and if you had a personal relationship with Him, you too would know He is real.

70

And the sage said: My brother, I do not question for a moment that you believe you carry on with God a personal relationship, and that it seems apparent to you that God is real. Yet deep personal conviction and intense mental and emotional experiences do not guarantee the accuracy of one's beliefs on what such convictions or experiences indicate about objective reality. Sadly, so many have been so wrong about so much. The human heart yearns for love, for guidance, for connection, for transcendence, for leadership, for security, for intensity, for intimacy, and for many other ideal and comforting qualities and states; and all these can seemingly be attained by means of a personal relationship with the Divine. And especially since relations with other humans are fraught with frustration, disappointment, abandonment, even betrayal, many of us are powerfully drawn to the notion of a relationship with God, and, when we attempt to create one, to the belief that we have succeeded.

Just as our dreams in the night seem compelling and real, and just as our daydreams and fantasies are, at times, intense and alluring, so too can anyone with a vivid imagination conjure an experience, and believe it to be real, of personal relationship with God—whether or not God in fact exists, or is in any way similar to what the imaginer envisions or thinks he experiences.

And, my gentle brother, what will you say to those who believe that they experience a personal relationship with Ahura Mazdah, with Buddha, with Vishnu, with Mohammad, with Zeus, with Poseidon, with Merlin, with the Sun or Moon, or with any number of other gods, prophets, spirits or wizards in which you do not believe—not to mention the many who are visited by voices and visions, and are sent to hospital where a few pills bring relief? Will you insist that their subjective experiences of personal relationship with their gods, prophets, spirits or wizards are less real than your subjective experience of a personal relationship with your Lord?[1] Is it not far more likely, devastating though such a letdown may

---

[1] Thoreau observed in *Walden*, "Every generation laughs at the old fashions, but follows religiously the new. We are amused at beholding the costume of Henry VIII, or Queen Elizabeth, as much as if it was that of the King and Queen of the Cannibal Islands. All costume off a man is pitiful or grotesque. It is only the serious eye peering from and the sincere life passed within it which restrain laughter and consecrate the costume of any people."

And while we may wish to quibble with Thoreau as to whether it is primarily the "serious eye" and "sincere life" that "consecrate" the clothing, or whether it is mainly familiarity and custom that make clothing seem right and reasonable, while unfamiliarity and lack of custom make clothing seem amusing or odd—in any case, what is true for fashions of clothing is equally true for fashions of worship and belief. The gods and prophets and dogmas and rituals of every religion—even living religions, and how much more so the dead religions of the past—appear, to nearly all followers of other religions or no religion, at best odd and unlikely to be true or reflective of any deity's will, and

be, that the devotees of various religions have all been mistaken in believing they had a personal relationship with a supernatural power, and in truth this fantasy was but fashioned through imagination and emotion, and other mechanisms of the mind quite natural?

Have you never, in merely human discourse, suddenly become aware that the person you thought was listening had already walked away, fallen asleep, or could no longer hear you—and yet, until you recognized this, you felt heard, but were, in fact, conversing with no one but yourself? And have you never seen a young child speaking intently to her imaginary friends?

My brother, when we perceive the presence or attention of another, such impressions arise, at times, more from our beliefs, imaginings, expectations, and emotional needs for bonding—the capacities and tendencies of a complex social animal's mind—than they do from the objective reality of whether anyone is truly there. And this holds true for all our experiences of connection—be they with mortals or with gods.

26. Argument that miracle stories prove the existence of God

And a devout man called out, saying: What of all the miracles done for the righteous? Do you think, then, that all is understood? Are there not accounts of wonders and supernatural events that astonish even the most brilliant of men? And do they not prove the existence of God, as my religion teaches?

And the sage lifted up his hands, spread his arms wide, and gazing all around him said: Indeed, wonders abound, from horizon to mesmerizing horizon. The shimmering warmth of yonder golden-leafed trees, and the sweet songbirds fluttering in their midst; the deep expanse of cerulean heavens, and the lingering hauntings on the fragrant winds; the tiny, perfect fingers of an infant's grasping hand, and the wide open eyes of the life-drenched young; subtle-wrought thoughts in the mind of man, and endless, enchanting words to send them forth: all these—and many, many more—are full of wonder. We know so little of how things happen, and of how all we see came to be. And too often our souls are distracted by tedium and deadened by familiarity and routine, and we trudge through our days with little astonishment or delight. My brother, would that our eyes and mouths could again fly open in awe, that the child's heart of amazement and spirit of innocence would evermore quicken within us, and live in harmony

---

often as silly or downright savage. Yet those rituals and dogmas to which we ourselves have been early accustomed, even if we should later question their truth, rarely strike us viscerally as absurd. But depend on it—for many accustomed only to other religious fashions, or to none at all, our native rituals and dogmas *do* seem absurd.

with maturity's vigilance and well-tutored knowledge. For so we might truly live while yet alive, and only grow cold when claimed by death.

All these wonders surrounding us, however, are of nature. As for supernatural miracles—have the universe's laws been shattered by benevolent gods, to save and exalt their favored elite? Have holy men worked miracles by divine agency and powers unknown? Has the sea been split or the sun delayed? Has stone brought forth water, or the Nile turned to blood? Has a man walked on the sea or, by supernatural powers, risen from the dead? To these questions, humility and honesty must answer: We do not know for certain, but reason suggests that such things never occurred. For do not all religions and peoples tell miracle tales of their own, though the heroes or gods to which these are ascribed differ, and the lands and ages in which they are supposed to have come to pass vary? The accounts are so numerous that they reflect not divine pleasure at any particular religion, nor even the intervention of God in human affairs, but rather the propensity of man to create and believe astonishing accounts of signs and wonders. Moreover, it has long been noted[1] that the factor which makes a

---

[1] Hume, in *An Enquiry Concerning Human Understanding* famously presents these arguments. He writes (section X, toward the end of Part I): "A miracle is a violation of the laws of nature…Nothing is esteemed a miracle, if it ever happen in the common course of nature…The plain consequence is (and it is a general maxim worthy of our attention) 'That no testimony is sufficient to establish a miracle, unless the testimony be of such a kind, that its falsehood would be more miraculous than the fact which it endeavors to establish; and even in that case there is a mutual destruction of arguments, and the superior only gives us an assurance suitable to that degree of force which remains after deducting the inferior.' When anyone tells me that he saw a dead man restored to life, I immediately consider with myself whether it be more probable that this person should either deceive or be deceived, or that the fact which he relates should really have happened. I weigh the one miracle against the other…and always reject the greater miracle. If the falsehood of his testimony would be more miraculous than the event which he relates; then, and not till then, can he pretend to command my belief or opinion."

See how boldness and candor speak to us, fresh and relevant, across the centuries!

And Thomas Paine, in his *Age of Reason*, says, in his vigorous style, something similar (though he seems to leave out the possibility of honest error, unless by the word "lie" he means untruth, irrespective of intent). He writes: "If we are to suppose a miracle to be something so entirely out of the course of what is called nature, that she must go out of that course to accomplish it, and we see an account given of such a miracle by the person who said he saw it, it raises a question in the mind very easily decided, which is—Is it more probable that nature should go out of her course, or that a man should tell a lie? We have never seen, in our time, nature go out of her course; but we have good reason to believe that millions of lies have been told in the same time; it is, therefore, at least millions to one, that the reporter of a miracle tells a lie."

miracle seem compelling—indeed, the very reason we would characterize an event as a miracle—is that it contradicts our repeated experience of what is possible or remotely likely. Thus, when we hear an account of a miracle, we must ask ourselves whether it would be more miraculous that the event took place as described, or that somehow the witnesses or tellers of this tale were one or more of the following: mistaken in their perceptions, errant in their interpretations, misinformed in their knowledge, or less than candid in their testimony. And so I ask you this: Would it not be more miraculous—less likely—for the purported miracles reported of gods and religious leaders to have actually taken place, than for the reports of the miracles to be incorrect?

And, my brother, it has further been noted that even if—contrary to our repeated experience of nature's laws—one thinks it more likely that the miracle took place than that the story of the miracle is inaccurate, an honest man's degree of confidence in the miracle story must be somewhat shaken and at least partially counterbalanced by the very fact that reality testifies every day, ten thousand times, against the likelihood that anything occurs in contradiction of nature's laws. Thus, belief in miracles cannot reasonably approach confidence, much less, certainty.

And, true, my brother: We cannot understand all; but if we are honest about what we *can* understand, must we not remain skeptical of all miracle tales?

27. Sub-argument: Why would miracle stories originate and spread if they were not true?

But the devout man shook his head and said: Surely the fact that we have so many miracle stories proves that miracles occur! Where would miracle stories come from and why would they spread if they were not true?

And the sage said: My brother, miracle stories sprout and flourish from the seeds borne on many winds. I shall mention ten and more of these causes and motives, but reflect on the matter and you will find more, still.

Yet Santayana, himself not a believer, illustrates the perspective of many believers in miracles, when he writes in his *Winds of Doctrine*: "The true Christian, for instance, will begin by regarding miracles as probable; he will either believe he has experienced them in his own person, or hope for them earnestly; nothing will seem to him more natural, more in consonance with the actual texture of life, than that they should have occurred abundantly and continuously in the past. When he finds the record of one he will not inquire, like the rationalist, how that false record could have been concocted; but rather he will ask how the rationalist, in spite of so many witnesses to the contrary, has acquired his fixed assurance of the universality of the commonplace."

Is it not a bit humbling and disturbing how a dash of eloquence almost makes primitive superstition seem reasonable?

First, the imagination often magnifies things, good and bad. See how early this begins, how the little boy in his make-believe games gives both his imaginary heroes and imaginary villains extraordinary powers—and if he is daring and hungry for approval, how he magnifies accounts of his own adventures and skills; and see, too, how the same boy instinctively spins and spreads grand and astonishing tales about the unequaled exploits not only of the athletes of stadium and arena, but of his father, his teacher, his elder brother, or even his tormenter and young foe across the road—and observe how his sister gazes up with awestruck eyes and fluttering, overflowing heart, at actors or singers, the heroes of stage and song. Even as adults, they will tend to magnify what they admire or what they fear, and describe, or believe descriptions of, performers or leaders or enemies wielding remarkable powers—be they physical, intellectual, military, or supernatural—and such stories spread quickly.

Second, and a related point: Young and old alike yearn for wonder, for magic, for astonishment and awe—for breaking through the tedious, the familiar and the limiting, to the heady, unbounded, and climactic consolations of super-natural favor or hope, even for a mere hint that something operates outside the purview of nature's humiliating laws. See how popular are tales of fairies and sorcerers and wizards and witches and ghosts and djinns, and other enchanted beings with special powers. See how the mind is eagerly enraptured and happily surrenders, how the eyes glow a bit brighter, how the blood flows a bit stronger, how the spirit feels a bit freer, when reading or hearing such tales—even when they are clearly known to be fiction, when not even the gullible believe the events actually occurred. And see how transfixed is the audience when a magician performs his tricks and illusions with cards and coins and rabbits and ladies sawed in half, although everyone knows that—notwithstanding the extravagant claims of the magician's assistant—nothing beyond the natural is taking place. Is it so difficult, then, to imagine the temptation many feel to hear and tell and believe stories of supernatural magic and wonder that are said to actually be true?

The belief and spread of miracle stories, then—whether astonishing feats performed by leaders, or directly by some spirit or god—is aided by the strong appetite found in so many, for being impressed by dramatic or exciting events, and for impressing others by recounting such events.[1] Many possess both the inclination to believe miraculous tales, and the urge to disseminate them.

---

[1] Again I quote Hume from his *Enquiry Concerning Human Understanding* (section X, toward the beginning of Part II): "The passion of surprise and wonder, arising from miracles, being an agreeable emotion, gives a sensible tendency towards the belief of those events from which it is derived. And this goes so far, that even those who cannot enjoy this pleasure immediately, nor can believe those miraculous events of which they

In this way, natural events are often enthusiastically—even if unwittingly—misinterpreted as miracles, and stories are, consciously or otherwise, embellished in their retelling so as to seem most impressive.[1] And once these tales of the supernatural have successfully spread within a society, they are believed by many, and recounted and bequeathed as sacred tradition to future generations. And in these subsequent generations, even one with a skeptical turn of mind, who may raise a disbelieving eyebrow at any miraculous tale originating in his own day, has long since accepted with reverence yesteryear's miracles, impressed upon him long ago with the authority of Scripture and sermon in the classroom and house of worship, fastened to him early with the fervent sentiment of story and song in the dimly recalled new world of kindergarten, even taken up into his marrow and bones in the forgotten whispers and lullabies of mother's cradle.

Third, many miracle stories involve spiritual leaders seeming to predict the future or know one's secret actions or thoughts. These can better be understood in light of how strong is the drive among many to achieve clarity and certainty, to recognize what will be, to know what to choose, indeed, to have someone choose for them. See how many earnestly consult psychics, fortune tellers, crystal ball gazers, readers of palms, tarot cards or, in other days and climes, tea leaves, Turkish coffee grounds, animal entrails, and more. Many feel such a great relief at being told what to do by one with supernatural knowledge, that they are eager to see in ambiguous circumstances evidence of just such supernatural knowledge, and if told stories of such things, will happily believe them.

Fourth, among the natural instincts of a social species is the instinct for hero worship.[2] This inclination to see one's leaders as remarkable and worthy of veneration, can help a group be more unified and confident; it can also increase the safety of followers, as the powerful leader basks in the flattery of their adulation and submission, and is less likely to harm them. And one manifestation of idealizing a leader is the readiness to believe that this leader is capable of supernatural deeds, or worthy of gods intervening on his behalf.

Fifth, stories gradually change with telling, and it has long been said that a dead mouse on one edge of town is, by the time the story reaches the other edge of town, a dead lion. Thus, many astonishing miracle tales began with far more

---

are informed, yet love to partake of the satisfaction at second-hand or by rebound, and place a pride and delight in exciting the admiration of others."

[1] Thomas Henry Huxley, in his *Lectures and Essays,* wrote: "Sir Walter Scott knew that he could not repeat a story without, as he said, 'giving it a new hat and stick.' Most of us differ from Sir Walter only in not knowing about this tendency of the mythopoeic faculty to break out unnoticed."

[2] See section 15.23 and its footnote for how the instinct for hero worship likely also functioned as one of the sources of religion, overall.

modest accounts—that were perhaps impressive but not at all supernatural—and, over the many years or tellings, grew to their present form.

Sixth, my brother—and this is not easy for some to accept—the history of miracle stories includes much deceit. True, many miracle stories were born of honest, though credulous error, or gradually assumed their supernatural dimensions; but, knowing human nature, many others likely had their origin in conscious lies. The temptation to strike fear into the hearts of the ignorant masses—or to excite their admiration, inspire their worship and submission, and elicit their gifts and generous offerings—was so strong throughout the ages, that many among the clergy, or their assistants and family members and others who would have benefited thereby, must have succumbed. And sometimes the deceit would have come from good intentions, too: Parents and leaders have often felt it more important to inspire or comfort the young and the masses with miracle stories than to hold to a strict standard of truth.

Seventh, uncommon events do occur—any one uncommon event will not happen often, but there are so many potential uncommon events that something extraordinary, of one kind or another, occurs fairly frequently. And people like to find explanations for events—and extraordinary events may seem to require extraordinary, even supernatural, causes. And so, in the aftermath of the unexpected death of one's husband, or even one's horse, or of a surprise improvement or deterioration in one's fortunes, or of an earthquake or any natural disaster or tragedy or war, or of many being harmed, or of many being spared, people look for reasons—was a god likely to be angered or pleased by something recently said or done, or was a holy man slighted or treated particularly well—or perhaps was he heard or seen saying or doing anything unusual? And stories begin to circulate about the supernatural cause of the uncommon event, and these stories are often elaborated upon in their retellings, to include further details that make the story more credible and impressive—and more satisfying to the many impatient minds more eager for explanation and drama than for truth.

Eighth, people want to believe that their spiritual leaders are exceptional, and capable of working transcendent wonders. This helps the common man feel proud of his people, and potent, too—for the weak feel a certain strength when aligned with the powerful, even if that alignment is limited to recounting the glory of the hero's feats, and claiming membership in his tribe.

Ninth, many invest great and desperate hopes in the expected wages of religion, and strain for years and decades laboring under her sacred yoke, yet taste little of the blessings promised to the long-suffering and the devout. For these frustrated souls, then, it becomes compelling to believe that while they themselves may not command any supernatural abilities demonstrating the power of their religious beliefs and practices, the clerics, the sages and the mystics, who they deem to be in possession of the greatest secrets and merits of their religion, can, indeed, work wonders. This serves to buttress religious belief, and spares the faithful from entertaining the humiliating proposition that all their pieties and devotions, all their toils and privations for the sake of God and religion, may have been devoid of supernatural meaning—and in error and in vain.

Tenth, the many are predisposed to believing that their priests or ministers or rabbis or shamans or monks or prophets or imams performed miracles, because belief in the supernatural power of leaders aids the masses in justifying their subordination to these leaders, and to their religious tradition, overall. For to believe in a miracle-wielding leadership is to ease the ever-present tension between, on the one hand, maintaining personal dignity and individual will and, on the other, submitting to the control of leadership and conforming to communal tradition.[1] It prevents dangerous thoughts of rebellion, and averts the perils of tribal instability. Thus, from the dark forests of our primal minds come forth the sacred poverty of eager credulity and all manner of miracle imaginings.

In addition, my brother, I will share with you another reason miraculous accounts have arisen so frequently. It has long been observed that humans instinctively animate and anthropomorphize—that is, we tend to see that which is non-living as alive, even as having humanlike characteristics or intentions. Thus we see fierce or funny faces in the passing clouds; giant profiles in craggy cliffs; and hulking bears in the boulders of twilight; and we hear, too, the ominous approach of unknown danger in the innocent rustlings of windblown leaves.

The natural functioning of the mind, then, often inclines us to find greater significance and intent in objects and events than circumstances warrant. And this is one reason we attribute natural and random events to supernatural powers wielded by humans, spirits, or gods—thus giving rise to miracle stories. When a plague strikes a city; when a family achieves unusual wealth; when a woman recovers from grave illness; when a superior force is defeated in battle; even when we notice unusual features in the physical landscape;[2] in short, when confronting anything remarkable or out of the ordinary—though it falls well within the domain of what may be unintending nature and indiscriminate chance—the human mind will often seize the occasion to inhabit the circumstance with characters of precise intent, even grand, supernatural powers.[3]

---

[1] This uneasy surrender of the prerogative of the individual to the constraints of the group is a central theme in Freud's *Civilization and Its Discontents*.

[2] As in the case of heavy salt concentrations forming pillars in the vicinity of the Dead Sea—a circumstance reasonably seen as having helped stimulate the belief reflected in the biblical story of Lot's wife being transformed to a pillar of salt.

[3] Many over the millennia—in Scripture and theology, in wisdom writings and fable, in philosophy and psychology, in literature and art, even in lyric and farce—have taught,

And why are humans inclined to animate and anthropomorphize? Those seeking a reasonable explanation have postulated this: that although anthropomorphic interpretations are often inaccurate, they have helped our ancestors survive longer and reproduce more effectively, thus propagating these instincts to us and through us. For if they saw a vague shape in the forest, and feared it was an enemy, they were on guard. If it turned out to be, in fact, only a tree stump, they lost little. And in the unlikely event that the shape was an enemy, they were more prepared and thus better able to escape or prevail. If, however, upon seeing the ambiguous shape, they always assumed it to be a harmless tree stump—and, inevitably, it will on occasion have been a tiger or bear or malevolent human— they may not have survived long to enjoy this complacent turn of mind, or to bequeath such reasoned nonchalance to future generations.

Similarly, if they heard a rustling sound and assumed it to be footsteps, they became vigilant, and turned to identify the source of the sound. If it was nothing but benign leaves blowing, they lost little by their false assumption. If, however, an animal or enemy were truly stealing up behind them, but our forebears always assumed such sounds to be blowing leaves, they may not have survived. Thus, our ancestors—the ancient ones who endured long enough to bring forth progeny—passed on, from their blood and bones to ours, this vigilant pattern-seeking, this animating and anthropomorphizing. And, again, it is this inclination—to suspect of ambiguous events that they are related to the intent and powers of living, thinking beings—that causes us, at times, to attribute natural events to miracle-working, whether by people, spirits, or gods.

My brother, I will tell you still another reason miracle tales abound. Supernatural stories are a way of naming and externalizing the indistinct fears we carry in the hidden chambers of our hearts and the deepest caverns of our minds. Tales of mysterious powers and irresistible forces provide a focus for unspoken anxieties over unidentified dangers. Indeed, they often provide relief, for as these miraculous tales usually involve the god or religious leader subduing or channel-

---

explicitly or implicitly, that anthropomorphism is *one* important source and feature of religion. For a recent work that narrows its focus and views religion primarily, if not exclusively, in terms of anthropomorphism, see S. E. Guthrie's *Faces in the Clouds*. He attempts to distinguish his theory from earlier observations of this kind, and elucidates admirably the role of anthropomorphism in human life overall, and sees it as the tendency that gives rise to religion. And no informed view can deny the significant role of anthropomorphism in religious sentiment and thought. Yet one may justly wonder whether anthropomorphism is, by itself, sufficient to explain religion's complex and varied forms, and seemingly diverse motivations, satisfactions, and means of perpetuation. I provide a layman's taste of such variety in sections 15 and 67, which discuss, respectively, why the search for truth is avoided, and some causes for religion's birth.

ing great powers, his followers can feel safe—protected from all manner of vague, unnamed terrors by his religion's authority and supremacy over whatever dark forces lurk unseen. Observe the young child proclaiming, and needing to believe, that his father is the strongest of all—and observe that child playing, too, with his toys of battle, and see how his side inevitably, often suddenly, prevails over its foes, whether otherworldly or human. The comfort of being on the side of the mighty begins early, and never truly ends.

And yet another reason miracle tales abound: Each of us has in our deepest and earliest memories the sense that powerful beings are engaged in mysterious or awe-inspiring acts. To the infant, all is miracle: being taken from one place and deposited elsewhere; father appearing when he cries, at other times disappearing; the unintelligible sounds of adult speech; the pleasant sensations of a warm bath, and the persecutions of troubled digestion; serenity at mother's lullabies, and terror at her screaming—all these and a thousand other common events of infancy are beyond the young one's capacity to grasp, an astonishing array of experiences and states with no discernible cause. And now, all these years later, miracles still seem familiar, echoes of our long-forgotten first tastes of living. And from the unquiet deep, vague memories stir and applaud fervent mystery, awakening the long-dormant but never-dead yearning for a return to the magical ignorance of Eden, to a time before life felt cursed with the banishments and burdens of autonomy, and the falls and sadness of mortal knowledge.

And observe that as mankind has matured beyond the frightened, fantasy-filled childhood of superstitious credulity, through the belligerent, reckless adolescence of crude rebellion or reactionary faith, and at last into the humbled adulthood of critical yet respectful thought, miracle reports have steadily become more moderate and subdued—from terrified grandiosity gushing of a parted sea and a stopped sun in the face of all the world; to simmering hubris whispering rumors of mystical wonders in some dark forest, and secret visits from angels and spirits; finally to besieged respectability conducting studies on the possible efficacy of prayer. My brother, is it not telling that miracles vanish in the light?

Oh, yes, perhaps there will always be innumerable claims of minor "miracles" which, upon scrutiny, are seen to be dubious, at best ambiguous, and which can be accounted for by various forms of perfectly natural explanation. Yet is it not odd that even the spokesmen of ancient traditions—those whose gods and saints, prophets and sages, purportedly in past ages were wont to alter the course of nature at will—claim no epic, spectacular, nature-conquering miracles by their heroes or deities today? Shall we not suspect, then, that supernatural events, though often spoken of by the unscientific ancients, never truly occurred?

Indeed, aboriginal peoples even in recent times and well-documented accounts have often misinterpreted unfamiliar natural objects or occurrences as miracles and omens. Is there any good reason to believe, as we smile in patient condescension at their credulity, that the miracle accounts of our own traditions, originating in ages of superstition and mass scientific ignorance, too, are not errors fed by the same human tendencies displayed by those peoples more recently ignorant of science, and more obviously mistaken in their superstitions?

Yet the temptation to believe in miracles is formidable. As we trudge through our days of burdensome tasks, mired in the gray muds of wonderless routine, how we ache for spectacular demonstrations of power that might awaken us to the colors of amazement; how we wish to feel again, as once we did in the distant mists of childhood, that we live in the presence of greatness— simultaneously seized by the fearful talons of awe and securely sheltered in safety's nest of down; how we long for the humbling and constricting laws of nature to be cast aside by nobler forces human and divine; how we yearn for the passionate confirmation that the natural is but an illusion blinding us to the other side, where lies our real treasure; and how it pleases our inner eyes and ears to catch glimpses and whisperings of the beyond—in miracle's momentary parting of nature's drapes—to reassure us in our deepest loyalties and most closely-held creeds. Still, my brother, are not these achings and pinings but the lusts of emotion and spirit—like all lusts, never to be mistaken for clear compass or dangerless delight?

28. Sub-argument that if God performed unmistakable miracles, we would lose freedom of choice

And the devout man spoke again, saying: Of course God does not perform indisputable miracles; if He did, His sovereignty would be too obvious, and we would no longer have the reasonable choice of whether to believe in Him and serve Him—we would all walk a righteous path. Therefore, God performs miracles that *can* be disputed, so as to preserve our freedom of choice, and enable us to earn the merit of faith. But, for believers, these miracles are enough, and show us in the events of this world the finger of a supernatural God.

And the sage replied: My brother, from incidents of which we can doubt whether they are truly miraculous, no responsible belief in God can be derived. To constitute proof of the supernatural, an event must allow for no other reasonable explanation. Indeed, if an alternative, non-miraculous explanation can be found, far from proving God's existence, such an event—along with its spectacle of eager and credulous interpreters—provides further cause to doubt all miracle claims, whether recorded in ancient scrolls or recounted by modern men. For if a natural explanation can be offered, it is by far the more likely one. Innumerable times have we witnessed the functioning of nature's laws; thus, we know they exist. And time after dishonorable time have we seen how hungry and gullible is the human heart for superstitious belief, and how objects of worship and horror have so often proved to be but the products of erroneous interpretation, anxious imagination, even empty legend. By contrast, not once has our society witnessed indisputably supernatural events. It is only with great skepticism, then, that we should entertain the zealous testimonies of the enthusiastic devout, who speak confidently of holy and unholy forces—whether gods, angels, or saints; devils, demons, or ghosts—violating nature's laws.

Moreover, if one must believe in God and miracles in order to see an event as supernatural, is it not circular reasoning to claim that the incident proves or even indicates God's existence? For then one has already accepted the conclusion—that God exists and performs miracles—before the ambiguous event could have been judged to be supernatural, and evidence for a God.

Furthermore, if without compelling evidence we attribute an action to God, we risk the unintentional blasphemy of making false claims about Him—and this is far from piety or loyalty to the Divine. Would you not wish for others to refrain from attributing actions to you unless they had sufficient cause to be certain it was you who committed them, the more so if numerous accounts of your deeds—confidently spread through the eager rumors mills of faith, and all manner of documents said to be sacred—not only contradicted each other, but brought upon mankind so much discord and hate?

And now, my brother, let us examine your premise—that if God performed indisputable miracles we would lose freedom of choice. Consider that even witnessing clear miracles, we would still retain the choice of whether to act on our knowledge of God's will or surrender to the beguiling whispers of temptation and the ever-present appetites clamoring for comfort. People, every day, act against their knowledge and wisdom, succumbing to desire instead. Why do so many incur debt for indulgences whose charms will pass long before their price is paid? Why do so few eat a healthy diet or engage in regular physical exertion when the benefits of such behaviors are widely known? And why do so many smoke or drink to excess or take into their body all manner of substances that provide temporary pleasure, but are known to later bring pain, even death? The reason, of course, is that temptation is well capable of seducing us away from acting according to our understanding of good and evil, of wisdom and folly. Intellectual knowledge, the awareness of what is and is not true and advisable, is far from the only influence on our behavior—indeed, for most it is but a feeble influence, when it conflicts with trepidation or lust, rage or sloth, hope or greed, ambition or pride, or any other of the many passions and illusions to which the flesh and spirit are heir.

The Bible itself, in the book of Exodus beginning in Chapter 7, speaks of how the Israelites witnessed the ten miraculous plagues being visited upon the

Egyptians, as well as the miracles performed during their travels out of Egypt, the splitting of the sea and the drowning of the Egyptian pursuers. Yet even after seeing these dramatic and repeated supernatural demonstrations, the Bible tells us in Exodus 32 that these same Israelites, upon being gripped by fears and passions, worshiped the golden calf. And later, as recounted by the Bible in Numbers 14, although they witnessed various miracles in the desert, the Israelites doubted God's promise that they would conquer the land of Canaan, and even wished to return to Egypt. The Bible, then, in these accounts and others—notably in its first story about humans, Adam and Eve succumbing to temptation and disobeying the Creator—illustrates its view that open divine revelation and clear miracles do *not* eliminate freedom of choice in obeying, or having faith in, God. It will not do, then, to argue in the name of the Bible's religions that such things *would* eliminate freedom of choice.

For these reasons and more, my brother, we must conclude that if God wished to communicate with humans by way of miracle, to show us His supernatural existence and will, He would not be constrained to perform only weak and inconclusive acts some choose to see as "miracles." Instead, He would either perform indisputable signs and wonders as clear messages to mankind, or He would not attempt such demonstrations at all. Thus, from mere stories of miracles we cannot know of God's existence. For in the case of ambiguous events, or acts and occurrences open to skeptical interpretation, our only responsible course is to assume that they are not supernatural, but belong rather to the natural order, which our patient and persistent inquiries have repeatedly shown to explain all that comes to pass beneath the sun—and beyond it, too.

29. Experiencing or witnessing miraculous healings after prayer

Then a devout woman spoke, saying: I have seen with my own eyes people healed by prayer, when physicians had given up all hope. I do not rely on some story told by others; I myself have witnessed these glorious events. God listens to prayers, and heals by miracle; therefore I know He exists.

And the sage said: My sister, I know how deep is the yearning for a God to heed our prayers when we plead for the lives of loved ones. And, yes, at times healing occurs in the aftermath of prayer. Yet do not unexpected recoveries occur in all diseases—without appeal to the supernatural? Does not the body often heal itself? How, then, can we know that any healing is due to prayer?

Second, even if prayer heals, must it be God doing the healing? If a believer prays, or knows prayers are being said on her behalf, surely this might inspire in her the belief that she will heal—and belief of healing itself has long been known by physicians to be powerful medicine.[1] Thus, even if prayer were sometimes to trigger healing in the believer, it need not involve any supernatural intervention.

And we have not responsibly found that prayer is effective in cases where the sick person is unaware of these efforts on her behalf.[2] And even if someday

---

[1] I refer of course to the placebo effect, which is so powerful that, for many years now, proposed medical treatments and drugs are almost invariably tested against placebos— pills or other substances or procedures that appear identical to the healing treatment but actually do not contain the curative element being tested. Moreover, such tests are generally conducted in a "double-blind" fashion; that is, not even the physicians or researchers directly administrating the placebos and the medicinal or curative substances or procedures being tested know which subjects are getting which. So potent is the expectation of healing, that even if only the physician or researcher knows which people have been genuinely treated, their positive expectations are understood to possibly result in better outcomes. Numerous research studies document the effectiveness of placebos, and indicate that such effectiveness, though varying by condition and other factors is, by nearly all accounts, very high—often estimated, for some ailments, at between thirty and sixty percent. For interesting discussion of this topic, see *The Placebo Effect: An Interdisciplinary Exploration*, published by Harvard University Press, 1999.

The mind is also well capable of producing negative effects if it believes the body has been subjected to a destructive agent or cause; this is often referred to as the nocebo response. Well before controlled scientific studies proved this effect, observant individuals noticed it. For one example among many, Joseph Addison, the English man of letters who lived into the early 18th century, wrote in his essay, *Household Superstitions*, "I remember I was once in a mixed assembly that was full of noise and mirth, when on a sudden an old woman unluckily observed there were thirteen of us in company. This remark struck a panic terror into several who were present, insomuch that one or two of the ladies were going to leave the room; but a friend of mine taking notice that one of our female companions was big with child, affirmed there were fourteen in the room, and that, instead of portending one of the company should die, it plainly foretold one of them should be born. Had not my friend found this expedient to break the omen, I question not but half the women in the company would have fallen sick that very night."

[2] Periodically, studies and books are published purporting to document that prayer is at least slightly effective even when those prayed for are not aware of prayers being said on their behalf. To date, none of these findings have withstood the rigors of sustained critique or unbiased replications of the experiments. Indeed, somewhat recently, a large scientific study, involving over 1,800 patients at six hospitals, was conducted to investigate the possible helpfulness of prayer for people undergoing heart surgery. The study was supported by the John Templeton Foundation, and significantly involved in the project was Herbert Benson, M.D. of the Mind/Body Medical Institute. Thus, there would not likely have been an anti-prayer bias to the study. The results were published as *Study of the Therapeutic Effects of Intercessory Prayer (STEP) in cardiac bypass patients*, an article in *The American Heart Journal*, Volume 151, Issue 4, (April 2006), and the abstract of the article concludes that "Intercessory prayer itself had no effect on complication-free recovery..." and that "...certainty of receiving intercessory prayer was associated with a

we were to find that it *is* effective, something other than God—other than any of the many gods of the many religions past and present—may account for such prayers' success.[1] Mystery does not constitute evidence, much less proof, that a specific attempt at explaining the mystery is true.

Third, my sister, if your argument were convincing, would it not prove too much? Do not all peoples and religions report successes in their attempts to heal the sick through prayer? Yet many of these religions teach that other religions are deeply mistaken in their foundational beliefs and, often teach, too, that other religions' gods do not even exist. If effective prayer proves divine intervention, it would seem to prove all these gods powerful, or all these spiritual belief systems capable of eliciting divine healing. And is this conclusion one that traditional religions would comfortably accept?

Most of all, my sister, is it not true that prayer usually does *not* heal, but rather leaves us pleading into silent skies, our calls unanswered, our tears shed in vain? Do not the majority of the gravely ill die, and not recover, though nearly all are prayed for? And has not your mother or sister, father or brother, friend or neighbor, perished—notwithstanding prayer vigils held on that poor soul's behalf?

---

higher incidence of complications." The study showed that not only among those who did not know whether they were being prayed for did the patients prayed for *not* have a better rate of smooth recovery (indeed, they had a slightly worse rate), even those who knew they were being prayed for did not benefit—they had a significantly worse rate of smooth recovery. These results seem to indicate no essential effectiveness of prayer, but a possible psychologically-based effect—in the case of the study, a negative effect—when one knows prayers are being said on one's behalf.

Nevertheless, even if that study's findings were to be consistently replicated and upheld, it would still be reasonable to consider that in many cases of prayer when, unlike the cases in the aforementioned study, a patient prays for himself, or is prayed for by friends, loved ones, or the prayer involves people and gods whose spiritual effectiveness he trusts, the psychological effects of such trust and positive expectation may well increase the likelihood of successful recovery.

[1] Various systems of metaphysics have long held that the focused mental powers and compassionate energies of those praying have salutary effects—by natural means—on the health and fortunes of those prayed for. This belief is speculation, of course, incompatible with current scientific knowledge, deserves our skepticism, and should not be accepted as truth until such time as compelling evidence is forthcoming in its support. The belief does illustrate, however, that God overall—and certainly any specific religion's notion of God—is not the only conceivable solution to the puzzle of why prayer might be effective beyond the placebo effect and other natural means—if indeed so it is ever shown to be.

Indeed, do not some become more ill, or even die suddenly, shortly after being prayed for, in cases where the physicians had expected them to recover? Shall we insist that prayer kills, merely because in those cases death followed prayer? If not, let us be consistent and, when recovery follows prayer, not insist that the healing was necessarily caused by the prayer. Rather, let us consider the more natural and humble causes of health and illness, and of life and death.

My sister, how desperately we wish to rescue our dying dear ones, for we lose pieces of our own heart when they go, and our loyalty is shown to be impotent, and our competence is sorely wounded, in our inability to save them from humiliating demise. And our own reflected mortality, too, causes us to cry out in childlike vulnerability for a Living God who might shepherd us away from the terrifying cliffs of death, or catch us softly when we, too, must take the inevitable plunge. And so it is that we yearn to believe in prayer and in its power of healing and salvation.

Yet as we walk through these fierce, withering wastelands, let us rather be noble and guard vigilantly against our weaker tendencies, lest desperate longings conjure, even in what may be a barren landscape, the phantom oasis of divine favor, and the pitiable mirage of eternal grace.

30. Personal prayers answered

And a voice in the crowd said: You may doubt the effectiveness of prayer all you like, but I know it works. I have prayed about many things, and my prayers were answered. Thus I know there is a God, and that He cares for me.

And the sage replied: My brother, every nation prays to its own gods and spirits, and every religion speaks of many prayers answered. Yet every major faith teaches that other faiths are mistaken in their foundational beliefs. If subjective conviction of answered prayers proves them truly effective, they have seemed to be so for every familiar religion and every discarded creed, too. Those who worshiped the sun and moon, or ten thousand now-forgotten goddesses and idols, also believed their prayers were answered. Is any belief system proved by all this? Shall we conclude that every obsolete object of pagan veneration is a true and living deity merely because her worshipers believed their supplications had elicited supernatural favor?

Moreover, my brother, what of the majority of your prayers—those not answered? Have you not prayed for the recovery of a desperately ill friend or loved one, and death still came? Have you not prayed many times for success and wealth, or friendship and peace, and on various occasions these did not come to pass? Do such results prove there is no God? If seemingly unanswered prayers do not indicate the lack of a God, why do seemingly answered prayers prove the existence of a God? If we are truthful must we not concede that those outcomes we confidently attribute to prayer are far from signed with God's unambiguous signature, and that our wishes and yearnings may come true, or be brushed aside by fate, for reasons unrelated to our fervent whisperings to a possible God?

Chance alone insists that at times we are kissed by success and adoration, at other times spat upon by failure and contempt. If two warriors battle to the death, one will win, by natural means, and the other lose. Nevertheless, if both prayed before the battle, the victor will be inclined to believe his prayer was answered. Or if a woman has three suitors in her town, and she must choose one, if all three prayed for her love, the one she chooses will suspect that his prayer was answered. Yet could not the blind, deaf, and mute idols of unsupervised randomness have answered prayers as well? Would not one of these have met with success without the existence or intervention of any deity?

And man's own actions, or natural events, often bring about good fortune. With effort and courage, preparation and skill, intelligence and charm, and other earthly attributes, many missions will meet with success. If one prays, performs well, and achieves good results, does it prove prayer effective, any more than does waking refreshed from a full night's sleep after praying for renewed energies? Many events and effects occur naturally.

And, my brother, another reason prayer seems effective is that it focuses the conscious mind upon goals. When we address a deity with our hopes and plans, the process brings the heart and mind into a state of concentration. This helps focus our actions; and focused action often leads to success. For this reason, those who teach the skills of achievement, speak—without any necessary reference to God or prayer—of the importance of identifying and remaining focused upon one's goals.

Moreover, there are the deeper, more subtle effects of prayer, that do their work in the unconscious mind, the farther caves of the soul, teaching the eyes what to see, the ears what to hear, and the brain what to think. Intense prayer—producing deep focus within—sets the filter of the spirit, and the compass of the bones, so that one finds oneself noticing the right people, saying the right words, and living in rhythm with success. All this is quite the natural process of providing focus for our complex, unconscious minds. We cannot consciously notice everything our eyes see, else our consciousness would be flooded. Instead, our unconscious mind brings to our attention that which it believes important. Intense concentration, such as prayer, teaches the deeper mind what are our goals, after which—through natural means—the deeper mind brings to our awareness all that is helpful for successful action. Then, our deeds seemingly charmed, we credit the gods.

Finally, prayer allows us to overcome our weak spirits. If we pray to God, and expect His help, we are no longer bound by what we perceive to be our poor abilities. Thus, we plant boldly, fertilize our richly-seeded fields with the gods' food of confidence, and gather in a harvest of abundance. And so it is that even secular teachers of achievement speak of the importance of believing in oneself and in the inevitability of one's success, and of affirming these beliefs several times daily.

For these reasons, and more,[1] my brother, although in the aftermath of seemingly answered prayers it is reasonable to wonder if some force hears prayer and intervenes in human affairs, we cannot honestly be confident of this pleasing hypothesis—much less can we trust that any such force there may be is the God of our particular creed.

31. Argument that religion must be true, because many scientists and philosophers have believed in God

Then a merchant stepped forward and said: I am no scholar, but a man of trade, who crosses the seas and returns to market. I have not studied these matters in depth, yet many intelligent men worship my God, and experts of great worldly knowledge argue His might—even some geniuses of mathematics and science and philosophy believe in my God. Therefore I may rest confident that my traditions are true.

And the sage said: My brother, the faith of able and learned notables might at first seem to add credibility to your beliefs. Yet let us consider the matter closely. Surely intelligence and knowledge are unreliable indicators of religious truth; for every tradition has its keen minds, and all gods and goddesses number among their worshipers collectors of worldly knowledge. Are there not exceptional men across the seas in the lands to which you travel, of advanced learning too, who kneel before gods you know not, and swear their allegiance to faiths you find

---

[1] Consistent with an earlier footnote regarding the possible effectiveness of prayer for healing, I would remind the reader that some, unsatisfied with purely psychological or conventional scientific explanations for the power of expectation and belief, claim that our minds, when focused, tap into great unspecified energies; that a metaphysical law causes us to attract what we expect—and that intense and confident prayer brings about desired results—even without God. To be sure, believers in such a metaphysical law have the heavy burden of proving this remarkable claim, before responsible thinkers could accept it as true. Nevertheless, if it should some day be found that confident prayer brings success in ways that transcend all apparent psychological and natural means, it would be well to remember that possible explanations exist which do not require us to postulate divine intervention. Thus, even if research were to prove prayer effective, humble open-mindedness on the reason for such effectiveness would seem the more honest stance than conviction that such effects result from the direct intervention of gods or spirits—especially those one is pleased to call one's own.

puzzling and strange? If the learned and scientific are to be followed on spiritual matters, why, then, do you not believe in these other gods?

My brother, intelligence is one thing; truth, quite another. When deprived of food, the bellies of the learned growl as does your own; and when lonely, their hungry hearts and empty arms yearn for yielding warmth, too. And so it is that the soul of man, whether simpleton, everyman, or sage, is often seduced by the fear-joy of belonging, the free-bondage of worship, and the overpowering allure of Hope, that sacred harlot who woos us from today's valor and candor with whisperings of salvation on a distant morrow.

My brother, honesty has never been the handmaiden of knowledge, nor courage the blood brother of brilliance. Many are the scholars among the mistaken and self-deceiving—and might we not spare them some compassion? For are they not chased by dread and hounded by conceit—would they not forfeit their status and position within their religious communities if they were to recognize and acknowledge that their beliefs are mistaken? And are they not held fast to their traditions by the tear-soaked knots of ancient tribe, and weighed down from escape by the awe of religion's heavy tomes, and by the marble and bones of their ancestors' tombs?

Moreover, my brother, you argue that men of science agree with your religious views. Yet if you would rely upon scientists' opinions on sacred matters, why rely on those who accept traditional religion? What of the many leading scientists who—though they may see within the fabric of the universe a weave of complexity undeniable—remain skeptical even that a Creator is the source of it, and how much more so of religions' claim that God has spoken to humans and has told us how He wants us to behave, and what He wants us to believe? Unless the great preponderance of scientists believe that science supports religion's claims—and, my brother, such is not the case—to rely upon religious scientists is not to build one's case upon science, but rather to fasten upon selective evidence so as to justify beliefs to which one is already committed.[1]

---

[1] Believers are often bolstered in their confidence in religion when coming upon God-fearing passages written by the famed and learned, such as Francis Bacon (1561-1626), who rightfully wore among other hats those of a philosopher and pioneer in scientific methodology, and who, in his essay *Of Atheism* writes: "It is true, that a little philosophy inclineth man's mind to atheism; but depth in philosophy bringeth men's minds about to religion. For while the mind of man looketh upon second causes scattered, it may sometimes rest in them, and go no further; but when it beholdeth the chain of them, confederate and linked together, it must needs fly to Providence and Deity."

Yet that essay advances poor arguments—e.g., atheists, Bacon insists, must not truly believe there is no God, because they talk so much about it, and try to get disciples, which, says Bacon, they would not feel the need to do if they believed their position; and

The foremost point, however, is that no scientist or philosopher or any other can do your thinking on ultimate spiritual concerns. Yes, it is wise to hear the arguments of the learned—but it is you who must finally render a verdict. As no other was born for you, and no other can travel the great mystery-trail of death in your stead, so too must you sit alone in the courthouse of your soul, and in sacred solitude weigh upon the scales of eternal justice the great questions of truth. You are the judge destiny has called to pass sentence upon belief systems ancient and recent; to hallow or forsake the many values and precepts offered by the world's established traditions and modern innovations, and to decide what principles will rule your life. My wisdom, too, cannot displace this glory-burden from the very center of your heart. Examine my words well, and if they prove false pronounce judgment against them. For neither the long words of scholars nor the thundering poetry of prophets can justly choose your life's course. It is

---

atheists will sometimes endure punishment rather than recant their views, a choice, Bacon says, they would not make if they believed there to be no God. But—and I say this as a non-atheist—did Bacon not notice that many among the religious are in the habit of talking about their beliefs rather consistently, too; and that they attempt to make disciples at least as energetically as do atheists? Was he not aware that people with passionate beliefs often desire to share them? And was it beyond his imagination that some, atheists included, prefer to suffer the blows of intolerance and hate, rather than forego their integrity, or even that men might resist their oppressors out of mere defiance and pride? Moreover, are there not many atheists who show no inclination toward speaking frequently on the matter, or gaining disciples?

Not only does this essay of Bacon reflect far from the best thinking of that very accomplished man, but the four centuries or so since its writing have seen the physical sciences, philosophy, and psychology gain vastly more knowledge and intellectual freedom than was available in Bacon's day, and with this increased knowledge and freedom the conclusions of many of our greatest recent and contemporary scientists, philosophers, and psychologists have been significantly at odds with the many supernatural teachings of traditional religion, and with Bacon's conclusion that depth in philosophy supports religious belief—even merely in "Providence or Deity."

Innumerable contemporary scientists and philosophers are non-theists, and even a very short list of well-known infidels of generations past includes Spinoza, Hume, Voltaire, Nietzsche, Schopenhauer, Freud, Dewey, Einstein, and Russell, a number of whom were outright atheists, and none of whom believed in the God of the Bible. And it is well to remember, too, that such towering ancient thinkers as Aristotle, Socrates, and Plato also did not believe in the Christ, Yahweh, or Allah of which today's popular religions teach.

To be clear, this or any other list of eminent non-believers does not prove the case for either atheism or agnosticism; but it does discredit the case for relying upon the religious convictions of others, no matter how scientifically or philosophically eminent, as valid indicators of religion's truth.

you who must learn; you who must see; you who must decide. And this is, perhaps, your greatest duty to the Universe and to your soul.

32. Argument that things work out for the best, sometimes in unlikely ways, and this proves the existence of a benevolent God

And a cheerful woman said: Things work out for the best in the end. We worry about so many small things, but our concerns prove unfounded. Even in big things and in surprising ways, God directs events for the best outcome. Have you not heard of the great ship that went down, and all the people aboard were rescued? And do you not know that octuplets were born and all survived, with perfect little fingers and hearts and kidneys and everything? These events tell me that a God, a compassionate God, exists, and orchestrates our lives for the best.

And the sage said: My sister, optimism is a pleasant philosophy of life, and often leads to practical success, too. We sleep easier and wake more eagerly when we believe each day dawns to bring us benefit; and we notice opportunities more quickly, and attain our heart's desires more often, when we expect good things to happen. To be sure, then, in most arenas of life we are wise to focus primarily upon what has gone well and what can be made to go well—and so to cultivate gratitude and confidence. But in the arena of ultimate issues—when we attempt to learn for our children and ourselves what we can honestly believe about God, religion, and life's meaning—it is degrading to distort our vision of truth in any direction, even toward the cheerful. And if we are to be honest, my sister, we cannot claim to know that everything works out for the best.

Yes, many of the small things about which we worry do not come to pass, but it is also true that many small difficulties, even fearsome and terrible things too, come to pass about which we did not even think to worry. And, my sister, yes, I have heard of the ship that went down and all were rescued, but have we not also heard of the many drowned even when their ship did not go down, and shall we pretend not to know of the myriads of uncounted corpses that through the ages have ever been tossed about on the cruel sea? And, yes, I know that octuplets were born and all survived; but do we not also know of babes stillborn or born deformed or gravely ill, even when they were the only ones in the womb? Should we not be embarrassed to look out at life so selectively? Is it, then, a virtue to think poorly, if only the conclusion we reach seems to us devout?[1]

---

[1] Though poor thinking abounds on every matter of engagement and discourse, such inferior reasoning is particularly shameful when applied to matters of greatest significance, such as claims about the existence or will of God. Recently I saw a sermon on film by perhaps the foremost Christian evangelist of the past half century. Confident and charismatic, he thundered forth with the following astonishingly poor claim. He said that the greatest mystery of the universe, which no professor could explain, was why there

My sister, tell history's innumerable sobbing mothers whose children lived short and miserable lives, and died terrible deaths of famine or disease; tell them that everything works out for the best. Tell the bowed and broken myriads who died in slavery and oppression; tell them that everything works out for the best. Tell the uncounted millions slain by bandits, by tyrants, by war or genocide; tell them that everything works out for the best. Tell the hosts of young and old snuffed out by swift-moving plague or slow-killing malady; indeed, tell the multitudes killed and maimed by millennia of religious violence. Tell them all, and their loved ones, too, that everything works out for the best.

If you, my sister, live in a land of prosperity and peace, and succeed at weathering the relatively small amount of suffering and defeat life throws in your path—or even if you have seen deep suffering, and still choose to look upon it brightly—do not insult the memory of the exiled and persecuted, the tortured, the crippled, the savagely murdered, the elderly abandoned and the too-young dead, for whom we dare not insist that everything worked out for the best.

Moreover, my sister, even if we lived in a universe in which all things did work out for the best, drawing religious conclusions from that circumstance would remain unwarranted. For how such a universe came about, and whether any God ever had—or continues to have—a hand in it, and what if anything such a God might want of us, and whether He approves of any religion, would yet remain, in our deeply honest moments, a sacred mystery.

---

was evil—why men had lust and greed and hate in their hearts. He insisted that the answer can be found only in the Bible, and was related to Lucifer's rebellion against God.

While it takes only a committed mind to believe the teaching that appetites and passions originated in a supernatural drama, it takes, for an intelligent man, a remarkably closed and well-defended mind to think, and certainly to say without shame in an address to a full stadium of spectators, that such natural inclinations constitute the universe's greatest mystery, and that no professor could offer a satisfactory alternative explanation. Indeed, the irony is that while calling everyone's attention to the supposed mysteries of lust and greed and hate—which, of course, are easily seen to be survival and reproductive advantages having their possible natural sources in evolution by natural selection—the reverend was loudly demonstrating another phenomenon at least as seemingly mysterious: the ability of an intelligent mind to be so taken with an idea, that it becomes blinded not only to anything that might call the idea itself into question, but even to elementary reason that might show why a particular argument in favor of the idea is unsound.

Such transparently poor thinking in the service of what one believes is God's will reminds me of the old woman living at the time the airplane was invented, who was strenuously opposed to the innovation, believing it was not man's place to fly, and citing in support of her case the Bible verse which says, "The heavens are heavens for the Lord, and the earth He gave to man." "Besides," she concluded with triumphant self-satisfaction, "if God had intended us to fly, He would never have given us trains."

33. Argument that ancestors in dreams prove God and religion

And a woman said: My dead father came to me in a dream, and spoke to me of things that did not happen until a later day. Surely this proves the existence of a spiritual world, and a God, and justifies my religious beliefs!

And the sage replied: My sister, your father appearing in a dream, seemingly from the other side of death, must have left you deeply moved, and I can see how this might lead you to feel more confident in traditional beliefs. Yet truth asks of us great care in how we interpret our experiences, no matter how moving they may be. Error is often but the overreaching cousin of accuracy—and the most seductive mistakes woo with the charms of partial truth. Although we may be puzzled, even astonished, by some dreams, it would be a mistake to derive from them specific spiritual or religious beliefs.

First, consider that so much of what our forebears found perplexing we now know to be natural, and to have reasonable explanations requiring no religious or occult beliefs. Among innumerable other superstitions, men have believed that thunder and lightning resulted from warring gods, that plagues were spread by dark angels and evil spirits, that crops failed because of witches' spells, and that the sun would only continue to rise if priests maintained their daily practice of human sacrifice. With our species guilty of such a long record of mistaking the bewildering for the otherworldly, does it not behoove us to be cautious in concluding that what is puzzling must be supernatural?

Second, let us here remember the distinction between perception and interpretation. Facts we can often accurately perceive, but our conclusions and our overall experience are based not upon facts alone, but upon the combination of facts and our interpretation of those facts. So, too, the mind often applies more than the bare "facts" of the dream in seeing predictions as accurate. A vague warning dreamed—for example, that suffering is coming—can later be applied to any of hundreds of possible events. Anything from failed romance to painful illness, from bodily injury to deep melancholy, from money losses to difficulties with children, even catastrophic war, can seem like the eerie fruition of a remarkable presentiment or prophecy. Indeed, we are likely to think back and remember the dream as specifically referring to what, in the end, occurred. And, of course, a prediction with innumerable possible fulfillments has no true fulfillment.

Furthermore, many dreams later remembered as foretelling specific events, neither directly foretold anything, nor were understood at the time as doing so. If a man has a vivid dream of walking through a large field, and a year later inherits a farm, he may look back at the dream and shudder at the uncanny accuracy of the prediction. But the dream did not predict anything, nor did he see it as doing anything of the sort at the time—and if he were never to have inherited a farm, he would not have looked back and considered the dream a false prediction.

When given the advantage of retrospect, the human mind can draw all manner of dubious connections between events and earlier "signs."

In addition, my sister, many of the predictions or warnings in dreams, which may seem unknowable by natural processes, are seen, upon critical reflection, to be well within the capabilities of our intuition and less-understood instincts. Students of the mind have often observed that the greatest portion of our mental functioning takes place below the level of everyday awareness. Indeed, dreams often present to us, sometimes in dramatic or symbolic form, ideas we avoid in our waking hours—but which are well known to the mind's deep regions. When the unconscious, that primal and powerful guardian, wishes to send a dramatic message, should we be surprised that in the theatre of dream it would communicate through some of the more fitting and emotionally resonant tools at its disposal—visions of our departed dear ones, those who, if they were able, would indeed speak to us on important matters?

Moreover, the deep, unconscious belief elicited by a dream—even in those who protest that at the time they did not believe in the power of dreams—may cause one to think and behave in ways that bring about the dream's realization. If a young lady dreams that she will meet her "soul-mate" soon, is she not more likely to groom herself to her best appearance, to ask friends for introductions, to notice available men in her environs, to return their glances with more confidence and cheer, to interpret words and gestures as perhaps leading to romance—and in a hundred other ways, by her own thought and behavior, to enhance the likelihood that she will, indeed, meet a lover? And, if she does meet one, is she not more likely to pour greater energies into the relationship, seeing it as a fulfillment of destiny?

In addition, my sister, by the laws of chance alone, some predictive dreams will come true. If ten thousand people dream they will be wealthy, will not several of them, with no more than usual effort, attain wealth in any case—by the unthinking, unfeeling, perfectly natural laws of chance? But will it not be tempting for these fortunate ones to suspect that the dream provided supernatural advance knowledge of their fate? Indeed, upon reflection, must we not concede that most predictive dreams remain unfulfilled—and are then quickly forgotten?

And even if no natural explanation for the dream's prediction seemed possible, would it prove that humans live on after death—much less that any particular religion is true? Or might we, in such a case, be honest and say that we do not understand how a dream predicts? Or, if one insists on speculating, might one not as easily and justly speculate that the living have intuitive powers the limits and workings of which we do not yet comprehend—powers that seem to enable the mind at times to tap into future events and speak to us of things to come, through the powerful symbolism and imagery of those we cared for, feared or trusted most—our deceased loved ones? This speculation one could not honestly and responsibly claim to know to be accurate, even if persuasive evidence of truly predictive dreams existed—and it does not. But it would be even more dishonest and irresponsible to jump to the conclusion that such dreams confirm religions' grandiose and detailed teachings on topics they have never proved to know anything about—a supposed supernatural God and His wishes of man.

Finally, note that people of all religions, and those of no religion too, have dreams like yours. Dreams, therefore, even those that are startling or impressive, do not prove any religion accurate. If you had a puzzling dream of your father, so have others had puzzling dreams of their fathers. If the Christian, the Hindu, the Muslim, the Buddhist, the Jew, the agnostic, and the atheist have all experienced fathers revealing information to them in dreams—what sacred beliefs could such dreams prove? Religions contradict each other on foundational matters and cannot all be accurate—yet adherents of each, and those without religion, too, have seemingly predictive dreams. Indeed, some have speculated that early religions incorporating ancestor worship were influenced, perhaps begun, by felt encounters like yours: a parent or ancestor appearing in a dream.

In summary, if we are to maintain our integrity, we must not allow mystery to shake us so, that we jump to unwarranted conclusions. Hasty interpretations, especially those agreeing with our deepest convictions or earliest influences, are often misguided. And, my sister, if your father's soul yet lives—and looks down upon you from the enlightened world of spirit many hope there may be—would he not be most proud of a daughter who exercised the nobility and courage to think honestly and with great care on these important matters, who resisted the seductive echoes of childhood and turned away from the persuasions of primal superstition?

34. Argument that something as complex as the human mind must survive death; therefore there must be a spiritual realm and a God

And a scholar said: I cannot believe that the human mind, in all its complexity, dies completely. A spiritual dimension must exist, where we live on after death. And so I hold fast to my beliefs in God and religion.

And the sage replied: My brother, the human mind is, indeed, a magical wheel upon which is spun the fine gold of skill, story, learning, and speculation, from but the common straw of matter and time. Tender poetry, magnificent art, inspired invention, brilliant mathematics, and libraries heaped up with knowledge and wisdom—all these have subdued and transformed for our species the wildness of our planet into enchanted imagination, civilized governance, and diverse and prolific craftsmanship. My brother, I join you in marveling at the human mind.

But come with me to the forests, the mountains, the jungles, and the fields—see how they blossom and bristle with innumerable forms of intricate life, too. Can you fashion the buzzing honeybee, or the soft, bright-hued flower from which she returns heavy with pollen? Can you craft the wings of feathery flight, or hone the skill of fangs on the hunt? Can you teach the tree to color her leaves in autumn, or the meadows to don their greenest in spring? So elaborately crafted are these flora and fauna. Shall we, then, insist that they live on for eternity, too?

And what of the famed industry of the ant; the silky engineering of the spider; the cooperative society of the wolf; the gentle communality of the giant elephant; the gifted mimicry of the sharp-witted parrot; and the keen minds of our strikingly familiar simian kin? Are all these not possessed of astonishing complexity, too—some, more so in various ways than are we? Yet do our hymns sing of an afterlife for all these remarkable creatures, too?[1]

---

[1] Seeing one's own species as especially blessed or deserving is natural. Montaigne, in Chapter XII of his *Essays*, in his *Apology of Raymond Sebond*, writes: "We must note that nothing is more dear and precious to any thing than its own being...Therefore *Xenophanes* said pleasantly, that if beasts frame any Gods unto themselves, as likely it is they do, they surely frame them like unto themselves, and glorify themselves as we do. For why may not a goose say thus? All parts of the world behold me, the earth serveth me to tread upon, the sun to give me light, the stars to inspire me with influence; this commodity I have of the wind, and this benefit of the waters: there is nothing that this worlds-vault doth so favourably look upon as me self; I am the favorite of nature; is it not man that careth for me, that keepeth me, lodgeth me, and serveth me? For me it is he soweth, reapeth, and grindeth: if he eat me, so doth man feed on his fellow and so do I on the worms that consume and eat him..."

And in his poem titled *Heaven*, Rupert Brooke addressed the familiar conviction of an afterlife, by way of parody:

> Fish (fly-replete, in depth of June,
> Dawdling away their wat'ry noon)
> Ponder deep wisdom, dark or clear,
> Each secret fishy hope or fear.
> Fish say, they have their Stream and Pond;
> But is there anything Beyond?
> This life cannot be All, they swear,
> For how unpleasant, if it were!
> One may not doubt that, somehow, Good
> Shall come of Water and of Mud;
> And, sure, the reverent eye must see
> A Purpose in Liquidity.
> We darkly know, by Faith we cry,
> The future is not Wholly Dry.
> Mud unto mud! — Death eddies near —
> Not here the appointed End, not here!

Or speak to those who have shared close bonds with a dog, a cat, a bird, or another animal; ask them if they did not experience in these relationships a deep connection to a complex being.

And allow not vanity to persuade you that, unlike man, these many other spirit-strands—bound up, all of them, in the sacred cord of life—are too simple in their consciousness to warrant eternity. For perhaps human complexity and self-awareness, though superior in important ways to simpler creatures, are still not sufficiently advanced to merit unending existence. Who can designate the complexity level at which mortal creatures end, and the supposedly immortal begin? Much as most of us do not see a great difference between the degrees of complexity distinguishing an ant from a bee—perhaps, from a possible Creator's perspective, apes and humans are not sufficiently different that one must be obliterated at death, and the other live on forever.

And what of man's machines? Shall we insist that these clever creations—in all their impressive complexity, performing many tasks more skillfully than we

---

But somewhere, beyond Space and Time.
Is wetter water, slimier slime!
And there (they trust) there swimmeth One
Who swam ere rivers were begun,
Immense, of fishy form and mind,
Squamous, omnipotent, and kind;
And under that Almighty Fin,
The littlest fish may enter in.
Oh! never fly conceals a hook,
Fish say, in the Eternal Brook,
But more than mundane weeds are there,
And mud, celestially fair;
Fat caterpillars drift around,
And Paradisal grubs are found;
Unfading moths, immortal flies,
And the worm that never dies.
And in that Heaven of all their wish,
There shall be no more land, say fish.

And, to be fair, though humans can think and write such things about fish, fish presumably cannot think and write such things for themselves—and this, argue some, is why the human spirit must be immortal and the fish spirit not. But as I ask in the text, what, aside from wishful thinking, persuades us that our powers of intellect and consciousness guarantee an afterlife—and is it not telling how we comfortably accept that various other forms of complexity and talent exhibited by other species do *not* afford such otherworldly durability?

do—when they lie broken and rusted, no longer functioning on earth, must live on for eternity in another realm?

My brother, as tragic as is the possibility that our minds—intricate, compelling, and suffused with meaning as they are—may perish and have no ongoing existence, it may, nevertheless, be so. And in seeking truth we must be willing to see what is, and ever restrain our fears and desires from representing reality to us in the familiar and delightful forms of our deepest longings.

And remember, too, that even if there were no doubt that man's mind was eternal, this would tell us nothing about whether any religion truly knows the existence or will of God. For many religions speak of an afterlife, yet they contradict each other on fundamental beliefs. Not only might *your* religion be mistaken about God and His will, *every* religion might be mistaken. And this, even if we knew man's mind to live on forever. But we know no such thing.

My brother, great is the glory of man. Everywhere—from flowing poetry to flowing canals; from brush-strokes of art to pen-strokes of wisdom; from war councils on the battlefield to legislative councils at the capital—is evident the genius of his incomparable mind. And upon spying man's inescapable, ignominious end, it is no wonder that indignant and tearful we plead: Is the wizard who wielded such magical powers, who held under the sway of his spells all that roamed the teeming plains of life, truly bereft of potion and prayer on the lonely precipice of death? Will none of his hard-won wisdom or well-wrought wiles enable him to cross over in power and peace?

In truth, my brother, we do not know. We cannot say if our minds live on; perhaps they do. Though there is precious little in the way of argument or evidence for such a proposition, we need not close ourselves to the possibility. But, my brother, your argument that our minds *must* live on, does not persuade. For as impressive as are the abilities of man, and as poignant as is our desire to avoid obliteration, sentiments cannot bend in the least the iron laws of reality—whatever such laws may be.

35. "Are you saying that my ancestors and the religious sages of every generation were all stupid or liars?" Argument that saintly religious leaders are intelligent and kind and would not lie—so their teachings about God must be true

Then a man grew irritated and said: Are you saying that my ancestors, and the religious sages of every generation, were all stupid or liars? Many of my community elders are intelligent and compassionate, and honest, too. They would not be deceived and they would not lie! And since they teach of my religion and God, I am confident these beliefs are correct.

And the sage said: My brother, not all who speak untruths are liars; even the most sincere may be mistaken. One who transmits errors, believing them to be truths—even one who is deeply misguided yet so committed to a belief system that he is unable to think clearly on such issues—is considerably different from one who intentionally and habitually fabricates tales to mislead others. And I am confident that most of our ancestors and religious sages thought their beliefs true, and did not intend to lead anyone astray on such matters.

And many elders are, indeed, gentle and kind, and for this it is well to accord them honor. Yet honor is different from unsighted reliance and unverified trust. We alone must be accountable for our beliefs and decisions on such matters as religion. My brother, the flower of gentle saintliness thrives not always in the same soil as the fruit of keen-questioning intellect. The greatest saints may be poor philosophers; and what they believe, with all intense sincerity, may not stand the test of critical, informed, and wide-ranging reason.

And observe the variety of claims made by the world's many spiritual traditions other than your own. Are not many of their leaders intelligent and well meaning, too? And do not all peoples have their priests or shamans, their scholars and saints? And surely you would not call all the religious notables of every faith other than your own stupid or liars. Yet each faith espouses beliefs differing from, even contradictory to, those of other faiths. Can good intentions, then, reliably indicate truth?

And, indeed, my brother, religious leaders throughout the ages have certainly not been stupid; they have, at times, wielded society's sharpest intellects. Nevertheless, intelligence is no substitute for accurate knowledge. It has long been noted that our wisdom is somewhat limited by the generation in which we live.[1]

Religious sages of yore were not stupid for being unaware of the scientific and technological advances of later days; not stupid for being blind to the best teachings of philosophy and of other religions; not stupid for not strictly applying modern standards of reason and evidence. They simply lacked knowledge, either because they lived before such knowledge was discovered, or because they were not educated on such things. And the most brilliant men of our day—had they lived in earlier days, or in certain insular communities—would have been saddled with much of this ignorance, too.

And in addition to insufficient knowledge, errant beliefs are maintained for another set of reasons—powerful unconscious allegiances to mother and father and history and tribe. And these, too, do not involve stupidity or intentional

---

[1] Thoreau said: "A man is wise with the wisdom of his time only, and ignorant with its ignorance. Observe how the greatest minds yield in some degree to the superstitions of their age."

lying—and they ensnare even the kindest and most intelligent among us. The unconscious mind, in an effort to protect us, prevents us from seeing ideas and understanding truths that too profoundly threaten our sensibilities, and employs all the mind's intelligence and skill—constructing elaborate defenses, distractions, and rationalizations—to avoid confronting thoughts too painful to bear. And as the swiftest runner does not overtake his sun-shadow more easily than does the slowest—for the shadow runs as fast as the foot, so, too, the intelligent man, not to mention the gentle and compassionate man, is no more immune than the simpleton to being deceived by his own mind.

My brother, do not the learned and sagacious begin life as we do—their world rocking gently in the nurturing tides of sweet mother's bosom, feeling her songs of faith reverberate through her very bones? And when they attain adulthood, are not their souls' ships ever more firmly moored to the island of tradition, held close by the steel anchors of social and vocational bonds, and powerfully dissuaded from exploratory voyages by the existential terrors of a vast and heaving sea?

Indeed, are not religious leaders more motivated—at many levels of awareness and avoidance—to retain their beliefs and loyalties, than are those with occupations unrelated to faith? When the dense clouds of identity and livelihood hang low to shelter belief, can the fine sunrays of truth easily filter through? Having invested so much more in religion than have others, are clergy more likely—or rather less likely—to vigorously challenge and carefully reconsider their sacred traditions?[1]

Moreover, my brother, the testimony of even the most trustworthy man is of little value when he speaks of matters he cannot know—such as foretelling the distant future or testifying in detail on events of ages past. Leaders who base their beliefs on ancient accounts of miracle or revelation cannot know that such events truly occurred. Instead, they rely upon the tales of others, who have relied upon the tales of still others—in a chain of trust whose beginnings are lost to the unquiet dusts of vanished antiquity. Perhaps many generations ago one of these accounts was mistaken, embellished, or misunderstood. Is it so unlikely that inaccurate tales have innocently evolved over hundreds of years, and were then carefully transmitted over hundreds, even thousands of years more—with no intent to deceive?

---

[1] Tolstoy is credited with this similar insight: "…most men, even those at ease with problems of the greatest complexity, can seldom accept even the simplest and most obvious truth if it be such as would oblige them to admit the falsity of conclusions which they have delighted in explaining to colleagues, which they have proudly taught to others, and which they have woven, thread by thread, into the fabric of their lives."

Also, let us not rule out the plain possibility that at some point in the succession of generations, long ago in the dark epochs of pervasive superstition, some well-intentioned religious leaders, in an effort to comfort suffering and inspire courage and faith, may have fashioned for the people tales of miracles and divine revelation—or perhaps some of these were not originally intended to be taken literally, but rather to be symbolic and motivational.[1] And these legends, accumulating over many centuries, may have gradually been accepted as literally true, and included in the Bible.

My brother, are not these natural theories on the transmission and persistence of religious belief—theories applying readily observed human tendencies—more likely to be true than are the various religions' contradictory accounts of supernatural beings, and astonishing tales of gods and prophets and saints repeatedly violating nature's laws?

In short, my brother, many religious leaders have been kind and meant well; yet neither gentle spirit nor good intentions are guarantors against error. Disoriented though this may leave us, we must answer to our souls and to the Universe for the beliefs we take as our own. No leader can speak for us in the privacy of our hearts, and no group can shield us in the grave intimacy of our moments of reckoning.

36. Argument that the beautiful, complex, and unifying concepts of theology are surely not wrong

And a young woman said: You have presented powerful and disturbing arguments—but I have read and heard theologians' beautiful discourses on my religion, tying together so many different concepts and seemingly unrelated points in a deeply satisfying way.[2] All those ideas and details fitting in to a unified theme, and causing me to feel so inspired, would be too much of a coincidence if they were not true. Therefore I know my religion is correct.

And the sage said: My daughter, I can well understand how intelligent people may be drawn to, and impressed by, eloquent and unifying explanations. I enjoy such thoughts, too. Yet if it is truth we seek, creativity and cleverness are not

---

[1] In *Reason in Religion*, Santayana says: "Religion is not essentially an imposture, though it might seem so if we consider it as its defenders present it to us rather than as its discoverers and original spokesmen uttered it in the presence of nature and face to face with unsophisticated men."

[2] Mencken said: "The average man does not get pleasure out of an idea because he thinks it is true: he thinks it is true because he gets pleasure out of it."

enough. We must distinguish between what is conceptually pleasing and what is accurate, between what is intellectually impressive and what is true.[1]

All sacred traditions have their theologians and unifying explanations. Indeed, all major religions have generated innumerable books filled with intelligent and creative elucidation, linking what had seemed to be unrelated pieces of information into cohesive systems of theology and homiletics. For thousands of years, Jewish scholars have weaved ingenious and conceptually elegant commentaries on the Hebrew Bible, its stories and commandments, and the indivisible Oneness of God—and even on Talmudic commentaries and commentaries on those commentaries. And for nearly as long, Christian scholars have put forth articulate, inspiring discourses on their extended Bible, and on the concepts of original sin, and salvation through the Lamb of God and the crucifixion at Calvary, and the Resurrection, and The Holy Trinity. And so with Islam, Buddhism, Hinduism and other religions: their scholars through the ages have produced intellectually impressive, emotionally satisfying theologies, homiletics, and exegeses on the beliefs and teachings of their respective creeds.

Yet these religions contradict each other not only on small matters, but on foundational beliefs. Indeed, if truth be told, much impressive intellectual output of any religion's scholars often contradicts not only the opinions and discourses of other religions' scholars, but even those of many of its own. Therefore, although often intellectually pleasing, can they possibly all be accurate? And, if not, why assume that the particular examples of such universal activity, when found in *your* religion are accurate, or indicate any form of supernatural origin or approval?

My daughter, intelligence is not to be mistaken for truth, nor creativity confused with deep honesty. Clever books have been written, and myriad connections drawn, not only supporting each of the major religions, but supporting various mistaken, even outlandish claims, too—to name but two of many: that extraterrestrial beings have been systematically abducting, and performing medical experiments upon, a significant proportion of the human race; and that Earth is hollow and its interior is home to cities of various advanced species and civilizations.[2] And such books and theories elucidate apparently intelligent

---

[1] The 18th century French writer Nicolas Chamfort is credited with saying: "There are well turned-out follies, just as there are smartly-dressed fools."

[2] Such paranormal or conspiratorial notions of creatures from space, or hollow Earth and its purported inhabitants of strange and sinister beings, may teach us nothing about the great beyond or about Earth's interior, but they do illustrate, if another illustration were needed, that strangeness indeed thrives—right here on the surface of our own humble planet.

explanations, seemingly meaningful observations, perhaps even remarkable coincidences—but for all this, their essential claims are no less preposterous.

Of course, not all untrammeled creativity is of equally poor quality. There are particularly egregious and silly examples of following unbridled imagination and spurning reason—but there are creative efforts more reasonable and impressive, too. Yet honesty never mistakes the intellectual mastery of conceptual weaving for even pedestrian accuracy, much less for sacred truth. For truth is not determined by the inspiring or impressive appeal, the elegant aphorism or eloquent turn of phrase—not even by association with brilliant analysis or profound insight. Truth is determined by what is. And some have spoken truth simply, and some have spoken error with great flair and beauty, even with genius.

My daughter, when affecting flirtations at the festival of the spirit, Religion sometimes winks at Reason, dances with Creativity, even embraces stout and sturdy Knowledge; inevitably, though, she returns home to the bosom of her husband Authority, or to that of her illicit lover, Faith.

37. Illustration of imaginative but false theology: God as chicken

And the sage continued, saying: My daughter, to illustrate that clever thinking on matters of the spirit need not be true, I will create for you some novel theology. Let us invent a religion that believes God is a chicken, and observe how many concepts and details then seem more meaningful and unified. And as we attempt this exercise, remember that if even the strange and silly notion of a divine chicken can be constructed into seemingly impressive theology and homiletics, how much easier it is to create such inspiring and seemingly persuasive ideas for ancient and familiar traditions hallowed by time and custom—and given many more concepts and symbols and stories to build with by centuries and millennia of previous contributions to that tradition— and, therefore, how much more must we question our tendency to be impressed by them.

Let us begin, then: In this imaginary religion, God, the Great Chicken, has created the Cosmic Egg—the Universe.[1] Humanity as a collective constitutes the chick, the most important life force, indeed the essential purpose, of the Cosmic Egg.

The egg's yolk, like the sun, is spherical and colored golden, while the egg white is oval. The yolk represents the sun, and the remainder represents that

---

[1] Many years ago, I contrived the notion of this chicken religion, which I thought original, in a mischievous diversion during a study period at seminary. But those familiar with such matters will recognize the conceptual ties to the Orphic egg of Greek mythology, as well as the egg's role in Hindu, Chinese, and other creation myths. Nature's common constituents are handy objects, characters, and metaphors—and ever have men lusted after tools.

which orbits the sun. Thus, the overall shape of the egg is not perfectly spherical, but oval and reminiscent of the elliptical paths of planets orbiting the sun. This physical metaphor of the energy and motion of the cosmos illustrates the divine significance of the egg, and its weighty implications for human affairs.

Moreover, both the sun and the moon—the two great heavenly bodies with strongest influence over our planet—are reminders of the Great Egg: the sunny gold of the egg's yolk, and the moon-like pale of the egg's shell. In fact, just as the sun has essential light, while the moon has no luminosity of its own, its brightness being only a reflection of the sun, so too is the egg yolk essentially productive, while the eggshell's importance is secondary, only in reference to the egg's interior. The Egg symbolizes not only the universe, but the cyclical nature of time and existence, too. The seasons turn, the planets turn, life turns. Universe within universe, truth within truth; and the wise will understand.

And have you wondered why our conception of angels envisions winged creatures? It is because we instinctively recognize that the spiritual sprouts wings—for deep in our souls we know that God is the Great Chicken. Indeed, angels, in theological terms, are little feathers—fragments of holiness, as it were—that fall off the Great Chicken God, and disseminate through the universe God's compassion and love.

And the chicken, though a bird and winged, spends much of its time on the ground, not soaring the heavens like the eagle. God being a chicken, therefore, symbolizes His selfless commitment to mankind, in that He remains involved in earthly affairs, and does not allow Himself to fly off for long into higher realms. The sages of the Chicken religion explain that this constitutes a critical distinction between their tradition and that of the Bible. The Bible compares God to an eagle,[1] but to the Chicken religion not only does the eagle signify an uninvolved deity, it is also the embodiment of an evil spirit, a predator who might eat young chicks if he could. And, incidentally, some scholars say that it is this deep awareness, that God has sacrificed Himself to remain humbly engaged with humans, which caused people to believe in the story of Jesus, a God or Son of God who sacrificed Himself by coming down to earth. Indeed, is any bird more often sacrificed to the needs of humans than is the chicken?

In addition, the egg represents hope, patience, and the miracle of creation—because what at first seems inanimate, gradually, with long patience, transforms itself into the miracle of new life, a chick.

Yet enlightenment and ultimate spiritual development are possible only when the shell cracks and new life escapes its limiting and obscuring prison. Thus, the shell represents the devil and his earthly seductions; it is the necessary evil at our

---

[1] Deuteronomy 32:11

beginning, but a smallness we must grow beyond. Observe how the shell cannot expand as the chick develops; instead, it cracks. And when it does, its fragments bear sharp and unforgiving edges—symbolizing the evil of underdevelopment.

And—say the ancient theologians of the Chicken religion—the moon, associated with the eggshell, symbolizes evil and darkness, and rules the realm of the night. Thus, they say, long human experience has shown that strange and evil events occur more frequently when the moon is full: Insanity and violence increase, as do all manner of perversion and malevolence.[1]

Observe, too, that the rooster—the male energy of the chicken species—awakens the morning and mankind. This is a metaphor for the voice of God calling out to humanity, attempting to rouse us from the snoring, deadening slumber of earthly engagement, to the waking splendor of spiritual awareness.

And the symbol for this religion is the oval, the shape of the egg. Adherents of this belief system explain that such a shape, unique among the many religious symbols, is simple and smooth, signifying wholeness and wisdom, unlike the cross, the crescent, or the star of David—symbols of other major religions—which have sharp edges or interrupted lines, and thus reflect their less advanced, less complete worldviews. Even those religious symbols incorporating the circle clutter it with all manner of complications—and thus diminish the beauty and wisdom of simplicity.

We must, say the wise ones of the Chicken religion, have compassion for those of other traditions, and treat their beliefs with ecumenical respect, for there are constructive and inspiring elements to all faiths. But, gradually, by politely witnessing to them on matters of feathery fulfillment, and perhaps most effectively by being shining examples of blessed and altruistic living, we can attempt to open their eyes to the light of truth and the incomparable joys of salvation—attainable only through walking the sacred path of the Great Chicken.

And now we can understand why one branch of the Chicken religion forbids its adherents to eat eggs and encourages them to eat chicken, while another branch forbids its adherents to eat chicken and encourages them to eat eggs. The

---

[1] And should one protest that such claims of full-moon behavior changes are not consistent with the findings of science, the adherents of the Chicken religion would—just as adherents of other religions—fall into different camps: Fundamentalists would insist by faith that such claims are true notwithstanding the "dubious," "biased," and "ever-changing" findings of science; rationalists and apologists would say that of course such things were never meant literally, and that deeper, more symbolic meanings were intended—and still others would wave away both those positions, and say that regardless of these words' original meaning, it is perfectly acceptable, even noble, to bring our own sensibilities to the analysis of such teachings, for meaning is always contextual, and the community of faith is the unfolding of an ongoing dialogue between man and the Divine.

one branch sees it as a benefit to eat of the chicken, the symbol of God, to take in the holy—similar to how some Christians practice the custom of eating the wafer and wine, in communion, as a means of eating of Jesus. And the egg, according to this branch of the Chicken religion, is forbidden, because it symbolizes the devil and his limitations, and should we take it in, it might spiritually pollute us. The other branch, however, believes that eating of a sacred animal is an offense to God, and therefore forbids eating of the chicken—similar to the Hindu prohibition against eating cows. Eggs, on the other hand, symbolizing the devil, and meriting no such sacred status, may be eaten. Indeed, they believe that consuming the egg symbolizes man defeating evil.

Another important concept of the Chicken religion is that of "Being-Becoming." An egg developing toward its future state as chicken, is the wonderful embodiment of something that exists, but whose entire existence is a process of becoming something else. And this, says the Chicken religion, is the most important aspect of a spiritual life—never-ending improvement, and the ongoing dedication of our life's energies to a brighter, more noble future.

And, my daughter, let us take our study of chicken theology further, and demonstrate that even simple, seemingly trite sayings are deeply significant—for those with eyes to see.

The old admonition not to count one's chickens before they hatch is actually a profound reference to the danger of overconfidence in matters of spiritual growth. God is the Great Chicken, and humanity's sacred objective is to develop from the egg stage to the God-like chicken stage, breaking through the devil's barrier of the eggshell, and assuming the mantle of true chickenhood. But when we see our students, our children, even ourselves, progressing spiritually, we may become complacent and assume that the course of continued development is assured. Thus, the wise maxim cautions us not to count those spiritual gains, those chickens, before they hatch. Instead, we are to remain vigilant in working toward spiritual maturity; for the devil employs devious deceptions and varying distractions in his attempts to stifle our spiritual growth and hold us captive in the cosmic eggshell.

Furthermore, have you never wondered about the expression, "Which came first, the chicken or the egg?" This is no idle conundrum. Contrary to what its common usage would suggest, it is a question brimming with theological and mystical implications—addressing, as it does, the essential identity of God. The question asks for resolution between two alternatives: One is that the Chicken we experience as God is only a limited notion of God, merely a metaphor to which we mortals can better relate, within the laws and limits of the physical universe— as Jewish and Christian theologians often say of the Bible's many human-like characterizations of God, that they are stated "in the language of man." In this case, the Chicken, it would be argued, is only a limited symbolic conceptualization of God, and does not adequately circumscribe His essential identity and powers. A second possibility is that the Chicken we know as God is truly the Ultimate and Unlimited God—even if we mortals are left puzzled, unable to perceive with our limited minds the boundless divinity and ultimate perfection of the Chicken.

Now hear the wisdom of that seemingly trite question, "Which came first, the chicken or the egg?" If the Chicken we know as God is only a limited, earthbound notion of God, then the "egg," which represents the universe, precedes the chicken—for only within the confines and limitations of the physical universe is God, in the minds of humans, conceived of as a Chicken. If, however, the Chicken we know of as God is the essential nature of the Ultimate and Unlimited God, then the "Chicken," came before the "egg"—because the Ultimate and Unlimited Chicken God created and preceded the universe. And this, my daughter, is merely the first layer of understanding on this involved matter; only with deep meditation and sustained focus, supplemented by long study at the feet of the masters, can one hope to unlock the spiritual treasures inherent to a comprehensive grasp of this sacred question.

And have you not heard another ancient question: "Why did the chicken cross the road?" Many dismiss this, too, as a silly riddle. The great mystics of the Chicken tradition, however, have revealed the deep significance of this query, and illuminated the powerful philosophical issues of which it speaks. As we know, the Chicken is God. Now let us consider the nature of a road: A road is a path from a beginning point to an end point. The road referred to in this sadly misunderstood question refers to the purpose and development of the universe. From the point of its creation in the distant past, to the point of its ultimate perfection in that future eschatological age, the universe must progress through a series of developments until it fulfills God's plan and attains its sacred and appointed goal.

Thus, we would expect to see God, the Great Chicken, on the road—that is, directing and leading the world according to His plan. Yet what we see, instead, is a world often gripped by confusion—even chaos. At such times, God does not seem to be on the road at all, but rather seems to be crossing the road—conducting history on a line incompatible with His original plan, and impeding those attempting to walk that good and sacred path—as if love and truth and compassion were not important to Him, as if He were traveling in a different direction entirely. Why does God, at times, seem to punish most severely those devoted to Him; why are houses of worship struck by lightning; why are the people of God visited with tragedies and persecutions? Thus have the mystics of the ages tearfully asked: "Why did the Chicken cross the road?"

Of course, it is no surprise that evil spirits have taken these holy and mystical teachings and turned them into trivial riddles and trite aphorisms. This suits their cynical designs of distracting us from what is most valuable; for they know that belittling or disguising wisdom so that it will not be taken seriously is often their most effective strategy. They know that if they can persuade us to perceive a saying as silly, its words will never be mined for their sparks of holiness and profound wisdom.

And as for the end of days, it has been prophesied that at the time of His divine and inscrutable choosing, the Great God Chicken will swoop down upon the earth, gather up the faithful, give glorious flight to their once hapless wings, and lead their ascent into heaven in final, majestic triumph—abandoning the unworthy to their just fate of tribulation and, ultimately, to fiery destruction on a doomed earth.

*****

My daughter, could not intelligence and creativity develop this system further, and make the absurd Chicken religion sound even more theologically impressive? And, again, if such simple and unfamiliar silliness can be so easily adorned with the glitter of intellect and the shine of enthusiasm, how very easy indeed must it be to do the same and better with religious beliefs and symbols revered for centuries and millennia, aided by scriptures comprising all manner of tales and characters and teachings—and buttressed by hundreds of commentaries and thousands of legends, and the contributions to religious literature of ten thousand scholars of every turn of mind. When given access to enough different pieces, there is virtually no limit to the imposing constructs and impressive connections that can be fabricated by creative thinking.

But clever concepts, even brilliant systems do not constitute truth. Truth is not merely what is intelligent, not simply what we find inspiring, not even what is clearly philosophically sophisticated. Instead, truth is that which is accurate. And accuracy is reliably gained neither by the intellectual virtuosity of theology nor by the sentimental genius of homiletics—but by the humble courage of the intrepid mind, hungry for the bittersweet clarity of knowledge, and willing to pay her often dear price.[1]

---

[1] The confident theologian speaking of God is like the little boy in the joke who sat in his class busying himself with pencil and paper. His teacher came over and asked, "What are you doing?" "I'm drawing a picture of God," said the little boy. "But," said the teacher, "Nobody knows what God looks like." Unfazed, the boy replied: "They will when I'm done."

38. What of brilliant theology and philosophy in support of religion—so brilliant it can hardly be understood?

And an earnest student said: All that you just explained, though creative, was not beyond my comprehension. But brilliant books—so complicated that I am not smart enough to understand them—have been written in defense of my religion. Surely, then, my religion must be true!

And the sage replied: My humble son, not every book you cannot understand contains brilliance too difficult for your mind. Some are written in a style unnecessarily tortured and obscure. If a writer has a point worth making, but does not make it in a way that most intelligent people can understand—the problem usually lies with the writer's poor skills at clear communication, perhaps even at clear thinking.[1]

Furthermore, brilliance is no guarantor of truth. Every major religion and belief system—atheism in its various forms, too—boasts treatises and manifestos that are weighty, imposing, and difficult to understand—and, we may suppose, among those many books each tradition has had its purveyors of brilliance. Yet clearly they cannot all be correct, for they contradict each other on fundamental points. Unintelligible writing, then, even when brilliant—and especially when merely opaque—in no way ensures accuracy.

That the imposing combination of complexity and obscurity should not be equated with truth, we can illustrate by creating some profound-sounding

---

[1] The centuries and millennia have not changed much in this regard. Nearly two thousand years ago, Epictetus stated in his Enchiridion: "When a man is proud because he can understand and explain the writings of Chrysippus, say to yourself, If Chrysippus had not written obscurely, this man would have had nothing to be proud of."

And Schopenhauer in his *Art of Literature*, in the section "On Style," writes, "If a man is capable of thinking anything at all, he is also always able to express it in clear, intelligible, and unambiguous terms. Those writers who construct difficult, obscure, involved, and equivocal sentences, most certainly do not know aright what it is that they want to say: they have only a dull consciousness of it, which is still in the stage of struggle to shape itself as thought. Often, indeed, their desire is to conceal from themselves and others that they really have nothing at all to say. They wish to appear to know what they do not know, to think what they do not think, to say what they do not say." He also states: "Nothing is easier than to write so that no one can understand; just as contrarily, nothing is more difficult than to express deep things in such a way that every one must necessarily grasp them."

And let us follow Schopenhauer's sweeping formulations with something more moderate and concise: Thomas Fuller, a 17th century preacher and historian, has been credited with saying: "One is not bound to believe that all the water is deep that is muddy."

theology ourselves, supporting the absurd notion, described earlier,[1] of God as the Great Chicken:

> Not only in its nomenclature but in its cosmogony and foundational constructs such an ideology singularly resonates to the ceaseless cry of man's spirit, *Altiora peto*. This should not be confused with, as Kant said in another context, "the paradoxical demand to regard oneself qua subject of freedom as a noumenon, and at the same time from the point of view of physical nature as a phenomenon in one's own empirical consciousness," for the encounter with existential flight is far more profound than mere consciousness—and it is evident that we need not wonder whether such an avian construct "assures reality to a supersensible object of the category of causality." And as it speaks to the eternal *anima mundi* at such an essential level the eschatological constituents of such a creed must, notwithstanding surface appearances, *a fortiori* be conceived of as transcending all affinities to the pervasive animism and anthropocentric projections endemic to other totemic cults if indeed such a complex symbolic framework can be adequately circumscribed by atavistic, categorical appellation; nor upon careful analysis can a charge of *deus ex machina* for the deployment of universal symbols and theological features of the contemporary theo-cultural gestalt in the efforts at effecting resolution of cognitive dissonance and attaining the ultimate satisfaction of mortal desideratum be legitimately substantiated; for such an approach would constitute an objection inconsistent with the truest epistemological spirit, though one must concede not the simplistic application, of Ockham's razor, and would as such be not only unsuitable for serving as intellectual foundation for dissent but smacking as it does of *ad hominem* vulgarities be inimical to the standards of normative scholarly expression; nor, indeed, would it be relevant to the logic of moral discourse nor to any germane ethical model, and, evidently, unperturbed by tensions between consequentialism and deontology, inasmuch as such a metalinguistic—as conceived of in the broad sense—approach to deconstructing myths denies any causal association between metaphysical processes and the justification and meaning of subjective existential truths constituting collectively the *sine qua non* of such paradigms when understood in the context of hermeneutics as applied, irrespective of whether its inferences are to be seen as ratiocinations, with appropriate modification to the mystical and symbolic realms foundational of the prosaic and the merely instrumental—by this we mean, of course, the continuum spanning the divide between individual mystical experience and the collective praxis. Nor must the illusion be indulged that other components of such a summary treatise pertaining to the avionic conceptualization of the Divine upon first encounter with the untutored psyche will find ready habitat; for the teleological impulse causative of the provision of energy to acquisitive conquest-oriented anthropocentric modernity is such that disciplines or indeed cognitive or affective patterns not lending themselves to the ready gratification of the many evidences of cultural decadence implicit in the retreat of theology from the numinous, *Thou-as-Thou*, theo-existential encounter to the *thou-as-that* humano-reductionistic intellectualized theocide, and finally to the *that-as-illusion* cultural-existential schism, the pathological repression-estrangement from, as

---

[1] Beginning in section 37.

it were, not only the much-trod Ground of Being but, in a sense, the phenomenological Firming of the Firmament, are perceived, or indeed suppressed, as dissonant strands of insignificant data. It becomes apparent, then, that when adjusting our inquiry to the fitting objects of our devotions as herein described, noting, too, the numerous instances of theological consilience, *mutates mutandis*, the proper analysis of theology can lead to but one conclusion: *Alis volat propiis.*

My son, what is the meaning of that interminable passage, and how many can comprehend it—that they may discern whether it contains any worthwhile ideas, or is little more than obscure babble, perhaps confused thinking hiding behind long, meandering sentences composed of opaque, maybe even misused, terms?[1] If it has any message worth conveying, would it not be my responsibility to clarify what that message is, and to state it in a way that can more readily be understood?

When walking in deep darkness, my son, one often stumbles not because the path is difficult but because the night is dark. When in the morning light the path can be seen, walking is likely to be far less challenging, perhaps even carefree and pleasant. So, too, with ideas: when obscured by the darkness of unclear writing, unfamiliar words, and rambling thinking, they can seem impressive and intimidating. And the opportunities and dangers for obscurity increase when the topics of

---

[1] One favorite technique of those who trade in obscurities and feigned profundity is that of creating nomenclatures, specialized systems of words and terms—and if they can be in a foreign or dead language, so much the better—which are then invested with the solidity and solemnity of institution, and are no longer to be questioned, but merely interpreted and built upon. But nearly two millennia ago, Diogenes Laertius wrote: "It was a common saying of Myson that men ought not to investigate things from words, but words from things; for things are not made for the sake of words, but words for things." And in the 18th century, Samuel Johnson, in the preface to his *Dictionary* wrote: "I am not so lost in lexicography as to forget that words are the daughters of earth, and that things are the sons of heaven."

And William Hazlitt, in the early 19th century wrote in his *Table Talk:* "Such is the use which has been made of human learning. The labourers in this vineyard seem as if it was their object to confound all common sense...They pile hypothesis on hypothesis, mountain high, till it is impossible to come at the plain truth on any question. They see things, not as they are, but as they find them in books, and 'wink and shut their apprehensions up,' in order that they may discover nothing to interfere with their prejudices or convince them of their absurdity. It might be supposed that the height of human wisdom consisted in maintaining contradictions and rendering nonsense sacred. There is no dogma, however fierce or foolish, to which these persons have not set their seals, and tried to impose on the understandings of their followers as the will of Heaven, clothed with all the terrors and sanctions of religion. How little has the human understanding been directed to find out the true and useful! How much ingenuity has been thrown away in the defence of creeds and systems!"

discussion are beyond the physical and natural—topics such as theology and metaphysics.[1] But most ideas upon which the light of straightforward explanation is allowed to shine are, by those of at least moderate intelligence, readily understood. And understanding provides a means of distinguishing the legitimately persuasive from the merely imposing.

This is not to say that all unclear writing is false, or all simply worded propositions true—rather that the vast majority of ideas worth discussing can be stated simply so that intelligent people understand them; and that opaque, scholarly-sounding writing in no way guarantees accuracy, much less profound truth.[2]

In summary, my son, scholars predictably produce great stacks of difficult-to-understand manuscripts in support of every major religion, and every significant anti-religious movement, too. The mere existence of such materials, then, cannot constitute good reason for following any specific set of beliefs about God or religion. Moreover, when writers do not express themselves clearly, they generally do not deserve access to our minds. And we must never mistake their lack of clarity for genius or deep thought, still less for accurate knowledge on ultimate issues, upon which we might responsibly rely to direct our lives. Instead—oh terrible joy of maturity—we are thrown back upon our own intellects, be they humble or grand. It is we who must think, attempt to clarify teachings that at first seem elusive, and arrive at conclusions by way of bracing, even painful honesty and the careful rigors of effortful study.

And turning to religions' most complex writings for authentic knowledge will be of little help. Too often, the obscure face of theology—alike bereft of the familiar features of clarity and the honest gaze of candor—offers but its averted countenance to the earnest inquiries of the seeker and to the humble reverence of the devout. My son, the heaviest books do not always carry the most wisdom—nor the longest words, the greatest part of truth.[3]

---

[1] Voltaire said: "When he that speaks, and he to whom he speaks, neither of them understand what is meant, that is metaphysics." And rarely outdone in acerbic commentary, Mencken observed: "Metaphysics is almost always an attempt to prove the incredible by an appeal to the unintelligible."

[2] Bertrand Russell is credited with saying, "Hegel set out his philosophy with so much obscurity that people thought it must be profound."

[3] "Wandering in a vast forest at night," says Diderot, "I have only a faint light to guide me. A stranger appears and says: 'My friend, blow out your candle so you can find your way more clearly.' This stranger is a theologian."

And perhaps it isn't stretching the point too far to say that much theology—but not only theology—uses the darkness of obscurity, wittingly or unwittingly, to similar ends as those to which literal darkness has often been employed by religion. Edmund Burke, in the 18th century, drew this same parallel between visual obscurity and literary or conceptual obscurity, in writing on how despots are often kept hidden from the people, when he

39. Sub-argument that intelligent and understandable books, too, are written in support of religion—and they must contain some truth

And a man said: Do not overstate your point. Yes, some theology is opaque, and unnecessarily complex. And yes, some of it is mistaken or at least cannot prove itself to be divine truth. But many books speaking for my religion combine intelligence and eloquence, perceptiveness and clarity. Will you not concede that they must contain some truth?

And the sage said: My brother, I appreciate your words for they allow me to clarify: It was not my intent to suggest that all religious books are opaque, or all theology gratuitously complex. Indeed, I readily concede that every major faith has its intelligent scholars and writers who make informed and subtle cases for their beliefs, and express themselves with clarity, even grace. And I readily concede, too, that many religious books contain some truth.

But consider this: Nearly every book, nearly every teacher, nearly every philosophy or belief system contains *some* truth. The most tragic errors, the most destructive lies, even the most hateful ideologies, include elements of truth, too—indeed, that is why so many find them persuasive, when they would quickly dismiss an approach consisting wholly of obvious errors, fantasies, and lies.

My Brother: In religious writings, that which is honest and reliably true is not supernatural knowledge, but human knowledge wearing religious robes. The lessons of practical and ethical wisdom, the insights of learning and art, and the intuitions and reflections of perceptive minds, all find their way into religious books. But they are earthly, human forms of knowledge, not born of religion's otherworldly realms, and certainly not evidence of her supernatural claims. Have we not seen religious leaders teach—in the name of the Bible—everything from the elementary financial wisdom of investing a portion of one's savings, to the basic psychological understanding that our thoughts affect our emotional states and influence our actions? Have we not also seen religious writings appropriate for the Bible the profound contemplations of modern philosophy and the keen insights of recent healers of the mind—even the latest speculative theories on chemistry and physics? My brother, any worthwhile lesson can be shoe-horned into one or more Bible verses, and be claimed by religion as one of its own. And,

---

added: "The policy has been the same in many cases of religion. Almost all the heathen temples were dark. Even in the barbarous temples of the Americans at this day, they keep their idol in a dark part of the hut which is consecrated to his worship. For this purpose too the Druids performed all their ceremonies in the bosom of the darkest woods, and in the shade of the oldest and most spreading oaks. No person seems better to have understood the secret of heightening, or of setting terrible things, if I may use the expression, in their strongest light, by the force of a judicious obscurity, than Milton."

of course, the same can be done with any other set of books, too, providing one is willing to read into their text what an objective eye does not there see.

And if you should need further reason to doubt the accuracy of religious beliefs held by those whose writings are learned and subtle, I remind you that all religions have such scholars and writers, and contradicting each others' beliefs as they do, most of them are—by all religions' accounts—mistaken.

Moreover, I call to your attention the numerous powerful reasons pushing and pulling even the most intelligent among us to supernatural belief.[1] Humans are versatile thinkers. On any topic, give us any set of premises or beliefs, and we can formulate clever thoughts supporting such positions. Every grave error—in science, medicine, even in the skills of everyday living, not to mention in governance and social policy—had among its premises and rationales some accurate and reasonable thoughts. To cite one example: In the days of old, when the most informed of men quite reasonably believed that a heavy craft could not fly through the air, they surely offered intelligent arguments for their certainty—or even considered it so apparent as to be unnecessary to support with argument. Still, they were wrong. In the arenas of political and moral life, many intelligent books have been written in support not only of beliefs naïve and misguided, but even of those oppressive and cruel. Slavery, Nazism, and Soviet communism had their intelligent and eloquent apologists, too. With the ubiquitous and continuous human commitment to religion, should it really surprise us that many keen minds, over the God-obsessed centuries and millennia, have devoted themselves to supporting and justifying—with creative and interesting arguments—the causes and claims of their favorite religions?

Again, let us never confuse intelligence with truth. That religious writers construct impressive systems of thought is undeniable—but upon what underpinnings? Exquisite mansions may be built atop foundations of sand. Nor let us be distracted by the profound and unifying concepts or the clever detail of their many writings; let us rather scrutinize their most important assumptions—that they know God exists, and that they know He wants mankind to follow the dictates of a specific religion. Exposed to such scrutiny, the weakness of their edifices becomes apparent.

And so I agree with you that religious thinkers—in their commentaries, theologies, sermons and more—often employ intelligence and reason. For although when defending faith or foundational principle religion often disparages reason, her scholars frequently apply reason, too—though of a subdued and trammeled

---

[1] See sections 15 and 67 for reasons affecting people, overall, and section 35 for a discussion on whether religious leaders and scholars can be depended upon for truth.

variety—using logical arguments and impressive apologetics when they can. And in the majority of cases this is well-meaning—any dishonesty is not consciously intended. But this should no more be confused with real and healthy reason than we would confuse the bearskin rug adorning a hunter's hearth for a live bear prowling the forest in primal freedom and power. As the hunter ensures the bear is quite dead before inviting it into his home, so too does Religion insist on killing reason—she knows her conclusions before beginning to think—and only then does she set about exploiting what she can of the valuable carcass.

And, my brother, religious literature comprises, among other things, much beauty, wisdom, and depth; but these were not necessarily inherent in the source documents or foundational principles of religion—and even in cases where they were, there is no reason to interpret this excellence as having originated in anything beyond the natural. Beautiful and wise and deep minds, giving their best to what they thought was sacred and divine, weaved what beauty, wisdom, and depth religious literature holds. These were not extracted from religion; they were fashioned into, and projected onto, religion.[1] Thus, my brother, books may

---

[1] I am reminded of the folk tale about spoon soup. (And similar folk tales are told of nail soup, stone soup, and the like.) One version has it that in days of shortage and war a hungry soldier came to a poor town, but nobody would offer him anything to eat—for they said they were hungry, too, and had no food to spare. So he reached into his bag and took out a pot, and told the townspeople he would make something wondrous and delicious—soup flavored only by a spoon. He filled the pot with water, took from his pocket a small spoon, and dropped it into the pot. He then set it upon a blazing fire, and when it began to boil he said: "Ah, how good it smells—so flavorful and warm, the perfect spoon soup—but it would be better still with a few carrots, for carrots bring out the best flavor of the spoon." An old lady, eager to share in the soup, brought out a few carrots, and they were added to the pot. Soon the soldier said: "What would make this excellent spoon soup downright special would be a little meat," and a farmer brought forth some meat—and it, too, was thrown into the pot. After a while, one villager asked, "When can we taste the soup?" "Not yet," said the soldier, "Everyone knows that salt brings out the best flavor of a spoon. Who has salt?" And a housewife brought salt, and it was added, too. And so it went, the soldier asking for "improvements" and the people providing, until the soup had potatoes, onions, garlic, and spices, too. At last, it was ready to his satisfaction, and the soldier shared the soup with the townspeople—and they shook their heads in wonderment at how such a tasty meal came from but a spoon, and what a marvel that spoon must be.

Yet both with the soup in the folk tale and with profound and complex religious literature, the flavor and nourishment came not from what was originally in the pot—a spoon or a supernatural message, but from what was *brought to* the pot, the bounty of the land or of the fertile human mind—in the case of traditional religions, many centuries of scholars' and poets' and sages' best work. And this applies even though these additions were supposedly only for elaboration, and to bring out the original flavor.

contain both religion and reliable truth; but what is reliably true is not strictly religious, and what is strictly religious is not reliably true.[1]

My brother, religions have long reinforced their credibility by writing profound commentaries on their sacred texts. But when the perceptive heart discovers that for such works of the creative imagination no divinely inspired texts are needed, it also begins to suspect that none exist. Then bereavement and liberation take each other's hands, and begin to move in a bittersweet tango.

40. Argument that numerology proves religion correct

Then a student said: Perhaps theology can be misused by creative, mistaken minds. But numbers do not lie; surely numerology is meaningful! There are many compelling examples of the letters in certain words adding up to very significant numbers, or equaling the same sum as the numerical value of other significant words. This should prove my religion true.

And the sage replied: My daughter, I know how impressive numerology[2] can seem; in my younger days I thrilled to such discoveries. But what I have since learned about numerology has been, though initially disappointing, instructive and grounding: Numerology may be inspiring and entertaining, but ultimately proves nothing—for its seemingly remarkable results do not stand up to critical investigation. I have seen that a creative mind can apply the charms of numerology to support any idea or belief. And that which can support every idea lends meaningful support to no idea.

More specifically, my daughter, in its attempts to claim religious significance, numerology simply adds up the number value of words and names until some significant relationship seems to have been discovered. But numerology has, in most of its applications, only several hundred numbers with which it deals. Even if such a system dealt with numbers of one to a thousand, that would constitute only a thousand possibilities. Yet language comprises millions of different words and word combinations. Therefore, almost regardless of the numerology sum of a particular word or phrase, it will be equal to the numerology sums of many, many other words and phrases. It is, therefore, natural and not particularly meaningful when a word or combination of words equals, or has another interesting mathematical relationship to, the numerical sum of another word or combination of words. Indeed, it would be quite unnatural—miraculous, in fact—if we did not find many thousands of such occurrences. And by the laws of

---

[1] Samuel Johnson famously commented in his review of a book: "This work is both original and good—but the part that is good is not original, and the part that is original is not good."

[2] Or "Gematria" in the Jewish tradition.

chance, some of those occurrences will involve words or phrases that seem conceptually significant to the realms of theology and religion.

Moreover, one can quickly demonstrate that numerology is unreliable. Observe that most words or sets of words with similar meanings, which would be expected to have similar sums—if, as numerology believes, meaning is to be equated with number—do not in fact have similar sums.

And to illustrate that numerology is far from an effective path to truth, I will provide you with examples of apparently intelligent numerological points—in support of the silly theology of God as chicken, the notion I recently introduced in our discussion and critique of theology.

Let us use a simple numerological system based on the English alphabet, wherein A = 1, B = 2, C = 3, and so on—all the way to Z = 26.[1]

Thus:

A = 1	B = 2	C = 3	D = 4	E = 5
F = 6	G = 7	H = 8	I = 9	J = 10
K = 11	L = 12	M =13	N = 14	O = 15
P = 16	Q = 17	R = 18	S = 19	T = 20
U = 21	V = 22	W = 23	X = 24	Y = 25
Z = 26				

First, observe that "THE EGG" equals "DEVIL." Both have a numerology sum of 52. This is consistent with the theology mentioned earlier. Since the egg is only a vehicle to create a chick, if it remains an egg—forever trapped by its shell in what was meant to be a merely temporary state—it is the devil's work of death and limitation. In other words, egg as developing chicken is noble; but egg as egg, seen as an independent end unto itself, is the devil's work. Thus, when preceded by "the"—which implies importance and separate identity—it is evil, and

---

[1] And the same point can be easily illustrated with most written languages, including those ancient biblical languages, Hebrew, Aramaic, and Greek. We can always discover words or groups of words that add up to the same number, but where the words or groups of words share no meaningful connection. And, conversely, in any of these languages, and for every idea we invent, we can discover many examples of what can be construed by partisans as significant numerological findings. English is used for this exercise simply to make this point accessible to more people.

therefore its sum is 52, the sum of "devil." But when "egg" stands alone, it is not at rest, not sufficient unto itself, even in language, but rather is missing something, and thus philosophically consistent with its intended temporary state of preparing to bring forth a chick—then it is good, and does not equate either to the work, or the numerological sum, of the devil.

Furthermore, this is consistent with much of traditional theology's understanding of evil—which represents it not as a force essentially bad, but as a force divorced from its proper use, "fallen" or otherwise misapplied, not fitting in as intended in its appropriate place in the Whole. So, too, the egg as an isolated being, outside its proper role of developing into a chick, is seen as evil.

Indeed, let us go deeper: "EGG" by itself equals "AND." Both have a numerology sum of 19. Because, reflecting our theology, the egg is properly seen as merely a temporary developmental stage, with no independent value of its own. So, too, the word "AND" is only a connecting word, which points to the relationship between one thing and another. The egg is the connection between God the Chicken, and our ultimate destiny as the cosmic chick.

Moreover, this same 19 is the numerological sum for "BEAK." For the beak, in this religion, has a very special significance: It is the tool by which the chick breaks through the limitations of the eggshell. The beak, then, is the instrument with which the chick transcends its earlier limitations. The beak embodies growth and movement—that which enables the next stage of development—and is therefore equivalent in both concept and numerology to the word "EGG" and to the word "AND."

The concept of becoming, of continuously improving toward a future and better state is, in this religion, stressed to a unique degree. The term used for this concept, as mentioned earlier, is "Being-Becoming." Thus, this religion considers the number 19 particularly important, and you will see 19 pillars supporting the temples of the Chicken religion, and if you look closely you may notice adherents wearing jewelry holding 19 charms. For this reason, too, young men of this tradition are initiated into full religious responsibility at 19 years of age.

Another numerological point to note is that "CHICKEN" equals "WING." Both have a numerological value of 53. The chicken, though it flies less than many birds, and one might therefore think it should be in conceptual terms less associated with its wings, is, to the contrary, because it is the most numerous and familiar bird whose wings are not used for prolonged, significant flight, most to be associated with the wing as an essential, not merely instrumental, part of its identity. That is, for most birds their wings are a means to an end—they help the bird fly. But to a chicken, the wings are not used for much flying, and are therefore to be understood as essential to the very identity of the chicken. It has wings not because wings give it the masterful flight of most birds; instead, it has wings because it is a creature of wings.[1] The wing symbolizes connection between the physical realm of earth, and the spiritual nature of heaven—and such is the ultimate purpose of God revealing Himself to humans: to help us transcend the physical, and relate to the realm of spirit. Thus, God the Chicken is associated with the wing, for both function in the role of symbolically lifting the earthbound heavenward.

Furthermore, "SATAN" equals 55, "SHELL" equals 56, "HUMAN" equals 57. This progression reflects the fact that Satan uses the egg's shell to reach humans. That is, if humans allow themselves to be held back from breaking through the eggshell of limitation and developing into their true potential, Satan has won. Our theology believes that Satan has no direct hold on people, except when he seduces them by means of the eggshell. That is, Satan can only hold a person down by convincing him that his current limited state is all there is, and that he should not continue to develop into something more.

Observe, too, the relationship between God and man. "GOD" equals 26, "HEN" equals 27, "MAN" equals 28. Note the progression. The energy of God is expressed through the Cosmic Hen, which then creates the chick, which is man.[2]

Additionally, "CHICK" equals "GRACE." Both have a value of 34. This signifies that humanity, the chick, is here by grace. And it reflects how deeply we are blessed by God the Chicken's love.

My daughter, I will stop here, in my possibly amusing, but obviously absurd illustration of numerology in service of the Great Chicken God. And if but one man's creativity and a very small portion of his time devoted to a silly exercise has cobbled together this, could not the scores of generations of your religion, with their tens of thousands of scholars devoting lifelong energies to the study of its texts and teachings—texts and teachings, mind you, that they truly considered

---

[1] And if you squint in skepticism at this questionable point, ask yourself whether it does not remind you of much apologetics and religious writing, in which a believer avoids calling into question his creed's foundational laws and principles, and instead turns every apparent weakness on its head, and attempts to connect those laws and principles to all knowledge and beauty, indeed, to construe them as the source and summit of all knowledge and beauty.

[2] Incidentally, those familiar with basic Hebrew numerology will note that 26, the numerological sum for the word "GOD" in English, is also the numerological sum for the main biblical, Hebrew name of God: the tetragrammaton, the 4-letter name often pronounced in English as Yahweh or Jehovah. That our approach of using English letters for numerology has "GOD" add up to 26, just as the Hebrew spelling of Yahweh or Jehovah adds up to 26 in the traditional Hebrew numerology lends further credence— say the proponents of the Chicken tradition—to our English numerological system, and its findings for the Chicken religion.

sacred—could they not have constructed, out of the elastic materials of ideas and numbers, homilies, even "proofs," far more impressive than those I have advanced today in favor of the Great Chicken God?

In summary, though some numerological points I have made in presenting the chicken as God may be creative, they are still false—and far from compelling evidence that God is truly a chicken. It is the same, my daughter, with all theologies and numerologies. Are many of them intelligent and creative? Yes. Are they intellectually enjoyable? To some. But does this necessarily mean that they illuminate a path to truth? No.[1]

41. Argument that we know of God's existence because mystics can experience a sense of divine communion

And a mystic began in a quiet voice, saying: When I meditate upon God, I tremble in awe, and have, at times, felt so overwhelmed by His presence that I could not remain standing, and fell to my knees. And these moments were more intense, more real, than anything I have ever experienced—so I know that God exists. And even the common man in hurried prayer feels a connection to God when he turns to His gracious presence. Thus, we can know God's truth, and be confident that He hears us when we speak.

And the sage replied: My gentle sister, sadly, in the enchanted kaleidoscope of the mind, what seems the solid marble of experience is often but the glossy vapor of imagination. Have we not felt the terrifying presence of an intruder in the night, when mere floorboards creaked, or when benign, aimless winds rattled at loose windowpanes? And, in the woods, have not our hearts startled at sudden sound, for fear of cruel men or savage beasts, when the silence was disturbed but by the falling of a harmless branch, or the innocent rustle of windswept leaves? And tonight, as you lie captured and bound in silken ropes of slumber, will you not experience mere fantasy as compelling reality, in the mind-magic realm of natural dream? And do not children create imaginary friends, and carry on lively

---

[1] I add one further illustration relating to numerology. Anagrams, being rearrangements of the very same letters as another word or phrase, must be equal in numerological terms to the other word or phrase. Yet when we examine some silly, nonsensical, or merely entertaining, anagrams, we see that numerological equivalence suggests nothing of relevance to underlying meaning or the search for truth. Some examples: Religion = "Igor Nile," "oil reign," or "no girlie." Sacred God = "Dodge scar," or even "scared dog." And my name, Michael W Posner, = "a prim Welch nose," "a chrome sewn lip," or "owl nip cashmere." And with reference to this section, let us not neglect to mention that "chicken religion" = "licorice hen king," "Glen kin ice choir," and "gecko in rich Nile." And because every word and phrase has numerous anagrams, it truly is meaningless, notwithstanding the knowing nods of some, that "dormitory" = "dirty room," or that "mother in law" = "woman Hitler."

discourse, their fantasies fashioning from the lonely sands of isolation glittering castles peopled with intense company?

Yes, my sister, the unaided human mind is quite proficient at weaving experiences and visions that seem real, but are not: They visit every man in his sleep, persecute many madmen even while awake, and transport the trembling mystic into states of transcendent devotion. Consider this: If a horrifying being chases me in my dream, and I awake sweating and screaming, but then feel immense relief upon realizing the danger is unreal, I am well. If, however, even after shaking off sleep I see the terrifying creature in hot pursuit, I may be in the grip of tragic lunacy. In both cases, though—healthy and unhealthy—it is but the human mind sparking the vision, and the winds of mortality inflaming the fear.

And consider this, too: Does not a child shaking in terror under the blankets for fear of an imaginary monster think it alive and real? Does the intensity of his fear—predicated upon the powerful conviction of a monster's presence—indicate that such a being truly exists? Surely not. Other emotions, too, are fashioned and experienced by the body and mind, with or without a connection to outside reality. Joy is not an objective state, necessarily reflecting good external circumstances or events, but an internal experience, that can occur regardless of life's conditions. Anger, too, can flare in the absence of any external provocation; and the emotion of love need not depend upon the worthiness or even the existence of a loved one. And so it goes: Our emotional and perceptual experiences reflect not necessarily external reality—but our own internal functioning. Thus, if we wish to arrive at responsible conclusions about what truly exists, and what our experiences truly teach us about objective reality, we cannot rely upon mere subjective certainty, or upon emotions, no matter how intense.

Moreover, my mystical sister, not only do the mind's imaginings often seem real, the intensity of the imagined can sometimes be greater than that of the real. Many of us have been more terrified in nightmares than in actual, waking dangers; more deeply moved to bliss by erotic dreams than by true, tangible encounters; and more euphoric during our delighted fantasies in sleep than during our most fortunate moments of real life. Purely internal experiences are often more powerful than those rooted in the external, perhaps because the latter are forced to do battle with the glaring and clamorous legions of sight and sound, and are sorely tempted by the distractions of victory and the dangers of defeat, ever besieging the mind on the field of vigilant consciousness. In the internal intensity of withdrawn and altered consciousness few other stimuli compete for the mind's attention—while in the waking state varied sensations, perceptions, emotions, and analyses all demand consideration. Thus, paradoxically, those emotions and experiences most pure in their intensity, are perhaps not more likely, but *less* likely, to be based upon the real, and we might suspect they are being generated—disconnected from the external—by an altered state of mind, whether dream, vision, meditation or trance.

True, most of what seems real is, indeed, real. But when what seems real would have us draw immensely important conclusions contrary to the observed laws of nature, such as the conclusion that we have experienced the supernatural, it is incumbent upon us to think through the matter very carefully.

And consider, too, that in the vast expanses of baking sands only the dehydrated traveler, with parched throat and desperate thirst, envisions the mirage of a heavenly oasis with cool, saving waters. A traveler well satisfied does not see such visions. My gentle sister, many who experience mystical encounters are those whose sensitive natures yearn for deep and intimate connection, but whose painful relationships with people have left such longings profoundly unsatisfied. Might not this powerful thirst for intimacy, left unquenched by fellow humans, conjure—even in a Godless universe—a mirage of overwhelming and intimate divine presence, an emotional oasis in the burning wasteland of an isolated soul?

In addition, my sister, what will you say to those whose gods you do not know—people who feel communion, too, in the intensity of *their* worship? What will you answer to the mystics and supplicating multitudes of other faiths; will you see their experience of divine presence as persuasive evidence of their gods visiting *them*? And what of our fathers in days of yore who were certain they felt supernatural union when bowing to sun or moon, or when kindling incense to ancestor or idol? Were all these gods truly supernatural and transcendent, worthy of worship and capable of providing assistance or salvation, simply because their adherents seemed to experience divine company and attention?

Whether an earnest worshiper in kneeling prayer, or a dreaming sleeper in twitching absorption; whether a pretending child in solitary play, or an awestruck mystic in fallen meditation; the mind projects onto imagined characters a sense of being and presence—and creates from the void a sense of communion.

And just as we rightly place the heavy burden of proof upon those claiming that lights in the sky, or patterns in grain fields, are evidence of flying craft from distant galaxies or alternative dimensions of existence; and just as we rightly require more than mere faith or inspiration, but convincing evidence, from, for example, followers of one who insists he channels the words of a teacher living thousands of years ago in the lost city of Atlantis—just so does reason demand that, in the absence of compelling proof, we remain skeptical of the claim that a mystic's experiences are sourced not in the natural functioning of the human mind, but rather in visitations from, or experiences of, a transcendent realm and a supernatural God.

My sister, in our deepest longings—though the flavor of our experiences will vary according to the nature of our minds, some being prone to more intensity than others—we are all mystics and theologians. The fervent religionist sees hidden divine meanings in Scripture and in the prose of daily events as the young lover sees sexual or romantic significance in the innocent discourse of the object of his affections, and in her every motion and glance; and is reminded of her by so many a stray sound or song or sight or scent; and is haunted and serenaded to a fever pitch by thoughts of her, even in his reveries and dreams.

Let us bear in mind, too, that the brain, a purely physical organ, is by itself capable of generating substances—chemicals, hormones, electrical energy and the like—that result in awe, trance, ecstasy, expansiveness, hallucination, and other unusual states. In dreams of the night it happens routinely, and even during wakefulness, while not very common, such unusual states of mind do occur spontaneously, and are well within the range of natural human experience.

My sister, when we observe that a small but undeniable portion of our species is afflicted with unusual brain functioning, causing such men and women to hallucinate, to hear or see, during waking hours, that which simply is not there; or to feel intense, manic confidence and energy—at times even leading them to believe they are God—when we see that such bizarre thoughts, emotions, and perceptions are regularly produced by mortal brains, is it really so hard to believe that the overwhelming emotional experiences you report may be the mundane result of mere natural—even if unusual—brain functioning, too?[1]

Moreover, various cultures have long since developed rites, practices, and meditations effective at inducing altered states of mind—some involving great intensity, even ecstasy. This, too, illustrates that unusual internal experiences need not reflect anything supernatural, and that the mystical adventure of seeming expansive, ecstatic unity with all, or overwhelming feelings of love and awe, constitute no more than natural, even if intense, colors in the human palate.

But, again, most of what we experience as intense and real is truly taking place. How, then, shall we mediate between our sacred convictions and cautious, responsible doubts? We do such holy work, my sister, by employing reason to

---

[1] Temporal lobe epileptic seizures are said to be associated, in many, with what subjectively seems like an overpowering experience of the Divine, or transcendent awe and wonder, or remarkable insights, or the sense of an outside presence, whether God or someone removed by distance or death. (Such seizures have also brought, to many, negative emotional experiences such as fear.) And whether or not a particular person feeling such things has been diagnosed with epilepsy, or has its other symptoms, the most likely accurate explanation for these seeming divine visitations is that such arresting, compelling, or ecstatic moments are related to the natural, even if uncommon, functioning of the brain—as illustrated by the somewhat similar experiences of many epileptics and others afflicted with neurological or mental disorders.

rigorously inspect the findings of our passionate moments—especially on matters of great consequence.

Let us speak, then, with reverence to a God, or to the Universe, and listen carefully for divine whispers; perchance they will come. But as we pray, and as we await a response, let us be humble, and lighthearted, and know that there may be nobody out there to hear our calls, and that what sound like heavenly answers may be nothing more than the reverberating echoes thrown back from the mortal canyons of our vast and lonely hearts.

42. Argument that there must be a God, because something must have started the planets and other things moving, and the Big Bang theory supports this (variation of the "First Mover" argument)

And a religious man said: Let us forget subjective feelings and speak about objective facts. Have you not heard God's existence proved by the need for a "First Mover"? Every moving thing moves only because it has been set in motion by something else. But this cannot stretch back forever. There must have been one First Mover, not moved by another—and this is God. Indeed, science has concluded that there was a Big Bang that started the universe, and that the universe did not always exist. Therefore, I have good reason to be confident of my religion's truth.

And the sage responded: My brother, let us first notice that even were such an argument correct and convincing, it would tell us only of a Creator billions of years in the distant past. We would not know if this Mover did anything more than simply set the first object in motion, nor would we know if He wanted humans to live in any particular way. Nothing of the nature, will, or worship of such a God would be known. Indeed, this argument, even were it compelling, would allow for many "unmoved movers" and, therefore, many gods: perhaps some things were set in motion by one god, and other things by a second or third god. And because this attempted proof tells us so little about God, it could be used—if it were persuasive—by all religions, including those whose teachings you might consider mistaken, even blasphemous.

It happens, however, that the First Mover argument is deeply flawed. First, my brother, why the insistence that things do not move without a mover to start them moving? Science has long since learned[1] that moving is as natural a state as stillness, and that movement will go on forever unless interfered with by other forces of resistance and friction. Indeed, even those who accept the currently ascendant Big Bang model—that an event occurred billions of years ago, which brought into effect the laws of the universe as we now know them—do not

---

[1] Famously in the works of Galileo and Newton

necessarily see it as precluding a phase preceding the Big Bang"[1] or perhaps even an eternal state, or series of states, of existence from which our current universe and its laws were born.[2] Moreover, some who see the universe as having begun with the Big Bang argue that it need not have come about by the intervention of anything outside the universe, such as a God, but rather could have resulted from the intrinsic laws that govern the stuff of which the universe is made. And some postulate that there may be a multi-verse or mega-verse, many universes, of which our universe and its laws are but one—and its beginning not necessarily the beginning of all reality.

But we need not depend for our healthy skepticism on the speculations or authority of any scientist who reassures us that the latest findings and theories allow for no God, no Creator of our universe or First Mover moving it. Because even if we postulate a God who initiated all motion, we must then ask: "What or Who moved God?" A God with no First Mover moving Him is as puzzling as a universe with no First Mover moving *it*. Can we say that our experience and instincts prepare us to expect anything, including that which you would call God, to begin moving without being moved by some force?

And, again, even if we rejected the thoughts of non-religious scientists, and insisted that there was a First Mover—what can we know of His will? Would the act of a God starting the universe moving tell us anything about whether He cares for any of the dogmas or devotions of human religions—or, indeed, whether He might instead resent them as, among other things, so much prema-ture certainty or cowardly conformity?

43. Argument that this world, in all its complexity, could not have come about by accident and random chance; therefore, evolution is wrong, God exists, and my religion is right

Then a religious teacher said: The sun warms all that lives, and provides light for our eyes; the rains quench the thirst of man, beast, and all vegetation—then rise to form clouds and fall again. And how wondrous are even the workings of a blade of grass as it feeds on the gifts of soil and sun; how perfectly designed are the paws and fur and ears of my dog, and how finely developed and complex are even the individuals and tribes of tiny ants! And what of the stupendous abilities of the human mind? You yourself admit that these things are full of wonder. Yet the theory of evolution wants us to believe that all this came about by accident,

---

[1] Sometimes referred to as "the period of inflation."

[2] Some physicists have expressed views along such lines, and suggested that the Big Bang may have been the beginning of our universe, but that our universe may be the offspring of another universe—and that this regression need not stretch back indefinitely, but that ultimately the original stuff of reality may have always existed.

by random chance. That is preposterous; there could not have been so many wonderful accidents. Surely the order and complexity and abundant excellence in nature shout, to every soul not deaf, the existence of a Creator! And for this reason I am confident of my religion.

And the sage responded: My brother, indeed, as we look about us we see the intricacies of nature, of which not only the large spectacles are worthy of notice, but even the dust we trample underfoot and the puddles we splatter in our passing, teem with manifold forms of life and substance, each of a complex nature comprising delicately synchronized components. Even the simpleton sees system surrounding us; the enlightened and the informed see this ever more as their knowledge deepens.

Still, my brother, I remind you that for purposes of seeking truth on matters of religion we must ask not whether nature is complex and precise, but whether such complexity and precision necessarily reflect a Creator; and, even if we should conclude that they do, whether we honestly know what, if anything, this Creator wants of us—whether we can have any legitimate confidence that this possible Creator is the God for which any Bible or religion speaks, claiming to know His will.

Complexity in nature, even if we were certain it reflected ongoing direct intervention by a Creator and that the theory of evolution were wrong, surely gives us no responsible basis upon which to accept any religion's claims that it knows this Creator's supernatural identity, powers, deeds, and wishes—the many teachings religions offer about God[1]—or that He expects us to believe in a Son of God, or in a divine revelation at Sinai, or in a greatest and final prophet appearing in Arabia.

Yet let us examine whether complexity indeed requires a Creator. My brother, we are short-lived creatures, with all our written histories spanning but a

---

[1] David Hume in *An Enquiry Concerning Human Understanding,* in section XI, writes: "Allowing, therefore the gods to be the authors of the existence or order of the universe: it follows that they possess that precise degree of power, intelligence, and benevolence which appears in their workmanship; but nothing farther can ever be proved, except we call in the assistance of exaggeration and flattery to supply the defects of argument and reasoning...You find certain phenomena in nature. You seek a cause or author. You imagine that you have found him. You afterwards become so enamoured of this offspring of your brain, that you imagine it impossible but he must produce something greater and more perfect than the present scene of things, which is so full of ill and disorder. You forget that this superlative intelligence and benevolence are entirely imaginary, or, at least, without any foundation in reason; and that you have no ground to ascribe to him any qualities but what you see he has actually exerted and displayed in his productions. Let your gods, therefore, O philosophers, be suited to the present appearances of nature..."

few flashes in time, and with each individual lifetime witness, in the context of the dizzying eons of the universe's existence, to the happenings of but an instant. Thus, our minds have no frame of reference for relating to changes that take place over myriads of millennia, and complexities that form over thousands of ages. And as an insect who lives but a day has no understanding of the oak tree's growth, and might consider it preposterous that it arose from an acorn, or that it ever grew or changed, so, too, our instincts and intuitions, refined for a creature living but several-score years, are not attuned to—and are unlikely to easily accept as existing—those processes whose effects are scarcely noticeable over the span of a hundred, even a thousand, human lifetimes.

And it is just this creeping pace of change that, according to some, has gradually developed into the complexity we now see. As life reproduced, the natural diversity of offspring, resulting from organisms reproducing their genetic material imperfectly, included some that were better suited than others to thrive and reproduce in specific environments. And when this better suitability resulted in more successful reproduction, their progeny, and their characteristics, gradually came to dominate—and therefore change—future generations of that species, or, indeed, developed into new species. And so the descendants of the earliest forms of simple life in time came to be both complex and diverse, numerous species of varied forms and innate skills. The organized ants of which you spoke, for example, may have become so by the slow natural selection of nature, as those with an instinct for organization survived better and reproduced more successfully. This is one illustration of the theory of evolution, as some see it.[1] And a great deal of evidence, from multiple disciplines and various lines of scientific inquiry, seems to support evolution's basic claims.

As our minds cannot easily grasp the vastness of outer space—the innumerable light years, the uncountable billons and trillions of miles separating us from various stars and other heavenly bodies—and yet our best evidence and repeated inquiries have shown these distances to be real, so too our minds are not well

---

[1] There are, of course, debates and innovations in theory and research in the field of evolution—including, in reference to the ant colony example, the question of whether and to what degree natural selection applies to groups, to individuals, or indeed, to genes—and, no doubt, if evolution remains the conventional view of science over the next number of centuries, it will be further refined. In this book—the primary focus of which is existential honesty, not the details of science—I do not attempt to explore the matter of evolution in any comprehensive sense, in part because as the text makes clear, whether or not one believes in evolution does not settle the question of God's existence, and even if one were to posit, as some fundamentalists amongst the religious do, that evolution is mistaken and a Creator fashioned every species directly, this would still provide us with no reliable knowledge about whether any one of the many speculative and mutually-exclusive religions is consistent with this Creator's will.

suited to easily grasp the vastness of time, the hundreds of thousands, millions, tens of millions, hundreds of millions, even billions of years that have apparently elapsed in the history of Earth and the universe, and just what processes and changes all this time may have naturally wrought.

Moreover, scientific research has begun to show that even small changes in genetic code can yield large changes in the color, form, or function of an animal or plant. If so, dramatic change can more easily be seen to be the result of unguided mutations, which, if they were helpful for survival and reproduction, came to dominate future generations.

And it is not accurate to say to that evolution claims all complexity in life developed by "accident" or by "random chance." Evolution does indeed hold that genetic mutations arise frequently, and these may be by accident or chance— but that what results in changes to future generations is not a process of accident or chance but rather the natural, expected outcome that any mutations which turn out to be an advantage for survival and reproduction will likely lead to greater survival and reproduction—and thus to future generations more resembling those "mutated" individuals. Therefore, growing complexity was the result not of inexplicable accident or chance, but of the ongoing refinement of competition between individuals and species as mutations arose naturally, and were either well-suited to their environment and thrived and reproduced and shaped future life, or were ill-suited to their environment and perished with little trace.

And, my brother, I know that there are some who argue with passion that evolution is mistaken and that evolutionists are influenced by the fashions and pressures of currently popular views in science and academia. Yet I also know that the great majority of scientists dismiss such critics as closed-minded, rooted in religious or other dogmas, and unwilling to accept what the near-consensus of scientific scholars say has been established, by several branches of science, beyond reasonable doubt—that evolution has occurred and continues to occur, is responsible for the diversity and functioning of life as we know it, and is, for all intents and purposes, to be seen as fact.

Indeed, because of this great preponderance of evidence, many religious factions and denominations[1] have long since accepted the basic premise of evolu-

---

[1] The Church of England has in recent years made clear that although it was initially vigorously opposed to Darwin's theory, it now sees much value in it. Even the Catholic Church does not completely oppose evolution; the most recent few popes have acknowledged that evolution seems to be supported by the scientific evidence, and apparently has validity. These churches and others—though they may have had to modify their formerly literal reading of the creation myth in Genesis—maintain their beliefs in God, and now do not find evolution to be incompatible with those beliefs.

tion,[1] and have come to believe that although God created life in all its variations, He did so through enabling, perhaps directing, the process of evolution.[2]

My brother: I understand that the prevailing views of science in each generation have been wrong on some issues, yet the many dissenting views rejected by the majority of experts have been wrong far more often. It is true that scientists, like others, are often reluctant to oppose widely held views within their field of knowledge, especially in cases where alternative views are seen as threatening or contemptible; indeed, the experts of any generation are often, unbeknownst to them, trapped in a web of perspectives that will to later generations seem limited and quaint.[3]

---

[1] One can, however, point out that this is consistent with the observation of the 19th century Swiss-American scientist Louis Agassiz—who, although along with his legitimate scientific contributions also promulgated some mistaken and offensive ideas, in this case astutely, even if in the over-generalized fashion of many aphorisms, maintained—that, "Every scientific truth goes through three states: first, people say it conflicts with the Bible; next, they say it has been discovered before; lastly, they say they always believed it." (Those interested in the art of aphorism may note that the model used here—not only in the structure of three, but also in the ironic progression from one opinion to its opposite—is the one used by Schopenhauer, too, in his comment about the three stages of truth, cited in a footnote about two thirds of the way through the preface of this book.)

[2] Darwin himself, toward the end of his *Origin of the Species,* writes: "I see no good reasons why the views given in this volume should shock the religious feelings of any one. It is satisfactory, as showing how transient such impressions are, to remember that the greatest discovery ever made by man, namely, the law of the attraction of gravity, was also attacked by Leibnitz, as 'subversive of natural, and inferentially of revealed, religion.' A celebrated author and divine has written to me that he has 'gradually learned to see that it is just as noble a conception of the Deity to believe that He created a few original forms capable of self-development into other and needful forms, as to believe that He required a fresh act of creation to supply the voids caused by the action of His laws.'"

[3] One of the influential, though controversial, books examining the process of scientific advance, including the historical, psychological, and social influences on that process, is Thomas Kuhn's 1962 work, *The Structure of Scientific Revolutions.* At the time of its publication it stimulated vigorous debate, and in the nearly half century since, it has continued to draw criticism from several quarters, including both those who think it gives too little positive distinction to the scientific method (and gives unintended ammunition and cover to postmodernists, creationists, and other denigrators of the scientific community) and those who think it gives too much.

And Max Planck, a German Nobel Prize winner in physics in the early 20th century, said—among other controversial things—"A new scientific truth does not prevail as the norm by persuading her opponents and teaching them enlightenment, but rather thus, that her opponents gradually die out, and the younger generation is, from the beginning, familiar with the truth."

Ironically, Darwin himself made a similar point, in Chapter XV of his *Origin of the Species,* when confronting what was then significant resistance within the scientific

But it is also true that intensely religious people who argue against evolution, likely have a bias against accepting the theory of evolution, because if it can be discredited, it would seem to render a Creator more necessary and prominent—and again allow them to bask, without cold shadow, in one of religion's traditional consolations: that humans have been directly created by God and that He finds worthy of notice the details of their lives. And it is also true that science, in the long term, honors those who break through misconceptions—especially misconceptions held by the scientific community—so there is some motive for scientists to reject evolution if they could show it to be mistaken. Science is far less harsh on its heretics than is religion. Still, for many—whether in the camp of evolutionists or anti-evolutionists—it is easier to accept the consensus of one's peers, and safe membership in the herd, than to pursue heroism and risk marginalization, not to mention the disillusionment and disorientation of a significant element of one's worldview being called into question.

My brother: In short, although all humans are fallible, and prone to self-deluding loyalties, the preponderance of expert opinion, based on several lines of inquiry and scientific study, seems to easily be on the side of evolution—and we are wise to take this seriously. Yet especially on matters about which the heart has misgivings, I can understand that one would not wish to close one's mind definitively to other possibilities. Indeed, then, do not close your mind; open it instead, and renew your efforts to research the matter and to understand it well.

But, again, my brother, and most to the point for our existential inquiry: Even if the great preponderance of scientific thinking and evidence on the matter were shown to be mistaken and evolution were proved wrong, and even if it were shown beyond any doubt that there was a Creator, we would still have no

---

community to his teachings on evolution. He writes: "Although I am fully convinced of the truth of the views given in this volume under the form of an abstract, I by no means expect to convince experienced naturalists whose minds are stocked with a multitude of facts all viewed, during a long course of years, from a point of view directly opposite to mine...but I look with confidence to the future, to young and rising naturalists, who will be able to view both sides of the question with impartiality."

My own view, as I try to convey in the text of this book, is that reason and empiricism should not be minimized (for my most direct comments along these lines, see the first several sections of this book, on relativism, intuition, postmodernism, and so on; also see Part V of the book for the entire series of sections on faith) nor equated with other more subjective means of supposed knowing—but also that all of us, including scientists, are prone to many forms of, often unconscious, bias, loyalty, and prejudice, and we should not underestimate the potentially distorting influence of these on our opinions, convictions, and conclusions. Experts, whether as individuals or groups, usually deserve the benefit of the doubt—but they are far from infallible.

responsible cause to believe that any of our human religions know this Creator's word or will.

44. Argument: "How can people be so quick to dismiss all the complexity and wonder of the world, as having come about by evolution?"

But the religious teacher said: After all the scientists' lectures, and after all your speeches, I still ask you: Do you honestly believe that all this, all we are, came about by itself? How can people be so quick to dismiss all the complexity and wonder of the world as nothing more than the product of evolution? And since evolution is preposterous, we must assume that religion is correct—that God created the world, and we should live the way He taught us to live.

And the sage said: Very well, my brother; this is not an issue that rests easy on the mind or heart, so I will say more. I can sympathize, in part, with your point of view. Our instincts do not resonate to the idea of intricacy forming without a designer. When we observe the astonishing complexity of life, the hawk's eye and the kangaroo's pouch; the bird's egg and the bear's winter sleep; the skunk's stench and the centipede's sting; the caterpillar's transformation, and the mockingbird's songs; the clicking language of the dolphins, and the behemoth families of the whale; the migrating, directional instincts of creatures as varied as salmon and geese; the dazzling, dizzying variety of flowers, and their buzzing and fluttering legions of pollinators; the spider's sinister weaving and the beaver's sturdy building; the poison factory of the viper and the confectionery of the honeybee; the color-changing magic of lizards and octopi, and the sound-seeing flight of bats in the night; the chemistry of a microbe, and the keenness of the human mind; the intricacy of cells and atoms, and all that is too small to see; the vastness of stars and galaxies, and all that is beyond our reach—and, with but a little knowledge, this list could extend longer than any man could recite—many find it difficult to avoid the conviction that these have been designed by a conscious intelligence.

Indeed, I do not mean to imply that we should dismiss out of hand the intuitive implications of life's spectacular sophistication, and—before understanding the various forms of evidence and rationale behind it—definitively attribute it all solely to the processes described by the theory of evolution, and other models that have no use for God. We must indeed take care not to make dogmas of the theories of some scientists, as once we made dogmas of the pronouncements of prophets and priests. Let us investigate such matters for ourselves, and let us refrain from premature and overconfident approval of ideas that sit poorly on our hearts and minds—even if the words of experts are long, and their credentials imposing. But let us investigate, and not sit content with our first reactions and anthropomorphic, untutored intuitions—and let us read the writings of

131

scientists themselves, not the arguments of science as represented, often unfairly, by her opponents.

And science, unlike the priests and prophets of old, marshals vast and varied evidence to support her claims. Let us not dismiss these accumulated lessons merely because they are, at first, difficult to absorb. Science has taught us many things the ancients never knew, things the earnest ignorant first saw as wondrous, even preposterous: that a heavy craft can fly and carry hundreds across the oceans; that voice or music or image can be sent through the air from the other side of the world, and even the long-since familiar lessons that Earth is a sphere and not flat, nor is it the center of the universe.

My brother, intuition and instinct can lead us astray, too, so we are wise not to appoint them our only counsel. Consider this humble example of evolution from our daily lives: Succeeding generations of bacteria change and become immune to the drugs that once defeated them—those bacteria resistant to the drugs survive and reproduce, thus populating future generations of bacteria with more resistant forms.

Still, some have argued that it is no small leap from such observations of limited intra-species, microevolution to the bold assertion of macroevolution, that new species arose from the old, and that all of life we see and all we are and shall be, results from nothing more than evolution's random mutations and the refining process imposed by the environment—the demands of survival and propagation. Yet mainstream science argues that the rise of new species by means of evolution has, indeed, been well demonstrated, or at least strongly indicated, by various forms of evidence including, among others, the fossil record, biogeography—where various life species are located—embryology, and genetic analysis.[1]

My brother, it is worthwhile for us all to learn about such an important idea as evolution. But because most are unlikely to spend the time and effort necessary to follow the detailed and sometimes complex arguments between the supporters and critics of evolution, I again remind you that for the purposes of finding the truth on matters of religion, committing to any specific set of conclusions on such matters is unnecessary. Because even in the unlikely event

---

[1] Books on evolution are plentiful and varied. A few of the recently published, helpful works explaining evolution for the intelligent layman are: On genetic evidence for evolution, *The Making of the Fittest: DNA and the Ultimate Forensic Record of Evolution*, by Sean B. Carroll, and *Relics of Eden: The Powerful Evidence of Evolution in Human DNA* by (a religious scientist) Daniel Fairbanks; and on evidence from the fossil record, *Evolution: What the Fossils Say and Why It Matters*, by Donald Prothero; and extending into anatomy and evolutionary biology, *Your Inner Fish: A Journey into the 3.5-Billion-Year History of the Human Body* by Neil Shubin.

that evolution were shown to be mistaken, and it were proved that all the varieties of life came about by means of direct intervention by a Creator, we still would have no responsible way of knowing His possible will on how we should lead our lives, and what if any religious propositions we should believe.

And, on the other hand, if evolution were proved correct, while it would force fundamentalists to modify some of their claims, and their understanding of certain biblical passages, it would not prove belief in God inaccurate. Indeed, as I have said, many among the scientifically-educated religious have long since accepted the theory of evolution, and see it as the mechanism by which God brings forth creation.[1]

My brother: Many intelligent people of a spiritual bent and cautious mind counsel us that on such matters we are wise to withhold hasty judgment—wise to resist being forced to choose between radical positions; that we need not believe any religion is correct in its claims that it knows God and knows what He wishes of us; nor must we believe that the multidimensional abundance of seeming design can be definitively accounted for by the unconscious forces of evolution, preceded by the unconscious forces giving rise to life in the first place, preceded by the unconscious forces responsible for the existence of the universe overall. And it is not unreasonable to wonder whether perhaps some intelligent being or beings began, or intervened in, or played some functional role in, the astonishing process of life developing on our planet—or on whichever planet or place from which Earth's life, or its precursors, may have come. Still, we should not refuse the lesson of today's evidence, which seems to teach that evolution by natural selection helped shape many of life's current functions and forms.

Once more: We must take seriously that the great preponderance of scientific opinion considers evolution to be supported by the evidence, yet even if we were to dismiss all this expert opinion and suspect that a Creator directly fashioned life in its varied forms, we are still far from the teachings of traditional religions. For how are we to know if this Creator has any continued interest in

---

[1] So long as a supernatural God stands behind evolution, causing or directing the process, the blow does not strike so harshly at religious sensibilities, not only because their accustomed beliefs can, in one form or another, be maintained, but because the flattering notion can still be salvaged that humans are the object of conscious, deliberate—even if indirect and non-immediate—creation by the Real and Living Divine, and are not merely the unintentional result of forces blind and uncaring.

Surely John Burroughs must have understood this, though he wrote, presumably for rhetorical effect, in his *Time and Change*: "We are willing to be made out of the dust of the earth when God makes us, the God we have made ourselves out of our dreams and fears and aspirations, but we are not willing to be made out of the dust of the earth when the god called Evolution makes us."

the universe? Perhaps we are but an artistic amusement long since discarded—a sculptor's practice-work of youth lying unheeded in the cosmic equivalent of a cellar closet. Indeed, if the Creator is all-powerful, might He not find creating such a universe as ours effortless, thus perhaps unimportant—and would it be so surprising if, therefore, it went unheeded and unguided?

Furthermore, if there is a God and He does remain aware of the universe overall, perhaps He has no interest in Earth's welfare; for our planet revolves around one star—our sun—among myriads of billions of other stars. And even if we postulate that the Creator cares about Earth, whence the indication that He cares very much about the human species? Has He not allowed so many other species, large and small, to go extinct? And even if we believe that God cares about humans as a species, why assume that He attends to the daily actions of the individual? Perhaps, much as most of us do not care about the actions of individual squirrels—though we may prefer that squirrels survive as a species—so too might the Creator neither monitor nor particularly care about individual humans.

What is more, even if God watches our individual behavior and wishes us to act in specific ways, must that mean He has communicated laws or values to our ancestors or to any humans? Instead, perhaps God waits hopefully for mankind to apply reason and compassion to guide our living. Indeed, perhaps this possible Creator wants mankind to rise above superstition, above craven worship, above ancient rumors, above valuing tribe over truth—perhaps He waits for us to attain the lofty peak of intellectual honesty. Thus, even if all notions of evolution were mistaken, and we knew for certain that life was designed by a Creator—we still would not know if He counted it as good or evil that a man submitted to religion.

More unsettling, perhaps this God wishes for those who are most powerful or cunning to rule, just as occurs in many other species—species which, if there is a Creator God, we might reasonably assume, in the absence of compelling evidence to the contrary, are functioning as He created them to function.

In summary, my brother, like you I am, in open-souled moments, astonished at nature's variety and complexity. Yet even with all this, much informed argument makes the case that such variety and complexity need not reflect a Creator's handiwork, but is, instead, the result of natural processes and events. And though many remain skeptical that all this could come about without an intelligent designer, if we are honest, we must confess that we do not know this to be impossible. These are matters the mind does not easily grasp—and science has presented us with many kinds of evidence in evolution's favor.

Finally, my brother, if you reject evolution, and solve the puzzle of nature's complexity and design by postulating a God, have you not traded a mystery for an insoluble enigma, and a sound in the night for a fearsome ghost? For if our complex world was too difficult for you to explain without fashioning for it a Creator, whom shall you find to create God?[1]

45. Sub-argument that evolution cannot explain the origin of life or of the universe; there must have been a creator; therefore, we must assume religion is true

But the religious teacher persisted and said: Numerous non-believers put their faith in evolution, but even if evolution thinks it explains how life developed from simple to more complex forms, it cannot explain how life began in the first place—and it certainly cannot explain how the universe itself began. Only religion can explain these, and the explanation is simple: God created everything. All your speeches are well and good, but I still refuse to believe that all this came to be by happenstance. Surely the universe is too complex for that—there must have been a creator! And therefore I stand with my religion.

And the sage said: My brother, if you cannot accept the possibility of a world uncreated, consider once more: If there were a Creator, would this tell us whether He wishes anything from man? And if we knew that He does, would we know whether He communicated those wishes to any of our ancestors, or to any others who claim, or about whom it is claimed, that God revealed to them His word or will?

And my brother, you are correct that the classic theory of evolution did not attempt to explain the beginnings of life or of the universe. And though some are not persuaded that the universe or pre-universe had an absolute beginning, this-- along with the beginnings of life—is, indeed, as of now not well understood. Still, some have put forward intelligent speculation on just such matters.[2]

But while it is true that the classic theory of evolution does not explain the beginnings of life or of the universe, neither does religion, in any legitimate sense. Instead, it merely assures itself that such baffling beginnings are solved by something named "God," without explaining the beginnings of this super-complex, super-baffling Being—a puzzle at least as challenging as the original puzzles of accounting for the beginnings of the relatively simpler universe and life. My brother, does one truly become free of debt when repaying a small loan by taking out another loan many times larger?

---

[1] As to the claim that the whole point of God is that He is not created, but rather sufficient unto Himself, see section 49.

[2] Two recent books dealing with and speculating on the natural means by which life may have begun are, *Genesis: The Scientific Quest for Life's Origins*, by Robert Hazen; and *The Origin of Life*, by Paul C. W. Davies.

And again I say that I share with you a sense of wonder for the complexity of the universe—yet I ask you: Why the need for dishonest certainties? Why abandon the open mouth of awe for dogma's pursed lips? Why not remain with honest unknowing, with the beautiful question, with sacred mystery?

One winter's night, my brother, a man is sitting in his home and hears several rhythmic taps at the door, and what sounds like a powerful voice speaking unintelligible words, then humming a haunting tune. He rushes to the door, opens it—but sees nothing. He calls out, again and again, but there is no response.

He says to himself, "That tapping, and that sound of a voice—of words and melody—these were no mere happenstances or random events. Someone must have been here." He decides that it must have been a tall man with a black mustache, dressed in a starched yellow linen suit; that his favorite color is therefore yellow; that he builds model ships as a hobby, and that he often eats blueberry pie. He further concludes that this dashing night-tapper meant to signal that we should set aside all other priorities and dedicate our lives to growing blueberries in model ships, and that we must paint these ships yellow—but never on Tuesdays—and that he will punish forever anyone who eats strawberries, or dares to paint their model ships red. A parable.

46. Argument that organized, goal-oriented functioning in nature proves God's existence (the teleological argument)

But the religious teacher spoke again and said: It is not only that things are complex. Do you not see how things were designed for a purpose? Everything accomplishes a specific end, even when it has no intelligence of its own. See how an apple seed grows into an apple tree, and how flowers make scent and color to attract bees for pollination. These organized, intelligent actions by unintelligent things prove that an intelligent Being, God, created them to help produce food for mankind. Therefore I know my religion is true.

And the sage said: My brother, I see why many find this argument appealing. When we look around us, so much does seem to function in a goal-oriented fashion. Yet, here too, even were this argument convincing it would tell us nothing about God's identity or nature, about what He may want of us—or even about the possible number of existing gods. Clearly, then, it cannot teach us which religion, if any, is pleasing to any deity there may be.

Yet is this argument from design convincing? If unintelligent things such as apple seeds and flowers require a creator, how much more does God—a super-intelligent being, capable of creating a universe—require a creator! I ask you, then, the child's question: "Who made God?" There is no gain in claiming that God is the creator of a universe that demands an intelligent cause—for the

Intelligent Cause would Himself require an even more Intelligent Cause, in a process stretching back with no beginning. And if there can be a Creator with no comprehensible source, perhaps there can be a Universe with no comprehensible source.

Furthermore, it is easy to notice the organized and good in nature, and project onto an imagined supernatural realm a goal-oriented, benevolent intent. But do we not also see much that either seems chaotic and unproductive, or even results in destruction or harm? Could we not infer, then, that many things have either not been designed, or have been designed for malevolence?[1]

Indeed, if this world was directly designed by a God, He does not seem to be the kind of God spoken of by popular religions. If your eye sees design and goal-orientation in how pollination uses bees and flowers and color and scent, so too will your eye, if honest, see design in the precision of the mosquito's complex blood-sucking apparatus spreading the powerful and efficient protozoan parasites that have helped malaria kill uncounted millions of children. And that is but one of the many dread diseases and disease-spreading mechanisms seemingly goal-oriented and well-designed.[2] And so, my brother, be careful what you argue for: If you credit a Creator with the design of nature's benevolent complexities, you shall have to credit Him with nature's monstrous complexities, too, and you shall then have to reconsider the notion of a merciful God.

My brother, let us not pretend that our lack of definitive knowledge about ultimate origins, and about the ultimate source of current complexity, is satisfactorily resolved by the teachings of traditional religion. For traditional religion,

---

[1] Those among the religious seeing supernatural intent to benefit humans in such phenomena as bees pollinating crops, are advised to bear in mind Oscar Wilde's irreverent witticism that "Missionaries are the divinely provided food for destitute and underfed cannibals."

[2] In *The Gods*, Robert Ingersoll writes with impassioned sarcasm of those who see evidence for God in the beauty and useful precision of sunshine, flowers, rain, and the like: "Did it ever occur to them that a cancer is as beautiful in its development as is the reddest rose? That what they are pleased to call the adaptation of means to ends is as apparent in the cancer as in the April rain? …By what wonderful contrivances the entire system of man is made to pay tribute to this divine and charming cancer! See by what admirable instrumentalities it feeds itself from the surrounding quivering, dainty flesh!...By what marvelous mechanism it is supplied with long and slender roots that reach out to the most secret nerves of pain for sustenance and life! What beautiful colors it presents! Seen through the microscope it is a miracle of order and beauty...Think of the amount of thought it must have required to invent a way by which the life of one man might be given to produce one cancer! Is it possible to look upon it and doubt that there is design in the universe, and that the inventor of this wonderful cancer must be infinitely powerful, ingenious and good?"

when formulating her ideas on such matters, did not have the benefit of the past several centuries of scientific discovery, including the theory of evolution—and even if religion were correct in insisting there was a Creator, the work of this Creator yields precious little evidence that religion understands Him, much less speaks for Him.

Still, my brother, nature seems to have the seeds of development within her bones, for plants and animals to spring up, and adapt to each other and the environment. And, indeed, we wonder Who sowed these wondrous seeds, for we suspect that such development does not occur without a Great Designer and Master Gardener. Imprisoned by our human minds—which have been shaped in, or designed for, the cause-and-effect environment, and the social context of our human lives—we can only relate comfortably to things with a beginning, and to complexity that has been sculpted by conscious intelligence. Yet if we strain to reach through the bars of our mortal cells we can begin to feel a bit of the Mystery that transcends human instinct.

My brother, although we are wise to never be too certain of speculations on earliest origins, many teachers, both ancient and modern, have suggested that the stuff of the universe, in some form, has always existed. And some have taught that cycles of development and destruction have occurred forever, as though time were on a sphere, going around and around: as the surface of the sphere has no beginning or end, so too time may have no beginning or end. And Science— the ever-learning student—is, as of this point in history, far from definitively knowledgeable on such murky matters as the possible beginnings of the current universe and its laws, and what if anything may have existed before.

Even those who accept the Big Bang model—that an event occurred, which brought into effect the present laws of the universe—do not necessarily see it as precluding an earlier version of existence, perhaps part of an eternal state of existence, from which our current universe, and its laws, was born. Indeed, some who see the universe as having a beginning in the Big Bang, argue that it need not have come about by the intervention of anything outside the universe. Further still, some suggest the controversial notion that there may be a multi-verse or mega-verse—many universes, of which ours and its laws are only one.

But, again, my brother, even if we neither accept nor understand natural or scientific theories as to how all has come to be, or exists, it would still be unwarranted to insist upon the unproved, even unexplained, claim that there was a Creator. And most important: Even if we assumed there was a Creator, the main claim animating religion—that this God wishes us to live by a specific set of laws or beliefs, which, conveniently, happens to be the set one's own tradition teaches—would remain unproved, irresponsible, and intellectually dishonest.

My brother, must we be so averse to humbly acknowledging that we do not know final answers to the mysteries of earliest origins, or to the question of what, if anything, a possible Creator might want of man?

47. Argument that the "fine-tuning" of the universe for human life proves God

But another man said: How can you doubt the existence of God? Scientists have discovered that in order for human life to exist, so many conditions must be balanced perfectly. Not only must the sun be only so far and so close to Earth for the temperature to be neither too cold nor too hot for life to develop and survive, but even the far less obvious laws that underlie all of reality—the fundamental constants of the universe, such as gravity, the nuclear weak force, the difference in mass between protons and electrons, among other examples— these laws are fine-tuned to allow for life. Had any one of these been slightly different, life could not exist. This "anthropic principle" proves that an intelligent Creator designed the universe, and that my religion is, after all, correct.

And the sage said: My brother, true, when studying the laws underlying reality one sees what seem to be specialized and unlikely combinations of factors, which appear to be necessary for life. So I understand the temptation to conclude that a Creator fashioned all this with the goal of producing life. Yet as with many complex matters, further study and contemplation show intuitive conclusions to be premature and overly confident. I will soon explain.

But first I remind you that even if we knew with certainty that the universe was designed with intelligent intent, we would still not be able to derive from this any knowledge about what, if anything, this force, or these forces, might want of humans—and which, if any, of the human religions is consistent with the will of this God, or these gods. Whom shall we pretend to know created the universe? Must it be the God of the Bible? What of Ptah? Nabu? Dagon? Zeus? These are but a very few of the legions of gods whose names scholars of history know, but whose reputations no longer inspire awe, sacrifice, or desperate prayer. And what of the additional innumerable gods whose worshipers never held sufficient military power, nor left behind written histories, that we would even know these deities' names and supposed powers and wishes?

Moreover, I remind you that finding complexity and apparent design in the universe, and then positing the existence of a God to solve the puzzle of a complex universe's origin, does not truly solve the puzzle, as it merely replaces a seemingly fine-tuned universe of mysterious origin, with an even more impressive, and surely more fine-tuned, deity of unexplained origin. For if we accepted religion's claim that a Creator exists, surely we must admit that this Creator is at least as impressive as His creation, and yet how shall we explain *His* origin?[1]

Furthermore, my brother, is it not as likely to displease any God there may be for us to jump to irresponsible conclusions about His identity and wishes, as it is for us to honestly state what we know and what we do not know? Do we have any good evidence that any Creator there may be is a sadist with an appetite for sycophants, enjoying the spectacle of humans falling to their knees, worshiping and humiliating themselves in the service of mere rumors of an inscrutable, yet demanding, heavenly lord?

Have we not taken this model from the ignoble example of weak, grasping, humans, who bolster their own confidence, or assuage their own wounded hearts, or attempt to compensate for their own inevitable demise, by subjugating or tyrannizing others? If we seek to project human models onto a possible Creator, why not project onto Him a far more noble model—perhaps that of a kind, confident, and autonomous elder? Why not consider that perhaps He wishes nothing more of His creations than that they live with as much honesty and dignity and compassion as they know how, and that they resist ardent self-deception and degrading submission on the strength of mere stories passed on to them from long-dead days of pitiful ignorance and pervasive superstition?

In practice, then, even if we knew for certain that the universe was designed by one or more supernatural powers, we would still have no good cause to follow the teachings of any religion that claims to know these supernatural powers' identities or wishes.

And, my brother, though your argument—from what seems the fine-tuning of the universe for life—even if true, would not lead to vindicating the rules and dogmas of any traditional religion, let us examine it closely and see if it is compelling even in proving a Creator. I shall speak of several points which have been explained by many others.

First, do we know that other forms of life, or other forms of impressive complexity, based on building-blocks far different from those of current reality, would not be possible if the universe were "fine-tuned" differently? My brother, if the universe were "fined-tuned" differently, and such forms of complexity or thinking life developed, they would be in position to make the same observation you have made. They too could exclaim: "See how the very laws underlying our universe are so narrowly fine-tuned as to make our complexity possible!"

---

[1] As to the claim that the whole point of God is that He is self-sufficient, and uncreated, see Section 49.

Indeed, many have suggested that the proof has things backward: that the universe was not fine-tuned to allow for life, but that life was fine-tuned to what was allowed by the conditions of the universe; that it constitutes no small amount of arrogance to assume that the universe was tailored to produce life, and that a more humble and likely scenario is that life evolved within the constraints of the universe's laws, and life is therefore fine-tuned to the universe, and not the other way around.

And computing the odds for the likelihood of certain events or conditions can be misleading. Consider, my brother, the combination of events and conditions necessary for me to have come into existence; they seem to have been fine-tuned. My parents met and built a family. But in order to have met, my parents had to be in the same country, their parents had to marry the specific people they married, and the three out of four of their parents who were immigrants had to arrive in the same land, and had to raise these two children, my parents, within several years of each other. Furthermore, my parents, being religious, had to be of the same religion, and needed a specific acquaintance in common who introduced them. They also needed to be drawn to each other after they met, among many additional considerations. But all that is just a beginning. All my parents' thousands of ancestors had to procreate with exactly the partners they did, in order for my parents to be who they were, and therefore for me to ultimately come into existence. Indeed, even after that very specific—"fine-tuned"—combination of a long, seemingly improbable, but exact sequence of ancestors' pairings that produced my parents, and after all the conditions and "fine-tuning" that resulted in my parents marrying and raising a family, only one specific sperm cell out of all the myriads of sperm cells released in that particular coupling, would have produced me. And the same incredibly small chance applies to every coupling by all my parents' ancestors. Vanishingly small sets of odds compounded by vanishingly small sets of different odds—these have resulted in my existence. That all this happened by chance seems, from that perspective, to be enormously unlikely, even preposterous.

But, my brother, the same is true of you, and of every human, and of every cat or honeybee, too. A very specific combination of factors resulted in any being coming into existence. Had my parents not procreated with each other, for example, I would not have come into existence; but whatever children either might have had, would themselves have been the result of a different long series of specific, and seemingly improbable conditions and events.

And this applies not only to living things. Any event—from a specific stone coming to rest at a particular spot on a riverbank to a specific drop of rain landing in one precise square inch of the Pacific Ocean—is possible only within the context of so long a chain of conditions and events, that it is tempting to characterize it as astonishing, even miraculous. But the same would be true of any alternative event.[1]

Yet perhaps the stuff of nature has within it the seeds of life, which, admittedly, can only sprout under very limited conditions. If so, with enough undirected cosmic events and explosions, occasionally such conditions may result. And our planet, perhaps with no supernatural interference or design, may have been one of those rare instances.

Indeed, as we look around us into the sky—with ever more powerful tools to enhance our vision and tutor our minds—at the planets and moons and stars and the varied enivronments and materials beyond our humble orb, we have not found, as of this time, another instance of conditions supporting advanced life forms, and we see innumerable surfaces across the inconceivably vast expanses of the universe where circumstances have not combined to make life possible. Even on our own fertile planet, immense areas are frozen or scorched, or in other ways hostile to life.

Thus, taken in whole, the picture seems to suggest either a process directed, but not designed with life as a prominent goal, or it suggests an undirected process that happened to produce, in a rare instance, the combination of factors necessary for life, but in the overwhelming majority of instances produced only barren places unfit for life. In neither case does it suggest a process directed by a supernatural, omnipotent being whose end in creating the universe was to cultivate life. For judging by the dim but honest light of our own perceptions, a possible Creator seems to have fine-tuned for life only parts of one tiny planet—or, at most, of a tiny minority of planets—within an unimaginably large universe, and for the most part created vast, unfathomable reaches filled with inhospitable expanses—of fire and ice and rock, and cold, unbreathable emptiness.

Moreover, as best we can tell, life developed only billions of years after the universe already existed, and human life developed many millions of years after many other forms of life. If life overall, or human life in particular, were the goal of an intelligent designer, such a designer does not seem to have been the combination of omnipotent and loving—because the process was seemingly terribly inefficient, taking so long to reach its goal, and was also stained with the blood and screams of uncounted legions of the many species who rose and fell, most going extinct, in the savage contest for survival in the eons preceding human life.

---

[1] Others have spoken of dice and coins: If one throws a die, or even flips a coin, fifty times, any resulting sequence of fifty numbers from 1 through 6, or fifty instances of heads or tails, will be only one possibility out of a dizzyingly large number. It could then be claimed that since the odds of this exact sequence occurring by pure chance are vanishingly small, it must hold supernatural significance.

Finally, these arguments I have so far mentioned are based on the assumption that other combinations of fundamental constants are possible—not for life to develop, but possible overall, and therefore it is seen as remarkable that precisely those constants necessary for life are the ones underlying our universe. Yet some have suggested that, based on certain inherent limitations, the underpinnings of reality cannot be constructed differently. In that case, the proof's entire premise—that our universe's combination of fundamental constants are highly specific and reflect an intelligent designer aiming at producing life, because without intelligent direction the odds of this combination of constants existing are very low—is undermined. For according to some, the very stuff of reality limits itself to these constants: No other set of constants is possible.

Yet, my brother, let us not pretend that we know which theories of current scientists will stand the test of time—of future discoveries and insights. But for purposes of your attempted proof let us remember that even if we knew the universe to have been supernaturally fine-tuned by a Creator, or evidence indicated this was likely, we would still have no responsible reason to believe that any religion knows His identity or will—and it could still easily be the case that such a Creator would strongly disapprove of those who accept religions' many claims about Him and His word, on such flimsy supports as faith.

My brother, anyone who blithely shrugs off the mystery of our complex existence—from abstractions of the universe's seemingly fine-tuned fundamental constants, to the more easily observable intricacies of so many aspects of nature and life—is either less than fully honest or less than fully aware; but so too is anyone who sees in the universe's complexity proof for traditional religion.

Let us, indeed, wonder at mysteries, and let us marvel at complexities—but let us not lie. Let us notice, and rejoice in, the many good and great offerings of life, and let us bear with dignity her many burdens and tragedies, too. But let us not claim to know what we do not know, about the universe's origins, or about the existence and will of a possible Creator. For is not simple honesty—admitting that we do not know what we do not know, and continuing in our efforts to discover—more respectful to our own humanity, and to any God there may be?

48. Argument that everything must have a cause; thus, the universe must have a first cause—which is God (The "First Cause" argument)

But the man pressed on, saying: Will you not agree that everything must have a cause? But this cannot stretch back forever; therefore there must be a first cause, which is God. And surely this is enough reason to subscribe to my religion!

And the sage replied: My brother, philosophers have noted that this "First Cause" argument can take two forms: One claims there must have been an

THE SAGE AND THE SEEKERS

earliest cause long ago, while the other claims that in each moment there must be a deepest underlying supernatural cause, supporting reality.

And many have observed that in either form such an argument, even if convincing, would teach us nothing of whether there was one cause or many, and even if one, whether this cause was alive or not, whether it was aware of anything, what the nature and other powers of this cause might be, and what if anything this cause might want of us—and thus, which if any of the religions we should follow.

Yet the "First Cause" argument has flaws similar to those arguments we have already discussed. Must we insist on an earliest cause outside the universe? Some scientists have postulated—as difficult as this may be to conceive of—that perhaps the universe as we know it came into being as a necessary and intrinsic result of its own laws, and was not created by a force outside it. And if the idea of a thing not caused by something outside it is too difficult to accept, how, my brother, will you accept the notion of God? How could God have not been caused by something outside of *Him*? Has the difficulty of a universe without an external cause been solved merely by moving our focus back one step, and attributing this quality to a mysterious being to be called "God"?

Moreover, some argue that the entire notion of cause is dependent upon time, that one thing precedes another, but that if the universe and its possible precursors were eternal they are outside the strictures of time—indeed, time would be one of the conditions within such existence, and subject to reality, and reality as a whole would not be subject to time. This, they say, is another reason the universe and its possible precursors, as a whole, need not have a cause.

And now let us speak of the claim that current existence must have a deepest cause in each moment, outside of natural laws. I ask you gently: What evidence have we for such a claim? How do we know that existing things require a supernatural force to maintain their existence?

And if you ask, "Why is there something instead of nothing?" I cannot answer. We do not know enough about reality and its determinants to say whether it is more likely that there be nothing than something. And even if we were to know that anything existing is unlikely, still we would not know that once a thing exists it requires ongoing supernatural support, nor would we have any basis to claim we know how things came about to begin with.

Again, my brother, is it not more honest and dignified to admit that we do not know, than to arbitrarily contrive an unintelligible cause and call it God, and then refuse to subject such a significant claim to the careful examination of straightforward reason? And again, even if there was, or is, a Creator, a First or Original Cause—what can we know of His will? Would the existence of such an

Entity tell us anything about whether He approves or disapproves of the beliefs and burdens of any human religion?

49. Sub-argument that the point of God is that He is not created, designed, or animated by anything outside Himself

Then a young philosopher spoke, saying: You dismiss these religious proofs by asking, "Who moved or caused God?" But that is precisely the point of God: that He exists of Himself, neither created nor designed by anything or anyone. And that is why we need to believe in God—so there can be a rational beginning to everything. For without a God who was not designed or created, we would be forced to say that things go back in an infinite series of steps, with each thing being designed or created by something still earlier or greater. And that would be irrational. Besides, God created time, so He is above the need for a beginning.

And the sage said: My brother, indeed, if God exists though neither created nor designed, the riddle of the universe's origins would seem, on one level, less puzzling. I therefore understand why so many eagerly adopt such a theory—especially as it is also consistent with their religious loyalties. Let us examine this approach, however, to see if it is worthy of our assent; for reason never distorts herself to honor our preferences, and reality never transforms herself to rescue us from our confusion.

First, mere convenience does not a legitimate answer make. If we were to dismiss all our puzzles by postulating previously unknown objects, concepts, or characters—and forbidding any critical examination of such speculations—those legions of invented theories would be irresponsible, dishonest, and likely false, even though they would, in the short term, provide the expediency and comfort of seeming to solve our conundrums. Thus, if a child lets go of a gas-filled balloon and sees it rise into the sky, and does not understand why it rises instead of falls, he might conclude that the nature and world of balloons is upside down compared to all else; that what is up for us is down for a balloon; and that although to us the balloon appears to be rising, the balloon is actually falling—for any child *knows* that every plaything let go of must fall. This seems to solve the problem, unless we have the temerity to ask that imaginative child how he knows that what is up for us is down for balloons. If he answers that it must be so because it solves the puzzle as to why the balloon rises, he confuses a speculative possibility with a real-life certainty, and he confuses, too, convenience with accuracy.

So, too, my brother, I say to you: Merely because the riddle of origins seems at first glance to be solved when you postulate an uncreated God who preexisted everything and created time—does not mean that such an answer to the riddle is true, any more than the child's upside down theory on balloons is true. Instead of insisting with confidence that there is an uncreated God, this argument at most justifies one to say: "*Perhaps* there is an uncreated God who created everything."

Moreover, and most to the point, the God "solution" does not answer the question; it merely states that the question will no longer be asked—that we shall postulate something called God, and invest Him with characteristics that preclude such a question. Has anything been explained? The original problem was, "How can the universe have come from nothing, when everything must have a beginning?" And the answer invents Someone who—for no demonstrated reason—does not require a beginning. Well, my brother, if we are abandoning the premise of the question, and are now willing to concede that not everything requires a beginning, why must we devise the notion of God? Why not simply postulate that the universe or its precursors, in some form, had no beginning? Do we have more reliable knowledge or experience of gods without beginnings creating time, than we do of universes without beginnings transcending time?

Indeed, if we are troubled at the bewildering origins of the universe—a universe that we at least know exists—have we really improved anything by introducing into the equation a God whose very existence we cannot honestly confirm, and are thus left unable to explain not the smaller problem of puzzling beginnings for something demonstrably real, but the far greater puzzle of the unfathomable lack of need for a beginning on the part of a mysterious, invisible Being we do not even know to exist?

My brother, against the confounding questions of earliest origins we have no easy remedy. Such mysteries shall neither be solved by solemn tradition nor silenced by authoritative pronouncement—neither will they be vanquished by evasion most cunning. And though we are tempted to turn away in dread and conceit from all evidence of our smallness, tempted to cleverly formulate all manner of mock certainties to cover our ignorance and deny our end, donning such armor only adds the unnecessary heaviness of self-estrangement to the already formidable burdens of our heartbreaking mortality. Instead, naked-souled and humble may we gaze upon the unknown heavens, and dance with her mystery in awed, wide-eyed wonder, our unfettered spirits humming the sacred melody of seeking, and our innocent hearts beating to the tender rhythm of the intimate and real.

50. "Contingency" or "Necessary Being" argument

But the young philosopher continued, saying: Have you not heard of the "Necessary Being" argument? Since each thing can be or not be, and its existence is, therefore, not essentially necessary, there must have been a time when there was nothing. And, if there was a time when there was nothing, it would have been impossible for anything to come into existence. And since we see things in existence, there must be a Being whose existence is not dependent on anything else, but is a necessary Being. And this is God.

And the sage replied: My brother, this argument is similar to the arguments for First Mover and First Cause, and shares their shortcomings. Even if convincing, this argument would teach us nothing of God's will, God's nature, how God should be worshiped or obeyed—or perhaps even how many gods there may be. Yet the argument is far from convincing. Consider that merely because all things have the possibility of not existing, does not mean there was a time when nothing existed. Instead, the existence of all things may well have overlapped with the existence of other things, forever—for although we witness individual things being impermanent, we do not witness reality as a whole being impermanent. Even those who accept the Big Bang theory as including a beginning to our universe, do not necessarily see it as the beginning of all predecessor universes.

And again, my brother, although it is difficult to comprehend the universe or the stuff of which it formed existing forever in some manner with no beginning in time and without being contingent upon anything else, this difficulty is not solved by moving the mystery back one step and claiming there is a Being called God upon whom everything is contingent—or who created all. For we would then remain with the question: Upon what is God contingent? And if we have abandoned the premise that everything must be contingent upon something else, and are willing to accept a being called God who is not contingent upon anything else, why not accept that the Universe itself, or its precursors, might not be contingent upon anything else?

And, again, even if we concluded that there is a God—upon whom all is contingent—would this tell us anything about whether He approves of the rules and rites, the dogmas and doctrines, of any human religion?

51. Argument that it pays to bet on God's existence, because we lose little if wrong, and gain everything if right (Pascal's Wager)

Then a gambler said: I am impatient with all these questions. Perhaps we cannot know for certain whether God exists. Nevertheless, I remain religious because it pays to live as if God exists. Listen: I lose little if I am wrong, but gain everything if I am right. Life is brief, and any pleasures I forego for God's sake would pale beside the rewards I might receive in heaven. And were I to deny God and refuse to follow His will, I would minimize my discomforts only slightly if right, and would bring upon myself eternal misery if wrong—because the fires of hell are a thousand times more painful, and endure ten thousand times longer, than any earthly discomfort I would bear in following religion.

And the sage replied: My brother, you believe it wise to follow your religion on a wager; indeed, many are persuaded by such arguments. But I ask you: Do not games of chance often flash bright, and wink seductively—only to turn one out with empty hands? This gamble, my brother, is no different: Its reasoning is mistaken on a number of grounds.

First, suppose we decide to believe in God—on a wager as you suggest—which faith should we follow, and how should we conduct our lives? The major religions contradict each other on essential beliefs and practices, yet this wager you speak of can be used to argue for any belief system that claims a God and an afterlife.[1] Moreover, our array of choices is not limited to existing religions; thousands of religions practiced by earlier humans are lost to history, yet your wager could be argued for them as well. And remember: The major religions agree that all but one are deeply misguided—only each claims that *it* is the one free of error. Thus, my brother, whatever your religion, a great many traditions clamor that you are mistaken. Perhaps, then, all religions are mistaken—and God, if He exists and cares about how humans live, wishes us to create a new, more correct system of beliefs and worship. How, then, shall we wager?

Second, since no religion enjoys the devotion of a majority of humankind, and all traditional religions contradict each other on essential matters, the preponderance of the faithful are mistaken in their foundational beliefs. Thus, if God wanted us to engage in the wager you speak of—and each remain with his own religion, for this argument works equally well for them all—most would be doomed to leading lives of deep error, at a minimum, and according to some religions, condemned to the eternal torments of hell. Only a cruel or irrational God would subject His handiwork to such injustice. And could we ever guess the will or whim of such an unfair deity? If it pleases Him to consign most of us to long odds on blind wagers, perhaps He would want us to worship mushrooms or reptiles or snowmen, or unimaginable absurdities—on pain of banishment to hell. And perhaps—as many of our ancestors believed—there are numerous small gods in addition to a Great Big God. And perhaps the Great Big God does not wish us to directly address Him, but rather to worship the smaller gods—and

---

[1] Pascal applied this wager to argue for his own, Christian deity. But William James, in his essay *The Will to Believe*, says: "As well might the Mahdi write to us, saying, 'I am the Expected One whom God has created in his effulgence. You shall be infinitely happy if you confess me; otherwise you shall be cut off from the light of the sun. Weigh, then, your infinite gain if I am genuine against your infinite sacrifice if I am not!' His logic would be that of Pascal; but he would vainly use it on us…"

And quite aside from whatever may be the merits of James's own philosophy on belief as expressed in that essay, or indeed of his merely psychological or pragmatic emphasis for why Pascal's argument would fail if used on Christians in the attempt to persuade them to believe in the Mahdi, James's colorful illustration shows why Pascal's argument—because it could be applied to any religion—if it were to prove anything, proves too much.

perhaps He punishes those with the audacity to think about Him, speak about Him, or are so arrogant as to worship and address Him directly. If God is unfair and unreasonable, attempting to please Him by guessing at His will is futile, and there is no way to figure a wager—for irrationality leaves no reliable clues.

Furthermore, my brother, and most to the point, discerning thinkers have long since noted that, even beyond the matter of which religion to wager upon, Pascal's wager is mistaken because there are *not* only two options—religion and dogmatic atheism—from which to choose,[1] and, indeed, we have *much* to lose, and not at all necessarily everything to gain, by subscribing to any traditional religion. For there is also the option of honesty—simply admitting that we do not know whether there is a God, or what such a God may wish of us.

If God is the moral force of which religion speaks, might He not prefer we choose the humble integrity of acknowledging our ignorance on these important matters, rather than deceiving ourselves and our children about what we know—and, if the dead are subjected to justice, might not the former strategy more likely gain us eternal reward, and spare us from eternal hell? If there is a God, and He values truth and accountability above gambling and chance, might not the hungriest flames of any possible hereafter await those who abuse their gifts of consciousness and reason—those who refuse to meet life on terms of stark, sometimes-troubling reality, and instead take refuge in comforting, simplistic wager?[2] Yes, what if eternal awareness and the sweetest delights of heaven are strictly reserved for those noble in earthly consciousness, those painfully honest souls who exercise the humility and courage, the spiritual authenticity, to admit what they do not know; who never cower from awareness though it bristles with the daggers of doubt; and who never turn aside from the path of seeking though it leaves them bloodied and weary, pierced by the arrows of disillusionment and wounded deep by despair's unspeakable sword?

---

[1] Pascal himself, in his *Pensées*, #233, gives a quick nod in the direction of this point when he acknowledges that some will protest that, "...according to reason, you can defend neither of the propositions," and that, "both he who chooses heads and he who chooses tails are equally at fault, they are both in the wrong. The true course is not to wager at all." But Pascal, instead of pursuing this line of reasoning, or conceding that there are not only many religious traditions aside from Christianity that one might weigh in the wager, but that the path of confessing honest not-knowing is a choice, too—arguably the most noble choice and the one that might satisfy any moral God there may be—brushes off all second thoughts about his wager, and merely says: "Yes; but you must wager. It is not optional. You are embarked. Which will you choose then?"

[2] Among the many who have offered this line of attack on Pascal's wager is Walter Kaufmann. And in section 49 of his *Critique of Religion and Philosophy*, he writes of Pascal: "Even an astounding competence in mathematics provides no safeguard against pathetic pitfalls when it comes to arguments about religion."

Moreover, my brother, there is another reason any God there may be might well disapprove of—and more likely punish than reward—those who accept religion on too little evidence: Religions say very specific things about God, some of which may be terrible slander. The Hebrew Bible has God commanding genocide and mass murder; the Christian Bible has God consigning people to the eternal tortures of hell; and Islamic holy and authoritative writings teach as God's will holy war, and the subjugation of other peoples. If God is loving and merciful—as religions paradoxically teach, too—and if none of these religions are accurate in their claims to speak in God's name, might He not reward those who restrain the impulse to conform and to believe things about Him which may be terrible and untrue, and might He not more likely find fault with those who too quickly accept such crude and common rumors?

Indeed, even if one of the traditional religions is accurate in its teachings about God, surely its adherents have no responsible way to be confident of this, and are thus accepting rumors about God on poor evidence.

Furthermore, my brother, another premise of the wager is unsound: Even if there were no God, or at least no God who interfered with or took much interest in individual human affairs, it is *not* true that in following religion there would be little to lose. For in the absence of a supervising God, human meaning is all we would have. And would it not be a terrible loss if we were to throw away everything we are on a desperate gamble for what would then be non-existent immortality? Would it not be tragic if we missed the opportunity to choose a noble life—based on human values, those principles and behaviors that allow us to live in harmony and pursue our dreams in dignity—and instead fell to our knees, groveling in submission to any of the legions of hearsay's gods? Would it not be ignoble to throw away our integrity in the only existence we would ever have, surrender our greatest gift, reason, and instead take up the banner of one of the many superstitious creeds, and its scriptures of diverse and divisive demands?

In light of these observations, my brother, even if one felt the impulse to wager, have not the odds become far less discernible, and has not the wisdom of wagering in this arena become far less clear? And if you insist that God rewards us for dishonesty and gambling, and demands that we be lucky and guess right; and if you believe He will punish us for being humble and leading an honest life; have you not made of Him a cruel and dishonorable fiend, a far cry from the God of deepest truth, most tender mercy, and unparalleled, redeeming love?

52. Argument that reason demands the existence of God and an afterlife (Kant's Postulate)

And a theology student said: Have you not heard the words of a famous philosopher who stated that reason demands the existence of God and an afterlife?

For the highest good is the combination of perfect virtue and perfect happiness, and reason demands that we attempt to achieve this. But, because perfect virtue cannot be achieved in a finite period of time; and since in our world we do not find the combination of perfect happiness and perfect virtue, reason demands[1] that there must be a God who will enable this combination in another realm.

And the sage replied: My son, even the great philosopher has a frail child in the bones of his memory, and a feeble old man, tottering toward death, ever casting an unshakable shadow across his distant imagination. As the brilliant grow tired and frightened and lonely, no less than others, so too do they long for transcendent meaning and immortal life. For desire seduces honesty, and desperation distorts reason. And many have observed that philosophers' questions are often far better than their answers.

The highest imagined good may, indeed, be the joining of perfect happiness and perfect virtue. But why should we believe that such perfection exists? Perhaps we shall never experience the joyous fantasy of all our wishes coming to pass. Indeed, if experience is any indication, we might more reasonably conclude that the ideal does not exist.[2] And since reason does not demand perfection in virtue and happiness, there need not be an afterlife for achieving this blessed union, nor a Great Power to bring such a union about.

My brother: The yearning for justice and the fear of death may desperately hope for a God and an afterlife; but surely unchained reason does not demand these, nor perhaps even consider them likely.

---

[1] To be fair to Kant (though philosophy as a field has long since rejected his postulate) he did not say these things could be proved by reason, or that we can know whether an afterlife existed—only that reason, or practical reason, demanded them.

[2] As Bertrand Russell argues in *Why I Am Not a Christian*: If one saw that in a box of oranges the top layer was spoiled, one would not assume that "The underneath ones must be good so as to redress the balance." Instead, Russell says, one might conclude, "Probably the whole lot is a bad consignment…"

And while those of optimistic or vigorous dispositions may protest that life, overall—or at least life as they experience it—is a good thing, and not to be equated with a bad lot of oranges, Russell's point stands: When, in practical daily life we find in any circumstance or situation an imperfection, we do not assume there must be a corresponding good to compensate for it; instead, we take things for what they seem to be. Similarly, there is no reason to assume that there exists some future life to provide compensation for the imperfections of this life.

53. Argument that one must believe before one can understand arguments for God

Then a devout woman spoke, saying: Unbelievers cannot comprehend the truth of God and religion. To them, no argument will be convincing. First one must believe; only then will one see.[1]

And the sage answered: My sister, I see how strongly you believe and how puzzling you find it that I would challenge such belief. Yet truth neither requires nor tolerates the manacles of pre-commitment. On matters one already holds in the embrace of what one feels to be sacred and virtuous belief, it is not easier to discern truth, but more difficult. For then, heavily invested, the prejudiced mind scorns the soft voice of honest questioning and eagerly nods its assent to the shrill cries of faith, and seeks but a censored reason's support for conclusions already arrived at by passion and will.

54. Argument that we cannot ponder forever, but must commit to a belief system

Then a merchant spoke, saying: We cannot spend our whole lives lost in philosophy, or we shall be unable to act. We cannot be stuck in analysis-paralysis. We must commit to a belief system and remain loyal to it.

And the sage responded: My busy brother, daily life pulls at us with many responsibilities, and it is true that we must act and not only think. Yet one need not choose between the two—action may be consistent with honest contemplation. Your mind and soul do not ask of you to sever your arms and legs, but rather to exercise them with intelligence and integrity. Neither should your arms and legs ask you to sever your mind and soul.

And knowing that most follow beliefs imbibed with mother's milk, and that religions agree that most are mistaken, is it reasonable to hastily dispense with careful thought on such matters?

My brother: It is not asked of you that you spend all your days, and the waking moments of your nights, in pursuit of truth. Would that one hour a week were spent meditating honestly upon the great questions. If there are endless hours for idle chatter, for numerous distractions and varied pleasures, ask your soul if there is not a little time remaining for deepest meaning.

---

[1] This elevating of belief over understanding has a long history in various traditions. For one example among many, Saint Anselm of Canterbury, toward the beginning of his *Proslogion*, says, "The believer does not seek to understand that he may believe; but he believes that he may understand. For without belief he would not understand." And a little later, "For I do not seek to understand that I may believe, but I believe in order to understand. For this too I believe—that unless I believed, I would not understand."

See part V of this book for an extensive set of arguments relating to faith.

My brother, is there virtue in staying loyal to beliefs? If beliefs are correct they are valuable, but because they are correct—not because they were stubbornly adhered to. And, if they are mistaken, it only does greater damage to perpetuate the error. Would a wise merchant quickly choose a venture and persist in it regardless of what he learns, simply because this would constitute a clear course of consistent action? Does a traveler quickly board a ship merely because it sails in a definite direction? Does he not inquire as to its destination—or if the ship is already underway, and he learns that he may be aboard the wrong vessel, does he not attempt to clarify the matter?[1]

Does virtue remain blindly loyal to what may be false? No, my brother: Authenticity and courage hold dear the loyalty of remaining committed to an ever-deepening awareness of what is true and meaningful and real—even if opinions and behaviors must, therefore, change with growing knowledge.

And consider this: We repeatedly attend to that which we value. He who values health cultivates by daily practices his own well-being, and perhaps regularly visits a physician. A careful shopkeeper takes consistent inventory of his merchandise, and an army patrols its borders regularly. Dare we, then, on the care of our deepest beliefs, our most precious wares, remain satisfied with a one-time decision—usually made by others, whose own decisions on such matters were generally made by still others? And even if one is among the small number of adult converts to religion, is it responsible to assume that one was optimally informed and optimally self-aware at the time of that decision?

My brother, convenience and satisfaction are indeed, for many, benefits of final decision on matters of religion, for questions are often unsettling, even frightening and disorienting—while answers seem confident, settled, and sound. But truth has no regard for convenience, and the soul grows lethargic on the plains of conformity. Only the rising cliffs of challenge call forth her strength, and enable her to see what the lowlands obscure. Come, then, be among the climbers, and manifest your instincts for clarity and loyalty—by pressing for truth, and never wavering on that sacred trail.

---

[1] William Kingdon Clifford, in his *Ethics of Belief*, addressed both the importance of being open to modifying one's beliefs and the matter of some claiming to be too busy to think through the issues relating to religious belief. He writes: "Inquiry into the evidence of a doctrine is not to be made once for all, and then taken as finally settled. It is never lawful to stifle a doubt; for either it can be honestly answered by means of the inquiry already made, or else it proves that the inquiry was not complete. 'But,' says one, 'I am a busy man; I have no time for the long course of study which would be necessary to make me in any degree a competent judge of certain questions, or even able to understand the nature of the arguments.' Then he should have no time to believe."

55. Remaining religious so that children have a connection to their tradition and culture

Then a mother said: My children need to feel connected to their heritage. Therefore, though I do not believe what it teaches, I will follow my religion.

And the sage said: My sister, you are a loving mother to think first of your children's welfare. Yet I ask you: Are the errors of their distant ancestors more grounding for them than their own mother's words of truth? Whatever the good lessons of Scripture and clergy, whatever the security of unwarranted convictions, and whatever the beauty of cultural identity, can any compare to the incalculable value of being raised with honesty, humility, and openness to reason? Why not embrace the truth, even with its burdens and discomforts, and teach your children not to fear the universe and all its uncertainties? Why not gaze with them unblinking into the stirring darkness of the mute heavens? My sister, can you teach your children to live with integrity by yourself living a lie?

Moreover, even in the absence of religion, our children need not go wanting; we can help them find culture and tradition in purer form. Let us create family rituals; let us ponder great mysteries in reverence alone, in groups, or in crowds; let us find meaning in love, and in the many forms of individual or joint creative expression—in writing, singing, building, and a thousand other blossomings— and let us find in authentic living a mission more orienting and ennobling than the dead past's heritage, with all its haunting, familiar lies.

And your little ones, being raised with only honest practices and beliefs, will be spared the common tragedy of a trammeled mind, and the self-loathing of a lying heart. For their sake, then, and for your own, let not your walk of mother-hood lead your children through the dank, constricted tunnels of tradition, but guide them, instead, across the open-aired bridges of forthright reason, and through the sun-brightened fields of flowering truth.

56. Remaining religious so that children belong to a community

And another mother said: I have no essential loyalty to one religion or cul-ture over another, and I do not believe my children need a connection to their heritage. Neither do I claim to know anything about gods or heavens or hell. But I do know something about people—especially children. A child needs to be part of a community. He needs to belong. And since communities are structured around religion, if I do not raise my children within a religious community, they may grow up feeling isolated and different—outsiders in society.

And the sage replied: My sister, I can understand that you wish to spare your children from what you fear might be a lonely existence. Yet I ask you: Cannot unity and kinship, friendship and affiliation, exist outside the parameters of religion? A hundred pursuits and activities beckon—from playing sport to playing music; from reading books to reading the skies—wherein children and families can come together and forge social bonds. And if you live where no community gatherings occur outside the framework of religion, why not bring such meetings to pass, thus helping yourself and helping others?

But even if there were no opportunities for community outside of religion, I remind you that every foolishness, every injustice, every practice degrading to the human spirit has, for a time, been accepted as the norm, even insisted upon by community. If it were still widespread practice to enslave fellow humans, would you teach your child to do so in order that he might feel more accepted in society? If it were still the custom for a bride to be deflowered by the pagan priest before she begins married life with her husband, would you encourage your daughter to submit to this, too? If it were still convention to kill one's firstborn as a sacrifice to the gods, would you exhort your children to do so, in order that they fit in with their community? And if it is still fashionable to stifle our greatest faculty, reason—by being dishonest with ourselves and each other on what we truly know of God and His will for our lives—and thus trample our deepest dignity and authenticity; if this is still the common, debasing behavior of the many, shall we walk the way of convenience and encourage our progeny along this corrupt and demeaning path? My sister, is not community sometimes too expensive?

Moreover, it is admirable that you hope to protect your children from the ravages of rootless isolation. Yet ask yourself this: Are there any stronger roots than those growing in the rich soil of courage and feeding from authenticity's deep springs? And is there any greater loneliness than being estranged from one's truest self—or any greater communion than confidently meeting one's own gaze on ultimate issues?

Let us forge community, then—without supernatural claims—around meaningful activity and honest ceremony. For shall we constrain fellowship's grace with the manacles of disgrace? Shall we come together and sing; and learn to live in harmony, and in wisdom and kindness, too; and give to our neighbors with our minds and hearts and purses and hands; and laugh, and celebrate each other's blessings, and support one another in our seasons of pain—shall we make such standing together in noble brotherhood contingent upon falling to our knees in ignoble submission to ideas we will not challenge and to gods we cannot know?

57. Remaining religious to preserve the family and protect children from suffering a broken home.

And a man said: It may be easy for one without children to leave a religious way of life. But I already have a religious wife and family, and, of course, I cannot consider divorce; because I agonize over how it would cause my children suffering.

And the sage said: My brother, I commend you for thinking of the most vulnerable, and for wanting the best for your children.

I ask you this, however: Is it so clear that when we continue to mislead and falsely educate a child on what we claim are the fundamental issues of human life, is it so clear that when we collaborate on perverting the intellectual development and integrity of a child, and, in all likelihood, in passing on this burden and blindness to the child's children, too—is it so clear that such grievous behavior is better than being honest, even if honesty is purchased at the price of pain?

And can one not be honest about one's religious beliefs without leaving a marriage or breaking up the family? Is it not possible to disagree about religion and still remain married? Yet if your wife refuses to continue wedlock with an unbeliever, and demands of you hypocrisy on the most important matters, and the continued betrayal of your children's defenseless minds and hearts, and insists that you go on indoctrinating them with what you have come to see as religion's dishonest and limiting claims—if this is what your wife demands of you as the price for keeping the family together, you may wish to reconsider whether such a shameful arrangement is worthy of your soul—or those of your children.

But, my brother, on matters that touch upon the tears of tender eyes, and the hearts of the yet-innocent young, we must not make sweeping pronouncements. Each case must be carefully pondered in light of its own unique conditions. Indeed, I would advise that no man or woman be hasty in disbanding a marriage—especially one in which children are being raised—assuming there looms no imminent, significant harm. Only after months of reflection and after seeking counsel from several wise people—from among the religious and the non-religious—would it be responsible to move forward with such a decision.

But even as I encourage you to agonize over the harm done to a child when his family is broken, so also do I encourage you to agonize over the compounding damage done to a child whose mind is ever more trammeled and whose heart is ever more twisted, being lied to by parents and teachers on what is truly known about foundational issues of existence: about God, religion, and life's meaning. So yes, my brother, let us agonize—but let not the agonizing go only one way.

58. Argument that religion provides a right and wrong and is therefore necessary

And a teacher said: I maintain my religion because it gives me a right and a wrong, values without which I would have no guidelines on how to live.

And the sage replied: My brother, many who desire clear direction are comforted by religion, which dictates how to act, how to speak, often even what to think and believe.[1] Sadly, however, not every system of rules is honest, dignified, or morally constructive. History's cruelest tyrants have often imposed clear rules, demanding of their people detailed obedience in word and deed—while some of the kindest souls, some of the noblest heroes, and many of the most intelligent thinkers, have been far more flexible and accepting of varying behaviors, and have even wrestled with disorienting doubts. Thus, though certainty may bring comfort and confidence, it has little to do with truth and spiritual integrity.

And remember, too, that by your standard, all religions are equally valid—for all teach confidently their own notions of right and wrong. Yet, does not your religion teach that other faiths are misguided? And if everyone remained loyal to his religion because it provided a right and a wrong, would not all religions agree that most people were mistaken in some of their foundational beliefs? Upon further reflection, then, is there any reason for confidence that your religion provides accurate knowledge about what a God may truly want of us? And does it not concern you that your system of right and wrong may actually be wrong?

My brother, not every collection of rules is worth following. Ultimately, each honest soul must reflect upon different sets of guidelines, and decide which he will abide by, and why. And while such self-direction may be our burden, it is also our great glory. Remember, too, that independent thought approaches heroism when conducted by one with an instinct for security and obedience. Reach for your excellence, then, and, impelled by your urge to know right and wrong, battle fiercely for true knowledge on what you may honestly be confident is right and wrong. For though some of us have the inclination to be followers and serfs, all have surging within us, too, the proud blood of spiritual autonomy, and the noble breath of sacred aristocracy.

59. Argument that religion helps one transcend the self, and feel connected to the universe

And a woman said: My religion helps me think of something bigger than myself, larger than my individual life, when it teaches me about God and His will. It helps me feel connected to the universe, and to all eternity.

And the sage said: My sister, I understand. At times we feel trapped in the smallness and brief quickening of our individual selves, and our spirits yearn to feel connected to all of life, to the past and to the future, and to the vast expanses of cosmic space.

Yet, my sister, without careful analysis by the lights of reason and experience how will you know if your feelings of being involved with something larger than

---

[1] For more on this topic, see Part IX of this book, titled, "Right and Wrong Without Supernatural Religion."

yourself are based in reality or merely in pleasant fantasy? And would it not be sad if you lived all your days following religion to escape smallness and isolation, but in truth you were not only deeply mistaken about the most important matters, and thus remained bereft of authentic spiritual connection, but your integrity was compromised, too, and your dignity decayed—and you were truly small?

Consider, too, that all religions help their followers feel a sense of larger purpose, of connection to the universe. If such a feeling indicated truth, everyone could justify her own religion on that basis. Yet religions contradict each other on the most essential and foundational matters—so they cannot all be true, though they all provide the feeling you covet. And religions themselves do not consider a sense of connection sufficient evidence for the truth of another religion. Should it justify yours?

My sister, is it not relevant to investigate whether religion can truly provide such eternal and unlimited meaning—or whether these are but vain promises? For surely you would not offer the finest fruits of all your days in exchange for a set of seductive pretensions! If a man promised you a mansion of unsurpassed elegance, unparalleled grandeur, and unlimited dimensions—yet offered you no evidence that such a magnificent structure existed, much less that he could provide it for you—would such a promise be better than the palpable reality of a charming though modest home whose solid bricks you might caress with your fingers, and whose familiar wooden floors would sound beneath your feet?

And if the price demanded for the promised mansion was your very soul all your life—your deepest allegiances and the foundations of your dignity and authenticity—and all this before you could possibly know if the man's promises were anything more than empty breath, would that manor of the imagination still seem so alluring? Yet religion speaks of mansions in heaven, and the price it demands is your very soul; and it offers no way to verify the existence of the promised reward until all that you have—all that you are—is already given in payment. Would any but the needlessly desperate strike such a deal?

My sister, is it a small thing to look up enchanted at the pink and purple sky; to tread with bare feet the soft grasses of spring, cushioned and tickled by the living sod; to catch the seductive scent of lavender, and the happy colors of dandelion and lily; to savor the heartiness of vigorous labor, and luxuriate in her keen appetites and ready slumbers; to feel the life-clinging grip of an infant's fingers; or to fall for a moment into the hungry eyes of eager passion or the welcoming arms of earnest love? Do you not feel connected to the universe when you drink the water fallen from clouds, eat the sun-ripened corn and squash with bread baked from the grains of the field, and drift off to sleep as our side of the planet spins into the dark of night? Can you not feel part of something greater than yourself when you sit in your home fashioned from the trees of the forest and plain, and from the sand and stones of Mother Earth?

And are you not part of a larger system of life? Do you not eat and drink and sleep and embrace, as do all who slither, crawl, walk, or fly upon the face of the earth? And will you not die as they do, too, to be replaced by the next generation, and they by the next? And do not all species live by the same good fortune of the sun being near enough to help all things grow, but not near enough to set everything ablaze? My sister, that you might know your connection to the vast universe—what more than these do you seek?

But perhaps you insist upon an unlimited connection to something eternal, beyond the bounds of the physical and the mortal. If so, I ask you gently if this is not a bit covetous and grasping, demanding of life more than a reasonable share. You would not demand unlimited wealth or unlimited power; why, then, demand unlimited connection? And can a dishonest dream, no matter how grandiose, truly connect you with the universe more than your own feet walking, your own heart pumping, in the perpetual procession of the cosmic parade?

My sister, why not assume, then, the noble posture of your most expansive self, heroic with courage, and large with truth? And though you grieve for the fanciful throne of imagined divine significance, rock yourself gently to consolation in the embracing hammock of profound humility, then sit in open-eyed dignity upon the immovable rock of enduring reason.

60. Religious observance to avoid hell

Then a blacksmith said: I follow my religion to avoid the fires of hell.

And the sage replied: My brother, the fiery punishment of which some religions teach is a fearsome proposition; I understand your wish to escape such a fate. Yet will you follow each religion—and each denomination of your own religion—that threatens hell for those who do not follow her teachings? If so, you have set yourself an impossible task, for a number of these belief systems contradict each other, and teach that hell awaits believers of other faiths.

And since you feel menaced by the heavy threat of hell, is it not especially important to learn whether the claims of any religion are well founded? To your great relief, you may after a reasoned investigation find yourself blessedly liberated from fears of eternal horror.

Moreover, if—as the doctrine of hell teaches—those with whom God is displeased suffer unspeakable agony, might it not be that accepting religion instead of independently studying what can truly be known of God's will may, more than many deeds religion forbids as sinful, kindle against you God's terrible wrath? For all of us know that various religions zealously insist upon widely differing claims about God; thus, we cannot plead ignorance as to the cacophonous multiplicity of such contradictory teachings. In avoiding a critical examination of religion, then, do we not show a negligent disregard for the possibility that we may be misquoting God, telling untruths about Him, misrepresenting His will, or worshiping the wrong being and calling it God? Might not a hell-wielding deity be enraged at such insolence and, on the Day of Judgment, speedily cast perpetrators of such offenses into the awful blazes of Beelzebub's fiery realm?

And so, my brother, we cannot avoid the threat of punishment in an afterlife by dutifully following religious dictates. For if God exists and is punitive and cruel, perhaps He punishes severely those who scorn vigilant reason and instead follow any of the many dubious religions men have fabricated from dread and hope, and a thousand lesser things. But if there exists a just and compassionate God, and we sincerely seek truth—and thus, when necessary, display the courage of honest ignorance—we may rest confident that such a God would not subject our well-meaning souls to the eternal tortures and torments of traditional religions' hells.

61. Argument that "God caused me to be born into my family and my tradition. Therefore, He must have intended for me to live this way."

And a man said: God has caused me to be born into my family and my tradition. Therefore, he must have intended for me to live this way. His will is that I be faithful to my people's religious beliefs, and trust Him about how I should live, instead of thinking myself so wise as to figure these things out for myself. No, I do not consider myself smarter than God. He placed me where I am, and He must want me to live as I have been raised to live.

And the sage replied: My dear brother, let us first note that your argument assumes both that there is a God, and that your specific circumstances are the result of His will. Therefore you believe it pleases God that you remain faithful to your native religion. But in truth, my brother, we have no reliable knowledge as to whether God exists—and, if He does, whether He holds us in sufficiently high esteem to arrange the specifics of our lives, including the family and religion into which we are born.

Yet even if we accept these assumptions—that a God exists, and that He plans, in detail, each human life—must we conclude that He wishes us to remain loyal to the religion of our fathers?

Has not the founder of your religion or sect abandoned or altered the creed of his family and culture? Have not Abraham, Buddha, Jesus, Mohammad, Luther, and all other trailblazers in the forest of sacred belief, brought innovation and change—and, to that degree, have they not forsaken the time-hallowed ways of their people?

And does not every religion teach that in our spiritual journeys we are confronted with battles in which we must conquer, and trials in which we must prevail? Thus, if there is a higher purpose for your life, intended by some supernatural force, who can say but that you were born for the struggle of resisting easy surrender to custom and tribe? And who can say but that, even now, God waits for you to transcend your beginnings? Does not heroism always demand some reaching beyond and reaching within; resisting the seductions of familiar circumstance and the indolence of comforting inclination—and does not heroism often ask the willingness to separate from family and friends? Did not Abraham leave his birthplace and his father's gods? Did not Moses renounce the palace of an Egyptian princess, and turn on the path at the prodding of his inquisitive mind? And did not Ruth, in her devotion to Naomi, abandon her people, and the worship of her Moabite gods?

Furthermore, my brother, most are born into religions other than your own. Do you truly believe that God approves of these varied and conflicting faiths, and encourages all to worship in the divergent traditions of their fathers—even when they reject that which you consider most holy? Would an intelligent and moral deity desire discord and confusion in our most sacred endeavors, and consider contradictory religions worthy of our highest aspirations for truth?

Finally, my brother, can circumstance of birth signal God's approval of one's native beliefs or practices? Do you, or other religionists, truly believe that God wants all those raised by atheists to remain atheists? And what of a child born into a clan of bandits, a family of slave traders, a dynasty of cruel monarchs—or to parents who advocate the genocide of neighboring peoples? Does God wish the child of a cruel man, or a foolish man, or a self-indulgent man, to perpetuate his father's inferior ways? Or might He not ask of us, rather, to think with our own heads and consult with our own hearts before we act with our own hands— and especially before we chart our own course, and heavily influence those of our children, on life's most meaningful matters?

62. Argument that there must be a heaven and a God, because many have reported near death experiences, even being dead, outside their bodies, and moving toward the light

And a man said: Many people have had near death experiences: Some have felt they were floating above, and looking down upon, their bodies; and some have felt they were moving toward a bright and warm light—and report this to have been an exquisite feeling. And many have been shown to be temporarily dead while this was occurring. Surely this speaks of a heaven and a God!

And the sage said: My brother, these things you describe are indeed experienced by many. And how comforting to believe that upon dying we all survive and go to a place of love and light. I, too, would like for this to be so. Yet can we reasonably assume it *is* so? Consider that our brains produce any number of intense, but purely subjective, experiences. All of us, in the dark and ready haven of a common night's slumber, are witness to the most astonishing theater of wild, even impossible, happenings realistically portrayed. In my dreams I have flown and levitated; I have been chased by giants, too. These things and more, some wonderful and some terrible, have I seen in dreams; and they felt real—though they were not.

Even in wakeful states, those under the influence of powerful drugs and medicines may see dazzling colors; or creatures crawling from their skin; or feel that they float upon clouds of ecstasy; or find plain objects to be remarkable, and simple thoughts profound.[1] And those unfortunate souls who bear the indignities and persecutions of madness see and hear and feel things that are apparently not there. Do all these subjective experiences prove such perceptions consistent with objective reality? Or do they not, instead, illustrate the varied powers of the human mind to conjure many different states of consciousness? So, too, near death experiences, for all their intensity, may be products of the human mind. Why assume them to be sourced in anything more?

Indeed, even without sleep, madness, or intoxicating potions, the mind hallucinates in sharp detail and profound intensity, especially in times of great stress. Consider the famished travelers in the desert who behold mirages of lush trees and cascading fountains: Is this, too, to be taken as proof that deserts are full of actual oases—or rather that desperately thirsty *minds* are full of *visions* of oases?

And, my brother, the common experience of moving toward an overwhelmingly loving light might be a natural occurrence, too. The human organism is well capable of creating bright images and feelings of ecstasy—as are readily experienced during intense imagination and sexual dreams. And the body produces natural pleasure chemicals and anesthetics to help us cope with stress and pain. Moreover, many have reported that a person gradually freezing to death often feels a powerfully seductive sleepiness—though perhaps without warm lights or spiritual images—pleasurably pulling at him to lose consciousness. It may be that for some, the process of dying under other conditions involves a similar—but perfectly natural—pleasurable pull into oblivion.

Moreover, anesthetic medication has been found capable of stimulating hallucinations. Some near death experiences—most of which involve the gravely ill

---

[1] Oliver Wendell Holmes is said to have awakened from an ether-induced spell of unconsciousness, with the conviction that he had at last understood the secret of the universe. Eager to capture the insight, he quickly wrote it down. Later, fully recovering awareness, he saw what he had written: "A strong smell of turpentine prevails throughout."

or injured, or those undergoing surgery, many of whom are under the influence of anesthetic medications—may have been caused by these substances.

And some say that the unusual perceptions of a near death experience may be caused by the shortage of oxygen-rich blood to the brain,[1] which results when the heart stops. The brain can survive for a short while even without the heart beating—during which time the person would be considered dead, yet may, due to insufficient oxygen in the brain, be subject to unusual perceptions, which can then be recalled when the heart resumes beating.

And other evidence exists that the feeling of floating outside one's body, and seeing oneself from above—oft-mentioned elements of a near death experiences—are rooted in the functioning of the human brain, and not the miracles of a divine realm.[2]

And even the startling claim that some people to whom these events occurred were clinically dead, is not all that it seems. Medical science is always learning and advancing, and its old understanding of what constitutes death is changing. Formerly, the combination of the heart no longer beating, the lungs no longer breathing, and the cessation of measurable brain activity, was enough for physicians to consider a person dead. But more recently, medical science has begun to see death not as a precise moment, but as a process, which can be brief or prolonged, and which is not complete in some cases until much later—because the dying process can often be reversed, and a person brought back to life. And simply because medical equipment has not always been sufficiently

---

[1] And this cerebral anoxia, or indeed the heart stoppage itself or other physiological crises, may trigger other neuro-chemical changes in the brain that cause or contribute to the unusual perceptions of a near death experience.

[2] A woman whose section of the brain known as the right angular gyrus was stimulated by electrodes during treatments for epilepsy reported a somewhat similar subjective experience of floating near the ceiling and seeing herself from above—as well as other illusions relating to her body. And these illusions were triggered repeatedly by such stimulation. See *Stimulating illusory own-body perceptions*, a paper by Olaf Blanke, Stepanie Ortigue, et al, published in *Nature*, Vol. 419, September 19, 2002.

Some researchers suspect that the right angular gyrus is involved in generating out-of-body experiences, overall, because that part of the brain analyzes and integrates signals on touch, balance, and vision.

Some researchers believe, too, that there are correlations and likely, therefore, possible similarities in physiological functioning between epilepsy, on the one hand, and near death experiences and intense religious experiences, on the other.

But, of course, medical science and theory change quickly; and whether these explanations are ultimately shown to be accurate, or other hypotheses on natural causes seem more consistent with later research, the overall point of this section stands—we simply have no responsible reason to conclude that near death experiences reflect anything supernatural, or provide any glimpse of an afterlife.

sophisticated to detect the subtle brain functioning occurring during the cardiac arrest phase of the dying process does not mean we should be surprised that the brain is functioning in many cases—so many, in fact, that a significant percentage of people, if their dying process is reversed, retain memories of this time.[1]

My brother: Another natural explanation is often suggested: Perhaps such visions are the brain's psychological defense against the anxiety over death; that the mind produces a subjective experience of surviving death and moving toward an afterlife—replete with a deep sense of well-being, the welcome of deceased relatives, and other comforting or expected religious figures or symbols. Nobody educated in the intricacies of human psychology and the power of subconscious defense mechanisms, would find it surprising that the mind is capable of this.

And observe that in a near death experience Christians tend to see Jesus or the apostles welcoming them, while adherents of other religions see themselves greeted by symbols or leaders of *their* religions—and those never exposed to religious beliefs may experience a non-religious, merely overwhelmingly loving presence. That people see their own familiar leaders and symbols is another indication that these experiences are creations of their own minds and not reflections of objective spiritual reality—for the major religions contradict each other on essential beliefs and practices, and consider each other to be terribly misguided. A real heaven, therefore—according to the teachings of most traditional religions and their denominations—would not send as a welcoming party the leaders and symbols of mistaken faiths. Thus, either these experiences do not indicate a true God or afterlife—or they teach that our traditional religions' dogmas are unnecessary to merit a heavenly afterlife.

My brother: I do not say that the possible explanations I have offered must be considered definitively true. I have merely illustrated that non-supernatural explanations exist for the intriguing strangeness of near death experiences.

---

[1] Early research into the matter suggests that those who had the conventional near death experience of seeing a bright light, feeling deep peace, and having out of body perceptions, were, even before this event, more likely to have difficulty keeping the waking and dream states separate—having rapid eye movements (REM) even while awake, though these are usually associated with sleep. But one need not chase down the details of each research study to notice the direction of the arrow of discovery moving from primitive intuitions seeing ancestors and spirits towards the more informed knowledge of nature and her complex ways. And such findings and others, though still in the early phases of study on the phenomenon known as near death experience, continue to confirm what those wary of superstition have long suspected—that the more closely we study this matter, and others, the more likely we are to understand the natural forces at work in the functioning of life and other constituents of our universe, and the less we will need to resort for our explanations to all manner of gods and ghosts.

Much is not yet understood about how our brains function, and why some have unusual visions and haunting ecstasies. It would be wise, therefore, to remain humble and attribute our puzzlement to our paltry knowledge of the human organism, rather than jump to the hasty, self-aggrandizing conclusion that our souls endure beyond physical death, and are welcomed with divine love and fanfare to a celestial realm. Moreover, even if we should leap, based on near death accounts, to the unwarranted conviction that there exists a spiritual world, and an afterlife, too, we would still have no responsible reason to believe in the many teachings and dogmas of any traditional religion.

Most important, my brother, remember that all of our human learning and ingenuity has been able to responsibly verify only natural events. No miracle or supernatural process, not one, has ever passed the careful scrutiny of science and reason. Thus, more is needed than a mere theory or possibility, in order to honestly draw supernatural conclusions. Indeed, so long as we can identify a plausible explanation of how an occurrence might be natural, the overwhelming burden of proof lies with those who say that this one phenomenon, unlike anything that has ever been responsibly investigated—and unlike the myriad of discredited superstitious beliefs in the long, benighted history of frightened and inspired error—is, indeed, supernatural.

My brother, sufficient honesty would have us say about such matters: "I do not know just what these people have glimpsed while on the road to death; these intense things may have been natural—perhaps a reaction to brain changes during the dying process, or a defensive psychological reaction against confronting death, or may be explained by any number of other plausible theories. Furthermore, even if I were to accept the unsubstantiated notion of a spiritual realm, these near death experiences give me no reliable lesson on whether there is a God in that possible spiritual realm, and whether such a possible God approves of any religion, or has any preference as to how I should live."

63. Argument that there must be a soul, because at the moment of death the body suddenly changes, as though something left it

And a physician said: I have seen that when a person dies, he instantly turns into a puppet. The life suddenly goes out of him, the arms and legs go limp, his face changes, and he seems very different. Clearly, then, it was the soul that left. And this proves the existence of a soul, a spiritual realm, and God.

And the sage replied: My brother, not only humans, but humbler forms of life, too—rats, mice, wasps, flies, ants, and cockroaches—go limp and seem to turn into "puppets" when they die. Shall we say, then, that they all have souls, too, that live on forever?

The many muscles giving the face its form, and making it recognizable to us, lose their natural tone upon death, and so the face does, indeed, appear different. But this change needs no assistance from the supernatural.

Moreover, even non-living things can appear to go suddenly limp when their energy runs out. An artificially powered machine or toy, as complex as it may be, goes suddenly silent and still if its energy is exhausted or its power source interrupted. The body—among other things—is an electro-chemical organism. It should come as no surprise that when it stops producing electro-chemical energy it suddenly loses animation and seems little more than a puppet.

My brother, this sudden change from a live human to a limp corpse is a sight most of us find disturbing. Yet much as it pains us, and much as we rebel against so undignified an end clearly in store for us, too—if we are honest we must concede that this transformation from alive to dead teaches us nothing about a soul or a spiritual realm. Moreover, even if we thought this sudden limpness at death sufficient to persuade us of a soul and an existence beyond, we would still not know whether God exists, and if so, what if anything He may want of humans—and thus, whether He approves or disapproves of any specific religion.

64. Argument that religion is ancient and therefore should be trusted

Then a man said: My religion is many hundreds, even thousands of years old. It teaches ideas that my ancestors believed, ideas that are the wisdom of the ancients. These things have stood the test of time and should be trusted. Therefore, I am confident that my religion is true.

And the sage replied: My brother, if we were to agree that a religion is true simply because it is ancient, we would encounter a perplexing question: Which of the many ancient religions should we follow? And do they not contradict each other on foundational points of belief and practice? And does not this show that many religions must be mistaken—ancient though they are? Thus, age confers upon religion neither the stamp of credibility nor the authority of truth.

In matters unrelated to religion, too, what is ancient is not necessarily true. My brother, would that the passing years were guarantors of accuracy, and the ancients, advisers infallible. Yet, in both knowledge and virtue, bygone ages and our esteemed forebears have been sorely deficient. In many ways, and for their epochs, they did well—and we would not likely have done better in their place. But was it the ancients whose knowledge conquered the oceans and skies, that we travel them now with ease? Was it the ancients who gave every man and woman across vast countries a voice in choosing government? Was it the ancients who banned slavery, and all but banished famine? Was it the ancients who enabled the near-sighted to see, or the deaf to hear—and who cured many dread diseases? And did not the preponderance of our ancestors—most of them religious—believe the earth to be flat, or, at least, that the sun revolved around the earth? O trusting one, would you sail the oceans on a vessel designed and built a thousand years ago, or on a ship designed by modern methods and crafted by modern tools? If time were short, would you travel across land in an ancient wagon over ancient roads, or in a modern vehicle on modern roads—or better yet, on a craft that flies through the air? If you were deathly ill, would you prefer to be treated by the error-stricken barbarisms of ancient witch doctors, or by the proven methods of modern medicine? Would you prefer to be tried by a court subject to the whims of ancient dictators and corrupt or superstitious judges, or by the relatively more fair justice systems of later, democratic ages?

My brother, many mistaken and evil practices have been with humanity for thousands of years: Hatred of other peoples and races; dictatorship, slavery, monarchy, and other abuses of power; wife beating and the abuse of children; illiteracy, witchcraft, and a remarkable diversity of crude superstitions. We do not say of these that they must be accurate and appropriate merely because humans have engaged in them for millennia. Instead, we attempt to learn and progress as a species. Might it not be possible, then, that traditional religion is mistaken, too, and that the findings of careful examination would counsel us to abandon it as but one more monumental error of the misguided ancients?

65. Argument that we should believe what religions agree upon—the common values and beliefs of all faiths—because such unanimity proves divine truth

And a man smiled warmly and said: Religions agree on the most important matters, and disagree only on details. We should accept the values and beliefs on which all faiths agree—for example, that we should love each other—because such unanimity of the world's faiths evidences divine truth.

And the sage replied: My brother, how pleasant is the spirit of brotherhood animating your thoughts. And would that all traditions agreed on essential matters, were indeed consistent with truth, and that honesty never had to initiate the discomfort of profound disagreement.

But what shall we do? Circumstances are otherwise. Religions differ not merely on trivial details, but on foundational beliefs and practices, too. One religion teaches that the Creator is indivisible and has not spoken through Jesus or to Mohammad; and that to believe the contents of the New Testament or the Koran is a serious perversion of God's will. Another religion states that not only has God spoken through Jesus, but that Jesus is the only way to approach God, or perhaps even is God; that holding this to be true is the only means to avoid eternal damnation—that those who do not believe in Jesus as the only begotten Son of God are doomed to hell. A different religion believes that God's greatest prophet was Mohammad; that all preceding divine commandments and prophecies were superseded by God's will spoken through Mohammad; that Jesus was not only not God, but that believing Jesus to be even the Son of God is blasphemy. Another religion says that myriads of gods exist, and that insisting on only one God, whether divided into a trinity or not, is a deep error. Still another religion may have originally taught little of supernatural beings, but encouraged its adherents to let go of attachments to life, and its pleasures and pains, in order to attain peace of mind. And, of course, innumerable other religions, of today and yesteryear, have inspired and blinded many in the long history of our species.

And as to how we should conduct ourselves, most religions have permitted, even instructed—at various points in their history—the persecution, the expulsion, even the killing of infidels. Thus, depending on whose scriptures or clergy are consulted, different people are marked for such abuse.

My brother: "Love thy neighbor as thyself" is a maxim to which many religions subscribe.[1] Yet the difficulty lies not only in agreeing on who comes under the category of "neighbor," but also in agreeing on what behavior is consistent with the commandment to "love." Religions have traditionally taught—and religious communities have often enacted—such passages to mean that one need only love those who subscribe to proper beliefs and practices: those of the true faith—one's own, of course. Indeed, it has often been taught by various religious sects that not even all members of one's own faith qualify, only those who practice it correctly—those who interpret scriptures and traditions exactly as do one's own favored leaders. And even those who chose to extend to non-believers the gift of "love," often held an unusual understanding of the word. Medieval inquisitors and their apologists, it is said, justified burning heretics at the stake by arguing that it was the loving thing to do in order to prevent worse suffering in hell—indeed, if one accepted their theology, such an argument seemed compelling—and even the more gentle amongst the religious have often looked down from their self-righteous perches, with a mixture of pity and scorn, at those who believed differently.

---

[1] Mistakenly thought by many to be the original teaching of Jesus, this is found in the Old Testament, in Leviticus 19:18. It is also taught, in one form or another, by many other teachers, religions, and traditions, among them Confucius (approximately 500 B.C.) in his analects 15:23; and Hinduism, Buddhism, and more. Indeed, the inclination toward fairness or generosity of a sort, at least to members of one's own group, is so pervasive and so basic an instinct for a social species that traditions not teaching this ideal in one form or another would surely be the exceptions, and we might postulate that if monkeys, even elephants and wolves, could write, undoubtedly some of them, too, would have left evidence of having taught—for practice within their immediate pack or group—some version of the golden rule.

It should not surprise us, then, that the Old and the New Testaments while commanding love and compassion in various ways—Jesus even going so far as to teach the loving of one's enemies—offer rather less loving lessons, too.[1] The Old Testament, along with its many teachings on justice and mercy, commands the genocide of various conquered peoples, and the death penalty for all manner of the insubordinate and the religiously disobedient; it also condones slavery. And the New Testament, far from being a consistent example of gentleness and love—as in some of its passages it is, notably the Sermon on the Mount—not only has Jesus railing against his opponents and calling them choice names,[2] but, far more important, threatens something the Old Testament never did— everlasting torture in the fires of hell.[3]

Moreover, my brother, far from all religions agreeing on the major issues, critical differences appear even within religions themselves. Consider Christianity—some have taught that to be considered virtuous and to merit heaven one need only have faith in certain propositions, while others have held faith to be insufficient, and taught that good works are necessary, too.[4] Indeed, even sects agreeing that belief alone assures entrance to heaven, have often bitterly disagreed on precisely *what* one must believe. Still others have taught that neither faith nor good works will ensure heaven, that mortal man can do nothing to achieve salvation, but must simply be one of the fortunate handful to have received God's unfathomable grace.

Moreover, even beliefs on which all religions agree—even such beliefs might be untrue. Consensus upon something we have no reasonable way of knowing, tells us little. If all the children in a schoolyard agree that monsters are real, but have very different beliefs as to who these creatures are, in what form they appear, and what powers they possess, should we confidently accept as true at least what they all agree upon—that monsters exist? No, not only because they have wide disagreements on substance, but because they have no credibility on the matter: They have no apparent means of determining the existence of such creatures; and they are driven, too, by emotional and imaginative urges to believe what they truly do not know.

---

[1] For greater detail and precise references, see sections 127 and 128, which deal with the morality of the Old and New Testaments.

[2] See Mathew chapter 23, for instance, where Jesus calls his opponents hypocrites, fools, blind, serpents, and a generation of vipers.

[3] For details, see section 128d, relating to the New Testament's teachings on hell, and the footnote there discussing the Old Testament's teaching on the same subject.

[4] Indeed, as many have observed, not even all the Gospels seem to agree that faith in Jesus' divine nature or sacrifice is a prerequisite to salvation. See section 123 where this issue is discussed.

Another example: Supposing all astrologers agreed that the position and movement of planets can determine or predict human events, must we accept this as true? Certainly not, because their credibility on the matter is far from compelling: We have no good reason to believe they can detect supposed mysterious connections between heavenly bodies and human events—and, as astrologers, they are pushed and pulled by many forms of self-interest and superstition to believe in such connections. So, too, my brother, with religion: Humans have shown no credible evidence that they know anything about a supernatural realm or being, much less that they know the specific will of a Creator God; and we have so many social, emotional, and other instinctual urges leading us to believe supernatural claims, that even if all religions were to be in harmony on essential beliefs regarding God—and, of course, they are not—we would still have no compelling reason to accept such notions as true.

Moreover, the contradictory accounts offered by religion, about God and His will, reduce the credibility of their testimony even on those details about which they are in accord; for if they so profoundly disagree with each other on many of the most central issues of who God is and what He wants—and their views, being mutually exclusive, illustrate by the account of every traditional religion just how erroneous the beliefs of most creeds can be—how reliable should we consider *any* of their testimony?

Thus, my brother, on supernatural matters—on the nature and will of a possible God—religions sharply disagree. And on how we should conduct ourselves while on earth, about this, too, the paths of religions diverge. And even without the authority of supernatural direction each society can arrive at common standards for behavior which are, in turn, built upon basic, shared values—and which may differ from the standards arrived at by other societies. Indeed, codes of secular law tend to be just that: communal standards of behavior, based upon widely accepted values, enforced by the power of the state. Stealing is designated a crime by nearly every group not because it is forbidden in the Bible; nor is murder designated a crime because of what religion teaches. Both are seen by most as serious violations they would not wish visited upon themselves, and which, therefore, they are willing—in common empathy, in enlightened self-interest, and in an implied social contract—to refrain from inflicting upon others. Without scriptures and clergy we, as societies of sane mortals, can and do arrive at such constructive judgments.

In sum, my brother, religious traditions as a group offer no unified guidance, for they contradict each other on fundamental teachings. Moreover, even if religions did not contradict each other so deeply and so often, they could not provide reliable guidance on the supernatural. For—conveyed to us by fallible men, natural beings all—religions' teachings have no reasonable claim to knowledge of matters beyond human ken. Nor do we need the guidance of such pretend expertise. For we, without ecclesiastical aid, can build societies of the reasonable, the courageous, and the kind, by reflecting upon and determining and legislating what amounts to beneficial, and what to injurious, behavior—and they, though mostly well meaning, always claimed to know what they did not know, and too often led us into ignorance and blood.

66. Argument that there must be a supernatural realm and a God, because all human societies have believed in the spiritual

And a woman said: Would you have us believe there is no spiritual realm? Every human society ever discovered has believed in supernatural forces! There must be truth to such a universal belief. And this is enough for me to remain with my God and religion.

And the sage replied: My sister, for many, the mysterious and ineffable moments of life have stirred them to suspect that something exists beyond the mere physical. And humans have, indeed, consistently created and perpetuated religions. Yet while it is perhaps true that most in every major society with which we are acquainted have believed in the spiritual and supernatural, it is also true that in most societies some have been sufficiently clear-thinking and candid to acknowledge not knowing what, if anything, a supernatural being might want of us—or whether, indeed, aside from the physical universe, anything existed.

Beyond the great majority of all humans who have never recorded their thoughts for posterity, and beyond the great majority of those who have recorded their thoughts but whose writings have not survived the ravages of time—or the censures of intolerant clergy—still extant writings and fragments of the ancients prove that thousands of years ago, in the biblical era, too, some suspended judgment as to the existence of gods, or refused to believe in the popular religions that taught of such notions as an afterlife, or of deities rewarding or punishing humans, requiring sacrifices of us, or working miracles.[1]

---

[1] In this category of ancients who turned a skeptical eye to some popular religious beliefs of their day we find Xenophanes, Aristophanes, Aristotle, Protagoras, Epicurus, Plato, Lucretius, Diogenes, Pliny the Elder, Cicero, Seneca, and more. Their original works—if available, and surviving fragments if not—help us understand their positions best. A fragment from Protagoras, from his work *On the Gods* provides a taste. In it he says that on the matter of the gods, he is unable to know whether they exist or do not exist, (and if they do exist, he) is unable to know what are their forms, because various considerations prevent such knowledge, including the subject matter's inherent obscurity, and the shortness of human life. For a sense of some of the ancients' thinking, see *Early Greek Philosophy* by Jonathan Barnes, *Ancilla to Pre-Socratic Philosophers* by Kathleen Freeman, and *The First Philosophers* by Robin Waterfield.

Indeed, the Bible itself records—in a negative light, of course—the existence of many who did not subscribe to religious belief. Psalms 14:1-3 states:

> The fool hath said in his heart, There is no God. They are corrupt, they have done abominable works, there is none that doeth good. The Lord looked down from heaven upon the children of men, to see if there were any that did understand, and seek God. They are all gone aside, they are all together become filthy: there is none that doeth good, no, not one.

The psalmist seems to indicate that it was rare in his day for there to be someone who truly believed in God. But even if the text engages in hyperbole when it says that not one person does good and seeks God, what is plainly stated—even if spoken of the foolish and the corrupt—is that some were of the belief that "There is no God." The Bible itself, then, documents disbelief in past ages.

Yet, my sister, even if humans of all generations were unanimous in holding supernatural beliefs, I ask you to consider that what is common to mankind reflects not divine truth, but human tendency. Indeed, the heart of man has been haunted by all manner of hopes, fears, and desires spurring him to kneel before ten thousand gods and to conjure innumerable, invisible realms. And we, and many before us, have identified and discussed a number of these motives. Yet such inclinations toward supernatural belief prove neither that such beliefs are noble nor that they are accurate.

What is common is not necessarily admirable, or even justified. See how many widespread instincts and behaviors are destructive! Has not war been a universal human endeavor? And is not dishonesty in the marketplace and infidelity in the bedchamber common to all societies? And have not tyranny,

---

And many collections of aphorisms and quotations include the skeptical words of the ancients. For specific references and quotations of this type conveniently gathered in one place, see the first chapter of J.E. Haught's *2000 Years of Disbelief.*

And I reference these wise men of old not as an appeal to authority, nor to argue that we should allow them to think for us, but to illustrate that leaping to unwarranted conclusions and fixed convictions about gods and their wishes is not only unnecessary today, but was unnecessary even in the ancient past—and, though such a temptation has ever been eagerly succumbed to by the masses, it has not been the universal condition. The careful, honest, and independent thinker of every age has conceded that when we contemplate possible realms beyond the natural, there is little if anything we can see, save reflections of our hopes, fantasies, and fears; and little if anything we can hear save the reverberating echoes of our parents' loyalty oaths, and the imagination's desperate songs of heaven and horrific screams in terror of hell.

slavery, religious persecution, female subjugation, and judicial corruption stained the hands of most civilizations throughout history? And have not ignorance and superstition darkened the vision and slowed the progress of all peoples? And have not all of us—at times, and to one degree or another—in the privacy of our own shame, surrendered to sloth, lust, fear, greed, anger, gluttony, arrogance, and all manner of self-destructive or self-serving passions? Indeed, does not religion herself in most of her forms teach that all are born into, or stumble into, sin?

Shall we insist that the aforementioned behaviors bespeak admirable human conduct, that they are sourced in transcendent truth—merely because they have been common to mankind? If not, I ask you to reconsider your conclusion that man's penchant for religion has its roots in either truth or wisdom.

My sister, there may be a realm beyond, of spirit and transcendence; the human propensity, however, to believe in and worship such a realm, sheds little light upon the question. Beliefs held by our species do not necessarily reflect, much less determine, truth. For Truth is strictly a matter of what is, and she answers not to custom no matter how widespread; she surrenders not to desire no matter how intense; and she gives no quarter to faith no matter how fierce.

And even if we accepted mankind's proclivity toward religion as proof of a spiritual world—we would yet remain ignorant of how to live that we might be in harmony with that world, how we might do its bidding or earn its approval or rewards. For human civilizations have believed very differently on such matters: We have worshiped one god and many gods; merciful gods and vengeful gods; warlike gods who demanded their enemies be vanquished, and gods of peace who despised the shedding of blood; gods who desired sexual worship, and gods who demanded strict chastity; gods hungry for human sacrifice, and gods who found such sacrifice an abomination. Indeed, nearly every action or belief considered sinful by one religion has, at some time by another religion, been seen as permissible, applauded as noble, even required as a matter of sacred obligation; and nearly everything deemed by one religion a great good has, at some other time by another religion, been branded a grievous sin.

In sum, my sister, that our species has always invoked the spiritual and worshiped some manner of divinity does not confirm the existence of a supernatural realm, for mankind has committed many universal blunders; moreover, even if we equated consensus with truth, the history of human religion provides only chaotic and contradictory guidance, and thus leaves us in the dark as to how we might go about pleasing or living in consonance with any gods there may be.

67. Causes for the birth of religion

And a man said: If there is no supernatural realm and God, tell us, then, what specific reasons have caused peoples throughout history to create religions?

And the sage said: My brother, we can only peer out at the world from within the house of flesh and blood. At times we are luxuriously enveloped in its sensual warmth, at other times painfully imprisoned by its punishing walls; but ever we remain in a tumultuous and distorting enclosure, our thoughts heavily influenced by primal fears and perpetual desires.

Many are the fathers of religion.[1] There are causes for the birth of belief, and sometimes-different causes for beliefs being maintained and passed down to succeeding ages. Humankind has many instincts toward religion; whatever path we walk, the gods seem to beckon, and whatever actions we take, the gods seem to respond.[2]

And many are the differences between the hearts of men, and multifarious are their worries and unnumbered their wants. And different religions may have had their beginnings in different causes—and even two who began worshiping in the same way may have been moved by different motives. And much of man's religion is driven by needs other than to know and worship God.[3]

---

[1] Every traditional faith will, of course, claim that her origins lie in the transcendent word and will of God, or in the metaphysical realities of ultimate truth. But as Gibbon said—in a witty blend of what may have been his own irreverent doubt and the circumspection required of him by the proprieties of his day—in a discussion of Christianity's rapid early growth, in Chapter XV of his *Decline and Fall of the Roman Empire*, "The theologian may indulge the pleasing task of describing Religion as she descended from Heaven, arrayed in her native purity. A more melancholy duty is imposed on the historian. He must discover the inevitable mixture of error and corruption which she contracted in a long residence upon earth, among a weak and degenerate race of beings…" A little later he continues: "…as truth and reason seldom find so favourable a reception in the world, and as the wisdom of Providence frequently condescends to use the passions of the human heart, and the general circumstances of mankind, as instruments to execute its purpose, we may still be permitted, though with becoming submission, to ask, not indeed what were the first, but what were the secondary causes of the rapid growth of the Christian church?"

And we might add that if such a "melancholy" duty falls to the historian, how much more does it fall to the seeker—and considering the greater freedom of thought and speech available to our age, this duty does not limit itself now to asking about secondary causes of religion, but extends to reflecting on her first causes, too.

[2] Ingersoll, in his *What Must We Do To Be Saved?* relates an amusing anecdote. A Jewish gentleman, he says, went into a restaurant to eat dinner and, unable to resist temptation, ordered some bacon with his meal and ate it with guilty pleasure. After finishing, he paid his bill and left the restaurant, only to find that a storm had moved in, ominous clouds hung low, lightning flashed and thunder exploded, frightfully shaking the ground all about. White-faced, he rushed back into the restaurant and said to the owner, "My God, did you ever hear of such a fuss being made over a little piece of bacon?"

[3] Thoreau—speaking in a different context—comes to mind: "Many men go fishing all of their lives without knowing that it is not fish they are after."

Some, but not all, are those reasons of which I earlier spoke in explaining why most do not vigorously question their religious beliefs.[1] Still, so important is it to understand the many human inclinations toward religion that I shall not be too careful to avoid repeating what has already been mentioned.

Perhaps you would have me speak of three or seven entirely separate natural causes for religion—but I ask your indulgence as I name many more, some overlapping with each other. For it is well to illustrate how many roads lead to belief, and how those roads begin in the humble dusts of the earth, not the ethereal clouds of heaven. Listen and I shall tell of many causes for the birth of belief—a score and more reeds woven into the cradle of God.[2]

67.1 Fear, and the desire for survival, safety, and success

All creatures seek survival and safety. But while most species merely attempt to manipulate or adapt to their immediate and tangible environments, we humans have powerful imaginations that conceive of forces distant and invisible. Thus, in fear of fang and foe, disease and disaster, famine and flood—and of a thousand smaller inconveniences—and in hopes of obtaining supernatural aid or favor on matters trivial and great, our ancestors attempted to influence events by bribing, appeasing, or appealing to divine powers desperately imagined.[3]

67.2 Desire for magical solutions

Life is often difficult, and rarely provides our needs and comforts without demanding of us a great deal of effort, frustration, and pain. Such a price many

---

[1] See section 15.

[2] My intention here is not to explore comprehensively the academic or classic—and sometimes abstruse–theories on religion's origins, but rather to offer a varied list of reasonable possibilities to which the layman can relate. For a more academic yet relatively brief and accessible treatment of some significant theories on religion's origins, exploring the ideas of Tylor and Frazer, Freud, Durkheim, Marx, Weber, Eliade, Evans-Pritchard, and Geertz, see *Eight Theories of Religion* by Daniel Pals. For valuable perspective, and intelligent and engaging reading, also see *Interpreting the Sacred* by William E. Paden.

[3] Many have made the point that the origins of religion lie in fear. For two eloquent examples, I offer Gibbon and Santayana. Gibbon, in his *Decline and Fall of the Roman Empire* writes: "Fear has been the original parent of superstition, and every new calamity urges trembling mortals to deprecate the wrath of their invisible enemies." And Santayana in *The Life of Reason* says: "That fear first created the gods is perhaps as true as anything so brief could be on so great a subject…The feeling with which primitive man walks the earth must…be, for the most part, apprehension; and what he meets, beyond the well-conned ways of his tribe and habitat, can be nothing but formidable spirits." And let us cite the poet Edward Young, too, who is credited with saying, "By night an atheist half believes a God."

find too high, and they long for a means of avoiding unpleasantness, of having things go well for them without submitting to the limiting laws of the natural. Religion, in many of its forms, holds out the promise of supernatural, even instant, blessings and solutions of all kinds, from wealth and healing to fertility and serenity. The faithful are pleased to believe that the glory of God can work magic and miracle and might swiftly rescue them from the tyranny of unlucky fortune or the consequences of their own poor choices.

67.3 Feeling soothed by answers to daily mysteries

Aside from all attempts at control and gain, the human heart desires to understand causes and effects. We are questioning creatures, and are soothed by answers. Even disturbing answers soothe, for they alleviate the greater discomfort of disorientation. And false answers often serve as well as any others, so long as they do not come under serious scrutiny. Thus, belief in a god, especially an inscrutable and overwhelmingly powerful God—becomes an emotionally effective answer for innumerable questions. "Why did war break out?" "Why did my neighbor become wealthy?" "Why did the little girl die?" "Why did my crops do so well this year?" These questions and so many others are efficiently quieted by the invention of the supernatural. When one tells oneself, "All that exists, and all that takes place, is because God wishes it so, and we cannot presume to understand or question God," the mind feels that it has been given an explanation—and its hunger for understanding is somewhat sated.

67.4 Desire for answers to the great mysteries of existence

Beyond the wish to understand daily events, humans have always confronted the great question of how the world came to be, and puzzled over what might be the mysteries underlying its functioning; and because they often created objects for specific ends, they expected that a purpose was intended for them, too—and they wondered what it might be. For most, such questions created occasional interest or disquiet, but for some they produced such consistent focus, that all manner of conjecture and speculation were born on possible gods and their secrets and designs. And some of our ancestors, either wholly conceiving of systems of their own or building upon millennia of earlier human imaginings, rushed to conclusions, persuading themselves that they knew how the world came to be, that they knew there to be gods, that they knew the names of these gods, and that they knew just what these gods wanted of humans. And such men were often driven by compulsion to teach their beliefs to others. In this way, we may surmise, have many religions been born, and many others spread.

67.5 Infant's experience of powerful Other

At the dawn of every human's awareness, deeply imprinted in the forgotten but formative days of early childhood, is the experience of being dominated by powerful beings—who were feared and obeyed, but who also provided food and satisfied many of our needs. Our first cries of primal pain brought forth the soft breast of comfort, and early rebellions were fraught with the danger of painful rebuke and retribution, or unthinkable rejection by the powerful and great. No longer children, we yet have the compelling anticipation that our cries in the night will be heard and that our misdeeds will bring upon us the wrath of mighty, inscrutable, forces. Thus, we expect gods.[1]

---

[1] It should come as no surprise that Freud, who traces so much of adult functioning to developmental roots, sees some of religion's beginnings along similar lines in his *Future of an Illusion*, explaining that impersonal forces and fates are unapproachable—thus we are powerless to influence them and many of our circumstances. But, he says, if all we experience is the result of conscious gods, we may hope to form a relationship with them and to exert influence upon them. "For once before one was similarly helpless; as a young child relative to one's parents..." Thus, says Freud, religious ideas are developed as a way of dealing with our weakness and smallness, memories of which we have from our "individual childhood, and the childhood of the human species."

Yet the connection between one's experience of parents and one's conception of God was recognized by many throughout history. For a perhaps less expected case than Freud, consider this from Amiel's January 6, 1853 entry in his *Journal*: "The mother represents goodness, providence, law; that is to say, the divinity...If she is herself passionate, she will inculcate in her child a capricious and despotic God, or even several discordant gods. The religion of a child depends on what its mother and its father are."

Also, the French philosopher Alain, in the often aphoristic and entertaining and always thought-provoking (even if frequently obscure, overstated, and sometimes offensive) *The Gods*, begins by recounting (in the name of the shade of Socrates) the tale told by the oldest nurse, and it is about giants. Once upon a time, goes the tale, there were giants who had an abundance of milk, fruit, and bread, and would share these with people, if asked in the right way. Also, if so inclined, these giants would carry people wherever they wished to go. And because it was so much easier to ask these giants for food than to attempt to find food on one's own, and because it was so much more convenient to be carried by these giants than to walk on one's own, and because it was dangerous to take the chance of angering giants, people did not learn how to find food or walk or fend for themselves, but instead spent all their cleverness and energies devising ways of flattering and imploring the help of the giants, through offerings and prayer. And so it was that even when there were no more giants, the people continued to hope for and expect their return, and kept calling for them. Alain follows by asking, "Who...has sufficiently weighed this phrase of Descartes: 'For we were children before we were men'?"

And lest we forget the obvious: Our Bibles and prayers are filled with references and appeals to our "Father in heaven." And though some may insist that knowledge of God was independent of the conception of father, and the figure of father was only used as an anthropomorphic aid in humans' attempts to relate to the Divine, the pervasiveness of

67.6 Longing for immortality

Knowing we will die, we long to escape this tragic and humiliating end. On most days, we succeed at blocking thoughts of death from encroaching upon our awareness, but always the terrible truth breaks through again—perhaps when we attend the funeral of a friend, or hear of the death of a leader, or see after some years the marked aging of those we remember as vital and young. And we are struck, if only for a disquieting moment, with the remembered horror that we, too, go the way of all flesh.

And we who have laid a loved one lovingly in the earth, can never forget the echoing screams of final silence, the terrible message of forever-silenced lips, the outrage of soil being shoveled over flesh, and the indifference of the everyday crowd, continuing unabated along a thousand paths, each winding unthinkingly to the same unthinkable end. And we wonder what is it all for, and how can we go on as though we have not seen, as though we do not know, as though even now the earth is not devouring those we have loved, and as though all too soon she will not have consumed us, too, and all for which we toil; and we ache for something to give meaning to the promise of our mornings, to justify the labor of our days, and to comfort us as we stand contemplating the gathering twilight.

And so our hopeful, even desperate, imaginations rebel against the specter of futility and obliteration, and conjure another realm, to which we go upon earthly death. What will a man not pay to extend his life for a few years, a few months, even a few days? How much more will he pay to extend his life for eternity! And what is the small cost of foregoing a little honesty and truth, when compared to the illusory allure of everlasting life?[1]

---

the parental metaphor in religion lends credence to the suspicion that for the common man the term "father" in referring to the Deity is not a weak attempt at fathoming the profound powers of God; rather, the conception of "God" is a universal echo of the profound influence of father.

[1] Alexis de Tocqueville, in his *Democracy in America,* writes: "The short space of three-score years can never content the imagination of man; nor can the imperfect joys of this world satisfy his heart. Man alone, of all created beings, displays a natural contempt of existence, and yet a boundless desire to exist; he scorns life, but he dreads annihilation. These different feelings incessantly urge his soul to the contemplation of a future state, and religion directs his musings thither. Religion, then, is simply another form of hope; and it is no less natural to the human heart than hope itself. Men cannot abandon their religious faith without a kind of aberration of intellect, and a sort of violent distortion of their true natures; but they are invincibly brought back to more pious sentiments; for unbelief is an accident, and faith is the only permanent state of mankind."

Yet we may add the obvious—that the seeker after truth does not consider a belief accurate or legitimate merely because it is most congenial to certain of man's inclinations.

And when our ancestors dreamed of the deceased, the dead seemed so alive to them, and real; thus, some say, originated—and all can see how was strengthened—the belief in a spiritual domain beyond mere physical life.[1] And such invisible and death-defying dominions seemed to require invisible and powerful forces to administer them—thus the gods.

67.7 Pride: the desire to feel important and meaningful

We hunger to feel important and noteworthy, to know that we matter, that our lives have consequence and our actions meaning. Yet this hubris is not easily satisfied; looking about us we are humbled and dwarfed by nature's immense power—towering mountains reverberating to the might of shattering thunderclaps; roiling storms on the vast seas tossing our great ships about like fragile toys; myriads of stars sprinkled across the incomprehensible distances of the heavens—and we feel small, indeed. And the cruel boot of the conqueror and the heavy yoke of the prince—and the tyranny of daily monotonies and mindless detail, and the terrible ticking of mortality's clock—teach us how little sway we hold even in human events. Thus, to cushion our wounded pride, our imaginations persuade us that there must be transcendent powers, gods, who monitor our existence and deeds; and as gods take us so seriously, we must be valuable in a grand sense. And though this supernatural belief in turn gives rise to guilt and fear, and demands of us various forms of worship and restraint, still our spirits find it a good commerce, for it feeds a deep yearning—the appetite for existential pride.

Moreover, there is an instinct, stronger in some than in others, for inspiration and deep meaning: the desire for an exalted sense of mission, an excited momentousness about one's actions—and the propensity to feel a sense of emptiness without such grand engagement. This drive makes some receptive to intuitions that life has profound significance, that the tedious routines and inconsequential details of their daily lives are given meaning by connection with

---

[1] If the superstitious of every land hold dreams in terror or reverence even today, how much greater must have seemed the power of dreams to our ancestors in earlier, more ignorant days—and many books and beliefs, inside and outside the fold of traditional religion, make this clear. For one prominent example, recall the Bible having God, or a spiritual domain, communicate with man through dreams—the first several examples being God's appearance to Abimelech in Genesis 20, Jacob's dream of a heavenly ladder in Genesis 28, and God's communication to Jacob and Laban in Genesis 31. And for one of the innumerable sources which describe the wide array of non-biblical peoples and belief systems seeing dreams as windows into a spiritual reality—see J.G. Frazer's classic, *The Golden Bough*.

Also see section 33 titled "Ancestors visiting in dreams," where the sage addresses a similar topic.

supernatural power and purpose. They are therefore inclined to believe in gods, spiritual realms, and perhaps an afterlife. And such people often attain their experience of inspiration by persuading themselves that their mission is to teach their spiritual beliefs to others. Thus have religions been born and propagated.[1]

67.8 Animism and Anthropomorphism: projecting living or human qualities onto the world

We have the instinct toward seeing life-like, even human-like qualities in events and circumstances, even when they do not exist. This is why we see all manner of creatures in clouds, bears in tree stumps, and large faces in profile on craggy cliffs; it is also why we hear the stealthy footsteps of enemies in harmless rustling leaves, perhaps even momentarily lash out in anger at a chair on which we stub a toe. Though usually mistaken, this instinct—to interpret our experiences as having been caused by intelligent intent and significant presence—was valuable for the survival of our ancestors. For if ninety nine times they startled unnecessarily at a sound in the woods, and the hundredth time it was truly an enemy's footfall, they may have owed their lives to this usually mistaken response. Thus, those with this instinct survived well, and passed to succeeding generations this heritage of over-cunning vigilance.

So when the blessed rains come, or the plague decimates, or the crops are bountiful, or a loved one falls ill, or the enemy conquers, or our hearts find love—in all events good and bad—we slyly suspect the cause to have been intelligent forces: gods or devils, or some manner of spirit unseen. And we enact prayers, rituals, sacrifices and prohibitions—to enlist and deserve the aid of benevolent powers, and to ward off or placate those of evil.[2]

---

[1] "Religion consists of believing that everything that happens is extraordinarily important. It can never disappear from the world, precisely for this reason." Even if we should wish to be more optimistic than Cesare Pavese, the author of those words, and hope that our species will ultimately forego this form of corrupt comfort, the overall point is well taken—many wish for their lives to be important, and religion provides this to a degree that other worldviews, and other forms of engagement, are hard pressed to equal.

[2] Many over the millennia have spoken of man's animating and anthropomorphizing tendencies. For one luminary, let us quote Shakespeare from Act V of *A Midsummer-Night's Dream*: "...Such tricks hath strong imagination/That if it would but apprehend some joy/It comprehends some bringer of that joy/Or in the night, imagining some fear/How easy is a bush supposed a bear!"

And many thinkers through the ages have noted anthropomorphic roots and functions of religion. For a recent and in-depth discussion of anthropomorphism and religion see *Faces in the Clouds* by S.E. Guthrie. Also, see section 27 of our book, and its footnote relating to anthropomorphism.

67.9 Magnification of the social instinct

Along with various species—ants, apes, bees, wolves, lions, monkeys, elephants, and others—humans are social beings. Every social being has the instinctual awareness that his actions relate to the wider group. In human beings, this social instinct, when combined with our conceptual minds, can intensify into a deep need for a mission far larger than the self, and larger, too, than the immediate group.

Just as we may imagine that mankind's musical abilities originated in instincts whose primal uses and benefits were far removed from performing symphonies in modern concert halls, so may we imagine that man's instinct for relating to a social context, though it may have aided the development of religion and the worship of gods, was useful in the primal setting for matters more terrestrial. But as humans have often channeled their instincts into endeavors a great deal more ambitious than those of other species—a lion may seek to conquer a neighboring territory, but men have sought to conquer the entire planet, indeed to extend their power to other planets and to regions of space unknown—the expansion of this social urge encourages thoughts of invisible realms of being, where human actions exert great effects on limitless spiritual worlds and beings. Thus, some of our ancestors were sorely tempted to imagine and devise religious systems, with gods, angels, devils, and more, interested in, and influenced by, humans.

67.10 The lust for power

Rulers and clergy have often taken advantage of the masses' superstition and fear of the unknown, and claimed authority over them by the unimpeachable will of the gods. Kings and prophets, princes and popes, have mandated, often with each other's cooperation, how the people were to worship and what they were to believe.[1] Even on a far more modest scale—with no papacies or scepters for prizes—a good living and no small amount of admiration has often been available to those who claim to speak for the deities. And the powerful elite have usually profited from the common man's fear and awe of gods, and have promoted and enforced the teaching of religion. Indeed, kings have often claimed not only to rule by the will of the gods—but to be gods themselves.[2]

---

[1] In his *Democracy in America,* Alexis de Tocqueville writes: "On close inspection we shall find that religion, and not fear, has ever been the cause of the long-lived prosperity of an absolute government. Whatever exertions may be made, no true power can be founded among men which does not depend upon the free union of their inclinations; and patriotism and religion are the only two motives in the world which can permanently direct the whole of a body politic to one end."

[2] That their rulers were gods was often believed true not only by the ancients, but even, until recently, by the masses of a relatively large country—Emperor Hirohito of Japan

That rulers have often helped institute religion and that the throne and the pulpit have often been in close collaboration are not the only connections between government and faith: Some have argued that a people's concepts of God and government are often strongly related.[1]

This hard truth, that religion has sometimes been a means to obtain or maintain power, is seen as repugnant and surely untrue by the fervent religious idealist who knows how sincere is her belief and how loving are her intentions. And,

---

was held to be such well into the 20th century—and only fire and steel and the devastation of a crushing military defeat, followed by new government and education, persuaded the people otherwise.

[1] Many have said this in one way or another. Elbert Hubbard, in *Love, Life, and Work,* addressed the point, saying: "Our idea of a Supreme Being is suggested to us by the political government under which we live. The situation was summed up by Carlyle, when he said that Deity to the average British mind was simply an infinite George IV. The thought of God as a terrible Supreme Tyrant first found form in an unlimited monarchy; but as governments have become more lenient so have the gods, until you get...to a republic, where God is only a president, and we all approach Him in familiar prayer, on an absolute equality..."

Alexis de Tocqueville, in his *Democracy in America,* illustrates the influence going in the opposite direction, too—from God to government. He says: "Every religion is to be found in juxtaposition to a political opinion which is connected with it by affinity. If the human mind be left to follow its own bent, it will regulate the temporal and spiritual institutions of society upon one uniform principle; and man will endeavor, if I may use the expression, to harmonize the state in which he lives upon earth with the state which he believes to await him in heaven. The greatest part of British America was peopled by men who, after having shaken off the authority of the Pope, acknowledged no other religious supremacy; they brought with them into the New World a form of Christianity which I cannot better describe than by styling it a democratic and republican religion. This sect contributed powerfully to the establishment of a democracy and a republic, and from the earliest settlement of the emigrants, politics and religion contracted an alliance which has never been dissolved."

To state what must be obvious—and to combine the insights of various luminaries—to me it seems that here, just as with many complex systems social and otherwise, reciprocal determinism is at work: Concepts of God and concepts of governance influence each other, and both are cause and effect. As the power and function of rulers change, so too do human conceptions of divine power and function—but, also, as perceptions of divine power and function change, so do perceptions of what powers and functions government should wield.

Furthermore, the factors involved in such cultural change are more than only government and religion: Other values and social norms—for one example, the balance of empathy and compassion vs. objective standards and justice—affect, and are affected by, notions of government and God. And while that line of inquiry is tempting to pursue here, it is too far afield from the primary focus of this volume to say much more on the matter than that wisdom has for good reason long spoken of the golden mean.

indeed, I think it reasonable to assume that the majority of clergy throughout history have not been intentional frauds. They were brought up within a belief system and—though perhaps exerting no extraordinary efforts toward intellectual honesty—upon taking on the role of shepherding their flocks they truly saw themselves as guiding the people by the received word of God.

Yet though it puzzles and hurts the gentle and merciful of this world to see it, do we not encounter selfishness, crudeness, and unprincipled ambition in many other arenas of life? Why, then, would the arena of religion be different—and free from significant fraud? Does not religion confer upon its leaders great power and influence, and thus offer a grand temptation to those of unscrupulous designs? And is not religion peopled by humans? And are not humans quite capable of so many forms of betrayal and greed? And cannot the lust for power on the parts of a guilty few set in motion, and periodically renew, traditions that get carried forth by large numbers of the innocent and the sincere?

67.11 Desire for fairness and justice

Seeing profound suffering and injustice in our own lives—or in the lives of those we love—leads many of us to yearn for a compassionate and fair Power who, in this realm or another, will compensate victims for their suffering and visit retribution upon the cruel. Thus, in our sorrow and bitterness, we long for a cosmic Judge who dispenses various forms of reward and punishment, who welcomes us and our dear ones to the blissful gardens of heaven, and drives our hated tormentors into the blazing fire-pits of hell.

67.12 Desire to see loved ones after death

How deep is the wound of losing a loved one, and how difficult to accept! Many of our ancestors have better weathered such agony, better regained some sense of orientation and composure, by insisting that their loved ones live on in another realm, and will, perhaps—especially if one walks the path of the just—be reunited with them, in the fullness of time. Indeed, have you not heard the bereaved comforting themselves by saying, "She is now in a better place," or, "Why should we cry? She is now with the Lord"?

And such consolations require an afterlife, with spiritual beings and gods or a God. Thus, the barren widow Death has at times given birth to—or at least suckled—various forms of religion and faith.

67.13 Desire to find meaning in suffering, or relief from guilt

When encountering pain or misfortune, many find a bracing species of comfort in seeing their suffering as punishment from God. Well has it been said,

"One who has a strong enough why, can endure almost any how."[1] And believing in any explanation that gives larger meaning to suffering is preferable, in the eyes and hearts of many, to facing the possibility that such suffering may be unrelated to anything more significant, and uncaused by any transcendent Power.

Moreover, those with a strong tendency toward guilt can have an almost primal conviction that suffering is punishment, and that punishment removes the stain of guilt. And because such individuals often walk the earth with a guilty gait, believing they have done wrong, they may find deep relief when they think they have paid for their transgressions, and that their sins have been expiated.

And to conceive of one's afflictions as divine punishment serves other purposes, too. It makes one's pain more understandable—for even an unhappy explanation at least ends confusion. And it also provides hope that future misfortunes may be prevented, by conducting one's life in such a manner that will please the exacting or angry gods.

67.14 Desire for clear instruction and direction
There are some in every group who believe—perhaps by instinct—that there is but one correct way to do anything; and they suffer the corresponding discomfort when lacking precise directions for carrying out a given task. This often spawns in such souls the intuition that there exists a supernatural being who knows the correct way of doing things, or has the authority to designate the appropriate way of doing things—has communicated this to humans—and will punish us if we do things incorrectly and reward us if we follow His rules.

67.15 Instinct for hierarchy
Related to the instinct for instruction and direction, some have the strong instinct toward hierarchy: to know who is the leader, and—of the others—who is above and below whom. Such an instinct, present to some degree in all social species, when combined with man's awareness of the world beyond his group leads many to the instinctive expectation that there exist great beings stronger than humans—or, ultimately, a Great Being more powerful than all, who controls everything. In turn, this belief often inclines such people to offer these gods, or this Great God, worship and submission. Thus, religion.

67.16 Desire for deep compassion, intimacy and love
In childhood, and during seasons of courtship and in moments of crisis, illness, or transition, many hunger for deep devotion and fervent love. Yet in every group there are some who yearn for such intense compassion and intimacy even

[1] Nietzsche

184

in the ordinary living of common days. In the face of nature's apparent indifference and mankind's frequent betrayal and cruelty, such souls nurture a strong intuition that somewhere, unseen, is a Great Loving Being who cares for them deeply, and wants us all to love one another.[1]

And one who believes in a God or gods always available to hear praise, prayer, or supplication—or to provide unlimited intimacy and love—such a one never feels completely alone, need never confront the primal terror of the totally isolated or the existential despair of the utterly abandoned.

67.17 Projecting from one's conscience

The conscience, an innate mechanism for a complex social being, triggers visceral reactions, signaling us that some actions are to be avoided. This sensitivity to good and bad behavior makes one likely to believe that some things are not merely socially dangerous, but intrinsically wrong, due to profound, unseen, forces—perhaps commandments of a Great Power who has written these laws on our hearts, or revealed His statutes to humans, and maybe even monitors our actions. Thus our ancestors imagined they knew God's will, or were receptive to those who taught that God considered certain actions good and others evil.

67.18 Desire to preserve success

On the surface, success seems an unadulterated blessing. But those who look deeper see that it can bring danger and discomfort, too. With success comes the anxiety over possibly losing the status or possessions one has gained, and fear of those who might have been made jealous or angry by one's good fortune. Many in such circumstances feel an urgency to placate those who pose a danger, or to gain assistance in protecting themselves against them. And invisible forces have often been seen, especially in ages of widespread ignorance, as the greatest threats, threats that must be appeased or successfully battled. And it was hoped that gods—the most powerful of the invisible forces—could be bribed or charmed into not harming one directly, and also into preventing various dangers

---

[1] The cerebral disciplines of science and reason can provide many excellent things, but they cannot provide the personal connection some seek in a God. As Kierkegaard is credited with saying, "Philosophy is life's dry-nurse, who can take care of us—but not suckle us." It is worthwhile to note, however, that profound honesty with oneself, meaningful engagement with life, and deep intimacy with other humans *can* provide much of the connection often sought in God, and this mortal, terrestrial solution to existential loneliness, though it suffers from the limitations of the real, also benefits from the blessings of the real: It leaves intact our integrity, and when we gaze into the mirror of self-assessment our soul can look back at us and smile, innocent and unashamed.

from befalling one's bounty, preventing rivals or enemies from taking it by stealthy theft, by violent force, by spiteful destruction, even by curses or spells of magic. Thus sacrifices and prayers were offered to the gods.

And, in a more subtle way, attributing one's success to a god can reduce the jealousy and competitiveness of others, because one is admitting that one is not especially capable or worthy—and is not attempting to outshine others. It may even increase others' fear of attacking the successful; for one does not wish to quarrel with the great unseen power who thinks so well of the person as to have given him success, and who may, by means of sacrifice and piety, have been recruited to his side. Thus, it has been of help both in one's heart and in one's village to attribute success to supernatural forces. Therefore, again, the gods.

67.19 Religion as a means to overcome low confidence, or low self-esteem

Threats to success come not only from obstacles or challenges external, but from enemies far closer yet less visible: dread and guilt and shame within—the legacy of life's early years. Most parents mean mostly well, but the child is so fragile and open, his mother's eyes bore so deep into his heart, his father's hands rest so heavy on his soul, his teacher's voice comes so loud upon his inner ears, his friends' smiles and sneers so deeply color his spirit, that it is but the uncommon child who receives the nurturing and guidance and acceptance he needs, and but the uncommon adult who lives largely free of childhood's chains.

Our distracted and troubled parents will often have inadvertently treated us in ways that injured our belief in ourselves, and caused us to doubt our goodness or strength. And though insecurity portends failure, many afflicted with this poison have discovered a handy antidote: attributing success and good fortune—either that for which one hopes, or that which one has already come upon—not to one's own doing, but to a Great Power's grace and will. Then, because the self is not seen as the one upon whose worthiness or abilities success depends, the internalized negative lessons of early life are silenced, self-sabotaging guilt and insecurity are avoided, and good fortune is predicted, pursued, attained and enjoyed. And when success is more often achieved and maintained after giving the credit to God—thus evading the dour-faced gatekeepers within—such beliefs are reinforced. Hence, saying and believing "By the glory of God!" or "This is all God's doing" not only brings a measure of inner peace, and relief from the humiliating limitations of low self-esteem,[1] but seems to ring ever more true.

---

[1] Whether religion, on balance, truly helps improve the average believer's self-esteem is quite another matter, and Nathaniel Branden in his *Six Pillars of Self-Esteem* argues forcefully that, at least in the cases of certain religious teachings, it does not.

67.20 Religion as the instinct to venerate and strengthen the group, or even to lose the limited self in glorious group and communal identity

Humans are a species with a delicate balance between individual and collective; though the one is wily and willful, he survives far better within a group. Thus, along with drives centered on our individual wants and needs, most of us have powerful instincts to think and feel and behave in ways that bring strength and cohesion to the group. Such social tendencies may not be as obvious as those in bees and ants—and with humans it is often difficult to distinguish instinct from learning—but they call from deep in our bones, nonetheless.

Suppressing the separate self in favor of identifying with the greater whole is readily observed to be not only an instinct for our species, but also for other beings who live in groups—wolves, lions, elephants, the aforementioned ants and bees, and many more. And whereas species less conceptual than us may confine the subordinating of individual for group identity to such behaviors as sacrificing themselves in combat, our species—though doing a good deal of that, too—has found in religion varied, expansive, and creative alternatives. Humans have long employed symbols and ceremonies and all manner of concepts and processes and substances and rituals to intensify their commitment to, and their common identity with, the group—and some scholars see in the broad set of social phenomena the real source and function of religion.[1]

And the urge toward group identity can be the cause of religion in another way, too. Beyond the peace of avoiding one's low self-esteem by individual devotion to God, one can relieve the worry and shame over one's own shortcomings by losing one's identity in a special form of communal whole, an intense religious group, a mass movement on a sacred quest and with exhilarating dreams of a glorious destiny.

Thus have men ever banded together in groups in pursuit of grand mission, to slough off the smallness and indignities of individual identity, and assume the resplendent mantle of dramatic and meaningful mass cause.[2] And is there

---

[1] Emile Durkheim was a pioneer in proposing the social source and function of religion—with his view often encapsulated by the words, "God is society, writ large"—but the work and theories of many others contributed, too. Durkheim's classic work on the matter is *The Elementary Forms of the Religious Life*. For two accessible books providing overviews of this and other approaches to religion, see *Interpreting the Sacred* by William E. Paden, and *Eight Theories of Religion* by Daniel L. Pals.

[2] This theme, of mass movements being an escape from individual identity, is explored by Eric Hoffer in his classic, *The True Believer*, where in the first chapter he explains that the attraction mass movements hold for people is not the opportunity for self-advancement, but rather for self-renunciation. He also writes, in his characteristically aphoristic style, "Faith in a holy cause is to a considerable extent a substitute for the lost faith in ourselves."

anything within reach more dramatic and meaningful than ideas of the supernatural, upon which man can project his wildest fears, his most inspiring ideals, and all manner of aspirations unfettered and grandiose?

67.21 Forced conversions

When a king or prince adopted a faith, he often forced it on all his subjects. Myriads were converted to religion not by the informed mind and the yearning heart, but by the billowing bonfire and the brandished sword.[1] And victorious armies and their often powerful churches or prophets readily imposed their religions upon conquered peoples—and we, the descendants of such subjugation, see these beliefs as our own, embellish them with the best of our cleverness, and defend them with alacrity and devotion.

67.22 Desire to feel superior

Observe a classroom of young children—or remember well your early years—and you will see how strong is the drive to be not just good, but special. Humans, along with, we may presume, members of other high social species, often want to be seen, and to see themselves, as superior. The young may wish to beat their classmates at arm wrestling, or be the prettiest, or score the highest grade on a test—and the seasoned, too, lust after distinction, in the realms of power, beauty, talent, knowledge, achievement, wealth, or fame.

Beyond the realms of obvious advantage, however, other opportunities for superiority beckon. One can be powerless and poor and without any other compensating charms, yet still look down at one's fellow man—if only one can devise or subscribe to a belief system in which power and wealth and beauty and knowledge and other advantages are seen as inferior to some other distinction within readier reach. The unlucky and the downtrodden, the timid and the weak—and even those who have much but wish for more—are ever prone to conceiving of ideas and philosophies that proclaim them, against all apparent evidence, to be the true heroes, the elect among men. And so they see invisible

---

And, one may add (upon noticing the fervor of youthful adherents to many forms of ideology and mass movement, religious and otherwise) that zealous faith in any ideology is often a substitute for *never-yet-developed* faith in ourselves. Hoffer, too, compares those involved in mass movements to adolescents, and draws several parallels.

[1] Machiavelli, in Chapter VI of *The Prince* states: "Hence it is that all armed prophets have conquered, and the unarmed ones have been destroyed. Besides the reasons mentioned, the nature of the people is variable, and whilst it is easy to persuade them, it is difficult to fix them in that persuasion. And thus it is necessary to take such measures that, when they believe no longer, it may be possible to make them believe by force."

gods railing against power and wealth, and they prophesy of coming days when the despised shall be raised up and the meek shall inherit the land, and when the wealthy and powerful will be sent to agony in everlasting fire, while they, the virtuous, on earth unlucky, will enjoy unimaginable bliss in paradise eternal.

And when a religion has succeeded at persuading a sufficient number of men to revere its teachings, and so has itself become an established and envied power, and wealthy—in perceived spiritual fortunes, or in the more obvious, formerly scorned currencies of money and land—new reformers and refiners rise up in turn, to found new sects or religions by assailing the idolatries and corruption of the religious status quo, proclaiming themselves more virtuous and pure, more true to God, or to the religion's original intent, than the entrenched ecclesiastical powers who, they say, have grown fat off the sacrifices of the people, and have abandoned God.

Thus can the forgotten one feel like the universe's favorite son, morally and existentially superior to those whose power he cannot more directly challenge. Religion has always been a subtle means of bettering one's betters, of redefining the rules so that one wins the game, all the while not having to admit—to others, or even to oneself—that one in any way wishes to compete. Religion offers this pleasing agriculture: not only the dream of reaping in song what was sown in tears, but the ready abundance of sowing humility and reaping pride.

67.23 Awe at nature's vast size, power, and beauty

When we gaze up at a mountain towering above us; when we confront the giant waves of the endless sea; when we stand alone in a star-filled night, contemplating the unimaginably vast distances of the dark heavens; we are gripped by awe—the spine-tingling sense of our smallness when measured against the overwhelming power and grand tapestry of the great and terrible Universe. This feeling of awe gives rise in many to the urge to worship. And, indeed, the ancients worshiped mountains, volcanoes, skies, waters, and trees, and deified all manner of other impressive natural forces. Over the centuries and millennia, as humans have become more knowledgeable, and have come to see nature as more unified, they have needed fewer gods—and monotheism has limited its object of awe and worship to only One.

67.24 Misinterpreting the products of unusual or puzzling mental and physical states as messages from gods

Unusual and puzzling states of sensation and consciousness are part of the human experience, and all manner of such states have been interpreted by our ignorant, credulous, and sometimes crafty forebears as being messages from the gods. We have already seen that some interpret dreams of ancestors as evidence of a spiritual realm.[1] But other types of dreams, too—the startling, the ecstatic, the terrifying or foreboding, the predictive or seemingly clairvoyant, among others—have ever made strong impressions on our kind, and were often interpreted as evidence of the gods. The Bible itself has several examples of people being visited by God in dreams. For one, the patriarch Jacob on his travels famously dreamt of the ladder between earth and heaven, of angels ascending and descending, and of God speaking to him—and he awakened and said,[2] "Surely the Lord is in this place and I knew it not…this is none other but the house of God, and this is the gate of heaven."

Mystical experiences, though they do not occur to the majority of any people, do occur to a small minority of every people, and these experiences can feel so powerful and otherworldly that those touched by them may believe they know God, and can forever after hold private belief in God, or even establish a new sect or religion.[3]

Another common occurrence that was often interpreted as being sourced in the supernatural is the epiphany, the sudden idea, the solution instantly crystallizing in the mind. To primitive men unaware of the complexity, and the mostly unconscious functioning, of the human mind, these flashes of understanding seemed to come from outside the self, and, they thought, from gods.

Trance states have also been discovered and induced by many peoples and cultures. In a state of trance—which we now understand to be natural, but which has been interpreted in some pre-scientific cultures as supernatural—a person may feel possessed by something outside himself, and this animating force has often been thought to be a spirit or god, and shamans and clergy took it upon themselves to explain what these forces wanted, and how they were to be communicated with and cajoled, placated, or worshiped.

Epileptic seizures are noteworthy, too, because they combine unusual experiences of a physical, mental, and often emotional nature. To the observer, and certainly to one whose body is afflicted with it, a powerful seizure can be frightening—at times involving falling to the ground, twitching, even losing consciousness. And when those prone to epileptic seizures also felt what seemed like ecstatic religious experiences, it should come as no surprise that many of our pre-scientific ancestors, both those who endured such seizures and those who witnessed them, saw such events as visitations from spirits or gods.

---

[1] For more on that topic see section 33.

[2] See Genesis 28:10-22.

[3] For more discussion on mystical experiences and whether they prove God's existence, see section 41.

And aside from epileptic seizures, other natural bodily occurrences such as fainting, momentary loss of consciousness, and comas, must have been puzzling to ancient man, for the life force seemed to go away and then return—and some would have interpreted these as being sourced in the actions or influences of a realm other than the physical, especially if such experiences coincided or were associated with, other meaningful actions or events—a battle, a birth, a death, an act of rebellion against parent or chief, and so on.

And then there is the entire thorn-field of mental illness. Several symptoms of some of these illnesses have clear connections to felt religious experience. Psychotic disorders often involve hallucinations—hearing voices, seeing visions, or feeling sensations that are not truly occurring in the objective world—and these have often been understood by ignorant, frightened, or deluded men as the voices and appearances and touches of gods or spirits, whether malevolent or good. And mania—the over-confident, highly energetic state of elevated mood—is often accompanied by delusions of grandeur, with the person feeling that he is exceptional and unparalleled,[1] perhaps a prophet, or even God. Extreme anxiety and panic attacks, or compulsions and obsessions one felt powerless to overcome, may also have been felt to be influences of the spirits, and depression and anger would have been interpreted—an apparent biblical example of which is included in the narrative about King Saul[2]—as visitation by evil spirits or abandonment by beneficial spirits. With scientific knowledge of mental illness we now dismiss such claims with pity or scorn, but in earlier days of our species some would have believed, or at least wondered, and superstition gained yet another toehold on the overrun mountain of man.

---

[1] Although for many years, now, I've worked almost exclusively with those who are well but wish to optimize their quality of life, in my early years in the mental health field I worked with the seriously mentally ill in an outpatient clinic affiliated with a mental hospital. I remember one charming and highly educated Catholic man diagnosed with bipolar disorder, who was prone to manic episodes when he stopped taking his lithium—which he repeatedly did because, at least toward their beginnings, the manic episodes brought him unbounded confidence and optimism. The progression of his episodes was evident by the extent of his religious delusions: In one case, the first indication that he was off his medication was his claim that he was made a priest; a week later, at his next visit, he said that various honors had been bestowed upon him and he was now to be addressed as Monsignor; and after missing his next appointment, upon being located by our mobile outreach team he glanced around quickly, lowered his voice, and in a conspiratorial whisper informed me that he had been contacted by emissaries of Pope John Paul II and was asked whether he would be willing to assume the papacy, because the pope wished to vacate the position in deference to him.

[2] See I Samuel 16:14-15, 23, where these evil spirits depart, and Saul is refreshed, when David plays for him the harp. See also I Samuel 18:10-12.

THE SAGE AND THE SEEKERS

*****

And the sage continued, saying: My brother, though we have spoken of one cause at a time, in most individuals and societies any number of causes combine to build and bolster religious belief. And this helps explain religion's persistence. A threefold cord is not quickly broken,[1] and the hundred-fold cord of supernatural belief has, in the human story, frayed ever so slowly, repeatedly mended itself—and we have yet to see if it shall ever be completely, and finally, severed.

Yet be not overly puzzled at the many causes for religion's birth, or for her continued tenacity; these can be entirely natural. Consider for how many reasons a man may be drawn to a woman, and for how many reasons—some different from those which drew him to her in the first place—he is persuaded to stay with her through the years. For several examples: he may initially be drawn to her by lust, by her charm, by loneliness, by the social current of his friends getting married, or by his image of masculinity which may require him to have a wife. And he may be persuaded to remain married by, among other reasons, the discomfort of too-great change, the shame of a failed marriage, the financial expense of divorce, the fear of losing friendships, compassion for his children, or the risk of diminished influence as a parent. Matters touching widely and deeply on human life often have many possible sources, and many ongoing supports.

And, my brother, I have spoken of the hundred-fold cord of faith, because although we have discussed many reasons for the widespread birth of religion, if you will but reflect upon the matter you will find many more. For in the fertile soil of the human mind there sprout not only the sweet apples of reason and the nourishing wheat of knowledge, but also the numberless weeds of error and the clinging brambles of weakness and superstition.[2]

---

[1] Ecclesiastes 4:12

[2] Baron d'Holbach, in the 18th century, spoke of the combination of causes giving rise to religion, and modifying and perpetuating religion, too. He said, "If we go back to the beginning we shall find that ignorance and fear created the gods, that fancy, enthusiasm or deceit adorned or disfigured them, that weakness worships them, that credulity preserves them; and that custom respects and tyranny supports them in order to make the blindness of men serve its own interests."

And Gibbon, who is said to have frequented d'Holbach's salon, throws a further handful of reasons for religion's birth and perpetuation our way when he writes in his *Decline and Fall of the Roman Empire:* "The different motives which influenced the reason or the passions of the barbarian converts cannot easily be ascertained. They were often capricious and accidental; a dream, an omen, the report of a miracle, the example of some priest or hero, the charms of a believing wife, and, above all, the fortunate event of a prayer or vow which, in a moment of danger, they had addressed to the God of the Christians." And though Gibbon was discussing barbarians adopting the already existent

68. Biases against believing in God

And a priest objected, saying: You have spoken of reasons men are drawn to believe in God—but there are reasons in the heart of man causing him to avoid believing in God, too, and to rebel against Him. Therefore, your citing of natural causes for belief as proof that religion is false, is itself misleading and false.

And the sage said: My brother, we have spoken of the many reasons for the birth of religion not because they prove religious belief false. They do not. Rather we have noted many all-too-human motives for supernatural belief to illustrate that religion's mere prevalence does not prove it accurate.

Yet some of your words are justified: there are, indeed, also inclinations in the heart of man drawing him away from belief in God. As some flee intimacy with fellow humans, having learned to fear the vulnerability of love, so there are those who dread being loved, even known, by a possible God—and thus avert their eyes from seeking God. And some are uneasy when not having all the answers; they fear dancing with mystery-clad truth, the graceful lover who moves in step only with the humble. Those who crave certainty, having seen the errors of organized religion, may too hastily conclude that there can be no God, and no cosmic purpose or meaning of any kind.

And untrammeled pleasure beckons with seductive wink and winning smile, promising easy ecstasy and sensual salvation. Deep yearnings for things forbidden—the pull of driving lust; the call to unprincipled glory, the urge to unbounded power, the rich luster of greed and the satin chains of sloth—all clamor and whisper against a God demanding obedience, and a clergy teaching restraint.

And some still wince at memories of being beaten by religious teachers, or bear with bitterness the soul-scars of an anguished childhood within the community of believers. And the unsated hunger of abandonment and the unsoothed sorrow of abuse, counsel avoidance or call for revenge. Others are lone spirits who feel caged by community ritual and trapped in conforming crowds. They may viscerally reject the notion of organized religion, and the gods of the herd irrespective of any truth such religion may hold. And some, in bitter resentment of smallness and mortality, shut prideful eyes tight against a possible God and His transcending power.

These and more can pull us away from considering whether there may, indeed, be a God who wants us to lead our lives in a particular fashion.

My brother, all of us, in the unexplored depths of our hearts, are pushed and pulled by conflicting fears and incompatible urges. Moreover, the diverse human

---

religion of Christianity, the motives he mentioned could apply, too, to superstitious beliefs not yet solidified into religion. Thus they may help explain, in some cases, religion's beginnings, too.

family comprises multitudes of individuals with widely varying spirits, inclinations, and life stories. Thus, for any number of reasons, some will be drawn toward belief, and for any number of reasons—sometimes the very same reasons—others will be drawn away from belief.

On matters of religion, then, though we seek the help of the wise and the sincere, we must in the end decide for ourselves—with the approval of reason and the best self-awareness we can muster. Disappointing though it may be, we cannot trust the impulses of our hearts, our intuitions and instincts, or the preponderance of human history or custom. For the chronicles of man, though they take in many admirable moments, also recount his ignorance and folly, his cowardice and credulity, his deceitfulness and his decadence. Let us, then, turn our eyes away from the dead library of the past and the familiar, and look instead to the daunting but living tome of honest seeking, whose ever-renewing ink never fades, whose just-milled paper never turns brittle, and whose every paragraph finds us engaged in a quest of noble daring.

And in living such authenticity our days will be our own, and our years the masterpieces of our spirit. And then, when night falls we shall surrender to the darkness with peace unparalleled; for the soul never gives herself over to sleep so contentedly as when her bedtime tale recalls how she emerged one day from hiding, cast away all her disguises, and danced fearlessly in the sunlight in all her tender beauty.

69. Argument that religion is necessary for society's survival

Then a town official protested, saying: Your words on religion may be true, but they are not wise. For without fear of gods, the hope of an afterlife, and religion's instructions on right and wrong, men would terrorize each other and civilization would crumble. Supernatural beliefs motivate mankind to behave with some measure of self-restraint. Religions are useful to society, and it is better not to study too closely whether they are true.[1]

---

[1] Gibbon, in his *Decline and Fall of the Roman Empire* provides examples of such usefulness when he writes: "They knew and valued the advantages of religion, as it is connected with civil government. They encouraged the public festivals which humanise the manners of the people. They managed the arts of divinations, as a convenient instrument of policy; and they respected as the firmest bond of society, the useful persuasion that, either in this or in a future life, the crime of perjury is most assuredly punished by the avenging gods." This comes in the same chapter as, and follows by a few pages, Gibbon's oft-quoted observation that, "The various modes of worship, which prevailed in the Roman world, were all considered by the people, as equally true; by the philosopher, as equally false; and by the magistrate, as equally useful."

In a similar vein, in his classic work on a young America, and speaking of its many religious sects, de Tocqueville says: "If it be of the highest importance to man, as an

And the sage replied: My brother, yours is a powerful challenge, one with which my heart, too, has grappled. Yet I put a question to you: Shall we attend to the clipped voice of pragmatism and ask merely what is useful—or listen, rather, for the warm melody of meaning and ask what is deeply worthwhile? Might it not be nobler for our minds and bodies to endure whatever ravages may be unleashed by truth, than to sell our souls for corruption's most paradisiacal calm? Can blindness or delusion, even if convenient, compare to awareness and vision, unquiet though such maturity may prove to be?

Would you pluck out the eyes of your neighbors, that they might no longer covet each other's possessions? Would you sever the arms of your friends that they no longer be capable of striking one another? A nation anesthetized by false religious security may sleep untroubled, but in its waking hours it sees not the lights of brightest understanding nor the darks of deepest sorrow; the colors of unadulterated authenticity nor the shadows of unadorned humility; the golden sunrise of expanding truth nor the sacred sunset of an honest death.

And all this holds, even if religion were only good and peaceful. But though the positive influences of religion are many, the agonized bloods of millions rise up from the earth in eternal protest: "Were we, the multitudes, not murdered by those seeking the glory of God, and were we, the myriads, not tortured by holy warriors and sanctified henchmen?" Look back at the historical landscape of

---

individual, that his religion should be true, the case of society is not the same. Society has no future life to hope for or to fear; and provided the citizens profess a religion, the peculiar tenets of that religion are of very little importance to its interests."

And Edmund Burke, Gibbon's contemporary, asks: "…is superstition the greatest of all possible vices?…Superstition is the religion of feeble minds; and they must be tolerated in an intermixture of it, in some trifling or some enthusiastic shape or other, else you will deprive weak minds of a resource found necessary to the strongest… Wisdom is not the most severe corrector of folly. They are the rival follies, which mutually wage so unrelenting a war…Prudence would be neuter; but if…a prudent man were obliged to make a choice of what errors and excesses of enthusiasm he would condemn or bear, perhaps he would think the superstition which builds, to be more tolerable than that which demolishes; that which adorns a country, than that which deforms it; that which endows, than that which plunders; that which disposes to mistaken beneficence, than that which stimulates to real injustice; that which leads a man to refuse to himself lawful pleasures, than that which snatches from others the scanty subsistence of their self-denial…"

But as I try to make clear in the text, not only are some of religion's societal benefits overstated by such opinions, and her costs not sufficiently taken into account, prudence is decidedly not the only measure of good. Nobility asks of us to consult values other than pragmatic gain—and the great values of honesty, authenticity, and truth beg of us not to fool ourselves or others or remain silent on life's most important matters, but to think and speak with courage, even at a price.

religion: her scarlet-running rivers—her mountains of grimacing skulls. If we have forgotten the innumerable smaller religious persecutions and massacres throughout the ages and lands, have we forgotten Joshua's conquering geno-cides;[1] the popes' Crusades and Inquisitions; the many Jihads and even today's legions of suicidal, indiscriminate murderers unleashing mayhem upon civiliza-tion in defense of religion's unlimited hubris and in pursuit of her promises of heavenly bliss? And shall we forget the days of old—before the birth of these world-spanning religions—the days of widespread human sacrifice to numberless hungry gods? And can our hearts rest easy when reflecting upon millennia of gentle and innocent martyrs, too—that vast and varied host of the eagerly slaughtered—who believed they were going to eternal reward? My brother, if society without religion frightens you, so, too, should society *with* religion.[2]

Indeed, for ages, now, the masses of those imprisoned for violent and hei-nous crimes were raised in religious homes, and maintained religious beliefs—and some who subscribed to no religion were gentle philosophers, generous philanthropists, and among the most helpful scientists and physicians. Thus, for ethical and socially beneficial living, religion is neither necessary nor sufficient.

---

[1] Or at least the tales of such in the Bible—for in addition to the obvious cause for skepticism on the miraculous elements of such stories, many scholars doubt that the biblical conquests and genocides of Moses and Joshua ever took place, and see such accounts, rather, as the attempts of later generations of ancient Israel's scribes, monarchs, and priests, to create what they saw as a unifying and heroic set of national myths, that might serve various political, religious, and inspirational ends.

Archaeologist William G. Dever, for one example, who, incidentally, argues insistently for the historicity of much spoken of by the later books of the Bible, including the existence of ancient Israel—and rails against revisionists who deny this—says in Chapter 4 of his *What Did The Biblical Writers Know and When Did They Know It?* that the overwhelm-ing archaeological evidence points to the conclusion that the stories of the patriarchs, and of an Israelite exodus from Egypt and a 40-year wandering in the desert, are simply not factual, and that the origins of the nation of ancient Israel were most likely the indigenous peoples of that very land.

Still, I do not mean to suggest that this is a settled issue. Perhaps the future will bring incontrovertible evidence, but for now other archaeologists, along with some scholars in other fields, too, defend the historicity of figures such as Moses, or even the Patriarchs, and events such as the exodus from Egypt and the conquest of Canaan. On matters of the dusty past and its interpretation, much controversy remains, and much ignorance; for the sands of antiquity have not preserved for us many footprints of fact, and have long since desiccated the meaning of ancient tears.

[2] To indulge for a moment in the bitter pleasures of dark levity, I remind the reader of Woody Allen's commentary that at this time in history our species is at a momentous crossroads, that "...one path leads to despair and utter hopelessness, the other to total extinction. Let us pray that we have the wisdom to choose correctly."

Yet let us address the argument that, overall, society would be far worse without religion. Is this true?[1] Consider that even without religion numerous motives remain for people to conduct themselves with civility. While this may initially seem inconceivable to those among the religious who see their morality and good behavior as based primarily upon religion's teachings, observe other social species—apes, elephants, monkeys and wolves—and see that without religious beliefs they live together with no more strife than exists amongst even religious humans. And consider, too, societies that have been, or are today, significantly atheist or agnostic: Have they not had their good and bad elements—as have societies that follow, or have followed, organized religion?

My brother: We are, by nature, social beings. Thus, instincts for peaceful interaction and group belonging lie deep in our bones, and drive most of us most of the time to treat each other well. Bonds of shame, fear, empathy, loyalty and altruism are secured in our sinews and flesh, too, and keep us from villainy more than any sacred tradition or superstitious doctrine ever could.[2]

To be persuaded of the strength of our social instincts, observe the intense desire to conform in basic ways—and how effective in shaping our behavior is the yearning to belong and the urgency to avoid losing the esteem of others. People wear what others in their society wear, not the type of garments worn in previous generations or in far away lands—a Roman toga, for instance, or even fashions a mere few decades outdated—though these other types of clothing are functional, too, and not prohibited by any Bible or Scripture, or even by any civil law. We choose our clothing so that we will not be seen as overly different from our group. Indeed, even those who fancy themselves rebels, and dress or groom in shocking ways, nearly always do so in a fashion that conform to the subculture, or alternative norms, with which they identify. They rarely rebel against one society without conforming to another.[3] And how many large and small things do most of us avoid, whether building an odd-shaped home or painting it an unusual color, or pronouncing words in different or frowned-upon accents, not

---

[1] For more discussion of right and wrong and social stability without religion, see Part V of this book, titled "Right and Wrong Without Supernatural Religion."

[2] Regarding basic social norms, James Q. Wilson, in the introductory essay to his *Moral Sense* puts it well. He says, giving the example of incest, that although rules may serve to keep the small minority in check, "...it is not the rule that explains the behavior of most people, but their behavior that explains the rule."

[3] Parents of teenagers often observe with frustration, and eventual resignation, that their youngsters, self-styled fierce individualists, tend to express their "individuality" in ways rigidly and anxiously consistent with the standards of at least a subset of their peers—and the healthy parent, stung by the loss of influence over his child, and wincing at recollections of his own awkward rebellions, grasps the warm hand of humility and walks further down the path of becoming fully human.

because any sacred text or Bible warns against such behavior but rather because we fear a neighbor's—even a stranger's—disapproval.

Observe, too, that laws about which the Bible has not spoken, but which society insists upon, such as traffic laws, tax laws, and drug laws, are obeyed by most people, whether religious or secular, most of the time—no less frequently, perhaps, than injunctions against such behaviors as adultery, stealing, and disrespecting one's parents, prohibitions found in the Bible's Ten Commandments. And does not the religious man sin in secret—though he believes God is everywhere and can see everything—thus demonstrating that he fears the disapproval of mortals more than the punishments of the Divine?[1] Indeed, even when people think they behave in certain ways to please God, in truth what likely most strongly pulls and pushes them to follow their religion is the natural instinct to conform to the rules they were early taught, or which are now valued by their group. And happily, societal rules and norms, to effectively influence people, need not be dishonestly taught in the name of phantom gods.

Let us neither overestimate the power of religion nor underestimate the power of society in using natural social instinct to shape the actions of men. For yes, some people at some times are restrained by invented notions of supernatural gods, but more people, more of the time, are restrained by the solid instincts and group norms of natural men.

My brother: Consider the isolated and overindulged man who, from infancy to adulthood, has always been carried by his father. As he never ventured to walk upon his own legs, he never learned to trust their strength. Instead, he feared that climbing down off his father's back would lead to all manner of stumblings, even catastrophic falls—and would therefore be dangerous and irresponsible. But is not such fear the result of having grown accustomed to so relying upon his father that he now sees this undignified dependency as necessary? And were he suddenly to find himself without such transport services, it may be that his own legs—so long neglected, and likely in a weakened state—would for a time not carry him well, and he may, indeed, fall. But should we then presume that he fell because he flouted the rule that men are not to walk on their own legs? Or shall

---

[1] In the 18th century, Baron d'Holbach wrote in *Good Sense*, "Almost every man fears...the judgments of men of which he feels the effects, more than the judgments of God of whom he has only fluctuating ideas. The desire of pleasing the world, the force of custom, the fear of ridicule and of censure, have more force than all religious opinions. Does not the soldier, through fear of disgrace, daily expose his life in battle...? ...The most religious persons have often more respect for a valet, than for God. A man who firmly believes that God sees every thing, and that he is omniscient and omnipresent, will be guilty, when alone, of actions, which he would never do in presence of the meanest of mortals."

we rather understand that he fell because he refused to use these legs for so long, and allowed them to deteriorate? Moreover, even factoring in a fall or two, will not the man, in the long term, after learning to use his own legs, move far better, not to mention with considerably greater dignity, than ever he could while being carried on another's back?

And so it is with religion: Many have grown so accustomed to relying upon her teachings for their motives to conduct themselves well, that they are unaware of natural human instincts inclining us to behave in ways good for society.[1]

And, true, human nature comprises not only instincts constructive for society, but instincts driving individuals toward selfish ends, too. For most people, however—in the majority of their significant choices—instincts preserving cooperative functioning prevail. And even at their best, religious societies can claim no better than similar results: most behaving well, most of the time.

And because humans are capable of violence and corruption and hate and not only of kindness, generosity and love, it is the high duty of every society to teach, and to hold up for praise and admiration, values leading to harmonious and prosperous living—and to strongly discourage, and vigorously punish, behaviors that threaten society's health. There is, of course, no exact code of laws that all societies would need to follow, but if each society were to devote itself to training its members to respect the rights and welfare of all, I daresay that mankind could do at least as well standing upright and acting from straightforward human-based motives, as it has done in its scheming and blood-soaked millennia of ignominious bowing and crawling, impelled by varied forms of avarice and fear into sometimes obeying the seductions and menacings of invisible gods.

My brother, in addition to the social instinct and its role in preserving civil behavior, the great majority of humans easily see the benefits of laws promoting safety and order in society—whether or not such laws are mandated by religion. Moreover, even those not moved by constructive instincts and emotions, and unconvinced of the value of social stability, will usually fear running afoul of civil authorities. For even without religion, those who fail to control their antisocial urges would be penalized by police and court, and—so long as institutions of power are stable, not overwhelmed by famine, rebellion, war, and the like, which create havoc in religious cultures, too—society would remain relatively safe.

Furthermore, in addition to social instincts and reasoned self-interest, a third element keeps most from behaving destructively: Their actions are guided by the

---

[1] Books dealing with this theme more extensively include: *The Moral Sense* by James Q. Wilson, and *The Moral Animal* by Robert Wright. And books that extend this theme to other species, too, include: *Good Natured* by Frans De Waal, and *Cheating Monkeys and Citizen Bees* by Lee Dugatkin.

internalized rules of society, rules they have absorbed, and now consider their own. This admonishing voice of the group echoing back as the individual's own voice, whether one labels it the superego[1] or the conscience, is an invisible but immensely powerful force integrated into the heart and mind of each seemingly autonomous person, and exerting great influence over his behavior. Thus, so long as a society raises its young with constructive values—upon any number of rationales, including reasoning on the common good—these values will be internalized in the next generation, which will usually not require logical or conscious decisions to avoid behaving destructively. Instead, most people, most of the time, will behave well reflexively: Inner controls—guilt, loyalty, anxiety, and other emotions triggered by internalized group norms—will ensure this. And is not a well-behaved majority all we can reasonably hope for, even with religion?

My brother: Children often require external rewards or punishments as inducement to behave well—while adults can learn to see the benefits in good behavior itself. A child may need the motivation of a candy or sparkling prize—or the threat of a toy being taken from him, or getting a lower grade—in order to learn his school lesson; an adult, however, studying knowledge he finds interesting or important, can find the learning inherently valuable, and not only does not require the likes of a candy to learn well, he might find such a reward insulting. So, too, with civility and civilization: Perhaps the human species in its childhood and adolescence required promises of external rewards and punishments—notions of gods and heaven and hell—in order to motivate it to constructive behavior. But in the adulthood of humanity it may be hoped that we can forego the shallow inducements of immaturity and see the inherent value and benefits of peaceful, productive, and cooperative society—and thus can do without religion's fables of a supernatural hereafter, and all its fictitious glory and flames.[2]

---

[1] A term famously popularized by Freud

[2] Many intelligent and well-intentioned men have believed not only that society, in order to survive, required religion, but that government needed to establish and maintain religion. Let us return to the 18th century Edmund Burke, who wrote: "The consecration of the state, by a state religious establishment, is necessary also to operate with a wholesome awe upon free citizens; because in order to secure their freedom, they must enjoy some determinate portion of power. To them therefore a religion connected with the state, and with their duty towards it, becomes even more necessary than in such societies, where the people, by the terms of their subjection, are confined to private sentiments, and the management of their own family concerns. All persons possessing any portion of power ought to be strongly and awfully impressed with an idea that they act in trust; and that they are to account for their conduct in that trust to the one great Master, Author, and Founder of society."

But the successful American example of separation of church and state over these past two centuries and the stable and civil examples of largely non-religious Scandinavian

70. Argument that people need superstition, the power and authority of the clergy should be respected, the customs of the people should not be challenged, and the rituals of religion should be performed regardless of whether the claims of religions are true

And a philosopher said: You mistake your first-level insights for final wisdom, and your anti-religious vendetta for a gift to mankind. But deeper wisdom knows that the customs of a people and the power of the clergy should be respected, the superstitious needs of the masses should not be underestimated, and their religious rituals should be performed, without subjecting them to the critiques of reason—for the great majority of people cannot handle the unfiltered truth, so religion for the masses cannot be expected to be the whole and literal truth.[1] But still it has value. Thus have many philosophers of old, though seeing

---

societies over these past decades, provide strong evidence that Mr. Burke was mistaken on the need for the state to establish religion, and some evidence, too, that, for society's wellbeing, even non-state-sponsored religion is unnecessary. And if future events should teach certain vulnerabilities or tragedies of non-religious societies, let us bear in mind, too, the vulnerabilities and tragedies that have ever plagued even the most religious of societies. And if neither religion nor irreligion guarantees all benefits and stability, at least the latter alternative does not sacrifice honesty on life's most profound questions.

[1] Schopenhauer, in his *Religion: A Dialogue*, has Philalethes say: "Religion must be regarded as a necessary evil, its necessity resting on the pitiful imbecility of the great majority of mankind, incapable of grasping the truth, and therefore requiring, in its pressing need, something to take its place."

And Thoreau, speaking not about religion in particular, but about being fully awake to life, intellectually, aesthetically, and more, gives a similarly poor grade to the great majority. In *Walden* he writes: "The millions are awake enough for physical labour; but only one in a million is awake enough for effective intellectual exertion, only one in a hundred millions to a poetic or divine life. To be awake is to be alive. I have never yet met a man who was quite awake. How could I have looked him in the face?" Yet Thoreau follows this with an optimism that better living is within reach if we would but exert ourselves. He writes: "We must learn to reawaken and keep ourselves awake…I know of no more encouraging fact than the unquestionable ability of man to elevate his life by a conscious endeavour…Every man is tasked to make his life, even in its details, worthy of the contemplation of his most elevated and critical hour."

Alexis de Tocqueville, for his part, insisted—like Burke who is quoted in the previous footnote—that society needs religion, especially a free society. In *Democracy in America* (speaking of certain developments in France) he wrote: "But there are others who look forward to the republican form of government as a tranquil and lasting state, towards which modern society is daily impelled by the ideas and manners of the time, and who sincerely desire to prepare men to be free. When these men attack religious opinions, they obey the dictates of their passions to the prejudice of their interests. Despotism may govern without faith, but liberty cannot. Religion is much more necessary in the republic which they set forth in glowing colors than in the monarchy which they attack; and it is more needed in democratic republics than in any others. How is it possible that society should escape destruction if the moral tie be not strengthened in proportion as the political tie is relaxed? and what can be done with a people which is its own master, if it be not submissive to the Divinity?"

Notice de Tocqueville's conviction that man cannot be trusted—that in order for society not to be destroyed, people need to fear some master, human or divine. And this is consistent with his discussion of early 19th century American slavery, a few chapters later in the same text, in which he says: "The negro enters upon slavery as soon as he is born: nay, he may have been purchased in the womb, and have begun his slavery before he began his existence. Equally devoid of wants and of enjoyment, and useless to himself, he learns, with his first notions of existence, that he is the property of another, who has an interest in preserving his life, and that the care of it does not devolve upon himself; even the power of thought appears to him a useless gift of Providence, and he quietly enjoys the privileges of his debasement. If he becomes free, independence is often felt by him to be a heavier burden than slavery; for having learned, in the course of his life, to submit to everything except reason, he is too much unacquainted with her dictates to obey them. A thousand new desires beset him, and he is destitute of the knowledge and energy necessary to resist them: these are masters which it is necessary to contend with, and he has learnt only to submit and obey. In short, he sinks to such a depth of wretchedness, that while servitude brutalizes, liberty destroys him."

Yet whatever difficulties may have occasioned a slave's encounters with freedom, surely freeing the slaves was noble—and, as it turns out, elitist arguments aside, the great majority of slaves were not destroyed by liberty. I believe the same will be said, someday, and with as much empirical evidence, on the matter of religion. Yes, there will be various difficulties to contend with as people grapple with the existential liberty of having lost their imagined divine master—but people can learn to handle liberty, even to cherish it, and to build a life of authenticity that would be impossible without it.

Elitist philosophers and noblemen, isolated from the masses—the former often by reclusive temperaments and unusually conceptual minds, and the latter by uncommon privileges and unearned wealth—have, through the ages, looked down from their libraries and castles upon the "common people" with disapproval and distrust, sometimes with a dollop of pity softening their disdain. And such pessimism is, no doubt, rooted in many reasoned arguments, and confirmed by the ever-abundant baseness that characterizes much of any society or culture. But in the grand narrative of history the victories for the human race are won not by those who disparage the abilities and virtues of the masses, but by those who call upon their better natures. For untold ages the elites insisted that human nature did not allow for the great majority to have a constructive say in their own governance, and that realism, and therefore wisdom, required monarchy or another variation of dictatorship or tyranny. And for unnumbered centuries and millennia it was argued that slavery was a necessary condition of human life, and that women, on the whole, were incapable of intellectual achievement or political participation, or even of managing their lives without the direction of a man. Choose your favorite or most infamous flavor of outdated bigotry—insisting upon the inherent inferiority and justifiable oppression of a group, based on gender, ethnicity, or any other distinguishing

the errors of religion, not only stifled their protests, but even stepped forward and played a prominent role in the worship rites of the people.[1]

And the sage said: My brother, you raise important objections, and make several interesting claims; let us discuss them in turn.

Customs, I agree, are important to a people, as is the stability cultivated by the elevating routines of formal ritual, and the respect accorded to wise leaders. Yet custom need not be the enemy of truth, nor stability and ritual the arms-bearers of error; and, decidedly, the wise cannot lead us into today's and tomorrow's battles riding upon the feeble chariots of yesteryear.

Change brings with it risk, or at least the fear of the unknown and the specter of chaos. But all progress depends upon change. Indeed, the very religion you wish to preserve, and protect from scrutiny—though you see it as necessary stability, was in its early days a heresy and a change.

And the "masses" to whom you refer were once thought—by those defending the old ways of monarchy and tyranny and slavery and other injustices and

---

characteristic—and there has been no shortage of teachers and experts arguing with passion and eloquence for the necessity of maintaining that bigotry.

But as this book goes to press, the United States has elected its first president of African ancestry, and his main rival for his party's nomination was a woman—as was the vice-presidential candidate of the opposing party. And it is obvious to the overwhelming majority of sane observers—including the great bulk of "whites," the "masses" which previous elites were certain could never tolerate, much less vote for, a "black" man as the country's leader—that whatever mistakes history will judge this president to have made will be due to his individual character, ideology, and judgment, and not to old, racist notions of inherent inferiority in dark skin color.

To be sure, the masses, and every other disparaged group, are far from perfect, and are often guilty of incompetence and worse—but so are their detractors, the privileged and the elite. To adapt a familiar aphorism: The sermons of those preaching that the masses are incapable of progress are often interrupted by reports of exactly such progress. And observe the irony: History peers out from her windows commanding the sweeping vistas of ages and lands, and looks down with disdain and pity upon the small-minded perspectives of the over-educated and over-privileged, with the same mixture of feelings with which these look down upon the greatest share of their brothers and sisters.

[1] "…in the age of the Antonines, both the interests of the priests and the credulity of the people were sufficiently respected. In their writings and conversations, the philosophers of antiquity asserted the independent dignity of reason; but they resigned their actions to the commands of law and of custom. Viewing, with a smile of pity and indulgence, the various errors of the vulgar, they diligently practiced the ceremonies of their fathers, devoutly frequented the temples of the gods; and sometimes condescending to act a part on the theatre of superstition, they concealed the sentiments of an Atheist under the sacerdotal robes." These wry and humane observations—marching in handsome, stately cadence—belong, of course, to Gibbon, in his *Decline and Fall of the Roman Empire*.

indignities—incapable of general literacy; incapable of governing themselves through democracy; incapable of resisting the crude appeals of slavery; incapable of accepting the equal rights under the law of all races and religions, incapable even of tolerating their own wives and daughters having rights equal to men. Yet history has proved such elitist pessimism mistaken. Why then must we accept, as any more warranted, that humanity cannot do without its misinformed religions?

Is significant change difficult? Surely it is. Is it frightening? Surely to some. But can it be achieved? Certainly it can be—and has been, repeatedly. In the long term and in the big picture, change, indeed life overall, involves balancing between the poles of absolute continuity and absolute chaos. We walk by keeping one foot in place, and moving the other to a new spot; and the very cells of our bodies are replaced over time by new cells, though they do not all change at once. And every radical transition, shocking as it may have seemed at the time, was built upon an already existent language, already existent concepts, and already existent people, material, and tools—not to mention an already existent Earth and cosmos. Complete change is no more possible for human life than is complete fixity. And so, my brother, when the day comes that our species will have shaken off the spell of pretending to know what it does not know on matters of God and the supernatural, such change will have occurred within a context of most elements in human life remaining the same.

Yet might not such important change occasion social upheaval and pain? It might, indeed—as have other important and noble transitions throughout history. Monarchy and oppressive traditions were dispensed with in some lands, and the industrial revolution birthed, but not without immediate instability and strife, and—one may argue—not either without the later, more terrible echoes of stability and authority making their temporary return in the form of fascism and tyranny. And, of course, one may argue that the modern era is littered with the victims of those seeking to regain a sense of security and pride, after being stripped of various forms of old certainties.

Still, was not the ancient world filled with corpses, too? Were not wars and massacres and revolts and myriad forms of strife the ever-present worries of our distant forebears, even in ages of unchallenged superstition? And would we choose to return to the days of ignorance and barbarism and slavery and plague?

Awakening to progress brings to the eyes the squint of pain, but also the gleam of inspiration and the brightness of hope; and willfully covering one's eyes with the blanket of the past may allow further comfort for a time, but only by hiding from the world in the darkness of slumber or escape—and only until such sleep or repose is interrupted, as it inevitably will be, late or soon.

My brother, you argue that we should respect the traditions and rituals and clergy of a people; I ask you, then: Is it not better to respect the people themselves? Shall we not value the conscience of a people over its customs? Shall we not cultivate keen-sighted integrity over glassy-eyed rote? And shall we not show the people that they can learn to dance on their feet for themselves, and need not crawl on their knees for their priests?

71. Argument that some, without religion, might find life meaningless, and thus behave destructively

And another man said: You yourself must see how meaningless some can find a life without religion. If we teach powerful honesty on such matters, and many lose their supernatural beliefs, some may find existence so devoid of meaning that they may take life and death lightly, and act in a destructive manner—without regard to the danger this poses to themselves or others.

And the sage said: My brother, so strong beats the life force within the mortal breast that the great majority will always cling to life, even if there remains—to their logical minds—no important reason to live.

Moreover, would it be the lack of supernatural meaning that might drive people to despair and worse—or would it be the letdown from the false meaning with which we have been indoctrinating our children for millennia? Perhaps if we were more honest with our children in the first place, and admitted that we did not know about things supernatural, they would base their lives, and happily so, on more natural and accessible goals and delights. And shall we continue to sow these dangerous religious illusions into the soil of future generations—when the truth is ever more available, and ever more likely to be discovered, and thus ever more likely to result in the destructive behavior you fear?

Further still, even if your concern is justified, and without religion some would take life less seriously and thus behave destructively, is that a persuasive argument in favor of religion? Has not religion itself been—in the millennia of its ascendancy—perhaps the most frequent cause people have scoffed at their own death while inflicting mayhem and ruin upon others? Has not the confidence in a heaven, where eternal reward awaits, provoked countless deeds of reckless cruelty and wanton destruction—in the name of God and religion? And has not the fear of hell, too, motivated untold numbers of decent men and women to follow the cruel instructions of misguided or unscrupulous clergy, instead of reaching out in compassion and assistance to those of different beliefs? Indeed, have not many who were categorized by religion as hell-bound sinners, thinking they had nothing more to lose, felt free to unleash their marauding or predatory passions upon their fellow man?

Civilization need not disintegrate without religion; the human species is more resilient than that. And while it may be that society without religion would be dangerous, we have seen society with religion—and it, too, is dangerous. Far from consistently preventing war, hatred, genocide, slavery, the subjugation of women, the multiplying of crippling fear and guilt, religion has—somewhere in the world, in nearly every generation—created or reinforced these, with the crushing weight of presumed divine decree.

My brother, perhaps no religion would yield the peace and benefits of honest, compassionate, not-knowing. Though rejecting religion is no panacea, who can say how magnificent and life-supporting would be the achievements of an age that knows it can only count on earthly existence, and whose energies are distracted neither by arrogant myths of chosenness nor by desperate visions of life eternal. And who can say but that unprecedented world unity might more easily arise when in the absence of religion there no longer existed divine causes for division and holy motives for hate. Ironically, it may be that religion's blood-red sun must set before the golden age she has long predicted might finally be allowed to dawn.[1]

72. Argument that taking religion away from people is cruel

Then a physician raised his voice and said: O sadistic sage, what good do you bring the people by robbing them of their hopes? Allow the dying to dream of heaven, and permit the wounded of soul their gods to lean on; allow the lonely their companionship of spirit, and permit the suffering meaning for their horrors.[2]

---

[1] One of the more touching examples of godless compassion comes not from some fainting romantic, but from the writings of an analytic, hard-headed logician, philosopher, and mathematician. Bertrand Russell, toward the end of an essay titled, *A Free Man's Worship*, writes: "United with his fellow-men by the strongest of all ties, the tie of a common doom, the free man finds that a new vision is with him always, shedding over every daily task the light of love. The life of Man is a long march through the night, surrounded by invisible foes, tortured by weariness and pain, towards a goal that few can hope to reach, and where none may tarry long. One by one, as they march, our comrades vanish from our sight, seized by the silent orders of omnipotent Death. Very brief is the time in which we can help them, in which their happiness or misery is decided. Be it ours to shed sunshine on their path, to lighten their sorrows by the balm of sympathy, to give them the pure joy of a never-tiring affection, to strengthen failing courage, to instill faith in hours of despair. Let us not weigh in grudging scales their merits and demerits, but let us think only of their need—of the sorrows, the difficulties, perhaps the blindnesses, that make the misery of their lives; let us remember that they are fellow-sufferers in the same darkness, actors in the same tragedy with ourselves. And so, when their day is over, when their good and their evil have become eternal by the immortality of the past, be it ours to feel that, where they suffered, where they failed, no deed of ours was the cause; but wherever a spark of the divine fire kindled in their hearts, we were ready with encouragement, with sympathy, with brave words in which high courage glowed."

[2] For more on meaning, see this book's entire Part X.

And the sage said: My compassionate brother, as earth and heaven are my witnesses, your question pierces deep, and I have asked it of my own heart. And so, I have not come to speak at the dying man's bed, nor at the shrines where the stricken gather desperate for cure. I have not argued unbidden at houses of worship, nor cajoled uninvited at schools of children. I have come to this field where all assembled have chosen to hear, and may walk their way at any time.

And, my fellow healer, is not truth the most life-giving of serums, and integrity the most healing of potions? Shall we show more concern for the palate than for the soul, by withholding desperately needed medicine, though bitter, from those who can bear it? And shall we not plead with drunkards to forego their poison, though today the bottle brings warm comfort?

Indeed, only strong and willing hearts will perceive the challenge of my words, or stagger beneath their burden. For ever the heart prevails: The keen ears of the heart rule the feeble ears of sound, turning deaf to what they find unbearable; the alert eyes of the heart shield the dimmer eyes of sight from perceiving that which looms too threatening; and the persuasive mouth of the heart hushes the mouth of mere words from speaking things too deeply troubling. And might a few of the strong and willing fall? Yes, in any worthwhile battle it must be so. But shall we not offer the intrepid spirit his encounter with destiny—remove the swaddling cloth from over his eyes, that he might at last behold his mortal foe?[1]

---

[1] Wrestling with the loss of one's religion is a serious and often agonizing ordeal; philosophy alone is often not enough to sustain one through the passage. Different people will be helped by different practices and resources. Non-judgmental social support is critical for most—a close family member or friend or lover or formal support group, or a network of friends and community connections who do not demand religious belief—and learning how to better manage one's emotions is important, too. Writing in a journal or diary, or other means of getting in touch with, and honoring and expressing one's deepest thoughts and emotions can be healing. Professional therapy or counseling can be helpful, too, so long as one chooses an open-minded therapist who does not attempt to impose a particular spiritual worldview. The therapist's exact clinical approach is less important than his or her accepting and intelligent presence. As for specific techniques to manage emotions, one well-tested approach is cognitive therapy (and the closely related cognitive-behavioral therapy)—the field dedicated to improving emotions through changing overly-negative thoughts. With or without therapy, books can be of help. A good, plain-spoken and research-based book to begin with is *Ten Days to Self-Esteem* by David Burns. Also worth seeing, two other books by the same author: *Feeling Good*, and *The Feeling Good Handbook*. Another helpful book for emotional management, as well as for developing a life orientation not based on religion, is *Six Pillars of Self-Esteem* by Nathaniel Branden. And to gain critical psychological and existential orientation by understanding one's own personality and temperament as compared to those of others, see *Please Understand Me II* by David Keirsey.

V. SHALL WE RELY ON FAITH?

73. Argument that faith is higher than reason

Then a gray-bearded religious teacher spoke, saying: Our Bible is the sacred word of the Almighty. In Him we have faith, and we see no need to doubt His Scripture. We have no right to question religion, for it would be sinful to doubt what has come from the Divine. Faith is higher than reason, and better than arguments or proof. Faith is the best kind of truth.[1]

And the sage spoke softly and said: My brother, faith is the ultimate and inevitable argument of the devout, for after these many centuries it is the last formidable barricade standing between the besieged castle of religion and the relentless advance of reason's liberating, though often fearsome, brigades.

My brother, it may be noble to have faith in the words of a Divine Almighty, and a grievous sin to doubt them—if only we knew what they were. Has the Almighty spoken in your ears or mine? Or have we merely been taught of divine revelation—taught by men? If we are agonizingly honest, must we not acknowledge that faith in religious teachings and laws is not faith in the Almighty, but faith in man and his stories? Perhaps the stories are true, and perhaps not, but they are *man's* stories.[2] And while faith in the Almighty may be a great good, faith in men is not to be esteemed so highly—certainly not to be valued above our best efforts at ascertaining truth.

Consider, too, my brother, that faith in religious teachings holds loyalty to human tradition above loyalty to God Himself. Would you think it virtuous and loyal if men were to say things in your name that they never heard you utter, but merely were told that you said? What if among the stories being spread of you were accounts that you instructed nations to kill or enslave each other, and that

---

[1] It is remarkable that although religions' notions of piety invariably include the virtue of being truthful, religions apparently see this duty of truthfulness as applying only to matters other than their own foundational claims. I'm reminded of the words of Simon Cameron, a 19th century American politician, who said: "An honest politician is one who, when he is bought, will stay bought."

[2] As for those who think they discern God communicating with them, they would not, strictly speaking, be relying on faith—but on a claim of knowledge based in experience. Of course, if they are honest they must concede that they do not responsibly *know* that the messages upon which they rely are coming from God. For perhaps their source is rather in hope, fear, guilt, ambition, intuition, religious training and expectations, even hallucination, or a thousand other forces welling up inside them, pretending to be the voice of God. These issues are dealt with directly in section 78.

you punished with death, or even horrific, never-ending torture, those who committed various minor offenses? Would you not want men to investigate whether you truly said and did these things?

And what of a possible God who observes masses of men accepting these things in His name, when all can see the many contradictory accounts religions teach of His wishes? Would such complacency satisfy Him? My brother, I beg you to reconsider what horrendous rumors you believe about God, and pass on to your children. As for me and my house, out of reverence for any God there may be—and out of respect for the dignity of the human spirit—we preach not of His will unless we know for certain what is His will, we say not words in His name unless we know for certain that He uttered those words, and we tell no tales of His deeds until such day as we can honestly know that those deeds were committed, and committed by Him.

Furthermore, my brother, I ask you this: Is it wise, even reasonable, to rely on faith, when all major religions agree that at least every religion but one is mistaken? If all walked in faith, all major religions would concur that the vast majority of us were terribly wrong in our beliefs. Would the Almighty be pleased with such recklessness, though it be blessed by the princes of tradition and garbed in religion's resplendent robes? Or would God rather prefer questioning caution, though dressed in the humble work clothes of honest inquiry?

And hear this, my brother: Even if we were to agree that faith is higher than reason, why not choose reason and reject faith? Because that does not follow? How would you know this, except by reason? So even the proposition that faith is higher than reason, and that we should therefore do away with reason when it comes to matters of faith—it, too, relies on reason! In short, only by the lights of reason can you even attempt to make your argument in favor of faith. For without reason and her sisters you could not be confident you were taught that faith is nobler than reason, nor could you conclude that if it were nobler, you should favor it over reason. Indeed, it is only by logic and experience that you know the words you read in your Scriptures today to be no different from the words in those Scriptures when you surrendered yourself to slumber last night.

Reason, standing on logic and experience, is not a trifle or luxury to be chosen when convenient. It is an indispensable foundation of our identity and of all we do. It allows us to be oriented to the world, to comprehend the basic laws of existence, and is necessary in any attempt to understand or speak intelligently on any matter, including faith. As strongly as we may yearn to defend tradition, it is futile to attempt this by attacking reason. Like the man who schemes to run his steed so swiftly that horse and rider might outrun the animal's very legs, the quest to fashion a belief or argument that dispenses with reason is self-contradictory.

For upon what are the horse and horseman riding, if not the horse's legs—and what makes any argument possible, if not the laws of reason?

Over these past few centuries, my brother, after thousands of years of mass and profound ignorance, we have at last beheld the rising sun of reason, and in her early light we have already seen many things more clearly. We now know that the merchant of faith, though wearing the countenance of earnest sincerity and attired in the costume of virtue and wisdom, was either deeply mistaken and unaware of the rust and mold in his wares, or was, at times, a wily swindler whose charming banter and commanding confidence found adoring spectators in our restless spirits, and eager buyers in our hungry hearts.

74. Argument that faith includes the faith to have faith

But the religious teacher pressed on, saying: Faith is belief beyond reason. Part of the challenge of faith is choosing faith precisely because faith is unreasonable! Faith in God includes having sufficient faith to have faith!

And the sage replied: My brother, I grant that such words have a satisfying ring, and the feel of creative thinking and deep conviction. But come, let us carefully examine what such words really mean. Then we shall see whether they are worthy of our souls.

If I ask you to believe that I am God, is it a virtue to believe as I ask you to? No religion would answer that question in the affirmative. Similarly, if I testify that God is a great whale, who wishes us to worship Him by praying toward the sea, no religion would want you to have faith in such a claim. Why? Because even religions agree that faith must stand upon a reliable foundation, and that unfounded belief is no virtue. Religions must concede that without reason and experience guiding our choice of beliefs, we could invest our faith in every charlatan and fool, every offered absurdity, at all times, on all matters. Thus, it will not do to claim that even without good reason to believe, faith in religion is legitimately based on nothing more than the decision to believe.

Furthermore, my brother, consider that only a minority of people believes in any one religion, and all major religions contradict each other on essential, often foundational, teachings about God, His will, or both. To illustrate, let us briefly examine what are often referred to as the three major Western religions. Traditional Christianity is based upon the idea that God either became man in the person of Jesus, or had a flesh-and-blood son by the name of Jesus. Traditional Islam and Judaism consider both these ideas blasphemy, and also disagree with the foundational notion of traditional Christianity that one needs to believe in Jesus in order to be saved from eternal damnation or to attain a heavenly afterlife. For its part, Islam believes that Mohammad was God's greatest prophet, that the Koran is the word of God as revealed to Mohammad and should be the basis of how we conduct our lives. Traditional Christianity and Judaism dispute these claims—believing neither that Mohammad was God's greatest prophet, nor that the Koran is God's word. Traditional Judaism, in turn, believes that God had no human offspring, is completely unified and not divisible into any notion of a trinity, and that Scripture closed and prophecy ended many hundreds of years before the birth of Mohammad. For obvious reasons, traditional Christianity and Islam, respectively, dispute such claims. And we have not even spoken of the far different beliefs of Buddhism, Hinduism, Zoroastrianism, and other non-Abrahamic religions.

Thus, even if one religion is the true word of God—but, for all we honestly know, perhaps none is—the greatest portion of humanity must be deeply mistaken; for no religion has more than a minority of humans as its adherents. I ask you, therefore: Would a just and merciful God want each of us to simply have blind faith in our own religion—even though, relying only upon faith, we would have no way to distinguish between the true and the false—thus condemning the majority to mistaken beliefs?

My brother, if there were but one ladder spanning the chasm between earth and heaven, and the unambiguous voice of God called out to us to climb the ladder, it might indeed be noble to have faith in God, to believe the ladder sound, and to begin climbing. Yet here we stand in the Great Silence; not one word have you or I heard from what we could responsibly know to be God—yet oh, how many ladders have men set up on earth, stretching heavenward!

When observing these many ladders, how shall we know which, if any, are sound? It would be one thing to trust our weight to the rungs if we tested a ladder ourselves or were directed by one with reliable knowledge about the soundness of ladders. It is quite another thing to climb a ladder when only assured of its soundness by those who have no direct way of knowing—but have only been told so by others, who were told so by still others—while, regardless of which ladder we choose, a majority of people insist that it is dangerously unsound. Under these conditions, is it not reckless to begin the climb toward heaven, without further investigating the questionable ladder?

And do we not betray our children when we begin climbing, clutching these innocents to our bosoms, insisting that trust is noble and that trusting a ladder includes assuming that it is sound—without checking?

My brother, although clever[1] and perhaps emotionally satisfying, the argument that faith is its own foundation does not persuade. Truth and Dignity turn

---

[1] Thomas Henry Huxley, in his *Lectures and Essays*, speaking of having read a particular philosophical essay as a boy, says: "…I could not possibly have understood a great deal of it; nevertheless I devoured it with avidity, and it stamped upon my mind the strong

away in sadness when frightened Hope comes upon perilous terrain high in the existential hills, and flinging herself carelessly into the arms of willful Blindness—calls such recklessness noble.

75. Argument that we cannot know everything, and must therefore have faith.

And a monk, looking down and blushing, said in a soft voice: Our minds are finite, our senses dull and few, our experiences are brief and our lives fleeting. Humility, even honesty, teaches that we must acknowledge how little we can understand. Do we not, then, need faith, to teach us what our own impoverished powers of observation and reason cannot know?

And the sage said: My gentle brother, indeed, our minds are feeble, our hearts hungry, our vision blurry, and our field of view narrow. So little *can* we see; still less *do* we see. Ever must we walk with humility, for all else is pretense, fleeing self-discovery.

Yet does not this same humility teach caution to those who would rely on the frailties of the varied and conflicting faith traditions? Did not merely finite human minds—your parents and teachers and spiritual leaders—instruct you in religion, and hungry human hearts press upon you loyalty to their beliefs? And have not the poor-sighted urged you to don the blindfold, and have not the nearly deaf eagerly stopped up your ears? And, I ask you in all gentleness, have not your priests and religious scholars encouraged faith and submission so that you may rely upon the convictions of their questionable traditions—convictions grown desperate or tyrannical, ambiguous or sentimental—with the dawning knowledge of their own infirmity?

My brother, each person's mind, though far from omniscient, must, on such matters, be the final arbiter. If God spoke directly to you or me and verified with indisputable miracles that the communication we received was, indeed, from Him, we might justly believe we knew of God and His will. Instead, see how many rely upon not a responsible and clear knowledge of God, but upon one of the many fable-filled, unproven traditions, or upon any of the myriads of intuitions, feelings, beliefs, and ambiguous signs—merely choosing to believe that these are communications from God.

And if men who teach religion were not limited by their own mortal minds, or even had they all presented throughout history but a plausible and unified account, we might, perhaps, make a stronger argument that we can justly follow

---

conviction that, on even the most solemn and important of questions, men are apt to take cunning phrases for answers."

their guidance. But from Almighty God we have heard but silence[1] and from the many who claim to speak for Him we have heard a cacophonous tumult of confident contradictions. Thus, although we yearn to rely upon something more than our own dim powers of reason, the alternatives are even less valid.

My brother, far from teaching submission to human religions, Humility looks to you with gentle eyes and the kindest smile, beckoning you to join her, and her sister Courage, on the journey of truth—a journey upon which you must not be carried or led, but ever must walk on your own trembling legs.

76. Argument that if reason were enough to know God, we would not need faith

Then a religious young man said: Reason is not sufficient to know God. If it were, we would not need faith! Precisely because we cannot know for certain— therefore we need faith!

And the sage replied: My son, astonishing though this may sound to your earnest ears, perhaps we truly do *not* need faith. Yes, religions encourage, even demand, faith; but this is no argument that faith is necessary, or even consistent with truth. We should not be mystified as to why religions have long insisted upon faith: They correctly surmise that reason will be their ruin, and thus they teach faith beyond all reason.

My son, how would we respond if others demanded faith in the manner religion demands faith? Behold, in the chaotic and colorful bazaar a merchant shouts above the din: My wares are priceless! Yes, it may seem that I offer inferior merchandise at a high price, but that is because you have made the mistake of trusting your own eyes and ears and have been seduced by the devil's whore of reason! Instead, you must have faith that the quality of my wares is high and that my prices are low. Faith is better than reason, and if reason were enough to buy my wares, you would not need faith![2]

Would we find such words at all persuasive? Yet how demeaning it is that numberless multitudes, who would not buy sandals on such a transparent swindle, eagerly kneel in submission to religious guidance both on life's daily details and on meanings deepest, even pin their fervent hopes for eternity on such baseless premises! How heartbreaking the ten thousand crimson rivers flowing with sincere martyrs' blood, and how maddening the hundred thousand

---

[1] As to those who think they have directly heard the voice of God, they must acknowledge, if they study the many natural phenomena that might explain such experiences, that they do not know it to have been the voice of God. See section 78 for elaboration.

[2] If faith is allowed to determine what we believe, anything is equally believable or unbelievable—as a charming saying of old has it: "When all candles be out, all cats be grey."

frenzied mobs of all religious ages and climes, who proudly slaughtered their neighbors in the glittering conscience of religious zeal, relying with confidence on such sacred double-talk! But worst of all are the uncounted myriads of religious flocks in every peaceful town and every sleepy village, where even in days of happy tranquility every man and woman suffers a withered soul from being too-long denied the waters of authenticity, and every child's spirit is blindfolded and bound, lest it happen upon the sad and beautiful truth.

So it is that in youth our hearts often become bonded to ideas and beliefs that are untrue, unhealthy, and unworthy of preserving. To mend the error of elevating faith above reason may bring agony—but it is heroic, too, and, in time, deeply healing. For one only becomes worthy of the glorious mantle of heroism by encountering danger or suffering, and responding with nobility and courage. Now, my son, in these days of fearful reflection, I urge you to reclaim your dignity and to behold the wonderful, terrifying, universe as it is—or as best we can honestly know it—your soul free of the shackles of dogma, and released from the bit and bridle of spiritual subjugation.

But I understand well that it is no simple task to shrug off this bliss-burden of belief. Faith is a word we have heard so often spoken intensely—with love, tears, anger, longing, devotion, even intimidation. And our parents and elders, sages and communal leaders, sacred Scripture and imposing theology, have all given faith their weighty approbations. Under the staggering influence of all these, is it any wonder that we shy away from challenging faith?

My blessing to you, my son: May you ponder without fear, and question without scripted conclusion, that the binding cloak of faith may at last fall away from the frail shoulders of your sheltered soul, and that your spirit's cold and cloistered skin may at last warm to the kisses of the springtime sun.

77. Argument that God is testing us, to see whether we will persevere in faith, even when plagued by doubt

Then a religious man with intense eyes said in a loud voice: Doubt is a test from God, to see how loyal is our faith in Him. My teachers have cautioned me many times not to be led astray by heretics. And I will maintain my faith, even though plagued by doubt and surrounded by unbelievers like you!

And the sage responded: My brother, indeed, it can seem noble, even heroic, to hold fast to faith and reject reason when one believes God views reason as a wicked temptress whose tawdry wiles we have been warned to resist.

Truly, if God spoke unmistakably in our ears, and told us the Bible was His word, and if God performed repeated and unambiguous wonders before our very eyes, and the eyes of all, to verify that it was His voice we heard—and not merely the product of our hopes, fears, ambitions, intuitions, education, expectations, hallucinations, or the many other imposters that have ever misled men into thinking they had heard from God—we might be justified to persist in faith, though burdened with doubts and confronted by doubters. Even when it seemed God was powerless or had abandoned us to a rudderless universe, we could still choose to have faith in Him—to trust that He is what He told us He is, and that He has spoken only truth. For this would be faith founded upon direct knowledge that God exists and that He told us about Himself and His wishes.

Religion, however, asks of us something very different: Most of her variations demand that we believe in a God that she does not claim we ourselves know, whose voice she does not say our own ears have heard, and whose signs and miracles she does not suggest our own eyes have ever beheld.

Yet religion wants us to testify falsely that we *know* God spoke His wishes to mankind hundreds, even thousands of years ago, and that of the many contradictory claims of divine communication and inspiration, we *know* that the tradition of our fathers is the correct one. My brother, not only do we pretend to know of a God, we compound this self-deception by amassing numerous detailed dogmas on the nature of God, on what He wants of us while we walk this earth, and on what He does with our souls when we are gathered unto death.

Such willful self-deception, which some are pleased to call faith, is neither faithful to God nor faithful to ourselves. Instead, it betrays any God there may be by accepting on poor evidence all manner of rumors about Him—and some of these rumors are dreadful. Such so-called-faith is traitorous, too, to our inmost soul who, neither distracted by crowd nor creed, is never fooled by our studied avoidance of these challenging matters, and keenly suffers the self-inflicted wounds of an inner life frightened and false.

And what kind of God would test us by demanding that we be dishonest with our innocent children and thereby so terribly deface both their souls and our own? Would not a good God love honesty and courage, and love deeply those who pursued these virtues? Would He not prefer that we acknowledge what we know and what we do not know, especially on life's most important matters?

Indeed, if there is a God and He tests humans, perhaps He looks at us tenderly even now longing for us to walk heroically in simple honesty, beset though we are by the heart's hunger for sacred conviction, burdened though we may be by the unceasing indoctrinations of clergy, and hounded though we often are by the crude and subtle coercions of conformist tribe.

78. Argument that "God speaks to me, so my faith is not unreasonable."

But another religious man said: Why do you say that religions ask us to believe in a God we have not experienced? My denomination teaches that God speaks to each of us as individuals. And God does speak to me regularly. When I pray, God responds by providing me with answers and with convictions about what I need to do. My faith in God, then, is not unreasonable, because I am believing in what I have directly experienced.

And the sage said: My brother, would that God responded to all our prayers, and spoke clearly to all our hearts. This teaching of your denomination, that even today God speaks directly to us as individuals—this, too, demands a great deal of faith strongly in conflict with reason. With but a little study of human nature we can identify many alternative—natural and earthbound—explanations for the subjective impression some have of receiving communication from God.

And not surprisingly, even your religious group, and others like it, does not believe that subjective impressions or feelings are sufficient to confirm it is God speaking; for if the message we hear is inconsistent with what your religion teaches, your church would have us conclude that it could not have been a communication from God—indeed, that it may have been of the devil.

If so, even when what seem to be divine communications *are* consistent with your religion's teachings, how can we be confident that they come from God? Is it not more likely that they have their origin in something more humble and close at hand, such as the internalized lessons of parents and teachers; our own best thoughts and intuitions galvanized by the conviction that God is the source of these messages; the eager receptivity on the part of members of a social species to experiences of interaction; the desire to believe we are sufficiently special for God to take an interest in us; the hopes for heaven and fears of hell—and a myriad of other obvious and less obvious considerations?

And so, if we were to exercise radical honesty must we not concede that we have no responsible basis for believing that our ears, or even the ears of our hearts, have heard the voice of God? And must we not also concede that we cannot responsibly insist that our leaders or teachers, parents or friends, or anyone we know, or even our distant ancestors, have ever heard the voice of God, or that their eyes have ever seen His glory?

79. Argument that even non-believers live by faith, and therefore we should have faith in God

And a baker-woman said: All people must have faith, and must at times trust what they do not prove. Even the non-believer has faith that when she bakes her dough in the oven today it will turn into bread as it has for all of human memory—and that when she eats her bread today it will satisfy her hunger as it did yesterday. Yet this cannot be proved in advance. Just so, I have faith in God.

And a farmer added: And all have faith that heavy rains will not fall out of blue skies, nor snow out of summer's sun—but this cannot be known with certainty in advance. For although experience has not shown this to occur, perhaps in the future it *will* occur.

And a frail, sickly man leaned on his cane and said in a hoarse voice: Yes, even the non-believer has faith in what doctors tell him and what experts teach, though he does not know with surety that they are correct.

And the sick man's wife hushed him, saying: Rest your voice; you must save your energy. And turning to the sage she said: My husband is right. Consider that even you, in using words to speak to us, have faith that words still mean today what they meant yesterday, and that we will understand your words. We need not—we cannot—prove everything. We all must have faith in so many ways in our daily lives. Surely, then, we may also have faith in God!

And the sage replied: My brothers and sisters, indeed, we all trust in things we have not proved. Thus, I can see why your argument may at first seem persuasive. Yet let us consider the matter more closely that we may know whether religious faith is truly comparable to the many ways we must daily rely on less than certain knowledge.

To trust that dough will transform to bread in the oven's heat, that this bread will satiate a gnawing belly, that rain will not deluge us from clear skies nor snow descend and cushion the earth in summer's heat, and to expect that words will continue to hold their meaning from one day to the next—these rely on our direct and repeated experience. Thus, such trust or faith is reasonable and responsible. Trusting in physicians and experts, too, is reasonable; for it rests upon the solid foundation of society's experience that its best information on earthly matters is usually in the hands of those recognized as knowledgeable.

Moreover, trusting our experience or our experts does not insist beyond the reach of reason that they must be correct; indeed, most of us understand that experts are often incorrect. Our trust in the counsel of the knowledgeable and our expectation that the repeated lessons of the past continue to apply today rely upon only the reasonable judgment that these are likely to be correct. We do not say: The physician is infallible and is certainly correct. We say: The physician knows much and is probably correct. This differs greatly from the absolute faith demanded by most forms of traditional religion.

And, significantly, all these examples that have been cited involve people trusting knowledge about which there exists no substantive evidence or argument to the contrary. We have not known dough to remain raw after baking long in the oven's high heat, nor seen bread fail to satiate healthy hunger; we have not seen blue skies bring forth floods, nor snows accumulating in summer's heat—neither does any sane and serious opinion suggest that these things are to be expected. Similarly, there is no reasonable argument stating that those with less knowledge generally give as good guidance as those with more knowledge.

This is very different from the faith demanded by most religion, which insists that we believe with certainty what our own experience, even the experience of all humans alive today, has not responsibly taught us, and what is vigorously disputed by most of the earth's population—for each religion is rejected by a majority of humanity. Yet priests, ministers, pastors, rabbis, imams, and religious leaders of all kinds enjoin us to believe, with certainty, propositions about God's existence, about God's will, about miracles performed in the past, about the metaphysics of spiritual realms, and about that which they say follows death. With none of these does any one of us have indisputable direct experience. Nor can we justifiably pretend to be unaware of the multiplicity of divergent, often incompatible accounts of different faith traditions. In which religious claims, then, shall we have faith—and why? Moreover, there are life views that make no religious claims. It would be irresponsible, then, to accept any religious tradition without subjecting it to vigorous, honest scrutiny.

Moreover, in light of the many ways humans are comforted or otherwise gratified by religion—even as we are frightened and controlled by her, too—and in light of the many ways religious belief seems to stem from natural human instincts,[1] we have sufficient cause to doubt the supernatural claims of all religion. Is it noble, then, to trust any faith without careful investigation?

And remember that religious faith is not anything so noble as trusting God. Most of us concede that God has not revealed Himself directly to us—in this lifetime—or asked us to remain faithful to Him. Instead, in abiding by religious faith we choose to trust certain opinions and teachings of *people*—on the subject of God. And even the small minority who believe God has spoken directly to them, must they not concede that there exist many other possible explanations for this subjective perception of divine communication, explanations that involve nothing supernatural, and that they have chosen to believe one explanation over the others—the one taught to them by the *people* of their religion, or perhaps by their own *human* imagination? Religious faith is, at bottom, faith in people and their stories and theories and interpretations, not faith in God.

Faith is trust. There is responsible trust and irresponsible trust. In the arena of religious belief, nearly all faith is irresponsible trust—because it has us shirk responsibility on our deepest beliefs and the meaning of existence; and it has us accept without sufficient scrutiny questionable, disputed traditions.

Brothers and sisters, it is valid to have faith that what we have experienced repeatedly to be true or proved logically to be true, remains true, unless we have good cause to believe that the facts have changed, or that our thinking or

---

[1] For more discussion on how religion stems from, and is perpetuated by, natural human inclinations, see sections 15 and 67.

perception was in error. It is also justifiable to rely upon the likelihood that an expert is correct—if we have no good reason to suspect that he is mistaken. It is not legitimate, however, to have absolute faith that something we have never reliably proven nor can responsibly believe we have experienced, is in fact true— especially when contradictory claims abound, as do numerous reasons for intelligent doubt. Nor is it legitimate to rely upon religious leaders, the supposed experts on matters of God and the spirit. For not only do such supposed experts contradict each other at every turn, the very type of knowledge they claim to hold is deeply suspect. They claim to know of supernatural beings in a different realm, and of supernatural acts in a long-gone age. In short, reasonable confidence on matters we can know is quite different from unreasonable certainty on matters we cannot know—matters that lie beyond any mortal's legitimate ken.

80. Argument that it takes more faith to deny God than to believe in God

And a religious man grew irritated with the sage and said: You criticize us for having faith, but it requires more faith to ignore the evidence for God than it does to believe in Him. Look around you at this grand and complex universe. How did it get here if not by God? You are employing faith, too; and I only wish my faith in God was always as strong as your faith *against* God!

And the sage replied: My brother, it is true that some are as dishonest in their certainty that there is no God, as others are in their certainty that there *is* a God and that they know what He wants of us.

Yet unlike those with closed minds, let us today examine the evidence, and think carefully about what it teaches, and what it does not teach; such honesty is far from faith against God. The windows in the searching spirit's abode are not—in arrogance or fear—shuttered against unfamiliar views, but are rather thrown open and vulnerable to the glorious light of reason and the refreshing winds of change. Let us peer out these windows with the wise naiveté of curious eyes, and with the eager innocence of a heart for learning. Faith, for or against, has no place in the house of truth.

And if, upon beholding nature, you are persuaded that a Creator must have fashioned the universe, I agree that such is one possible conclusion—but I would have you add that you do not know for certain it was so fashioned, and that there are other explanations for the existence of the universe, even if you think them unlikely to be true. And add, too, that if a Creator is responsible for the universe, not only does the evidence point to a Creator rather different from the omniscient, all-merciful deity of our religions, we are also then baffled as to how the Creator came to be.

Yet, my brother, even if we were to ignore other possibilities and assume there was a Creator—and even if we were to ignore the obvious problem of explaining how a Creator, even more complex or impressive than the universe, came to be—what can we truly know of this Creator, and of how He might wish us to live? No religion in particular is proved, nor is religion in general proved; for perhaps the Creator weaved the universe from silken strands of void, and fashioned mankind in all our subtle complexity, but never spoke to us or directed us to live by any particular statutes. Consider that even those who believe God commanded humans on how to live do not believe that God spoke to wolves or honeybees or other creatures on how *they* should live. Have the beasts of the forests, the deserts, the mountains, the plains, the waters, and the air, been given Bibles, Korans, or other sacred scriptures? Have apostles or prophets been sent to enlighten our fellow inhabitants of the earth who crawl and fly and gallop and swim? Yet we see it as quite natural that these species live guided only by their innate natures and the conditions of their environments. Why must we insist that man is different and has received special instruction from God?[1] And as no religion has compelling evidence to prove its tradition of divine communication, we are left with sincere doubt as to what if anything a Creator wishes of us. All this, even if we knew for certain there was a Creator, which we do not.

My brother, humbling and confusing though it may be, would not Honesty say: I think there may have been a Creator, but I do not know; and if there was a Creator I do not know how He might have come into existence or whether He still exists and observes the lives of men, and, if He does, what, if anything, He may want of me?

81. Argument that "We have faith in ourselves, why should we not have faith in God?"

And a merchant said: When I started my business I did not know for certain that it would succeed, but I had faith that it would. I had faith in myself. Why should I not have faith in God?

And the sage said: My brother, it is a matter of honesty. If you were honest at the beginning of your business you did not insist you knew for certain it would succeed. Rather, based on your knowledge and experience, you thought it likely that it would. And if you did claim to know with certainty that your business would succeed, that was less than honest—but was, in any case, different from religion, in that the outcome of your business was within your power to strongly influence. The faith you had in yourself was hope and confidence, with energy

---

[1] As to the argument that a Creator would not create a species as intelligent as humans and then fail to give them direction on how to live, see section 96.

and effort for its hands and feet. By contrast, we hold no sway over whether there is a God and, if there is, over what He might have revealed to humans.

Yet for most of its centuries and in most of its variations religious faith has demanded that we lie to ourselves and insist that we know what we do not know. It has not asked us to believe that *probably* there is a God. It has insisted we proclaim with conviction that *certainly* there is a God, and that we know when, and how, and to whom, He revealed Himself, and just how He wants us to live, and that our particular religion is accurate, and other religions are mistaken. Yet, in truth, we know none of this.

And, again, my brother, having religious faith is not anything so noble as trusting God. God has not revealed Himself to any of us and asked that we remain faithful to Him—in any language or message we can responsibly consider reliable. Instead, people have taught us what to believe, and how to interpret, based on what other people have said God wishes, based on what still others have taught about events that were said to have occurred many, many years ago, in days obscured by the opaque mists of ancient history, which no mortal eye can pierce but every mortal imagination can embellish. Or else we have experienced that which we think, but have no responsible way to know, are messages from God. Religious faith, then, is not sincerely following God, but choosing to trust opinions and teachings of *humans*—perhaps including ourselves—on the *topic* of God. And opinions and teachings of humans should not be considered sacred and beyond scrutiny.

And so, my brother—to return to your question—religious faith is not to be compared with trusting in your own future success as a merchant. Let us not confuse *confidence* in an outcome we *can* influence, with *certainty* on that about which we have *no* direct knowledge, and not even the faintest shadow of an influence.

82. Argument that doubt is appropriate only before making a decision about religion, but not once a decision has been made

Then a man shook his head impatiently and said: All this doubting and questioning is appropriate before making a decision about religion. But since I have already made a decision I must ignore all doubts and press forward.

And the sage replied: My brother, I understand how uncomfortable it may feel, and how inefficient it may seem, to continue questioning one's views after having made a decision. Yet I ask you, on these most important of issues, what other course is truthful and wise?

Remember, one's decision does not actually settle what is true; it only means that one has stopped thinking carefully on the matter. What is true is true, and what is false is false, regardless of whether, when, or what, one decides. A conclusion neither changes nor determines reality, and if we feel certain of our decision, our certainty is but a subjective feeling. Numberless confident decisions are made in error, every day, in every arena of life. Thus, knowing that our decisions are often unsound, perhaps we might exert the humility and courage to reconsider.

My brother, to walk in authenticity we must be open to correcting our course, even after choosing a path. This is especially true for matters deeply meaningful, on which it is all the more important that we strive for accuracy. It is also especially true on matters controversial, when arguments against our chosen path are easily accessible—for then we have less justification in persisting willfully along our habitual tracks. Matters of religion and life's meaning, being both deeply meaningful and controversial, call for careful and ongoing examination. Traveling swiftly and confidently is well and good, my brother, but should we not also pay heed that we are moving in the right direction?

83. Argument that faith is a blessing only some are given

Then a devout man smiled and said: Faith is a blessing bestowed by grace upon some and not upon others. Those who have faith know they have been given a blessing and can only feel sorry for those who have not received this gift. I pity you, because your heart is hardened in rebellion against the Lord, and you have not been given the grace of faith.

And the sage said: My brother, perhaps you are right. But how does one distinguish between this form of divine gift and ten thousand forms of pleasant self-deception? And if faith is a gift from heaven, how can you protest against those who have faith in gods other than your own, or our ancestors who professed faith in the sun, the moon, or paganism's and witchcraft's many objects of worship and spell? Can they not also claim their faith to be a gift from heaven bestowed only upon some—and that this is why you do not share their faith?

And if faith is a gift that cannot be explained to those who have not received it, is it not pointless to teach faith, or to ask anyone to have faith? Yet do not so many of the religious do these things—to their children, even to strangers—in the attempt to save souls?

Moreover, if one insists that faith has been sent from some supernatural source—a premise I believe mistaken—cannot one as easily argue that not only is faith not a gift from God, but that it is an insidious temptation crafted by the devil? Might it not be the darkest objective of evil that mankind, thinking it is being noble, voluntarily revoke its greatest gift—the careful thinking mind—surrender to intellectual bondage and slavish obedience, and stoop to groveling before dogma, doctrine, and priest?

Consider, too, my brother, that the desperate fear cast by dawning awareness upon the deeply mistaken can sometimes assume the guise of condescending compassion, that claims it need not persuade or even engage in searching discourse with the object of its pity. It is not for me to tell you whether your pity is noble sympathy or terrified rigidity—or even the offspring of mere indolence and pride. It is rather for each of us, when we feel ourselves pitying another and disregarding his arguments, to look deep into our own hearts, in the privacy of conscience and in the fullness of time, and to pass judgment upon ourselves.

And remember, my brother: In erecting even the most ornate and beautiful barriers against others' arguments we deprive ourselves deepest. For the same gilded walls and watchtowers that lock out unpleasant objections, imprison the minds of their complacent masters in stale-aired smallness. And is not prison a curse, and freedom a blessing, even if one names one's dungeon Salvation and labels liberty the Mother of All Abominations?

84. Argument that faith is a different form of knowledge than is scientific reason, that it comes from a time before there were widespread notions of scientific evidence, and that asking faith to be rational confuses two categories of knowledge

And a religious philosopher said: Traditional religious faith does not require evidence, at least not the evidence of direct experience or careful reasoning. Traditional religions were founded at a time before such notions of scientific evidence were widely known. Instead, traditional religions base themselves upon faith in sacred stories or writings. Traditional religions make no scientific claims, but rather point to their foundational documents and the word of God as the basis for their knowledge. Therefore, it is a mistake, a confusion of categories, to apply the standards of science to religion. They are two different systems of knowledge.

And the sage said: My brother, I agree that, historically speaking, and for purposes of tracking the development of ideas, it is relevant to note that religions were founded at a time when the scientific method, and the standard of strict reason, was not yet widely accepted. It is an entirely different matter, however, to suggest, therefore, that whatever ideas or claims originated back then should be seen as justifiable even if they do not stand up to reason or experience. That would be akin to saying that because knowledge of preventing infection did not exist in ancient medicine, it would be acceptable for a physician today to follow ancient medical practices, and perform surgery with unsanitary implements. Would you subject your body or the body of a loved one to such treatment, merely because this old method was originated at a time when scientific knowledge of infections was unavailable?

Reality is reality. If previous ages did not yet develop an effective and reliable way of understanding truth—and, my brother, truth is another word for reality[1]—then their ancient conclusions are to be reviewed with great skepticism, certainly not accorded equal credibility to conclusions based upon superior knowledge, the accumulated reason and experience of more advanced ages.

Another illustration: If many in the ancient world believed our planet Earth to be flat, but now we know it to be spherical—shall we say that we cannot challenge their assertion that Earth is flat because, after all, that belief was originated in a day before scientific proof was available? Certainly we do not avoid correcting their error—even if we do so respectfully—because their assertion was a statement about objective reality, and reality does not conform itself to the limitations of anyone's knowledge. It is well to hail the ancients for remarkable achievements considering the limited knowledge and tools at their disposal. But what is most important in our attempt to find truth is whether their conclusions were accurate. And of those who believed Earth was flat, we must say simply this: They were mistaken.

It is only intelligent and responsible to take a similar approach when examining the claims of religion. When a story is told as historical fact, a claim is being made about reality. When the Hebrew Bible states that God revealed himself to Abraham and Isaac and Jacob and Moses and Joshua and Samuel and many others; and when it states that God performed numerous astonishing miracles and wonders for the ancient Israelites; and when the New Testament states that Jesus performed various wonders and was raised from the dead, and upon the veracity of such accounts the Scriptures stake their laws and teachings—including their demands for faith—these Scriptures and traditions are making assertions about what are the facts. They are saying that these events truly occurred, in the real world. Of course, the Bible does not use scientific or philosophical or mathematical words, or terms of formal logic. But all her miracle stories, and accounts of God revealing Himself and legislating laws—or speaking His word through prophets or apostles—are founded on the basic premise that these stories actually took place, in ways that were observed by the eyes and ears of those who, we are told, witnessed or experienced the events.

And, yes, in later generations—after challenges from science and philosophy—creative religious scholars toyed with the meaning of verses to turn nearly every plain statement of the Bible into a metaphor or symbolic message. But the major streams of traditional religion have always seen the plain text of biblical stories as literally true—even if these passages were said to contain additional

---

[1] For discussion on the meaning of the word "truth," see section 3, and Part I of the book, overall.

layers of meaning. And cannot any imaginative mind turn any plain statement in any book into mere metaphor and homily?

In short, my brother, knowledge is knowledge. What is true is true. There may be different ways we can try to determine what is true, but these different means of acquiring knowledge cannot claim immunity from challenge by each other. Either miracles occurred as the Bible recounts, or they did not. Either God commanded what the Bible says He did—or He did not.

Religion does not speak to us only about a different world, where the laws of reality may be different; she speaks to us about our world, too, and makes claims upon us and our children, upon our best energies and most earnest tears. There is, therefore, no good reason to grant her exemption from persuading us that her stories and teachings are accurate.

One common form of dishonesty is pretending to know what one does not, in fact, know. Religion clothes this form of dishonesty in priestly robes, introduces it with solemn chants, calls it faith, and asks us not only to tolerate it, but to venerate it above all else we know to be honesty and truth.

My brother: If in light of our better understanding of the many ways humans have been gullible and mistaken; if in light of our growing comprehension of the social and subconscious forces shaping religious belief; if in light of our greater awareness of the sweep of history and the variations of culture and religion—if in light of all these advances, and more, we find ourselves in a far better position to question the religious traditions of yesteryear and their notions of our beginning and end, is it not our intellectual and moral responsibility to do so? Shall we seek pretexts and justifications to remain in a state of intellectual infancy, to relieve ourselves of the burden-blessings of the tree of knowledge in order that we may continue to dwell in our small conceptions of Eden, or shall we not behold this tree's peerless fruit with delight, and eat our fill, savoring the acquired taste of autonomous vision, ever trying to distinguish between what is worth believing and what we have no responsible right to believe—and enduring with noble resolve whatever falls may come?

85. Argument that faith is not against reason or facts, it is above them

And the religious philosopher said: Be that as it may, you are making a simple error. You speak of faith as though it is against reason or facts. It is not. Instead, faith begins where facts end—and it shows us how to think about that for which we have no reason or facts. Indeed, it shows us a higher way to think.

Faith is not irrational—it is non-rational and supra-rational. Indeed, it is the path of reason that is sadly deficient, not the path of faith.[1]

And the sage said: My brother, even if I could agree that faith does not oppose reason, I would challenge you on your belief that religious faith is a valid way of thinking or knowing.

But does faith not oppose reason? Has faith not demanded of our ancestors and us supernatural beliefs that savage reason? For when skeptical men of science are present to act as witnesses, have we ever known nature's laws to be broken even in small ways—much less in the manner of the Nile turning to blood or the splitting of the sea or the sun being stopped or a man walking on water or rising from the dead?

Yet even if faith did not oppose reason, but only spoke of things about which reason had nothing to say, would this make faith responsible? Deciding to accept as true that which we have insufficient basis to take as true—and which, instead, we should be honest enough to concede is mere speculation or theological imagination or rumor or ancient and not quite reliable tradition—this decision does not reflect a noble or higher way, above fact and reason, but rather reflects a hasty and pitiable way if entered into oneself and, especially when imposed upon the ignorant and the young, a downright ignoble and lower way, far beneath fact and reason and their honest though bracing standards.

86. Argument that scientific knowledge is based on faith, too—and that the sage's faith is logic

But the religious philosopher persisted, and said: Scientists often claim that their evidence and logic are true sources of knowledge whereas knowledge based on faith is false. However, the claim that scientific evidence and logic are truthful is ultimately an assumption taken on faith just as all assumptions are ultimately taken on faith. Therefore, scientists also have a faith, and it is called Logic. And you seem to bow down to the God of Logic, too![2]

---

[1] Whether by conscious professions of "faith" or by imperviousness to reason, the many fervent, closed-minded partisans of not only religion, but of political and secular ideological causes, too, illustrate every day the astute observation of Montaigne: "Men are most apt to believe what they least understand" (and, at times, even the statement attributed to Tertullian, "I believe it just because it is unbelievable").

On the great issues orienting men to life, belief is rarely fathered by the virtuous means of sober-weighed evidence or careful thought; instead, much takes place in the dark of night and in the terrible shadow of the mob's stampede—and a rightful heir, should one be born, would have little resemblance to the numerous bastard progeny of fear and lust; we should not be surprised, then, that they, taking one look, reject him as illegitimate.

[2] Walter Kaufmann addresses this point in the prologue of his *Faith of a Heretic*, where, speaking about those who claim that everyone is irrational and that those who think they

And the sage said: My brother, although we can never completely rule out the possibility of error—no matter what the source of our knowledge—it is misguided to see as equally valid, logic and empirical evidence on the one hand, and faith, on the other. The critical distinction between responsible thinking and irresponsible thinking lies in how much honest effort one has expended in getting at the truth, at the reality of the matter. It is mistaken, though usually well-intentioned, to equate a person trying as hard as he can to get at the truth—carefully using the most effective methods available—with someone choosing not to think critically to the end of things but, instead, sooner or later in his arguments taking refuge in something he calls faith.

My brother, to say that believing in scientific knowledge or logic requires faith is to stretch the meaning of the word faith considerably. Let us avoid the mistake of all-or-nothing thinking. Of course, any scientific knowledge, or any apparently logical thought, may ultimately be discovered to be false, and something believed by faith may ultimately turn out to be proved true. There is a great deal of difference, though, in how responsible are such different means of acquiring what we hold as knowledge. Scientific knowledge is based on what humans have reliably observed or experienced or witnessed with our own eyes and ears, bolstered by what our best efforts at reasoning and challenge and ongoing experience have confirmed to be true. And logic is our best attempt to use reliable, repeatedly tested rules for thinking effectively about reality. These are standards of knowledge far different from those of religious faith. Traditional religion asks us to accept as true that which we have not reliably observed or experienced, that which we are not free to truly challenge with new or outside evidence, and that which we are strongly discouraged from exposing to even the compelling questions of innate reason.[1]

Indeed, faith is usually what others—who themselves are relying on others, who in turn were relying on still others, in a chain stretching back deep into the dark ages of ignorance and superstition—are said to have said is true. And no matter how impressive a veneer we raise around faith's house of twigs—with the imposing brick of learned or clever rationalizations and the artistic filigree of evocative apologetics—her flimsy underlying structure remains unsound as ever.

---

are being rational are merely shallow, he says that such an appeal to modesty is popular because it is compatible with lazy thinking, and far easier than being deeply honest.

[1] Eric Hoffer in *The True Believer*, section 56, writes: "…how much unbelief is necessary to make belief possible." And he credits Bergson with the insight that faith's power "manifests itself not in moving mountains but in not seeing mountains to move."

And the winds of truth never cease; and they are never turned aside by mere facades; and woe to the soul who inhabits such a house on the day it falls.

My brother, if I run with eyes closed, it is yet possible that I might reach my destination safely; and if I run with eyes open I might, nevertheless, fall and break my bones. But does this mean that it is all the same whether I run with eyes open or closed? And does running with eyes tightly shut seem any wiser if I point out that were I to run with open eyes, and believe what my eyes were telling me, I would still be relying on vision—which is, after all, just another form of faith; and that, therefore, keeping my eyes closed and having faith that everything will be fine is just as responsible? Would you willingly have me carry your fragile crystal as I run without seeing? And can you imagine using this argument—that all knowledge is only faith, therefore all sources of information are equally valid—in any important arena of life other than religion? Would you allow a physician to operate on you with knowledge gained by that premise? Would you have your adviser give you business counsel on that approach? Would you want a builder to plan the foundation and pillars of your home with design principles gathered by a method that assumes all thoughts to be equally true? Would you consent even to your young child's school lessons being formulated with information indiscriminately collected?

And again, it is not a matter of absolutes. No respectable scientist claims that knowledge based on faith is automatically false, or that knowledge based on scientific evidence is automatically true. Instead, the widespread view among men and women of science is that something known by faith *may* turn out to be true, but that we should not count on it being true—because faith is not a reliable way of coming to knowledge. Conversely, those things which we know by the evidence of our senses, or our persistent attempts at reason, are not automatically true, but these are the best methods we have of gathering knowledge, and therefore—subject to our continued openness to new evidence and argument—relying upon such knowledge is responsible and advisable.

And, my brother, even religions asking us to rely upon faith build their faith upon something other than faith. Thus, it would be more accurate to say that faith attempts to base itself on logic and knowledge of the senses—than it would be to say that logic and knowledge of the senses base themselves on faith.

Consider this: If I were to proclaim, Have faith that I am your Great God, and follow My commandments, to do diligently whatsoever I shall instruct you, religions would warn you not to have faith in me. But why? Is not faith enough by itself? No, my brother, it is not, and even religions do not argue that it is. Instead, religions make claims based upon logic and experience, to establish with credibility their demands for faith. They say: God revealed himself at Mount Sinai and commanded our ancestors to live according to these laws; therefore have faith in God. Or, Jesus died on the cross and rose from the dead; therefore have faith in Jesus. Or, Mohammad was God's last and greatest prophet, and the Koran is God's word; therefore have faith in what Mohammad taught.

Religions, then, decidedly do not encourage all faith—only faith in their particular beliefs. How, then, shall we discern which faith, if any, is truly consistent with God's will? To answer this question religions must resort to arguments based on experience or logic in one form or another—or else concede that they have no good claim on your loyalties. Thus, we are back to the freedom and responsibility of judging for ourselves whether the basis upon which a faith rests—and all religions rest upon some basis of argument or claimed experience—is sufficiently credible to compel our belief, along with all the ramifications of such belief.

And yes, my brother, science makes its share of mistakes, and is sometimes peopled by those with various self-serving agendas and a distaste for painful honesty. And in many cases traditional knowledge is accurate and helpful—such as selected ancient moral and psychological wisdom, or even some expertise in the healing arts. Yet there is a critical difference between the premises of traditional faith and the premises of reason and science. The approach of reason and science—even if not the practice of every individual scientist or logician—is to hold nothing beyond question and challenge. Thus it promotes an ever-refining knowledge of what is true. By contrast, faith-taught knowledge may at times be true, but religion does not in general tolerate—much less encourage—the challenging of its "authoritative" views. It is therefore far less likely to be accurate. This is a profound distinction between the worldviews of science and religion, and their systems of arriving at knowledge.

In summary, then: Supposed knowledge arrived at by faith makes many claims not only about spiritual dimensions, but about the physical, objective world in which we live—the same reality about which logic and scientific approaches have acquired much understanding. Faith, for example, demands that we believe various supernatural events occurred, at the hand of God or His emissaries, to real people in real places, here on earth. Faith is, therefore, not immune to the challenges and objections of what reason and experience have demonstrated to be true, and what they have repeatedly shown to be false.

My brother, many would find it comforting if the claims of religion could be absolved from the rigors of reason. Yet daylight will not be denied; we must, if we are to live with integrity, now or later shake off our slumber, kick aside the blankets, and encounter life on its own terms. For the morning sun intrudes upon even the most seductive of dreams, and its rays throw glaring light upon even what wishes to remain undisturbed, lost in kaleidoscopic visions of other realms, and forever cloaked in the blind obscurity of merciful night.

87. Argument that faith capable of being proved would not be faith; therefore it is not desirable to prove religious belief even if we could; and no logical argument should dissuade us from faith

And a religious woman said: I reject the very idea of trying to defend faith by logic. It is futile to do so. Faith cannot be proved by logical arguments; if it could, it would not be faith. The point of faith is to hold as true that which cannot be known by experience or logic. Even those religious people who use apologetics and reason to defend their faith are gravely mistaken, for they undermine the very point of faith. As for me, I maintain my faith as my heartfelt gift to God—and no logical argument will sway me.

And the sage replied: My sister, yours is a bold and creative argument. Let us examine the matter, however, and see whether it holds up to honest review. The first thing to note is that, ironically, you just used reason in the attempt to explain why faith should not be subject to reason. Even you, then, would concede that at least your argument—as to why we should not attempt to prove faith by logic or experience—should be subject to reason's lights.

And aside from your use of reason in arguing your position, it is clearly untenable for us to accept, without scrutiny, all claims for religious faith. For then we would have to subscribe to all religions at once—Christianity, Islam, Judaism, Buddhism, Hinduism, Jainism, Zoroastrianism, and many more, not to mention the many denominations within religions—and this would be self-contradictory, for these belief systems disagree with each other on foundational matters, and many of them insist that all other religions are mistaken or unnecessary.

Thus, one who believes in the legitimacy of faith also requires a responsible method for determining which faith God would have one choose.

Moreover, my sister, even if the concept of faith—as taught and explained by man's religions—requires one to believe without regard to reason or experience, this would not necessarily make such a requirement responsible, or pleasing to any God there may be. If I maintain that one should not be reckless because recklessness is irresponsible, it is no argument in defense of recklessness to point out that the very concept of recklessness entails being irresponsible; for we could all agree that recklessness entails irresponsibility, but still conclude that recklessness is unwise and ill advised.

The same is true about faith, even if the concept of faith—as taught by religions—requires one to abandon reason. For without reason not only would we not know which religion to follow—and to follow all would be self-contradictory and against various faiths—we would not even know if God approves of the whole notion of faith. For if we are truthful, must we not concede that *people* have taught us that God demands faith? Has God, then, told us directly—in any way we can responsibly know was really God's communication—that He wants

230

us to cling to faith, to believe things without the benefit of reason or experience? No, my sister, all talk of faith is transmitted to us by human traditions or intuitions. And might not these human sources be mistaken? And might not a possible God strongly disapprove of one who shirked the responsibility of thinking carefully about what He may truly want of us?

And so, my sister, how do you propose that we discern whether God truly wants us to have faith beyond reason—and if He does, which one of the many incompatible bundles of religious beliefs, which particular objects of faith, He would have us choose?

Furthermore, must it be that the only kind of faith of which we can conceive is faith beyond reason? Cannot faith be based upon solid knowledge? Consider this: If God revealed Himself unambiguously to all in our generation—foretelling and carrying out repeated and dramatic miracles that flouted the laws of nature— and told us to believe that He would provide us sustenance for the coming year, and that we should neither sow nor reap, but rather wait upon His salvation—we could then choose to have faith in that promised salvation, about which we could responsibly believe God told us, even though we would not know for certain that God would keep His promise. In such a case, the exercise of faith would consist in trusting God, though some of our mortal vigilance and skepticism would tempt us to lay up provisions for ourselves. But we would not have to trust with gross irresponsibility that the message to avoid doing so—to avoid sowing and reaping, and simply wait for God's salvation—came from God. For in the case described, we would have witnessed powerful and repeated evidence sufficient to responsibly establish that the message did, indeed, come from God.[1]

---

[1] Even in such a case—with dramatic and repeated apparently supernatural demonstrations—the message may not have come from what any particular religion considers God. Theoretically, the message, and the wonders, could have been the work of other advanced beings.

And this opens another interesting line of thought, leading to the question of whether beings immensely more powerful than us should be seen as worthy of worship—or whether in order to merit worship—if anything at all merits worship—superhuman power must be matched with lofty morality and good. The implications of this question are great even for traditional religion: Is it necessarily moral or right to follow God's wishes—even if we could responsibly believe we know what they are—or do we have a moral responsibility to weigh the commands of God against other standards of right and wrong? And as heretical as that question may sound, a straightforward reading of the Old Testament suggests that Abraham, in negotiating with God and attempting to persuade Him not to destroy Sodom and Gomorrah, and Moses, in persuading God not to destroy the Israelites after they worshiped the golden calf, grappled with the matter of maintaining an independent moral conscience even in the face of God's word and will (See Genesis 18 and Exodus 32).

Indeed, such reasonable faith was the biblical faith of Abraham in the story,[1] of God speaking to Abraham directly, promising him innumerable progeny— though he was childless and old—and Abraham believing God.[2] But had Abraham indiscriminately trusted what others told him God wanted him to believe, would he not have remained with the religion and gods of his clan, instead of breaking from tradition and believing in One God?

Thus, my sister, not all conceptions of faith are at war with logic and experience—not all require belief beyond responsible reason. But even if one believed that true faith *does* require a complete dismissal of reason, we would be lost if we did not at least use reason to choose between the many different faiths, and their truth-claims demanding our allegiance. I urge you, then, to investigate which if any religious tradition offers compelling reason to choose her faith.

Moreover, my sister, perhaps you might consider that fervent and sincere offerings are not necessarily pleasing if one misreads the desires of the gift's recipient. When a cat brings her master a dead mouse as daily tribute, he does not find the proffered feast appetizing—indeed, he is likely repelled. At best, he is touched by her intent, for the cat cannot know any better; and she brings at least a real and fresh corpse she has killed with her own honest effort. But can we be sure that a Cosmic Master would be pleased with our gifts of secondhand or unsubstantiated faith without us bothering to determine whether He finds this desirable—when we could have looked into the matter and perhaps known better? Though we might offer it up in fierce loyalty or tender and sacred love, what if God is repelled and offended by all this faith, and sees it as the willfully ignorant dragging in mere rumors and tales of the long-since dead?

88. Argument that faith is a leap

Then a man said: They call you a sage? I call you a simpleton! Even a child knows that faith is a leap. If we had logical reasons for faith it would not be a leap. We need not worry about finding justification for faith. God wants us to take the leap of faith for Him—and I am happy to do so.

And the sage turned, pointed to a distant mountain and said: My brother, would you climb that mountain and leap to the rocks below? No—because it would be reckless and jeopardize your life. Then why do you so quickly assent to taking this leap you call faith—a leap that might savage your soul? Of old you have been taught that faith is a leap—verily I say unto you today that leaping off

---

[1] By contrast, one may, of course, question whether the Bible's portrait of Abraham's willingness to slaughter his son Isaac—based on what he perceived to be the word of God, but which the Bible gives no indication he took any pains to verify—can be characterized as a reflection of reasonable and responsible faith.

[2] See Genesis chapter 15.

a mountain is a leap, too. Do you wish to take a leap with your integrity, your deepest beliefs, your very soul—and those of your little children—but not with your legs? My brother: Is only faith a leap? Is not a leap a leap, too?

And yes, some leaps are responsible, even noble and tender. Hardened eyes might well mist over upon witnessing the flowering of trust—a young girl hesitating at the edge of the water, then taking her first leap into outstretched arms, the arms of a father yearning to be believed in, a father longing to don for even a brief moment the mantle of the strong and loving hero.

Yet that little girl sees, waiting to catch her, a real father in the real water, with outstretched, real arms. She has every good reason to take the leap. By contrast, traditional religion tells us of a Father we have never seen; speaks to us of divine promises and assurances we have never heard Him utter; and insists that we leap into an existential abyss without looking, into what we are told are the eternal hands of this Father, outstretched to us, waiting in perfect love.

My brother, some leaps are wise and noble, and some are inadvisable, even dishonorable. Merely because many have called faith a leap does not mean it is a worthwhile enterprise. When religion claims that God wishes us to engage in such apparently risky conduct, the burden is hers to persuade us of this—and not by threats or emotional appeals or circular arguments or calls to obedience or obscure claims of mystery. Rather, by a straightforward explanation that withstands the challenges of reason. Would you ask anything less of one urging you to leap off yonder mountain of stone?

And if there is a God similar to the one religion describes—a God who holds the soul to be our most precious essence—would He not want us to be vigilant stewards, protecting our incomparable treasure from any danger of corruption or harm? And might He not be immeasurably saddened to see how many of us eagerly renounce our deepest integrity by naming recklessness Faith, and dressing irresponsibility in the guise of sacred loyalty? My brother, if there is a loving Creator, how shall we comfort the Father who longs for his children to be safe, and all around Him they blindly leap off hazardous cliffs into rumors of heavenly clouds and hearsay of salvation-bearing arms?

89. Argument that doubt is a necessary part of faith, because only in persisting in faith despite doubt do we prove the strength of our faith in God

And a man said: Doubt is normal. Indeed, it is a necessary part of faith. It is a poor faith indeed that has not been leavened by serious doubt.[1] Only when we

---

[1] Many intelligent religious thinkers have expressed this view. Thomas Merton, for one, is quoted as saying, "You cannot be a man of faith unless you know how to doubt..."

are attacked by doubt, yet persist in faith despite that doubt, do we demonstrate the strength of our faith. Therefore, doubt does not concern me—and it certainly will not cause me to relinquish my faith. To the contrary, I rejoice in the doubt because it enables me to hold fast to my faith in spite of questions and challenges, thus showing how unshakeable is my faith in God.

And the sage replied: My brother, if I should ask you to believe that I am God, and if I should further admit that you may have doubts—since I seem quite human—but if I point out that only in persisting in your faith in me despite your doubts would you be proving your loyalty and love for me as God, would this persuade you? No? And why not? Because when there is no good reason to believe something, one who chooses to believe it anyway is not more noble, more responsible, or more likely to be accurate in his belief, merely because he appeals to the notion of faith despite doubt; he is, rather, less noble, less responsible, and less likely to be accurate. The same applies to faith in religions' gods.

90. Argument that faith is like love, and does not need to be proved by reason

And a man said: Must you, or can you, prove by reason why you *should* love—or that you *do* love—your wife and children? Of course not! So, too, faith does not need to be proved; it is a form of love for God.[1]

And though I argue in this section against the position that any religious faith has already taken a satisfactory accounting of doubt, I think it obvious that for most believers this point is less than immediately relevant—because the great majority of those who claim to have religious faith are not aware of the best reasons to doubt their religion's teachings, nor educated in why such doubt may be the most honest and noble course. To be fair, let us note, too, that most people holding any strong belief—political, ideological, aesthetic, etc.—are insufficiently educated on their opponents' best arguments, and unlikely to honestly expose these favored positions to rigorous challenge.

[1] In his *Reason in Religion,* toward the end of Chapter VI, Santayana writes: "Matters of religion should never be matters of controversy. We neither argue with a lover about his taste, nor condemn him, if we are just, for knowing so human a passion. That he harbours it is no indication of a want of sanity on his part in other matters. But while we acquiesce in his experience, and are glad he has it, we need no arguments to dissuade us from sharing it. Each man may have his own loves, but the object in each case is different. And so it is, or should be, in religion. Before the rise of those strange and fraudulent Hebraic pretensions there was no question among men about the national, personal, and poetic character of religious allegiance. It could never have been a duty to adopt a religion not one's own any more than a language, a coinage, or a costume not current in one's own country. The idea that religion contains a literal, not a symbolic, representation of truth and life is simply an impossible idea. Whoever entertains it has not come within the region of profitable philosophising on that subject."

While Santayana's beautiful mind was, overall, a fount gushing with stimulating ideas and observations eloquently expressed, I cannot, of course, agree with all his points and positions. And the passage I have just quoted is one of those instances where I would venture to take issue with him. To me it seems that unlike religion, but like hunger and sleep, romantic love holds within its natural cycle its own inevitable cure, once the ends of this trick of nature are achieved. Possession of, and consistent exposure to, one's idealized beloved reliably transforms this fantasy of the perfect angel to the reality of the flawed mortal—even, at times, to the nightmare of the vile and diabolical. Religion, by contrast, in that it reaches for an ideal it can never achieve, for a lover it can never possess or truly know—thus a lover whose spell need never fade—does not carry its own cure, and constitutes therefore a more persistent seductress leading us off the wide and airy paths of truth, into the fetid caves of insular and contagious ignorance or the steep cliffs of dangerous fanaticism. And while love is an appetite that finds its satisfaction in a physical object or process, and thus its ambitions are bounded by the predictable abatements and limits born of satiety, religion, by contrast, as its objects are intangible, need not lead to satiety. We may here apply Eric Hoffer's insight that one can never have enough of what one does not truly need. And, beyond degrading the individual, the dangers to society of these insatiable quests have been many and bloody.

Moreover, again like food or sleep, in the normal course of events each man's different preferences for love can coexist with those of nearly every other man, because no man's satisfaction of these appetites need be threatened when another man satisfies such appetites by different means or objects—different foods, a different type of bed, or a different woman. By contrast, not only are religion's central claims about the objective reality we all share—how the world came to be, by what values and practices we must live, and what happens to us when we die—religion also represents her teachings and concerns as far more significant than mere earthly concerns, and worth not only living for but dying for. Religions' exclusive claims, when combined with her insistence that her dogmas dwarf all natural considerations, make for great danger to society. Thus wars and persecutions—not to mention coercive community programs for educating children and controlling adults—have often been launched because a man insisted that everyone worship his God, and rarely if ever because a man insisted that everyone love his woman. Love tends to be personal in its ambitions; religion, communal—even global.

For these reasons and more, I must protest when Santayana says that we should look upon the religion of a fellow citizen and "acquiesce in his experience," and certainly I cannot agree that we "are glad he has it." Instead, I believe that our families and friendships and communities and societies will be more authentic and noble when we engage each other in gentle compassion—but with deep honesty, too—on the great matters of existential meaning, and strive for the standards of integrity and truth. (Indeed, even in the private matter of love, those who care about a man should attempt to warn him if they believe they have compelling evidence that he is investing his affections in one who is not in his best interests, who does not love him—or who may not even exist.)

And that religions, for lo these millennia have been making universal claims about their gods, claims incompatible with the claims of other religions, is, in retrospect, as natural and predictable as it is tragic. The development of monotheism—a universal God, in contrast to merely national or personal deities—is not, as Santayana has it, a "strange and

And the sage replied: My brother, you raise an interesting idea. You say that faith is love, and thus need not be proved. Yet in comparing faith in God to our love for humans, consider this: In the case of our wives or children, we know—by the responsible means of direct sensory experience—that the objects of our love are real. We are not insisting, in the absence of evidence, that we have invisible wives and children. And because the existence of these humans is not in question, in loving them[1] we are not making an unsupported claim about objective reality. Instead, we experience emotions or passions about, or choose to be loyal or devoted to, beings demonstrably real. And on such matters, reason and logic are not definitive—people feel love when they feel love, and they are entitled to invest their energies and loyalties in anyone they choose. Again, loving someone is not making unsupported claims about objective reality; therefore we have no responsibility to justify our love by means of reason.

Faith in God, by contrast, is a different matter: There we are choosing to pretend—without responsible evidence—not only that we know He exists, but that we know who He is and what He wants. Thus, religious faith, unlike love, is

---

fraudulent pretension." As well say that the urge toward developing fewer and universal laws of science, instead of innumerable personal and local guesses and theories and formulas and magics and exceptions in the functioning of nature, was "strange and pretentious." Monotheism was a natural, and not at all strange, development in the human story. True, this development—like many others in every field of endeavor—first arose in one nation, and only later was emulated by many; and, true, unlike other religious systems, the exclusive nature of its claims often led to dangerous intolerance. But these are no reasons to consider the development of monotheism strange, any more than the development of nuclear weapons, though dangerous, and at first uncommon, was strange. Humans, at least those with ambitious minds, will seek to unify and generalize into ever greater and more over-arching principles, and to gather—for themselves and their gods—ever more power.

And Santayana is surely wrong, too, about there being "no question among men" in pre-monotheistic times that religion held only symbolic or poetic truth. Perhaps he makes the philosopher's generous error of mistaking his own easy rejection of notions of actual gods, for the maturity and insight of all. Yet the great majority of every ancient people likely saw their gods as real and alive—though perhaps limited, and ruling only one land—and the claims of their religions as more than merely symbolic or poetic. We may presume that most men have always been, as they are today, more sensory and practical and literal than conceptual or poetic. And the fact that each nation—including the Israelites—had poets and shrewd thinkers who saw beyond surface and convention, and transcended a literal and simplistic view of the gods, did not, we may be confident, make skeptical philosophers of—or engender "profitable philosophizing" in—most teachers and priests, much less the great bulk and crush of any bygone age's superstitious masses.

[1] This point holds true whether the love referred to is the bond between parent and child, the romantic infatuation of early mating, the more enlightened commitment to another's highest best interests—or other forms of human connection and loyalty.

not merely a matter of subjective feeling or a commitment to voluntary action; instead, it is a set of claims about objective reality. Faith, therefore, comes along with the responsibility to explain the legitimate basis for such a position.

My brother, this loving of something we do not even know to exist, we may call many things—grand and earnest fantasy; devotional, conjured intimacy; fervent flight of fevered imagination—but we cannot responsibly call it knowledge. And treating it as knowledge is a grievous error, because then one speaks without sufficient basis to humankind's deepest identity and ultimate destiny.

Indeed, if a human were to love another human in the way traditional religions have often demanded we have faith, it would be analogous to a woman today claiming that she loves the legendary King Arthur—who, she insists, is alive but invisible—that she talks to him daily, though he never talks back; that she dedicates her life to him and finds her deepest meaning in this relationship; and that she raises her children to love him, too, and to center their lives around him. In such a case, would you not think it incumbent upon her—if not for her own benefit, at least for the welfare and dignity of her children—to support, with reason or empirical evidence, this "faith" in King Arthur?

Mind you, this example sounds foolish, notwithstanding that in the case of King Arthur, though we are persuaded he is not alive today, and may even wonder whether he ever did live, at least we know that his kind—human kings—existed. We know that monarchy was a common form of government through many generations of well-recorded history—and there are no intelligent challenges to such accounts. But in the case of God, we have no responsible knowledge that the deity of any religion has ever existed.

My brother, many who have faith in religious teachings do, indeed, feel love for the gods they believe in. But the emotion of love can be generated whether or not the object of one's devotions and affections actually exists; the imagination is more than capable of providing an endless supply of beings to love. And when it comes to religious faith in gods, if you call it love, this love is predicated upon the claim that such gods exist. And this is a claim about objective reality—which is not up to each of us to choose, and is certainly not a matter of emotion. It is not their love we ask those of religious faith to prove, but rather their claims about reality—that the object of their love, the God of their religion, actually exists, and has commanded what they say He has commanded.

91. Argument that if faith were able to be proved it would be too easy, and boring

And a woman raised her voice and said: How boring it would be, and how easy, if we knew about God with certainty, and God did not have to be accepted on faith!

And the sage said: My sister, difficulty and excitement have little to do with truth. The simple proposition that two and two equals four may be boring and easy to prove—but it has the charming advantage of being accurate. Conversely, that a tooth fairy collects the baby teeth of children, or that Santa Claus flies upon a reindeer-drawn sleigh from the North Pole and comes down every chimney once a year to give presents to children—these are more exciting possibilities, and far from easy to prove; they are also burdened, however, by the inconvenient characteristic of being false.

And then there are truths that are exciting and challenging, and lies and superstitions that are unimaginative and boring. Truth may be exciting or boring in any particular case, but either way that is aside from the point when we seek to understand, and possibly realign, our deepest commitments. And today we speak about what we can believe is true—not about what provides the most drama.

Yet, my sister, I hasten to assure you that the quest for truth—the tense, risky, and unpredictable investigation into what we can believe to be true in the realm of our foundational beliefs—can be one of the more exciting adventures one might ever know. Indeed, most avoid this quest precisely because, at some level, it is anything but boring, and instead is recognized as a challenge too terrifying.

92. Argument that since reason cannot tell us whether there is a God, it is legitimate to rely on faith

And a man said: Why do you say that faith is against reason? Faith goes where reason cannot go. Since reason cannot tell us one way or another whether there is a God, faith is a legitimate choice.

And the sage said: My brother, I agree with you that reason cannot, with our current knowledge, tell us definitively whether there is a God or not. Yet this does not mean that it is honest to simply choose one of those positions and pretend to know it to be true.

My brother, faith, as the word is often used, is another word for lying—first and foremost to ourselves—about what we know and what we do not know, on the most important matters. Do you think that any God who respects honesty and courage would want us to lie to ourselves and to our children about what we know about Him—and about the most meaningful issues in our lives?

When Honesty does not know something, she says: I do not know. When Religion does not know something, she says: I *do* know, and all who disagree with me—even those who are merely skeptical as to whether my unsupported claims are true—are either deeply mistaken or evil, and are to be the objects of ridicule, rejection, even hatred or, at a minimum, condescending pity and prayer.

93. Argument that religious faith is beyond logic, like theatre and literature, and allows one to suspend disbelief

And a writer shook his head and said: You miss the point when you try to use logic to prove or disprove faith. Religious faith is beyond logic; like good fiction and good theatre, it allows one to suspend disbelief, and to experience a grand narrative and rich encounter with existence.

And the sage replied: My brother, you raise a subtle and provocative protest, and religion does have certain similarities to the arts. Yet let us examine the matter carefully.

Consider that even those who lose themselves in the enchantment of good literature or theatre remain aware that such voyages of the imagination are not to be confused with reality. Would an actor be the object of admiration—or of pity or scorn—if, going home after a performance, he banishes doubt and believes that he is not merely playing Julius Caesar, but truly *is* Julius Caesar? And would one who encouraged such delusion be offering a healthy influence? Does not theatre turn to tragedy or farce if the spectator walks home from the playhouse and believes that the events he witnessed on stage constituted not entertaining simulation, but contemporary real life? And does not fiction become horror if the reader turns the last page, closes the book, and truly cannot distinguish between the pretend literary scenario that recently seduced his imagination, and the unblinking reality to which he is forever wed? My brother, recognizing the difference between fantasy and reality is what separates art from madness.[1]

Let us not confuse the deadly serious with the artistic and whimsical. A murderer is not to be set free, even admired, simply because his actions have a certain similarity to the actor who plays a murderer on stage. Neither do we applaud heartily when a loved one takes her last gasping breath, merely because it is similar to a job well done by an actress portraying a dying woman. What is real is real, and what is fantasy is fantasy. To completely obscure the line between the two is the tragic distortion of the insane, the avoidant rationalization of the craven, the degrading manipulation of those seeking psychological tyranny—or

---

[1] This point—though flouted by a few apologists for religion, or even for secular escapism—is so basic that it will have been made by many. Years after writing the above passage I was browsing through a newly-acquired set of antique volumes of John Ruskin's works and, in his *Seven Lamps of Architecture*, found this: "For it might be at first thought that the whole kingdom of imagination was one of deception also. Not so: the action of the imagination is a voluntary summoning of the conceptions of things absent or impossible; and the pleasure and nobility of the imagination partly consist in its knowledge and contemplation of them as such, *i.e.* in the knowledge of their actual absence or impossibility at the moment of their apparent presence or reality. When the imagination deceives it becomes madness."

the second birth of naiveté—in the over-educated.[1] In short, I say in all gentleness: Equating fantasy with reality is the counsel of only the mad or the cowardly, the sinister or the sadly mistaken.

My brother, if religion merely asked of us to indulge our imaginations—as we do in literature and theatre—and encouraged us all the while to remain honest and aware that her teachings and beliefs are not to be confused with reality, I could find religion quite agreeable, and compatible with integrity and authenticity. But religion does not encourage us to see her beliefs as fiction. To the contrary, she insists that they constitute the most important aspects of reality.

Indeed, because religion says of herself that she is not merely fiction or theatre, not merely an imaginative and grand narrative allowing one to temporarily suspend disbelief—but rather insists that she and her dogmas and dictates are the most meaningful aspects of the real—religion is not only less than honest, not only less than responsible, not only less than morally courageous, but is also degrading to the human spirit, for she demands that we destroy the mind's deepest foundation: the sound awareness of what is real.

And, my brother, I know that your words were a well-intended effort to deflect unwelcome scrutiny from religion and her adherents. But is it not ironic that in your defense of her, you render religion a mere imaginative fiction? Not only might one have to search extensively to find religious people even in our day who agree with your eviscerating characterization of religion, but for much of her history religion would have hanged, burned, crucified, or drowned you for daring to suggest that her sacred beliefs were anything but the most real and literal truths. And although such capital penalties would make for better theatre, would constitute a more gripping narrative, and would provide the crowd a richer encounter with existence, are you not glad that we shall have none of that here today—glad that we restrain our appetites for intensity and imaginative drama, and subordinate these to a clear-eyed vigilance of the perilously real?

94. Argument that God's truth transcends earthly matters and therefore requires faith to be understood or accepted

Then a religious woman shook her head and said: You are trying to understand a higher truth—God's truth—with your inferior and earthly intelligence. It should be no surprise that you are not succeeding. Unlike earthly truths, God's truth requires faith and belief in order to be understood or accepted.

And the sage said: My sister, let us think about your words to see if they truly persuade. First, consider that most religions base their authority on accounts of

---

[1] Montaigne is credited with saying, "I prefer the company of peasants because they have not been educated sufficiently to reason incorrectly."

miraculous events taking place in the observable, earthly world—whether divine revelation at Sinai, Jesus rising from the dead, or God's incomparable word being spoken to Mohammad. And religions say that the witnesses of the day—using sound and unbiased judgment—concluded that these events were evidence of divine communication or will.

My sister: Religions teach that these witnesses depended upon their experience and reason to recognize the miracles and form their belief in God. For if they first believed in the new religion and in the miracles and only then interpreted the events as miraculous, their judgment and testimony would be questionable. Is it not fitting, then, that we, too, employ our experience and reason to examine the claims that such events indeed took place, and were miraculous? For these dramatic accounts either accurately reflect events as they occurred, or not. And if they do, these events either compellingly point to the conclusion claimed by religion, or they do not. And since the miraculous events a religion says occurred—and upon which it bases its claims of supernatural truth—are said to have taken place in the actual earthly world, why should our assessment of earthly reality require the aid of faith? Would you tell a child she could not see that two added to two equals four—unless she first believed it? And would you trust a merchant, who insisted that you must first have faith in his wares and only then would you understand why you must buy them? Would you tell yourself you must believe a conjurer to have magical powers before you were able to understand and accept that the rabbits and doves he seemingly produced out of thin air were truly products of his supernatural spells?

And as to religions that do not base their claims upon miracles other than revelation, remember this: Not one among us has directly heard the voice of God or witnessed His revelation—in any way that can be responsibly relied upon. Instead, our beliefs about God are what we have been taught by other humans— or those we have arrived at with the aid of our own imagination and interpretation. Thus, it is a collection of *human* claims and conclusions *about* God that religion asks us to believe—not claims we know God to have made Himself.[1]

---

[1] Thomas Paine, in his *Age of Reason*, makes the point this way: "No one will deny or dispute the power of the Almighty to make such a communication if he pleases. But admitting, for the sake of a case, that something has been revealed to a certain person, and not revealed to any other person, it is revelation to that person only. When he tells it to a second person, a second to a third, a third to a fourth, and so on, it ceases to be a revelation to all those persons. It is revelation to the first person only, and hearsay to every other...It is a contradiction in terms and ideas to call anything a revelation that comes to us at second hand, either verbally or in writing. Revelation is necessarily limited to the first communication. After this, it is only an account of something which that person says was a revelation made to him; and though he may find himself obliged to

And we do not responsibly know whether these human claims are accurate. Is it not, then, incumbent upon us to carefully scrutinize such claims—lest we risk committing the grave error of believing false things about a possible God?

Moreover, have you not heard those of other religions making the same argument: "Believe in our God and then you will understand that He is the Lord"? Why, then, my sister, do you not adopt the beliefs of these other faiths, so that you might realize they are true? Have you not said that only by first believing a religion's claims can you understand its truth? Indeed, even an atheist might argue that you must first believe there is no God and then you would understand atheism to be true; would you find that argument reasonable? If not, I ask you in all gentleness whether your argument is any more persuasive.

My sister, when one believes strongly, it is simple to find or manufacture what one persuades oneself are rational justifications. This applies to all objects of belief: from one's country's claims when at war, to arguments for the superiority of one's native culture, to the cause of one's favorite team in the athletic arena, and even to the dubious claims of the occult—of astrology, clairvoyance, numerology, and more. However, the finding of reasons for what one already believes is more a function of searching for vindication and reassurance than it is a legitimate effort at searching for truth. Moreover, my sister, the issues of God and religion are harder to think about clearly and honestly than nearly any other, because our social and emotional lives are often so heavily intertwined with religious identity. Thus, when searching in the spiritual landscape we must be especially careful—not less careful—to employ unbridled reason, free from the overpowering enticements of emotion and tribe, and the fierce constraints of sacred allegiance.

And, my sister, what sort of God would have us use your argument as a basis for belief? According to all major religions, most humans are deeply mistaken in their faith. Yet all belief systems, once committed to, can seem persuasive. Would a compassionate, or even reasonable, God want us to first believe in our religion, then feel convinced, and thus follow a course that condemns the vast majority to false beliefs on matters most sacred?

In short, we cannot come closer to truth by accepting a bias and thinking less critically—such a path leads not to clarity and authenticity, but to blindness and self-deception. My sister, when one runs from oneself there is no place to hide, and when chasing after truth there is no escaping reason.

---

believe it, it cannot be incumbent on me to believe it in the same manner, for it was not a revelation made to me, and I have only his word for it that it was made to him."

94.5 Argument that faith is warranted because Jesus Christ fills an emptiness that nothing else can fill, and transforms lives in ways nothing else can

And a church pastor said: You may be persuading some with your crafty logic and pretty words, but you do not persuade me. I have seen, time after time, the rich and successful man, having amassed the wealth he so long sought, and having achieved the fame he so desired, and having satisfied his lusts and pleasures, too—having collected all the prizes of the natural world—remain with a feeling of emptiness, even of despair, and wonder: Is that all there is? And I have seen that when a man like this accepts Jesus Christ as his Lord and Savior, the emptiness is filled, and life again feels worthwhile, and this time with a value that no earthly disappointments can diminish. And I have also seen people with ruined lives—criminals, or those addicted to whiskey and drugs, or those unable to control their gambling or their rage—have their lives transformed once they accepted the love and sacrifice of Jesus Christ. So you may have clever arguments and fancy words, but I have seen too much evidence of what the Lord can do. I know He is real, and that my religion is true.

And the sage said: My brother, your religion has, indeed, brought a feeling of fullness to many who felt their lives empty, and has helped many others turn from their destructive ways. Yet ask yourself this telling question: Is my religion the only one that brings fulfillment to those who feel their lives empty, or the only one that helps people turn from destructive ways?

My brother, if you seek the answer to this question honestly—and its implications, too—you will recognize that every significant religion with which we are acquainted helps people in these same ways. Many have felt that their empty lives became full when dedicating themselves to Judaism or Islam or Buddhism or Hinduism or any of the numerous other religious traditions our species has seen fit to create. Thus, when a man accepts Jesus Christ as his Lord and Savior and then feels a fuller life or turns away from destructive acts, these positive changes no more prove Christianity to be the true word and will of God than Judaism, Islam, Hinduism and Buddhism are proved to be the true word and will of God when some of their adherents rededicate themselves to *their* religions and undergo similar positive changes. Indeed, since different religions have filled this emptiness some people feel and have helped many turn aside from destructive ways, yet each religion teaches that the other religions are wrong—if transforming lives makes a religion's teachings accurate, they all prove each other false.

Moreover, my brother, not only is yours not the only religion that can turn lives around, this emptiness of which you speak has been prevented and filled for many by things other than religion. True, the chase after wealth or prestige or physical pleasure tends, after a time, to leave one unfulfilled, but deep engagement, especially with a cause greater than the self, can banish emptiness and bring new enthusiasm and meaning to life.

And though religion—nearly any religion—provides one such means, other means have been effective, too. And it has long been observed that if a man can lose himself in a great cause, especially in a mass movement, he can discard his ruined sense of self, and feel invigorated and fulfilled, and prepared for great sacrifice. And so we find that the true believer,[1] he who dedicates himself to an ideology or a group, whether it be a cause animated by religion or nationalism or politics or war, or any other deeply felt common cause, often becomes energized, even exhilarated, by his new identity—or, indeed, the liberation from individual identity.

And for purposes of banishing the feeling of emptiness, the truth and moral content of the cause are less important than its intensity. Those in Germany of the 1930's, swept up in the social tide of marches and parades and grand spectacles and fierce dedication to the Fuehrer, and to his fervent hatred, racist ideology, and military aggression, felt their lives more full than many a bored and lonely high school student in England of the same day, who hated nobody and wished everyone well.

Thus, not only is that which brings fullness to empty lives not proved to be the word and will of God, such transformative power does not even prove it to be a cause for good. Because, my brother, if faith fills empty lives, it is not due to the nature of that in which we place our faith, but rather due to our faith itself— and nearly anything that can arouse our willingness to give ourselves over, to trust and be dedicated to something outside ourselves, will prove sufficient.

But one need not choose religion or mass political movements, or the like, in order to fill one's life and ward off emptiness. Less dramatic, more common, and often deeply constructive pursuits are available, which, when compared to chasing pleasure, fortune, and fame are more authentic—yet honest and with no supernatural pretensions—and the sense of engagement they offer can endure, even deepen over time.

My brother, I shall speak of some of the many ways people fill their lives without pretensions to supernatural knowledge: Loving, helping, and connecting

---

[1] *The True Believer* by Eric Hoffer is a classic study of the phenomenon of mass movements, written with aphoristic eloquence. The book was published only several years after WWII, the establishment of the State of Israel, and the beginning of the Cold War. In 1951 these insights on the mass movements of Nazism, communism and (neither he nor I compare this following example to the first two in any moral sense) Zionism were particularly resonant. But even today it is well worth reading, for its style, yes, but for its substance too: Mass movements are always, somewhere in the world, about to reappear; and our predilection toward such movements teaches many lessons on human nature.

with others, in romance, family, friendship, and community; expressing oneself creatively through various means, from the writer's pen to the craftsman's hammer to the potter's wheel; learning and thinking and discovering, relishing the voyages of the mind, through books and teachers and discussion and solitary reflection; going into nature and encountering the animals and the trees, the skies and the winds, the suns of different seasons and the many different moods of the clouds, the drama and beauty of the mountains and the deserts and the rivers and the seas; traveling to distant lands and seeing new masks upon the human face, the varying cultures into which has been poured the spirit of man; these and other avenues are open to those who wish to avoid emptiness in their days and a restless foreboding in their nights. Observe the artist or artisan bringing forth his visions, or the scientist wresting from nature another of her secrets; see the glint in the scholar's eye as he understands something new, or the gentle purpose in the teacher's face as she helps others to understand; see the busy mother dressing her little child, the friend carrying a meal for one taken ill, and the lover, with blessed anticipation, buying a tender gift.

My brother, if you will but refrain from preaching long enough to observe and listen to the great sermon of Man, you will notice the many natural labors and laughters, the many natural commitments and liberations, the many natural blossomings and becomings, the many natural sacrifices and joys, that have kept innumerable lives so engaged and busy and full that Emptiness dared not knock at the door, much less enter and attempt to speak of despair.

*****

And the sage turned his gaze from the pastor, looked out across the gathered crowd, and in a gentle voice said: Brothers and sisters, my innards ache for you: I know how crushing can be disillusionment. Mere philosophical assurances, and even the warmest of consolations, cannot much ease the way for a spirit first spying the abyss that seems to yawn for the devout who lose their footing in faith. But from one who has walked that path, know that new and solid footing, surer than any faith, can gradually be gained on the cliffs of life, and that after a few treacherous turns the way becomes wide and generous, a trail of expanding peace and existential poise—even of meaning and inspiration.

Then in a loud voice he continued: On the question of faith, brothers and sisters, after all has been heard, the end of the matter is this: In our search for truth, faith's seductive dark renders us blind. Though destiny deprives us of the noonday sun on matters of God, religion, and life's meaning, if we would live with integrity we must attempt to illuminate the intellectual night. We dare not shut our eyes tightly, and tell ourselves that the lights and colors we then see shall guide us home. We must, rather, scrutinize the paths we walk and when necessary blaze new ones, always shining upon our beliefs two noble forms of light—the leaping torch of experience, and the calm candle of reason. And in searching out truth well, we shall see what reason says about our experience, and what experience reveals about our reason—then will the candle have gifted the torch with vision unblinking, and the vitality of the torch will have made the candle dance.

VI. ON THE BIBLE

95. Claim that studying the Bible will make all truth clear

And a man said: All this general talk about religion and faith misses the main point—that God has given us His word through the Holy Bible. Let us discuss the Bible. For if we study God's word and His teachings, all truth becomes clear.

And the sage said: Yes, my brother, Scripture has for millennia been believed by many to be the word, or inspired message, of an almighty God. As we seek truth, then, it is fitting that we examine these books to see what we can honestly believe about them—books for which many have died and for which many more have lived.

And a possible Creator who may have written a Bible would surely want us to investigate its qualities and claims so that we may distinguish *His* Bible from the blizzard of books written by mere mortals, many of which have been falsely attributed to powers supernatural. Therefore, such questions we now discuss, and any challenges we might present, are in keeping with reverence for the Great Mystery, or any gods there may be.

96. Argument that God would not create an intelligent species such as humans without giving them directions on how to live—and this must have been the Bible and religion

And the man continued and said: I cannot believe that God would create human beings, such complex thinking creatures, and then not give them instruction on how to live. Therefore, it is clear to me that God has communicated his truth to us through the Bible, and that is why I follow my religion.

And the sage said: My brother, humans are, indeed, complex thinking beings. And to some it seems that such intelligence cries out for instruction from above. Yet if we are painfully candid must we not admit that we have clear knowledge neither about whether a God exists, nor about whether such a possible God would think it necessary to communicate with us?

First, even should we assume there is a God, consider that other species are intelligent, too, yet seem to be living without special, supernatural revelation. Does not the lion pride, without benefit of words, coordinate a collaborative ambush on the deadly hunt? And do not the apes engage in complex strategies, and the elephants in intelligent living, too? And what of the sharp-minded crows, ravens, and parrots—and what of the dolphins and whales?

And if you have raised dogs you know that members of the family of wolf understand when they disobey their leader's will. Thus humans are not the only species with the capacity to choose to follow direction. Yet you do not puzzle at how there is no Bible for the beasts of the earth, no divine revelation for navigators of the air, and no saints or apostles for creatures of the sea.

And let not your heart be tempted to respond that since humans are more intelligent than these other species, we therefore require divine instruction. For if these species are not sufficiently complex thinkers to merit God's communication, perhaps we, though in some ways more complex, are still too simple to be spoken to by God. Perhaps only beings even more complex than humans would warrant divine guidance.

Moreover, might we not argue the exact opposite of your argument? Might we not as persuasively suggest that precisely because humans are so intelligent, a Creator would have intended them to employ this intelligence to discern appropriate ways of living? After all, is requiring instruction a sign of great intellect—or rather of inferior intellect, the inability to draw one's own conclusions?

Furthermore, according to the Bible and its major religions, God did not reveal a detailed way of life for humans until millennia of human history had passed. The Bible makes clear that God waited thousands of years after creating Adam before giving a people—the Israelites—systematic and detailed instruction on how to live. If even according to the Bible God waited so long, why must we insist that He would not wait longer still? Have you considered that even if there is a God, and it is His plan to reveal a way of life to humans, that He may not have done so yet?

Finally, my brother, when examining the Bible we find so much that is unlike anything an omnipotent and compassionate God would be like or teach—an insecure and volatile deity commanding slavery and genocide, and punishing people with eternal torture, and more—that either our religions are mistaken about the nature of God, or God did not originate the Bible's teachings.

97. The wisdom and depth of the Bible, compared to other writings and law codes

Then a religious teacher said: Surely the wisdom of the Bible cries out that it must have been written or inspired by God. No unaided human could have written the Bible! Every time one reads its passages one sees new insights and learns further lessons!

And the sage said: My dear brother, as a groom sees unparalleled beauty in the countenance of his bride while others see but an ordinary face; as a woman hears music in the words of her lover while others hear but common chatter; and as a mother finds the magic of dance in her young one's first faltering steps while others see but the graceless gait of another stumbling child; so too do we find our sacred scriptures remarkable, in ways others do not.[1]

My brother, let us speak, then, of wisdom. Have not all traditions produced wisdom? Can it not be argued that the ethical teachings of Confucius, the psychological insights of the Buddha, the depth and expanse of the Bhagavad-Gita, the long-incubated lessons of ancient Egypt, the autonomous ideals of the stoic philosophers, even the sages, poets and scholars of every age, taught wisdom as impressive as the Bible's? For who shall arbitrate between wisdom and wisdom?[2]

And have not the Greeks—Socrates, Plato and others—developed a tradition of philosophy, the ideal of honestly searching for non-dogmatic wisdom,[3] in ways the Bible has not? And has not science provided the touchstone for how to discern and attain reliable knowledge and, in so doing, offered us the great gift that enables humanity to escape the dark caves of ignorance and the sinister confines of superstition—a form of wisdom absent from the Bible?

Moreover, not only is it unconvincing to argue that the Bible's wisdom is unparalleled, many of the Bible's laws seem to have actually been based upon earlier law codes,[4] and many of the Bible's poems and proverbs seem to have been influenced by older Egyptian wisdom and poetry.[5]

And, my brother, as to your claim that unending wisdom and insights can be found in the Bible, I ask of you to bear your aching heart, and answer whether the same cannot be said of any text considered wise—the more so of one considered sacred. For is it not human nature to project onto admired texts our most excellent and elevated thoughts?[6] Do not literary scholars find as many new profound ideas in Shakespeare's plays as theologians do in the stories of the Bible? Do not Muslims find as many new, inspiring notions in each sura of the

---

[1] Partisan eyes—clouded by greed, fear, lust, pride, or any of the many impediments to clear vision—are only too capable of seeing excellence invisible to others. Samuel Johnson, in *Marmor Norfolciense*, speaking on British royalty and their sycophants, said: "Our monarchs are surrounded with refined spirits, so penetrating that they frequently discover in their masters great qualities invisible to vulgar eyes, and which, did they not publish them to mankind, would be unobserved for ever."

[2] In his *Devil's Dictionary*, Ambrose Bierce says: "SCRIPTURES, n. The sacred books of our holy religion, as distinguished from the false and profane writings on which all other faiths are based."

[3] Not that these were perfect models of critical thinking and intellectual honesty in all instances, but they did take giant steps in the direction of subjecting beliefs to reason.

[4] See section 116 where this is discussed in greater detail.

[5] See section 117 and its footnotes for more detail.

[6] For more on this point of excellent thoughts being projected onto religion and its texts, see section 39 and its footnote recounting the story of spoon soup.

Koran as Christians find in each chapter of the New Testament, or Jews find in each parsha of the Torah?

In short, there *is* wisdom in the Bible; but there is wisdom elsewhere, too. And the Bible's wisdom is not so evidently superior to that of other books that we need believe it was authored or inspired by a force transcendent or omniscient. Consider the Bible's many repetitive verses; her seemingly irrelevant, obscure genealogies; her dearth of systematic or clear psychological teachings; and, with respect to practical wisdom, her apparent ignorance of many medical, mechanical and general scientific principles. My brother, limited human wisdom, as it existed in ancient days, is evident in the Bible—but, if we are honest, the hand of a supernatural, All-Wise Author is not.

98. Sub-argument that the Bible contains supernatural wisdom that we mortals cannot see

But the religious teacher persisted, saying: It may be that we cannot see the extent of the Bible's wisdom. But this is due to our own defects, our weak and mortal powers of perception. Could we but see clearly and deeply enough, we would discern that the Bible truly teaches remarkable, supernatural wisdom.

And the sage said: My brother, does not this argument undermine your earlier words? If our mortal minds cannot perceive the supernatural wisdom of the Bible, then these same mortal minds cannot reasonably claim to see in the Bible evidence of its divinity—and, for those who do, the conclusion that the Bible is of divine origin has already been assumed before investigating the matter with any degree of honest deliberation.

My brother, could your words not be employed to argue for the divinity of any religion, including those you believe misguided? Indeed, could not your argument be used in the service of any secular book, too, to claim, for example, that Aesop's Fables issued from the sacred finger of God? And if one should protest that that the work, though containing some wisdom, does not seem supernaturally wise, you have suggested a ready answer—that our mortal minds cannot see through its apparently unremarkable contents to its transcendent wisdom. My brother, would you find such an argument persuasive in that case? If not, does the same argument in favor of the Bible persuade any better?

99. Supernatural knowledge in the Bible

And a man said: Some biblical verses contain knowledge only discovered by science many generations later. Surely this proves the Bible was written by God!

And the sage said: My brother, would that you beheld your eyes as they beheld Scripture, that you might examine whether they glisten like the eyes of a lover seeing naught but enchantment—or open wide like the eyes of the besieged, desperate for survival and escape. Yet the eyes of truth are neither infatuated nor fearful; they squint into the bright lights of reason, though this sometimes stings; and though yearning for beauty, such eyes turn not away from necessary horror.

A poet whispered to me that the eyes give lesson on how to live: They see, and they also cry; they teach us to seek what is true, though it oft brings sadness. The soul cries to wash away failed visions of reality—outdated maps of security, comfort, and love. And after the hot tears, comes renewal; a luminous rainbow stretched across the sky of the spirit—across the inner eye—the sun of knowledge mixes with the mist of the soul, painting a fragile vision of beauty and hope. The rainbow fades, but honesty's tears collect into a mirroring pool within, and reflect a truer vision of the self, of the world, and of our yearnings for mortal and immortal gods, and for various forms of heaven. Thus whispered the poet.

My brother, let us scrutinize, with as much objectivity as we can muster, our cherished scriptures, the scriptures of others too, and the surviving legends and teachings and records and works of ancient peoples who left no scriptures. Does the Bible reveal secrets of biology, chemistry, or physics? And does the Bible give lesson on the numerous achievements of the modern age—does it teach us how to fly through the skies, or instruct us on replacing a diseased kidney or a failing heart? Does it tell us how to print books, improve eyesight, illuminate the night, capture moving pictures, replay music without musicians, travel over land with horseless chariots, conduct conversation across oceans and continents, or the innumerable other advances in arts and science that the minds of men have discovered and developed without supernatural revelation?

And what of the science you believe impressive in the Bible? Does it compare to the advances of the modern age? Would not an Author of infinite intelligence demonstrate in His book far more scientific knowledge than appears in the Bible?

And look, too, at other ancient peoples. Perhaps in our conceit we underestimate the achievements of those civilizations that did not produce the Bible. Did not the Egyptians embalm their dead, and construct pyramids, with an expertise unknown to the science of industrial ages three millennia later? And have not other ancient peoples devised astronomical calendars with baffling precision, constructed metal plumbing systems, originated complex agricultural practices, manufactured advanced weaponry—and arrived at other knowledge not taught, and apparently not known, by the Bible?[1]

---

[1] One small but telling biblical passage shows that even the heroes of the Bible, God's chosen people in the days of their ascendancy, did not always have access to the technology available to others of the day—let alone knowledge of advanced technologies

My brother, if the Bible is the word of God, its divinity surely cannot be deduced from its scientific content, which is far short of divine. And even if such content is sometimes impressive, it is no more so than the scientific knowledge of other ancient peoples—and falls far short of the standard of what would constitute the unambiguous signature of an omniscient God.

100. Argument that as science learns more, the Bible's knowledge becomes ever more clear

And a Jewish man protested, saying: That man was right. Even in modern times, the more science learns, the more we see how knowledgeable the Bible truly is. This shows the supernatural origin of the Bible. For example: The Bible in Leviticus[1] forbids us to eat pork and shellfish. Only many centuries after the Bible was written did science discover that the disease trichinosis comes from pork, and that many are allergic to shellfish.

And the sage replied: My brother, if it is truth we seek, we must read the Bible with unenchanted eyes, and reflect upon her with an unbetrothed heart. It may indeed be that the Bible prohibited certain foods for reasons of health—though the Bible's stated reason for these prohibitions does not refer to health.[2] Yet even if we were to assume that the Bible prohibited certain foods due to health concerns, must we conclude that what seems like medical knowledge on the part of the Bible indicates divine authorship? If the Bible was written by human religious authorities who saw their role as protecting and guiding the people, might not these authorities have included in the Bible rules incorporating considerations of health? Indeed, the Talmud, and other later Jewish writings, even Maimonides's works on religious law, include much medical advice. And my

---

universally unknown to their age. Judges 1:19 says: "And the Lord was with Judah; and he drave out the inhabitants of the mountain; but could not drive out the inhabitants of the valley, because they had chariots of iron." So the Israelites of that day apparently did not have, and could not produce, iron chariots or the weapons or strategies to overcome such chariots. And if the heroes of the Bible in the first few generations following Moses—those we might expect to have best understood the Five Books of Moses, and have best gleaned its teachings—were behind in technology, surely it would be unreasonable to claim that the Bible was so far ahead of its day in scientific knowledge that it must be supernatural.

Incidentally, that passage in Judges 1 is striking for another reason: In so many biblical stories, God's help guarantees success against any odds, yet this passage suggests that even though "the Lord was with Judah" Judah could not overcome iron chariots.

[1] Chapter 11.

[2] See Leviticus chapter 11, especially verses 44 and 45, where the Bible seems to indicate that these foods are being prohibited for reasons of emulating God's holiness—there is no mention of health considerations.

brother, do not all peoples develop a set of medical beliefs, about what is healthy and what is not? And does it require great, much less supernatural, scientific advancement to notice a pattern, wherein many become ill from certain foods, and thus to conclude that they are inherently dangerous—or that consuming them displeases God—and to forbid them to the people?

And has not the Old Testament forbidden many foods that we have no cause to believe are unhealthy? Moreover, has not the Old Testament allowed certain foods that sicken people as often as do pork and shellfish? The Bible does not prohibit eggs, yet they have caused many incidents of salmonella poisoning. And milk is not only permitted by the Bible, but held up as a symbol of promise and blessing: How often the Bible speaks glowingly of the "land flowing with milk and honey!" Yet a great many people are either allergic to milk, or unable to digest it. And peanuts have been, for many, a deadly allergen, too; but the Bible does not prohibit them—perhaps did not even know of them. Thus, if you are correct that the Bible warned us away from foods that might prove harmful, the evidence suggests that the Bible was rather limited in its knowledge of which foods could be harmful—and this reflects a level of knowledge far from divine.

Moreover, have not other peoples and religions taught many health practices of their own—practices the Bible did not teach, and that science is only now confirming to be healthy? What of the religions and traditions of the East that have taught Yoga, Tai Chi, and other forms of physical exercise and relaxation, and a myriad of disciplines and meditations for peace of mind—matters on which the Bible is silent? Yet relaxation, meditation, and physical exercise have been proved by modern science to be of significant help in maintaining the health of body and mind. And, my brother—tell me in all candor—had the Bible taught these, would you not have cited them as further evidence of the Bible's supernatural scientific wisdom?

Reflect upon the matter further and you may conclude that the Bible does not offer an exhaustive prescription for health; that non-biblical ancient traditions taught equally helpful lessons for well-being—and that what guidelines the Bible does teach could easily have originated in the minds of intelligent men, and in the collective, cumulative experience of a cautious and literate people.

101. Argument that science has not been able to disprove one story in the Bible; thus, the Bible must be true

And another man said to the sage: Will you at least admit that science, in its hundreds of years of attempts, has not been able to disprove any story in the Bible? Surely this should persuade us that the claims of the Bible are true!

And the sage said: My brother, it is very difficult to prove that any story written about the ancient past did *not* occur. But this does not mean that it *did* occur.

When accounts contradict the laws of nature, a fair-minded thinker considers them fanciful—not accurate—unless such tales can be supported by compelling evidence. Is this not how you view ancient Greek mythology? Its stories, too, have not been conclusively demonstrated to be false. Can we prove that the immortal children of Uranus and Gaea did *not* exist and were *not* the Hundred-Handed Giants and the one-eyed Cyclopes? Can we prove that Persephone, too, did *not* exist, was *not* the daughter of Demeter and Zeus, and was *not* abducted and taken to Hades? No: These, and a thousand other myths, cannot be disproved. Yet do we, therefore, believe them accurate in the literal sense, as many ancients did—and worship the colorful, contentious assembly of archaic gods?

For that matter, my brother, neither have children's fairy tales or the most whimsical of fables been incontestably refuted: Can you prove that no talking pigs or flying witches inhabited Europe's forests medieval? Can you prove that no peasant maid was assisted by a bitter and covetous dwarf in spinning straw into finest gold? Can you prove that no pumpkin was transformed to a grand stagecoach and delivered in noble style a deserving damsel to the prince's ball? Can you prove that no young boy scaled the heights of a magic beanstalk and barely escaped the wrath of a child-eating giant? And can you prove that no gallant knight ever battled a fire-breathing dragon to win the hand of a pale princess in a castle enchanted? Yet do we accept such fanciful tales as true, merely because we cannot definitively prove them false?

Indeed, my brother, if a man in the next village tells us that he went without food or water for forty years; and that in seasons past he grew fields of wheat and corn without sowing seeds, but rather by chanting magical incantations; and that, for his amusement, he regularly transports himself in an instant across oceans and continents by use of a magic carpet—but that he has no wish to demonstrate his great powers by replicating these things in the presence of responsible witnesses—could science prove his claims false? No: Science could merely point out that the feats he describes go against the laws of nature as we know them, and that he has done nothing to persuade us that his astonishing claims are true. And I dare say that you would not find science's inability to prove his claims false, any good reason to believe them likely to be true.

Moreover, even in the arena of religion, a story merely not having been disproved remains far from sufficient cause to invest that story with sacred credibility. Consider that the story of Jesus being the Son of God, dying on the cross and being resurrected, has not been shown to be false; yet Jews and Muslims, Buddhists and Hindus, and those of other religions—not to mention agnostics and atheists—find this no compelling reason to convert to Christianity. And the story of Mohammad being God's greatest prophet, and conveying God's will to mankind in the holy Koran, has not been disproved; but Christians and Jews,

Hindus and Buddhists, and those of other religions or no religion, do not find this sufficient reason to adopt the religion of Islam. And so it is with the foundational beliefs and supernatural tales of each religion: The majority of the world's population is not persuaded to believe such claims, though they cannot prove them false. The burden of proof lies, and should lie, with each religion to do what none has ever done—prove its supernatural assertions true.

In summary, my brother, when considering a story, we must distinguish between it being true, and it having merely not been proved false. And the miracle stories and religious claims of the Bible, along with innumerable other non-religious tales, belong in the latter, crowded category—they have merely not been proved false.

102. Argument that archaeological discoveries prove the Bible true

But the man pressed on, saying: It is not only that the Bible's stories have never been disproved. More and more discoveries are being made that prove the Bible true! Archaeologists have discovered ancient inscriptions, and have done scientific tests proving that kings mentioned in the Bible actually existed; that battles recounted in the Bible actually were fought; and that even specific tunnels and other projects were built at the time the Bible specifies. That is why I say the doubters are wrong, and the Bible is the sacred and perfect word of God.

And the sage replied: My brother, you are quite right that science has verified certain elements of the Bible's historical account. And, indeed, critics of the Bible and religion have often unfairly assumed that even the Bible's non-supernatural narratives were all intentionally fabricated or otherwise grossly inaccurate.

We must, however, make the important distinction between the Bible being truthful in many natural, historical accounts—and the Bible having credibility in its claims of supernatural causes and events. For to be accurate about names of cities and kings, or the dates of battles and building projects, does not in any way challenge the laws of nature; it simply involves accurate record keeping, of the sort incorporated into thousands of history books written today. By contrast, to believe the Bible's supernatural claims of miracles and divine communication requires abandoning foundational, daily-confirmed laws of nature.

My brother, answer me this: Is it truly beyond the realm of probability that over the hundreds of years following the natural events having been recorded, popular imagination or religious leaders embellished with supernatural elements these stories, and that the Bible's authors or editors included in the sacred texts these enhanced accounts? And would we not still expect that these stories' natural, historically accurate elements would be verified by archaeology?

And, my brother, by saying that the Bible's authors recorded enhancements to well-known natural events, I do not insist that they, or the religious masses who may have developed the supernatural elements of these stories, intended to teach inaccuracies. Legends grow from kernels of truth. Intelligent and well-meaning people, fervently believing in God, would have interpreted many events as having been ordained by God. Thus, if Joshua and the Israelites were known to have captured and destroyed the city of Jericho, and especially if the remains of the wall seemed to the eyes of later generations to be positioned in unusual formations, the legend may have grown that the victory was miraculous and involved communication or intervention from God. And when the Bible's writers chronicled the story for posterity, perhaps hundreds of years later, they would have written, with honest intent, what may by then have been the accepted version of events. They would have recorded the story as follows:

> And it came to pass, when Joshua was by Jericho, that he lifted up his eyes and looked, and, behold, there stood a man over against him with his sword drawn in his hand: and Joshua went forth unto him, and said unto him, Art thou for us, or for our adversaries? And he said, Nay; but as captain of the host of the Lord am I now come, And Joshua fell on his face to the earth, and did worship, and said unto him, What saith my lord unto his servant? And the captain of the Lord's host said unto Joshua, Loose thy shoe from off thy foot; for the place whereon thou standest is holy. And Joshua did so...And the Lord said unto Joshua, See I have given into thine hand Jericho, and the king thereof, and the mighty men of valor. And ye shall compass the city, all ye men of war, and go round about the city once. Thus shalt thou do six days. And seven priests shall bear before the ark seven trumpets of ram's horns: and the seventh day ye shall compass the city seven times, and the priests shall blow with the trumpets. And it shall come to pass, that when they make a long blast with the ram's horn, and when ye hear the sound of the trumpet, all the people shall shout with a great shout; and the wall of the city shall fall down flat, and the people shall ascend up every man straight before him...So the people shouted when the priests blew with the trumpets; and it came to pass, when the people heard the sound of the trumpet, and the people shouted with a great shout, that the wall fell down flat, so that the people went up into the city, every man straight before him, and they took the city.

And so, indeed, is it written in Joshua 5:13—6:20.

Thus, if archaeologists find scientific evidence proving that the wall at Jericho was destroyed in battle at about the time of Joshua, it only confirms the natural historical account—that such a battle took place at around the time the Bible says it did, and that the wall was destroyed. The archaeological evidence, however, in no way confirms the supernatural claims—that God and the captain of the host of the Lord spoke to Joshua, or that the wall was felled by circling priests blowing rams' horns, and by shouts from the people.

Let us illustrate the point with a more recent example. Toward the end of the twentieth century C.E. the infamous Berlin Wall, separating the two countries of East Germany and West Germany, was torn down, followed by the reemergence of a united Germany. A supernatural account could be written as follows:

> And the Lord God heard the cries of the persecuted children of Germany of the East, and he heeded their screams; and he remembered his servant Luther and all that he had done for the glory of God. And the Lord God said unto his heart: No longer shall I allow Luther's people to be persecuted by heathens who know not my name, and call not upon the God of the heavens. And the Lord God sent an angel unto the communist government's leader and said unto him: Thus saith the Lord: Let my people go. And if thou wilt not let my people go, then behold, in three days time I will bring forth against thee the hosts of the heavens and the mighty forces of the winds, and thy wall shall crumble to dust and pebbles before the awesome power of the Lord. But the leader of the communists said unto his ministers and advisers: Who is God that I should hearken to his voice? I do not know God, neither will I set the people free. And it came to pass on the third day, that the wrath of the Lord God waxed hot, and He sent forth the angel Gabriel, and all the legions and hosts of heaven, against the wall of the tormentors at Berlin. And the angel came forth out of a flaming cloud against the barrier, beating his wings with a furious force. And thunder shook the ground and lightning flashed from the heavens, and a great whirlwind blew out of the north and descended upon the wall; and the angel Gabriel sent forth his hand against the pride of the enemies of the Lord; and the great wall crumbled to the ground, before the terrifying might of the God of heaven, fulfilling that which the Lord had spoken. And the people of Germany rejoiced and praised God, and held feasts and merriment for many days.

My brother, if archaeologists a thousand years hence confirm that the Berlin Wall indeed existed, and that it was, indeed, torn down at about the time of which this passage speaks—would it prove the miraculous account of angels and whirlwinds? No: It would confirm only that the Berlin Wall existed and, in a certain era, was torn down.

The same applies to biblical history: We can believe that many historical events mentioned in the Bible truly occurred, and still assume that they took place by natural means. Reason would counsel that we remain skeptical of any story's supernatural elements. Thus, if archaeology confirms the historical existence of a Moses, a David, or a Jesus, we need not jump to the irresponsible conclusion that the miracles claimed for them actually transpired. Rather, we can simply accept what the evidence would then have taught us: that those people existed. And when we find compelling evidence for specific battles, let us accept that those battles were fought; but all this is far different from believing that such battles involved the miraculous intervention of God, and constituted events that shattered the laws of nature.

My brother, although we are tempted to apply the findings of science to confirm what we desperately wish to believe, integrity demands that we carefully consider which elements of a story have been proved, and which remain unproved. And if the miraculous aspects of an account have not been proved, our vast experience with never having responsibly verified a supernatural event should teach us to remain, at the very least, skeptical that anything supernatural did, in fact, occur.

And mourn not too bitterly, my brother, the loss of the supernatural. The untutored spirit's ears yearn to hear of miracles, strain for the distant echoes of infancy's terrible joy—again to tremble in abject submission to irresistible force, once more to suckle unvigilant, unarmed, at the unspoiled breasts of early bliss. But wisdom teaches a healthy horror for such sheltered feebleness—and urges, instead, a vigorous encounter with life on its own terms, asking neither the advantage of magic nor the dispensation of miracle. And though our haunted, overburdened spirits long to return to the sunny fields of half-remembered beginnings, shall we not remember the wise observation that what is charming in the boy is often grotesque in the man?

103. The beauty of the Bible

Then a preacher spoke, saying: Can you deny the beauty of the Bible? Could anyone but the Divine Almighty have penned words of such loveliness and majesty?

And the sage said: My brother, the Bible is, indeed, graced with many beautiful and evocative passages—to name but several: the banishment of Adam and Eve; the heartache and glory of Joseph; the deathbed blessings of Isaac and Jacob; and the poetic prophecies of Balaam, son of Beor. Moreover, strong and subtle characters populate the Bible, and many of her verses are rich with metaphor, symbol, and more. As a young child, I was captured by this ancient spell. My heart pined with melancholy longing to meet her ancient characters—a longing I knew could never be fulfilled this side of death. Yet I sought refuge and inspiration in the Bible's accounts of these men and women; my spirit surged with their triumphs, my eyes winced at their failings, and my innards ached in sympathy with their sufferings. And these rich narratives of heroism and tragedy colored my psyche with hues both passionate and subtle, and taught my spirit to dance with the stately cadences of sacred poetry. Far more than the prosaic one inhabited by my body, this was a world that appealed to me; a world long lost and forever gone—and so, paradoxically, beyond the disappointment and decay of the real—but ever accessible between the covers of the eternal Book.

My brother, the Bible contains some beauty; on this there is no intelligent, informed debate. The question at hand, however, is whether the Bible's beauty is so unparalleled that it could only have been written or inspired by a Being supernatural. To this question we must answer: No. For consider the fine and beautiful passages of other literatures; I ask you this, my brother: If the exquisite poetry and grand folk tales of any land or people were taught as God's holy word, would they not seem transcendently lovely? And are there not within the Bible many dry, difficult, and repetitive passages, too, quite unlike anything else we call beautiful?

Have you read Numbers chapter 7, which repeats the very same series of verses twelve times, describing the identical sacrificial offerings of the 12 princes of Israel? And have you seen that beginning in Exodus 25, the Bible uses several chapters to describe God's commandments on how the tabernacle should be built—and that in chapters 35-40 the Bible uses another several chapters to essentially repeat itself by describing in detail that in building the tabernacle the Israelites followed God's instructions?

And tell me, my brother, do most Bible verses bring tears to your eyes—for their beauty—as often as do the words of your favorite poets, the sentimental scenes of evocative theatre, or even the popular lyrics of sad-sweet songs?

My brother, I have agreed that the Bible contains some beauty. But I shall cite several passages of another sort—from the Five Books of Moses no less. Let us answer to ourselves, with uncorrupted candor, whether such words would be deemed beautiful if found not in the Bible, but in any other book.

The following verses are found in Exodus 21:

> If thou buy an Hebrew servant, six years he shall serve: and in the seventh he shall go out free for nothing...And if a man shall sell his daughter to be a maid-servant...And he that smiteth his father, or his mother, shall be surely put to death. And he that stealeth a man, and selleth him, or if he be found in his hand, he shall surely be put to death. And he that curseth his father, or his mother, shall surely be put to death...And if any mischief follow, then thou shalt give life for life. Eye for eye, tooth for tooth, hand for hand, foot for foot. Burning for burning, wound for wound...

Leviticus Chapter 5 states:

> Or if a soul touch any unclean thing, whether it be a carcase of an unclean beast, or a carcase of unclean cattle, or the carcase of unclean creeping things, and if it be hidden from him; he also shall be unclean, and guilty.

Leviticus Chapter 13 states:

> When a man shall have in the skin of his flesh a rising, a scab, or bright spot, and it be in the skin of his flesh like the plague of leprosy…And the priest shall look on the plague in the skin of the flesh: and when the hair in the plague is turned white, and the plague in sight be deeper than the skin of his flesh, it is a plague of leprosy: and the priest shall look on him, and pronounce him unclean. If the bright spot be white in the skin of his flesh, and in sight be not deeper than the skin, and the hair thereof be not turned white; then the priest shall shut up him that hath the plague seven days...

Numbers, Chapter 5 begins:

> And the Lord spake unto Moses, saying: Command the children of Israel, that they put out of the camp every leper, and every one that hath an issue, and whosoever is defiled by the dead. Both male and female shall ye put out, without the camp shall ye put them; that they defile not their camps…

Tell me, my brother, are those biblical passages truly beautiful?[1] And would any objective assessment characterize them as *supernaturally* beautiful? Yet these verses are not rare exceptions; for although there is beauty in the Bible, there is also a great deal—ritual law, mundane statutes, lengthy genealogies, and more—possessed of little grace, much less of peerless beauty.

And even the poetic, grand, or evocative biblical passages are by no means clearly superior to the beautiful passages in various forms of secular literature, or other nations' sacred writings. Compare the Bible's beauty to that of Homer, Sophocles, Virgil, Rumi, Shakespeare, Dante, Milton, Gibbon, Johnson, Scott, Longfellow, Byron, Keats, Wordsworth, Whitman, Browning, Blake, Swinburne, Gibran, Tagore, or a thousand other writers and poets, of various styles and

---

[1] The translation used here is that of the King James Bible, whose archaic English makes even these verses sound at least stately. But in the original Hebrew of the Old Testament, and in many English translations, these specific verses are quite plain—neither beautiful nor stately.

tastes, both the famous and the lesser known, whether prized by the literary, or by the masses. Wide and fair-minded reading—in the Bible and outside it—provides sufficient evidence to call into grave doubt the proposition that the Bible's beauty exceeds the capacities, or even the extant and varied handiwork, of mere men.

And how is it, my brother, that you are not persuaded by the Muslim who speaks of the supernatural beauty of the Koran, and the Hindu is not persuaded by your talk of the supernatural beauty of the Bible? Might it not be for the same reason that a woman can better judge the beauty of a child not her own?

And let not your heart be tempted to say that the Bible is written with transcendent beauty—thus proving its divine origin—but that we cannot appreciate its loveliness with our crude, mortal minds. For not only could such an argument be advanced to claim supernatural beauty for any text, it would be groundless, too: assuming in advance what it aims to prove—insisting before looking, and after apparent contrary evidence, that the Bible must be uniquely beautiful.

104. Argument that biblical prophecies have been fulfilled

Then a man said: Many prophecies in Holy Scripture have been fulfilled. I am a Bible teacher, and I know this. How can you doubt that the author of the Bible was God, and that its teachings are His will?

And the sage replied: My brother, the hopes and hauntings of prophecy have animated great portions of the human race for centuries and millennia. The ardent pursuits of nations and men and the grand sweep of ages and time are suffused with the echoes of voices calling in the wilderness and crying out in the night, sounding terrible warnings of wrath and destruction, and proclaiming passionate consolations of glorious rebirth. My brother, the influence of prophecy over the sons of men is undisputed. The question, however, is this: Can we responsibly believe that such prophecies have been communications from God—that they evidence supernatural prediction or supernatural fulfillment?

To understand the issue well, let us first note that when one says biblical prophecies were fulfilled, one could be making two different claims. First, that the Bible recounts prophecies it says were already fulfilled by the time those biblical passages were written. Second, that the Bible foretold events that are said to have occurred—and thus fulfilled biblical prophecies—after these biblical passages were written. Let us examine both claims.

The Bible does, indeed, recount many tales of prophecies fulfilled—everything from the destruction of Sodom and Gomorrah to the sacking of ancient Jerusalem. Yet surely, saying that a prophecy came to pass does not make it so. Only those prophecies foretold in the Bible whose fulfillment is vouched for by reliable witnesses outside the Bible can be represented as evidence at all helpful in arriving at the truth of what actually transpired.

Moreover, events known to have occurred, and claimed by the Bible as prophecies fulfilled, must be shown to have been foretold—predicted by the Bible or its heroes before the events took place. For even a blind man will prove a flawless marksman when the target is drawn after his arrow has already come to rest—and anyone can write tales of remarkable prophecies, when writing of the foretelling, only after the events have already come to pass.[1]

My brother, I can write, today, a miraculous account of a prophet living a thousand years ago predicting your name, the date of your birth, that you would be a Bible teacher, and that you would attend this gathering today and challenge me on the issue of biblical prophecy—as you have just now done. And we might be astonished by the accuracy of these predictions—had we not known that this "prophecy" was written after the events took place.

As to biblical prophecies claimed by some to have been fulfilled in post-biblical days, consider the following. Prophetic predictions must be specific and unambiguous for us to responsibly see any supernatural cause in their fulfill-ment—indeed, in order to credibly argue that they have been fulfilled at all. For anyone can prophesy that at the end of days children will not respect their parents; that there will be great changes and difficulties; that armies will come from across the seas; that there shall be great battles with fire and smoke; that earthquakes and storms will ravage the earth; that wisdom will be lost; and that people will return in great numbers to the word of God. And in every generation many have claimed that all signs pointed to their own times being the foretold realization of such sacred predictions. Always they say, All these things are coming to pass in our day; surely this is the fulfillment of the holy prophecies, and these are the end of days. Yet the faithful and weary have been saying this in every generation, for centuries and millennia. And a prophecy that is always coming true, can never come true. Instead, it functions as a mere sacred inkblot on whose ambiguous form one projects one's deepest fears or yearnings.

Then, too, my brother, there are self-fulfilling prophecies, which tell more about the strength of earthly belief, than about these prophecies' divine origin or miraculous fulfillment. If a man believes he is fated for failure, will he not surely stumble? And if a man believes he is destined for glory and success, will he not persevere and prevail? And if a man believes he is doomed to suffer a violent

---

[1] Winston Churchill is credited with saying: "I have always avoided prophesying be-forehand. It is much better to prophesy after the event has already taken place." And this point has been made through the ages by many, including Horace Walpole who wrote in an 18th century letter, "Prognostics do not always prove prophecies—at least the wisest prophets make sure of the event first."

death, might not the depths of his heart propel him to acts that bring him to such an end? And if each individual in a nation fasts several times a year, and recites prayers and blessings many times each day for two thousand years hoping for the day his people returns from exile; and if untold generations of children see their mothers crying and their fathers earnestly chanting, all for the fulfillment of the prophecy that they will return to their land—shall we find it remarkable that such intense belief, given enough time for opportunity to blossom, eventually brings the prophecy to pass?[1]

And, my brother, it is not enough to say that this war or that peace may possibly be the fulfillment of prophecy. To claim the status of supernatural prophecy, an event must shout the definite truth of a specific prediction. If the Great Mystery would choose to reveal Himself through prophecy, surely He would not limit Himself to vague, or potentially self-fulfilling, predictions. Instead, He would have a prophet proclaim, in the eyes of all the people, that specific events will take place at precise times—events not vulnerable to alternative explanations of self-fulfillment or natural, random occurrence.

And an intelligent and reasonable God would not expect us to believe in Him based on miracle stories from the distant, superstitious past, accounts likely to be rife with error and worse. Instead, He would demonstrate miracles in the present—miracles beyond doubt. Perhaps He would have a prophet predict that one week hence, at midday, every dog on earth will chant, for one hour, original poetry in the human language of its native land. Surely, with a few similarly remarkable wonders, no sane man would deny that a Supernatural Force was the source of those prophecies.

And let not your heart be tempted to respond that faith in biblical prophecies is a noble choice precisely because there are alternative explanations available. For if alternative, non-supernatural, explanations are available, not only is it not necessary to invoke divinity, it disrespects the Great Mystery, any God there may be, by speaking in His name words one does not know He has spoken, and attributing to Him actions one does know He has taken.

And, my brother, do not say that if miracles were clearly performed man would have no choice but to obey God. For the Bible itself teaches that temptation must ever be battled—even by those who have seen the miraculous or received direct communication from God. The Bible recounts how Adam and Eve succumbed and disobeyed the clearly spoken words of God. In the biblical Exodus, too, the Israelites stooped to idolatry in worshiping the golden calf shortly after witnessing the miraculous plagues on Egypt and the splitting of the

---

[1] I refer, of course, to the 20th century CE reestablishment of a Jewish state in the biblical land of Israel.

Red Sea—and even after witnessing divine revelation at Sinai, they doubted God's promise that they would conquer the land of Canaan.

And, my brother: We need not accuse the biblical prophets of fabricating prophecies for their own glory, or even of engaging in the pious fraud of nurturing a nation's hope and faith by claiming to have received for them communication from God. Instead, such prophets may have sincerely, but mistakenly, believed they were experiencing contact with the Divine. For have you never been gripped by a powerful intuition, or poetic compulsion, or frightening reverie, or haunting dream, or surging inspiration, or profound despair? And had you been living in a culture that interpreted such intensities to be communications from God, and especially if you were of a passionate temperament and had inclinations toward doing momentous work, might you not be persuaded that you were the recipient of divine messages, prophecies you were meant to convey to the people?

And as disconcerting as this may be to the devout, is it not possible that some prophecies, beyond mistaken interpretations of normal minds, had their source in unhealthy states? Have you considered the disturbing similarity between the prophetic experience and the visions and voices that stalk the unwell mind? Today, too, many hear the voices of gods or demons; many see spectacular visions. But if they believe strongly that such communications issue from the supernatural, they are—regardless of their intelligence or level of education—given medication and admitted to hospital, and the voices and visions subside. Should we not speculate on whether in superstitious, less informed ages some we would now consider psychotic were then seen as prophetic? Should we not wonder whether some prophecies were no more from God than are the contemporary hallucinations of the mentally ill, and whether compassion would have been a more appropriate response than reverence and faith?

105. Claim that the Old Testament must be accurate and divine because it was transmitted perfectly by Jews, from generation to generation, since its writing; that every Hebrew Bible text throughout the world was always identical; and that this justifies the basis of biblical religion

And a Jewish scribe said: The Hebrew Bible, what some call the Old Testament, has been perfectly transmitted by my people, with great care and sacrifice, from generation to generation—and I, and many other rabbis and scribes, continue that legacy today. And throughout the world, and all through these thousands of years, all Jewish communities have exactly the same text. Such an extraordinary transmission is supernatural, and proves that God wrote or inspired the Hebrew Bible, and oversees its integrity. It also proves the biblical accounts of God's miraculous revelation at Sinai, and all other biblical stories and laws, to be God's sacred truth—because each generation has testified to the next, of those events' accuracy.

And the sage said: My brother, this matter you raise is of greatest importance to Jews, but it is important, too, to Christians and Muslims—because these faiths rely in great measure upon the credibility and narrative of the Old Testament. The New Testament teaches that Jesus was the fulfillment of various Old Testament prophecies and was the Son of the God of the Old Testament, and Muslims have taught that Mohammad was the greatest and final prophet in the chain of prophets first introduced to us by the Old Testament. Thus, if the Old Testament—the Hebrew Bible—is not the word of God, then not only Judaism, but Christianity and Islam too, find themselves on shaky ground. Let us all consider the claim, then, that the Old Testament was perfectly transmitted, and is, therefore, divine, or accurate in its supernatural accounts.

My brother: The Jewish people have, indeed, accomplished a remarkable transmission of the Hebrew Bible for over two thousand years. And I have little reason to doubt your sincerity and effort—and those of the great majority of your fellow scribes throughout these long centuries. Yet loving and careful devotion do not necessarily preserve a text perfectly over millennia, much less do they prove divine intervention, or a text to be of supernatural nature or origin. Scholars have done long and courageous work on these matters, and have much to teach us.[1]

---

[1] On this topic of the integrity of the biblical text, there is much scholarly common knowledge going back at least to the time of Spinoza—who himself credits the earlier Rabbi ibn Ezra for having seen that some verses in the Five Books of Moses were written by someone other than Moses—and it is difficult to identify the origins of particular facts and insights. And while I would like to give credit to each scholar for his specific contributions, this is not always possible when the beginnings of ideas and information are obscured, and numerous articles and books and informed verbal and written discourse make mention of many of the same points, which have now become part of a body of well-recognized facts and arguments of the arena.

To be clear, I do not claim any original contributions to technical knowledge about the biblical text's transmission. And I would like to mention the names of a few important scholars and their works on these topics, who are quoted and referenced in many secondary works on such matters—and, indeed, sometimes reference each other—and who have, among others, directly or indirectly, taught much of the content in this section: Let us begin with a few early works, the aforementioned Benedict de Spinoza in his *Theologico-Political Treatise,* and (the less heretical) Thomas Hobbes in *Leviathan,* and the bold Thomas Paine in his *Age of* Reason, and then skip centuries of learned contributors to the field and note contemporary and recent scholars and works such as Emanuel Tov's book, *Textual Criticism of the Hebrew Bible;* B. Barry Cohen's book, *Fixing God's Torah;* Menachem Cohen's articles, "The Idea of the Sanctity of the Biblical Text and the Science of Textual Criticism" and "On the Number of Verses, Words and Letters in the

One point to recognize is that even if the transmission of the first and most authoritative part of the Hebrew Bible, the Five Books of Moses, were perfect for the past more than two thousand years—and, my brother, it was not—we would still have no convincing evidence that this accurate transmission began any earlier than several hundred years after the days of Moses and, therefore, several hundred years after foundational miracle events described in that part of the Bible, such as the ten plagues visited upon Egypt, the manna in the desert, and the divine revelation at Sinai, were supposed to have taken place. Indeed, the Bible itself seems to tell us[1] that no unbroken chain of biblical transmission stretched back to Moses. And a period of hundreds of years—especially in superstitious ages—is more than enough time for inaccurate stories to develop, spread, and finally become incorporated into sacred texts.

My brother, by analogy, suppose an ancient legend spoke of an emperor living three thousand years ago, who was magically taught wisdom by five flying lions and seven golden doves, and who received instructions from these supernatural beings to write a scroll of this wisdom. And further suppose we had evidence that for the past two thousand, five hundred years a specific book was claimed to be this ancient emperor's wisdom text, and was guarded carefully, and its text transmitted perfectly. Could we be at all confident that earlier than two and a half millennia ago, in the first five hundred years after the days of the emperor—but before we have any record of it having been guarded and carefully transmitted—theft, error, accident, pious fraud, or gradual evolution of the legend, did not modify, or add significantly to, the ancient text, or even entirely invent the tale of the emperor and his supernatural wisdom? Would we not be wise to doubt this ancient legend of the emperor's wisdom scroll, especially since believing it would require us to accept supernatural claims, the premise of which is so similar to the superstitious thinking of all ancient cultures, and contradicts our repeated experience of reality—and the results of all our scientific inquiry?

Is the case of our Bible so different? Even if the Five Books of Moses remained perfectly preserved since the days of Ezra,[2] a period of hundreds of years would still have elapsed between Moses and Ezra. And how can we be confident that the transmission of the Bible was perfect during those hundreds of years? Indeed, how can we be confident that natural causes—imagination, legend, superstition, and more—did not give rise to the writing of the Bible over those

---

Bible," and Ernst Wurthwein's book, *The Text of the Old Testament*. Also see Jeffrey Tigay's article indirectly addressing these matters: "The Bible 'Codes': A Textual Perspective."

[1] See sections 111 and 112 for specifics.

[2] See sections 112 and 113 where Ezra's role is discussed in greater detail.

hundreds of years, even a Bible subsequently transmitted through the generations very carefully?

But even without directly calling into question the veracity of the Bible's accounts, and even setting aside what changes may have occurred to the text—or even whether it was first created—during the hundreds of years between Moses and Ezra, I say again that even the transmission of the Five Books of Moses over the latest two thousand years, the years after the last books of the Hebrew Bible were written, has been far from perfect. And this refutes the claim that the Bible must be supernatural because its transmission has been perfect. It simply has not.

My brother, ample testimony from a variety of authoritative Jewish sources through the ages, including the Talmud, makes it clear that errors and uncertainties crept into the biblical text over the past two millennia. The premise of your argument—that every Torah was identical throughout the world and over the generations—is mistaken. Rather, notwithstanding the great efforts of Jewish scribes and rabbis to preserve the text, errors proliferated. Such widespread errors in the Torah's transmission are, in addition to being suggested by various clues, clearly indicated by several types of evidence, as scholars have shown.

One type of evidence: A change in the alphabet used to write the Hebrew Bible scrolls.

Another type of evidence: Existing Hebrew Bible scrolls—ancient and more recent—whose texts are in conflict with each other. Our own eyes can see that no perfectly uniform text endured through the ages.

Another type of evidence: Authoritative rabbinic writings over the centuries explicitly stating that the Bible's text had by their time become errant, or at least uncertain, and that various Bible scrolls of their day differed from each other.

Yet another type of evidence: Authoritative rabbinic writings that include spellings or quotations of biblical words and passages differing from the text of current versions of the Hebrew Bible—thus indirectly illustrating that the Hebrew Bible's text has not always been consistent.

Let us examine each of these categories of evidence more closely.

a. Change in the Bible's alphabet

First, my brother, do you know that the very alphabet in which the Hebrew Bible is written has changed—to one with markedly different characters? For the past more than two thousand years scribes have been writing the Bible in "square" Assyrian characters, known in Hebrew as "K'tav Ashurit." In earlier days, however, the Hebrew Bible was written in a vastly different, ancient Hebrew alphabet. Not only have fragments and manuscripts from ancient Israel been found which are written in such characters, indicating this was their alphabet, and suggesting that Bibles of their age were likely written in this earlier script, the Talmud itself—the venerable collection of authoritative Jewish rabbinic writings stretching back fifteen centuries and more—testifies to this change of the Bible's alphabet.

The Talmud in tractate Sannhedrin, 21b states:

> Said Mar Zutra, and some say it was Mar Ukva: In the beginning, the Torah (Bible) was given to the Israelites in Hebrew letters and in the holy language. It was again given to them in the days of Ezra, in the Assyrian script and in the Aramaic language. They chose for the Israelites the Assyrian script and the holy language...

Contemporary Jewish Bibles have only one script—Assyrian. Writing Bibles in the older Hebrew letters is a practice lost to history, along with any notion of a perfectly preserved, unchanging Bible. For if the most sacred writings of a people were, over time, no longer even written in their original alphabet, it stretches credulity to believe that the centuries giving rise to such a dramatic change in the writing would have been scrupulously careful to preserve without change everything else about the texts.

Yet some may argue that although the Bible switched alphabets, perhaps its text was not changed in the slightest, and that every letter in the original ancient Hebrew alphabet of the Scriptures was carefully replaced with its equivalent in the Assyrian. Let us, then, illustrate from other evidence, beyond alphabet, that the Bible's text was not kept absolutely consistent and uncorrupted—and thus that its transmission provides evidence neither for a supernatural conservation of a perfect text nor for the credibility of its foundational miracle tales.

b. Existing Bible versions with different texts

Scholars explain that several significantly different ancient text versions of the Hebrew Bible still exist. The main texts are: The Septuagint, the Samaritan, and the Masoretic.

The Septuagint is an ancient Greek translation of the Hebrew Bible, written around the year 200 B.C.E. It differs in so many ways from the other two main text forms—the Masoretic and Samaritan—that many scholars believe the Hebrew Bible from which it was translated must have been a third text tradition.

The Samaritan text is the Bible version used by the Samaritans, an offshoot sect of Judaism that considered Mount Gerizim—and not the temple mount in Jerusalem—God's chosen, holiest ground. Their text contains some specific differences reflecting such beliefs, and these can be attributed to changes the Samaritans themselves made to the text. There are, however, many differences between the Samaritan text and the Masoretic text that are unrelated to Samaritan beliefs; furthermore, many of these same differences are found in the Septuagint texts, too. Yet the Samaritan text also differs in many instances from the Septuagint. All this, some scholars say, indicates that during the Second Temple era of ancient Israel there was another Bible text—different from both the Masoretic version and the text used to create the Septuagint—from which the Samaritans created their final version.

The Masoretic text is the version accepted today and for the past two thousand years throughout Judaism, and is the version upon which are based most modern-day Christian translations of the Hebrew Bible, the Old Testament. Yet manuscripts from the middle ages, as well as manuscripts found at Qumran—the collection known as the Dead Sea Scrolls—show that even Bibles written in this Masoretic tradition have quite a few differences in spellings and words, and are far from precisely the same as the currently accepted and nearly uniform text.

One cause of change over time even in the early Masoretic text was the gradual change in spelling in Hebrew due to the growing use, in Bibles, of vowel letters א, ה, ו, and י—referred to by scholars as the *matres lectionis*. Many biblical Hebrew words can legitimately be spelled with or without vowel letters, and these letters may have been added to help the reader more easily recognize each word's proper pronunciation and meaning. Scholars cite evidence that vowel letters were introduced later in the development of the Hebrew language, that this introduction was gradual, and that earlier scrolls, therefore, had fewer vowel letters used in fewer ways. This is one reason for variations in spelling—especially over the centuries—between different Masoretic Bibles.

Also, attempts by Jewish scribes through the ages to record instructions on the proper writing and precise text of Torah scrolls constituted a body of material known as the Masorah. Among the information recorded are more than two hundred differences in spelling between the Bibles of the east, the *M'dinhai*, and the Bibles of the west, the *Ma'arbai*. And differences between *K'tiv*, the way a word is written, and *K'ree*, the tradition on how the word is to be pronounced—sometimes as a completely different word—seem to indicate the attempt in Jewish biblical scholarship to unify different traditions of what was originally written in the Bible text.

But even were we to disregard the evidence of Bible's quite different from the Masoretic text—such as the Samaritan and Septuagint texts—and even were we to disregard the evidence, from the scrolls found at Qumran, and from Masorah writings of Jewish scribes, of different variations within the Masoretic text itself, and even were we to disregard the implications of the many differences between the way a word is written in the Hebrew Bible and the way it is supposed to be read—*K'tiv* as compared to *K'ree*—and even were we to forget that by the Talmud's own account the very alphabet in which the Bible is written has changed drastically, we would still be left with extensive evidence from rabbinic writings that the transmission of the traditional biblical text was not precise. Rabbinic writings throughout the ages directly discuss the prevalence—within and between Jewish communities—of ignorance, confusion, and disagreement about the Bible's precise text.

c. Direct rabbinical writings testifying to biblical textual error

Accounts from the Talmud and the writings of later Jewish rabbinic authorities bemoan how the Torah scrolls of their days were rife with error. A few examples will suffice.

The Talmud in tractate Kiddushin, 30a, in explaining why it would do no good to count the letters in an actual Bible scroll to determine the exact halfway point, has Rav Yosef state:

> They (the scholars of another region) are experts on the issue of missing (short) and full[1] (with vowel-indications) spellings (in the Bible). We are not experts.

Thus, the Talmud seems to concede that the Bible scrolls and the scholars of their region could not be depended upon for precise spellings of many biblical words.

Elsewhere,[2] rabbinic literature speaks of three Torah scrolls that were found at the Temple in Jerusalem, and how when discrepancies were noted between them, the rabbis settled these matters one at a time by adopting the text or spelling present in any two of the three scrolls. Thus a rabbinic tradition teaches of differences in Torah scrolls existing as far back as the period of the Jerusalem temple, two millennia ago, and also teaches that determinations of the proper text were made by no more definitive a method than following a simple majority of two out of three.

Hundreds of years later, the rabbi known as Rabbeynu Tam says in his *Hilchot Sefer Torah* that in his generation the scribes are also not expert in writing properly, and that the Bible scrolls of his day could only be considered religiously acceptable by applying the concept that one must sometimes act against the law in the larger mission of service to God.

---

[1] The academic terms for "missing" and "full" spelling are, respectively, "defective" and "plene."

[2] The story is told in the tractate of *Sofrim* (6:4), generally understood to have been written in the early centuries after the close of the Talmud.

Generations later, Rabbi Yom Tov Lippman Milhausen wrote in his *Tikkun Sefer Torah*, that although he labored to find a Bible scroll written properly, or which was accurate in its 'missing' or 'full' spellings, he could not—and he concluded that these were matters lost to his generation.

And these are but a small sample of the many rabbinical statements directly speaking of the imprecision of biblical texts in their day.

d. Discrepancies between rabbinical references to biblical text and current biblical text

There is also indirect evidence of disagreements between texts of different Bibles, or changes to the text over time, in that verses are quoted by the Talmud and later rabbinic writings which differ from the wordings or spellings of those verses in current versions of the Bible.[1]

One example: The Talmud, in tractate Shabbat, 55b,[2] specifies the spelling of a particular word in the Bible, and the rabbinical commentary *Tosafot*, noting that in Bible scrolls of his day the spelling was different, says in admirably direct fashion:

> Our Talmud disagrees with our Bible scrolls.

And *Tosafot* there also mentions another instance in a different tractate of the Jerusalem Talmud where the Talmudic text speaks of the Bible saying that Samson ruled for forty years, but, *Tosafot* notes, in the Torah scrolls of his own day, the verse says Samson ruled not forty, but twenty, years.

Another example: The Talmud, in tractate kiddushin 30a, states:

> For this reason the scholars of old were called *sofrim*, because they counted all the letters in the Torah (Five Books of Moses). They would say that the letter *vav* in the word *gahon* (Leviticus 11:42) is the halfway point of all the letters in a

---

[1] Again, for more discussion and detail on these and related themes on the Bible's text, see the following books: *Fixing God's Torah*, by B. Barry Levy; *Textual Criticism of the Hebrew Bible* by Emanuel Tov; and *The Text of the Old Testament* by Ernst Wurthwein. Also see Menachem Cohen's "The Idea of the Sanctity of the Biblical Text and the Science of Textual Criticism," an excellent and accessible article. As of this writing the article was posted on the Internet at: http://cs.anu.edu.au/~bdm/dilugim/opinions/CohenArt/

[2] Those readers capable of reading Talmudic commentaries in their original Hebrew, and wishing to pursue many more examples of discrepancies between biblical texts evident in rabbinic writings, including several instances from the works of *Rashi*, are encouraged to refer to the *Gilyon Ha'Shas* entry on the above-mentioned Talmudic passage in tractate Shabbat, 55b.

Torah scroll; that (the words) *darosh darash* is the halfway point of all the words (in a Torah scroll)…

Yet an actual count of the letters of current Torah texts shows the halfway point of the letters to be many hundreds of letters away from the *"vav* of *gahon."*

In summary, my brother, the Bible's text was not supernaturally prevented from changing. Changes arose—different changes in different communities and in different scrolls. Throughout the centuries, many rabbinic decisions were made as to which version would be considered authoritative—and all existing texts found to differ from the new decisions were taken out of circulation. Indeed, even with such efforts at repeatedly establishing consistency, Torah scrolls often differed significantly from each other in the same generation, even within communities and regions—and all the more so did Torahs separated from each other by much time or distance show variations.

With the advent of the printing press in the fifteenth century C.E., however, Jewish scribes and rabbinical authorities were better able to establish and propagate a more uniform text, by having scribes, in the process of writing a Torah scroll, consult an authorized, uniform, widely distributed printed version, to ensure they were creating each new scroll in complete agreement with the then-approved text, and by having rabbis check their own communities' Torah scrolls against such authorized printed versions—and removing from circulation any nonconforming scrolls.

This process amounted not to a miraculously unerring transmission, but rather to a quite human system for repeatedly reestablishing consistency—but not necessarily fidelity to the original version—in a text that frequently became corrupted.

My brother, the Jewish people have done a remarkable thing in transmitting the Torah—the Five Books of Moses, and in a larger sense, the entire Hebrew Bible—through the centuries, with a great degree of accuracy. Through wars and plagues, forced migrations and horrendous persecutions, and in so many different cultures and lands, they have kept the Torah text mostly intact. Preserving the integrity of these texts was an admirable feat, requiring deep commitment, extensive education, painstaking effort and discipline, and, often, great personal courage and sacrifice. But these heroic efforts did not result in an error-free transmission. Nor did this remarkable transmission necessarily begin anytime within many hundreds of years of Moses—in whose day the religion's foundational events and miracles are supposed to have occurred. Thus, no persuasive case can be made for the transmission being miraculous, divinely guided, or proof of the Bible's truth.

My brother, it is human to yearn for the existence of sacred words inspired, perhaps even spoken, by God. It is human to yearn for unshakeable certainty about the veracity of a text for which one's ancestors have lived and often died. It is human to hastily assent to any argument that confirms one's way of life to be correct, and one's holy books divine. And while all these things are human, my brother, and might justifiably awaken our sympathies, they cannot prevail upon our fair-minded reason to see them as anything more than human.

And my brother, the heart of a devoted scribe bleeds with the ink of his writing, and his quill runs with the lifeblood of his scrolls. Much more can be said about these matters of biblical transmission, and one like you would, perhaps, gladly give them many hours. But other questions are weighing upon the hearts of teachers and bakers and builders and singers and farmers and poets, and all manner of others. Let us, then, leave further knowledge on biblical transmission for you to seek on your own—in the writings of learned scholars[1] who have exerted the courage to examine heritage and legend with an unblinking eye.

106. Argument that the Hebrew Bible is accurate in all its important content, even if not perfectly transmitted in every letter or word—and therefore can be trusted as a reliable eyewitness account of God's revelation, His miracles, and His will for our lives

And a religious man said: Of course not every word or letter was accurately transmitted. And I agree that the transmission was not miraculous. But all the evidence tells us that that the biblical transmission was accurate on the Bible's significant points, over the past two thousand years. Words and letters may have been lost or changed, but no ideas or laws or stories were changed. And this tells us that the Bible can be trusted as reliable eyewitness testimony. Therefore I can believe that all the events of the Bible, the divine revelation at Sinai, as well as all the miracles performed for God's people, the wonders of the prophets, and so on, truly took place—and that the laws of the Bible are God's will for my life.

And the sage said: My brother, even if there were no significant changes in the past two millennia, can we speak to what happened earlier still? We simply do not know whether any ideas or laws or stories in the Bible have changed, since first it was written—indeed, we do not know when first it was written.

Moreover, even if nothing of import changed in the Bible since it was written, this would still give us no reason to believe that its contents are either accurate or divine. Have not many fables and legends—Aesop's stories of

---

[1] As indicated in footnotes above, see the writings of Professors Menachem Cohen, Emanuel Tov, and Ernst Wurthwein, and B. Barry Levy, among others.

donkeys and dogs and all manner of beasts, and fairy tales of talking pigs and scheming wolves, and the like—remained significantly unchanged for many hundreds, perhaps thousands of years, too? Yet do we think this sufficient reason to consider them either factual or supernatural?

Yet we have good evidence from the Bible itself that important changes were made to its text, new laws and the like—and I shall speak of these soon.[1]

Overall, my brother, there is good reason to strongly suspect that the Bible is neither completely accurate in its claims, nor the will or word of God. It comprises a set of books coming to us from deep within the ages of rampant superstition; and though it contains much beauty and wisdom, even much that is historically accurate, it also tells many tales the events of which violate the laws of nature; and it contradicts itself on numerous occasions, too, both on small facts and on substantive teachings. And we shall soon speak more on all these.

107. Argument that the biblical account of mass divine revelation at Sinai must be accurate—and therefore belief in the God of the Bible is justified—because no generation of Jews would have accepted that version of their ancestors' history, unless their parents knew of such a tradition (The "Kuzari" proof)

And a gray-bearded scholar said: The Bible tells us of God's revelation to mankind at Mount Sinai—from which follow the three religions of Judaism, Christianity, and Islam. And this revelation I think must have taken place. Consider this: Some generation of Jews was the first to receive the Bible. If it was the generation of Moses, as I believe it was, the accounts of revelation must be true, because the Bible states it happened to them, and they would never have accepted a Bible that told a story they knew was false. And even if the Bible was written in a later generation than that of Moses, the accounts of divine revelation still must be true, because if those accounts were fabricated, how would any generation of Jews have accepted such a Bible, which states that the whole nation of Israel—each person's ancestors—witnessed that divine revelation? If the story were untrue, they would have known this, because none of them would have heard about this momentous event from their parents—as there would have been no national memory of this. And this event, had it occurred, would surely have been known to some of their parents from the lore and traditions of their forebears. Clearly, then, that the Jews accepted and transmitted this Bible proves

---

[1] See sections 111 and 112 which deal with the book Hilkiah found, and with Ezra's return from exile.

that the mass divine revelation truly took place.[1] And do not say that such a claim can be made even if false. No other religion claims such mass revelation to an entire people. This proves such a claim cannot be made unless it is true.

And the sage said: Dear father, your argument is intelligent and creative, and I can see how some find it appealing—especially as it supports what is time-honored and beloved. And the picture I paint will not be pleasant for the believer to behold. The sight of a majestic tree being put to the ax makes poetic eyes sting—and the awful spectacle of an ancient,[2] sacred heritage being felled can wound far deeper. Yet the corpses of trees can sometimes build warm homes for the living—and at times even the stately oak of tradition must be cleared to grow the necessary bread of authentic and noble existence.

Meditate upon the following, father, though your heart breaks. Perhaps the current text of the scroll of Moses has not been with the Jewish people since the days of Moses and the generation of which the scroll speaks. Rather, perhaps the text developed gradually—from varied and conflicting tales and traditions—and the current version became final only hundreds of years after the death of Moses. And only then were its tales of revelation and miracles declared by a unified leadership to be the authoritative word of God, thereafter to be faithfully preserved by the Jewish people for millennia.

Father, the human mind—or the minds of a certain number within every group of humans—has a natural affinity for tales of magic, or a yearning for transcendental significance. Is it any surprise, then, that such tales of revelation developed and grew? Perhaps, over the course of hundreds of years after the death of Moses, deep in the ages of magic and superstition, miraculous accounts were born and spread—mostly by the honest gullibility of wonder and gossip,

---

[1] A version of this argument has been presented at least as early as the 12th century by the Jewish rabbi and mystic Yehudah HaLevi in his book *The Kuzari*, which argues for the truth of Judaism (or at least the superiority of its claims when compared to those of Christianity and Islam) and uses as its setting a Jewish legend about an 8th century king of the Khazars—a tribe said to have lived in the vicinity of what is now eastern Russia— converting to Judaism along with many of his people after considering the evidence.

[2] What is long gone takes on the enchantment of nostalgia and the hues of reverence and meaning. It is difficult to idealize the present; much easier to do so with the past, or even the future—and religion does so with both: her legends and miracles and Garden of Eden of old, and her messiahs and raptures and golden ages yet to come. Scottish poet Thomas Campbell wrote:

Why do those cliffs of shadowy tint appear
More sweet than all the landscape smiling near?
'Tis distance lends enchantment to the view
And robes the mountain in its azure hue.

but in part by pious fabrication and sacred deceit—because they bolstered claims of the people's chosen status; reinforced the credibility of religious laws; comforted many at times of great loss; and infused a nation's history with the drama and justification of miracle. Thus, no generation need suddenly have accepted all these embellishments. Instead, as is the case with many ideas, they likely spread gradually, were accepted by some and undoubtedly dismissed by others—until permanently canonized, by religious authorities of a later day, as definitive truth. And by that time, the legends would have been very old, and nobody—especially in those days of rampant superstition and scientific ignorance—could state with certainty that they were *not* true.

And, father, to conclude that tales of revelation at Sinai are not credible, one need not even insist that nothing took place at Sinai that gave rise to the legend. Instead, it may well be that some awe-inspiring event—a volcano, perhaps, or a great storm—was witnessed by a group of several hundred or several thousand ancestors of some portion of what later came to be the people of Israel,[1] and that a charismatic leader such as Moses helped these terrified primitives—even recently freed slaves, as the Bible has it—to interpret this as a direct visitation from God, followed by Moses delivering to them various commands he said God taught him on the mountain. Then, over several centuries, this legend could easily have grown to its final form as seen in the Bible—of an entire nation including 600,000 adult males camping at the foot of the mountain, preparing three days for the revelation, and all witnessing the spectacle in unison.

And so, father, there need not have been one generation to whom a completely new Bible was presented, that they could have asked their parents whether its tales of miraculous divine revelation were accurate. Instead, by the time such tales were recorded in the Bible, they had likely long been circulating as folklore—perhaps originally as entertaining stories told to excite children's imagina-

---

[1] It has been pointed out that a nation often identifies with a tradition of its "ancestors," or founders, even when the ancestors or founders being referred to were only the progenitors of a small percentage of the population. One example is the American holiday of Thanksgiving, a common ritual of which is telling the account of the Pilgrims landing at Plymouth Rock and being helped by the "Indians" to survive their first winter in the "New World." For another example: the American Founding Fathers not only were not the ancestors of most contemporary Americans, the ancestors of the great majority of Americans were not even in America until long after the new country was founded. Still, when the United States is healthy in its unity, the nation as a whole identifies with such stories of its origins. It is not difficult to imagine, then, that the legend of Moses and the ancestors escaping Egypt and witnessing divine revelation may have originally been the tradition of only a small group, but was later adopted as the broader national story of what came to be known as the Israelites—and eventually the entire nation believed they had a common ancestry spoken about in the Bible.

tion, but later adopted by earnest and credulous adults oriented to worship and astonishment, and only gaining general acceptance generations later. Thus, even if not everyone would have believed such stories upon first seeing such accounts in a Bible, no definitive popular rejection would have been evoked—for, again, by the time such things would have been recorded in the Bible, these stories would have been old and familiar, and nobody could state with certainty that such things had not taken place. And following the Bible's canonization by religious authority, no dissenting voices on such a matter would have long been tolerated—much less transmitted to future generations.

And as to why other religions have not made claims of an entire nation witnessing a revelation, I offer the following points. First, anytime we see one nation, or movement, or individual, incorporating a unique element, this does not prove that others could not have done the same, and it certainly does not prove the involvement of anything supernatural. Consider that the ancient Greeks developed science and philosophy and democracy to a degree unparalleled by nations of their day, or even of many centuries to follow. And the ancient Egyptians built pyramids and preserved the bodies of their dead with knowledge unknown to other nations. Does this make those achievements supernatural? Shall we argue that if such things were natural other nations would have developed these same ideas and practices to the same degree at the same time?

Moreover, the many centuries by which Judaism and its early myths preceded the birth of Christianity, and the even larger number of centuries by which Judaism preceded the rise of Islam, helps explain the difference in the magnitude of the claims. As the prevalence of writing and literacy, and organized record-keeping, and wider, easier travel, grew over the centuries—it became increasingly difficult to make claims about mass events, when not true. Judaism had many centuries to develop; its beginnings are shrouded in the mists of ancient legends and forgotten days. By contrast, Christianity and Islam had well-documented, and relatively sudden, beginnings. Instead of half a millennia or more in the darkness of lost ages which would have allowed Judaism to gradually develop an account of a mass revelation before its Bible was canonized, Christianity and Islam began in the glare of more watchful history against the backdrop, and represented as a refinement, of the Jewish religion—and these later religions produced their scriptures relatively quickly. Indeed, the Jewish influence of zealously guarding the integrity of their Bible, a practice that may well have taken hold only hundreds of years after Moses, likely made it more difficult for either of her two powerful monotheistic offspring—Christianity and Islam—whose clergy followed, to some degree, the Jewish example, to allow, once their scriptures were written, changes to their accepted version of events, including such changes as lesser tales developing into accounts of mass revelations to an entire nation.

Furthermore, in addition to a claim of revelation to an entire people being admittedly more difficult, and, if not intentionally manufactured, requiring more time to develop naturally among a people, there may be other cultural or ideological reasons why Judaism developed the teaching of mass revelation, while other—even equally ancient—religions did not. The Greeks and various others, though they believed in the existence and power of gods, did not necessarily believe that such gods were interested in communicating directly to humans on an organized system of how we must live. The Jews did. Thus, arguably, divine revelation overall, was more important to Jews than to other ancient peoples. And, being more important to them, the legend about such divine revelation was developed in impressive form.

Further still, although the Jews, like other nations, eventually developed a priestly hierarchy—indeed, one to which access was only gained by the accident of being born into a priestly family—and which at times held great power and influence, the Jews also had a strong sense of spiritual egalitarianism, as evidenced by seeing themselves as a "kingdom of priests and a holy nation;"[1] and as evidenced by the rebellion of Korah and two hundred and fifty princes against Moses and Aaron, in which they complained[2] that Moses and Aaron were improperly raising themselves up as spiritually superior to the rest of the people; and as evidenced, too, by various books in the early Bible speaking of private sacrifices to God by individuals—without priestly assistance—and later biblical books bemoaning the far from consistently successful attempts to limit worship to a centralized temple in Jerusalem. Thus, one may argue that the egalitarian, anti-priest-class attitude amongst the early Israelites, or the religious leaders' awareness of such an attitude, in combination with the prophetic notion of spirituality—that God speaks to humans—helped in the development and acceptance of the legend that God had revealed himself to the entire people.[3]

---

[1] Exodus 19:6

[2] Numbers 16:1-3. And, though the Bible unambiguously portrays Korah as in the wrong and Moses and Aaron's priesthood as in the right, we may learn from scholars to ask what this story meant, and why—from a non-supernatural perspective—the priests or other powers would have included such a story in the Bible. One theory, as I indicate in the text, is that the Jewish people did not comfortably accept the notion of hierarchical spirituality presided over by a special class, and thus, the Aaronite priests felt the need to reinforce the lesson of the descendents of Aaron being the only legitimate priests.

[3] In this context it is worthwhile to note that not only with regard to the priesthood did the early Israelites chafe against authority and hierarchy, but even with regard to government. The books of the Hebrew Bible make clear that the early Israelites were ambivalent about the institution of monarchy. Among other clues, the book of Judges speaks of a pre-monarchical age with no centralized government, when the Israelite tribes aided each other in battle when needed, and accepted the temporary leadership of various

Other peoples, perhaps less fiercely resistant to hierarchy, or not as imbued with the model of prophetic spirituality, may have had less reason to develop a tradition of God revealing Himself to the entire nation.

108. Sub-argument that everyone chooses what to believe, everyone is biased; that believers choose arguments that support the Bible, including its account of God's revelation at Sinai, while skeptics choose arguments that cast doubt on the Bible and its teachings

And the scholar said: Your words are all well and good, but they are arguments just like my arguments. We each choose which arguments to rely upon. Skeptics like you pretend to be objective, but choose arguments against the Bible, just as believers like me choose arguments for the Bible, and for its teachings on the revelation at Sinai. Why do you think your bias is better than mine?

And the sage said: Father, it is not a question of legitimate choice between two reasonable alternatives. The Bible's version of events asks us to believe in the occurrence of numerous supernatural events. But in light of thousands of years of human error and superstition—where all manner of what were thought to be supernatural events are now seen to have been natural events misinterpreted, even accounts woven out of nothing but pious imagination or worse—and in light of our knowledge of how vulnerable are humans to the seductions and terrors of religious belief; and in light of how common it is for legends to begin, travel, and grow; and in light of not one supernatural event ever having been credibly proved to the standards of responsible evidence; in light of all this, must not the honest seeker be exceedingly suspicious of supernatural claims?

And so, Father, to responsibly disbelieve the story, those skeptical of the Bible's account of supernatural revelation at Sinai need only suggest one non-supernatural scenario in which such a story could have ended up in the Bible and beliefs of a people.

Remember, although human history has always and everywhere been rife with tall tales and miracle claims, when such things are examined closely, not one

---

heroes or judges, and the book ends, by saying (Judges 21:25) "In those days there was no king in Israel: every man did that which was right in his own eyes."

And the Bible has God see the people's request for a king (in 1 Samuel 8:7) as a rejection of God's direct rule over the people. Generations later, upon King Solomon's death (in 1 Kings 12) the people were unhappy with the heavy service he exacted from them, and demanded from his son Rehoboam, as a condition of accepting him as king, that he lighten the burden. When he refused, they said (verse 16) "What portion have we in David?...to your tents, O Israel..." and the Bible relates that most of Israel rebelled and chose another king, and the kingdom was split from that day forward into Judah and Israel.

supernatural event has ever been shown to have taken place. Thus, the overwhelming burden of proof lies with those who claim that anything—including the account of revelation at Sinai—truly involved the supernatural.

109. Did Moses write the Five Books of Moses?

The scholar squinted, stroked his beard slowly, and shaking his head from side to side, said: No; these stories did not develop gradually. I have no reason to believe that the Five Books of Moses were not written by Moses, and received by the very generation that witnessed those events. Thus we can trust that those miracles occurred, and that the Bible speaks the word of God.

And the sage replied: Dear father, I understand that what you have just said is what your tradition has taught for many centuries. Many among the faithful have believed that Moses wrote the Five Books of Moses, wherein the story of divine revelation is recorded—and that the Jews have transmitted the Bible from the very generation of Moses. Yet there are many reasons for the honest and thoughtful to question this tradition.

First, nowhere does the Five Books of Moses claim that Moses wrote its entire text. When Deuteronomy 31:22-24 speaks of Moses writing down a song and a book of teaching, it is not at all clear to what this refers. It seems to be referring to some sections of Deuteronomy, and to the song that directly follows within a few verses—the song of "Ha'azinu," which begins: "Give ear, O ye heavens, and I will speak: and hear, O earth, the words of my mouth." The plain context of the verses indicates that the book being referred to is not the entire Five Books of Moses. After all, several chapters of Deuteronomy remain after the account of Moses writing the song and book of teaching. And when the Bible speaks of someone having written a book, that book could not have been the Bible. A book cannot discuss, in the past tense, the completion of its own writing—all the more so when the passage in question is well before the book's end.

And courageous men[1] have, for hundreds of years, urged that plain reading of the Five Books of Moses suggests, to eyes not closed by a committed heart, that Moses was not its sole author, but that its final version was written by a writer or writers living much later. Let us discuss a number of their observations.

And, yes, religious commentaries attempt to answer these problems in various ways. But reflect upon the matter and ask yourself honestly, in a quiet moment, whether the evidence suggests Moses truly wrote those verses, or not.

---

[1] Spinoza, Hobbes, Paine, and others—some before them, and many after them.

Deuteronomy 34:5-10 states:

> So Moses the servant of the Lord died there in the land of Moab, according to the word of the Lord. And he buried him in a valley in the land of Moab, over against Beth-peor: but no man knoweth of his sepulchre unto this day. And Moses was a hundred and twenty years old when he died: his eye was not dim, nor his natural force abated. And the children of Israel wept for Moses in the plains of Moab thirty days: so the days of weeping and mourning for Moses were ended. And Joshua the son of Nun was full of the spirit of wisdom; for Moses had laid his hands upon him: and the children of Israel hearkened unto him, and did as the Lord commanded Moses. And there arose not a prophet since in Israel like unto Moses, whom the Lord knew face to face.

The death of Moses, the people mourning for him, and their subsequent loyalty to his successor Joshua, are described in past tense. Moses would not have witnessed these, nor written about them.

Second, in that account of Moses' death, Deuteronomy 34:6 states:

> …But no man knoweth of his sepulchre unto this day.

The phrase "unto this day" implies that a great deal of time had passed since Moses had been buried. Is not the only straightforward conclusion that this verse was written many years, even generations, after Moses' death?

Third, that passage states, in 34:10:

> And there arose not a prophet since in Israel like unto Moses…

Here, too, one would only make such a claim many generations after the days of Moses. Thus, this does not seem to have been written by Moses.

Fourth, Deuteronomy 3:14 states:

> Jair son of Manasseh received the whole Argob district…and named it after himself, Havvoth-Jair, unto this day.

The plain meaning of this verse implies that its author was writing many years after the generation of Jair, who lived in the days of Moses—and remarking that the place still carried the name given to it by its founder in the distant past.

Fifth, Deuteronomy 10:8-9, states:

> At that time the Lord set apart the tribe of Levi to carry the Ark of the Lord's Covenant, to stand in attendance upon the Lord, and to bless in His name, unto this day. Therefore the tribe of Levi received no hereditary portion among his brothers: the Lord is his portion.

The writer, when he uses the phrase "unto this day," seems to be referring to the Levites doing sacred duties well after the days of Moses. If it were Moses speaking to his own generation, why would he mention that the Levites are still attending to the duties their own generation had seen them undertake at the word of God?

Sixth, the apportionment of the land is discussed in past tense, when it is explained that the tribe of Levi "received no hereditary portion among his brothers…" But the land was not apportioned until after the death of Moses; thus, the writer of these verses seems to have lived after Moses' death.

Seventh, Genesis 36:31 states:

> And these are the kings that reigned in the land of Edom, before there reigned a king for the children of Israel.

One generally refers to a time "before" a certain set of events, only after that set of events begins. When the writer of this verse in Genesis refers to a time before Israel had kings, it suggests the writer lived after there *were* kings in Israel—a period the Bible itself makes clear began hundreds of years after Moses.

Eighth, Deuteronomy opens as follows:

> These are the words that Moses spoke to all the people of Israel on the other side of the Jordan, in the desert…

The term "the other side of[1] the Jordan," when referring to the land across the Jordan from the rest of biblical Israel, is only accurate from the geographical, cultural, and temporal point of view of someone writing after Moses' death—someone in the land of Israel after it was settled by Jews. The Bible makes clear that during the lifetime of Moses, neither he nor the Jews crossed the Jordan into

---

[1] Oddly, the King James translation renders the phrase as "this side" of the Jordan. The Hebrew word is "b'ever," and the straightforward meaning of "b'ever" is "across" or "on the other side of." And this meaning, of "on the other side of," has been the traditional and contemporary translation of most Bible versions and commentaries.

Israel; thus, in the lifetime of Moses the land across the Jordan from Canaan-Israel would not have been referred to as the "other" side of the Jordan. It was "this" side of the Jordan.

Ninth, Genesis 12:6 states:

> And Abram passed through the land unto the place of Sichem, unto the plain of Moreh. And the Canaanite was then in the land.

The straightforward implication of this is that it is written from the perspective of a time when the Canaanites were no longer in the land. Yet Moses died before the Israelites crossed into, and conquered, the land of Canaan—before the Canaanites were driven off the land. Thus, Moses apparently did not write this verse.

Tenth, at many times the text speaks of Moses in the third person. One example is the opening of Deuteronomy:

> These be the words which Moses spake unto all Israel...

Yet at times the text has Moses speaking in first person, as in Deuteronomy 1:9:

> And I spake unto you at that time, saying, I am not able to bear you myself alone.

Moses does not appear to have written the entire text, for the parts where Moses speaks about his own actions are surrounded by a narrator speaking of Moses in third person, Moses apparently being someone other than the narrator. This back and forth changing of point of view appears to be not the work of an author writing of himself, but rather the work of an author writing about the words and deeds of another.

Father, these clues, and more, discerning and courageous men have noticed and spoken of for hundreds of years—in the effort to illustrate that someone other than Moses composed the final version of the Five Books of Moses. To be sure, religious scholars committed to Moses' authorship of the entire Five Books of Moses have attempted to answer these observations. Indeed, none of the clues and indications I have mentioned is *proof* that Moses was not the sole human author of the entire Five Books of Moses, nor are they intended as proof—merely as relevant evidence. On this matter let every one of us seek the truth with an open heart, and see which side's arguments appear persuasive, and which like but desperate defenses of besieged dogma.

And let not your heart be tempted to respond that perhaps Moses did not write all of the Five Books of Moses, but that he did write the account of the divine revelation at Sinai, events of his own day—thus lending credibility to these supernatural claims. For if Moses did not write all of the text, how can we know which parts he wrote, and which not? And without compelling evidence, why should we believe that passages speaking of supernatural events, which contradict our extensive knowledge of reality, were truly recorded accurately—that is, by Moses himself, speaking to his own generation of miracles they all witnessed?

Now, then, as there is no compelling evidence outside the Bible that Moses wrote the entire text of the Five Books of Moses—and considerable evidence even within the Bible that he did not—perhaps you might consider that these texts, and the revelations and miracles they recount, may have been developed into their current form only hundreds of years after Moses, and are thus likely inaccurate in their claims of miraculous events about which their writer or writers would have had no firsthand knowledge.

110. Sub-argument that all anachronisms in the Five Books of Moses, including all instances of the phrase "unto this day," are consistent with Moses being the author, because they are supernatural prophecies

And the religious scholar persisted, saying: Only those without faith would think your evidence convincing. Those of us with faith know that Moses wrote the Five Books of Moses—and that all instances where its text seems not to be reflecting the generation of Moses are simply prophecies God instructed Moses to include in the Bible. And whenever the Bible says, "unto this day," those statements are prophetically worded that way because they will be true regardless of when in history that passage is read. And so, as is indeed true, nobody knows the burial place of Moses until this day, no prophet like Moses has arisen in Israel until this day, and the Levites are still set aside to serve God in Jewish worship services until this day. And so, you see, you have been too quick to dismiss the Bible and her believers. You do not realize the depth and subtlety involved in the sacred text. It is not we who are naïve and mistaken, but you.

And the sage said: Father, you offer an interesting protest about some of the examples I cited. You say that although by plain analysis of the text Moses does not seem to have written the entire Five Books of Moses, he could still have done so if the anachronistic passages were written by supernatural prophecy.

Yet consider several points: First, the Bible never claims that such passages are prophecies—nor does it, in those cases, use the future tense, the natural way to refer to predictions or assurances about the future. And especially since the plain phrasing of those passages seems to indicate that they were meant for the people of the day, it would have been strange and incongruous to have conveyed

284

words that were not yet relevant to those people—such as uses of the term "unto this day," in reference to the Levites still being set aside for sacred service, and the name of the city still being Havvoth-Jair, implying that a great deal of time had passed since the consecration of the Levites and the naming of the city—both of which happened in the very generation of Moses and those to whom he was speaking. Is it truly reasonable, then, for us to conclude that such instances of "unto this day" are anything but straightforward writing, intended to reflect what was true in the days of the author?

More damaging to your argument, however, are examples of the Bible using the words "unto this day" in cases where the verses clearly have not applied for all time. Thus, these passages either do not mean to be prophecies to apply for all time, but speak rather of what held true in the author's day—or they do mean to be prophecies applying for all time, and the prophecies have been proved false. The first example is from the Five Books of Moses. Genesis 47:26 states:

> And Joseph made it a law over the land of Egypt unto this day, that Pharaoh should have the fifth part; except the land of the priests only, which became not Pharaoh's.

Father, it has been many long centuries since any Pharaoh ruled Egypt. The fifth-part tax for Pharaoh, then, which Joseph is said to have initiated, has clearly not held for all time. Thus, at least in this case, the phrase "unto this day" either was not intended as prophecy, or is a false prophecy. As to the other instances of "unto this day" from the Five Books of Moses, which, when read in their plain context seem to indicate that their writer was not Moses, why should we assume that in those cases the words were written by Moses and intended as prophecy for all time? Is the Bible so inconsistent and unclear as to sometimes use the phrase "unto this day" in its plain meaning, to denote what is true in the day of the author, yet at other times—without any indication, and without employing the future tense—uses the phrase to predict a prophecy for all time? Now that we have seen The Five Books of Moses to use the term "unto this day" and apparently not be prophesying for all time, but rather referring to the day of the writer—is it not reasonable to conclude that those passages in the Five Books of Moses referring to points in time later than Moses, and using the phrase "unto this day," were not written by Moses in prophecy—but by a later author speaking in quite natural terms of his own day?

And since parts of the Five Books of Moses were, therefore, apparently written by those living in generations later than Moses—are we not justified, indeed are we not responsible, to react with skepticism to claims of a perfect and reliable testimony transmitted through all generations beginning with Moses—a claim based upon the seductive yet seemingly inaccurate notion that Moses himself wrote all the miraculous accounts of the Five Books of Moses, including those of divine revelation at Sinai?

And as further support for the argument that the biblical phrase "unto this day" does not denote prophecy, I shall cite several examples of other books of the Bible using this same phrase and clearly not prophesying for all time, but rather speaking about the day of the author. Joshua 9:27 states:

> And Joshua made them that day hewers of wood and drawers of water for the congregation, and for the altar of the Lord, even unto this day...

Father, ages have passed since the Jews assigned to any particular people the roles of hewing wood or drawing water. Indeed, these tasks themselves are largely unnecessary in modern life. Moreover, the "altar of the Lord" is no longer existent, let alone functioning and requiring supplies of wood and water. Clearly, then, this passage in Joshua was not making a prophetic statement for all time, but rather describing conditions as they existed in the writer's day.

Another example, I Samuel 5:5 states:

> Therefore neither the priests of Dagon, nor any that come into Dagon's house, tread on the threshold of Dagon in Ashdod unto this day.

Father, the ancient god Dagon is no longer worshiped; thus, there are neither priests of Dagon nor any visitors to the house of Dagon who would observe such cautions; that passage, therefore, when using the phrase "unto this day" clearly has not prophesied for all time. Instead, as with the other passages, this verse speaks of what held true in the author's day.

Still another example is II Chronicles, 5:7-9 which states:

> And the priests brought in the ark of the covenant of the Lord unto his place, to the oracle of the house, into the most holy place, even under the wings of the cherubims... And they drew out the staves of the ark, that the ends of the staves were seen from the ark before the oracle; but they were not seen without; And there it is unto this day.

Father, the ark is *not* there unto this day. Over the past two millennia, the ruins of the Jewish temple were raided and searched repeatedly by all manner of conquerors and thieves. And a heavily attended mosque has later occupied the site for hundreds of years, too. Perhaps, when the temple was about to be sacked, the Jews concealed the Ark of the Covenant elsewhere, or perhaps hostile armies plundered it for its gold. In any case, the ark is certainly not in the Holy of Holies where originally placed. When the Bible says, "And there it is unto this day" it was not prophesying that such will remain its location for all time; instead, it spoke from the author's perspective, describing the circumstances of his day.

And so, father, these verses and others illustrate that when the Bible used the phrase "unto this day," the conditions it described have often not applied for all time. And this supports the argument that this phrase when used in the Five Books of Moses similarly does not intend prophecy, but rather straightforward description of conditions in the author's day. And since those passages reflect a time later than Moses, it seems that Moses, at minimum, did not write the entire Five Books of Moses. And since he did not write all of that text, we cannot reliably know how much, if any, of the text he did write. Thus, we have little responsible support for confidently relying upon notions of accurate and uninterrupted Jewish traditions of biblical miracles and divine revelation. Who can say but that many accounts in the Bible were written by generations hundreds of years after the days of Moses, holding no first-hand knowledge—thus offering no reliable testimony—of supernatural events and divine revelation.

111. The book found by Hilkiah and presented to King Josiah: evidence from later books of the Old Testament that there was no continuous and reliable transmission, dating back to Moses, of the Five Books of Moses—and that the Jews' acceptance of a Bible with accounts of mass miracles does not prove such accounts true

Then the old scholar lifted a trembling hand and said: I do not concede the point, but even if you are correct that Moses did not write the entire Five Books of Moses, my claim may still stand—that the Jews have an unbroken chain of tradition testifying to God's supernatural revelation at Sinai and to other great miracles of the Exodus from Egypt. I still maintain my principal point: Regardless of who wrote the Bible, no generation of Jews would have accepted as authoritative a book claiming that all their ancestors saw those miracles—unless knowledge of such monumental events was long since seared into their national memory, and passed down from father to son in a sacred transmission beginning in the days of Moses and the wandering Israelites. Thus, that the Jews embraced the Bible must mean its astonishing accounts of mass witnessing of nature-defying miracles are true, even if the final version of the Bible was written later than Moses. And I do not consider your alternative explanations persuasive.

And the sage replied: Therefore, father, I shall speak of direct evidence from the Bible that the Jews did *not* have a continuous and reliable transmission of the Five Books of Moses—even long after it was said to have been written. And I will illustrate not only that a nation might embrace a Bible containing previously unknown accounts of their ancestors, I will show that the Jewish people actually did this—and more than once.

The Bible in two separate accounts relates the story of the book of the Torah of Moses, or the book of the law or covenant, being found by the high priest Hilkiah, in the eighteenth year of the reign of King Josiah, around 620 B.C.E., 600 years, or so, after the days of Moses who—assuming the events occurred— would have led the Israelites out of Egypt between 1200 and 1300 B.C.E. Listen to the words of the Bible recounting the story, read them in your own Bible's text, and judge for yourself whether it seems that the king and the people were familiar with the contents of the found book—claimed to be the book of the covenant written by Moses—or whether its teachings were, to them, heretofore unknown.

II Kings, Chapter 22, beginning in verse 8 says:

> And Hilkiah the high priest said unto Shaphan the scribe, I have found the book of the law in the house of the Lord. And Hilkiah gave the book to Shaphan, and he read it...And Shaphan the scribe showed the king, saying, Hilkiah the priest hath delivered me a book. And Shaphan read it before the king. And it came to pass, when the king had heard the words of the book of the law, that he rent his clothes...And the king commanded Hilkiah the priest...saying, Go ye, inquire of the Lord for me, and for the people, and for all Judah, concerning the words of this book that is found: for great is the wrath of the Lord that is kindled against us, because our fathers have not hearkened unto the words of this book, to do according unto all that which is written concerning us.

And II Kings Chapter 23 begins:

> And the king sent, and they gathered unto him all the elders of Judah and of Jerusalem. And the king went up into the house of the Lord and all the men of Judah and all the inhabitants of Jerusalem with him, and the priests and the prophets, and all the people, both small and great: and he read in their ears all the words of the book of the covenant which was found in the house of the Lord.

The story continues with King Josiah enforcing and renewing the covenant as it was written in the book found in the house of the Lord.

Father, the entire account reflects the discovery not of an additional copy of already familiar knowledge, but of a message new to the people. For if the scroll found in the temple were merely an older copy of a familiar text, why would this have caused great alarm, or resulted in religious awakening, in mass gatherings and teachings? And why would King Josiah exclaim that their "fathers" had not kept all the words of the book—if the current generation already knew of these biblical words they should have been obeying these laws themselves, irrespective of their ancestors' actions. Moreover, how would the finding of this additional copy have told the king anything of what the forefathers did or did not do? For these reasons, it is evident that the generation of Josiah was surprised to learn of the scroll—which contained words of God they had never before heard. And therefore King Josiah reacted with surprise and alarm to the contents, and intended by his remarks to blame previous generations—those to whom he refers as "our fathers"—for not following the teachings of this book, and for not transmitting knowledge of these teachings to their posterity.

The story is told a second time in II Chronicles, Chapter 34. Verse 14 begins:

> And when they brought out the money that was brought into the house of the Lord, Hilkiah the priest found a book of the law of the Lord given by Moses.

The ensuing verses complete the same story as the one in II Kings. Here, too, the clear implication is that neither Josiah nor his people were previously familiar with the contents of the book.

Whether this newly discovered scroll constituted what we now refer to as the Five Books of Moses, or whether it was, instead, Deuteronomy or another significant portion of the Torah, this story indicates that there was no unbroken tradition, no reliable transmission, from the days of Moses, of the entire Five Books of Moses or its laws. And it further demonstrates that the people of Israel not only could, but actually *did,* accept laws of God previously unknown to them, laws they were told their forefathers had known. The high priest Hilkiah claimed the book was the newly recovered word of God to Moses; King Josiah believed this and commanded the people to follow the book's teachings—and they did.

Thus, we have not only reasonable conjecture, but direct evidence from the Bible itself indicating that accounts in the Five Books of Moses may well have been written, collected, and accepted by the people as sacred, hundreds of years after the events they purport to describe.[1] And this greatly weakens the claim that the acceptance and transmission, by the Jews, of the Five Books of Moses down

---

[1] And, to be clear, this is a widely-held scholarly view—that the book, probably Deuteronomy, was put together hundreds of years after Moses, placed in the Temple perhaps by religious reformers, and was subsequently "found" and attributed to Moses. For one example of many who speak of this prevailing scholarly view, see Chapter 4 of William G. Dever's *What Did The Biblical Writers Know & When Did They Know It?*

through the ages constitutes reliable testimony of God's revelation, His Miracles, or His will.

112. Ezra's return from exile: further biblical evidence that the transmission of the Five Books of Moses by the Jewish people was interrupted, and thus unreliable

And the sage continued, saying: Father, Hilkiah's discovery of the book of the Torah of Moses is not the only biblical evidence that the Five Books of Moses was not transmitted uninterruptedly down through Jewish history. Generations later, Ezra—an important Jewish leader and scribe—came to Israel at the head of thousands of Jews returning from many decades of Babylonian exile. At this time, the Bible recounts, Ezra presented to the Jewish people the Book of the Torah of Moses—and again they were unfamiliar with significant portions of its contents.

Nehemiah Chapter 8 recounts that all the people gathered to hear the book of the law. Beginning in Verse 8, the Bible states:

> So they read in the book in the law of God distinctly, and gave the sense, and caused them to understand the reading. And Nehemiah, which is the Tirshatha, and Ezra the priest the scribe, and the Levites that taught the people, said unto all the people, This day is holy unto the Lord your God; mourn not, nor weep. For all the people wept, when they heard the words of the law. Then he said unto them, Go your way, eat the fat, and drink the sweet, and send portions unto them for whom nothing is prepared: for this day is holy unto our Lord: neither be ye sorry; for the joy of the Lord is your strength. So the Levites stilled all the people, saying, Hold your peace, for the day is holy; neither be ye grieved. And all the people went their way to eat, and to drink, and to send portions and to make great mirth, because they had understood the words that were declared unto them.

Verse 13 continues:

> And on the second day were gathered together the chiefs of the fathers of all the people, the priests, and the Levites, unto Ezra the scribe, even to understand the words of the law. And they found written in the law which the Lord had commanded by Moses, that the children of Israel should dwell in booths in the feast of the seventh month... So the people went forth, and brought them, and made themselves booths, every one upon the roof of his house... And all the congregation of them that were come again out of the captivity made

booths, and sat under the booths: for since the days of Joshua the son of Nun unto that day had not the children of Israel done so.

Father, all this describes a people who required special efforts to help them comprehend the Bible and, by the Bible's explicit account, a people that had not known about the commandment to dwell in booths, and had not followed the practice for hundreds of years, since the days of Joshua.

And note: The law of dwelling in booths each year at the feast of the seventh month was unfamiliar not only to the masses of the Jews, but even to the chiefs of the fathers—the leaders of the people. And remember that if the purported original Torah from Moses had truly included this commandment, as Ezra claimed, it would not have been easily forgotten; for dwelling in booths annually for a full week of feast and festival is such a dramatic and engaging practice, that its observance every year would have come at great effort, change of routine, and emotional intensity—the very sort of ritual that endures in the national memory. Thus, this annual practice would, arguably, have been more likely remembered than mere stories of the past, stories such as a revelation at Sinai.

The Jews' ignorance of the law of dwelling in booths, along with the implication that the people hearing the reading of the Torah had never understood the Bible before—and were therefore crying at not having kept the law of God—leaves us with two possibilities. Either these Torah texts—and particularly, the passages speaking about God commanding the Jews to dwell in booths—did not exist before Ezra, thus explaining why nobody seemed to be familiar with them, or they did exist in past generations as Ezra claimed, but—for hundreds of years—were forgotten, which would indicate that the great bulk of the Jews, even their leaders, did not know, for hundreds of years, what was in the Bible.

Either way, the Jewish people accepting from Ezra this law as the word of God illustrates how easily they might have accepted stories of the exodus from Egypt and God's revelation at Sinai, even if they did not hear such accounts from their parents. For it is reasonable to surmise that people will more easily accept a miracle story about their founding heroes, or a flattering account of their ancestors being addressed by God—than they will accept unfamiliar obligations and burdensome commandments in God's name. And the Bible itself states that the people accepted obligations and commandments, new to them, in the reign of King Josiah, and later in the days of Ezra. Remember, too, that in both cases the people were told that these laws, laws known neither to them nor to their parents, were originally commanded by God through Moses, to the entire Jewish people—to all their ancestors. Yet although they had never heard from their parents of these laws, they still accepted, as authentic, Scriptures in which was written that their ancestors were taught these things.

And scholars have noted, too, that in the cases mentioned, those reeducating the people on what the Bible said—King Josiah, and later Ezra—wielded the legislative and police powers of government; and they were supported, too, by the formidable authority of the priesthood and clergy. These circumstances would have enabled them to promulgate, and if necessary enforce, these new religious practices, and to ensure that the people would, indeed, accept these books as the ancient and authentic books of Moses.

And, father, allow me to remind you that Ezra lived over seven hundred years after Moses. Seven hundred years[1] is a very long time, more than enough time for fables and stories to be created, developed, or significantly embellished. Think back to seven hundred years ago: What year would that have been? And even though the past seven hundred years have been the most skeptical, the most scientific, the most technology-assisted years in human history—and even though for many of those years we have had access to printing presses—do you have great confidence that supernatural stories told about events of seven hundred years ago are accurate? Would there not have been numerous opportunities for the stories to have been inflated, distorted, even invented, or to have otherwise evolved—with or without the intention to deceive? So, too, even if the text of the Five Books of Moses we see today is relatively unchanged since the time of Ezra and the scribes, there would still have been a very long period of seven hundred years for this part of the Bible to have gradually grown and changed, long after the days of Moses, before Ezra presented it in its current form.

Another element to consider is the great turbulence of the generations preceding Ezra, generations defeated in battle, decimated by war and disease, and exiled to distant lands. When Ezra led a return from exile, the once proud and independent Israelites were reduced to a tenuous vassal state. As scholars have pointed out,[2] so much had been destroyed and uprooted, that it was an historical moment with great opportunity for introducing the new as if it was old, and for the people to desperately welcome Ezra's Book of Moses and its accounts of a

---

[1] Even if we were to assume that some significant portion of Ezra's version of the Torah existed before he came on the scene—indeed some scholars see evidence for some passages, eventually incorporated into the Torah, having originated as early as the 9th century, or so, B.C.E—this essential point remains: Several hundred years may well have elapsed between the supposed events foundational to Judaism (the miracle-filled exodus from Egypt, the divine revelation at Sinai, supernatural sustenance while wandering 40 years in the desert, etc.) and the final formulation of the Bible, the text from which we learned those stories. This would have allowed more than enough time for various forms of inaccuracy to have developed and to have been mistakenly canonized as sacred fact.

[2] R.E. Friedman, for one, makes these and related points in *Who Wrote The Bible?*

glorious and meaningful past, and its promises for both natural and supernatural success. It was also a document whose laws and stories could unify a people suffering from a tarnished identity and little direction—and the people may have felt this in their bones and eagerly committed themselves to its disciplines and myths.

And we must not forget that the Bible comes to us from epochs of superstition and scientific ignorance. The peoples of ancient days—including the Jews of biblical times—were hounded by terror at the thought of angry gods or evil spirits, and seduced by hopes for generosity and benevolence on the part of forces they deemed supernatural. Our ancestors readily believed all manner of— what to more knowledgeable ages seem—ridiculous things, and were wont to spread all sorts of wild tales and rumors. Thus, accounts of wonders and signs originating in such periods—including the miracle tales of the Bible—should raise the eyebrow of suspicion on the face of every honest and responsible soul.

Finally, father, let us remember that in generations of yore, long before the advent of printing and commonly available books—and long before mass literacy—the only copies of the Bible were those painstakingly handwritten by a relatively small number of highly educated scribes, and these scrolls were kept mostly by the few in religious or executive authority, thus placing these texts beyond not only the intellectual ken, but even the physical reach, of ordinary people. The elite few would, therefore, have been able to wield great influence in shaping what the people believed about the contents of the sacred books—and effectively suppress the tiny minority possessing the knowledge to oppose them. For remember, too, that in days bygone—days when nearly everyone subscribed to their people's supernatural beliefs—religious community was often powerful and pervasive, encompassing the social, economic, and political arenas of life, and one could not be confident of success, or even survival, if incurring the wrath of religious leaders and being rejected by the community of faith.

And these reasons for being skeptical that the Bible was accurately transmitted from Moses all the way to the present day do not even take into account the evidence and theories suggesting that multiple, and sometimes contradictory, early texts were combined by one or more editors or redactors into the current form of the Old Testament. We shall speak of this soon.[1]

And so, my father, we stand on firm ground when remaining skeptical of supernatural accounts—including that of mass revelation at Sinai—and when remaining skeptical, too, of claims of an inerrant transmission of sacred tradition. For if the Bible itself testifies that the Jewish people of Ezra's day accepted what they had never heard before, and what their parents never knew—a scriptural

---

[1] See section 114 for discussion on theories of biblical origin.

account of their ancestors being commanded in the name of God, many hundreds of years previously, to dwell in booths for a full week each year—why should we have any confidence that a people, including the Jewish people of any number of generations in the ages of pervasive superstition and easy credulity, would not accept the far more gratifying, and far less demanding, story of their ancestors being chosen by God for mass divine revelation?

113. Account, from the Apocrypha, of Ezra writing the Torah after it was forgotten

And the sage continued, saying: My father, for hundreds of years now, scholars have noted the existence of an ancient account telling of how Ezra rewrote the Torah after it was forgotten and, therefore, that the present version of the Hebrew Bible can be assumed to be no older than the days of Ezra.[1]

I will share with you passages from the Apocrypha—religious texts written by Jews and early Christians two thousand or so years ago—which suggest that even back then many accepted that no unbroken chain of knowledgeable generations transmitted the Torah from Moses to their generation; indeed, that in the days of Ezra the Torah had been largely forgotten by the people of Israel. Now, I grant you that not everyone considers the Apocrypha a legitimate part of the Bible, but it cannot be denied that these writings are ancient. Thus, one does not have to consider these books a rightful part of the biblical canon to see that even two millennia ago some taught of Ezra rewriting the Torah after it was destroyed and forgotten. If that tradition is accurate—and it seems to be consis-

---

[1] Thomas Hobbes, for an early example—using the Greek name for Ezra, Esdras—in Chapter 33 of Leviathan, a book first published in the mid-17th century, says: "And if the books of Apocrypha (which are recommended to us by the church, though not for canonical, yet for profitable books for our instruction) may in this point be credited, the Scripture was set forth in the form we have it in, by Esdras; as may appear by that which he himself says, in the second book, chapter 14..." Later Hobbes writes: "For, as the books of the Old Testament are derived to us, from no higher time than that of Esdras, who by direction of God's Spirit retrieved them, when they were lost..."

Spinoza, too, in "A Theologico-Political Treatise" suggested that the current version of the Five Books of Moses reached its final form in the days of Ezra. In Chapter VIII of that work he wrote: "The putting together, and the order of the narratives, show that they are all the work of one man... I suspect that he was Ezra, and there are several strong reasons for adopting this hypothesis..." Later, he continues: "I think Ezra set himself to give a complete account of the history of the Hebrew nation from the creation of the world to the entire destruction of the city, and in this account he inserted the book of Deuteronomy, and...he called the first five books by the name of Moses..."

tent with the biblical passages already cited, showing Ezra introducing a Torah unfamiliar to the Jews—it follows that miracle stories of divine revelation at Sinai could easily have been inserted at that time, because Ezra was reintroducing a Torah to a people that had forgotten the original text, and had no way of knowing whether the contents of Ezra's version were ancient or newly invented.

II Esdras, Chapter 14, verses 19-26, has Ezra speaking to God:

> Then I answered before thee and said, Behold Lord, I will go, as thou hast commanded me, and reprove the people that are present: but they that shall be born afterward, who will admonish them? Thus the world is set in darkness, and they that dwell therein are without light. For thy law is burnt, therefore no man knows the things that are done of thee, or the works that shall begin. But if I have found grace before thee, send the Holy spirit into me, and I will write all that has been done in the world since the beginning, which was written in thy law, that men may find thy way, and that they which shall be in the later days may live.

The rest of the chapter continues the story of how Ezra—also referred to as Esdras—wrote the sacred books, with the help of five assistants. Thus, even close to two thousand years ago, some recorded that the Bible had been lost and forgotten, and that Ezra wrote it anew. If that was the case, even had there followed a perfect transmission of the Torah for the more than two millennia since Ezra, we could not responsibly rely on the transmission having accurately stretched back to the days of Moses—seven hundred years, or so, before Ezra.

In summary, father, from the biblical text itself we have evidence that Moses did not write the entire Five Books of Moses—and we therefore have good reason to suspect that such is the case for most, perhaps all, of these books' texts—that they were not written by Moses—including the account of a supernatural divine revelation at Sinai. And, as explained, we have good cause, and some evidence from the Bible itself, and other sources, to believe that the Jewish people did not have an unbroken tradition of the entire Torah, and that tales of miracles may well have had the opportunity, over many years, to develop and gain credibility, and ultimately to be canonized as "God's Truth" by religious authorities making final the biblical text many hundreds of years after Moses.

Ask yourself this: Would I today accept as accurate, supernatural tales told by other nations about events they say happened to their ancestors hundreds, even thousands, of years ago? If not, what compelling evidence exists for divine revelation or dramatic miracles as described in the Bible about the ancient Israelites?

Moreover, even if the text of the Bible provided no evidence that Moses was *not* its author, we would still have no good reason to believe that Moses *was* its author. After all, many a book contains no internal proof of its author's identity—but this does not mean we can simply claim a specific person of our choosing to have been its author. Nor can we responsibly rely on legend or tradition to decide who wrote which books. And note that more biographies are written than autobiographies, and that most books about heroes are not written by the heroes themselves, but by admiring writers often living many generations later. Thus, a book about Moses could quite naturally have been written by someone other than Moses.[1] Furthermore, many have pointed out that in ancient Israel it was a common practice—either as a sincere gesture of dedication and discipleship, or as a means of lending legitimacy to the work—to attribute a book to, or name a book after, a well-known hero of the past.

And, father, I must impress upon you that in order to believe in the biblical account and in any of the religions based on the Bible, we would need *compelling* evidence of divine revelation and miracles—and not merely the theoretical possibility that such things may, after all, have occurred. For our daily experience, and all we have learned of how the universe operates—as the slowly cultivated fields of knowledge have gradually beaten back the jungle of frightened, ecstatic, or habituated ignorance—has taught that the laws of nature never get broken or suspended. None of us has witnessed, nor does any of our knowledge or verified experience allow for, dramatic, nature-defying, miracles of the sort described in the Bible. Neither can any of us be legitimately confident that we have received prophecies or direct communication from God. Thus, the burden of proof should lie heavy not upon the defender of experience and reason to persuade us that supernatural biblical tales are inaccurate, but rather upon the defender of dogma and tradition to show that what superstitious ages wrote about and believed, that what seems to contradict every standard of reason and contemporary experience, that what clashes with our basic knowledge of the laws of nature—actually took place.

---

[1] And this is the straightforward supposition of Spinoza in his *Theologico-Political Treatise* as to the reason for the names of of the Bible's various books—that the first five books were named for Moses because he is their chief character, and that the same reason applies to the naming of the books of Joshua, Samuel, Kings, and so on. And Hobbes, in his *Leviathan* expresses the same opinion, that the name of a biblical book does not indicate its author, and sums it up by saying: "For in titles of books, the subject is marked as often as the writer."

114. If Moses did not write the Five Books of Moses by the word of God, who was its author?

And a woman asked: If the series of books we call the Five Books of Moses was not written by God dictating its text to Moses, who *did* write it?

And the sage replied: My sister, we will likely never know all those responsible for the Hebrew text of the Five Books of Moses. As others have explained, untold thousands of believers, among them numerous scribes, scholars, and religious teachers, lived during the many centuries of ancient Israel. Any of them could have written stories, teachings, and prophecies that were later incorporated, along with folk traditions, into the Bible's text. But though we cannot know these matters of authorship with certainty, we may hope to gain some insight by closely studying the words of these ancient texts, and by considering the varied religious, historical, and political contexts in which the Hebrew Bible was written.[1]

Before discussing theories on biblical authorship, let us put the matter in perspective: I speak about who may have written the Five Books of Moses not because a specific human author need be named or else we must believe its verses to be God's infallible word. Many books' authors are unknown, yet we do not therefore assume them to have been written by God. And numerous reasons counsel us to doubt that the Bible is of divine origin. Indeed, speculations regarding its possible contributing authors, or final editor, provide only a small, but interesting, support to the argument against religion's supernatural claims.

---

[1] *Who Wrote The Bible?* by Richard E. Friedman is an accessible and intelligent book on these matters. In it, the author discusses the documentary hypothesis (an important and controversial theory of biblical authorship) and supplements it with his own scholarship and creative conjecture. His book deals with the matter of biblical origins in far greater depth and detail than does this volume—and one need not agree with all his premises and conclusions in order to find the material stimulating and educational.

Another book dealing extensively, and accessibly, with biblical authorship, among other issues, is *How to Read the Bible*, by James Kugel, in which many biblical stories are illuminated from two perspectives—the traditional, religious point of view, and the newer way informed by non-traditional research and influences. Although religiously observant, the author in no way minimizes the secular scholarship and scientific findings about the Bible which create difficulties for the traditional religious point of view. Kugel, in this book, and in others, evidences wide knowledge, creative insight, and a native and loving familiarity with the Hebrew Bible's texts—and writes in an engaging style that the intelligent layman will have no difficulty following.

And the documentary hypothesis is far from the only view of the Bible's origins, even amongst secular scholars. Many reject the entire notion of the documentary hypothesis—that extensive and distinct documents were combined into one, to form the Pentateuch—let alone any specific attempt to identify each verse's author. Instead, some say that one primary document was supplemented by later editors, and others believe that numerous fragments, but not extensive, distinct texts, were combined to form the Bible.

For purposes of pursuing truth on matters of religion, the real value of biblical authorship theories—including attempts to illuminate the social, religious, political and historical roots of the Bible—lies not in whether all their details are correct. This, perhaps, we shall never know, for events of days long bygone may be forever beyond any sure knowledge. Rather, the value of such theories lies in their painting for us a plausible picture, consistent with a great deal of evidence inside and outside the Bible, of a book given its final form not by a transcendent God high in an unfathomable heaven, but by humans, solidly rooted in the passions, power contests, and varied foibles pervading humble earth—in addition to the natural inspirations and belief systems firing their hungry spirits and creative imaginations. And thus our minds and hearts may be better prepared to consider afresh whether Scripture contains the word or will of any deity.

And as we speak in greater detail about the Five Books of Moses, let us note that these are the first five books of the Bible—the Bible upon which are based in significant measure the religious foundations of Judaism and Christianity, even Islam. The Five Books of Moses, also known as the Pentateuch, or the Torah, are: Genesis, Exodus, Leviticus, Numbers and Deuteronomy.

Many scholars have adduced evidence they say indicates that the Bible, even the Five Books of Moses, is a combination of several documents, incorporating the writings of various authors living at different points in history—edited into its final form hundreds of years after Moses. Although not all scholars agree with this theory, and there are intelligent arguments against it,[1] especially against some of its immoderate applications, it is, nevertheless, intriguing, and its claims—disturbing to the traditional frame of reference—must be pondered by all who respect the Bible enough to study to their best ability its many layers and facets.

As we have earlier discussed, it has long been observed that Moses does not seem to have written the complete text of the Five Books of Moses—for some

---

[1] See, for one, Walter Kaufmann, in *Critique of Religion and Philosophy* section 88, who points out that this school of thought would presumably conclude that *Faust*, actually written by Goethe alone over a span of sixty years, must have been written by several authors and editors—due to its multi-faceted and sometimes inconsistent elements.

For a taste of other biblical scholars who take issue with some of the arguments and conclusions of the documentary hypothesis, see Umberto Cassuto's *Documentary Hypothesis*, Robert Alter's *Art of Biblical Narrative* and his *Art of Biblcial Poetry*, and R.N. Whybray's *Making of the Pentateuch*. And, dear reader, this humble book you now read, also composed over a number of years by one person, avails itself of several styles, too, everything from an archaic and lyrical style, to one more contemporary and analytic—and, it must be confessed, to a pedestrian one at times, too. While some passages were intentionally expressed in a specific style, other passages received their particular sound and savor based simply on the author's state of mind while writing. The same landscape has its different seasons, even its varying weather patterns in the same season.

of its passages speak about his death, and include names and phrases that would only have been used by later generations. It has also long been noted that the Bible, especially in Genesis, tells many of its stories twice, and in slightly different versions; and that the two versions often use different names for God, one using the name "Elohim," and the other, the name "Yahweh." This, say the proponents of one point of view, suggests there were at least two original and somewhat similar sources[1] from which were pieced together the current text of the Five Books of Moses. Scholars of biblical criticism name these: "E," the source using "Elohim," and "J," the source using "Yahweh."[2]

Some scholars eventually came to believe that the Five Books of Moses were composed of more than two source documents. A third source, they said, was a text dealing heavily with law, religious guidelines, and priestly worship rites; this became known to scholars of biblical criticism as the "P" document, for its priestly contents. And Deuteronomy is believed by many to have its source in a separate document, too—largely because its style and content are so unlike the first four of the Five Books of Moses. They refer to this Deuteronomy source document as "D." These several sources are said by some to have their distinct style and "voice," not only in favorite words used, but also in emotional tone. And scholars differ on how many source documents may have been combined into the final form of today's Five Books of Moses. Some insist there are several more than the four we have mentioned.[3]

And it has been suggested by a number of scholars that two of the source documents for the Torah may have been the similar—but slightly differing—sacred texts of the two kingdoms of Israel and Judah. The Bible recounts how

---

[1] Yet to be fair, traditional Judaism has taught for ages that God interacts with creation in at least two important modes, justice and mercy—and that these two characteristics of God are often associated with the names Elohim and Yahweh. When one considers the necessary duality of objective/subjective, (and traditionally male/female) in achieving balanced judgment; and when one considers that 3-dimensional vision requires seeing the same scene from two slightly different perspectives; and when one remembers that much of biblical poetry involves the "parallelism" of saying things in two slightly different ways, it may not be stretching credulity too far to postulate that one unified biblical tradition may have intentionally presented important biblical tales in two slightly different forms. The line between creative apologetics and profound truth is not always easy to discern.

[2] It is widely explained that the "J" designation originates at a time when the Hebrew "Yahweh" was transliterated to other languages as "Jahveh" or "Jehovah." The letter "J" in German (and related languages) spoken by a number of historically influential Bible critics, carries the sound of the letter "Y" in English.

[3] See James Kugel's *How to Read the Bible*, and Richard E. Friedman's *Who Wrote The Bible?* for accessible and more detailed discussion of these themes.

the Israelites split into these two kingdoms after the death of King Solomon.[1] Each kingdom developed its own priesthood, and, in all likelihood, over time, its own sacred texts with, it may be assumed, at least slightly differing wordings and slightly differing emphases on many central stories and heroes of the Jewish tradition. Indeed, some have suggested that certain biblical stories, and their echoes in other biblical accounts about later periods, reflect the differing politics and allegiances between the priesthood of Judah and the priesthood of Israel.

One example is the pair of stories about Aaron's golden calf in Exodus 32, and Jeroboam's golden calves hundreds of years later, when Israel split from Judah, in 1 Kings 12. In these stories, both Aaron and Jeroboam, living centuries apart, are quoted as saying, remarkably, almost the very same words, "These are your gods, O Israel, who have brought you up out of the land of Egypt," or "...behold your gods, O Israel, who have brought you up out of the land of Egypt." Yet the Bible says in Exodus that God became so angry at the Israelites for worshiping the golden calf that He nearly destroyed them. Why, then, would Jeroboam and the people of Israel consider it a good idea to do the same thing hundreds of years later? Because of these and other peculiarities, some scholars see in these stories evidence of competition between rival priesthoods: the priests of Judah, descended from Aaron, and the priests of Israel, of the tribe of Levi but not descended from Aaron—and speculate that the story about the golden calf in the days of Aaron originated in later generations, for political reasons.[2]

---

[1] See 1 Kings chapters 11 and 12 for the beginnings of this schism, and later biblical chapters and books for its manifestations over generations of ensuing biblical history.

[2] R.E. Friedman, in chapter 3 of *Who Wrote the Bible?* postulates that certain priests of Israel, perhaps descended from Moses—and, unlike the priests of the kingdom of Judah, not from Aaron—were hopeful of being returned to institutional power when Jeroboam split off from Judah and established the kingdom of Israel, but that when Jeroboam created the golden calves as objects of worship, they felt betrayed. Thus, an Israelite priest, feeling excluded from the priesthood in Judah by the figure of Aaron—from whom he was not descended, and therefore not considered a legitimate priest in Judah—and excluded from the priesthood in Israel by the figure of the golden calves, must have created the story of Aaron forming, to God's great wrath, a golden calf in the days of Moses, and of Jeroboam doing the very same evil deed in a later generation.

James Kugel, in *How to Read the Bible* mentions another theory of biblical scholars on this story, namely that the use of golden calves in the worship of God was not originally seen as a sin—for, after all, did not even the tabernacle and the later temple at Jerusalem, both contain, by the Bible's own account, cherubs, animal forms, in the Holy of Holies?—but that a later "Deuteronomistic historian" misrepresented the calves as direct objects of worship; Kugel also relates the theory that the story about Aaron reflects a conflict between P and D (postulated biblical source documents) as to who is a legitimate priest, and that a non-Aaronite priest wrote the story critical of Aaron—the progenitor and hero of those who insisted that priests must be descended from Aaron.

And centuries later still, after the fall of Israel, these two sources—the texts of Judah and Israel—may have been combined, preserving the different versions of the same stories, in the attempt to unify the Jewish tradition. This, it has been suggested, explains, among other things, the "couplets," the frequent biblical examples of twice-told tales.

It has also been stated, implied, or postulated by many scholars[1] that only in the days of Ezra was the Five Books Of Moses established as authoritative and canonical for all time; and that perhaps Ezra himself was the redactor, or editor, of the Five Books of Moses, or even of the entire Old Testament, giving it its final form, which has since remained nearly unchanged. Among other points, it is noted that Ezra was the only prominent figure of his era—the era during which the current form of the Old Testament was apparently set—characterized by the Bible as possessing both the scholarly knowledge and the political power to succeed at the task. As mentioned, it has also been observed that the Jews of the day would have been receptive to the presentation of an authoritative Bible with a grand narrative, returning as they were from exile, desperate for a renewed sense of unity and national pride.

In short, my sister, many scholars suspect that the current text of the Five Books of Moses was written neither by God nor by Moses, but instead represents the cumulative work of several unknown writers and editors—perhaps further modified by long transmission and evolution—in ancient Israel, over hundreds of years. Some of its passages may have existed in some form in the 9th century B.C.E., or even earlier—but the Five Books of Moses as we now know it was likely first woven together into one text many hundreds of years after the death of Moses. Thus, the foundational miracle stories would have been canonized in the Bible centuries after the events they purport to describe—and the credibility of such accounts is, therefore, heavily compromised.

To be fair, and as stated earlier, there are those who argue that different writing styles, different subject matter, even duplicate and differing accounts of the same story, are compatible with the possibility that the Bible had only one author—even if this author was mortal and speaking his own words. And some have charged that many scholars eager to butcher what is sacred to religion have gone to unreasonable lengths in carving up the Bible, even individual verses, into more and more supposed source documents. And there is some justice to these protests, too. For is it so rare that one author writes on many topics, and in many styles—especially over the course of a lifetime? And would it really be impossible that, for various reasons, one person would have told an important story in more

---

[1] From Hobbes in *Leviathan* and Spinoza in *A Theologico-Political Treatise*, hundreds of years ago, to R.E. Friedman, recently, in *Who Wrote The Bible?*

than one fashion—for purposes of emphasis, or paradox, or to create a multifac-eted set of legends, or even in an evolving sense of creativity or insight—and either himself recorded the multiple versions, or such multiple versions were recorded by a loyal assistant or scribe? It is, therefore, wise and humble not to pretend we know with certainty from which source documents any particular verse or phrase derives, or even that multiple authors of distinct, extensive texts wrote the Five Books of Moses—though the occasional anachronistic phrase we might reasonably assume points to interpolation at the hand of one or more later scribes or editors. The evidence and theory arguing for multiple authors for the bulk of the Five Books of Moses may be characterized as interesting, even impressive, but—at least at this point—not conclusive.

Yet remember, my sister, even if one postulates that the Five Books of Moses had only one author or one early compiler or editor—would it be respon-sible to believe, without compelling evidence, that the text was written or inspired by God? After all, millions of books have had only one author each; but do we, therefore, believe that each of these authors was either God or a writer to whom God had granted inspiration supernatural? Thus, if the Five Books of Moses did indeed have only one author or early compiler or editor, must we grant this person unquestioned credibility? Since we have already illustrated[1] that parts of it were apparently written well after the generation of Moses and the foundational miracles it describes—which writer would have been the hypotheti-cal sole author, and why should we accept his stories of events long before his time, and his supernatural claims and demands, without careful scrutiny?

And again, my sister, we mention the possible source documents from which the Bible may have been weaved, and the historical and political contexts of ancient Israel that may have played a role in shaping various passages of the Bible, not because without such theories and elements we would be forced to accept the Bible as the word of God. Rather, we discuss these matters so that we who have been taught that the Bible is a Holy, Mysterious, Authoritative, Inerrant, and Self-Contained Book presented by God Almighty to our Incompa-rable Forebears in the Sacred and Inaccessible Past, may begin to glimpse the clues suggesting human sources for these texts, and the very real passions and power struggles that prevailed during the period in which the Bible came on the scene—and thus be more prepared to contemplate whether its origins must necessarily be divine, or whether they might, in fact, be merely human.

---

[1] See sections 109 and 110.

115. Argument that the Bible is divinely inspired, even if not written by God's direct word through Moses

And a religious teacher said: Let us not be so simple-minded. Of course the Bible—whether the Five Books of Moses or any other part—was not written directly by God through the hand of Moses. But God inspired the Bible, and it is, therefore, God's will. I believe that God's spirit guided all the many writers who contributed to the Bible over the centuries, and therefore your arguments casting doubt on the notion that God or Moses directly wrote the Bible do not at all disprove religion.

And the sage replied: My brother, your position does seem to offer comfort to the believer faced with powerful evidence that humans wrote the Bible. But let us consider several points. First, since the Five Books of Moses was apparently given its final form, much later than Moses,[1] its story of God's revelation and miracles for Moses and the Israelites—a story upon which traditional Judaism's confidence in her religious tradition is based, and a story providing foundational support to Christianity, and some support to Islam, too—would likely have had hundreds of years to develop, does not have a direct generation-to-generation transmission from eyewitnesses, and thus loses much of its credibility.

Second, the Bible contains many errors and contradictions—of which we shall in due course, speak—and God would not have inspired errors and contradictions. And if some biblical passages are not inspired, how can we know which, if any, *are* inspired? Perhaps those sections containing the core elements of any religion's teachings are bereft of God's spirit or direction, too.

Third, although the Bible teaches some excellent things, it also teaches some terrible things. And since the morality of the Bible is far from what even we less than all-loving humans would consider acceptable—at times commanding genocide, condoning slavery, and so on, and in the New Testament, condemning sinners to eternal fire—it would not have been inspired by anyone we could honestly characterize as compassionate or even fair. Thus, either those sections of the Bible—and, reasonably we may assume that other sections, too—are not sourced in God's spirit and will, or they are, and He is far from the just and loving deity of which religions often speak.

Finally, and most important, my brother, it is not enough to claim that the Bible is inspired by God; anyone can make such an assertion about any book. Such an astonishing claim—that the Creator of the universe intervened and guided texts produced by human authors—requires not merely the insistence upon our grandparents' traditions, but compelling evidence. Yet the Bible shows

---

[1] See sections 109-114.

no supernatural qualities: It is not supernaturally beautiful or poetic;[1] it is not supernaturally compassionate or moral;[2] and it is not supernaturally advanced in its practical knowledge or science, either.[3] The Bible's stories, laws, and poetry, though at times inspiring and impressive—and, it must be said, at times horrific, repulsive, repetitive or dull—are quite within the realm of what man is capable of producing on his own, without divine inspiration. Indeed, many stories, and collections of knowledge, laws, and poems—similar in various ways to the Bible—were written earlier than the Bible, by people and civilizations that the Bible characterized as abominable idol-worshipers.[4] In the absence of compelling contrary evidence, then, why should we see the Bible as anything but humanly written and humanly inspired?

116. The Code of Hammurabi: Was the Bible unique, and completely original—or was it influenced by earlier traditions and laws?

But the religious teacher persisted, saying: I disagree. If you study the Bible closely you will see how unprecedented it was, how it is utterly unlike anything that came before, and completely incomparable to anything in the cultures of the

---

[1] For more discussion on the Bible's beauty, see section 103.

[2] The Bible's morality is dealt with in sections 127 and 128.

[3] Sections 99 and 100 address the matter of the Bible's scientific knowledge.

[4] For one example, see the following section (116) where the Code of Hammurabi is discussed. For another, the extensive and systematic records of Egyptian hieroglyphics stretch back far earlier than the days of Moses. For a rich set of resources on ancient writings relevant to the Bible, see the following works: *Old Testament Parallels* by Matthews and Benjamin; *Myths From Mesopotamia* by Stephanie Dalley; *The Treasures of Darkness* by Thorkild Jacobsen; and *From Distant Days* by Benjamin Foster.

Also, most civilizations did not make a central focus of writing things down and preserving them for posterity on scrolls to be continuously read by future generations, as did the Jews. This does not mean that such civilizations were bereft of laws and stories, merely that because they were not as effectively preserved, we no longer have access to them. Consider this: If we were to find cookbooks of one ancient civilization but not another, would we really conclude that only the former prepared meals and had recipes? And if we were to find a dictionary in the remains of one civilization but not another, would we really infer that only the former used language? No: As basic as some things are to human functioning, we can safely assume that every civilization, every people, has made use of, among other things, not only language and food, but games and war and intrigue, and forms of poetry and wisdom and law, too, notwithstanding the sometimes scant surviving evidence of these. And by saying this I do not mean to suggest that all cultures are equally constructive, admirable, and accomplished: Differences, important differences, do exist. But it is simply wishful and self-congratulatory thinking on the part of some religionists to claim that the Bible was the radical beginning of knowledge, poetry, beauty, and law, or that its examples of these reflect something supernatural.

peoples surrounding ancient Israel. This alone should tell you that it could not have come by the hand of unaided man, but was, instead, inspired by God.

And the sage said: My brother, even if the Bible were utterly unique, unlike the books of any other nation, such a circumstance would not prove divine origin. As I have earlier stated, neither the Greeks' unparalleled advances in science, philosophy, and government, nor the unusually advanced building and preservation skills of the Egyptians, indicate anything supernatural. Yet the Bible is *not* utterly unique. Not only, as I said, have scholars found much evidence of similar laws and practices and stories and poetry produced by cultures surrounding Israel in the biblical and pre-biblical eras, we have remarkable evidence that the Bible—the Five Books of Moses, no less—may have been directly influenced by an earlier Babylonian law code, or by other traditions and tales.[1]

Let us first speak of Hammurabi—also called Hammurapi—a Babylonian king, who is understood by scholars to have reigned for a number of decades, somewhere between the years 1736 and 1848 BCE,[2] several hundred years before the generally accepted estimates of when the biblical Moses would have lived. Hammurabi taught a set of laws, and these were engraved on large stones.[3] This Code of Hammurabi addresses issues such as property, business, personal injury, and marriage and family relationships.

My brother, I will now relay what many others have illustrated[4]—passages from the Code of Hammurabi, along with biblical verses that seem to borrow

---

[1] See final footnote in section 115 for reading recommendations on this topic.

[2] Sources cite varying dates for Hammurabi's reign, but most fall within this range—and some date it significantly earlier. For one among many sources, see James Kugel's *How to Read the Bible*, p. 270. For another, see materials published by the Louvre (including its website, www.louvre.fr) which holds in its collection a surviving basalt stele of the Code of Hammurabi, where Hammurabi's era is given as 1792-1750 B.C.E. (And as early as was Hammurabi, his laws are not the earliest of which we know—let alone the earliest in fact—as is made clear by those same Louvre materials which explain: "Two Sumerian legal documents drawn up by Ur-Namma, king of Ur (c. 2100 BC) and Lipit-Ishtar of Isin (c.1930 BC), precede the Law Code of Hammurabi." So the informed and conceptual mind, upon perceiving the intercourse and evolution of ideas and practice across borders and generations, sees that the earliest influences upon the Bible apparently predate it not only by many centuries, but are, indeed, lost to the mists of early history.

[3] In the first few years of the 20th century a stone engraving of these laws, comprising thousands of lines of cuneiform, was found, in excavations supervised by Jacques de Morgan, at Susa. As mentioned, the Louvre holds an ancient stele of Hammurabi's Code.

[4] Who deserves credit for which of these observations is difficult to ascertain. Doubtless, many familiar with the Bible's teachings, upon perusing Hammurabi's Code, notice, independent of other scholars and educated laymen, some of the very same similarities. Thus, many, in various media, from early books on the subject, such as the 1905 work, *The Codes of Hammurabi and Moses*, by W.W. Davies, to numerous more recent works such

from or respond to these passages. Interestingly, scholars have shown that a section of Exodus, Chapters 21 and 22, seems especially influenced by the Code of Hammurabi.

We shall not speak of all the similarities between Hammurabi's Code and the Bible, but let us speak of some.

First, on the matter of punishing false witnesses, in Section 3, the Code of Hammurabi states:

> If a man, in a case pending judgment…has not justified the word that he has spoken, if that case be a capital suit, that man shall be put to death.

The Bible teaches something similar, in Deuteronomy 19:16-21:

> If a false witness rise up against any man to testify against him that which is wrong…and, behold, if the witness be a false witness, and hath testified falsely against his brother; Then shall ye do unto him, as he had thought to have done unto his brother…And thine eye shall not pity; but life shall go for life…

Second, on the criminal paying multiple times the value for something he has stolen, the Code of Hammurabi states, in section 112:

> If a man stays away on a journey and has given silver, gold, precious stones, or treasures of his hand to a man, has caused him to take them for transport, and that man whatever was for transport…has taken to himself…that man shall give to the owner of the transported object fivefold whatever was given him.

The Bible also speaks of the thief, in certain circumstances, repaying multiple times what he stole. Exodus, 22:1 (or 21:37)[1] states:

---

as *Old Testament Parallels* by V.H. Matthews and D.C. Benjamin, and innumerable articles and discussions, draw similar comparisons between the Bible and Hammurabi (whether or not they conclude that the Bible was influenced by Hammurabi). I simply acknowledge that most of these ideas and observations are not mine—and surely none are uniquely original to me—and, regrettably, do not know to whom is owed the earliest credit for each point.

[1] This is one of those instances in which different Bible versions are organized slightly differently in regard to their division and numbering of chapters and verses. The King James translation, as well as various other Christian Bibles, has Exodus 21 having only thirty-six verses, and has the verse we quote (on the payment of five oxen for one who

If a man shall steal an ox, or a sheep, and kill it, or sell it; he shall restore five oxen for an ox...

Third, on the matter of temporary slavery, the Code of Hammurabi states in Section 117:

If debt seized a man, and he has given his wife, his son, his daughter for the money, or has handed over to work off the debt, for three years they shall work in the house of their buyer or bondmaster. In the fourth year they shall regain their liberty.

The Bible also speaks of temporary slavery, but instead of three years of service, it prescribes six years. Exodus 21:2 states:

If thou buy an Hebrew servant, six years he shall serve: and in the seventh he shall go out free for nothing.

Fourth, when a man leaves property with another for safekeeping, and the property goes missing or becomes damaged, both Hammurabi and the Bible legislate an accounting in court or "before God" to settle the matter. Note the similar use of the term "before God" used both in the Code of Hammurabi and in the Bible. The Code of Hammurabi states in Section 120:

If a man has heaped up his corn in a heap in the house of a man, and in the granary a disaster has taken place, or the owner of the house has opened the granary and taken the corn, or has disputed as to the total amount of the corn that was heaped up in his house, the owner of the corn shall recount his corn before God, the owner of the house shall make up and return the corn which he took and shall give to the owner of the corn.

---

steals and slaughters an ox) as the first verse of Chapter 37. Many Jewish Bibles, however, have this verse as the thirty-seventh, and final, verse of Chapter 36.

To be clear, though, the chapter or verse number of the biblical passage in question is unimportant in the context of the point here being made—that the Bible shares many similarities of content with Hammurabi's Code.

The Bible for its part states in Exodus 22: (6)7-8:[1]

> If a man give to his neighbor money or utensils to guard, and they are stolen from the man's house, if the thief is found he shall pay double. If the thief is not found, the owner of the house should come close before God if he has not sent forth his hand in his neighbor's work.

And in verses (8)9 and 10, the Bible again legislates the use of coming "before God"[2] to settle similar situations.

Fifth, both Hammurabi and the Bible legislate that one in possession of another's property must pay the owner if the property is stolen. The Code of Hammurabi states in Section 125:

> If a man has given anything of his on deposit, and where he gave it, either by housebreaking or by rebellion, something of his has been lost, along with something of the owner of the house, the owner of the house who has defaulted all that was given him on deposit and has been lost, he shall make good and render to the owner of the goods, the owner of the house shall seek out whatever of his is lost and take it from the thief.

The Bible, in that same chapter of Exodus 22, after stating that an animal who dies or is injured in the safekeeping of another, requires only an oath of innocence, but no payment to the owner, states in verse (11)12:

> But if it is actually stolen from him, he shall make restitution to its owner.

Sixth and seventh, as scholars[3] have observed, there is an extraordinary similarity in the juxtaposition and sequence of two laws: Both the Code of Hammurabi and the Bible discuss inheritance laws relating to a man with children by two wives, and then immediately discuss a different law—that of punishing or rejecting a bad son.

---

[1] On this verse I use my original translation, because the King James Version translates the Hebrew Bible's verse to say that the parties should be brought "unto the judges." And though that is likely the practical intent of the verse (and perhaps the practical intent of the corresponding law in Hammurabi's Code) the straightforward literal translation of the relevant Hebrew Bible's phrase "el ha'Elohim" is "unto God" or "before God." And when translated literally, the parallel to the translated passage I have quoted from the Code of Hammurabi is more evident.

[2] Or, according to less literal translations, before judges. (See previous footnote.)

[3] Many make this point, including *The International Standard Bible Encyclopedia*.

The Code of Hammurabi states in Sections 167:

> If a man has taken a wife, and she has borne him sons, that woman has gone to her fate, after her, he has taken to himself another woman and she has borne children, afterwards the father has gone to his fate, the children shall not share according to their mothers, they shall take the marriage portions of their mothers and shall share the goods of their father's house equally.

Immediately following this, in Section 168, the Code of Hammurabi states:

> If a man has set his face to cut off his son, has said to the judge "I will cut off my son," the judge shall enquire into his reasons, and if the son has not committed a heavy crime which cuts off from sonship, the father shall not cut off his son from sonship.

The Bible, for its part, in Deuteronomy 21:15-17 states:

> If a man has two wives, the one loved and the other unloved, and both the loved and the unloved have borne him sons, if the firstborn son belongs to the unloved, then it shall be in the day he wills what he has to his sons, he cannot make the son of the loved the firstborn before the son of the unloved, who is the firstborn. But he shall acknowledge the firstborn, the son of the unloved, by giving him a double portion of all that he has, for he is the beginning of his strength; to him belongs the right of the firstborn.

And immediately following this, beginning in verse 18, the Bible states:

> If any man has a stubborn and rebellious son who will not obey his father or his mother, and when they chastise him, he will not even listen to them, then his father and mother shall seize him, and bring him out to the elders of his city at the gateway of his hometown...

Eighth, on punishment in kind, the Code of Hammurabi, Section 196, says:

> If a man has caused the loss of a free man's eye, his eye shall be caused to be lost.

And in Section 197:

> If he has shattered the limb of a gentleman, his limb shall be shattered.

And, in Section 200:

> If a man knocked out the tooth of a man equal to him, one shall make his tooth fall out.

The Bible, in Exodus 21:24-25 famously—and similarly—states:

> Eye for eye, tooth for tooth, hand for hand, foot for foot. Burning for burning, wound for wound, stripe for stripe.

And, in Leviticus 24:19-20, the Bible states:

> And if a man causes a blemish in his neighbor; as he hath done, so shall it be done to him. Breach for breach, eye for eye, tooth for tooth; as he hath caused a blemish in a man, so shall it be done to him, again."

Ninth, on the matter of paying the medical bills of those one has injured, the Code of Hammurabi states in Section 206:

> If a man has struck another in a quarrel and caused him a wound, then he shall swear, "I did not wound him knowing," and he shall pay the doctors.

The Bible, in Exodus 21:18-19 states:

> And if men strive together, and one smite another with a stone, or with his fist, and he die not, but keepeth his bed: If he rise again, and walk abroad upon his staff, then shall he that smote him be quit: only he shall pay for the loss of his time, and shall cause him to be thoroughly healed.

Tenth, on the matter of monetary payment for causing the loss of a fetus, the Code of Hammurabi states in Section 209:

> If a man has struck a gentleman's daughter and caused her to drop what is in her womb, he shall pay ten shekels of silver for what was in her womb.

The Bible in Exodus 21:22 similarly states:

> If men strive, and hurt a woman with child, so that her fruit depart from her, and yet no mischief follow: he shall be surely punished, according as the woman's husband will lay upon him; and he shall pay as the judges determine.

310

Eleventh, on the distinction between damages due from the owner of an ox with no history of aggression, and an ox that does have a history of aggression, the Code of Hammurabi states in Sections 250 and 251:

> If a wild bull in his charge has gored a man and caused him to die, that case has no remedy. If the ox has pushed a man, by pushing has made known his vice, and he has not blunted his horn, has not shut up his ox, and that ox has gored a man of gentle birth and caused him to die, he shall pay half a mina of silver.

The Bible, in Exodus 21:28-32 states:

> If an ox gore a man or a woman, that they die: then the ox shall be surely stoned, and his flesh shall not be eaten; but the owner of the ox shall be quit. But if the ox were wont to push with his horn in time past, and it hath been testified to his owner, and he hath not kept him in, but that he hath killed a man or a woman; the ox shall be stoned, and his owner also shall be put to death. If there be laid on him a sum of money, then he shall give for the ransom of his life whatsoever is laid upon him. Whether he have gored a son, or have gored a daughter, according to this judgment shall it be done unto him. If the ox shall push a manservant or a maidservant; he shall give unto their master thirty shekels of silver, and the ox shall be stoned.

Twelfth, the Code of Hammurabi uses a slave's ear to symbolize submission to his master; the Bible follows suit. The Code of Hammurabi states in Section 282:

> If a slave has said to his master 'Thou art not my master,' as his slave one shall put him to account and his master shall cut off his ear.

The Bible in Exodus discusses a Hebrew slave who does not wish to go free after six years, but wishes to remain a slave. Exodus 21:6 states:

> ...he shall also bring him to the door, or unto the door post; and his master shall bore his ear through with an aul; and he shall serve him for ever.

And other similarities between Hammurabi's ancient Code and the Bible can be illustrated, but the twelve we have discussed should suffice to make the point.

Now, my brother, to be clear: The Five Books of Moses comprises stories, poetry, prophecy, and other material—in addition to laws. Thus, the great majority of its text deals with matters not addressed by the far-briefer Code of

Hammurabi and its far more specific focus. It is also true that on many matters the Bible's laws are different from those of Hammurabi. But the examples we have cited should be enough to illustrate, even acknowledging the many differences, how similar and related are many of the Bible's laws to laws of earlier civilizations. Thus, the Bible begins to look rather more human than divine. Indeed, it seems that many of the Bible's laws are not only similar to earlier laws of other peoples, but drew from them direct influence.

Moreover, many scholars believe that the Code of Hammurabi itself borrowed heavily from still earlier law codes. Indeed, we know of such earlier law codes.[1] Thus, some of the Bible's laws are apparently not only not unique, they seem to have originated not with God, Moses, or later Israelites inspired by God—but with Babylonians and other peoples living many hundreds of years before Moses. And this provides further cause for sincere and intelligent doubt as to whether the Bible is sourced in God, or merely in man.

And, true, the similarities illustrated do not prove beyond all doubt that the Bible was influenced by Hammurabi's code, for perhaps both Hammurabi and the Bible borrowed from a third, earlier code of laws, or drew upon a set of rules and expectations of those ancient cultures in the part of the world they both shared. In any case, whether the Bible was directly influenced by Hammurabi, or simply shares many similarities to Hammurabi for other reasons, the Bible is not a unique, entirely new message, originating in God's heavens, nor must her laws be seen as rich with sacred and divine meaning.

And my brother, I do not mean to suggest that the Hebrew Bible was in no way original, and made no important contributions to the advance of human ideals.[2] The Bible and the civilizations that produced the Bible—along with other

---

[1] See chapter 17 in J. Kugel's *How To Read The Bible* where he cites similar laws and wordings in other ancient Mesopotamian law codes, such as the Laws of Lipit-Ishtar (ca. 1930 BCE) and the Sumerian Laws Exercise Tablet (ca. 1900 BCE).

[2] Walter Kaufmann, in his *Faith of a Heretic*, in the context of a very sympathetic treatment of the Old Testament, acknowledges the "tremendous influence" of Hammurabi's Code on certain biblical teachings (as well as the influence of the Egyptian, Sumerian, Babylonian and Assyrian cultures) but says: "The historically ignorant believe in absolute novelty; those with a smattering of history…in no novelty at all…" and he follows through by saying that away from these two mistaken extremes lies the more mature perspective of noticing "small, but sometimes crucial differences."

He is right on this, of course—his thinking here, as on many other points, being sharp and subtle. Yet traditional religion takes little consolation from what she sees as the faint praise that her Bible made important contributions and advances. She wants her Bible to be supernatural, and utterly unlike anything humans ever created, or ever could create, without divine assistance. And this standard, as Professor Kaufmann would surely have agreed, is one the Bible, with all its excellence and innovation, falls well short of, as

---

books and civilizations—have contributed mightily. But only with a rash disregard for reason, evidence, and experience could we characterize these contributions as supernatural.

My brother, one can employ creative arguments in the attempt to maintain traditional religious views on the Bible even having seen the evidence from Hammurabi's code. One might argue that the similarities between the texts are nothing more than a series of remarkable but meaningless coincidences, or that, contrary to available evidence, perhaps Hammurabi's code was actually written later than the Bible and *it* was influenced by the Bible, and not the other way around—or that Hammurabi's code is nothing more than an elaborate archaeological hoax. But, my brother, investigate the matter further, and when you have done so, ask yourself in a quiet moment whether you can be confident of such defenses, or whether honesty must not acknowledge at least significant doubt.

117. The Epic of Gilgamesh, Egyptian wisdom writings, and other apparent influences on the Bible

But the religious teacher said: This Code of Hammurabi is only one example, and perhaps there is some mistake in your claims. Do you have other examples of the Bible being influenced by earlier human sources?

And the sage said: My brother, indeed, the Code of Hammurabi is not the only source from which the Bible may have drawn influence. The Epic of Gilgamesh is a widely known set of stories preserved on stone carvings older than any known copies of the Bible, and the tales it tells are set many centuries earlier than the days of Moses. In some versions it tells the story of a great flood, and the story in many, though not all, of its details is remarkably similar to the account of Noah's flood as described in the Bible's book of Genesis.

For several examples: In both stories a flood was brought upon humankind because of divine wrath; only one human was saved with his family or companions and assistants; he was told to build a craft to survive on the waters; the dimensions or shape of the craft are described; it was sealed with pitch; the seed of all living things was taken aboard; as the flood subsided the craft came to rest on the top of a mountain; a dove and a raven were sent out to see whether the waters had gone down sufficiently to uncover the land; the survivor, upon disembarking on dry land, brought a sacrifice, and God, or the gods, smelled the

---

evidenced by many indicators, among them not only its striking similarities, in some passages, to the Code of Hammurabi, but the many advances of law and ethics—not to mention of science and technology—that came only after the close of the Bible, such as the abolition of slavery and the conceiving of genocide as an abomination and war crime.

pleasant fragrance, whereupon the deity or deities in question considered the matter of never again bringing a flood upon all the earth.

My brother, here too one can claim that the non-biblical story was based on the original story of Noah, which religious people might claim is more accurately told in the Bible. But honesty reminds us that we have no compelling evidence to believe that, and it may as likely be true that the Bible borrowed the Noah story from the Epic of Gilgamesh, or that both the Bible and the Epic of Gilgamesh borrowed from another source or earlier tradition. Of one thing we can be certain: The biblical story of Noah is not unique in the ancient world, for a remarkably similar story was carved in stone, by other peoples, long before our currently known oldest copies of the Bible, before the days of Ezra, too—indeed, perhaps even centuries before Moses.[1]

Other examples of influence upon the Bible are reflected in the many covenants and treaties the Old Testament speaks of God entering into with the ancient Israelites. These agreements and ceremonies, scholars explain, betray their mortal origins in that they are similar to the format and wordings of treaties between kings and their vassal states in the ancient Near East.[2]

Even many of the worship rituals of the temple, most obviously animal sacrifice, but others, too,[3] as described in the Bible—indeed, the architecture of the

---

[1] Scholars note that extant copies of the Epic of Gilgamesh date to the 7th century BCE, and copies of another flood story, the Epic of Atrahasis are dated to the 17th century BCE. By comparison, Ezra is understood to have lived—and perhaps edited the final version of the Old Testament—in the 5th century BCE, and Moses is generally understood to have lived in the 13th century BCE.

[2] James Kugel in Chapter 15 of his *How to Read the Bible* provides an excellent overview of scholars' findings on these Suzerain treaties of the Hittites in the ancient Near East, on the convention form of these treaties, and on how these conventions seem to be followed in various covenants and treaties of the Old Testament—including the Ten Commandments. There is some controversy, as Kugel explains, on whether the Hittite connection is a valid one—some scholars point to Assyrian treaties which they say are closer in time and in form to biblical writings, and others, especially some religious scholars, deny any non-Israelite influence on the relevant biblical passages. Still, for the purposes of our discussion, whether the Bible was directly influenced by earlier and nearby cultures or merely arrived at similar conventions on its own, such similarities provide one more illuminating example of how the Bible, and its collection of laws and teachings, was not a complete innovation—much less is it unexplainable without resort to supernatural revelation. It demonstrably resembles, in many ways, what has been produced by strictly human means, and in cultures that did not share the Israelite religion.

[3] See, for example, Kugel's discussion, and citations, on the rituals for purifying a temple, and for priests washing themselves and donning linen garments—the latter especially reminiscent of biblical prescriptions for temple rituals on the Day of Atonement—in Chapter 20 of his *How to Read the Bible*.

temple itself[1]—were quite similar to the rituals and temples of other peoples, the Canaanite-Phoenicians, the Babylonians, and others, in the ancient Near East.

Moreover, various poetry and wisdom sayings in Psalms, Proverbs, and other books of the Bible seem to echo earlier texts of the Egyptians and others.[2] And remember, too, that the apparent influence of Hammurabi's laws and other texts on the Bible is by no means the main reason to conclude that the Bible is man-made. Rather, this constitutes only one small, though interesting, indication—among the heaps of arguments and evidence that the Bible's authors and inspirations, though sometimes exceptional and noble, were mortal, not divine.

118. Errors and contradictions in the Bible

Then a young religious man said: I have no knowledge of these other writings, so I do not know what to say about them. But I do know the Bible. And earlier you claimed that the Bible contains contradictions. I challenge you to name even one. The Bible never contradicts itself. It is perfect, and consistent in its message and facts, because it comes from God.

And the sage responded in a soft voice, saying: My son, blessed are you for requesting evidence of biblical fallibility, for this boldness leaves you vulnerable to being deeply pained if such evidence is forthcoming. May the rewards of honest inquiry see you through whatever falls may come.

To begin, my son, even if the Bible held no contradictions, such internal consistency would neither prove its stories accurate nor its origin divine. Myriads

---

[1] See William G. Dever's discussion on "The Temple in Jerusalem" in Chapter 4 of his *What Did the Biblical Writers Know and When Did They Know It?* where (in the cause of defending the historicity of the biblical temple against those who claim it never existed) he writes: ...We now have direct Bronze and Iron Age parallels for *every single feature* of the 'Solomonic Temple' as described in the Hebrew Bible..."

[2] See, for example, *Old Testament Parallels* by Matthews and Benjamin, especially their sections on the similarity of Psalm 104 to the Egyptian *Hymn to Aten,* and the similarity of certain verses in Proverbs to the Egyptian teachings of Ptah-Hotep. To be clear: No responsible scholar would deny that the Bible—just as the literature, sacred or otherwise, of any culture—has its distinctions giving it a separate identity and demonstrating that it and the cultures from which it arose are not exact duplicates of other writings and cultures. Still, the extensive influence upon the Bible, from earlier and surrounding cultures, is evident—and this influence hurts the fundamentalist religious notion of the Bible as a totally unique and necessarily divine work.

And a final citation on the matter: Ambrose Bierce, in one of his definitions of "Babe" in his *Devil's Dictionary*, touches with characteristic sarcasm on the matter of the Bible's similarity to the traditions of surrounding cultures. He says: "...little Moses, from whose adventure in the bulrushes the Egyptian hierophants of seven centuries before doubtless derived their idle tale of the child Osiris being preserved on a floating lotus leaf."

of books—including those of fables, and magical fairy tales for children—contain no internal contradictions but are neither the word of God nor accurate accounts, and are certainly not worthy of our highest allegiance and most fervent submission.

Yet daring and intelligent men—in days when such observations endangered their community status, their freedom, even their lives—have long since noted that the Bible contradicts itself numerous times. And although a Bible free of contradictions is not necessarily of divine origin—nor even necessarily accurate—still, a Bible containing contradictions is *not* of divine origin, or at least demonstrates that God does not prevent errors from creeping into the biblical text. And errors in any part of the biblical text put the credibility of the remainder of the Bible in question.

Also, before recounting any biblical contradictions, I must clarify an important point. Many claims of supposed contradiction raised against the Bible are misguided and unconvincing. Indeed, in some cases, the answers of those defending the Bible are probable, even definitive.

Here is one example of many: Those who raise as a contradiction that the Bible, in the Ten Commandments, teaches not to kill, but in other passages mandates that the courts put to death those guilty of various sins or crimes, and that the Israelites kill their enemies, are making a simple error—they have not understood the original Hebrew of the Old Testament, in which it does not forbid killing. It does not say *Lo taharog*, which would have been the ancient Hebrew words for "Thou shalt not *kill*." Instead, it says, *Lo Tirtzach*, which are the ancient Hebrew words for "Thou shalt not engage in *unjustified killing*." And the consistent and plain message of the Bible on such matters is that unjustified killing—the killing of one private citizen by another, unless in self-defense or other special circumstances—is strictly forbidden; but that killing of various kinds, in battle and by the courts, or by command of the king or prophet, is allowed and even mandated.[1] We may not agree with the morality of the Bible on all matters of killing, but the above claim of a biblical contradiction is mistaken.

Another example of a misguided attack on the Bible is the claim that Leviticus 11:19 is in error, and lists the bat as one of the "birds" forbidden to eat. Since

---

[1] Those familiar with biblical Hebrew may find it interesting to note that the word "retzach" (and its other forms such as tirtzach and rotzeach) cannot accurately be translated as "murder," though it often is. In Numbers 35:25-28 the Bible repeatedly refers even to the unintentional killer as "rotzeach," and the Bible does so again in Deuteronomy 4:42. Thus, it seems to me, the biblical "rotzeach" is best translated—as I indicate in the text—not as one who murders, but as one who commits an act of *unjustified* killing—that is, killing one who was not deserving of being killed—and this can, indeed, be compatible with doing so unintentionally.

the bat is a mammal, not a bird, some say the Bible has here shown its scientific ignorance. But for those who can read the original Hebrew of Leviticus, this matter poses no difficulty. They see that the Hebrew word translated as "bird" is "*owf*," which literally means "flyer" or "flying thing." Using that means of categorization, the bat does indeed belong in the group, for it is a "flying thing." The modern categorization of birds and mammals was simply not used. Instead, the Bible employed a different and perfectly reasonable approach to organizing and referring to various creatures—by their means of locomotion, in this case flying, instead of by their means of birthing or nourishing their young, characteristics which help define the category of mammal. Indeed, the context of this verse is not a biblical lecture on biology, but a practical set of instructions for a people's dietary laws; and it stands to reason that categorizing animals by their most obvious characteristics—whether they stay on the ground, in the water, or fly through the air—would be not only an acceptable basis for characterization, but perhaps a preferable one. Moreover, if one looks in the first chapter of Genesis, in the account of the creation of all living things, one can see them being described by their means of locomotion and where they are found—on land, in the sea, or in the air. Thus, the Bible—in its original Hebrew—has not said that the bat is a bird; it has merely referred to the bat as a flying creature.

This explanation is consistent with the rest of that Leviticus chapter 11, which begins by speaking of the land animals:

> And the Lord spake unto Moses…These are the beasts which ye shall eat among all the beasts that are on the earth.

It continues in verse 9 to speak of creatures from the water:

> These shall ye eat of all that are in the waters…

Then, in verse 13 it speaks of flying things:

> And these are they which ye shall have in abomination among that which flies.

Moreover, even if the Bible meant the word "birds," and not the more general term of "that which flies,"[1] the bat is the last item on that biblical list, and

---

[1] The King James Bible and other translations do, in this verse, use the word "fowls" or "birds." But I maintain that, especially seeing the ordering of the chapter and the terminology used to identify the other categories of animals, one has more than enough justification to translate the word "Ha'owf" as "that which flies." Indeed, later in the very

being an unusual animal, a flying mammal, there would be no proof the Bible thought it was a bird, merely because it appended it to the end of a list of birds. Indeed, the fact that it comes as the very last item on the list might indicate that the Bible considered it somewhat different from the earlier items.

And many other passages cited by some Bible opponents as errors or contradictions are easily understood by the fair-minded and informed investigator to be correct after all, or at least quite possibly consistent with the biblical passages they supposedly contradict.

Yet, my brother, although some objections raised by overeager, misinformed Bible critics are mistaken, and can justifiably be shrugged off by the believer, other apparent biblical errors and contradictions should be seen by the believer as more troubling—for, in many cases, even a thorough familiarity with original biblical languages, and a clear understanding of context, does not offer the objective mind easy answers.

Remember, the honest religious soul is not relieved of the duty to investigate the many serious charges against the Bible merely because some objections are based in ignorance or worse, and invalid. Would you accept the same defense if anti-religious beliefs were in question? If some religious people raise misinformed and unconvincing objections to agnosticism and atheism—as some do—would you say that non-religious people can responsibly assume that *all* religious protests against secularism are equally invalid? Surely not; for in every camp of ideas there are arrayed, along with the thoughtful and the scholarly, the vulgar and the foolish. And since no cause can avoid attracting to its ranks some unfit for battle, the noble warrior seeks out from among the "mixed multitude" his truly worthy opponents.

And because many supposed criticisms of the Bible are not valid, for this reason I do not pass along any and all instances claimed by some to be biblical errors and contradictions, but have rather chosen carefully. And if you believe that one or several of the contradictions I raise are misinformed, can you truly say the same of them all? Can you really, in good conscience, wave off all the examples I cite of biblical contradiction and error as misinformed?

Indeed, my son—and all of you, brothers and sisters—if you think you have persuasive rebuttals to the biblical contradictions I mention, please speak. Then,

---

same chapter, in verses 21 and 23, the Bible discusses other winged creatures such as the locust, and uses a combination term—"Sheretz Ha'owf"—and there the KJV translates the word "Ha'owf" as "flying...thing," with the combination term being translated as "flying creeping thing." This provides clear indication that even the authors of the KJV saw the word "Ha'owf" as meaning not necessarily "fowl," but "flying thing" or "that which flies."

the sparks of contending bedrock and flint—the lights of intense but honest debate—may illuminate the paths of all.

And if it is truth you seek, do not rely on the fact that apologists for religion have provided "answers" or "solutions" to every possible biblical error and contradiction. Any creative mind can provide "answers" or "solutions" to any challenge. Ask not, "Has an answer been given?" Ask, rather, "Has a reasonable and convincing answer been given, one that leaves me persuaded that the Bible is the word or will of an omniscient, perfect God?"

119. Errors and contradictions in the Old Testament

And the sage continued, saying: As for the contradictions and errors in the Old Testament, I shall not mention them all, but rather a sufficient number to illustrate their existence beyond a reasonable doubt.

Let us begin with contradictions and errors of fact, number, and event, for these are harder to explain away by determined apologetics than are contradictions on matters more open to conceptual interpretation and creative explanation, such as those of theology and law—though I shall, in due course, offer examples of those kinds of contradictions, too.

a. Sequence of creation

What was the sequence of creation? Were other animals created before humans, or humans before other animals? The Bible gives two contradictory accounts. In Genesis 1:25-27, other animals are created first. There the Bible states:

> And God made the beast of the earth after his kind, and the cattle after their kind, and every thing that creepeth upon the earth after his kind: and God saw that it was good. And God said, Let us make man in our image, after our likeness: and let them have dominion over the fish of the sea, and over the fowl of the air, and over the cattle, and over all the earth, and over every creeping thing that creepeth upon the earth. So God created man in his own image, in the image of God created he him; male and female created he them.

But in Genesis 2:18-19, the Bible seems to say that the first man was created before other animals. There the Bible states:

> And the Lord God said, It is not good that the man should be alone; I will make him a help meet for him. And out of the ground the Lord God formed every beast of the field, and every fowl of the air; and brought them unto Adam

to see what he would call them: and whatsoever Adam called every living creature, that was the name thereof.

b. Were animals created between the creation of Adam and the creation of Eve?

Was the creation of man and woman uninterrupted by the creation of other animals? Or was Adam created, then other animals, and then Eve created from Adam's rib? In Genesis 1:26-27 the Bible says man and woman were created together—after the other animals:

> And God said, Let us make man in our image, after our likeness and let them have dominion over the fish of the sea, and over the fowl of the air, and over the cattle, and over all the earth, and over every creeping thing that creepeth upon the earth. So God created man in his own image, in the image of God created he him; male and female created he them.

But in Genesis 2:18-22 the Bible states:

> And the Lord God said, It is not good that the man should be alone; I will make him a help meet for him. And out of the ground the Lord God formed every beast of the field, and every fowl of the air; and brought them unto Adam to see what he would call them: and whatsoever Adam called every living creature, that was the name thereof. And Adam gave names to all cattle, and to the fowl of the air, and to every beast of the field; but for Adam there was not found a help meet for him. And the Lord God caused a deep sleep to fall upon Adam, and he slept; and he took one of his ribs, and closed up the flesh instead thereof. And the rib, which the Lord God had taken from man, made he a woman, and brought her unto the man.

Thus, in one biblical account Adam was created first, then all other animal species, and finally Eve. But in another biblical account all other animal species were created before Adam, and only later were created Adam and Eve.

c. What was the sequence of the Israelites' journeys after the exodus from Egypt?

Numbers 33 provides a comprehensive list of the journeys the Israelites undertook after leaving Egypt and before arriving in the Promised Land. One section of this list is of interest to us here. Beginning in verse 31, the Bible states:

And they departed from Moseroth, and pitched in Benejaakan. And they removed from Benejaakan, and encamped at Horhagidgad. And they went from Horhagidgad, and pitched in Jotbathah.

Yet in Deuteronomy 10, the Bible weaves into the address of Moses to the Israelites the sequence of these journeys—and the sequence of the first two is reversed. Notwithstanding the slightly different pronunciations or translations of the places, there is no mistaking—for those who read the original Hebrew of the Old Testament—that they speak of the same journeys. Verses 6-7 state:

And the children of Israel took their journey from Beeroth of the children of Jaakan[1] to Mosera: there Aaron died, and there he was buried; and Eleazar his son ministered in the priest's office in his stead. From thence they journeyed unto Gudgodah;[2] and from Gudgodah to Jotbath.

d. What were the genealogies of the early Israelites?

The Five Books of Moses provides several inconsistent accounts of early Israelite genealogies. Genesis 46 speaks of Jacob's children and grandchildren, and Numbers 26 speaks of a later time when these sons of Jacob had grown into clans and tribes.

Of the several inconsistencies between these two accounts,[3] two examples will suffice. The first relates to the name of the only son of Dan—Dan being one of the patriarch Jacob's sons. Genesis 46:23 states:

And the sons of Dan; Hushim.

But Numbers 26:42 states:

These are the sons of Dan after their families: of Shuham, the family of the Shuhamites. These are the families of Dan after their families.

---

[1] The word "Benejaakan" of the King James translation of Numbers 33 is, in the original Hebrew Bible, two words, "(me')bene Jaakan" which literally means "the children of Jaakan." It is therefore seen to be the same place mentioned in Deuteronomy 10.

[2] The word "Horhagidgad" of the King James translation of Numbers 33 is, in the original Hebrew Bible, two words, "Hor Hagidgad," which literally means "the mountain of Gidgad." And the Numbers 33 word "Gudgodah" literally means "to Gudgod" or is the feminine form of "Gudgod" (or Gidgad). Again, those familiar with biblical Hebrew will have no trouble seeing that these verses refer to the same places.

[3] For further inconsistencies, study the lists of names given, by these two biblical accounts, for Jacob's sons, and note not only discrepancies in names, but also omissions.

Thus, Genesis and Numbers agree that Dan had only one son, but Genesis has him named Hushim, and Numbers has him named Shuham.[1]

A second example concerns the names of the children of Issachar, another of Jacob's sons. Genesis 46:13 names them Tola, Phuva, Job, and Shimron; but Numbers 26:23-24 names them Tola, Pua, Jashub, and Shimron.

Thus, the third son of Issachar is by Genesis named Jashub, and by Numbers named Job.[2]

e. How many horse stalls did King Solomon have?

In 1 Kings 4:26[3] it is stated that King Solomon had *forty* thousand stalls for horses and chariots. Yet II Chronicles 9:25 states that Solomon had *four* thousand stalls for horses and chariots.

f. How large was the pool at the temple?

In describing Solomon's building of the Temple, 1 Kings 7:26 says he built a pool containing *two* thousand baths, while II Chronicles 4:5, describing the same project, says it contained *three* thousand baths.

g. How many of Haddadezer's men and chariots did David capture?

In recounting the battle victories of King David over Haddadezer the king of Zovah, II Samuel 8:4 says—if we translate literally from the ancient Hebrew—that he captured one thousand and seven hundred horsemen; or, if we follow the loose translation of a widely popular English version[4] of the Bible, that he captured one thousand chariots and seven hundred horsemen. By contrast, in I Chronicles 18:4 in telling the same story, the Bible states that David captured one thousand chariots, seven thousand horsemen, and twenty thousand footmen. Neither the literal translation of the verse in II Samuel, seventeen hundred

---

[1] To those who read the passage's original Hebrew, an obvious cause for the inconsistency suggests itself: The first two non-vowel letters—the *shin* and the *het*—were, somewhere along the line and by one of the accounts, or the document or tradition from which it stemmed, transposed. Yet this likely explanation does not serve the purposes of those who insist that the Bible is without error.

[2] And although the KJV translates the 2nd son's name in Numbers as Pua, which differs from its translation of that son's name in Genesis as Phuva, I do not consider this a contradiction because in the original Hebrew of this Bible's passage both Genesis and Numbers name the 2nd son Phuva. By contrast, as regards the name of the 3rd son—which I *do* raise as an inconsistency—the Bible, even in its untranslated Hebrew gives two different names.

[3] In the King James version—and 1 Kings 5:6 in some Jewish Bibles

[4] The King James version

horsemen, nor the loose translation, seven hundred horsemen, is consistent with the seven thousand horsemen mentioned in II Chronicles.

h. In a battle with Syria, how many chariots did David destroy, and were the forty thousand men he slew horsemen or foot soldiers?

The Bible has different accounts of one battle King David waged against Syria. II Samuel, 10:18 says:

> ...And David slew of Syria seven hundred chariots and forty thousand horsemen...

By contrast, I Chronicles, 19:18 says:

> ...And David slew of Syria seven thousand chariots and forty thousand foot soldiers...

These biblical accounts contradict each other on two matters: the number of chariots destroyed as well as whether the forty thousand additional killed were horsemen or foot soldiers.[1]

i. How old was Ahaziah when he began to reign over Israel?

In II Kings, 8:26 the Bible states that Ahaziah was *twenty*-two years old when he began to reign over Israel. Yet in II Chronicles, 22:2 the Bible states that he was *forty*-two.

j. Did Michal, the daughter of King Saul, ever have children?

In II Samuel, 6:23 the Bible states: "Therefore Michal the daughter of Saul had no child unto the day of her death." Yet in II Samuel, 21:8 it states: "...and

---

[1] In an apparent attempt to avoid this contradiction, the King James translation inserts a few words into both texts—different words into each text—which are not present in the original Hebrew. In II Samuel the text is made to read: "And David slew *the men of* seven hundred chariots," while in I Chronicles, the text is made to read: "And David slew of the Syrians seven thousand *men which fought in* chariots."

Two points bear remembering: First, the original Hebrew text shows no justification for these extra words to be inserted—especially since different insertions are chosen as convenient for the two texts—and virtually any contradiction between any texts can be resolved by adding different words to each text. (I'm reminded of Henny Youngman's joke that when he told his doctor he couldn't afford an operation, the doctor offered to touch up the X-rays instead.) Second, even after those questionable words are added, the contradiction still remains as to the identity of the forty thousand—were they horsemen or foot soldiers?

the five sons of Michal the daughter of Saul whom she bore to Adriel, the son of Barziliai the Mecholathite."[1]

k. What was the census of soldiers, counted by Joab for King David?

In two biblical accounts of the same census of soldiers—commanded by King David, and overseen by Joab, and for which David was later punished—the numbers are contradictory. II Samuel 24:9 says there were eight hundred thousand of Israel, and five hundred thousand of Judah. Yet I Chronicles 21:5 states there were one million, one hundred thousand in Israel, and four hundred and seventy thousand in Judah. When comparing these two biblical accounts, neither the numbers for Israel nor for Judah are consistent—nor are the total sums for Israel and Judah combined.

l. How many did David's chief of the captains kill with his spear at one time?

II Samuel 23:8-9 says eight hundred:

> These be the names of the mighty men whom David had: The Tachmonite that sat in the seat, chief among the captains; the same was Adino the Eznite: he lift up his spear against eight hundred, whom he slew at one time. And after him was Eleazar the son of Dodo the Ahohite, one of the three mighty men with David, when they defied the Philistines that were there gathered together to battle...

---

[1] The King James Version, though using the same name Michal for both verses, in this verse substitutes "brought up" for what is more accurately translated from the Hebrew as "bore" or "gave birth to." This was, presumably, an attempt to avoid the contradiction. But at best this is commentary and not translation—and to be candid, it is worse: It is commentary passing itself off as translation.

Another translation, the New International Version (NIV), does not even use the name Michal in this verse, but instead uses the name Merav—in an apparent attempt to avoid the contradiction about Michal—following what it acknowledges is not the text of most Hebrew or Septuagint sources. Interestingly, this use of the name Merav here is, indeed, consistent with the Bible's narrative in 1 Samuel 18:19 where it is stated that Merav (not Michal) was married to Adriel, and that Michal was married to David.

Yet even if we conclude that the word Michal in II Samuel 21:8 is mistaken, and should really be Merav, and therefore there is no contradiction, we are still left with an error in the authoritative text of the Hebrew Bible—which proves at the very least that errors have crept into Scripture, and that we cannot be confident that what we read in the Bible are the actual, or even the inspired, words of God.

By contrast, I Chronicles 11:11-13 says three hundred:

> And this is the number of the mighty men whom David had; Jashobeam, an Hachmonite, the chief of the captains: he lifted up his spear against three hundred slain by him at one time. And after him was Eleazar the son of Dodo, the Ahohite, who was one of the three mighties. He was with David at Pasdammim, and there the Philistines were gathered together to battle...

And note that both books of the Bible are either speaking of the same man, and contradict each other as to the number he slew at one time with his spear, or they are speaking about different men, and contradict each other on who was David's chief of the captains. And these biblical passages seem to be different versions of the same tradition, because both introduce their man as David's chief of the captains, and both immediately follow the account of the chief of the captains with the account of the son of Dodo the Ahohite.

m. How many chief officers supervised Solomon's building projects?
In discussing King Solomon's chief officers supervising his building projects, I Kings 9:23 states there were *five* hundred and fifty, while II Chronicles 8:10 says there were *two* hundred and fifty. And in both I Kings 9 and II Chronicles 8, the verse preceding the mention of chief officers for building says that Solomon did not make servants out of the children of Israel, and the verse following speaks of the daughter of Pharaoh, confirming that these are versions of the same story.

n. How much gold did Hiram provide for King Solomon's temple?
The Bible gives two accounts of how much gold King Hiram provided for the construction of King Solomon's temple. I Kings 9: 27-28 states:

> Hiram sent in the navy his servants, shipmen that had knowledge of the sea, with the servants of Solomon. And they came to Ophir, and fetched from there gold, four hundred and *twenty* talents, and brought it to King Solomon.

By contrast, the Bible in II Chronicles 8:18 states:

> And Huram sent him, by the hands of his servants, ships, and servants that had knowledge of the sea; and they went with the servants of Solomon to Ophir, and took thence four hundred and *fifty* talents of gold, and brought them to King Solomon.

o. How tall were the two pillars at the front of the temple?

The Bible has two different accounts of the height of the two pillars—called Jachin and Boaz—at the front of the temple at Jerusalem. I Kings states in 7:15 that the height was eighteen cubits:

> For he cast two columns of brass; of eighteen cubits high apiece…

Later, after describing the carvings and decorations of the pillars, the Bible, in verse 21, names these pillars:

> And he set up the pillars in the porch of the temple: and he set up the right pillar, and called the name thereof Jachin: and he set up the left pillar and called the name thereof Boaz.

In II Chronicles 3:15-17 however, the Bible states that the pillars' height was thirty-five cubits:

> Also he made before the house two pillars of thirty and five cubits high…And he reared up the pillars before the temple, one on the right hand, and the other on the left; and he called the name of that on the right hand Jachin, and the name of that on the left Boaz.

A careful reading of these biblical texts makes it clear that they both refer to Solomon's building of the one temple for God at Jerusalem, and they both refer to the same pillars.[1]

---

[1] Apologists have answered that perhaps the verse giving the greater height to the pillars was referring to the sum of both pillars' height in that number, or was including in its measurement something (quite tall) upon which the pillars may have stood, or that it was a copyist error. But if these are the answers upon which defenders of the Bible rely to deal with inconsistencies like these, even if we were to accept their answers, they make the Bible a confusing document which cannot be taken at face value because it could easily mean something different from what it appears to say—is it not misleading, at best, to describe the height of pillars by adding them together and giving the sum of their heights, without making clear that it is their sum one is stating? What if one were to say that the average giraffe's legs are 24 feet tall, and neglected to mention that he was not referring to what we would expect—the height of each leg—but was rather stating the sum of the legs' heights? Or, if the disparity in numbers is due to a copyist error, it shows the Bible to be a fallible text, a far cry from the perfect divine document spoken of by our forebears' traditional religion.

p. How old was Jehoiachin when he began to reign, and who succeeded him to the throne?

The Bible in II Kings 24:8 says that Jehoiachin began to reign at age eighteen, and, in verse 17, that he was succeeded on the throne by his uncle. In contrast, II Chronicles 36:9-10 says that Jehoiachin began his reign at eight years of age, and was succeeded by his brother. These different accounts contain two contradictions: Jehoiachin's age, as well as his family relationship to his successor.

q. When did King Baasha die?

The Bible in I Kings 16:6-8 states:

> So Baasha slept with his fathers, and was buried in Tirzah: and Elah his son reigned in his stead...In the twenty and sixth year of Asa king of Judah, began Elah the son of Baasha to reign over Israel in Tirzah...

But in II Chronicles 16: 1 the Bible states:

> In the six and thirtieth year of the reign of Asa, Baasha king of Israel came up against Judah...

So I Kings states that Baasha died in the twenty-sixth year of Asa's reign, while II Chronicles says Baasha was still alive—for he was leading a battle-siege—ten years later, in the thirty-sixth year of Asa's reign.

r. When was Jehoiachin released from prison?

The Bible in II Kings 25: 27 states that it was on the twenty-seventh day of the month:

> And it came to pass in the seven and thirtieth year of the captivity of Jehoiachin king of Judah, in the twelfth month, on the seven and twentieth day of the month, that Evilmerodach king of Babylon in the year that he began to reign did lift up the head of Jehoiachin king of Judah out of prison.

But in Jeremiah 52:31 the Bible states that it was the twenty-fifth day of the month:

> And it came to pass in the seven and thirtieth year of the captivity of Jehoiachin king of Judah, in the twelfth month, in the five and twentieth day of the month, that Evilmerodach king of Babylon, in the first year of his reign, lifted up the head of Jehoiachin king of Judah, and brought him forth out of prison.

s. How many of the family of Arah returned to Israel from the Babylonian exile?

The biblical books of Ezra and Nehemiah both tell of the return of the Jews from Babylonian exile to Israel. Much is consistent between these accounts, but there are also many contradictions in their different census numbers of returning Jews. Here are the first several examples: Ezra 2:5 says that the sons of Arah, were seven hundred and seventy-five. In contrast, Nehemiah 7:10 says they were six hundred and fifty-two.

t. How many of the family of Pahath-Moab returned?

Ezra 2:6 says that the children of Pahath-moab, of the children of Jeshua and Joab, were two thousand, eight hundred and twelve.

In contrast, Nehemiah 7:11 says that the children of Pahath-moab, of the children of Jeshua and Joab, were two thousand, eight hundred and eighteen.

u. How many of the family of Zattu returned?

Ezra 2:8 says the children of Zattu were nine hundred and forty five, while Nehemiah 7:13 says they were eight hundred and forty five.

v. How many of the family of Bebai returned?

Ezra 2:11 says the children of Bebai were six hundred and twenty three, while Nehemiah 7:16 says they were six hundred and twenty eight.

w. How many of the family of Azgad returned?

Ezra 2:12 says the children of Azgad were one thousand, two hundred and twenty two, while Nehemiah 7:17 says they were two thousand, three hundred and twenty two—almost double the amount listed in Ezra.

My son, Ezra 2 and Nehemiah 7 contain more such contradictions. To find them, simply compare the names and numbers of the families—even singers—listed in those two chapters. And to be clear: Both Ezra and Nehemiah are talking about the same events, the same time period, the same families. To illustrate this, I will quote the introductory verses in those sections of Ezra and Nehemiah, leading up to, and beginning, their census numbers. Ezra 2:1-4 states:

> Now these are the children of the province that went up out of the captivity, of those which had been carried away, whom Nebuchadnezzar the king of Babylon had carried away unto Babylon, and came again unto Jerusalem and Judah, every one unto his city. Which came with Zerubbabel, Jeshua, Nehemiah, Seraiah, Reelaliah, Mordecai, Bilshan, Mizpar, Bivgai, Rehum, Baanah. The number of the men of the people of Israel: The children of Parosh, two thousand, a

hundred seventy and two. The children of Shephatiah, three hundred seventy and two. .....

And the book of Nehemiah introduces its census in a way that makes it clear that it refers to the same return as that described in the book of Ezra. Nehemiah 7: 6-9 states:

> These are the children of the province, that went up out of the captivity, of those that been carried away, whom Nebuchadnezzar the king of Babylon had carried away, and came again to Jerusalem and to Judah, every one unto his city. Who came with Zerubbabel, Jeshuah, Nehemiah, Azariah, Raashan, Mispereth, Bigvai, Nehum, Baanah. The number, I say, of the men of the people of Israel was this. The children of Parosh, two thousand, a hundred seventy and two. The children of Shephatiah, three hundred seventy and two...

Both books of the Bible are clearly describing the same events. Indeed, for many of the families Ezra's totals agree with those of Nehemiah.[1]

And do not answer as some apologists have, that the contradictory numbers between Ezra and Nehemiah are merely because one counted those planning to return, and the other counted those who actually returned. Note that both Ezra and Nehemiah give the identical sum for the total number of returnees—forty-two thousand, three hundred and sixty. Are they not clearly speaking of the same group?

Ezra 2:64 states:

> The whole congregation together was forty and two thousand three hundred and threescore.

---

[1] A close examination also shows that the lists of notables returning with Zerubbabel are also inconsistent between Ezra and Nehemiah. But this is not necessarily a contradiction, because—unlike some biblical contradictions where one account leaves out critical elements present in another account, or mentions different and incompatible numbers or places than the other account—here it can be argued that the author of the Ezra passages, for whatever reasons, mentioned some of the returning notables, and the author of the Nehemiah passages mentioned other notables, but that no disagreement need be inferred.

And Nehemiah 7:66 states:

> The whole congregation together was forty and two thousand three hundred and threescore.

My son, this is not a complete list of the Old Testament's errors and contradictions, but it should be sufficient to stimulate an open mind to consider whether the Old Testament might indeed be less than perfectly accurate or consistent.

120. Errors and contradictions in the New Testament

Then a man spoke, saying: As a Christian, I am more interested in the New Testament than the Old Testament. Show me contradictions or errors there!

And the sage responded: My brother, as a result of the contradictions and errors in the Old Testament, even if the New Testament were free of all contradiction and error, its credibility would still be suspect, because—along with the more basic reasons for skepticism, such as it claiming supernatural knowledge and miracles, with insufficient evidence—the New Testament draws considerably upon the authority of the Old Testament, quoting it, and claiming that Jesus was the Messiah predicted by Jewish tradition and was the fulfillment of various Old Testament promises and prophecies.[1] Still, the New Testament *does* contain many apparent contradictions and errors. Let us, then, speak of them.

And, my brother, as I have said in regard to the Old Testament, not all that are claimed by the Bible's critics to be errors or contradictions in the New Testament truly are those things. Still, as I have also earlier said, when you hear my challenges ask not whether religious teachers and apologists have offered answers—for any intelligent and creative teacher can formulate at least a weak answer to any question or contradiction, especially if given the freedom to add meanings not present in the text, and to resort to other clever but dubious devices. Ask instead, then, whether the answers of religious teachers are truly persuasive to that most eager and impartial student—Honest Reason.

And do not be complacent either, my brother, if you believe you have a valid response to one or more of the contradictions and errors I raise. Remember, to cast doubt on the notion of a perfect Bible it takes but one apparent flaw.

First let us speak of errors and contradictions on facts and numbers, matters which are more plain to assess, and more difficult to explain away by creative

---

[1] For several of many examples of how the New Testament confirms its belief in the Old Testament's veracity and supernatural origin, see Matthew 1:22-23; 2:15; 2:17-18; Mark 15:28; John 12:38-41; and James 2:23.

apologetics. But if you wish me to cite contradictions on matters of teachings and beliefs, I shall be happy to do so, in due course.

And I shall not mention all the errors and contradictions of the New Testament. But that we may have apostles of honesty, let us speak of twelve.

a. Genealogy of Jesus

First, consider the two biblical genealogies of Jesus, found in the first chapter of Matthew and the third chapter of Luke. There are several ways in which these accounts are contradictory. Matthew lists twenty-eight generations from David through Jesus; Luke, by contrast, lists forty-three. Moreover, Luke has Jesus descending from David's son Nathan, while Matthew has him descending from another of David's sons—Solomon.

And do not say that Luke was merely more detailed and included more generations, generations that Matthew left out—for nearly all names in one account differ from names in the other account. And, as mentioned, the two genealogies attribute the lineage of Jesus to different sons of David.

And let not your heart be tempted to answer, either, that perhaps one list refers to the lineage of Mary the mother of Jesus, while the other refers to the lineage of Joseph. Both genealogies specifically trace the ancestry of Jesus through Joseph.

b. Where was Jacob buried, and who bought which burial field from whom?

Second, the New Testament seems to confuse where Jacob was buried, and who bought which field from whom for a burial place. Acts 7:15-16 states:

> So Jacob went down into Egypt, and died, he and our fathers. And were carried over into Sychem, and laid in the sepulchre that Abraham bought for a sum of money of the sons of Emmor, the father of Sychem.

Yet the Old Testament earlier made it clear that Jacob was not buried there, but in field of Machpelah, at Mamre, a piece of land Abraham bought not from the sons of Emmor, but from Ephron the Hittite. Genesis 50, speaking of Jacob's death, states in verse 13:

> For his sons carried him into the land of Canaan, and buried him in the cave of the field of Machpelah, which Abraham bought with the field for a possession of a buryingplace of Ephron the Hittite, before Mamre.

331

According to the earlier Old Testament, Jacob was not buried in Sychem,[1] but at Machpelah, and it was not bought from Emmor[2] the father of Sychem, but rather from Ephron the son of Zohar, the Hittite. And the burial place of Machpelah was at Hebron, not Sychem. These points are clear from Genesis 23. First, in verses 8 and 9 Abraham speaks to the people of Heth: "…Entreat for me to Ephron the son of Zohar, That he may give me the cave of Machpelah…" Then in verses 16-19 it states:

> …And Abraham weighed to Ephron the silver…And the field of Ephron, which was in Machpelah, which was before Mamre…were made sure unto Abraham for a possession…And after this, Abraham buried Sarah his wife in the cave of the field of Machpelah before Mam're: the same is Hebron in the land of Canaan.

As to the field—mistakenly mentioned in Acts as the burying place of Jacob—bought from the sons of Emmor, it was Jacob who bought this field from them, not Abraham. Genesis 33:18-19 states:

> And Jacob came to Shalem, a city of Shechem…And he bought a parcel of a field…at the hand of the children of Ha'mor, Shechem's father, for a hundred pieces of money.

And this field, the field that Jacob bought, eventually became the burial place for his son Joseph, many years later. The Old Testament states in Joshua 24:32:

> And the bones of Joseph, which the children of Israel brought up out of Egypt, buried they in Shechem, in a parcel of ground which Jacob bought of the sons of Hamor the father of Shechem for an hundred pieces of silver; and it became the inheritance of the children of Joseph.

In summary: The New Testament text in Acts seems to have confused the two separate incidents of Abraham and Jacob buying land, and mistakenly stated that Abraham bought the field in Shechem. Furthermore, aside from the matter of who bought the field at Shechem, the New Testament in Acts mistakenly has Jacob being buried in that field, when the Old Testament states clearly that *Joseph* was buried in Shechem, and that Jacob was buried at the burial place Machpelah, at Hebron.

---

[1] This place is sometimes spelled "Shechem."
[2] This name is sometimes spelled "Emmor."

c. How did Judas die, who bought the field, and why was it called the "field of blood"?

Third, in discussing the end of Judas, the disciple who betrayed Jesus, the New Testament seems to contradict itself in several ways—on how Judas died; on who bought the "field of blood"; and even on how the field got its name. Matthew 27:3-8 states:

> Then Judas, which had betrayed him…repented himself, and bought again the thirty pieces of silver to the chief priests and elders…And he cast down the pieces of silver in the temple, and departed, and went and hanged himself. And the chief priests took the silver pieces, and said, It is not lawful for to put them into the treasury, because it is the price of blood. And they took counsel, and bought with them the potter's field, to bury strangers in. Wherefore that field was called, The field of blood…

Thus, the Matthew text seems to say that Judas died by hanging himself; that the chief priests bought the land; and that it was called "field of blood" because it was bought with blood money.

In the book of Acts, by contrast, the New Testament seems to say that Judas died by falling, bursting open and his innards gushing out; and that Judas himself bought the field; and it seems to say that it was called "field of blood" because of the bloody end of Judas—falling and bursting open. Acts 1:16-19 states:

> …concerning Judas, which was guide to them that took Jesus…Now this man purchased a field with the reward of iniquity; and falling headlong, he burst asunder in the midst, and all his bowels gushed out. And it was known unto all the dwellers at Jerusalem; insomuch as that field is called…The field of blood.

d. How much time passed between the resurrection being discovered, and Jesus ascending to heaven?

Fourth, how much time passed between the resurrection and Jesus' ascension to heaven? Luke 24:2-50 seems to teach that the ascension occurred on the very day Jesus was discovered risen. It states:

> But they found the stone rolled away from the tomb. Then they went in and did not find the body of the Lord Jesus. And it happened, as they were greatly perplexed about this, that behold, two men stood by them in shining garments. Then, as they were afraid and bowed their faces to the earth, they said to them, Why do you seek the living among the dead? He is not here, but is risen!

...Now behold, two of them were traveling that same day... So it was, while they conversed and reasoned, that Jesus Himself drew near and went with them... Then He said to them, Thus it is written, and thus it was necessary for the Christ to suffer and to rise from the dead the third day, and that repentance and remission of sins should be preached in His name to all nations, beginning at Jerusalem. And you are witnesses of these things...and He lifted up His hands and blessed them. Now it came to pass, while He blessed them, that He was parted from them and carried up into heaven.

And the account in Mark 16[1] does not make clear about how many, if any, days passed between the resurrection and ascension.

But Acts 1:1-10 teaches that it was forty days after the resurrection. It states:

...of all that Jesus began both to do and teach, Until the day in which he was taken up...had given commandments unto the apostles whom he had chosen: To whom also he shewed himself alive after his passion by many infallible proofs, being seen of them forty days... And when he had spoken these things, while they beheld, he was taken up; and a cloud received him out of their sight...they looked stedfastly toward heaven as he went up...

e. How many of the thieves were against Jesus?

Matthew 27:38-44 says both thieves were against Jesus:

Then were there two thieves crucified with him, one on the right hand, and another on the left. And they that passed by reviled him...The thieves also, which were crucified with him, cast the same in his teeth.

Mark 15:27-32 agrees, stating:

And with him they crucify two thieves; the one on his right hand, and the other on his left... And they that passed by railed on him... And they that were crucified with him reviled him.

But Luke 23:33-42 apparently contradicts this, and teaches that only one was against Jesus, and the other rebuked his fellow thief. Luke states:

---

[1] Much of which, say some scholars, is in any case unreliable as it does not appear in the earliest manuscripts of Mark.

...there they crucified him, and the malefactors, one on the right hand, and the other on the left... And one of the malefactors which were hanged railed on him, saying, If thou be Christ, save thyself and us. But the other answering rebuked him, saying, Dost not thou fear God, seeing thou art in the same condemnation? And we indeed justly; for we receive the due reward of our deeds: but this man hath done nothing amiss. And he said unto Jesus, Lord, remember me when thou comest into thy kingdom.

f. What were the last words of Jesus?

Sixth, the New Testament contradicts itself on what were the last words of Jesus. Luke says they were: "Father, into thy hands I commend my spirit." In contrast, John says they were: "It is finished." Here are the relevant verses.

Luke 23:46 states:

And when Jesus had cried with a loud voice, he said, Father, into thy hands I commend my spirit: and having said thus, he gave up the ghost.

In contrast, John 19:30 states:

When Jesus therefore had received the vinegar, he said, It is finished: and he bowed his head, and gave up the ghost.

g. Angels at the sepulcher

Seventh, how many angels were in the sepulcher at the discovery that Jesus had risen, and how were they situated? Mark 16:5 says:

And entering into the sepulcher they saw a young man sitting on the right side.

In contrast, Luke 24:4 says:

...behold, two men stood by them in shining garments.

John 20:12 gives a third version:

And seeth two angels in white sitting, the one at the head, and the other at the feet, where the body of Jesus had been.

Thus, Mark, Luke, and John contradict each other on how many angels there were, whether they were sitting or standing, and if sitting, where?

h. Mistaken attribution of prophecy

Eighth, The New Testament attributes a prophecy incorrectly. Matthew 27:9 states:

> Then was fulfilled that which was spoken by Jeremy the prophet, saying, And they took the thirty pieces of silver, the price of him that was valued…

But this prophecy appears nowhere in Jeremiah. Matthew seems to be referring to a prophecy by Zechariah. Zechariah 11:12-13 states:

> And I said unto them, If ye think good, give me my price; and if not, forbear. So they weighed for my price thirty pieces of silver. And the Lord said unto me, Cast it unto the potter…[1]

i. Who told Mary Magdalene that Jesus had risen?

Ninth, who told Mary Magdalene—and others, depending on which Gospel account one reads—that Jesus had risen? Mark 16:5-6 says it was the "young man" angel sitting on the right side. Luke 24:4-6 says it was the two angels standing. John 20:15, by contrast, does not have any angels inform Mary of Jesus having risen, but says Jesus himself spoke to Mary, whereupon she understood that he had risen.

j. What was written on the cross?

Tenth, the New Testament contradicts itself on the text of the inscription written by Pilate, placed on the cross above Jesus. This contradiction may seem minor, but if—as some believe—the Gospels are the inspired word of God, one would think they would not contain several conflicting accounts of precisely what was written above Jesus on the cross—a foundational story of Christianity. Indeed, the four gospels teach several different versions. Matthew 27:37 says it was: "This is Jesus the king of the Jews."[2] Mark 15:26 says it was: "The king of

---

[1] Matthew seems to be referring to this prophecy, because this verse of Matthew is stated within the context of the story of Judas' end, and the story has the chief priests buying "the potter's" field with Judas' blood money. This would explain Matthew's claim that it was a fulfillment of the old prophecy which mentions giving 30 pieces of silver to "the potter."

[2] Even taking into account the different translations of Greek, Aramaic, Latin, or other languages from which these words—of the Bible or the original inscription on the cross—have been translated, the multiple accounts of what was written there cannot adequately be explained.

the Jews." Luke 23:38 says it was: "This is the king of the Jews." And John 19:19 says the inscription was: "Jesus of Nazareth the king of the Jews."

k. How many blind did Jesus heal, and how, as he departed Jericho?

Eleventh, what were the circumstances of Jesus healing the blind as he departed Jericho? How many blind people did he heal, and how? Matthew 20:29-34 states that there were two blind men and that Jesus healed them by touching their eyes. In contrast, Mark 10:46-52 states that it was one blind man and that Jesus healed him by speech, saying "Go thy way; thy faith hath made thee whole."[1]

l. What was the sequence of the devil's temptations of Jesus?

Twelfth, in the books of Matthew and Luke the same story is told of the devil tempting Jesus—after Jesus had been without food in the wilderness for forty days, and after the devil challenged Jesus to turn stones into bread—by bringing him to a pinnacle of the temple, and by bringing him to a high mountain. But where did the devil bring Jesus first, to the temple pinnacle or to the mountain? Two New Testament books contradict each other on that point. Matthew 4:1-11 says to the pinnacle of the temple, and Luke 4:1-13 says to the mountain.

*****

And the sage continued, and said: My brother, I have now illustrated twelve contradictions and errors of the New Testament; and these twelve barbs are but a hastily-grabbed handful from a field which, though blessed with many flowers, is thick with thorns, too.

121. Sub-argument that such contradictions are only about numbers, dates, and events, and may be copyist errors, and also do not touch on the main teachings or message of the Bible.

But a man said: All the contradictions you have cited, both in the Old Testament and the New Testament, relate only to trivial matters—of number, date, or exact event. Not one of these deals with the important teachings or main messages of the Bible. These simple errors of fact you cite probably crept into the text over the many centuries as these texts were copied from one parchment

---

[1] And an examination of the texts in Matthew and Mark makes clear that the same event is being described: The verses immediately preceding and immediately following the story are the same in both texts.

to another. I do not insist that the Bible is inerrant in all its details—only that its message on important teachings is accurate, consistent, and divine. Therefore, your contradictions and errors do not disturb my faith. You have only raised trivial inaccuracies because the Bible contains none that are significant.

And the sage said: My brother, as I have earlier said, I will be happy to raise biblical contradictions and errors on what all must concede are significant matters, too. But first I ask you to consider that if one defends the Bible by claiming that such inaccuracies which you refer to as trivial are but errors of scribes who copied from an original Bible free of such inaccuracies, one must still concede that God did not prevent the current biblical text from becoming inaccurate. And if God would not intervene to ensure the Bible's accuracy for these contradictions and errors, how can we be sure that He has prevented the Bible from being adulterated by inaccurate miracle stories and man-made laws and beliefs?

And if one should respond that small facts and details of numbers are not important, and therefore God did not prevent them from being copied wrong, then answer why the Bible—the Word of God—would include so many unimportant details in the first place. Is it not reasonable to assume that information deemed important enough for inclusion in the Bible, to be seen and treated as Holy Scripture, is not to be dismissed as unimportant to God? Moreover, if God allows small errors in the Bible, who can decide what constitutes a small error and what, a large error—where shall we draw the line, and which parts of the Bible can we be confident are not in error?

122. Old Testament contradictions and errors on important teachings

And the sage continued and said: My brother, because many among the religious *do* insist that the Bible is inerrant even in its particulars relating to numbers, dates, and exact events, to speak to their beliefs I have cited the first group of contradictions.

Moreover, anything other than a bald fact or number can be interpreted and explained to mean almost anything one wishes it to mean.

Yet in response to your challenge, let us indeed speak of contradictions that go beyond numbers, dates, and details of events—contradictions and errors on matters more significant.

a. Does God change His mind?

Genesis chapter 1, beginning in verse 26, speaks of the creation of man:

> And God said, let us make man in our image…So God created man in his own image…And God saw everything that he had made, and, behold, it was very good.

But in Genesis chapter 6, beginning in verse 6, the Bible says:

> And it repented the Lord that he had made man on the earth, and it grieved him at his heart. And the Lord said, I will destroy man whom I have created from the face of the earth…for it repenteth me that I have made them.

The Bible goes on to recount how God brought a flood upon the earth, killing all living things—except for Noah, and the animals Noah sheltered in the ark. Then, after the flood, in Genesis 8, beginning in verse 20, the Bible states:

> And Noah builded an altar unto the Lord…And the Lord smelled a sweet savor; and the Lord said in his heart, I will not again curse the ground any more for man's sake; for the imagination of man's heart is evil from his youth; neither will I again smite any more every living thing, as I have done.

In this series of events, God is originally satisfied with His creation of man, then regrets having created man and decides to flood and destroy all life because of man's wickedness; and, finally, God changes His mind again, and decides never to do again what He had done—never to punish the earth and all living things because of man, and never again to bring a flood upon all the earth—apparently because of something God had not realized or taken into account before, that man is a creature whose "heart is evil from his youth."

Another example of God apparently changing His mind is in Exodus 32, relating to the Israelites having worshiped the golden calf. After first recounting that God told Moses He would like to destroy the Israelites, and that Moses pleaded with God not to do so, the Bible states in verse 14:

> And the Lord repented of the evil which he spoke of doing to his people.

A similar interaction between God and Moses is recounted in Numbers 14, in the aftermath of the return of the scouts, or spies, which God had Moses send to the land of Canaan. When they brought back reports of giants, the Israelites complained that it would have been better for them to die in Egypt or in the wilderness than to face the fierce peoples of Canaan. The Bible then says, beginning in verse 11:

> And the Lord said unto Moses, How long will this people provoke me? and how long will it be ere they believe me, for all the signs which I have shewed among them? I will smite them with the pestilence, and disinherit them, and will make of thee a greater nation and mightier than they.

Moses then pleads for God to be merciful—and in verse 20 the Bible states:
> And the Lord said, I have pardoned according to thy word.

In the book of Jonah, too, the Bible illustrates that God can and does change His mind. The Bible recounts that God sent Jonah to prophesy to the city of Nineveh because of their wickedness. Chapter 3, verses 1-4, states:

> And the word of the Lord came unto Jonah the second time, saying, Arise go unto Nineveh, that great city, and preach unto it the preaching that I bid thee. So Jonah arose, and went unto Nineveh, according to the word of the Lord…And Jonah began to enter into the city a day's journey, and he cried, and said, Yet forty days, and Nineveh shall be overthrown.

The people of Nineveh, led by their king, fasted and prayed to God, and the Bible states in verse 9 that the king of Nineveh said:

> Who can tell if God will turn and repent, and turn away from his fierce anger, that we perish not?

And in verse 10 the Bible continues:

> And God saw their works, that they turned from their evil way; and God repented of the evil, that he had said that he would do unto them; and he did it not.

We have seen several instances in the Bible, then, where God changed His mind.

Yet in the book of Numbers, chapter 23, Balaam states that God does not change his mind. In verse 19, the Bible states:

> God is not a man, that he should lie; neither the son of man, that he should repent; hath he said, and shall he not do it? Or hath he spoken, and shall he not make it good?

In the first book of Samuel, too, the Bible, in one story, seems to give conflicting messages about whether God changes His mind. In chapter 15 of I Samuel, the Bible recounts how King Saul sinned by not following God's instructions to completely eradicate the nation of Amalek—Saul did not kill quite the entire nation and its animals, as God commanded, but instead, though killing nearly everyone, took Amalek's King Agag alive, and also spared the best of Amalek's sheep and oxen. Beginning in verse 10, the Bible states:

> Then came the word of the Lord unto Samuel, saying, It repenteth me that I have set up Saul to be king…

The Bible goes on to recount that Samuel then prophesied that God had taken the kingdom away from Saul. Verses 28-29 state:

> And Samuel said unto him, The Lord hath rent the kingdom of Israel from thee this day, and hath given it to a neighbour of thine, that is better than thou. And also the Strength of Israel will not lie nor repent: for he is not a man, that he should repent.

God chose Saul, and then regretting the choice, took the kingdom away from Saul—and the Bible has Samuel say that God, unlike man, will not change His mind—and thus Saul has no hope of prevailing upon God to allow him to retain his kingdom. But not only has God changed His mind—relented from planned punishments—at least twice in the case of Moses and the Israelites, and in the case of Jonah and Nineveh, too, the Bible also has God change His mind with respect to Saul himself, in first choosing him as king and later rejecting him.

b. Does God punish sons for the deeds of their fathers and grandfathers?

And the sage continued and said: My brother, a second Old Testament contradiction on important substance relates to guilt and punishment. In several passages the Bible teaches that God punishes people for the sins of their forebears. In Exodus 20:5 the Bible states:

> …for I the Lord thy God am a jealous God, visiting the iniquity of the fathers upon the children unto the third and fourth generation of them that hate me.

In Exodus 34:6-7 the Bible states:

> And the Lord passed by before him and proclaimed, The Lord, The Lord God, merciful and gracious, long-suffering, and abundant in goodness and truth. Keeping mercy for thousands, forgiving iniquity and transgression and sin, and that will by no means clear the guilty; visiting the iniquity of the fathers upon the children, and upon the children's children, unto the third and to the fourth generation.

In Numbers 14:18 the Bible states:

> The Lord is longsuffering, and of great mercy, forgiving iniquity and transgression, and by no means clearing the guilty, visiting the iniquity of the fathers upon the children unto the third and fourth generation.

In Deuteronomy 5:9 the Bible states:

> ...for I the Lord thy God am a jealous God, visiting the iniquity of the fathers upon the children unto the third and fourth generation of them that hate me.

In those passages, the Bible states that God punishes us for the deeds of our parents, grandparents, even great-grandparents. Yet in Ezekiel chapter 18, the Bible says otherwise—that each man is accountable for his own sins only. In verse 19-20 the Bible continues, and says:

> Yet say ye, Why? Doth not the son bear the iniquity of the father? When the son hath done that which is lawful and right, and hath kept all my statutes and hath done them, he shall surely live. The soul that sinneth, it shall die. The son shall not bear the iniquity of the father, neither shall the father bear the iniquity of the son: the righteousness of the righteous shall be upon him, and the wickedness of the wicked shall be upon him.

And a religious man replied: Perhaps the passage in Ezekiel is referring to the justice that the Israelites were supposed to enforce in their court system—that is, humans must only punish a man for his own sins; and that is why they differ from the passages you cited in Exodus, Numbers, and Deuteronomy, in which God speaks of His own standards of divine punishment.

And the sage said: My brother, your answer is intelligent—but, I believe, incorrect. I urge you to read Ezekiel chapter 18, and see for yourself that its plain meaning speaks of God's own justice—not of Israelite courts.

Indeed, because of this very distinction you mention—the standards for human courts possibly being different from the direct justice of God—for this reason I did not quote as a contradictory passage the verse in Deuteronomy 25:16, which states:

> The fathers shall not be put to death for the children, neither shall the children be put to death for the fathers: every man shall be put to death for his own sin.

My brother, that passage is found in middle of a chapter dealing with practical laws and statutes which God is commanding the Israelites. Thus, it can reasonably be seen as dealing with guidelines for human justice only—and as not contradicting the passages where God says He punishes to the third or fourth generation for the sins of forebears. But the extensive set of verses in Ezekiel 18 is not speaking to the Israelites about how they should administer justice in their courts—rather about how God punishes.[1] And in Ezekiel, unlike in other parts of the Bible, we are taught that a man is punished only for his own actions.

And do not attempt to answer, as some have, that the verses stating that God will punish later generations for sins of the fathers refer to when later generations persist in wickedness. First, if they persist in wickedness, why mention the sins of the fathers? They would be liable for punishment for their own sins. Second, if they are to be punished more severely due to their father's sins, this would still be unfair, as well as contradictory to the spirit of what Ezekiel says: "The son shall not bear the iniquity of the father, neither shall the father bear the iniquity of the son: the righteousness of the righteous shall be upon him, and the wickedness of the wicked shall be upon him."

And do not either answer that the verses speaking of later generations being punished for the sins of their forebears refer only to natural consequences—that the lifestyle and actions of one generation will likely have strong repercussions for the following several generations. For although it is true that all manner of health and blessings, or illness and curses, of the body as well as of the mind and spirit, get passed down through the generations, the biblical verses we have quoted from Exodus, Numbers, and Deuteronomy do not speak of such natural consequences, but have God actively punishing the later generations, as Deuteronomy 5:9, for instance, makes clear:

---

[1] In addition to the plain context and meaning of the chapter, specific clues confirm that Ezekiel 18 is not discussing human justice—at least as taught elsewhere in the Bible. Some of the sins mentioned as being punishable by death, such as taking usury and increase, are not sins for which the Bible had legislated the death penalty (in human courts) in its extensive law codes in the Five Books of Moses. Thus, either it isn't speaking of human courts, or it is—and it constitutes a different inconsistency.

...I the Lord thy God am a jealous God, visiting the iniquity of the fathers upon the children...

c. Should miracles be trusted as evidence of divine approval?

And the sage continued and said: A third important contradiction in the Old Testament, my brother, relates to the meaning and credibility of miracles. Throughout the Bible, humans are given signs and wonders as proof that God was behind the message of the one calling forth the signs and wonders. And those who would not obey the ones wielding miracles, were considered to have sinned gravely. Thus—for only a few of many examples—when God sent Moses to free the Israelites from Egyptian bondage, the Bible, in Exodus 4:1-5, states:

> And Moses answered and said, but, behold, they will not believe me nor hearken unto my voice; for they will say, the Lord hath not appeared unto thee. And the Lord said unto him, What is that in thine hand? And he said, A rod. And he said, Cast it on the ground. And he cast it on the ground, and it became a serpent, and Moses fled from before it. And the Lord said unto Moses, Put forth thine hand, and take it by the tail. And he put forth his hand, and caught it, and it became a rod in his hand That they may believe that the Lord God of their fathers, the god of Abraham, the God of Isaac, and the God of Jacob, hath appeared unto thee.

And over the next several verses the Bible has God telling Moses that if the Israelites will not believe that sign, Moses should perform a second sign—turning his hand leprous by placing it into his bosom, and curing it instantly by repeating the motion. Then the Bible has God telling Moses that if the Israelites will still not believe even in the second sign, Moses should take some water from the Nile and turn it to blood.

And in Exodus 10:2 the Bible has God saying:

> And that thou mayest tell in the ears of thy son, and of thy son's son, what things I have wrought in Egypt, and my signs which I have done among them; that ye may know how that I am the Lord.

And in Numbers chapter 16 the Bible speaks of Korah's challenge to Moses, and the miraculous punishment suffered by Korah and his group, being swallowed alive by the earth. And in verses 28-30 Moses tells the people:

> ...Hereby ye shall know that the Lord hath sent me to do all these works; for I have not done them of mine own mind. If these men die the common death of

344

all men, or if they be visited after the visitation of all men; then the Lord hath not sent me. But if the Lord make a new thing, and the earth open her mouth and swallow them up, with all that appertain unto them, and they go down quick into the pit; then ye shall understand that these men have provoked the Lord.

Again, then, we see the Bible teaching that a sign or miracle is deemed sufficient to prove that the one wielding or foretelling the miracle is speaking the word of God.

And in Judges 6, beginning in verse 11, the Bible speaks of an angel of the Lord visiting Gideon and the Lord speaking to Gideon, and Gideon asking for a sign that it was, indeed, the Lord speaking to him,[1] and, for a sign, God sending fire up from the rock to consume Gideon's offering.

And in I Kings 18 the Bible speaks of Elijah and his contest with the priests of Baal to demonstrate whose God is real and powerful, and when the fire of the Lord miraculously burns Elijah's sacrifice, verse 39 states:

> And when all the people saw it, they fell on their faces: and they said, The Lord he is the God; the Lord he is the God.

Yet persuasive and binding as miracles are supposed to be, the Bible does not consider them persuasive and binding if they are wielded by those teaching that which the Bible does not wish to be taught. Indeed, the worker of signs and wonders who, if verifying with his signs and wonders what the Bible wishes to be verified, is worthy of reverence and shown to be speaking for God, is, if teaching something counter to the Bible's message, not only not to be revered or believed—but is to be put to death.

Deuteronomy chapter 13 begins:

> If there arise among you a prophet, or a dreamer of dreams, and giveth thee a sign or a wonder. And the sign or the wonder come to pass, whereof he spake unto thee, saying, Let us go after other gods, which thou has not known, and let us serve them. Thou shalt not hearken unto the words of that prophet, or that dreamer of dreams: for the Lord your God proveth you, to know whether ye

---

[1] For an interesting discussion on how several Old Testament stories introduce an angel of the Lord yet continue with the Lord Himself as a direct actor or speaker—without a clear distinction between the angel and God Himself—see Chapter 2 of James Kugel's *The God of Old*.

love the Lord your god with all your heart and with all your soul...And that prophet, or that dreamer of dreams, shall be put to death...

But the veracity and authority of the Bible's heroes were based on signs and wonders. So if signs and wonders can be from sources other than God, how shall we believe that the miracles of the Bible's heroes necessarily bespeak the approval or intervention of God? How shall we know that the miracles said to be done in the name of the Lord were not really done by a different god, to test the people's loyalty and love? Indeed, perhaps such signs and wonders might have been performed by a God who "proveth" you, to know whether you love *honesty* with all your heart and all your soul, and to see whether you will stand in simple courage and say, "I do not know what such signs mean, and I cannot say that they speak unambiguously of the will of any god there may be."

In summary, then, the Bible contradicts itself on the important matter of whether signs and wonders are to be seen as valid indication of God's will.

d. Do the righteous prosper and enjoy a good life, and are the evil punished with failure and suffering?

And the sage continued, saying: My brother, another discrepancy in the Bible is on the matter of whether the good are rewarded, and the evil visited with retribution, in this world. The Bible tells many stories featuring the victories and successes of the righteous, and the failures and punishments of the wicked. Yet reality—in the small brushstrokes of individual lives or the grand tapestry of world history—and perhaps even a few Bible verses, argue against such a conclusion.[1]

First let us review how the Bible teaches the terrestrial success of the good and the terrestrial downfall of the bad. The very first man and woman in the

---

[1] To be clear, I do not deny that living a "good" life, in the sense of treating others well, and not abusing one's appetites, will often result in a better quality of life—especially if one lives in a stable and just society, a condition not especially common in the annals of history. But these are simply matters, among others, of social, psychological, medical, and economic dynamics: Do good unto others, and you are likely to sleep better and meet with more success, not only because those well-treated others are less likely to seek ways to avenge themselves upon you, and you are less likely to be plagued by fear and guilt, but also because you are likely to internalize a higher value for human life, and thus have greater respect for yourself. And, yes, if you treat your body and resources wisely, you increase your chances of reaping health and prosperity. But these likely natural consequences are far from what the Bible seems to be teaching—guaranteed punishment and reward, administered by the ongoing supervision of God.

Bible are famously punished for disobeying God's command. Adam and Eve eat from the tree of knowledge, and are banished from the Garden of Eden.

The story of Noah, beginning in Genesis 6, tells how a righteous man is saved, while his evil generation is destroyed. Genesis 6:5-9 introduces the story:

> And God saw that the wickedness of man was great in the earth, and that every imagination of the thoughts of his heart was only evil continually. And it repented the Lord that he had made man on the earth, and it grieved him at his heart. And the Lord said, I will destroy man whom I have created from the face of the earth; both man, and beast, and the creeping thing, and the fowls of the air; for it repenteth me that I have made them. But Noah found grace in the eyes of the Lord. These are the generations of Noah: Noah was a just man and perfect in his generations, and Noah walked with God.

And, of course, the story continues with Noah being told to build an ark; Genesis 7 begins by saying:

> And the Lord said unto Noah, Come thou and all thy house into the ark; for thee have I seen righteous before me in this generation.

Later, in Genesis 18, God notifies Abraham that Sodom and Gomorrah are sinful, and implies they will be destroyed. Abraham then bargains with God as to how many righteous residents it would take for Sodom and Gomorrah to be spared. In Genesis 19, Sodom and Gomorrah are destroyed, yet Lot, Abraham's nephew, and a hospitable resident of Sodom, is led by an angel to safety. Lot's wife, however, disobeying the angel's directions not to look back, is transformed to a pillar of salt.

In another example of the good and innocent being rewarded, Joseph was sold into slavery by his brothers, resisted the temptation of engaging in adultery with his master's wife, was unjustly sent to prison—but triumphed in the end, being appointed viceroy of Egypt, becoming a hero to his father and brothers, and prospering into old age. His tale is told in Genesis chapters 37-50.

Other instances of good being rewarded in life, and evil punished, include the following: Exodus 22:22-24 states:

> Ye shall not afflict any widow, or fatherless child. If thou afflict them in any wise, and they cry at all unto me, I will surely hear their cry; And my wrath shall wax hot, and I will kill you with the sword; and your wives shall be widows, and your children fatherless.

And Deuteronomy 28:1-7 states:

> And it shall come to pass, if thou shalt hearken diligently unto the voice of the Lord thy God, to observe and to do all his commandments which I command thee this day, that the Lord thy God will set thee on high above all nations of the earth: And all these blessings shall come on thee, and overtake thee, if thou shalt hearken unto the voice of the Lord thy God. Blessed shalt thou be in the city, and blessed shalt thou be in the field. Blessed shall be the fruit of thy body, and the fruit of thy ground, and the fruit of thy cattle, the increase of thy kine, and the flocks of thy sheep. Blessed shall be thy basket and thy store. Blessed shalt thou be when thou comest in, and blessed shalt thou be when thou goest out. The Lord shall cause thine enemies that rise up against thee to be smitten before thy face: they shall come out against thee one way, and flee before thee seven ways...

And the blessings for good behavior continue for several verses more. Then in Deuteronomy 28:15 the Bible continues:

> But it shall come to pass, if thou wilt not hearken unto the voice of the Lord thy God, to observe to do all his commandments and his statutes which I command thee this day; that all these curses shall come upon thee, and overtake thee: Cursed shalt thou be in the city, and cursed shalt thou be in the field. Cursed shall be thy basket and thy store. Cursed shall be the fruit of thy body, and the fruit of thy land, the increase of thy kine, and the flocks of thy sheep. Cursed shalt thou be when thou comest in, and cursed shalt thou be when thou goest out. The Lord shall send upon thee cursing, vexation, and rebuke, in all that thou settest thine hand unto for to do, until thou be destroyed, and until thou perish quickly; because of the wickedness of thy doings, whereby thou hast forsaken me...

And the punishments for not heeding God's word continue for many verses. Furthermore, Psalms 5:12 states:

> For thou, Lord, wilt bless the righteous; with favour wilt thou compass him as with a shield.

And the entire Psalm 37 expresses the same theme of the good being rewarded and the wicked being destroyed:

Fret not thyself because of evildoers, neither be thou envious against the workers of iniquity. For they shall soon be cut down like the grass, and wither as the green herb. Trust in the Lord, and do good; so shalt thou dwell in the land, and verily thou shalt be fed. Delight thyself also in the Lord: and he shall give thee the desires of thine heart... evildoers shall be cut off: but those that wait upon the Lord, they shall inherit the earth. For yet a little while, and the wicked shall not be: yea, thou shalt diligently consider his place, and it shall not be. But the meek shall inherit the earth; and shall delight themselves in the abundance of peace. The wicked plotteth against the just, and gnasheth upon him with his teeth. The Lord shall laugh at him: for he seeth that his day is coming. The wicked have drawn out the sword, and have bent their bow, to cast down the poor and needy, and to slay such as be of upright conversation. Their sword shall enter into their own heart, and their bows shall be broken... The steps of a good man are ordered by the Lord: and he delighteth in his way...I have been young, and now am old; yet have I not seen the righteous forsaken, nor his seed begging bread... Wait on the Lord, and keep his way, and he shall exalt thee to inherit the land: when the wicked are cut off, thou shalt see it...

And Psalms 92:7-15 states:

When the wicked spring as the grass, and when all the workers of iniquity do flourish; it is that they shall be destroyed for ever: But thou, Lord, art most high for evermore. For, lo, thine enemies, O Lord, for, lo, thine enemies shall perish; all the workers of iniquity shall be scattered. But my horn shalt thou exalt like the horn of a wild ox: I shall be anointed with fresh oil. Mine eye also shall see my desire on mine enemies, and mine ears shall hear my desire of the wicked that rise up against me. The righteous shall flourish like the palm tree: he shall grow like a cedar in Lebanon. Those that be planted in the house of the Lord shall flourish in the courts of our God. They shall still bring forth fruit in old age; they shall be fat and flourishing; To shew that the Lord is upright: he is my rock, and there is no unrighteousness in him.

And many more passages in the Hebrew Bible teach the earthly rewards of the righteous and the earthly punishments of the wicked.

And Psalm 73 and Job 24 wrestle with the question of the apparent prosperity of the evil and the suffering of the good, but seem to teach that, contrary to appearances, the wicked are punished.

Yet anyone who has lived with open eyes has seen that righteousness is no guarantor of prosperity, delight, or long life, and that evil is no guarantor of poverty, suffering, or early death; that some of the good and innocent die young, too, after much agony, and that some of the evil and guilty are among the prosperous and famed, and live on in health into ripe old age.

Life alone provides such powerful and constant testimony against the afore-mentioned biblical teachings of earthly blessings for the righteous and earthly punishment for the wicked, that more is not needed to disprove them. Interest-ingly, though, the Bible itself seems to contradict those teachings. Ecclesiastes 9:2 seems to minimize any difference between the fate of the good man and the fate of the evil man when it states:

> All things come alike to all: there is one event to the righteous, and to the wicked; to the good and to the clean, and to the unclean; to him that sacrificeth, and to him that sacrificeth not: as is the good, so is the sinner; and he that sweareth, as he that feareth an oath.

And, my brother, do not be tempted to answer that the rewards of the right-eous and the punishments of the wicked are to be enjoyed and suffered in an afterlife. First, the plain meaning and context of the Old Testament passages I have quoted indicate no such thing. Indeed, Moses and the prophets never taught anything about rewards or punishments in an afterlife, and the Old Testament cannot reasonably be interpreted to teach a heaven and hell after death where humans go to punishment or reward.[1]

Moreover, Ecclesiastes, in 9:5-11 continues and teaches that time and chance happen to all, and that the dead have no knowledge or reward:

> For the living know that they shall die: but the dead know not any thing, neither have they any more a reward; for the memory of them is forgotten… Whatso-ever thy hand findeth to do, do it with thy might; for there is no work, nor de-vice, nor knowledge, nor wisdom, in the grave, whither thou goest. I returned, and saw under the sun, that the race is not to the swift, nor the battle to the strong, neither yet bread to the wise, nor yet riches to men of understanding, nor yet favour to men of skill; but time and chance happeneth to them all.

---

[1] Heaven, when mentioned in the Old Testament, is the abode of God and angels; and the dead—whether good or bad—are said to go to "Sheol." Neither place is spoken of as a place of punishment or reward. Anyone with a feel for the Old Testament, especially in its original Hebrew, and with the willingness to encounter it free of the forced interpreta-tions of later dogma-bound commentaries, will find this obvious. For those who would like third-party confirmation of this view, see, for two examples of many, the entry under "Heaven" in the Oxford Companion to the Bible, and chapter 32 of James Kugel's *How to Read the Bible* in his discussion on the resurrection of the dead, in the context of Ezekiel's vision of dry bones.

Still, even this same book of Ecclesiastes follows up such unvirtuous talk by summary assurances—though some have speculated that these were added by a censor's hand—that there is, indeed, divine judgment, and by charging us to obey God's laws.

Ecclesiastes 11:9 says:

> Rejoice, O young man, in thy youth; and let thy heart cheer thee in the days of thy youth, and walk in the ways of thine heart, and in the sight of thine eyes: but know thou, that for all these things God will bring thee into judgment.

And the very last two verses of Ecclesiastes, 12:13-14 say:

> Let us hear the conclusion of the whole matter: Fear God, and keep his commandments: for this is the whole duty of man. For God shall bring every work into judgment, with every secret thing, whether it be good, or whether it be evil.

And again, my brother, though later religious teachers assured their flocks that accounts would be squared in a world to come, if any afterlife of heaven and hell exist, they will have come as a great surprise to Moses. For such concepts are clearly not taught in the Five Books of Moses, nor even hinted at in the great majority of the remainder of the Old Testament. Yet do not be puzzled at this; for religions are significantly shaped by the ever-changing customs, cultures, and politics of peoples, and are far from exclusively loyal to original, unchanging spiritual ideals or theological beliefs. Ironic though it may seem, religions have long been openly contradicting—all the while noisily, and for the most part sincerely, reverencing—books they say were authored by God.

123. New Testament contradictions and errors on important teachings

And a Christian said: The Old Testament does not interest me as much as the New Testament. Can you show me any contradictions or errors there, on important teachings?

And the sage said: My brother, has not Christianity traditionally believed the Old Testament to be the earlier word of God, even as it believed the New Testament to be the later word of God? Surely, then, Christians cannot be unconcerned about claims of contradictions or errors even in the Old Testament. But to address your question directly: Yes, just as with the Old Testament, there are, indeed, a number of contradictions and errors on important teachings in the New Testament.

a. How does one attain salvation?

Perhaps the central aim of Christianity is attaining salvation. Yet precisely how does one go about this? Faith in one's heart? Faith spoken aloud? Faith even without works, or only with works? If faith alone, does that mean only belief? If so, belief in what? Or perhaps belief in combination with baptism in water? And is repentance necessary? And can anyone attain salvation, or is salvation predestined and not guaranteed through any means including faith or works?

The New Testament not only leaves much room for confusion on these matters, it seems to contradict itself repeatedly.

Let us speak of specifics. The Bible in several places teaches that salvation by faith is not based upon works—even explaining that such is the case in order that no man should be able to boast. Yet in other places the Bible teaches that faith is not enough, and that works are important for gaining salvation.

Ephesians 2:8-9 states:

> For by grace are ye saved through faith; and that not of yourselves: it is the gift of God: Not of works, lest any man should boast.

And Romans 3:28 says:

> Therefore we conclude that a man is justified by faith without the deeds of the law.

And after speaking in Romans 9 and 10 of Christianity's teaching that the law cannot save, but faith in Jesus can, the Bible says that if we can achieve salvation through faith by grace, then it must be grace alone, and if works are needed, it must be works alone. Romans 11:6 states:

> And if by grace, then is it no more of works: otherwise grace is no more grace. But if it be of works then is it no more grace: otherwise work is no more work.

And Galatians 2:16 agrees, definitively, that we are saved by faith, and not by works. It states:

> Knowing that a man is not justified by the works of the law, but by the faith of Jesus Christ, even we have believed in Jesus Christ, that we might be justified by the faith of Christ and not by the works of the law: for by the works of the law shall no flesh be justified.

And Acts 16:30-31 states:

> ...Sirs, what must I do to be saved? And they said, Believe on the Lord Jesus Christ, and thou shalt be saved, and thy house.

In another passage, however, the New Testament seems to say that silent faith—in the proposition that Jesus is Lord—is not enough, but must be combined with saying it aloud. Romans 10:9 states:

> That if thou shalt confess with thy mouth the Lord Jesus, and shalt believe in thine heart that God hath raised him from the dead, thou shalt be saved.

Thus far we have seen biblical verses teaching that faith saves, and works are not necessary. Yet Jesus himself, in speaking of the Old Testament law, is quoted in Matthew 5:19-20 as teaching that if one wishes to get to heaven, works are absolutely necessary:

> Whosoever therefore shall break one of these least commandments, and shall teach men so, he shall be called the least in the kingdom of heaven: but whosoever shall do and teach them, the same shall be called great in the kingdom of heaven. For I say unto you, That except your righteousness shall exceed the righteousness of the scribes and Pharisees, ye shall in no case enter into the kingdom of heaven.

And in Matthew 7, too, Jesus says explicitly that works are necessary. Matthew 7:21 has Jesus say:

> Not every one that saith unto me, Lord, Lord, shall enter into the kingdom of heaven; but he that doeth the will of my Father which is in heaven.

And James makes it clear that faith alone is not sufficient. James 2:14-26 states:

> What doth it profit, my brethren, though a man say he hath faith, and have not works? Can faith save him?...Even so faith, if it hath not works, is dead, being alone...But wilt thou know, O vain man, that faith without works is dead? Ye see then how that by works a man is justified and not by faith only. Likewise also was not Rahab the harlot justified by works, when she had received the messengers, and had sent them out another way? For as the body without the spirit is dead, so faith without works is dead also.

And I John 2:1-4 also seems to require works. It states:

> ...And if any man sin, we have an advocate with the Father, Jesus Christ the righteous...And hereby we do know that we know him, if we keep his commandments. He that saith, I know him, and keepeth not his commandments, is a liar, and the truth is not in him.

And Hebrews 5:9 also seems to teach that faith is not enough, but works—in the form of obedience—are necessary. There the Bible, speaking of Jesus, says:

> And being made perfect, he became the author of eternal salvation unto all them that obey him.

And the above passages do not speak of repentance. But Luke 13:3, has Jesus saying that repentance—thus, apparently not merely faith—is necessary.

> I tell you, Nay: but, except ye repent, ye shall all likewise perish.

And Luke 24:46-47 also speaks of repentance being necessary:

> And said unto them, Thus it is written, and thus it behoved Christ to suffer, and to rise from the dead the third day: And that repentance and remission of sins should be preached in his name among all nations...

And Acts 17:30 states:

> ...commandeth all men every where to repent.

And II Peter 3:9 states:

> ...not willing that any should perish, but that all should come to repentance.

And all the aforementioned biblical passages speaking of salvation do not mention anything about baptism. Yet a number of New Testament verses do seem to say that baptism is required for salvation. Mark 16:16 states:

> He that believeth and is baptized shall be saved; but he that believeth not shall be damned.

And John 3:5 states:

> Jesus answered and said unto him, Verily, verily, I say unto thee, Except a man be born of water and of the Spirit, he cannot enter into the kingdom of God.[1]

And Acts 2:38 states that both repentance and baptism are necessary:

> Then Peter said unto them, Repent, and be baptized every one of you in the name of Jesus Christ for the remission of sins, and ye shall receive the gift of the Holy Ghost.

To further complicate the matter of salvation, let us ask this question: Does the New Testament consistently teach that faith is at all necessary for salvation? The answer may surprise you. In the book of Matthew, a young man asks Jesus this very question—how to achieve salvation—and Jesus tells him.

Matthew 19:16-19, recounts the story:

> And, behold, one came and said unto him, Good Master, what good thing shall I do, that I may have eternal life? And he said unto him…if thou wilt enter into life, keep the commandments. He saith unto him, Which? Jesus said, Thou shalt do no murder, Thou shalt not commit adultery, Thou shalt not steal, Thou shalt not bear false witness. Honour thy father and thy mother and, Thou shalt love thy neighbor as thyself…

In that story Jesus said nothing about believing that he, Jesus, was the Son of God, or came to atone for the world's sins, or that in order to enter eternal life one had to believe such things.[2]

---

[1] A case can be made that this verse does not refer to baptism in actual water, but refers instead to a metaphor for physical birth—an interpretation which, in the context of that story in John, is not unreasonable. But anyone having even a passing familiarity with controversial theological issues within Christianity, and the bases for the differences in doctrine between Christian denominations, knows how many Christians read this verse in its literal sense, to mean baptism in actual water. At best, then, the lack of clarity in the New Testament on such a foundational matter has led to great confusion and discord among Christians. Moreover, other biblical verses mentioning baptism, and which I cite in the text, seem to require baptism in water in the literal sense. And, as this section illustrates, the New Testament is inconsistent, too, as to other requirements for salvation.

[2] True, the story continues with the young man saying that he has always kept the commandments, and asking for something further he can do; Jesus then tells him that in order to be perfect he should give away all his possessions and follow him. But this

Then, in Matthew 25:31-46, the Bible has Jesus speak about the sheep and the goats—the righteous and the unjust—and how the former go to life eternal because of their good deeds, of feeding the hungry and clothing the naked and visiting the sick, and so on, and the latter go to everlasting fire because they did not do these things. Nothing is mentioned about faith in Jesus being a way—much less the only way—to salvation.

Yet in John 3:14-18, the Bible seems to say that in order to attain salvation, belief in Jesus is necessary:

> ...even so must the Son of man be lifted up. That whosoever believeth in him should not perish, but have eternal life. For God so loved the world, that he gave his only begotten Son, that whosoever believeth in him should not perish, but have everlasting life...He that believeth on him is not condemned: but he that believeth not is condemned already.

And some passages of the New Testament seem to take the matter yet further, teaching that salvation is predestined according to God's will.

Acts 13:48 states:

> And when the Gentiles heard this, they were glad, and glorified the word of the Lord: and as many as were ordained to eternal life believed.

And Ephesians 1:4-11 speaks of predestination even more clearly:

> According as he hath chosen us in him before the foundation of the world, that we should be holy and without blame before him in love. Having predestinated us unto the adoption of children by Jesus Christ to himself, according to the good pleasure of his will...In whom we have redemption through his blood, the forgiveness of sins, according to the riches of his grace...In whom also we have obtained an inheritance, being predestinated according to the purpose of him who worketh all things after the counsel of his own will.[1]

---

should not be construed as Jesus telling him that in order to be saved he had to believe that only through Jesus was there salvation, or anything of the sort. To the contrary, Jesus had already answered the question on how to get eternal life: he answered that the young man should keep the commandments. If more were necessary, he would have said so in the first place. The later suggestion to give away all his possessions and follow him was, as it were, for extra credit—to be "perfect."

[1] And against the obvious unfairness of predestination—and its contradiction to the other instructions the New Testament prescribes for salvation—it will not do to answer that God knows who will choose what, but that He does not determine what we will

In short, my brother, on perhaps the most central concern of the New Testament—achieving salvation—the Bible seems rife with confusion and contradiction—not the sort of teachings we would expect from anything sourced in, or inspired by, an omniscient, omnipotent God.

b. Was Jesus God?

And the sage continued, and said: My brother, another important contradiction or confusion in the New Testament relates to the identity of Jesus. Mainstream Christians have for these many centuries seen Jesus as God or the Son of God. But what does the New Testament itself say on the matter?

In the book of Matthew, Jesus admonishes a young man for addressing him with a descriptor that Jesus thinks should only be used when referring to God. This implies that Jesus did not see himself as God, and wished to correct any such mistaken notion.[1]

Matthew 19:16-17 states:

> And, behold, one came and said unto him, Good Master, what good thing shall I do, that I may have eternal life? And he said unto him, Why callest thou me good? there is none good but one, that is, God...

Similarly, Mark 10:17-18 states:

> And when he was gone forth into the way, there came one running, and kneeled to him, and asked him, Good Master, what shall I do that I may inherit eternal life? And Jesus said unto him, Why callest thou me good? there is none good but one, that is, God.

---

choose, and thus the teaching of predestination does not contradict free will, and allows all to choose salvation. That answer might, with some generosity, be allowed to suffice for the question of how God can see into the future and yet we are held responsible for our actions—but it cannot account for a God predestinating only some to salvation "after the counsel of his own will." Will denotes not merely a knowledge of the future, but a shaping and determining of the future—and when events are determined by God's will, man cannot reasonably be said to enjoy freedom of choice.

[1] In the three cases I cite on this matter, one can, of course, choose to understand Jesus' admonitions as a coy or clever attempt to call attention to the possibility that by their own "admission" these people were calling him God. But this not only would be straying from the straightforward meaning of the text as to what Jesus seemed to have said, it would also paint Jesus as an eccentric, over-clever, even manipulative (or possibly delusional) character, forcing self-serving, grandiose interpretations into the words of others—interpretations they, by using the common term "good," almost certainly did not intend.

And Luke 18:18-19 states:

> And a certain ruler asked him, saying, Good Master, what shall I do to inherit eternal life? And Jesus said unto him, Why callest thou me good? none is good, save one, that is, God.

And Matthew 27 has Jesus crying out in complaint to God. The clear implication is that God is something separate from Jesus. Matthew 27:46 states:

> And about the ninth hour Jesus cried with a loud voice, saying, Eli, Eli, lama sabachthani? that is to say, My God, my God, why hast thou forsaken me?[1]

And John 5 also implies that Jesus is not God, but rather was sent by God. John 5:30 has Jesus say:

> I can of mine own self do nothing: as I hear, I judge: and my judgment is just; because I seek not mine own will, but the will of the Father which hath sent me.

And John 14 seems to say the same. John 14:24 has Jesus say:

> ...and the word which ye hear is not mine, but the Father's which sent me.

---

[1] This verse, among others, cannot easily be seen as consistent with the mainstream Christian teaching of the Trinity—which entails, among other things, that Jesus is God as much as the Father is God—and that the crucifixion was God's plan to bring salvation to mankind. If these were true, why would Jesus insist on not being called "good," out of concern that this term was to be reserved for God; why would he not know of the plan for his sacrifice; and if he did know, why would he think he was being forsaken, and complain about it?

In theology, however, all things are possible. Some theologians have taught the concept of "kenosis," explaining that although in every way as powerful and unlimited as God the Father, Jesus temporarily took on some of the limitations of mortals when he became flesh. And such theologians correctly caution that we should not be surprised if the nature of a supernatural God—and how He seems to manifest in the Bible—remains to us something of a confusing mystery. But here is the rub: How shall we distinguish between the "true" and legitimately opaque divine mystery, and the myriads of confusing mysteries claimed to be divine or true by all the accumulating superstitions and all the false religions and all the creative charlatans and all the closed-minded but clever theologians of all the ages—as they defended their dogmas and hunches and traditions against contradictory evidence and sharp-eyed reason, and conveniently took shelter behind the skirts of claimed divine mystery?

Then, in verse 28, Jesus says:

> …my Father is greater than I.

And Acts 2 speaks of Jesus as a man, not God. Acts 2:22 states:

> …Jesus of Nazareth, a man approved of God among you by miracles and wonders and signs, which God did by him in the midst of you.

The aforementioned passages do not place Jesus on an equal level with God.[1] Yet other passages in the New Testament are less clear, and leave room for confusion, and for the development of the teaching that Jesus was God—or even seem to say so outright.

John 1:1-17 states:

> In the beginning was the Word, and the Word was with God, and the Word was God…And the Word was made flesh, and dwelt among us, (and we beheld his glory, the glory as of the only begotten of the Father,) full of grace and truth. John bare witness of him, and cried, saying, This was he of whom I spake…And of his fulness have all we received, and grace for grace. For the law was given by Moses, but grace and truth came by Jesus Christ.

John 8:58 states:

> Jesus said unto them, Verily, verily, I say unto you, before Abraham was, I am.

John 10:30-38 has Jesus speaking and saying:

> I and my father are one…The Jews answered him, saying, For a good work we stone thee not; but for blasphemy; and because thou, being a man, makest thy-

---

[1] Many passages in the New Testament seem consistent with the teachings of Arius, and Arianism, who saw Jesus, though superior to mortal man, as not quite on the level of God. And these passages seem at odds with the creed adopted as authoritative by the Council of Nicea, which, in 325 A.D., condemned Arianism and, supporting the notion of the Trinity, described Jesus as: "God of God, Light of Light, very God of very God, begotten, not made, being of one substance with the Father."

self God…Jesus answered them…that ye may know and believe, that the Father is in me, and I in him.

And John 20:28-29 has Thomas speaking to Jesus and calling him God, and Jesus does not protest. Indeed, he approves:

And Thomas answered and said unto him, My Lord and my God. Jesus saith unto him, Thomas, because thou hast seen me, thou hast believed: blessed are they have not seen, and yet have believed…

And Titus 2:13 states:

…the glorious appearing of the great God and our Saviour Jesus Christ

And Colossians 2:9 states:

For in him dwelleth all the fulness of the Godhead bodily.

And Hebrews 1:8 has God the Father speaking, and states:

But unto the Son he saith, Thy throne, O God, is for ever and ever: a sceptre of righteousness is the sceptre of thy kingdom.

And I Timothy 3:16, speaking of Jesus, states:

God was manifest in the flesh, justified in the Spirit, seen of angels, preached unto the gentiles, believed on in the world, received up into glory.

My brother, these are some, but not all, of the verses in the New Testament dealing with the matter of whether Jesus was God. Yet they are sufficient to show that in the New Testament we have Jesus himself, in some passages, rebuking someone for addressing him in a way that Jesus thinks should be used only when speaking of God; we further have Jesus explaining that he is less than God. In other passages, however, we have Jesus not only not protesting when he is explicitly called God; we are taught outright that he is God, and that he and the Father are one—or else that he is the Son of God.

And so, as with the contradictions and confusions on the matter of how one attains salvation, the New Testament seems to contradict itself—and certainly speaks far less clearly than many humans easily could—on the question of just who was Jesus. And since salvation has often been seen by Christianity as

360

attainable only through Jesus and by believing very specific things about him, this set of biblical inconsistencies or lack of clarity on just who was Jesus is a grievous flaw. Tell me, my brother, should we not wonder whether a supernatural being would have taken any part in producing such a welter of obscurity or contradiction?

c. When will the Son of Man return in glory?

And the sage continued, and said: My brother, one of the more important teachings of Jesus was that the end of days was coming, with great tribulations, when the Son of Man would return in glory, and the righteous would be saved. But Jesus taught that this would happen in that generation, and it clearly did not. Matthew 24:3-34 states:

> And as he sat upon the Mount of Olives, the disciples came unto him privately, saying, Tell us, when shall these things be? and what shall be the sign of thy coming, and of the end of the world? …Immediately after the tribulation of those days shall the sun be darkened, and the moon shall not give her light, and the stars shall fall from heaven, and the powers of the heavens shall be shaken: And then shall appear the sign of the Son of man in heaven: and then shall all the tribes of the earth mourn, and they shall see the Son of man coming in the clouds of heaven with power and great glory. And he shall send his angels with a great sound of a trumpet, and they shall gather together his elect from the four winds, from one end of heaven to the other…Verily I say unto you, This generation shall not pass, till all these things be fulfilled.

And Mark 13:24-30 similarly states:

> But in those days, after that tribulation, the sun shall be darkened, and the moon shall not give her light, And the stars of heaven shall fall, and the powers that are in heaven shall be shaken. And then shall they see the Son of man coming in the clouds with great power and glory. And then shall he send his angels, and shall gather together his elect from the four winds, from the uttermost part of the earth to the uttermost part of heaven…Verily I say unto you, that this generation shall not pass, till all these things be done.

Likewise, Luke 21:27-32 states:

> And then shall they see the Son of man coming in a cloud with power and great glory. And when these things begin to come to pass, then look up, and lift up

your heads; for your redemption draweth nigh...Verily I say unto you, This generation shall not pass away, till all be fulfilled.

Indeed, this mistaken notion that the end of days was imminent, is reflected in many other verses in the New Testament, among them Matthew 4:17, which states:

From that time Jesus began to preach, and to say, Repent: for the kingdom of heaven is at hand.

And Matthew 10:22-23 states:

And ye shall be hated of all men for my name's sake: but he that endureth to the end shall be saved. But when they persecute you in this city, flee ye into another: for verily I say unto you, Ye shall not have gone over the cities of Israel, till the Son of man be come.

And Matthew 16:27-28 states:

For the Son of man shall come in the glory of his Father with his angels; and then he shall reward every man according to his works. Verily I say unto you, There be some standing here, which shall not taste of death, till they see the Son of man coming in his kingdom.

And I Peter 4:7,13,17 states:

But the end of all things is at hand: be ye therefore sober, and watch unto prayer...But rejoice, inasmuch as ye are partakers of Christ's sufferings; that, when his glory shall be revealed, ye may be glad also with exceeding joy...For the time is come that judgment must begin at the house of God...

And I John 2:18, 28 states:

Little children, it is the last time: and as ye have heard that antichrist shall come, even now are there many antichrists; whereby we know that it is the last time...And now, little children, abide in him; that, when he shall appear, we may have confidence, and not be ashamed before him at his coming.

And the book of Revelation speaks repeatedly of the imminent coming of Jesus. Indeed it begins as follows: Revelation 1:1-7 states:

The Revelation of Jesus Christ, which God gave unto him, to shew unto his servants things which must shortly come to pass…Blessed is he that readeth, and they that hear the words of this prophecy, and keep those things which are written therein: for the time is at hand…And from Jesus Christ, who is the faithful witness, and the first begotten of the dead, and the prince of the kings of the earth…Behold, he cometh with clouds; and every eye shall see him…

And Revelation 22:6-7, 12, 20 states:

…and the Lord God of the holy prophets sent his angel to shew unto his servants the things which must shortly be done. Behold, I come quickly…And, behold, I come quickly…He which testifieth these things saith, Surely I come quickly. Amen. Even so, come, Lord Jesus.

But the miraculous and cataclysmic end of days did not come, and the Second Coming did not take place in that generation. Neither did it take place for the ensuing two thousand years and more—and many, many believers are still waiting.

My brother, if the holy book of any religion other than your own repeatedly promised in the name of its founder and its god that an important prophecy would be fulfilled in its first generation, yet it did not come to pass within the promised time, and even two thousand years after that generation the prophecy has still not come to pass—would you give much credence to that religion?

If Jesus and his disciples were so confident that the end of days would come in that generation, as would the glorious return of the Son of Man, yet it did not happen then, and has not happened for another two millennia, why should we not suspect that they were mistaken, too, about the prediction overall—and about their entire belief system? Why should we believe that the Son of Man will ever return, and why should we believe any other teachings of Jesus, or anything else the New Testament says?

For, my brother: Either Jesus and the apostles did not say these things, and the New Testament is untrustworthy—or Jesus *did* say these things and he, not to mention the apostles, was wrong on such a central teaching, and quite fallible. Do we have any responsible basis, then, to insist he could not be equally wrong about his other teachings?[1]

---

[1] Santayana, in his *Winds of Doctrine*, writes: "The prophecy about the speedy end of this wicked world was not fulfilled as the early Christians expected; but this fact is less disconcerting to the Christian than one would suppose…This world must actually vanish very soon for each of us; and this is the point of view that counts with the Christian mind…" This line of thinking Santayana illustrates may have reassured the doubts of

d. Should one believe because of signs and wonders?

And the sage continued, saying: My brother, the New Testament seems to teach a double standard, a logical contradiction, on whether one should believe in those who perform signs and wonders: that when performed by Jesus or his disciples, such acts should be sufficient to establish God's approval, but when performed by others, such acts should be taken not as a sign of divine approval, but rather the opposite—as grounds for suspicion of false prophecy.[1]

First I will quote for you New Testament passages supporting, at times demanding, belief in signs and wonders. John 20:30-31 states:

> And many other signs truly did Jesus in the presence of his disciples, which are not written in this book: But these are written, that ye might believe that Jesus is the Christ, the Son of God...

That passage makes clear that merely reading about signs should cause us to believe.

And Acts 2:22 states:

> Ye men of Israel, hear these words; Jesus of Nazareth, a man approved of God among you by miracles and wonders and signs, which God did by him in the midst of you, as ye yourselves also know...

In that passage, men of Israel are criticized for seeing miracles, wonders and signs, yet still not believing in Jesus.[2] The passage demands that they interpret signs, miracles and wonders as God's signals that He approved of Jesus.

---

many Christians ancient and modern. But for those not already bound to Christian loyalties—or even those among them who hear the protest of deep honesty—two problems remain: First, Jesus himself specified, in speaking of the Second Coming in Luke 21, "Verily I say unto you, This generation shall not pass away, till all be fulfilled." The vanishing of the world for each of us by individual death does not, it seems, satisfy that specific prediction; and second, by allowing for such a metaphorical "fulfillment" of prophecy, no prophecy can ever be found false, and thus its claimed truth or fulfillment means little.

[1] The Old Testament is vulnerable to the same charge of double-standard on this matter, as I have detailed in section 122.

[2] They had him executed, too, presumably as they understood the Old Testament to require. Deuteronomy 13 explicitly warns against following a miracle worker or prophet who seeks to get the people to change their religion. Indeed, that passage ends by mandating that such a prophet or dreamer—though he performed miracles or signs—be put to death. Moreover, by the account of the New Testament, Jesus was seen by the Jews as desecrating the Sabbath as well as being insubordinate to the religious authorities,

Mark 16:15-20 discusses Jesus addressing his disciples, and states:

> And he said unto them, Go ye into all the world, and preach the gospel to every
> creature. He that believeth and is baptized shall be saved; but he that believeth
> not shall be damned. And these signs shall follow them that believe; In my
> name shall they cast out devils; they shall speak with new tongues; That shall
> take up serpents; and if they drink any deadly thing, it shall not hurt them; they
> shall lay hands on the sick, and they shall recover. So then, after the Lord had
> spoken unto them, he was received up into heaven, and sat on the right hand of
> God. And they went forth, and preached everywhere, the Lord working with
> them, and confirming the word with signs following.

In the foregoing passage, too, the New Testament teaches that miraculous
signs indicate God's approval of the words being preached by those performing
the signs.

And Acts 5:12, 14-16 states:

> And by the hands of the apostles were many signs and wonders wrought
> among the people...And believers were the more added to the Lord, multitudes
> both of men and women; Insomuch that they brought forth the sick into the
> streets, and laid them on beds and couches, that at the least the shadow of Peter
> passing by might overshadow some of them. There came also a multitude out
> of the cities round about unto Jerusalem, bringing sick folks, and them which
> were vexed with unclean spirits: and they were healed every one.

That passage celebrates how multitudes were added to the ranks of believers
after they were shown signs and wonders.

Thus far we have cited several New Testament passages indicating that signs,
wonders, and miracles are not only legitimate reasons to believe in the message
of those performing such acts, but that people who see signs and wonders and
do not believe are to be criticized, perhaps condemned.

In contrast, consider the following passages from the New Testament. In
Matthew 24:24-27 Jesus states:

> For there shall arise false Christs, and false prophets, and shall show great signs
> and wonders; insomuch that, if it were possible, they shall deceive the very

---

two additional offenses for which the Old Testament mandates the death penalty. Yet
contravening explicit teachings of the Old Testament, the New Testament faults the men
of Israel for not seeing Jesus' miracles and wonders and signs as proof of God's approval.

elect. Behold, I have told you before. Wherefore if they shall say unto you, Behold, he is in the desert; go not forth: behold, he is in the secret chambers; believe it not.

In this passage Jesus warns his disciples *not* to believe in those who perform great signs and wonders, if their statements are at odds with his.

Similarly, in Mark 13:21-23 the New Testament quotes Jesus as saying:

And then if any man shall say to you, Lo, here is Christ; or, lo, he is there; believe him not: For false Christs and false prophets shall rise, and shall show signs and wonders, to seduce if it were possible, even the elect. But take ye heed: behold, I have foretold you all things.

Here, too, Jesus warns his disciples not to believe in the signs and wonders of others if their messages are inconsistent with what he has foretold. My brother, is it logically consistent, is it fair-minded and reasonable, for the New Testament to insist that only the miracles of Jesus and his disciples are signs of God's approval, but that anyone who performs miracles and teaches against what Jesus said should be considered a false prophet?[1]

*****

And the sage continued and said: Brothers and sisters, these contradictions and errors I have mentioned are by no means the only contradictions and errors in the New Testament, but they are enough to illustrate that this part of the Christian Bible, too, is not completely accurate or internally consistent.

And—as I have also said with regard to the Old Testament—even if some of these difficulties are attributed merely to the errors of later scribes and copyists, it undermines the New Testament's credibility. For if God did not protect the biblical texts from being corrupted by small and medium sized errors, how shall we be confident that larger errors, even critical, unwarranted additions, were prevented? Moreover, some of the items I have cited—such as the frequent but inaccurate predictions of a quick Second Coming—cannot reasonably be attributed to copyist error.

---

[1] This is all the more striking in light of Christian teachings which have understood Jesus and his disciples to be abolishing important teachings and covenants of the Old Testament—yet, as mentioned, the Old Testament gave similar warnings not to believe prophets who taught against the Old Testament's religion, even if such renegade prophets should perform signs and wonders. (See Deuteronomy 13:1-5)

And, again, the most important arguments against Bibles and religions are not the contradictions they may contain; nor are the most important arguments against Bibles and religions the great harm they bring upon society by episodically unleashing all manner of barbarism enacted in the glittering conscience of self-righteousness. Rather, the greatest arguments against Bibles and religions are the damages they wreak upon the individual soul and upon the souls of families and communities by insisting that we lie about what we know and what we do not know on life's most important and perplexing questions.[1]

Moreover, as mentioned with respect to the Old Testament, even if the New Testament contained no contradictions, such internal consistency would not prove it accurate, and certainly would not prove it of divine origin. Millions of books, including tales of fantasy and magical fables for children, contain no internal contradictions; but this does not confer upon them the status of God's word and will, or even the credibility of accurate accounts—neither are their passages deemed sacred counsel, nor their characters the objects of reverence and earnest emulation. Yet it is instructive to speak of the Bible's contradictions, for although an absence of contradictions would not have proved divine origin— the presence of contradictions in the Bible *does* prove that those contradictory portions of the text are not all correct and did not all originate with God, and therefore casts significant, intelligent doubt upon the accuracy and source of the remainder of the Bible, too.

124. Sub-argument that such seeming contradictions and errors can be explained and interpreted to have meanings different from what they seem to have on the surface—as religious scholars and theologians have done for ages

But a religious man who had spoken earlier said: Such passages are open to interpretation; they are not outright contradictions. They only appear to be contradictory to the eyes of one who does not know the correct traditions on how to understand the Bible's holy words and complex ideas. Religious commentaries and apologists over the ages have offered answers to the supposed problems you raise.

And the sage said: Indeed, my brother, anything short of simple contradictions of fact—such as numbers, dates, or precise account of events—can be explained away, if only we exercise enough ingenuity and pay insufficient heed to the voice of honesty. Therefore I first recounted simple contradictions of fact—

---

[1] And I have earlier, in Part II, sections 13 and 14, spoken of religion's gifts—and they are many—but I have also expressed the opinion that her gifts come at too high a price.

of number, date, or event. Yet in response to those contradictions, a religious point of view said that we need not be troubled, because these were mere details of fact, and did not touch on the Bible's important teachings. And now that I have spoken of contradictions more substantive—yet necessarily more involved, leaving more room for avoiding or evading straightforward meanings—you now say that other interpretations are possible. My brother: Cannot any text, any religion, any ideology no matter how foolish or destructive, be defended by the same maneuvers?

Is it fair or reasonable for believers to have it both ways—to say that contradictions of "mere" fact are not disturbing, either because they are copyist errors or because they do not affect the Bible's essential message, and that all contradictions other than plain fact—for which "answers" are always possible if one is willing to value creativity over candor—will be considered solved by any and all rebuttals, no matter how implausible they may appear to an objective eye, and no matter how little they are supported by a plain reading of the text? Does not such a double standard prevent the believer from ever taking an honest look at the texts he considers most holy?

And, my brother, though the centuries of sacred scholarship cast for believers a commanding and comforting shadow and, as you say, religious apologists have addressed many challenges against the Bible, let not your heart be tempted to dismiss the many biblical errors and inconsistencies by saying: These are old challenges; surely the wise men of religion have long since considered them and provided answers. Instead, go you and investigate whether they have indeed provided answers and, if they have, whether those answers are satisfactory. For, notwithstanding the protestations of some believers, religions have generally not come about their sacred traditions by way of reason, and generally do not consider the objections of reason sufficient cause to abandon these traditions; rather, most cling to the familiar with a tenacity that only increases with every terrifying glimpse of just how mistaken may be their foundational beliefs, and just how feeble are tradition's attempts at a rational defense.

Thus, believers will often put forward imaginative and clever answers to apparent biblical errors or contradictions. But, my brother, I ask you in gentle candor whether an honest and unbiased arbiter would find such responses persuasive—or whether many of these apparent errors and contradictions are, likely, what they appear to be, and the hastily proffered solutions but desperate attempts to make reality conform to cherished beliefs.

And ask yourself these telling questions, too: "Would I find the arguments of Bible defenders persuasive in defense of another religion's scriptures—even in defense of a secular or atheistic text? And, if not, is it fair of me to put them forth in favor of my own?"

Finally, my brother, I remind you: The most important considerations against traditional religions are not the contradictions contained in their Bibles or other sacred texts. Rather, the strongest arguments against traditional religions are the dearth of evidence supporting their foundational teachings; the terrible dangers to the human race of fostering exclusive and other-worldly belief systems that have repeatedly given rise to wars and persecutions; and, even when peaceful, the profound wound inflicted upon the human spirit by encouraging us all—and for all our lives, from stumbling infancy through tottering old age—to flee from honesty on matters most vital.[1]

125. Further argument that answers have been given to these apparent biblical errors and contradictions

And another religious man said: You have not convinced me. I, too, believe that there are answers to all these contradictions and apparent errors. These questions and challenges only come about because people do not understand, or do not wish to understand, the true meaning of the Bible—including reading it in its original language, and not being bound by this generation's cultural assumptions. Many religious scholars and apologists have addressed these supposed contradictions, and have provided answers. Thus, one can still see the Bible as perfectly consistent, and without error. And that is what believers must do.

And the sage said: My brother, as I have stated at the outset of examining the matter of biblical accuracy or inaccuracy,[2] many claims of supposed biblical error or contradiction are, indeed, misguided and unconvincing. For this reason I have not passed along all such challenges, but have, instead, chosen carefully, and spoken only of errors and contradictions that *do* seem, to me, justified.

And my brother, yes, if one is sufficiently imaginative one can generate what some would consider adequate answers to all the seeming biblical errors and contradictions. For that matter, one who is sufficiently imaginative can manufacture "answers" to any contradiction in any book, or any error on the part of any person or any theory. The question is, however, whether such answers would be honest and credible or, rather, forced and unconvincing.

Indeed, my brother, what, if anything, would be, even in theory, for the believer, an adequate contradiction—what would the Bible have to say for the devout to concede that the Bible *does* contradict itself? And why would that kind of contradiction be any different from those already identified? Could we not use our creativity to generate "answers" to such challenges, too? If so, if to the believer nothing would constitute an indisputable biblical contradiction, or cause

---

[1] For more on the dangers and damages of religion, see sections 141-145.
[2] See section 118.

him to doubt the Bible's inerrancy, is not the impartial observer justified in concluding that such a man does not consider the evidence with an open mind—but uses every means of mental agility, honest or otherwise, to formulate defenses for his beleaguered beliefs?

To illustrate how easy it is for the human mind to spin creative interpretations, let us pretend that the Bible contained additional inconsistencies that it does not truly contain—and we shall see how simple it is to invent "answers."

First, consider an imaginary historical claim: If in one verse the Bible were to say that God brought the Israelites out of the bondage of Egypt, and elsewhere the Bible were to say that He did not, would not religious apologists answer that the first verse refers to a physical bringing out from a position of persecution and deprivation, while the other refers to a spiritual bringing out, which, they would say, every man must do for himself by choosing to have faith and to follow the Lord; or else, might not apologists claim that one verse refers to most Israelites who did, indeed, leave Egypt, while the other verse refers to those Israelite sinners who died in Egypt, or perhaps to earlier generations of Israelites who died before the Exodus; or, if all else failed, might not apologists claim that God's ways are beyond us and we must simply have faith that there is an answer to this inconsistency, even if we do not yet see it?

Now, let us consider a moral claim. If the Bible were to say in one verse that slavery is permitted, and in another verse that slavery is forbidden, would not religious apologists claim that the Bible did not truly mean that slavery is permitted, only that in our fallen state, we indulge in the sin of slavery; or that the permitted slavery refers to a spiritual servitude to God, and not actual physical slavery to man; or that God specifically taught against slavery in one verse in order to tell us His view, but, in the other verse, permitted slavery in order to allow humans, with their freedom of choice, the opportunity to eventually take the initiative in rising above the moral error of slavery—an error which He knew they were not yet sufficiently morally developed to overcome?

Now let us consider another example. If the Bible were to say in one verse that God wants humans to live virtuous lives, and in another verse say that God does not care how men lead their lives, would not religious apologists claim that the first verse is spoken to good men, while the second verse is spoken to evil men, upon whom God wishes to visit punishment in the hereafter; or that the first verse was spoken in the literal, straightforward meaning, while the second was meant as a sarcastic commentary, obviously understood by the people of the day to have been intended to prod the wicked into reconsidering their ways?

Now let us consider a matter relating to simple fact. If the Bible were to have said in one verse that David was a man, and in another verse that David was a woman, would not religious apologists claim that the first verse was clearly literal, while the second was meant in the metaphorical sense—to convey that David was the bride of God, just as elsewhere in the Bible the entire people of Israel is referred to as God's bride; or that it was a copyist error; or that there were actually two Davids, one of whom was a man, and the other, a woman?

Let us further consider a numerical claim. If the Bible were to say in one verse that the earth was created ten thousand years before Abraham, and in another, that it was created one hundred thousand years before Abraham, would not religious apologists claim that it was a copyist error; or that one verse referred to certain features of the earth, while the other verse referred to other features; or that the earlier date referred to the planet itself, while the later date referred to humans, who are taught in Scripture to have come from earth—and, indeed, the name of the first human, Adam, comes from one Hebrew word for earth—"adamah"?[1]

Finally, we shall consider a theological matter. If one Bible verse taught that God was omnipotent, while another taught that He was limited in His powers, would not religious apologists claim that the first verse is meant as it sounds, but the second was referring only to His self-limiting powers in conducting human affairs, in order to allow us freedom of choice; or that in the second verse the Bible was actually not referring to the truth, but rather to the view that some wicked people have of God; or, in the absence of a better response, that the ways of God are beyond us, and we cannot expect to understand the meaning of every last verse of His Holy Bible?

If, to believers, no *hypothetical* apparent inconsistency in the Bible could ever constitute a contradiction or even a cause for significant doubt as to the Bible's inerrancy or divine authorship or inspiration, can their minds be considered truly open to examining without bias the biblical text as it now exists? And are we not, on these matters, justified in receiving their answers and reassurances with great skepticism?

126. A Bible for the beasts: further illustration that "answers" can easily be suggested for any text we will not truly question

But the religious man said: I am not persuaded by your words. Our sages and theologians have given many answers to the problems raised by heretics. I still believe the Bible is perfect.

---

[1] Strictly speaking, the Bible uses the word "adamah" to denote the meaning of earth as in soil; while the meaning of earth as in as in "God created heaven and earth," is denoted by the word "aretz." But the reader will perhaps excuse this imprecision in the context of a parody of apologetics by noting that the forced quality of this scholarship is, indeed, reminiscent of a good deal of apologetics.

And the sage said: My brother, allow me to offer a different illustration. Let us pretend there is a religion that believes God has revealed himself to non-human animals, and provided them with a Bible whose main characters are animals—although a few humans are included in the stories to provide interest for the other species, as we find it interesting when non-human animals populate human stories. Indulge me in a farcical exercise, as I recast a familiar child's fable as sacred Scripture—so that we may demonstrate how easy it is to "answer" apparent contradictions. Yes, it is playful, some might say absurd, but perhaps it will be illuminating, too.

Let us suppose that the animal Bible contains the following two seemingly contradictory accounts: Mammals chapter 6, beginning in verse 5, states:

> And God spoke to the three little pigs, and said unto them: Get thee out of thy mother's house and find thee building matter with which to build homes for yourselves, and you and your seed shall know my blessings. And the pigs did according to God's word, and went out to seek their fortune. The first pig found a man with straw and said: May I have your straw to build me a house? But the man said: No, for I shall use the straw myself. And God said unto the pig, Kill that man, him and his wife and his children and his animals; fear not, neither have mercy upon them, for I shall be with you and give you strength. And the pig did according to the word of God: he killed all these souls, leaving nothing alive, and then built him a house of straw.

Yet in describing the same story elsewhere, the hypothetical animal Bible states in Pigs 12: verse 3-8:

> And God spoke to the three little pigs, and said unto them: Get thee out of thy mother's house and find thee building matter with which to build homes for yourselves, and you and your seed shall know my blessings. And the pigs did according to God's word, and went out to seek their fortune. The first pig found a man with straw and said: May I have your straw to build me a house? And the man said: No, for I shall use the straw myself. And God said unto the pig, Go, then, and gather your own straw; for he who gathers his own straw is warmed twice: once in the gathering, and again by its shelter.[1] And the pig did according to the word of God: he gathered his own straw and built him a house.

---

[1] This, say the apologists for the animal Bible, is the inspiration for the aphorism which states, "Who splits his own wood, warms himself twice."

We see, then, that the first version has God commanding the pig to kill the man, while the second version has God commanding the pig to gather his own straw. When challenged with this seeming contradiction, the parrots—the animal kingdom's loquacious but less than authentic spokespeople—respond with all manner of answers. First, they say, there is no proof that in the first account God did not tell the pig to collect his own straw, or that in the second account God did not tell the pig to kill the man; perhaps God said both things to the pig, but each story tells only part of what God said.

Second, they say, perhaps when the first account tells of God commanding the pig to kill the man, it is not to be taken literally. Instead, it simply means that the pig should blot out of his mind all thoughts of the man and his straw, and rather go and gather his own straw—thus, they say, even in the human Bible, when commanding the Israelites to kill every member of the nation of Amalek, the term "blotting out the memory" is used to denote killing.[1] Here, then, in the animal Bible, in the first account of the pigs, killing is used to denote blotting out of the memory; and the first passage is really saying the same thing as the second passage—erase this man completely from your life, kill all memory of him from your mind, and find straw independently.

Third, say the parrots, perhaps it was an entirely different set of three pigs in each story, and both stories took place. Fourth, they say, even if we cannot arrive at a satisfactory answer, we must trust that God has an answer. After all, we must not be so arrogant as to assume that merely because something is puzzling to us, it is necessarily mistaken.

And so, in this illustration the parrots have done with the pigs as well as humans have done with all manner of biblical characters and passages.

And, my brother: Upon whom should rest the burden of proof? Should skeptics reasonably be required to prove beyond all doubt that apparent errors and inconsistencies in the Bible are, indeed, what they seem—when nobody can ever prove beyond all doubt, for any book, that seeming mistakes and contradictions are insoluble problems? Or should religionists rather be expected to persuade us that the Bible's scores of apparent errors and inconsistencies, in a book passed down to us through ages of superstition and scientific ignorance, a book that—mingled with its noble and inspiring passages—makes claims of talking snakes and donkeys, and of seas splitting or being turned to blood by the pointing of a staff—and all manner of stupendous, nature-defying events, the likes of which we have not only never seen, but which all our best knowledge tells us is impossible; and a book that has God speaking to men and condoning

---

[1] Deuteronomy 25:19, "When the Lord thy God has given thee rest from all thy enemies... thou shalt blot out the memory of Amalek from under heaven; do not forget."

slavery, and commanding the wholesale slaughter of men, women, children, even animals;[1] and torturing people in fire forever,[2] something the most evil men have never done, nor could ever do; and still the Bible calls this God merciful—to decide on the veracity of such a book as this, upon whom should rest the burden of proof?

And my aim in recounting some of the Bible's apparent inconsistencies, and seeming contradictions, is not to prove the Bible mistaken, but rather to bring before my brothers and sisters one more reason—among many others—to examine with a more critical eye the teachings of religion. For no apparent inconsistency in any book is absolute proof of contradiction; one can always suggest various possible explanations. But if, in a quiet moment, hushing the haunting echoes of tradition and pondering far from the pride-filled rancor of debate, we ask ourselves whether all these inconsistencies do not warrant at least a closer look, and whether they might not be one more indication that religion may not be the word of God it claims to be—if we strain our inner ears at such a moment, I believe the answer may be faint, but it will be unmistakable.

And so, when reading a biblical text and deciding whether it seems to be consistent with, or contradictory to, another biblical text, we cannot decide the matter based upon whether someone has offered an answer. For there is always an answer: to biblical incongruities, for the Christian and Jew; to incongruities in the Koran, for the Muslim; to incongruities in political positions, for the party faithful; and, theoretically, to real or hypothetical incongruities in any tale, any position, any book—so long as loyalty trumps intellectual honesty. In short: The question we must ask ourselves is not whether there are answers, but whether such answers would persuade untrammeled reason.

My brother: Do the attempted answers to the Bible's errors and contradictions truly make the Bible perfect? Or does the Bible only seem perfect if we contort our sense of consistency and logic, twist our natural sense of reason and fairness, and turn ourselves into intellectual and spiritual cripples, hobbling along faith's well-worn paths?

I am reminded of a little tale.[3] A man's daughter was engaged to be married, and for the wedding he needed new clothes. So he went to a shop and tried on a

---

[1] In the case of the Old Testament

[2] In the case of the New Testament

[3] Although I may have later come across this joke elsewhere, if memory serves well I heard it first from a rabbi whose lectures I attended in my years of seminary study in Jerusalem, a man who believed strongly in the integrity and profundity of religious texts. He, being brilliant and intellectually nimble, was often able to solve apparent difficulties in the texts by offering novel, yet compelling, conceptualizations. Others were not as gifted, and he didn't always suffer them gladly. When a young man attempted to solve a

suit, but noticed that the coat was overly long. The clothier, seeing the customer's displeasure, reassured him, saying: "Simply hunch up your shoulders and the coat length will be right."

But the trousers were long, too. "All is well," said the merchant, "only crouch down, bending your knees deeply as you walk, and keeping your legs far apart, and they, too, will fit." Finally the man noticed that the left coat sleeve was a good deal shorter than the right. The clothier pressed on, saying: "Simply pull your left hand up and in as far as you can, in addition to following my other instructions, and the suit will fit you just fine." The man peered into the mirror and, indeed, when he did all that the clothing merchant said, the suit *did* seem to fit. So he paid his money and walked out wearing the clothes, following the advice he was given—hunching his shoulders, crouching down as he walked with his legs far apart, and keeping his left hand pulled up and in. From the barbershop across the street, two men saw him hobbling home. One said: "Look at that poor crippled man." "Yes," said the other, "but what a perfect suit!"[1]

126.5 Argument that the Bible must be true and divine, because if humans would have fabricated a text to serve as the basis of a religion, they would not have made its heroes so flawed

And a religious man said: Well, you make all kinds of arguments against the Bible, but I know it is both true and divine, for a simple reason: If the Israelites fabricated the Bible to be the most sacred and foundational document of a religion, they would never have included so many deeply flawed characters and claimed them as their ancestors and heroes. The Bible tells of Abraham banishing his son Ishmael into the desert, tells of Jacob only giving his famished brother Esau some food after Esau sells him the rights of the first-born, and tells, too, of Jacob lying to his father Isaac in order to get the blessings intended for Esau. And the Bible tells of Joseph's brothers selling him into slavery, and of Aaron making a golden calf which the Israelites worshiped, and of Moses hitting the

---

textual problem in the Talmud by resorting to a combination of multiple, far-fetched "answers," the rabbi looked at him with disbelieving eyebrows and a half frown, then after trying unsuccessfully to disabuse the young man of his prized theory, he broke out in a half-smile of pity and disappointment, and recounted this story about the father of the bride and his perfect suit.

[1] To be clear: I do not rely on humor to make this argument. The issue itself I have already discussed in all seriousness, and by appealing to reason and conscience. That is, we should distinguish between credible, honest answers on the one hand, and forced, partisan answers on the other. Now I merely elaborate on the point, by illustrating, with an entertaining little tale, the inappropriateness of unnatural solutions—even when they seem, like the clothier's suggestions, to address all objections.

rock to get water for the people instead of talking to it as God had commanded. The Bible also tells of the flaws of King Saul, and even of the misdeeds of David—and I can cite many other examples, too. Indeed, the Bible repeatedly criticizes the Israelite people overall, for being stiff-necked, and for worshiping strange gods. This pattern proves that the Bible was not a fabrication, but was rather true, and from God, because if humans fabricated it they would have portrayed their heroes and ancestors as glorious and perfect.

And the sage said: My brother, you raise an interesting point; let us examine the matter from several angles. First, one can believe the Bible to be man-made without believing that its stories were fabricated wholesale. We need not be forced into an all-or-nothing proposition on matters of the Bible's truth. The Bible may well contain stories which were originally based on true events. But the supernatural elements—which I argue we should consider enormously unlikely to be accurate—could have been gradually added to the stories over the years. Many of these stories may have developed gradually, and may have been included in the Bible only decades or centuries after they were first told; and by the time the Bible was being formed into its final, current version, such elaborations were already well-accepted elements of the stories, and were therefore incorporated into the sacred text.[1] This is one possible reason many of the Bible's characters are imperfect: they may be, at root, the stories of real people, and real people are imperfect.

Second—and a related point—stories that were eventually included in the Bible were not necessarily originally written for the Bible. Indeed, they may well not have originally been written at all, but may have been folktales that circulated for generations before being written down, and for generations more before being included in the Bible. This may be a second reason there are flawed characters in the Bible: The stories were not necessarily originated in order to contribute to the foundational text of a religion.

Third, my brother, it is well to bear in mind that we see the Bible but "through a glass darkly,"[2] obscured to some degree by millennia of religious biblical commentaries forcing the text to mean what their own laws and theologies taught, and obscured still further by our own unacknowledged cultural

---

[1] This matter of avoiding the false choice between absolute truth of everything in the Bible vs. sudden or devious fabrication of everything in the Bible, is elaborated upon elsewhere in the book, including sections 102 and 107, which deal, respectively, with archaeological findings seeming to corroborate the Bible's accounts, and the argument from the seeming implausibility of any generation of Israelites accepting an invented, and therefore unfamiliar, account of all their ancestors witnessing God's revelation at Sinai.

[2] These memorable and oft-used words are from I Corinthians 13, King James translation.

assumptions of good and evil, and of other things, too. And so I will tell you what many scholars have suggested: Some stories eventually included in the Bible may well have originally been told and accepted because they advanced the interests of one Israelite faction over another—by speaking poorly of the other faction's heroes or ancestors.[1] For several examples: the kingdoms of Judah and Israel against each other, relishing stories that spoke of faults of the other's progenitor, Judah or Joseph; the Aaronite priests of Jerusalem and the Levite priests of Shiloh against each other, each retelling stories unflattering to the their adversaries' claimed progenitors or heroes, Aaron or Moses; the forces loyal to the prophets against those loyal to the kings, each seeking to cast less than flattering light on predecessors or ancestors of the other group's leaders. And many generations after the partisan passions animating such tales may have died, when the Bible was put into its final form, the stories may have come to be considered familiar and beloved national history to many of the people, and were thus incorporated into the sacred text.

Indeed, that some stories ultimately included in the Bible originated as propaganda against enemies is strongly evidenced by the Bible's accounts in Genesis 19:30-38 on the origins of Amon and Moab—the progenitors of two nations, of those same names, hostile to ancient Israel. The biblical story has them being born from incestuous couplings of Lot with his two daughters, after fleeing the destruction of Sodom. If the origins of some stories included in the Bible, then, seem clearly motivated by propaganda against international enemies, it should not surprise us that propaganda may have been the motivating force, too, behind some biblical stories reflecting poorly on *domestic* foes.[2]

A fourth reason why we need not see flawed biblical characters as proof of the Bible's divine origin, is that many of the practices we now consider improper, even evil, were in ages past seen as acceptable, perhaps admirable. For one clear example, the Bible says that the genocide and mass murder of certain Canaanite peoples was commanded by God, to Moses, Joshua, Samuel, and others. Slavery, too, was explicitly allowed by God. When such accounts are given in the Bible, it should be clear that the generations during which these stories originated did not find such teachings and deeds improper—for they not only have their heroes doing such things, they have God commanding them.

---

[1] Among others, Richard E. Friedman, in his book *Who Wrote the Bible?* addresses this matter, and does so in an interesting and accessible fashion.

[2] And for evidence of this all-too-human inclination to besmirch the reputation of one's adversaries by the use of story, one need only observe the extreme partisans at work in nearly every important political contest—even in what we are pleased to think of as our far more civilized times and lands—spreading damaging, often false, rumors about the candidate of the other party, or his spouse or children.

And for more subtle examples, let us turn to the matter of Jacob using Esau's hunger and weariness to extract from him the sale of his first-born rights, and of fooling his father Isaac into bestowing upon him the blessings intended for Esau. To the modern sensibilities of some, lying is deeply wrong. But to the hardened culture of a tribal people surrounded by hostile tribes, such lying to procure advantage was likely to have been seen as admirable cleverness and daring. And so the Bible has many characters resort to trickery, when confronted by an opponent of greater strength or numbers. Recall the deceit practiced by Simeon and Levi in killing all the males of the city ruled by Hamor after his son Shechem raped their sister Dinah in Genesis 34; or the deceit practiced by the Gibeonites in eliciting a treaty and oath of safety from the princes of Israel in Joshua 9; or the deceit practiced by Ehud in assassinating the Moabite king Eglon in Judges 3; or the deceit practiced by Jael when killing the general Sisera in Judges 4; or the deceit of the infamous Delilah in entrapping Samson; in these cases and more, the Bible reflects how wiliness was, especially in service of a great or necessary cause, or when operating against a militarily superior foe, not seen as immoral.

Indeed, even modern societies who think themselves greatly civilized would never be so naïve as to demand of their agents of military intelligence that they tell only the truth to their adversaries, and never engage in deceit. To the contrary: When circumstances call for it, daring deception is admired, even by those who see themselves as far more ethically advanced than the ancients. Moreover, in the part of the world in which these stories were set, one can still go to the marketplace, nearly any Middle Eastern *souk*, and observe—more than two millennia after these stories were incorporated into the Bible—how it is expected that one engage in haggling, which routinely involves dishonest claims and feigned poverty and pretend emotion in the service of striking one's best deal. It is likely, then, that many of what modern readers see as flaws in biblical characters, would have been seen by the original tellers and hearers of these tales as entertaining, perfectly acceptable, perhaps even cause for pride and admiration.

Fifth, the ancient Israelites were a fiercely independent and iconoclastic people, not comfortably submitting to being ruled or dominated—not by a too-proud monarchy, nor by a too-exclusive priesthood, not even by a too-jealous God, whose case the Bible's prophets and narrator repeatedly plead in the face of a populace that time and again reverts to worshiping other deities.

Bringing down the high and mighty and raising up the low and the scorned, is a consistent theme running through the Bible, beginning with God favoring the offering of the younger Abel over the older—and in ancient Near-East societies, therefore—more important and powerful Cain. God tells Abraham that his true progeny will come not from Ishmael the older son, but from Isaac the younger son. And Joseph is favored over his older brothers by their father Jacob, as is Joseph's son Ephraim, over his older brother Manasseh. Moses is chosen over his older brother Aaron for the primary leadership of the Israelites, and a despised slave nation of Hebrews is chosen to prevail over the power of Pharaoh and the ancient civilization of Egypt. The people's first leader Moses and his brother Aaron the high priest are far from consistently respected, and are the targets of a rebellion by Korah and other notables.

Recall that even into the days of the prophet Samuel, the Israelites are depicted in the Bible as a loose confederation of tribes, without a monarchy, and only when fearing growing military threats did they ask for a king. Even then Samuel rebuked them harshly, seeing this as disrespectful to God, and, indeed, not all the people welcomed their first king.[1] Saul is chosen from the smallest tribe of Israel, and later loses the kingdom to David, who is chosen above his older, taller brothers. Once David abuses his power, he is censured by the prophet Nathan, and over the course of his kingdom was subject to rebellions by his sons, and jeering disloyalty from others; and though David succeeds at retaining the crown, his dynasty is significantly diminished after his son Solomon's death, when the people insist that the king has treated them too harshly. Most of the tribes refuse allegiance to the Davidic line, and thenceforth the nation was broken into two separate kingdoms: Judah and Israel. And the Old Testament prophets and narrators repeatedly criticize various kings that ruled over the subsequent biblical history.

Indeed, at times this aversion to elitism went so far as to challenge the notion of Israel's superiority, or uniqueness before God, as in the entire thrust of the Book of Jonah, where the generosity and compassion of the pagan sailors, and the humility and ready repentance of the people of Nineveh, contrast sharply with the frequent biblical complaints about an Israelite people seeing themselves as superior, and slow to heed the voice of the prophets. Indeed, the only character in the book of Jonah painted negatively, as disobedient, ungenerous, and callous—in attempting to run from his duty to prophesy, and in being unhappy at the salvation of the myriads of Nineveh—was Jonah himself, a prophet, and presumably the cream of Israel.

And this challenging of Israel's special status before God is most directly expressed in Amos 9, where in verse 7 the Bible says:

> Are ye not as children of the Ethiopians unto me, O children of Israel? saith the Lord. Have not I brought up Israel out of the land of Egypt? and the Philistines from Caphtor, and the Syrians from Kir?

---

[1] See 1 Samuel 10.

This puncturing of special privilege and pride and the knocking down of heroes may well have been one consistent thread in the tapestry of Israelite culture, and would, therefore have naturally emerged in their stories, some of which were eventually included in the Old Testament.

Even the New Testament continues this thread of bringing down the powerful and elite and raising up the low and the scorned—for several examples—in the protests of Jesus against the religious powers of the day, the Pharisees and the priests at Jerusalem; in an echo of the technique used in the story of Jonah, the contrasting of the ungenerous priest and Levite with the good Samaritan; and, most prominently, in the paradox that the one the world saw as captured and humiliated, and put to death like a common criminal, was said by Christians to have really been the Messiah, even the Son of God or God Himself.

This theme of the high and mighty being brought low, and the low being elevated to unexpected heights, in addition to perhaps having been native to the fiercely independent spirit of the ancient Israelites, may also have been magnified by, and enlisted in the aid of, religious teachings of human frailty and of the ideal of submitting only to God, and may even have been further, and unintentionally, stimulated by accumulated centuries of stories introduced to the culture for the political reasons mentioned earlier—to shed unflattering light upon opponents' heroes—but stories which, when gradually integrated into the cultural heritage of a people, helped magnify their distrust of power, and their inclination to find fault with leadership. These attitudes, then, will have naturally emerged in their later stories, some of which may have been incorporated into the Bible, too. And this iconoclastic aspect of Israelite culture is a fifth reason we need not interpret the many flawed heroes in the Bible's stories as proof of the book's divine origin.

Sixth, storytelling is an ancient art, does not depend on modern technology, and may well have been quite advanced in ages past. One elementary rule of storytelling is to make one's characters credible and realistic, and one application of this rule is to mar each one, at times significantly, at times only slightly, with some fault or misdeed; to paint a few clouds in a sky of blue; to set a night for every day, and to cast a shadow for even the strongest sun. If we have allowed our eyes to see, we have all observed that our neighbors, our friends and families—and we ourselves, too—are far from perfect. The only perfect people are the people one does not know well. And so, some of the many storytellers of ancient Israel, and those who contributed to the final text of the Bible, may have understood the narrative power and literary advantage of creating flawed heroes—and such imperfect characters need not be evidence of supernatural authorship. Indeed, if one insists that the ancient Israelites were incapable of grasping this elementary rule of storytelling, can one be justly confident that the religious heritage of what would have been such a primitive-thinking people is valid and true?

In short, my brother, we are left with the choice of understanding flawed Bible characters as either having arisen naturally, by any of the many means— some of which I have discussed—that can contribute to such an end, and which neither prove all the Bible's stories true nor any of its contents divine; or, in contradiction to everything our species has learned about the universe and how it operates, and dismissing the numerous plausible natural explanations, we can choose to insist that the presence of flawed heroes in the Bible proves that its contents are all true and its origins can be traced only to a supernatural God. My brother, is there any doubt as to which option is more reasonable?

127. Is the Old Testament a perfect guide for morality?

And a man raised his voice and said: Surely you must admit that the Bible is our great source of morality, thus giving credence to the claim that it is of divine origin, and that its teachings are God's instructions on how we should live!

And the sage replied: My brother, the Bible has taught many instructions on righteous principles and ethical behavior, and many kind and virtuous people have considered the Bible the sacred source of their admirable goodness. Some just and noble laws are taught in the Bible, and some touching and compassionate lessons, too. It is fitting that we speak of a few of the Bible's many good lessons, before we speak of biblical passages more troubling.[1]

Genesis Chapter 4 tells the story of Cain and Abel, and how Cain was punished for killing his brother.

---

[1] The average religious person in our day—and undoubtedly in other ages, too—reads the Bible, or whatever is his sacred scripture, not as an instruction book for immediate action, but rather as an idealized text, which may or may not relate in any literal sense to his daily life. The average Christian no more seriously thinks of turning and offering the other cheek when hit on one, than does the average Jew consider slaughtering an animal to atone for a sin. And the most gentle among the religious, who might become ill at the sight of blood or suffering in real life, may, nonetheless, blithely pass over, even read with reverent piety, passages in the Bible commanding genocide, or promising eternal fiery punishment in hell. So I do not challenge religion on horrendous biblical passages out of the fear that its average adherent will immediately act upon those passages. Instead, I challenge religion on these matters for several other reasons—among them, that religion has episodically put to terrible use the violence and persecution inherent in her Bibles, and will likely episodically stoop to doing so in the future; and, that even when people do not take action on what they read, their hearts are invariably influenced by these teachings purported to originate with God; and, lastly, that it is simply intellectually dishonest to hold up a text as the pinnacle of moral perfection, when by any discernible standard it clearly is not.

And Genesis 39:9 tells of how Joseph, who was invited to commit adultery, resists the temptation and says:

> ...how then can I do this great wickedness, and sin against God?

And in Exodus chapter 20, and Deuteronomy chapter 5, in two accounts of what are popularly known as the Ten Commandments, the Bible teaches the importance of honoring one's parents, and prohibits murder, adultery, stealing, bearing false witness, and coveting what belongs to others.

And in the following passages in Exodus, the Bible teaches the considerate treatment of strangers, of widows, and orphans; that money should be lent to one's community without usury; and that one must be sensitive to the needs of the poor. Exodus 22:21-27 states:

> Thou shalt neither vex a stranger, nor oppress him: for ye were strangers in the land of Egypt. Ye shall not afflict any widow, or fatherless child. If thou afflict them in any wise, and they cry at all unto me, I will surely hear their cry; And my wrath shall wax hot, and I will kill you with the sword; and your wives shall be widows, and your children fatherless. If thou lend money to any of my people that is poor by thee, thou shalt not be to him as an usurer, neither shalt thou lay upon him usury. If thou at all take thy neighbour's raiment to pledge, thou shalt deliver it unto him by that the sun goeth down: For that is his covering only, it is his raiment for his skin: wherein shall he sleep? and it shall come to pass, when he crieth unto me, that I will hear; for I am gracious.

And a bit further in Exodus, the Bible teaches kindness to one's enemies, and to animals; fairness and justice; truthfulness; the avoidance of bribes; and the prohibition against mistreating strangers. Exodus 23:4-9 states:

> If thou meet thine enemy's ox or his ass going astray, thou shalt surely bring it back to him again. If thou see the ass of him that hateth thee lying under his burden, and wouldest forbear to help him, thou shalt surely help with him. Thou shalt not wrest the judgment of thy poor in his cause. Keep thee far from a false matter; and the innocent and righteous slay thou not: for I will not justify the wicked. And thou shalt take no gift: for the gift blindeth the wise, and perverteth the words of the righteous. Also thou shalt not oppress a stranger: for ye know the heart of a stranger, seeing ye were strangers in the land of Egypt.

And Leviticus 19 teaches against revenge or bearing a grudge, teaches the famous dictum "Love thy neighbor as thyself," and teaches the Israelites to love the strangers living among them. It also teaches respect for the old, justice, and honesty in business dealings. Leviticus 19:18 states:

> Thou shalt not avenge, nor bear any grudge against the children of thy people, but thou shalt love thy neighbour as thyself: I am the Lord.

And Leviticus 19:34 states:

> But the stranger that dwelleth with you shall be unto you as one born among you, and thou shalt love him as thyself; for ye were strangers in the land of Egypt: I am the Lord your God.

And Leviticus 19:32-36 states:

> Thou shalt rise up before the hoary head, and honour the face of the old man, and fear thy God: I am the Lord. And if a stranger sojourn with thee in your land, ye shall not vex him. But the stranger that dwelleth with you shall be unto you as one born among you, and thou shalt love him as thyself; for ye were strangers in the land of Egypt: I am the Lord your God. Ye shall do no unrighteousness in judgment, in meteyard, in weight, or in measure. Just balances, just weights, a just ephah, and a just hin, shall ye have: I am the Lord your God, which brought you out of the land of Egypt.

And in Deuteronomy 1, Moses recounts how he charged the Israelites to render justice fairly and fearlessly, with no regard for kinship, status, or wealth. Deuteronomy 1:16-17 states:

> And I charged your judges at that time, saying, Hear the causes between your brethren, and judge righteously between every man and his brother, and the stranger that is with him. Ye shall not respect persons in judgment; but ye shall hear the small as well as the great; ye shall not be afraid of the face of man; for the judgment is God's...

And Deuteronomy 16:18-20 again stresses the importance of honesty and fairness in justice:

> Judges and officers shalt thou make thee in all thy gates, which the Lord thy God giveth thee, throughout thy tribes: and they shall judge the people with just judgment. Thou shalt not wrest judgment; thou shalt not respect persons, neither take a gift: for a gift doth blind the eyes of the wise, and pervert the words

of the righteous. That which is altogether just shalt thou follow, that thou may-
est live, and inherit the land which the Lord thy God giveth thee.

And Isaiah 1:17 also teaches of justice and compassion:

Learn to do well; seek judgment, relieve the oppressed, judge the fatherless,
plead for the widow.

And Ezekiel 45:9-10 speaks against violence and unfairness and for honesty
and just treatment when it states:

Thus saith the Lord God; Let it suffice you, O princes of Israel: remove violence and spoil, and execute judgment and justice, take away your exactions
from my people, saith the Lord God. Ye shall have just balances, and a just
ephah, and a just bath.

And Amos 5:24 also teaches justice:

But let judgment run down as waters, and righteousness as a mighty stream.

And Proverbs 31:20, teaches charity when, in praise of the virtuous woman,
it states:

She stretcheth out her hand to the poor; yea, she reacheth forth her hands to
the needy.

My brother, these and many, many more passages in the Old Testament
teach good and positive moral lessons. None of what I say is intended to negate
the positive messages the Bible has taught.

One[1] important question before us, however—as we address certain traditional religious beliefs—is not whether the Bible contains some positive ele-

---

[1] Another important question is whether even those more liberally-minded among the
religious, who concede that the Bible is a human product—but look to it as a cherished
work of tradition documenting the human quest to understand the universe and its
meaning, and to wrestle with the notion of a Creator—whether even those with such
relatively open minds are complicit in crimes against the human spirit, and are too quiet
in defense of dignity and reason and truth, in that they do not clearly enough separate
themselves from both the historical and contemporary masses of believers who have
revered, and continue to revere, the entire Bible as God's word; and whether they may
also be in some way complicit in any future horrors visited by Bible believers upon each

ments, even many kind and inspiring teachings, but rather whether the Bible is a pure and inerrant source of morality, the living word of a perfect God.

And if we answer this question with painful honesty, we must concede that in addition to its good and ennobling lessons, the Bible also teaches much that today nearly everyone, including many religious leaders, would consider horrendously immoral. Thus, either the Bible's accounts of God's word are inaccurate, or God taught what we, today, would consider far from highest morality.

My brother, we have been so accustomed to conceiving of the Bible as moral and holy, that if one claimed that the Bible commanded or condoned genocide, mass murder of civilian women and children, slavery, polygamy, religious persecution, the death penalty for homosexuals, unequal rights for women, and other such practices, we might angrily accuse this person of dishonesty, ignorance, and of defaming and misrepresenting the Bible. Yet I ask you in all gentleness and honesty to hear the direct quotes and the evidence and judge for yourself whether these are, or are not, included in the Bible's teachings. Though your head shakes no; though your arms cross in defense; though your lips turn down in frowning disapproval; I ask you to indulge me and examine my citations from the Bible, and then tell me where I am wrong.

a. Mass murder and genocide in the Old Testament

First let us speak of mass murder and genocide. Such deeds, including the killing of civilian women and children, are commanded several times in the Bible. Most dramatically there is the case of Amalek—a people who, the Bible relates, attacked the Israelites on the road, after the Exodus. For this provocation, the Bible states, God commands Moses to direct the Israelites[1] to commit genocide

---

other or upon "non-believers"—complicit because they do not take a strong stand in repudiating the seeds of exclusivity and persecution that remain in the biblical text which throughout the past two millennia and more have repeatedly sprouted, giving religious approbation and fervor to intolerance and hate, passions and behaviors the likes of which we have good reason to fear will haunt future centuries, too. Sam Harris, in his book, *The End of Faith*, argues strongly that the answer to this question is yes.

[1] It should be noted that as of this writing, the stories of massacres overseen by Moses and Joshua cannot be verified as having actually occurred—indeed, many scholars doubt they did. It should also be noted that the Jews, the people who gave the world the Old Testament, the people that have always considered it God's only Bible or sacred Scripture, have—for all of currently verifiable history—been far more often the victims than the perpetrators of violence, and have, as a rule, over the past two millennia turned their ambitions not toward physical aggression but toward intellectual and mercantile achievement, and other non-violent pursuits. And since they have been emancipated from the ghettoes they have, quite often, in their interactions with others, been idealistically inclined, seeking as much as any people—and arguably more than most—universal

against them, even if this should only be feasible to carry out in a future generation, at a time when all of the perpetrators of the attack on the Israelites were
long since dead. In Deuteronomy 25:19, the Bible states:

> When the Lord thy God has given thee rest from all thy enemies... thou shalt
> blot out the memory of Amalek from under heaven; do not forget.

And, generations later, in I Samuel Chapter 15, the prophet Samuel conveys
God's word to King Saul as follows:

> Thus saith the Lord of hosts... Now go and smite Amalek, and utterly destroy
> all that they have, and spare them not; but slay both man and woman, infant
> and suckling, ox and sheep, camel and ass.

My brother, would you consider women and children deserving of genocide
because the military leaders of their people decided to attack your people? And
what can be said for the morality of a Bible, and its God, that insists upon even
the great grandchildren of these women and children being exterminated for the
attack committed generations ago by their forebears—people they never knew?

But this matter of Amalek is far from the only example of genocide commanded by God according to the Old Testament. When the Israelites were on
the march, conquering the "Promised Land," warring with nations in and around
what was later to be called the land of Israel, they were commanded by God to
kill defenseless women and children as a matter of course.[1] For example, after

---

justice and compassion; and they have engaged to an uncommon degree in altruistic and
philanthropic enterprises. So this criticism of parts of the Old Testament is no indictment
of Jewish people, overall, any more than my criticism of parts of the New Testament is
an indictment of Christian people, overall.

[1] The objection may be raised that women and children are, at times, active and dangerous enemy agents. Recent events—ironically, especially in that part of the world in
which the ancient stories of the Bible were set—include the repeated incidence of female
suicide bombers, and of youngsters being sent off on such missions of mayhem, their
own eagerness for violent and malevolent death surpassed only by the fanatical commitment of their mothers, some of whom, after the fruit of their own wombs have been
obliterated in the zealous and hate-filled objective of indiscriminately obliterating others,
have been observed passing out candies and singing wedding songs in celebration.

It is, of course, an overly convenient and naïve assumption that women and children,
and those presenting themselves as civilians, are necessarily innocent and harmless, and
that treating them as enemies is, in every case, barbaric. Indeed, those so restricted by the
out-of-date, chivalric, categorical distinction between "dangerous adult men in uniform"
and "innocent women and children in civilian dress," put many truly innocent women

doing battle with Midian, and killing all their men, the Israelites had not yet killed the women and children. The Bible in Numbers 31:17-18 states that Moses gave instructions as follows:

> And therefore kill every male among the little ones, and kill every woman that hath known man by lying with him. But all the women children, that have not known a man by lying with him, keep alive for yourselves.

These Midianites were, according to the Bible's account, treated better than most victims of the conquering Israelites. Listen to Moses recounting what was done to other peoples they vanquished. With regard to Sihon the king of the Emorites, the Bible quotes Moses as saying in Deuteronomy 2:34:

> And we took all his cities at that time, and utterly destroyed the men, and the women, and the little ones, of every city, we left none to remain.

Far from God disapproving of this genocide, the Bible recounts that when the Israelites prepared for their next battle, against King Og of Bashan, God commanded Moses to do the same. In Deuteronomy 3:2 God tells Moses:

> And the Lord said unto me, fear him not: for I will deliver him, and all his people, and his land, into thy hand; and thou shalt do unto him as thou didst unto Sihon king of the Amorites, which dwelt at Heshbon.

And beginning in verse 6, Moses reports that the Israelites exterminated all civilians in King Sihon's sixty cities:

---

and children, and quite a few truly innocent men, too, in grave danger. As the Talmudic saying has it: "He who is merciful to the cruel, in the end is cruel to the merciful." Instead, each case must be assessed for its actual risks and dangers, not decided by arbitrary factors such as clothing, age, or gender.

Still, it would be quite a stretch to explain the commands of God and Moses and Joshua and Samuel in the Bible—for genocide and mass murder—as arising from similar and legitimate concerns. In the first place, the Bible in its accounts of Moses and Joshua commands the Israelites to slaughter the infants, even the animals, of Amalek and other condemned nations of Canaan. Yet these surely posed no military threat. Moreover, generations later, when God has Samuel direct King Saul to kill every human and animal of Amalek for the explicitly stated reason that their ancestors wronged the ancestors of the Israelites hundreds of years earlier, neither can this reasonably be explained as legitimate self-defense—nor, by our contemporary standards, as anything approaching high morality.

And we utterly destroyed them, as we did unto Sihon king of Heshbon, utterly destroying the men, women, and children, of every city. But all the cattle, and the spoil of the cities we took for prey to ourselves.

Joshua, the immediate successor to Moses in leadership of the Israelites continued this policy of genocide. In telling the story of Joshua conquering Jericho, the Bible, in Joshua 6:21, says:

And they utterly destroyed all that was in the city, both man and woman, young and old, and ox, and sheep, and ass, with the edge of the sword.

Again, God approves of the genocide and commands Joshua to repeat the performance in future battles. After Jericho, the next city to be captured by Joshua was Ai. In Joshua 8:1-2 the Bible states:

And the Lord said unto Joshua…And thou shalt do to Ai and her king as thou didst unto Jericho and her king: only the spoil thereof, and the cattle thereof, shall ye take for a prey unto yourselves: lay thee an ambush for the city behind it.

And Joshua obeys God's word; Joshua 8:26-28 states:

For Joshua drew not his hand back, wherewith he stretched out the spear, until he had utterly destroyed all the inhabitants of Ai. Only the cattle and the spoil of that city Israel took for a prey unto themselves, according unto the word of the Lord which he commanded Joshua. And Joshua burnt Ai, and made it an heap for ever, even a desolation unto this day.

Later, Joshua conquered Makkedah, and killed indiscriminately again. Joshua 10:28 states:

And that day Joshua took Makkedah, and smote it with the edge of the sword, and her king thereof he utterly destroyed, them, and all the souls that were therein; he let none remain: and he did to the king of Makkedah as he did unto the king of Jericho.

This genocide, the killing of civilians, even women and children, continues throughout the Bible's account of the Israelites' conquest of the land—at Livnah, at Lachish, at Eglon, at Hebron, at D'vir, and on and on. And note: The Bible repeatedly states that this policy was carried out at the instruction of God.

Moreover, this was by no means the work of a renegade commander. Moses himself took the lead in directing genocide, and Joshua, the next Israelite leader, continued this practice. Nor were these seen as sinful anomalies: The Bible recounts all these exterminations as the proper and fortunate conquering of the Promised Land at the command of God. Mass murder and genocide were—at least in the Old Testament—the policies of the God of the Bible.

I ask you, my brother: If your land was attacked by a foreign people claiming to be God's chosen nation, would you not take up arms in defense of your property and homeland? Would it be morally acceptable if you and your family, your entire city—men, women, children, the tottering elderly, too—were killed unless you immediately surrendered your land to a people claiming to have God's permission to seize your country, without you having any way of confirming such a supernatural claim? And can you honestly believe the Bible to be moral, yet reserve your outrage and moral condemnation for other mass murderers of later generations who, in their lands and for their reasons, implemented a policy of killing defenseless civilians, too?

And, my brother, do not be tempted to justify such slaughter by saying that God and the Israelites were concerned that the people of Canaan would have exerted a morally negative influence upon the Israelites. For although peoples living in close proximity do influence each other, does this justify genocide? If so, every nation could justify committing such atrocities upon its neighbors by claiming to be concerned about negative influence.

And let not your heart be tempted to excuse such mass murder, either, by claiming that God's will must be done; for every religion can teach it to be God's will to kill one's neighbors—and many religions have. We have not heard God command us to murder, and neither do we know the Bible to be the word of God. It is of our own free will, and without good evidence, that we choose to believe that God commanded such atrocities.

My brother, I know how shocking it can be to confront the possibility that the Bible contains not only imperfect elements, but even some that are, to modern sensibilities, downright barbaric and despicable. And one test of our spiritual strength and nobility on these matters is whether we can and will admit to what is, instead of denying consistency and conscience by stubbornly insisting that mass murder of civilians—when commanded by the Bible—is a fine and righteous thing.

b. Slavery in the Old Testament

And the sage continued, saying: Moreover, the Old Testament condoned slavery.[1] Indeed, the early heroes of the Bible were slave masters. The twelfth chapter of Genesis tells how Abraham journeyed to Egypt in consequence of the land of Canaan being struck by famine, and how the Egyptian king took an interest in Abraham's wife, Sarah—who pretended to be Abraham's sister. Genesis 12:16 says:

> And Abram benefited because of her, and he had sheep and cattle, male donkeys, male and female slaves, female donkeys and camels.

Abraham received more such gifts from another king, Avimelech, who was also interested in his wife, as she again pretended to be his sister. After Sarah's true identity was discovered by the king, the Bible states in Genesis 20:14:

> And Avimelech took sheep and cattle and male and female slaves and gave them to Abraham, and returned to him his wife Sarah.

In none of these cases does the Bible suggest that it was immoral for Abraham to own slaves. To the contrary, the Bible devotes extensive coverage to stories involving a male slave of Abraham named Eliezer, and a female slave named Hagar. Indeed, when Eliezer went in search of a wife for Abraham's son Isaac, and decided upon Rebecca, the Bible makes clear in his speech to the girl's family that Abraham continued to own slaves and saw them as property. Genesis 24:34-35 recounts Eliezer's presentation:

---

[1] Among several other instances, in discussions of slavery I depart from my standard practice of using the stately King James translation, because it does not (with a rare exception) use the word "slave," even when the Bible is clearly referring to humans as property to be bought and sold; instead the King James translation uses the word "servant." Example: Exodus 12:43-44 discusses who can eat of the Passover sacrifice: "And the Lord said unto Moses and Aaron, This is the ordinance of the Passover: There shall no stranger eat thereof: But every man's servant that is bought for money, when thou has circumcised him, then shall he eat thereof." Another example: Deuteronomy 5:15, "And remember that thou was a servant in the land of Egypt, and that the Lord thy God brought thee out thence through a mighty hand and by a stretched out arm..." Of course, the Bible begins the story of the Israelite nation with them being captive slaves, in persecuted bondage. Since in contemporary English usage, speaking about a slave but using the word servant would be less than clear, I have used the New International Version and the New American Standard Bible, or original translation, instead, when citing verses dealing with slavery.

And he said, I am a slave of Abraham. And God has blessed my master exceedingly, and he has become great. And he has given him sheep and cattle and silver and gold and male and female slaves, and camels and donkeys.

Note that the slaves are listed between, on one side, sheep, cattle, silver—and, on the other, camels and donkeys. All these are possessions.

And when God commands Abraham to circumcise himself and all the males of his household, slaves—clearly characterized as being "bought with money"—are included. Genesis 17:12 states:

And he that is eight days old shall be circumcised among you, every man child in your generations, he that is born in the house, or bought with money of any stranger, which is not of thy seed.

Jacob, the third of the patriarchs is also documented by the Bible to have owned slaves. After describing how Jacob bred Laban's sheep in an unusual way so as to become the owner of most of their offspring, the Bible describes Jacob's wealth by stating, in Genesis 30:43:

And the man expanded exceedingly, and he had many sheep, female slaves and male slaves, and camels and donkeys.

There, too, notice that human slaves are listed between sheep and camels.

Moving out of Genesis, and stories of the patriarchs, into the books dealing with the Israelites as a nation, we continue to see the Bible accepting slavery. In a Leviticus passage, God tells the Israelites not to treat Israelite slaves the same as slaves of non-Israelite origin. In Leviticus 25:39-46 some of these differences in treatment are specified—for example: an Israelite slave, unlike a non-Israelite, cannot be owned forever, but must be set free in the jubilee year. Also, unlike a slave of another nationality, an Israelite slave is not to be worked at hard labor. In verse 44 the Bible states:

...From the nations which surround you, from them you may buy male and female slaves. And also from those native peoples who live with you, from them buy and from their families which are with you, which have been born in your land. And they shall be for you an inheritance. And you shall bequeath them to your sons after you, to inherit; forever you shall work them, but with your brothers of the children of Israel, a man shall not work his brother in hard labor.

Moreover, the Bible makes it clear that a slave's life is not as important as a free man's life, and a slave's death is not to be treated as the death of a fully human being, but primarily as a financial loss. Exodus 21:29-32 states:

> If, however, that ox has been a habitual gorer, and its owner has been warned but has not guarded it, and it kills a man or woman, the ox shall be stoned and also its owner shall be put to death. But if the ox gores a slave, male or female, he shall pay thirty shekels of silver to the master, and the ox shall be stoned.

Exodus 21:20-21 provides another example of the Bible not considering a slave's life or death to be as important as that of a free man:

> If a man strikes his slave, male or female, with a rod and he dies immediately, he shall be avenged. But if he survives for a day or two he shall not be avenged, because he is his money.

And, reflecting the Bible's acceptance of slavery as a normal part of life, the following passage discusses eligibility rules for eating the Paschal sacrifice, which each Israelite family prepared for the Passover holiday. Exodus 12:43-44 states:

> And God said to Moses and Aaron, this is the law of the paschal sacrifice: all strangers shall not eat of it. And every slave belonging to a man, bought by money, you must circumcise him and then he may eat of it.

The Bible also demonstrates its acceptance of slavery in a passage discussing the Sabbath. Deuteronomy 5:14 states:

> And the seventh day is Sabbath for the Lord thy God; do not do any work; you, your son and your daughter, your male slave and female slave, your ox and your donkey and all your animals…

My brother, would you accept slavery as moral—to buy or capture another human being, to own him, and to consider his life less than fully human? If not, can you honestly accept the Bible as teaching and embodying ideal morality?

c. Religious intolerance in the Old Testament

And the sage continued, saying: The Old Testament commands religious intolerance: the destroying of other religions' sacred places and shrines, and even the death penalty for an Israelite who worships, or attempts to persuade another Israelite to worship, the god of another religion.

392

The Bible tells of how God commanded the Israelites not to make peace with the peoples of the land of Canaan, but to utterly destroy them, and to destroy their religious places of worship. Deuteronomy 7:1-5 states:

> When the Lord thy God shall bring thee into the land whither thou goest to possess it, and hath cast out many nations before thee, the Hittites and the Girgashites and the Amorites and the Canaanites and the Perizzites and the Hivvites and the Jebusites, seven nations greater and mightier than thou. And when the Lord thy God shall deliver them before thee thou shalt smite them, and utterly destroy them; thou shalt make no covenant with them, nor show them any mercy... But thus shall ye deal with them; ye shall destroy their altars, and break down their images, and cut down their groves, and burn their graven images with fire.

And the Bible mandated that even amongst the Israelites, if someone attempted to persuade another to worship a different god, no tolerance was to be shown. Deuteronomy 13:6-10 states that such a person is to be stoned to death:

> If thy brother, the son of thy mother, or thy son, or thy daughter, or the wife of thy bosom, or thy friend, which is as thine own soul, entice thee secretly, saying, Let us go and serve other gods, which thou hast not known, thou, nor they fathers; namely, of the gods of the people which are round about you...thou shalt surely kill him; thine hand shall be first upon him to put him to death, and afterwards the hand of all the people. And thou shalt stone him with stones, that he die; because he hath sought to thrust thee away from the Lord thy God...

Deuteronomy 13:12-18 goes even further and states that if a city has been persuaded to worship another god, the entire city, all humans and animals, are to be put to death, and everything in the city is to be burned—and it is to remain an everlasting ruin.

Even the solitary act of worshiping another god on one's own—without involving anyone else—is punishable by death. Deuteronomy 17 states that one who worships any other gods in the heavens, such as the sun or moon, is to be stoned to death.

My brother, if a set of laws in our days condemned to death anyone caught worshiping a different god than the one in which the majority believed, or even if laws merely directed the majority to systematically burn or demolish other religions' sacred objects and houses of worship, would we consider these laws examples of perfect morality—or rather of cruel intolerance? Would it not be honest, then, to pass similar judgment against the Bible?

393

d. Death penalty for rebellious adolescents

And the sage continued, saying: The Bible states in Deuteronomy 21:18-21:

> If a man have a stubborn and rebellious son, which will not obey the voice of his father, or the voice of his mother, and that, when they have chastened him, will not hearken unto them: Then shall his father and his mother lay hold on him, and bring him out unto the elders of his city, and unto the gate of his place; And they shall say unto the elders of his city, This our son is stubborn and rebellious, he will not obey our voice; he is a glutton, and a drunkard. And all the men of his city shall stone him with stones, that he die...

My brother: Would not all contemporary civilized nations charge with murder those who stone to death an adolescent who would not obey his parents? And how then shall we characterize as perfectly moral a book that legislates such a practice?

e. Inequality of rights for women in the Old Testament

And the sage continued, saying: In various ways the Bible teaches that the rights of a woman are less than those of a man.

First, the Bible makes it clear that a woman is to be subservient to her husband.[1] In Numbers Chapter 30, the Bible teaches God's laws relating to vows. The Bible states that a woman who lives with her father or husband, cannot independently make a vow or follow through upon it. Rather, her father—or, if married, her husband—is the one who decides whether the vow stands or is to be nullified. But nowhere does the Bible suggest that a mother or wife has the privilege of nullifying a man's vow. Numbers 30:13 states:

> Every vow, and every binding oath to afflict the soul, her husband may establish it, or her husband may make it void.

Moreover, throughout the Bible, men—especially the Bible's greatest heroes—have more than one wife at a time, or, and perhaps also, additional concubines; but a woman is never allowed to be married to more than one husband at a time, or enjoy the privilege of the equivalent of male concubines. Abraham had one wife, Sarah; and two concubines, Hagar and Keturah. Jacob

---

[1] Indeed, the biblical word for husband is "Baal" which is the same word for owner. And those familiar with the Old Testament will recognize the word "Baal," from another usage, also denoting the meaning of lord, as in the name of Canaanite gods. (And the word "husband," too, has its roots in a culture that saw woman as subordinate to man.)

394

had two wives, Leah and Rachel, and two concubines: Bilhah and Zilpah. Esau, his brother, also had several wives. King David had eighteen wives; King Solomon had several hundred wives and several hundred concubines. Additional cases of multiple wives are mentioned in the Bible, too.

In a related case of inequality, the Bible legislates that in the case of a married woman who has sexual relations with any man other than her husband, even if those relations are with an unmarried man, both parties are punished with death, while in the case of a married man who has sexual relations with a woman other than his wife, there is no death penalty legislated, unless it involves incestuous or other forbidden unions, or the wife of another man.

Leviticus 20:10 states:

> And the man that committeth adultery with another man's wife, even he that committeth adultery with his neighbour's wife, the adulterer and the adulteress shall surely be put to death.

But nowhere in the Bible is the death penalty taught for the married man having sexual relations with an unmarried woman outside his marriage—so long as it does not involve one of a few forbidden unions.

Divorce rights are also unequal to the extreme. Biblical law allows a man to divorce his wife, but does not allow a woman to divorce her husband. A marriage is ended only by a man writing his wife a document of divorce. Deuteronomy 24:1-2 states:

> When a man hath taken a wife, and married her, and it come to pass that she find no favor in his eyes, because he hath found something unclean in her; then let him write her a bill of divorcement, and give it in her hand and send her out of his house. And when she is departed of his house, she may go and be another man's wife.[1]

Inheritance rights are inequitable in the Bible, too. Only if a man does not have sons do his daughters inherit his land. Numbers 27:8 states:

---

[1] And to this day—along with a good number of dignified and compassionate religious laws—many Orthodox Jews follow this biblical law, too. In such cases, if a woman's husband refuses to give her a document of divorce, she can never marry again—even if she lives apart from her estranged husband for years and desperately wants to be divorced. And though in many cases community pressure is exerted upon such a husband to grant the divorce, if he chooses not to—perhaps evading community pressure by moving to another city or country—the woman has little effective recourse.

> And thou shalt speak unto the children of Israel, saying, If a man die, and have no son, then ye shall cause his inheritance to pass unto his daughter.

My brother, if you consider a society unfair which denies equal rights to women, would it not be honest to admit that the Bible was unfair in its treatment of women, too—or at least is a poor guide for us on such matters today?

f. Selling a daughter into servitude condoned by the Old Testament

And the sage continued, saying: The Bible even permits a man to sell his daughter as a maidservant. In addition to working for her master, the master has the right to marry her himself, or marry her off to his son. Exodus 21:7-9 states:

> And if a man sell his daughter to be a maidservant, she shall not go out as the menservants do. If she please not her master, who hath betrothed her to himself...And if he have betrothed her unto his son...

My brother, what opinion would we hold about a society that allows a man to sell his young daughter into servitude, or into marriage? Would we consider such laws to reflect appropriate treatment of a child—would we even see them as consistent with basic human rights? And would any of us characterize a society legislating such laws as exemplifying the pinnacle of morality? What, then, shall we say of the Bible? Can we truly venerate it as a perfect moral compass?

g. Death Penalty for Homosexuality in the Old Testament

And the sage continued, saying: The Bible punishes homosexual behavior with death. In Leviticus 20:13 the Bible states:

> And a man who shall lie with a male in the way one lies with a woman, they have both committed an abomination, they shall both be put to death; their blood is upon them.

Would not a contemporary nation punishing homosexual behavior with death be considered barbaric and cruel? Why then, my brother, should we not pass the same judgment upon this teaching of the Bible?

In all these matters, my brother, shall we weigh with two standards? Or shall we have one honest measure?

And although judging the morality of previous ages is a complex and difficult endeavor, vulnerable to the errors of myopia and oversimplification, we can—without involving ourselves in the messy matter of condemning the past by the lights of the present—confidently state that revering a set of books today, which along with its good and neutral teachings has God commanding slavery, geno-cide, mass murder, and religious persecution, is inappropriate, degrading to the human spirit, and, in the fullness of time, threatens to strangle in the cradle every nascent hope for human brotherhood and peace.

My brother, whatever one thinks of Moses and Joshua and Samuel as men—whether one judges them, in the context of their day, as good or evil or some balance of the two—is it not clear that some of their teachings and deeds would today be seen as stooping to lowest immorality? And dare we continue to look for moral guidance to the books that glorify them, and have them behaving atrociously on the word of what we say is a just and loving God?

128. Is the New Testament a perfect guide for morality?

And a devout Christian said: I have long heard that the Old Testament is full of wrath, so those examples do not surprise me; but is not the New Testament the perfect model for all that is moral and good?

And the sage replied: My brother, we can easily see the flaws of other relig-ions and their sacred books, but on our own religion and our own sacred books such clear vision is harder to come by.[1] And indeed, my brother, along with the Old Testament, the New Testament teaches many good lessons that are compas-sionate and moral. But, as with the Old Testament, it has its flaws, too. First let us review a few examples of the good, for there are many.[2]

One important teaching of Jesus, in line with some of the Hebrew prophets, was to equate righteousness not with ritual, but rather with treating others well. And Jesus taught forgiveness—and even on the cross forgave others.

The importance of people forgiving each other is taught in the New Testa-ment in other ways, too. Matthew 18:21-22 states:

---

[1] Two people zealously debating the merits of their respective religions appear to the non-religious observer—or even to an adherent of a third religion—to be far from persuasive, even if one's arguments are slightly less poor than the other's…like the man in the joke who comes to his friend, swears him to secrecy, and asks if he would help him recover a sunken treasure. He explains that he had rented a boat from the many available at the dock, and had gone out to sea and, while diving, happened upon chests of gold coins on the ocean floor. "Did you mark the spot," asks the eager friend, "so you can find it again?" "Yes," says the man, "I made a mark on the bottom of the boat, exactly where it went over the treasure." "You fool!," shouts his friend, "Never in my life have I heard anything so stupid! What if when we go to the dock, we don't get the same boat?"

[2] For further examples of the New Testament's positive lessons, see section 137 titled, *The Character of Jesus in the New Testament.*

Then came Peter to him, and said, Lord, how oft shall my brother sin against me, and I forgive him? till seven times? Jesus saith unto him, I say not unto thee, Until seven times: but, Until seventy times seven.

And Luke 17:4 also teaches repeated forgiveness:

And if he trespass against thee seven times in a day, and seven times in a day turn again to thee, saying, I repent; thou shalt forgive him.

Mark 11:26 teaches forgiveness, too:

But if ye do not forgive, neither will your Father which is in heaven forgive your trespasses.

Ephesians 4:25-32 teaches against lying, against anger, against stealing and bitterness, and teaches instead, kindness, tenderness, and forgiveness:

Wherefore putting away lying, speak every man truth with his neighbour: for we are members one of another. Be ye angry, and sin not: let not the sun go down upon your wrath: Neither give place to the devil. Let him that stole steal no more: but rather let him labour, working with his hands the thing which is good, that he may have to give to him that needeth. Let no corrupt communication proceed out of your mouth, but that which is good to the use of edifying, that it may minister grace unto the hearers. And grieve not the holy Spirit of God, whereby ye are sealed unto the day of redemption. Let all bitterness, and wrath, and anger, and clamour, and evil speaking, be put away from you, with all malice: And be ye kind one to another, tenderhearted, forgiving one another, even as God for Christ's sake hath forgiven you.

Collosians 3:8-14 also teaches similar good lessons, against anger and malice and blasphemy, against ethnic and other forms of discrimination, and for mercy, kindness, humility and charity:

But now ye also put off all these; anger, wrath, malice, blasphemy, filthy communication out of your mouth. Lie not one to another, seeing that ye have put off the old man with his deeds; And have put on the new man, which is renewed in knowledge after the image of him that created him: Where there is neither Greek nor Jew, circumcision nor uncircumcision, Barbarian, Scythian, bond nor free: but Christ is all, and in all. Put on therefore, as the elect of God, holy and beloved, bowels of mercies, kindness, humbleness of mind, meekness, longsuffering; Forbearing one another, and forgiving one another, if any man have a quarrel against any: even as Christ forgave you, so also do ye. And above all these things put on charity, which is the bond of perfectness.

And Philippians 2:2-4 teaches humility, peacefulness, and caring for the best interests of one another:

Fulfil ye my joy, that ye be likeminded, having the same love, being of one accord, of one mind. Let nothing be done through strife or vainglory; but in lowliness of mind let each esteem other better than themselves. Look not every man on his own things, but every man also on the things of others.

And Galatians 6:2 teaches of helping one another:

Bear ye one another's burdens, and so fulfil the law of Christ.

My brother, these and many other passages in the New Testament teach good morality. Still, for those who hold it to be the direct or inspired word of an all-loving, all-merciful, perfect God, it is not enough that much of the text is admirable: All of it must embody values beyond reproach. And if an informed and intelligent claim is advanced that some passages of the New Testament are tainted with serious moral failures, good Christians, who take their Bible seriously, dare not avoid investigating the matter.

And again, the New Testament's credibility rests, in part, upon the credibility of the God of the Old Testament. The New Testament repeatedly teaches that Jesus and his message constitute the fulfillment of Old Testament prophecies and the will of "the Father," the God of the Old Testament.[1] Therefore, if the Old Testament—intermingled with its positive elements—teaches some lessons deficient in morality, Christianity's message is built upon a questionable foundation, even if no immoral teachings were to be found in the New Testament itself. Yet listen to the following citations, and judge for yourself whether some immoral teachings are, indeed, to be found in the New Testament.

---

[1] In John 5:39 Jesus says, "Search the scriptures...they are they which testify of me." And many times throughout the New Testament, the text explains events occurring in the life of Jesus as fulfillment of what was prophesied in the Old Testament. For a number of examples, see Matthew 1:22-23; Matthew 2:15; Matthew 2:17; Matthew 2:23; Matthew 4:14; John 12:38; John 19:24; and John 19:28.

a. New Testament condoning slavery

First, my brother, although slavery was practiced in the days of Jesus and his disciples, the New Testament does not condemn slavery,[1] nor teach masters to free their slaves. This alone can be seen as a striking moral failure.

True, Paul in I Timothy 1:10-11 disapproves of stealing men:[2]

> ...for men-stealers and liars and perjurers—and for whatever else is contrary to the sound doctrine that conforms to the glorious gospel of the blessed God...

But far from not forbidding or even merely protesting the practice of slavery, the New Testament, in the very same book of Timothy, encourages slaves to work diligently for their masters. I Timothy 6:1-2 states:

> All who are under the yoke of slavery should consider their masters worthy of full respect, so that God's name and our teaching may not be slandered. Those who have believing masters are not to show less respect for them because they are brothers. Instead, they are to serve them even better, because those who benefit from their service are believers...

And Colossians 3:22-23 states:

> Slaves, obey your earthly masters in everything; and do it, not only when their eye is on you and to win their favor, but with sincerity of heart and reverence for the Lord. Whatever you do, work at it with all your heart, as working for the Lord, not for men.

---

[1] As elaborated upon in a footnote in section 127, relating to slavery in the Old Testament, the word for an owned human being is rendered by some Bible translations, including the KJV, as servant, and by other Bible translations as slave. And in the New Testament, too, the correct translation for contemporary English would seem to be "slave." If studied in context of the verses and of history—slavery was rampant in Roman times, and several verses urge the slave to behave with obedience and reverence for a master, and even to respectfully submit to his beatings—the Bible seems to be referring to, and to condone, outright slavery. In order to avoid any confusion, on the matter of slavery I depart from my normal practice of quoting the King James translation and usually quote instead from the New International Version and the New American Standard Bible. For more on this topic see the above-referenced footnote.

[2] Some translate this verse to speak of "slave traders." In any event, the owning of slaves was clearly not prohibited.

And Colossians 4:1, in speaking to masters, also clearly condones slavery:

> Masters, provide your slaves with what is right and fair, because you know that you also have a Master in heaven.

In addition to condoning slavery, the New Testament commands slaves to submissively accept their treatment, and not rebel, even when being treated harshly and unjustly. I Peter 2:18-21 states:

> Slaves, submit yourselves to your masters with all respect, not only to those who are good and considerate, but also to those who are harsh. For it is commendable if a man bears up under the pain of unjust suffering because he is conscious of God. But how is it to your credit if you receive a beating for doing wrong and endure it? But if you suffer for doing good and you endure it, this is commendable before God. To this you were called, because Christ suffered for you, leaving you an example, that you should follow in his steps.[1]

In Luke 17, the disciples ask Jesus to "Increase our faith!" In his response, Jesus makes it clear that he condones slavery, implies that slaves are to consider themselves unworthy, and certainly does not tell his disciples to free their slaves. Jesus states in Luke 17:7-10:

> Which of you, having a slave plowing or tending sheep, will say to him when he has come in from the field, Come immediately and sit down to eat? But will he not say to him, Prepare something for me to eat, and properly clothe yourself and serve me while I eat and drink; and afterward you may eat and drink? He does not thank the slave because he did the things which were commanded, does he? So you too, when you do all the things which are commanded you, say, We are unworthy slaves; we have done only that which we ought to have done.[2]

---

[1] Though some Bible versions speak, in this passage, of servants, by any translation this is clearly referring to something more than a butler-like, free employee. It explicitly refers to being beaten, and enduring suffering.

[2] This translation is from the New American Standard Bible. Some other translations make this teaching of Jesus sound less harsh. But the general acceptance of slavery—and certainly of treating other humans in a less than dignified and loving fashion—is evident in the verse regardless of translation.

And Ephesians 6:5-8 not only condones slavery, but commands slaves to obey the master as they would obey Christ:

> Slaves, be obedient to those who are your masters according to the flesh, with fear and trembling, in the sincerity of your heart, as to Christ; not by way of eyeservice, as men-pleasers, but as slaves of Christ, doing the will of God from the heart. With good will render service, as to the Lord, and not to men, knowing that whatever good thing each one does, this he will receive back from the Lord, whether slave or free.

And Titus 2:9-10 states:

> Urge bondslaves to be subject to their own masters in everything, to be well-pleasing, not argumentative, not pilfering, but showing all good faith so that they will adorn the doctrine of God our Savior in every respect.

And Luke 12:36-48 states:

> Be like men who are waiting for their master...Blessed are those slaves whom the master will find on the alert when he comes...Whether he comes in the second watch, or even in the third, and finds them so, blessed are those slaves...Blessed is that slave whom his master finds so doing when he comes...And that slave who knew his master's will and did not get ready or act in accord with his will, will receive many lashes, but the one who did not know it, and committed deeds worthy of a flogging, will receive but few...

My brother, would a book of perfect morality teach slaves to submit happily to their masters, or even refrain from crying out against the evils of humans holding each other in degrading bondage? And if we would today condemn, even wage war against, a nation practicing slavery—can we honestly label the New Testament's acceptance and support of slavery anything other than immoral?

b. New Testament teaching women subservience

And the sage continued, saying: The New Testament, in several passages, teaches that woman is to be subservient to man. I Timothy 2:11-14 states:

> Let a woman learn in silence with full submission. I permit no woman to teach or to have authority over a man; she is to keep silent. For Adam was formed first, then Eve. And Adam was not deceived, but the woman was deceived and became a transgressor.

402

Colossians 3:18-19 states:

> Wives, be subject to your husbands, as is fitting in the Lord. Husbands, love your wives and never treat them harshly.

Unlike their wives, husbands are told to be considerate and loving—but not submissive.

After commanding slaves to obey their masters in I Peter Chapter 2, women are addressed at the beginning of I Peter Chapter 3. Specifically, I Peter 3:1-6 states:

> Wives, in the same way, accept the authority of your husbands, so that, even if some of them do not obey the word, they may be won over without a word by the wives' conduct...It was in this way long ago that the holy women who hoped in God used to adorn themselves by accepting the authority of their husbands. Thus Sarah obeyed Abraham and called him lord.

The New Testament states not only that a woman should be subject to her husband, but that her submission should go so far as obeying him as she would obey Christ. Ephesians 5:22:

> Wives, be subject to your husbands as you are to the Lord. For the husband is the head of the wife just as Christ is the head of the church, the body of which he is the Savior. Just as the church is subject to Christ, so also wives ought to be, in everything, to their husbands.

And, again, while that Bible chapter tells men to love their wives, it does not tell them to submit to their wives—but does tell wives to submit to their husbands.

And Titus 2:4 states:

> ...So that they may encourage the young women to love their husbands, to love their children, to be self-controlled, chaste, good managers of the household, kind, being submissive to their husbands...

And I Corinthians 11:3 states:

> But I want you to understand that Christ is the head of every man, the husband is the head of his wife...

And in verses 7-9 it continues:

> For a man ought not to have his head veiled, since he is the image and reflection of God; but woman is the reflection of man. Indeed, man was not made from woman, but woman from man. Neither was man created for the sake of woman but woman for the sake of man.

And I Corinthians 14:34-35 states:

> Women should be silent in the churches. For they are not permitted to speak, but should be subordinate, as the law also says. If there is anything they desire to know, let them ask their husbands at home. For it is shameful for a woman to speak in church.

And if today we consider backward and barbaric a people that forces its women into submission, and requires them to obey their husbands, how can we consider the New Testament a good moral guide for our day?

c. New Testament teaching submission to dictatorship and tyranny

And the sage continued, saying: Moreover, far from encouraging people to oppose injustice and tyranny, the New Testament equates resistance to government with resistance to God. Romans 13:1-3 states:

> Let every person be subject to the governing authorities; for there is no authority except from God, and those authorities that exist have been instituted by God. Therefore whoever resists authority resists what God has appointed, and those who resist will incur judgment.

My brother, if this teaching of the New Testament were followed, no nation would ever rebel against tyrants or repressive governments. The United States of America, with her beginnings in revolution, would never have come into existence, nor would all other democracies born of resisting, changing, or overthrowing despotic authority. The great advances in human rights in recent centuries have come about only when people challenged and rose up against unfair or repressive government. Yet the New Testament would, it seems, have us all submit to authority, no matter how cruel or unjust. For the New Testament teaches that all authority comes from God, and that resisting authority will incur judgment. Can a book that includes such guidance be considered a reliable source of perfect morality?

d. New Testament teaching eternal fiery punishment for sinners

And the sage continued, saying: If a society punished its criminals by roasting them alive in fire until death, we would be horrified at such barbarism and cruelty; for although the criminal's agony would be over within minutes or hours, the suffering would be unspeakable. Consider then, the depths of cruelty and immorality reflected in the torturing of a person in everlasting fire—suffering without end! Can any crime be deserving of never-ending agony? Yet this is what Jesus teaches to be the punishment for sinners. And this is the same Jesus widely represented as the most loving and kind spirit ever to walk the earth in a human body. Is this not, instead, cruelty beyond anything mentioned in the Old Testament,[1] and beyond anything practiced by the most barbaric sadist?

In describing the day when "The Son of Man" judges the nations, Jesus says, beginning in Matthew 25:31:

> When the Son of man shall come in his glory, and all the holy angels with him, then shall he sit upon the throne of his glory. And before him shall be gathered all nations; and he shall separate them one from another, as a shepherd divideth his sheep from the goats. And he shall set the sheep on his right hand, but the goats on the left...Then shall he say also unto them on the left hand, Depart from me, ye cursed, into everlasting fire, prepared for the devil and his angels...And these shall go away into everlasting punishment, but the righteous into life eternal.

And let not your heart be tempted to answer that Jesus was only stating a fact—that sinners suffer in hell—and not originating this policy, and that Jesus should, therefore, not be held accountable for the cruelty of hell. For if Jesus was God, as some Christians teach, then this answer is evidently unsatisfactory. And if Jesus was the Son of God—without powers to make policy on such matters as hell—or even a mere compassion-filled mortal, he could still have protested the

---

[1] The Old Testament, in its original Hebrew, does not speak of hell, or of everlasting punishment of any sort. *Sheol* is the word used in the Old Testament to refer to where the dead go; it seems to mean a shadowy underworld, even a poetic synonym for death, but it is not associated with horrific or eternal pain. The KJV, in translating *Sheol* from the Hebrew, sometimes uses the word "hell," but at other times uses the word "grave," (see, for example, these two instances of *Sheol* in the Old Testament: Deuteronomy 32:22, and I Samuel 2:6. In the former, *Sheol* is translated as "hell," and in the latter, as "grave." Those unable to read the Old Testament in its original language would not know that the same word, *Sheol* was used in both verses of the biblical Hebrew. And considering traditional Christian teachings about hell, the different translations imply a great difference in meaning—a misleading difference not present in the original text.

matter with God, as the Bible says Abraham protested the impending destruction of Sodom and Gomorrah[1] and Moses protested and successfully prevented God's threatened destruction of the Israelites after they worshiped the golden calf.[2] Yet not only does the New Testament not represent Jesus as protesting the policy of punishing sinners in everlasting hell, it seems to portray him as quite comfortable with sinners going to an eternal fiery fate—indeed, seemingly satisfied with this—when he says in Matthew 25:41: "Depart from me, ye cursed, into everlasting fire, prepared for the devil and his angels."

e. New Testament teaching collective guilt and using inflammatory language

And the sage continued, saying: A well-accepted rule of fairness and morality is that each individual should be judged on his own merits, and not lumped into a group as one of "those," based on religion, skin color, national or ethnic origin, and so on. If someone were to speak poorly of others and say, "The Blacks think this," or "The Polish are such and such," or "The Irish are that way," it would reflect unfairness, and sloppy thinking too—the more so when the overgeneralization is employed not only to disparage, but to cast blame on entire peoples. If one were to say "The Italians are lawless and have built organized crime," or "The Greeks killed Socrates and have persecuted philosophers," these would be unfair, gross overgeneralizations.

That *some* Italians have supported, even celebrated, *some* organized crime leaders is true. But to lump all Italians into that category and say "the Italians" are against law and support crime—this is inaccurate and unfair. Similarly, that *some* Greeks in power in the days of Socrates sentenced him to death is true; but to blame his death on "the Greeks" is inaccurate and unfair. To say that in the day of Jesus, *some* Jews—by the account of the New Testament—wanted Jesus executed, for what they perceived to be blasphemy and insubordination, among other offenses, would be true.[3] But to lump an entire people into one category and say "the Jews" killed Jesus is inaccurate and unfair. Yet the New Testament repeatedly speaks of "the Jews" with just such unfair, gross overgeneralization.

I shall cite several examples. And reflect honestly, if you can, upon how you would judge a writer or journalist writing or saying such things today: Would you

---

[1] See Genesis 18:20-33.

[2] See Exodus 32:9-14 and Deuteronomy 9:13-19.

[3] See John 5:16-18 quoted presently in the text. And this, incidentally, would be similar to the behavior of the leadership in other religions—perhaps most famously, Christianity—which at various points in history persecuted and executed not only rebellious personalities perceived as a threat to their leadership, or those openly defying religious convention, but even countless private individuals accused of secret unbelief.

consider him to be engaging even in fair and ethical communication, much less in all-loving kindness and perfect morality?

I Thessalonians 2:14-16 states:

> ...for you suffered the same things from your compatriots as they did from the Jews, who killed both the Lord Jesus and the prophets, and drove us out; they displease God and oppose everyone by hindering us from speaking to the Gentiles so that they may be saved. Thus they have constantly been filling up the measure of their sins; but God's wrath has overtaken them at last.

And John 5:16-18 states:

> Therefore the Jews started persecuting Jesus, because he was doing such things on the Sabbath. But Jesus answered them, "My Father is still working, and I also am working." For these reasons the Jews were seeking all the more to kill him, because he was not only breaking the Sabbath, but was also calling God his own Father, thereby making himself equal to God.

And John 10:31 states:

> The Jews took up stones to stone him. Jesus replied, "I have shown you many good works from the Father. For which of these are you going to stone me?" The Jews answered, "It is not for a good work that we are going to stone you, but for blasphemy, because you, though only a human being, are making yourself God."

And John 19:12 states:

> From then on Pilate tried to release him, but the Jews cried out, "If you release this man, you are no friend of the emperor..."

And in verses 14-15:

> Now it was the day of Preparation for the Passover; and it was about noon. He said to the Jews, "Here is your King!" They cried out, "Away with him! Away with him!" "Crucify him!"

Those are examples of the New Testament's negative and grossly generalized use of the term "the Jews." All of these accounts of reported actions by a small number of people, and by some religious leaders, are referred to as "the Jews" said this or "the Jews" did that. This collective term was used even though, in those days, nearly two thousand years before the advent of modern means of transportation and communication, the vast majority of Jews spread across ancient Israel—not to mention the many Jews living in other lands—would have had no idea about the religious revolutionary being executed along with petty criminals in the capital city.

The great majority of Jews living in Jesus' day not only had nothing to do with his demise, in all likelihood they never even heard of him. Many itinerant preachers and prophets plied their intense trade across ancient Israel, and were similarly unknown to the vast majority of the populace. This may come as a surprise to some devout Christians—who read the New Testament to be teaching that Jesus was the central focus not only of heaven, but of all the earth, too—yet there is no good reason to insist that Jesus was particularly well known while he was alive. Only many years after his death did Christianity, by the authority and sword of the Roman Empire, make the name Jesus famous across the world. Thus it is unlikely that many, outside the relatively small group of people involved in the events, were even aware of who Jesus was, much less of his agonizing end.

My brother, the labeling and attacking of an entire group of people, as the New Testament does, is not only inaccurate, not only unfairly implicates innocents, and not only is in its own right far from a shining example of perfect morality and love, such incontinence has borne bitter and evil fruit—incitement and persecution, murder and mayhem—for many ages[1] and, sadly, may continue to bear such fruit for many generations more. And while the authors of the Bible's irresponsible and crude speech cannot in fairness be held directly accountable for the atrocities such passages have spawned, neither are they completely blameless. And we may certainly conclude that such unkind, unjust words are far, indeed, from reflecting perfect morality.

---

[1] Of course, many Christians—especially in the United States, and especially in recent decades—are admirably tolerant and kind to all groups, including Jews. Indeed, some Christian denominations are more supportive of the State of Israel than are many Jews. And official church policies of all legitimate denominations have long eschewed anti-Semitism. Danger yet lurks, however, in some of the teachings of the New Testament, as evidenced by long and shameful history—history that, if the Bible continues to be taught as sacred, it is not unreasonable to fear may someday repeat itself. And documentation of Christian anti-Semitism over the centuries is extensive and beyond question. For one important book on the subject, see Malcolm Hay's *Europe and the Jews: The Pressure of Christendom on the People of Israel for 1900 years.*

f. New Testament teaching religious or political intolerance, even murder

And the sage continued, saying: Although most of the punitive messages of the New Testament were focused on a future, eternal life, and not on this earthly existence—likely because Jesus and his disciples wielded little to no military or political power in their day[1]—we do find a striking instance in which Jesus directs his disciples to kill those who do not wish to be ruled by him. Luke 19:27[2] has Jesus state:

> But those enemies of mine who did not want me to be king over them—bring them here and kill them in front of me.

And this phrase "who did not want me to be king over them" likely refers to religious kingship, in other words, those who did not believe in Jesus' teachings. But perhaps some would understand the verse to be referring to actual political

---

[1] An interesting parallel and paradox exists in the contrasts between, on the one hand, the disparity in violence and religious persecution in the Bibles of Judaism and Christianity and, on the other hand, the disparity—going in the other direction—in violence and religious persecution in Judaism and Christendom during the two millennia of history, or so, following the close of the Bible. Some Christian apologists point to the religiously-ordained violence in the Old Testament, and see in the mostly terrestrially peaceful approach of the New Testament evidence of Christianity's moral superiority. Some Jewish apologists, for their part, prefer to point to the two millennia following the Bible's close; they note how relatively peaceful Jews have been in post-biblical times, and how frequently were campaigns of religious war and persecution waged by Christians, in the name of the Prince of Peace—and infer from this a moral superiority for Judaism.

The truth on this matter, however—and the solution to the paradox—seems to be related far less to identifying and weighing the sublime contents of either religion's Scriptures or creed, than to the crude reality of opportunity and power. The Old Testament's heroes and immediate audience were—in real life, or at least in the Bible's tales—often in positions of military strength: Moses and Joshua and Samuel and David, and other leaders and prophets and kings, had armies, and the institutions of the state, at their command. So did many Christian countries over the past two millennia. And since power is often abused, it should come as no surprise that Judaism in many ages of the Old Testament, and Christianity in many ages after the close of the biblical era, wielded their power in abusive fashion. But Christians, including Jesus, in the days and pages of the New Testament—and Jews, in the two millennia of post-biblical history—lacking temporal power and unable to make the compelling argument of the sword, spoke instead of peace and compassion, and limited their aggression to promises and fantasies of divine retribution.

[2] I cite this verse from the NIV translation because it makes the meaning most clear to the modern reader, but its treatment of this verse does not differ in substance from other mainstream translations.

rule—that Jesus wanted killed those who would not have him be their political ruler. In any case, whether religious or political, we see in this instance an extreme form of intolerance—perhaps vengefulness—even to the point of advocating murder.

129. Argument that the Bible was morally advanced for its day, so criticism of it is unfair

And a religious man said: You judge the Bible harshly, but its teachings are less cruel and less unfair than those of many other laws and practices of ancient peoples. We must see it in context: For its time, and judged against the cultures of its own day, the Bible was enlightened and moral.

And the sage said: My brother, I agree that we must not be too quick to judge previous ages by the standards of today. Moreover, the Bible has taught many good and kind lessons, and as I have earlier stated and illustrated it is not my aim to characterize it as completely immoral. My objective on this point, my brother, is not to condemn the past, but to help in what small ways I can, to improve the present and the future. I have no interest in branding the Bible or its heroes wholly evil—but I do have an interest in imploring the yet living to more clearly see the range of lessons in the Bible, and to recognize the indignities and dangers of some of its teachings. So in addition to examples of biblical compassion and constructive morality I have cited examples of biblical harshness and extremism to illustrate that—contrary to the earnest claims of many religionists—the Bible, for all its good points, is far from a model of ultimate morality, and far from a text to which we should today look for unerring guidance.

And for those who see the Bible as manifesting the flawless morality of a perfect God, a book whose teachings we and our children must strive to fulfill, and whose heroes we must attempt to emulate, is it truly satisfactory to argue that the Bible was merely less cruel, less unfair, and less immoral than the teachings and practices of many further depraved societies in its barbaric day? If the Bible is truly the word of a transcendent God, is it sufficient for its morality to only somewhat exceed the competing moralities of its deeply flawed age? Should it not be absolutely moral? Moreover, are there not many teachings and teachers—aside from the Bible and its heroes—who were morally advanced beyond most of their generation? Shall we, then, worship these, too?

No, let us rather say with mature candor: Some writings and teachers, inside and outside the Bible and from various cultures and belief systems, have at times kindled lights of wisdom and compassion that partially dispelled the prevailing darkness of their day, but other writings and teachers, inside and outside the Bible, have at other times extinguished what candles were already lit, and spread fear and hatred in the unnecessary dark. And thus it is that we may learn but cautiously from these imperfect sources, not holding up such texts as ideal guides for conduct—nor overly reverencing their authors, nor confidently emulating their heroes, nor worshiping with the eager masses their gods.

130. Sub-argument that the Bible was given to people who would not have accepted true morality, and for this reason teaches less than perfectly moral behavior

But the religious man persisted and said: When you say the Bible should be perfectly moral, you speak like a starry-eyed idealist. The Bible was originally given to people steeped in a backward culture, people who would not have accepted true morality. We must recognize the limitations of human nature; nations cannot transform their ways in an instant. Therefore, the Bible only mandated partial improvements—even though these do not represent the truly perfect moral sense of God.[1]

And the sage responded: My brother, the argument you raise seems, at first glance, intelligent and subtle. Yet if we examine the matter closely, does it truly persuade? First, remember that the Bible has God burdening the Israelites—during those forty years in the desert, between exiting Egypt and entering Canaan—with all manner of difficult and restrictive new laws. Does it truly stand to reason that the people were capable of accepting those hundreds of laws encroaching on every area of their lives, but that they would not have accepted laws against atrocities, such as slavery, mass murder, and genocide?

Let us listen in on a conversation between two ancient Israelites. Says Nahbi to Amiel: "Amiel, my friend, all these new laws are hard to accept and to remember—who would have thought that freedom from Egyptian slavery would bring so many new obligations and restrictions?—but I can abide by them. I may no longer cut my hair a certain way? Very well. I cannot have my way with various relatives, or anyone else's wife? I will abide by that. Even when hungry I cannot eat pig or camel or eagle or various other animals and birds and sea-food—nor can I partake of fat or blood? Fine. I have to be rid of all bread and yeast for a week of Passover every year, and instead eat flat bread? All is well. For

---

[1] Ingersoll, in chapter 6 of a short work titled *Some Reasons Why*, responded to a similar argument as follows: "I suppose if we now wished to break a cannibal of the bad habit of devouring missionaries, we would first induce him to cook them in a certain way, saying: 'To eat cooked missionary is one step in advance of eating your missionary raw. After a few years, a little mutton could be cooked with missionary, and year after year the amount of mutton could be increased and the amount of missionary decreased, until in the fullness of time the dish could be entirely mutton, and after that the missionaries would be absolutely safe.'"

another week out of the year I must live in a hut? This is no problem. I am required to travel across the country to God's one temple three times a year for worship? Fine. I have to leave various parts of my harvest in the field for the poor? Very well. I cannot eat the fruit of my trees during their first few years? This is no problem. I have to cut the foreskin off each of my baby sons? That is easy. I must abstain from enjoying my wife at various times? Fine. I must wear reminders of God on my arm and head? That is no difficulty. I must bring animal sacrifices to the priests at the temple, for various causes and occasions? Fine. I need to put blue strings on the corners of my garments? Fine. I need to post sacred scrolls on the doorposts of my home? Very well. I am required to fast on the Day of Atonement? Good. I am no longer allowed to worship other gods? Very well. If I accidentally touch a dead person or animal I am ritually impure for a time, and must undergo elaborate rituals, and bring a sacrifice to become acceptable again? Fine. One day each week, the Sabbath day, I am forbidden to do work, and if I do work I am to be put to death? Also fine. For various other sins I get put to death, too? This is no problem. Every seventh year I am not allowed to plant my fields, but must keep them lying fallow—though I do not know where I will get food to eat? This is no problem. I cannot oppress the widow and orphan? Fine. I cannot charge interest when loaning money to my neighbor? Very well. As a judge I am forbidden to take bribes, and can favor neither the rich man nor the poor? Good. I must even be kind to my enemy's donkey? Fine. And the hundreds of other commandments God has given us? I say to these, all is well. But I tell you, Amiel, even I have my limits. Can you believe that God has now forbidden slavery, genocide, and mass murder? I will not agree. I cannot agree! This time, God has gone too far!"

Come, now, my brother, let us not stretch credulity.

Furthermore, even if you continue to claim, for reasons I cannot see, that these commandments would have been harder for the Israelites to accept than the others the Bible says they did accept, could not God have performed astonishing miracles, impression upon the people an overpowering terror at His might? The God of the Bible, who split the sea, turned the Nile to blood, and killed Egyptian first-borns at the stroke of midnight, along with various other awe-inspiring feats—would this Great God, this Father in heaven, with powers unlimited and love unbounded, not have even one miracle remaining for the great mission of forbidding his people to engage in atrocities and oppression?

For one example: Surely, in the immediate aftermath of the great drama of the supernatural, God could have mandated to the terrified Israelites even as culturally alien an innovation as the complete and sudden abolition of slavery, and a people in the grip of miracle's wonder—especially a people recently themselves the victims of slavery—would have obeyed.

And Jesus and the apostles in the New Testament, too, with as many signs and wonders as they are said to have performed, and in such ways as to have convinced so many of the divine truth of their words, could they not have spared a few miracles to teach against slavery, against collective guilt and scapegoating, and against notions of eternal torture?

And, for any nation, only the first generation or two requires reeducation. Had the Israelites or the early Christians been taught higher standards of morality, their progeny and ensuing generations, who would have been born into societies prohibiting human bondage and other injustices, would have accepted such existent laws as familiar and reasonable, and would no longer have required extreme measures to support these pillars of individual dignity and social morality—for the only societies they would have known would have been those in which such deeds were forbidden and considered immoral.

Furthermore, and perhaps most compelling, if we accept your argument—that the Bible includes teachings inconsistent with God's true will; teachings inferior and incomplete, reflective of the cultural limitations of biblical ages; teachings that do not constitute moral standards for later generations including our own—how, then, can we be certain that any of the Bible's teachings are relevant instruction for our day? Perhaps all manner of other biblical lessons are also not meant for contemporary times, but were merely necessary to deal with the relatively uneducated and backward cultures of the distant past.

Indeed—to extend the argument to its ultimate and provocative application—perhaps the very notions that God wants us to follow His laws or have faith in Him are, in light of our current advancements, limited and outdated. Just as a good father insists on obedience from his son only until the boy is grown, now that large portions of humanity have attained the maturity of ethical democracy and enlightened individualism, perhaps God prefers that we take responsibility for ourselves, that we not eagerly surrender our freedom to masters and kings and gods, but rather that we understand our accountability, as individuals and societies, to cultivate wisdom and sound judgment and to decide for ourselves—with no help or interference from the Divine—on how best to live.

My brother, in light of the examples of the cruelty and immorality commanded or condoned in the Bible, it would seem that believers are left with only two choices: Either the Bible cannot be the word of God, because God is fair, merciful, and all-loving—or the Bible *is* the word of God, and He is apparently not always fair, merciful, and loving.

131. Argument that if we were able to see what God sees, we would realize that the entire Bible is moral

And another man said: We should be humble and realize that we cannot understand God's intentions and value judgments when He lays down His laws and teachings in the Bible. But if we could see what God sees, we would realize that the entire Bible is not only moral, but is the expression of highest morality.

And the sage said: My brother, in considering any matter, we must separate what we know from what we hope to ascertain or wish to prove. In this case, we must concede that we do not know—in any responsible sense of the word—that the Bible was written or inspired or approved by God. Indeed, these are some of the central points a seeker attempts to determine.

In our discussions on these matters, I have, among other observations, called attention to some of the Bible's cruel and apparently immoral teachings—in both the Old Testament and the New—to illustrate that many of the sensibilities upon which the Bible was based are not what we today would consider moral. And these observations should, in turn, cause us to examine far more carefully how we came to be so confident, and whether we can continue to justifiably believe, that the Bible is the literal or inspired word of an all-loving God. Such caution is all the more warranted if we respect a possible God and wish to avoid falsely attributing to Him degrading or destructive teachings.

Thus, my brother, your argument falls short unless one already assumes the conclusion that the Bible is the word of God, after which one may wish to insist that God has reasons we cannot understand, and that even what seem like His atrocities—not to mention His instances of mere unfairness—are perfectly moral. But do such arguments illustrate anything more than how vulnerable we are as humans to unjust and inconsistent thinking in defense of our cherished beliefs?

For we are now engaged in exploring whether we can believe the Bible derives from God. And as part of that process we are examining the Bible's morality. To say, then, that its teachings are from God, and they are moral, and that if we only had the vision of God we would see their high morality, is assuming as your premise a conclusion on the very matter we are attempting to determine—whether God wrote the Bible. Is this not circular reasoning?

132. Argument that even if it does not seem so to us, the Bible is moral, because whatever comes from God is, by definition, moral

But another religious man said: You can question God's actions in the Bible, if you like, and condemn His commandments and call them immoral. But your judgments about what is moral have no bearing on whether God wrote the Bible. God is the very source and arbiter of morality. Therefore, whatever God does or says is, by definition, moral. Thus, since God wrote the Bible, the Bible is, by definition, moral.[1]

And the sage replied: My brother, at first hearing—especially if we set aside the obvious problem that you are assuming what you cannot possibly know: that the Bible was written by God—your words seem to ring with creative logic. Let us, however, listen more closely.

Consider this: Even if unassailable proof of the Bible's divine origin or inspiration were forthcoming, and one insisted that God defines morality, and that the Bible is, therefore, regardless of its contents, moral, this would lead to the inevitable conclusion that genocide and slavery, and many lesser outrages, can be moral. But upon a moment's further reflection, does defining morality this way not become a mere confusion of words, a game of semantics?

And, yes, some of what may be designated as good or bad behavior is arbitrary, and subject to differing interpretations. Whether one may work on the Sabbath, indeed, whether there should be a Sabbath, and if so, which day of the week should it be; what forms of assistance the community must provide to the individual, and what forms of deference and conformity the individual must provide the community; which crimes are to be punished, and what should those punishments be; these and many others are matters about which the moral judgments of different cultures can legitimately differ. For such rules are not based upon any inherent laws of human nature and, as such, different positions on them may be compatible with stable societies and peace between nations.

Some behaviors, however, such as the aforementioned genocide and slavery, so deeply violate human instinctual needs, so predictably bring about suffering and enmity, and so undeniably degrade the human spirit, that especially with the advance of humanistic values—including seeing those of other nations as fully human—we may confidently classify such deeds as improper, and very unwise.

For whatever else we may wish to subsume under the category of wise and appropriate behavior, surely we must include that which fosters peaceful and stable interactions between men and nations. Men and nations—unlike religion's gods and their heavens and hells—we responsibly know to exist, and the seeking of guidelines for constructive living requires that we find ways for humans to coexist with far more harmony than strife, and to inculcate in themselves and each other a sense of dignity for what it means to be human.

And so, if in characterizing behavior as appropriate, we mean, among other basic principles, doing unto others as we would have them do unto us—the most

---

[1] This relates to what Plato has Socrates asking Euthyphro (in Plato's work by that name): "The point which I should first wish to understand is whether the pious or holy is beloved by the gods because it is holy, or holy because it is beloved of the gods."

straightforward rule for goodwill, and the self-evident basis of the social contract inscribed on each of our hearts—is it not clear that owning fellow humans as one owns cattle, and most especially putting to the sword every man, woman, child, and beast of conquered cities, cannot be consistent with an admirable approach, regardless of who it is that commands or condones such behavior?

Thus, even if we knew that God wrote the Bible, would this preclude some of its teachings from being legitimately seen, especially in later generations, as inappropriate? True, if God exists, He can overwhelm us with His power—but does that necessarily make all His actions and teachings admirable? Can we truly consider ourselves high-minded if we believe that might makes right? Neither does high intelligence, even omniscience, guarantee moral superiority.

Indeed, even Abraham, the first of the patriarchs in the Old Testament did not assume that all God's deeds must axiomatically be appropriate; for this reason he implored God, in the case of Sodom, to be just and not kill the good along with the wicked, saying in Genesis 18:25:

> Far be it from you to do such a thing—to kill the righteous with the wicked, treating the righteous and the wicked alike. Far be it from you! Will not the Judge of all the earth do right?

Clearly, then, Abraham, one of the heroes of the Bible, in attempting to influence God into changing His mind and doing "right," was not assuming that everything God wished to do was, by definition, right.

My brother, if we can agree upon certain bare basics of morality—behavior conducive to human coexistence and wellbeing—such as seeing genocide and slavery and vindictive torture as bad, then the Bible, a book commanding or condoning genocide and slavery, even eternal torture, should be designated as far from perfectly moral for us, regardless of who was its author.[1]

133. Argument that all systems of morality are subjective and equally valid, and therefore it is shallow and misinformed to judge the morality of the Bible

And a religious university professor said: You speak as though there is some objective standard of morality. But once you reject God's teachings you must concede that all systems of morality are subjective, and therefore equally valid. So by your own secular standards it is nothing but shallow and misinformed for you to say that the Bible's morality is inferior to any other system of morality.

---

[1] For more discussion on morality without supernatural religion, see Part IX, beginning with section 159.

And the sage said: My brother, let us agree that the matter of morality and its bases is complex, and does not lend itself to easy formulations. It is too easy to judge the morality of one age or culture by the myopic lights of another,[1] and deceptively easy, too, to assume we can find logically compelling first principles.

Yet we need not judge another age to make wise decisions about our own. Whatever may have been the moral judgment of days bygone, my brother, we need not conclude that what the Bible teaches is, today and for us, equal in its morality to every other standard—especially when, on some matters, the Bible includes words or deeds or teachings that if uttered or enacted or taught by men today would be excoriated by nearly everyone, and seen as deeply immoral.

My brother, many have argued that all morality is subjective, that morality cannot be absolutely decided for all time, but is dependent upon the changing sensibilities of each culture and age, and that all systems of morality are equally valid. Others have argued, however—even without basing themselves on religion—that at least some tenets of morality can rest upon bedrock foundations approaching a standard of objectivity, tenets widely agreed to be conducive to human coexistence and wellbeing.

Even if one holds that morality cannot be founded upon unchanging principles, but depends upon shifting and evolving views of right and wrong, this does not mean that, in any given context or age, one must see all things as equally good and bad, with no behaviors better or worse than any others.

I ask you: Is it not our duty today to engage—as the noble of previous generations have, and as the best of our posterity will—in serious thought as to what our highest efforts and instincts, our best understanding and evidence, tell us is right? And would it not be irresponsible to evade such existential labor by

---

[1] Thoreau, in *Walden*, writes: "Whatever my own practice may be, I have no doubt that it is a part of the destiny of the human race, in its gradual improvement, to leave off eating animals, as surely as the savage tribes have left off eating each other when they came in contact with the more civilised." If he is correct, and such a vegetarian ethic takes firm hold upon the practice and conscience of most humans, those generations will look back at an era such as ours—an era that has long since judged the mass murder and slavery of humans as atrocities, but blithely owns and slaughters cows and chickens and other animals for our food and comfort—as benighted and barbaric. And, indeed, if the collective moral judgment of an age concludes that eating animals is wrong, a book permitting animal slaughter for food could not be considered a morally perfect light for that later age, or for all time. Thus, though we cannot in fairness judge the writers of the Bible to have been, for their time, immoral and blameworthy—and we cannot prevent future ages from possibly seeing our standards of morality as inferior to standards that may develop decades and centuries after we are gone—we can state with confidence that for ourselves, our children, our neighbors and our societies, the Bible, in teaching slavery, mass murder, eternal hell and more, cannot be a perfect moral guide for our time.

pretending to know that the Bible was written by God, and that its unchanging contents remain the best morality for all time? Indeed, have not even the Bible-believing religions changed their moral teachings a good deal over the centuries, by issuing religious rulings and providing legalistic or theological justifications to forbid what the Bible allowed, and to allow what the Bible clearly forbade?[1]

And if, on the other hand, one believes that morality can, indeed, rest upon at least a few objective or close-to-objective standards which are universally seen to be beneficial to humans as individuals and societies and conducive to human coexistence and wellbeing—such that, to name several examples, clear violations of morality would include slavery, mass murder, and genocide—then the Bible fails as an unerring guide to morality even in its own day, but certainly in ours.

And, my brother: If a book approving even of mass murder and genocide and slavery and eternal torture can be held up as a moral exemplar, what possible book—or what possible ideology or teaching—can ever be said to be immoral? And if humans will consider such atrocities moral merely because an unproved and much disputed tradition—originating deep in the ages of widespread ignorance and rampant superstition—says that a supernatural being taught these things, I ask you my brother, how far have we really advanced from barbarism, and how shall we avoid sliding back into its violent and brutish pit?

Yet as repugnant as are some passages of Scripture, religions do not generally edit their foundational documents, or even criticize their historically significant authorities or heroes—perhaps because once one begins to concede flaws in a tradition, the entire premise of the tradition being unquestionably correct comes into doubt, a prospect many find terrifying. So it should not surprise us that religious Jews and Christians and Muslims—and those aligned with all manner of other faiths—will reflexively defend, with whatever admixture of reason and

---

[1] Selected examples, from among many, of each: In Jewish religious law these past many centuries polygamy has been forbidden, a practice the Bible implicitly and explicitly condoned; Jewish religious law has also allowed, through legalistic maneuvers, the charging of interest on loans—something the Old Testament explicitly forbids. As for Christian religious teachings, while the New Testament directs women to be silent in church, and criticizes divorce, some denominations have "strayed" so far as to have female pastors or ministers regularly give speeches to the entire congregation; and many churches accept divorce and even provide divorce support groups. Yet slavery, nowhere prohibited in the New Testament—indeed several passages actively encourage slaves to be loyal and respectful to their masters—has been for generations deeply abhorrent to mainstream Christian religious sensibilities, and anathema in practice.

passion they can generate, the foundational texts and venerated writings their people have historically held dear.

Religion is, for many, in the storm of complexity and strife, a boat keeping them afloat on the high existential seas; when shown the rotting boards beneath their feet, most will choose any alternative over removing these boards; perhaps they can be painted, or covered with pleasing fabric, or, better yet, interpreted not as rotted, but instead the very epitome of what good wood should be—if only one knew the real nature of wood, which surely the builders of the boat knew, but which we should not be so arrogant as to assume we know. Religionists very much suspect that removing any original or integral part of the boat will commence the waters rushing in—and perhaps in this they are correct. But they are mistaken for assuming that they must remain on the old boat. They can learn to build more sea-worthy vessels, perhaps even walk on water.

134. The character and nature of God in the Old Testament

And a man said: Perhaps there are laws or stories in the Old Testament that do not reflect the highest morality for all time. But surely the nature and character of God Himself, as described in the Old Testament, is perfect, all-powerful, all-knowing, all-loving, and beyond reproach!

And the sage replied: My brother, if we are to believe the Bible that God commanded certain laws and actions which we would consider immoral, does that not reflect upon the moral character of God?

Still, I agree with you that many biblical passages in the Old Testament speak of a loving and just and perfect, all-knowing God. I will mention several such passages—but then I shall ask you to consider other passages, which seem to tell a different story.

The following several passages speak of God's goodness and mercy. Exodus 34:6 states:

> And the Lord passed by before him, and proclaimed, The Lord, The Lord God, merciful and gracious, longsuffering, and abundant in goodness and truth...

Exodus 22:26-27 states:

> If thou at all take thy neighbour's raiment to pledge, thou shalt deliver it unto him by that the sun goeth down: For that is his covering only, it is his raiment for his skin: wherein shall he sleep? and it shall come to pass, when he crieth unto me, that I will hear; for I am gracious.

Deuteronomy 4:31 states:

> For the Lord thy God is a merciful God; he will not forsake thee, neither destroy thee, nor forget the covenant of thy fathers which he sware unto them.

Isaiah 54:7-12 speaks of God's mercy and benevolence:

> For a small moment have I forsaken thee; but with great mercies will I gather thee. In a little wrath I hid my face from thee for a moment; but with everlasting kindness will I have mercy on thee, saith the Lord thy Redeemer. For this is as the waters of Noah unto me: for as I have sworn that the waters of Noah should no more go over the earth; so have I sworn that I would not be wroth with thee, nor rebuke thee. For the mountains shall depart, and the hills be removed; but my kindness shall not depart from thee, neither shall the covenant of my peace be removed, saith the Lord that hath mercy on thee. O thou afflicted, tossed with tempest, and not comforted, behold, I will lay thy stones with fair colours, and lay thy foundations with sapphires. And I will make thy windows of agates, and thy gates of carbuncles, and all thy borders of pleasant stones.

Joel 2:13 states:

> ...and turn unto the Lord your God: for he is gracious and merciful, slow to anger, and of great kindness, and repenteth him of the evil.

Jonah 4:2 states:

> ...Therefore I fled before unto Tarshish: for I knew that thou art a gracious God, and merciful, slow to anger, and of great kindness, and repentest thee of the evil.

Psalms 86:15 states:

> But thou, O Lord, art a God full of compassion, and gracious, long suffering, and plenteous in mercy and truth.

Psalms 103:8 states:

> The Lord is merciful and gracious, slow to anger, and plenteous in mercy.

MICHAEL WILLIAM POSNER

Psalms 111:4 states
...the Lord is gracious and full of compassion.

Psalms 116:5 states:

Gracious is the Lord, and righteous; yea, our God is merciful.

Psalms 145:8-9,17 states:

The Lord is gracious, and full of compassion; slow to anger, and of great mercy.
The Lord is good to all: and his tender mercies are over all his works...The
Lord is righteous in all his ways, and holy in all his works.

And Psalms 139:7-13 seems to speak of God's omnipresence when it states:

Where can I go from your Spirit? Where can I flee from your presence? If I go
up to the heavens, you are there; if I make my bed in the depth, you are there.
If I rise on the wings of the dawn, if I settle on the far side of the sea, even
there your hand will guide me, your right hand will hold me fast. If I say,
"Surely the darkness will hide me and the light become night around me," even
the darkness will not be dark to you; the night will shine like the day, for darkness is as light to you. For you created my inmost being; you knit me together
in my mother's womb.[1]

My brother, these and many other passages in the Old Testament speak of
God's greatness and love, and present Him to us as holy and moral and of great
knowledge and power.

Yet, my brother, what shall we do if truth insists we look not only at that
which agrees with our views, but also at that which challenges our views—
whether or not we wish such things were so? In our honest seeking we have no
choice but to examine everything the Bible says about God, not only those
passages that reinforce our theology or whisper to us of consolation and love.

My brother, the nature of God as described in the Bible is far from always
omnipotent or omniscient, and far from always what we ordinarily mean when

---

[1] This passage is from the New International Version's translation of the Bible. I
depart from my usual (aesthetic) preference for the King James translation because in
verse 7 KJV translates the Hebrew word "Sheol" as "hell." This is confusing, perhaps
misleading, because, as discussed elsewhere in this volume, the Hebrew Bible, unlike the
New Testament—and, incidentally, unlike later rabbinic Judaism, too—does not teach of
an afterlife where people get rewarded or punished.

we use the word moral—on the whole, rather unlike the good and all-powerful deity of which many religionists speak.

Genesis 6:5-7 states:

> And God saw that the wickedness of man was great in the earth, and that every imagination of the thoughts of his heart was only evil continually. And it repented the Lord that he had made man on the earth, and it grieved him at his heart. And the Lord said, I will destroy man whom I have created from the face of the earth; both man, and beast, and the creeping thing, and the fowls of the air; for it repenteth me that I have made them.

God is not here depicted as omniscient: He apparently did not foresee that man would be evil, for upon such a turn of events God became profoundly sad, reflecting surprise and disappointment. Furthermore, had God originally foreseen mankind's descent into evil, He would not, when such wickedness became manifest, have regretted creating them.

Second, the aforementioned passage, in which the story of the flood is introduced, recounts how God chose to obliterate civilization—rather than attempting to teach humans right from wrong. The Creator deluges the world, causing horrible suffering, and killing an untold number of souls with nary an attempt to reform mankind for the better.

Third, answer me this my brother: Could infants and animals have knowingly chosen evil, and been deserving of punishment? Yet were they not all destroyed, according to the biblical story of the flood, in an act of indiscriminate, collective "justice"?

Fourth, God is portrayed as a being of fickle judgment, easily influenced by sensual delight—and, perhaps, by the flattery of worship: On the great moral issue of whether to destroy all life, He is shown changing His mind—upon smelling a pleasant aroma. Noah and his family, after disembarking from the ark, had built an altar and sacrificed a burnt offering to God. Genesis 8:21 states:

> And the Lord smelled a sweet savour; and the Lord said in his heart, I will not again curse the ground any more for man's sake; for the imagination of man's heart is evil from his youth; neither will I again smite any more every thing living, as I have done.

Fifth, God seems to have learned from these events and changed His view about the appropriateness of bringing a catastrophic deluge upon the entire world. And the reason God gives for committing to no longer curse the ground is a reason an omniscient being would have known before smelling the "sweet savour"—indeed, before bringing a flood upon earth. Does this God of Noah's flood seem all knowing? Does one who has always known everything ever learn new things, and does an omniscient, omnipotent being ever regret past decisions?

Sixth, as recounted in Genesis 18:20-32, God was apparently willing to destroy the city of Sodom-Gomorrah and have the righteous perish along with the guilty. Abraham intercedes with God and persuades Him to spare the city if within it could be found fifty righteous people. When God consents, Abraham pleads for the city's safety even if fewer than fifty were to be found. Gradually Abraham influences God to spare the city even if it held only ten good people. Throughout this incident, however, it is Abraham, not God, who tries to prevent the good from being destroyed with the evil.

Seventh, would a God of boundless compassion and unlimited knowledge allow people to suffer under the cruelty of slavery and persecution, including the murder of all their infant sons, and not help them until they cried out? Would a man be considered perfectly moral who withheld desperately needed assistance until he heard screams and groans? Yet in first two chapters of Exodus the Bible describes the terrible suffering endured by the Israelites over a period of many years, including harsh slavery and Pharaoh's decree that all male Israelite children be put to death. Either God knew about it and did nothing and was therefore not merciful, or He did not know about it, and was therefore not omniscient. Only when the Israelites cried out did He seem to take an interest in their plight. Even then, God apparently intervened only because He had, generations earlier, entered into a covenant with their ancestors. Exodus 2:23-24 states:

> And it came to pass in process of time, that the king of Egypt died: and the children of Israel sighed by reason of the bondage, and they cried, and their cry came up unto God by reason of the bondage. And God heard their groaning, and God remembered his covenant with Abraham, with Isaac, and with Jacob.

Eighth, throughout the course of the ten plagues God brought upon Egypt, it was not only the Egyptian king and others in power who were punished, but the common and powerless people who had little or nothing to do with keeping the Israelites in bondage were punished, too. In addition, not only the adults of Egypt were made to suffer terribly, but also the children. The miraculous punishments of blood, frogs, lice, swarms, plague, boils, hail, locusts, darkness, and the dying of first-borns affected all non-Israelites in Egypt, indiscriminately; even prisoners and cattle lost their first-born to death. Exodus 12:29-30 states:

> And it came to pass that at midnight the Lord smote all the firstborn in the land of Egypt, from the firstborn of Pharaoh that sat on his throne unto the first-

born of the captive that was in the dungeon; and all the firstborn of cattle. And Pharaoh rose up in the night, he and all his servants, and all the Egyptians; and there was a great cry in Egypt; for there was not a house where there was not one dead.

My brother, would not a compassionate and omnipotent God have rather targeted His punishments only at Pharaoh, his officers, and other guilty parties?

Ninth, the Bible recounts that shortly after the Israelites left Egypt, Moses went up on Mount Sinai, and that when his return was delayed the people fashioned a golden calf and worshiped it. For this, God wished to destroy all the Israelites, but Moses begged and persuaded Him not to do so. Exodus 32:9-12:

> And the Lord said unto Moses, I have seen this people, and behold it is a stiff-necked people. Now therefore let me alone, that my wrath may wax hot against them, and that I may consume them; and I will make of thee a great nation. And Moses besought the Lord his God and said Lord, why doth thy wrath wax hot against thy people, which thou hast brought forth of the land of Egypt with great power, and with a mighty hand? Why should the Egyptians speak and say, For mischief did he bring them out, to slay them in the mountains, and to consume them from the face of the earth? Turn from thy fierce wrath, and change your mind of this evil against thy people.

The Bible recounts that God did, indeed, change His mind and refrain from destroying the Israelites. Yet note that Moses did not even appeal to God's mercy. Rather, he argued that God, if He killed the Israelites, would ruin His own reputation with the Egyptians. So it happened, once again, that a human needed to persuade God not to kill indiscriminately. And, to protect His reputation God might refrain from killing an entire nation, but to be merciful and non-murderous was apparently insufficient cause to restrain Himself. In this story God comes across as neither compassionate nor confident, but as cruel, prideful, and insecure. He is also portrayed as being prone to fierce anger that flares unpredictably and can be soothed by a diplomatic human. In this biblical story, God is a picture not of rock-like stability, but of emotional volatility. Nor does the God of this story seem to possess foreknowledge and omniscience—or He would not have initially wished to do one thing and later, after hearing the arguments of Moses, changed His mind.[1]

---

[1] Moses repeats this story to the Israelites in Deuteronomy, as part of his long farewell set of addresses to the Israelites. This indicates that, consistent with the plain sense of these verses, the original event was not merely a leadership lesson or test for Moses, in

Tenth, as mentioned in our discussion of the Hebrew Bible's morality, God commands and condones the genocides of various populations—the native peoples of Canaan, as well as the people of Amalek for all generations. Does this not reflect a set of values, which if espoused by humans, we would consider barbaric?

In addition, as discussed, God condoned slavery; God allowed the selling of one's daughter; God commanded the death penalty for homosexual acts; God commanded extreme religious intolerance, including smashing the altars and worship objects of other religions, and putting to death any Israelite who worshiped another God; God commanded inequality of rights for women; and God commanded, too, the death penalty for rebellious adolescents, for anyone working on the Sabbath, for those committing adultery, practicing witchcraft, or engaging in various other behaviors seen as sinful.

In sum, my brother, the God portrayed in the Old Testament is far from the all-powerful, all-knowing, all-loving deity of which some religions teach. Yes, there are passages in which He is portrayed as powerful and knowledgeable and loving, the protector of widows and orphans, and responsive to earnest prayer. But these same books of the Bible portray Him, too—at times—as intolerant, quick to kill, prone to fits of anger, open to persuasion and flattery, surprised at the consequences of His actions, and approving of various injustices, degrading practices, even atrocities.

135. Defense of God in the Old Testament: Argument that the Bible "spoke in the language of humans," and far from being flawed, is actually a superior manuscript

And a religious scholar said: Your arguments are simplistic and unfair. For two thousand years and more, religious commentaries have explained that when the Bible describes God becoming angry, changing His mind, or being surprised at how events turn out, the Bible was simply using figures of speech to which humans can relate. The Talmud and other commentaries repeatedly state in discussing biblical verses that the Bible was merely speaking in the language of

---

which a compassionate God who never would have killed the Israelites only threatened to do so in order to give Moses the opportunity to advocate for his people. Moses—by the Bible's characterization the most humble of men—would not have recounted the story in order to brag of the excellence of his leadership. Instead, he tells the story as straightforward history and as a means of reinforcing the warnings against idolatry, in reminding the people of God's readiness to kill the entire nation save Moses as the natural consequence of the worship of the golden calf.

humans.[1] Thus, any biblical descriptions of God as less than all-powerful and all knowing do not disturb me. For God is truly omnipotent and omniscient—and the Bible was speaking not about God's true nature, thoughts, or feelings, but rather about how human beings might conceive of such matters. So not only are there good answers to all your questions, but the very things you see as problems in the Bible are actually ways in which the Bible was superior to other texts. In this case, the anthropomorphic passages may seem to depict a less than perfect, less than all-powerful, less than all-knowing God, but that is only to make God's word, the Bible, more accessible to its human audience, which relates better to human-like characters. In truth, however, God and His word are perfect.

And the sage replied: My brother, yes, intelligent believers have for long centuries insisted that any indication from the Bible that God is less than omniscient, omnipotent, and all loving, is not to be taken literally. Yet such a defense on the part of philosophically educated believers is not necessarily accurate. Consider the matter closely, and judge for yourself what seems reasonable. If the God of the Five Books of Moses is above experiencing emotions, and if He always sees into the future, why could the Bible not tell us these things? Why disguise the truth in inferior costume? Humans are certainly capable of more elevated understanding—indeed, as you point out, theologians and believing philosophers have been teaching God's omniscience and omnipotence for ages.

And if the greatest part of early generations—those who are said to have witnessed the miraculous events of which the Bible speaks—were so primitive

---

[1] The Talmud states this many times, and in a number of tractates—a few examples being Berachot 31b, Yebamot 71a, and Ketubot 67b—though usually in the service of explaining why the Bible was not as concise as it could have been in a particular phrase, and justifying why one need not infer that the Bible meant to teach additional lessons by each seemingly unnecessary word.

Yet many religious commentaries have undeniably offered creative and non-literal explanations for everything from the Bible's seeming redundancies to its unlikely miracle tales. For one prominent and ancient example, Philo of Alexandria, a Jewish contemporary of Jesus, famously explained many accounts of the Bible in allegorical fashion, an approach significantly influenced by Greek philosophy.

And down through the centuries, alongside their more literalist brethren and fellow scholars, some religious teachers have emphasized reason and symbol and allegory and metaphor over strict adherence to the naked meaning of the text.

Deviating from a literal understanding of the Bible, then, is far from a modern innovation. But the relevant question for the seeker on such matters is not whether, and for how many centuries, creative, non-literal interpretations have been advanced in defense of the Bible, but rather whether, when seen in the light of our best reason and evidence, such defenses would truly cause us to be persuaded that the book is the word of a supernatural Creator.

that they could only conceive of a God manifesting the character and intelligence of a tribal despot, and so were taught in anthropomorphic ways instead of the plain truth, why should we trust such underdeveloped minds in such backward cultures to have effectively understood the events they witnessed, and to have accurately transmitted to their descendents God's word and will?

Moreover, if in various stories the Bible did not tell us the truth about God—but rather painted gross distortions of God for literary effect, or so that some could better relate to the text—how can we trust the Bible's accuracy on anything else? Perhaps many or all of the Bible's accounts of miracles, commandments, and ethics supposedly ordered by God are not true either; perhaps the Bible spoke inaccurately on its central principles, too, in order to speak "in the language of humans" of more primitive days, or to reach and exert influence upon a wide audience of the simple-minded in every age.

Indeed, if previous eras—and the unsophisticated masses of every era—could not relate to the truth of God's transcendence, and therefore the Bible spoke to them inaccurately, perhaps the entire Bible and its teachings were only meant for such primitives, those of inferior intellect and education, unable to conceive of an omniscient and transcendent God—perhaps none of the Bible is meant for sophisticated people in our more enlightened age.

In short, my brother, ask yourself whether it will truly do to explain away the Bible's straightforward words; for can we in all fairness and good intellectual conscience pick and choose when the Bible means what it says and when it does not? And, my brother, does offering such "answers" truly satisfy the questions, much less replace doubts with evidence of superiority and excellence?[1]

---

[1] A traditional Jewish joke tells how a persistent matchmaker tries to interest a young man in a particular girl. After hearing the name, the young man asks, "Isn't her family poor? I'm also poor; so how will we raise a family?" "Yes," replied the matchmaker, "she is poor, but she'll therefore all the better appreciate your income." "But," protested the young man, "I hear that she's an angry person who constantly screams." "Well," said the matchmaker, "but that's an advantage, because if you marry her you won't be visited as much by pesky peddlers. They'll want to avoid her." "I don't mean to be unkind," said the young man, "but she's not at all attractive." "True," said the matchmaker, "but don't you see? That's better, because other men won't be envious of you." "But," said the young man, "she's a hunchback!" "So?" answered the matchmaker, "Your house will be clean. She's already bent over, so if something drops it will be easier for her to pick it up." "But," said the young man, "she's been married already three times and all of her husbands died within a year of marrying her! I'm afraid she's bad luck." "Yes," said the matchmaker, "her first three husbands died quickly, but surely this means if you marry her you'll live a long life; because what are the odds of that happening to four husbands in a row?" Exasperated, the young man said, "But she has only one leg!" At this, the matchmaker throws up his hands and says, "What—*everything* you want?"

136. Argument that God of the Bible is fair, merciful, and all-loving but that we cannot comprehend His ways

And a kind woman said: Do not speak such words. God is indeed just, merciful, and all-loving but we simply do not comprehend His ways. Perhaps what seems cruel to us is actually compassionate, when understood in the deepest, broadest sense—a perspective only visible to God.

And the sage said: My dear sister, I applaud the earnest gentleness from which such a statement arises, but I must differ with the statement itself.

It would be another matter if we knew for certain that the deity described in the Bible truly existed, and was who the Bible says He was, and said and did the things the Bible claims He said and did. But we have no such legitimate certainty. We know of the Bible's God only from the Bible. Thus it is from the Bible that we must form our opinion of this supposed God. And what else can we do but use our best understanding to see how the Bible describes its God?

If it is legitimate for a Christian or Jew to disregard what the Bible says about its God, and instead cling to what later apologists and theologians have said, why is it any less legitimate for Muslims to disregard any reservations about what the Koran actually says, or members of the Church of Jesus Christ of Latter Day Saints to shrug off reservations about what the Book of Mormon actually says, indeed why cannot anyone disregard what any book actually says—and instead insist that its apparent flaws and incongruities, and its apparent lack of supernatural qualities, are only due to our own faulty and meager minds, and that its "true" meaning is wonderful and ideal, but beyond our abilities to comprehend?

My sister, if biblical accounts of God mandating slavery and genocide, and being appeased by the aroma of burnt sacrifices and deciding to never again extinguish all life, and being persuaded not to kill the entire Israelite nation lest the Egyptians think less of Him, are to be judged compassionate merely because the Bible is believed to be God's word—when if found in other books such laws and behaviors would be seen as primitive barbarism—then surely the Bible's God is not just, merciful, or all-loving in any reasonable sense of those terms. And is it not merely twisting words, and our own integrity, to claim that He is?

137. The character of Jesus in the New Testament

And a Christian woman said: I have heard that the God of the Old Testament was cruel and full of wrath, but surely the character of Jesus, as presented in the New Testament, is exemplary and pure!

And the sage replied, saying: Indeed, my sister, many passages of the New Testament portray Jesus as embodying gentleness, compassion, and love—courage, too. Let us speak of these, but let us also speak of other passages more troubling. First, let us note some of the good:

John 15:9-13 speaks of Jesus and his love:

> As the Father hath loved me, so have I loved you: continue ye in my love. If ye keep my commandments, ye shall abide in my love; even as I have kept my Father's commandments, and abide in his love. These things have I spoken unto you, that my joy might remain in you, and that your joy might be full. This is my commandment, That ye love one another, as I have loved you. Greater love hath no man than this, that a man lay down his life for his friends.

Matthew 9:35-36 shows Jesus healing others, and feeling compassion:

> And Jesus went about all the cities and villages, teaching in their synagogues, and preaching the gospel of the kingdom, and healing every sickness and every disease among the people. But when he saw the multitudes, he was moved with compassion on them, because they fainted, and were scattered abroad, as sheep having no shepherd.

Matthew 14:14 also speaks of Jesus feeling compassion and healing others:

> And Jesus went forth, and saw a great multitude, and was moved with compassion toward them, and he healed their sick.

Matthew 15:32 again speaks of Jesus feeling compassion:

> Then Jesus called his disciples unto him, and said, I have compassion on the multitude, because they continue with me now three days, and have nothing to eat: and I will not send them away fasting, lest they faint in the way.

Matthew 20:34 speaks of Jesus having compassion on two blind men and healing them:

> So Jesus had compassion on them, and touched their eyes: and immediately their eyes received sight, and they followed him.

Matthew 21:14 also speaks of Jesus healing others:

> And the blind and the lame came to him in the temple; and he healed them.

And Mark 6:34 again speaks of Jesus and compassion:

> And Jesus, when he came out, saw much people, and was moved with compassion toward them, because they were as sheep not having a shepherd: and he began to teach them many things.

Matthew 21:12-13 has Jesus demonstrating the courage to take bold action in challenging what he saw as wrong:

> And Jesus went into the temple of God, and cast out all them that sold and bought in the temple, and overthrew the tables of the moneychangers, and the seats of them that sold doves, And said unto them, It is written, My house shall be called the house of prayer; but ye have made it a den of thieves.

And Luke 23:34 teaches how Jesus, even while being crucified, was forgiving:

> Then said Jesus, Father, forgive them; for they know not what they do.

My sister, these verses and many more in the New Testament show Jesus, in both word and deed, embodying various traits of noble character.

Yet there is another side to the story, another face to Jesus, even in the New Testament.

And my sister, I beg you to remember that those who have been raised to think of Jesus as the epitome of holiness, purity, and love—from listening to sweet mother's lullabies at the cradle to singing Christmas carols in the glow of moonlight—may be incredulous at the notion that his character might, especially in passages of the Bible, embody anything less than perfection.[1] Thus, some

---

[1] Indeed, even so independent a thinker and courageous a writer as Thomas Paine, in Chapter III of his *Age of Reason*—the very book in which he savages religion—still writes: "Nothing that is here said can apply, even with the most distant disrespect, to the real character of Jesus Christ. He was a virtuous and an amiable man. The morality that he preached and practiced was of the most benevolent kind; and though similar systems of morality had been preached by Confucius, and by some of the Greek philosophers, many years before, by the Quakers since, and by many good men in all ages, it has not been exceeded by any."

One has to be puzzled by Paine's words. The only extensive accounts we have of Jesus are from the New Testament; and these speak of one in whose teachings was prominently featured the notion of eternal punishment in fire for sinners, as well as other objectionable items I will presently mention in the book's text. Still, Paine either could not bring himself to give up on the unwarranted cultural bias that the character and morality of the "real" Jesus was at least as elevated and benevolent as those of any other

Christians, upon hearing evidence associating Jesus with negative character traits, might object with righteous indignation and dismiss such evidence with outrage or contempt, while others might respond with condescending skepticism, or mere polite rationalizations. And, indeed, on such matters—early in life pounded heavy into the heart and receiving the sworn allegiance of the mind—nothing can be proved to everyone's satisfaction, and nobody can be compelled, against their fierce loyalties, to change views. Yet in the privacy of your own conscience ask of yourself the fortitude to seek the truth on these things, and the courage to bear whatever implications such seeking may yield.

And, my sister, before we discuss specific citations from the Bible on Jesus' words and actions that shed a less positive light on his character, let us bear in mind the historical and sensible context. We shall not find stories of Jesus killing entire nations or legislating harsh punishments into earthly codes of law. To some, therefore, it might seem that compared to the God of the Old Testament, Jesus was far less destructive and cruel. Yet such a point misses the critical consideration of just what options were available to Jesus.

When judging the character of an ancient king, a man who had power over the very lives of his subjects, we look to see if he abused such power by killing unjustly or instituting immoral laws; by contrast, when judging the character of a man without significant temporal power, we must look at how he wielded the limited power at his disposal—how kindly he treated others, whether his actions were consistent with his words, and whether his wishes and views were moral—even if he lacked the power to carry them out.[1]

Unlike the God of the Old Testament, Jesus—in his earthly form as a man—is not depicted even by the New Testament as having military or political power. Thus, he simply was not in a position to engage in acts such as genocide or cruel legislation. His destructive potential was generally limited to the words and deeds available to an itinerant preacher. The greatest potential power he wielded was the threatening of torture in the afterlife—and this he did, and if one believes such threats were credible, they make all the callousness and cruelty of the Old Testament fade to insignificance. For the worst of temporary injustice, even murder, cannot compare to the unending suffering and horror of eternal punishment in fire—a teaching nowhere found in the Old Testament, but vigorously preached and threatened by Jesus.

---

man in history—or (and this would be, I think, the worse possibility, and I trust it is not true) he was not gripped by this illusion, but even in a book devoted to speaking unpopular truth on ultimate issues, he chose to flatter the figure of Jesus so as to come across to his Christian readership as at least slightly less objectionable.

[1] Philemon the ancient Greek similarly said that a just man is not he who does no evil, but he who with the power to do evil chooses not to.

Remember, too, my sister, that you and I and the great majority of humans in every generation are not mass murderers and have not legislated cruel laws. If we do not find Jesus to have done such horrific things either, he would simply be similar, in that regard, to most humans—who are acclaimed neither as deities nor as sons of deities. The question we are now investigating is not whether Jesus was an abominable villain—rather, whether we can honestly and intelligently claim that he was morally perfect. For this is what many Christians over two millennia have believed, and what some affirm to this day. And to put this claim, that Jesus was perfect, in severe doubt we need not show him to have committed atrocities; we need only show that—even by the account of the New Testament, and even in the relatively few acts of his life recorded therein—he engaged in behavior, or held values, that fell short of the ideal.

I shall cite for you ten examples from the New Testament, of the character of Jesus apparently deviating from the standards of love, gentleness, and moral perfection.

First, as mentioned, Jesus taught and supported everlasting torture in fire for sinners, such as those who did not feed the poor. In describing the day when "The Son of Man" will judge the nations, Jesus says, beginning in Matthew 25:31:

> When the Son of man shall come in his glory, and all the holy angels with him, then shall he sit upon the throne of his glory. And before him shall be gathered all nations; and he shall separate them one from another, as a shepherd divideth his sheep from the goats. And he shall set the sheep on his right hand, but the goats on the left...Then shall he say also unto them on the left hand, Depart from me, ye cursed, into everlasting fire, prepared for the devil and his angels...And these shall go away into everlasting punishment, but the righteous into life eternal.

My sister, infinite torture for a finite crime is not only grossly unjust, but is obviously lacking in compassion, too. How terrible we would think a dictator who punished thieves by roasting them alive for even brief moments! How much more abominable must we consider the character of one who would roast people alive *forever*, simply because they were not generous, and did not give of their property to the poor! And, as mentioned, nothing in all the stern punishments of the Old Testament comes anywhere close to the unreasonable and extreme cruelty of everlasting torture in fire. The "vengeful" God of the Old Testament never threatens eternal hell, but Jesus does.

And, my sister—as earlier mentioned—do not be tempted to argue that Jesus was only speaking God's word, and did not originate the idea of everlasting hell. For if, as some Christians teach, Jesus is God, then such an argument offers no defense. And if he is not God, or did not know he was God, why did he not—as, by the account of the Old Testament Abraham and Moses *did*—argue with God, and plead for Him to be more compassionate; in this case, not to burn people for eternity? Instead, he says with no evident empathy, and with seeming satisfaction: "Depart from me, ye cursed, into everlasting fire..."

Second, Jesus humiliated a woman who begged him to heal her daughter. He referred to her, in her presence, in degrading language. Mark 7:25-29 states:

> For a certain woman, whose young daughter had an unclean spirit, heard of him, and came and fell at his feet. The woman was a Greek, a Syrophenician by nation; and she besought him that he would cast forth the devil out of her daughter. But Jesus said unto her, Let the children first be filled: for it is not meet to take the children's bread, and to cast it unto the dogs. And she answered and said unto him, Yes, Lord: yet the dogs under the table eat of the children's crumbs. And he said unto her, For this saying go thy way; the devil is gone out of thy daughter.

Thus, my sister, Jesus humiliated the woman by comparing her to a dog because she was not of the people of Israel, and only helped her when she accepted the humiliation and agreed that she was comparable to a dog. My sister, if you saw a man treat a woman this way, would you wish your daughter to marry him?

Matthew tells the story similarly, with Jesus first ignoring the woman because she was not of the people of Israel, then humiliating her by comparing her to a dog—and only healing her daughter after she agreed she was comparable to a dog and begged for help in any case. Matthew 15:22-26 states:

> And, behold a woman of Canaan came out of the same coasts, and cried unto him, saying, Have mercy on me, O Lord, thou son of David; my daughter is grievously vexed with a devil. But he answered her not a word. And his disciples came and besought him, saying, Send her away for she crieth after us. But he answered and said, I am not sent but unto the lost sheep of the house of Israel. Then came she and worshipped him, saying Lord, help me. But he answered and said, It is not meet to take the children's bread, and to cast it to dogs. And she said, Truth, Lord: yet the dogs eat of the crumbs which fall from their masters' table. Then Jesus answered and said unto her, O woman great is thy faith: be it unto thee even as thou wilt. And her daughter was made whole from that very hour.

Third, as evidenced in this tale, Jesus discriminated against non-Jews, considering them of lesser importance—comparable to dogs—and not worthy of helping. My sister, what would you think of any other man who taught that his people were above others, and that other peoples were like dogs?

Fourth, although Jesus taught a lot about the importance of love, he was not moved by compassion to heal a supplicating woman's daughter. In this story, Jesus initially ignores the woman's pleas, and even when he relents, after the woman begs and persists, he does not heal the woman's child out of compassion, but rather as a reward to the woman, as Jesus said: "O woman great is thy faith: be it unto thee even as thou wilt." My sister, what would you think of a physician who was unmoved by a child's suffering, refusing to heal the child, and only relenting when the mother begged and persisted, and subjected herself to his humiliations—thus proving her faith in the physician? And what would you think if you heard that this physician was revered as the most loving man of all time?

Fifth, the story seems hypocritical. Jesus at first refuses to heal the woman's child because such an act fell outside what he considered his religious mission. Yet in Mark Chapter 3, Jesus gets angry at the "hardness of the hearts" of the Pharisees who will prosecute him if he heals a man's hand on the Sabbath—an act considered by them to be a violation the Sabbath, an important religious law included in the Ten Commandments. Mark 3:1-5 states:

> And he entered again into the synagogue; and there was a man there which had a withered hand. And they watched him, whether he would heal him on the Sabbath day; that they might accuse him. And he saith unto the man which had the withered hand, Stand forth... And when he had looked round about on them with anger, being grieved for the hardness of their hearts, he saith unto the man, Stretch forth thine hand. And he stretched it out: and his hand was restored whole as the other.

Thus, my sister, Jesus became angry, judging the people as hard-hearted for disapproving of the man's hand being healed on the Sabbath—though healing on the Sabbath was forbidden by their religious laws. Yet, as the other story illustrates, Jesus himself was unwilling to heal a child even after being begged by its mother, because she was not Jewish—and therefore was not one of the people to whom he believed he was sent. In other words, he would not heal because it was not within what he saw as his religious obligation. Was that not a hardness of heart, too—of the same sort that elicited from him anger and righteous indignation when engaged in by his religious adversaries, the Pharisees?

Sixth, Jesus, in another case, seems not to have followed his own teachings. In Matthew 5:39 Jesus says:

But I say unto you that ye resist not evil; but whosoever shall smite thee on thy right cheek, turn to him the other also.

But when Jesus is actually hit he does not respond by turning and offering the other cheek. Instead, he protests and demands an explanation. John 18: 22-23 states:

And when he had thus spoken, one of the officers which stood by struck Jesus with the palm of his hand, saying, Answerest thou the high priest so? Jesus answered him, If I have spoken evil, bear witness of the evil: but if well, why smitest thou me?

My sister, if it were someone else who taught one thing but then did another, would we not charge him with hypocrisy? And is it fair and reasonable to come to a different conclusion here?

Seventh, Jesus was, at times, far from gentle and forgiving and generous, even though he is regularly quoted as teaching gentleness and forgiveness and generosity—even to one's enemies. In Matthew 5:44-46 Jesus is quoted as saying:

But I say unto you, love your enemies, bless them that curse you, do good to them that hate you, and pray for them which despitefully use you, and persecute you. That ye may be the children of your Father which is in heaven; for he maketh his sun to rise on the evil and on the good, and sendeth rain on the just and on the unjust. For if ye love them which love you, what reward have ye? Do not even the publicans the same?

Yet did Jesus consistently display the magnanimity and gentleness which he teaches to others? Matthew 10:33 states:

But whosoever shall deny me before men, him will I also deny before my Father which is in heaven.

And in Matthew, Chapter 23, Jesus hurls insults and angry words against the Pharisees who have not accepted him. He repeatedly calls them "hypocrites," and "fools and blind." Verse 33 is especially intense:

Ye serpents, ye generation of vipers, how can ye escape the damnation of hell?

Worse, in Luke 19:27 Jesus actually demands that those who did not wish to be ruled by him be killed:

> But those mine enemies, which would not that I should reign over them, bring
> hither, and slay them before me.

I ask you, my sister, if you did not know these stories were speaking of Jesus, or if you were not already a committed Christian, would you really characterize the one engaging in these behaviors and uttering these statements as gentle, peaceful and loving—much less the most gentle, peaceful, and loving person ever to have walked the earth?

And is it not ironic that in his angry insults Jesus calls the Pharisees hypocrites, but that these very outbursts contradict his own teachings—and seem to render *him* hypocritical?

Eighth, in the story of Jesus turning water into wine, Jesus treated his mother with what, if we observed any other man behaving so, we would characterize as rudeness and disrespect. John, Chapter 2 begins as follows:

> And the third day there was a marriage in Ca'na of Galilee; and the mother of
> Jesus was there. And both Jesus was called, and his disciples, to the marriage.
> And when they wanted wine, the mother of Jesus saith unto him, They have no
> wine. Jesus saith unto her, Woman, what have I to do with thee? Mine hour is
> not yet come.

My sister, even if Jesus wanted to demonstrate that he could perform miracles by turning water into wine, could he not have been gentle and loving, or at least respectful, to his mother—and then performed his miracle? Would not a mature and kind man—much less a divine and perfectly loving being—have smiled and gently said: "Dear Mother, true, by natural means there is no wine; but see what the glory of God can provide: we shall have wine by miracle, and by God's grace." Especially in light of the Ten Commandments requiring respect for one's parents, would not a paragon of morality have said some such words— instead of, "Woman, what have I to do with thee"?

Ninth, the Bible relates that Jesus cursed a tree and killed it for not bearing fruit out of season when he wanted fruit. Matthew 21:18-19 states:

> Now in the morning as he returned into the city, he hungered. And when he
> saw a fig tree in the way, he came to it, and found nothing thereon, but leaves
> only, and said unto it, Let no fruit grow on thee henceforward forever. And
> presently the fig tree withered away.

And Mark 11:12-13 in beginning to recount the same story makes clear that it was not even the season for figs:

And on the morrow, when they were come from Bethany, he was hungry. And seeing a fig tree afar off having leaves, he came, if haply he might find any thing thereon; and when he came to it, he found nothing but leaves; for the time of figs was not yet.

My sister, would it not have been a more compassionate and constructive use of miraculous powers to command the tree to produce figs out of season, instead of cursing it with death because it properly did not have figs? And was not this behavior of Jesus needlessly destructive and his intentions vindictive, even irrationally vindictive? Indeed, even the common man—no saint and no teacher of morals—does not destroy a tree simply because it has no fruit for him when he is hungry—especially when the tree is out of season. And if we observed a man destroying a tree for so irrational a reason, what would think of such a man? Would we have him cultivate our property? Would we trust him to care for our children? Would we wish him to marry our daughter? I ask you then, my sister, is it fair to judge Jesus differently?

And do not be tempted to answer that this story is mere metaphor or allegory. For absent compelling indication to the contrary, we must take the Bible at its literal word. And are we to understand that all miracle stories in the Bible were also mere metaphors or allegories—none of them claiming the occurrence of true miracles? This would be inconsistent with the overall message of the New Testament which directly states that many were brought to belief after witnessing miracles by Jesus and his disciples. And since some of the miracle stories are clearly meant as literal descriptions of events, upon what reasonable basis are we to assume that this story is meant to be understood otherwise?

Moreover, even if it *were* mere metaphor or allegory, the author of such a tale has the responsibility to construct it in such a form that it reflects and teaches values he upholds—especially when it would be easy for many readers to assume the tale to be literal. Indeed, my sister, as wise men have taught, even an allegorical tale insensitive to injustice says something about its author.

Tenth, as mentioned, Jesus never protested in the New Testament against slavery, though slavery was widely practiced in his day. He even constructed analogies that clearly condoned the subjugation and harsh treatment of other humans. Jesus states in Luke 17:7-10:[1]

---

[1] This rendering is from the New American Standard Bible, and not all translations of this passage use the word "slave." Some use the word "servant." Yet even if the verse speaks of a servant, does one embody the height of morality and kindness if one cannot imagine that a person might invite a servant to eat with him, or at least thank the servant for his service?

Which of you, having a slave plowing or tending sheep, will say to him when he has come in from the field, Come immediately and sit down to eat? But will he not say to him, Prepare something for me to eat, and properly clothe yourself and serve me while I eat and drink; and afterward you may eat and drink? He does not thank the slave because he did the things which were commanded, does he? So you too, when you do all the things which are commanded you, say, We are unworthy slaves; we have done only that which we ought to have done.

I ask you, then: Is it the pinnacle of loving morality to condone slavery, to have no gratitude for the services rendered by a slave—and even, according to some translations, to consider a slave worthless—as Jesus teaches?

My sister, not only is Jesus' attitude on slaves far below our contemporary moral standards, even in his day there were those more sensitive to a slave's plight. Compare Jesus' views on the matter to those of Seneca, the Roman pagan philosopher and orator, who lived while Jesus walked the earth—and who is not held up by any religion as the epitome of compassion and love. Seneca laughed at those who considered it degrading for a man to dine with his slaves. He taught that a man should treat his slaves the way he would want his superiors to treat him; that slaves were just as human and worthy of dignity as were free men.[1]

My sister, the kind and virtuous inclinations within us, often besieged by myriad forms of temptation, disappointment, and despair, yearn for a shining example to whom we can look, the heroic embodiment of moral perfection and gentlest love, who can be said to have manifested these in earthly life, and whose words and deeds can provide us with guidance and inspiration. Yet shall we allow such longings to obscure or overpower our search for truth? Although the New Testament portrays Jesus as demonstrating courage and righteous indignation in rebelling against some entrenched, legalistic religious powers of his day, and although it speaks of him as teaching, and at times embodying, love and forgiveness and other virtues—if we cleave to deep honesty must we not conclude that he was by no means, judging from the very biblical account, in his own behavior a paradigm of purest consistency, compassion, gentleness or love?

And as I have explained in earlier footnotes, including those to sections 127b and 128a, the historical and textual contexts make clear that both the Old and New Testaments condoned what we would today refer to as slavery.

In discussions of slavery I have not used the King James translation, because it does not (with a rare exception) use the word "slave" to refer to slaves, even when the Bible is clearly referring to humans as property to be bought and sold; instead the King James translation uses the word "servant." For elaboration, see footnote in section 127 on slavery in the Old Testament.

[1] See *The Stoic Philosophy of Seneca* translated by Moses Hadas: letter 47, "Slaves."

And let not your heart be tempted to say, as some have, that the real Jesus was perfect, but that the New Testament misrepresents him—or that the passages where Jesus is depicted as imperfect are due to later redactions or interpolations. For our primary source of the good and loving teachings of Jesus, or of the claim for the divinity of Jesus, or the status of Jesus as the Son of God, is the New Testament. If we cannot trust the New Testament's accuracy on the stories that portray Jesus as less than loving, how can we trust the New Testament's accuracy on the other stories—those in which Jesus *is* portrayed as loving? Indeed, if we cannot trust the New Testament in all its accounts, how do we know we can trust it in any of its accounts—including the basic story of who Jesus was, and what he came to teach? Because if such significant passages are mistaken, yet were allowed to become part of the New Testament, even the Christian must concede that God does not prevent the text from becoming badly compromised. How, then, shall we trust any part of it?

But remember too that even if it were not clear from the New Testament that Jesus' character was significantly flawed—even if by the accounts of the New Testament Jesus seemed exceptionally moral and kind—this alone would still give us no good reason to believe the New Testament's religious and miraculous claims. For do not many books portray their heroes in a very favorable moral light, yet we often do not know if such accounts are true? And even when we take such favorable accounts as true, do we worship any one of these heroes as God or the Son of God?

138. Argument that we cannot use logic to understand the Bible, because God's ways are beyond us

Then a religious woman said: You make the basic mistake of trying to understand the Bible through logic and human reason. Of course human reason cannot fathom the ways of God. The only thing we can do is wait for God to open our eyes so that we can comprehend His ways, and His word in the Bible. In fact, we do not even need to understand why God would say or do certain things. All we need to know about the Bible is that He said it, we read it, and that should be enough for us.

And the sage said: My sister, a book written by God deserves to be taken seriously even if we do not understand it. On this we agree. And if the time ever comes that we possess a book we can responsibly believe to have been written by God, I will treat it with great respect. The problem, my sister, is that we do not honestly know the Bible to be the word of God. Instead, a *human* tradition makes this claim—a tradition with its beginnings lost to the mists of ancient history, and its many subsequent stages influenced and invigorated by ages of widespread ignorance and terrified superstition.

Oh, to be sure, many act as if they know God to have written the Bible, and out of religious zeal vigorously dispute or summarily dismiss any questioning of whether the Bible is truly the word of God. But subjective conviction should never be confused with accurate knowledge. Indeed, it is readily apparent that even the most intense certainty is an unreliable indication of what is and what is not God's word: Observe, for example, how many Muslims feel with subjective certainty that the Koran is God's word, and how many adherents of other religions feel a subjective certainty that it is not. And observe how many Christians feel subjectively certain of the New Testament's divine nature, and how many Hindus, Buddhists, Jews, and others are quite skeptical of that belief.

My sister, as a Christian, would you agree with the argument of a Muslim who claimed the Koran to be God's inspired word, and who further claimed that you must adopt this belief without persuasive evidence and simply pray to Allah to be given the wisdom to understand His words? If you were to accept this argument, you would have to convert to Islam; but, of course, since every religion could make this argument, you would have to convert to every religion—yet your beliefs would then be self-contradictory, because most religions contradict each other. And since you do not accept this argument in support of Islam or other religions, how is the same argument, when advanced it in support of *your* religion, any more legitimate? Is it not evident that subjective certainty is inadequate as a means of determining whether a text is the word of God?

Moreover, it is far from admirable piety to ascribe to God what may not be of His authorship. It does not show respect to a man if we honor a document appearing to show his signature, when there are loud and credible claims that the signature is forged. To the contrary: We show him respect by investigating whether the signature is truly his. Is it not conceivable, then, that any God there may be would strongly disapprove of humans saying things in His name without bothering to investigate well whether these words are truly His—especially since there are so many intelligent arguments to the contrary?

My sister, would you be delighted, or perhaps disappointed, if your friend spread rumors that you were unkind? How much worse if your friend spread rumors—because someone told her so—that you not only directed others to kill thousands of women and children; that you not only sentenced people to death for small offenses like not honoring the Sabbath; but that you also arranged for people to be tortured and burned for eternity unless they were lucky enough to have heard of an itinerant preacher and they were willing to suspend critical reason and believe that he was your supernatural Son and that he rose from the dead! This portrait is one that no kind, or even reasonable, person would want painted of herself. Is it right, then, that we paint this portrait of God, without trying very hard to determine if it is accurate?

And thus, my sister, it is not enough to assume that the Bible is God's word, and simply pray for divine guidance in understanding it. First we must do the uncomfortable work of investigating whether the Bible is, indeed, God's word. Out of decency and fairness to God—not to mention awe, love, or reverence—shall we not at least, in our dealings with Him, apply the golden rule, supported by the Bible and so many other traditions: "Do unto others as you would have others do unto you"?

And, my sister, if you examine it well, with honest eyes, you may find that the Bible will seem far from the perfect word of a flawless and all-merciful God. Instead, it may read more like a collection of passionate works created by inconstant, mottled men, reflecting in its various beauties, incongruities, and flaws a wide range of human characteristics, incorporating into its legends and poems and laws man's best instincts and his worst. And what else, then, can one expect but that the One in whose name the Bible claims to speak, has been made into a mottled character too, a suspiciously familiar amalgam of the transcendent and the base?[1]

My sister, if the Bible and its religions have largely succeeded in removing the manufacture of gods from the carver's chisel and the smelter's flames, they have only transferred the license for such production to the prophet's frenzy, to the scribe's quill, and to the brazen imagination of every lonely theologian.

139. The "Bible code"

And a student said: You have many seemingly clever and logical arguments against the Bible. But all your arguments will come to nothing because there is scientific proof that the Bible is supernatural. Have you not heard that codes have been discovered in the Bible, codes that include meaningful clusters of hidden words, which miraculously predict events happening in our days, thus proving divine authorship of the Bible?

And the sage replied: My son, I have heard much about what is called the Bible code. Some have claimed that in the Bible are found remarkable words and messages encoded with consistent spacing—such as every twelfth letter, forty-ninth letter, seventy-first letter, or letters found at any other repeating interval. And some of these messages are claimed to be predictions that were fulfilled hundreds, even thousands, of years after the Bible was written. Moreover, other messages related to the same topic—and either encoded, or written in the plain text—seem to be situated, in the Bible's words and letters, nearby these codes.

---

[1] As Voltaire observed, "If God created us in his own image we have more than reciprocated."

My son, all this sounds impressive, even astonishing, but consider the following: The average person, though perhaps fascinated by an illustration of supposed Bible codes, does not understand statistics, probabilities, and other elements of advanced mathematics, and is unable to discern whether these codes of which we speak are legitimately supernatural, or merely an impressive but purely natural phenomenon, similar to a parlor trick—a clever but ultimately unimportant demonstration.

Most of us—not having specialized knowledge on such matters—would need to call upon experts to tell us whether these claims are credible, and why or why not. And, my son, the consensus in the scientific, statistical community is that these code findings are not supernatural, but can rather be accounted for by causes quite natural—which they explain.[1]

My son, if a magician waves his wand, conjures a white rabbit, tells us this constitutes a supernatural sign, and that we must follow his divinely ordained instructions, the dissenting opinions of professional magicians become very important on the matter—especially if they explain how the trick was done—even if to our unknowing eyes the feat seemed inexplicable. If the overwhelming majority of magicians say the trick is well within the bounds of the natural, we have no reason to believe that anything supernatural took place. And if a member of the audience chooses to believe that the trick *was* supernatural, his belief would not be based upon sound evidence but upon his own untutored astonishment, and upon his willingness to trust the integrity and judgment of a maverick magician claiming supernatural powers.

Similarly, that the great majority of scientists see no validity in the codes is important. Conversely, it is not significant in our search for truth that the codes seem impressive to the average layperson—because he is unable to distinguish between natural occurrences that merely *seem* supernatural, and any possible phenomena that might truly be operating against the known laws of nature.

In short, the Bible codes are presented as a proof based on science and mathematics. Scientists and mathematicians are the ones who know these fields—and they have pronounced this proof invalid, and have explained why.[2]

And do not be tempted to argue that many scientists are anti-religious and would, therefore, not believe any evidence for God. Although there may be, within the ranks of science, a number of stubborn, dogmatic atheists who would willfully ignore even incontrovertible evidence of God's existence, the vast majority of scientists would acknowledge the truth of responsible proof for a supernatural Bible, should any such proof be presented. In fact, mainstream

---

[1] See following section for references, and further discussion on Bible codes.

[2] See following section and its footnotes, for further detail and references.

science would be willing to recognize many theoretical examples of encryption as intentional and miraculous, but the findings known as the Bible code do not meet such standards, for several reasons.

Thus, even if a supernatural being *did* encrypt the seemingly random and natural messages referred to as the Bible code, He could not reasonably expect us to believe from this inconclusive evidence—with which the great majority of scientists are not impressed—that a divine message had been sent. Would not God have to be unfair, even sadistic, to demand that we accept evidence of the type that only experts know how to interpret—when the nearly unanimous view of these very experts is that the evidence in question is unsound, and the proof it attempts fallacious?

Indeed, my son, even if the scientific community were significantly divided on whether there are supernatural codes in the Bible—and it is not—this would still constitute insufficient reason to believe that the Bible is God's word. For why would an all-powerful God communicate His existence in such a questionable and unclear manner—when He could so easily perform miracles undeniable?

And let not your loyalties urge you on to argue that skeptics will doubt all miracles, and that God cannot send us signs unless we have an open heart to notice them and believe. To the contrary, if we must believe before we would recognize signs, they are not signs but inconclusive phenomena from which it would be irresponsible to draw conclusions. And is it beyond the power of God to send unambiguous messages of His presence? Is anything too difficult for omnipotence? Could God not send a voice from heaven, proclaiming that in seven day's time all housecats in the land will sprout wings and fly around their masters' homes seventy times, before landing and immediately presenting their masters with seven white doves while reciting, in the language of the land, the twenty-third psalm? If all heard this prophecy with their own ears, and if all with their own eyes witnessed the promised events coming to pass—would this not be a conclusive sign for all alive at that time?

And are there not a thousand other signs you and I could suggest, that would be astounding, compelling, and anything but ambiguous and unconvincing? Would such signs be difficult for a God who is said to have created the heavens and the earth, and all their intricate hosts—from the vast exploding stars in the unfathomable expanses of space to the invisible complexities of the tiniest cells?

Thus, my son, do not be tempted to say that although inconclusive, the evidence for a Bible code is sufficient for the faithful; because if evidence is sufficient only for the faithful, what persuades the faithful is not evidence, but a bias toward their preexisting convictions. And belief resting upon questionable evidence is—for both the devout and the sincerely uncommitted—neither noble nor responsible.

And can it be virtuous to believe too quickly that God wrote the Bible? Such belief necessarily accepts the many harsh assertions of the Bible including, among others, that God commanded genocide, that God condoned slavery, that God decreed unequal rights for women, and that God legislated the death penalty for numerous nonviolent offenses. Would we be gratified, or offended, if friends believed such things about us—in the absence of unassailable poof? Would we not rather expect our friends to investigate carefully before believing about us such immoderate testimonies? And do we not owe a possible God the same courtesy?

Thus, we must not say that the Bible code, though it does not offer conclusive proof of the Bible being written by God, is impressive enough to justify the risk of believing. We must not say such a thing, because without compelling cause for belief we would be treating God in a way we ourselves would not wish to be treated. And this would constitute not elevated piety, but ignoble injustice and indolence. If a God exists and watches over human affairs, might He not strongly disapprove of mankind claiming to know His intent and communications—on the strength of such flimsy and refuted evidence?

Moreover, consider a further moral dimension. If the Bible code were true—and the basis upon which we are supposed to be persuaded of the Bible's supernatural origins—what would this say about God? Why would a benevolent Almighty condemn thousands of years of honest seekers to tortured uncertainty and spiritual confusion simply because they were born before the age of computers, when the Bible code could finally be discovered—and before the age of advanced statistical knowledge when complex probabilities could finally be computed? Again, in the absence of compelling evidence that the code is supernatural, we dare not assume that it is, and, therefore, that God wrote the Bible—for then we place ourselves in great danger of slandering a possible God.

Finally, my son, in all of human history no supposedly supernatural event has ever passed the withering test of wide-ranging reason and the inexorable trials of accumulating human knowledge. Rather, once the age of science dawned and humans better distinguished between reality and superstition, nothing has ever been demonstrated to operate beyond the purview of the natural.[1]

---

[1] Of course, even some natural phenomena are not yet understood—that is, science has not yet discovered the mechanisms by which they operate. But most of what scientists understand today, they did not understand a mere century or two ago; and there is no good reason to believe that what they observe but do not yet understand will remain beyond the ken of science some centuries hence. And such phenomena are quite different from that which dramatically transcends and flouts our understanding and repeated experience of natural laws—and could reasonably be seen as miraculous—

When encountering any impressive feat, puzzle, or supernatural claim, therefore, our overwhelming assumption must be that the object or event or process in question is natural—unless we have *conclusive* evidence to the contrary. And such evidence has never been forthcoming.

On the matter of the Bible code, too, since we lack anything approaching definitive proof that it is supernatural—indeed, the great majority of those with the expertise to know, mathematicians and scientists, who have investigated and addressed these matters, have responded with persuasive rebuttals and clear rejections of such claims—our only responsible supposition must be that any apparent code in the Bible is, in fact, nothing transcending the natural.

For repeated human experience has taught that what too easily brought our forefathers to their knees in awed worship of sacred mystery, is later seen by their shamefaced descendents to be merely the unfamiliar—governed, all the same, by predictable features of natural law. Our astonished and credulous ancestors, reacting fearfully to the novel and the misunderstood, imagined lightning bolts to be the spears of angry gods, and plagues the attacks of evil spirits; accordingly, they engaged in rituals designed to placate the gods and ward off the spirits. Their descendants, however, seeing by the light of greater knowledge, have largely abandoned such superstitions. Let us, then, spare our progeny the burden of correcting, even pitying, their forebears for believing this piece of willful ignorance, too.

140. Further detail on why the "Bible code" does not prove divine origin or inspiration for the Bible

But the student said: It is all very easy and convenient to say that scientists dismiss the Bible code. But you have not at all explained why they do, and why I should not believe that the Bible contains miraculous codes, thus proving the Bible to be from God.

And the sage said: My son, now that we have explained that belief in God cannot responsibly be based on controversial claims of supernatural codes in the Bible—claims that only statisticians and other such experts could verify—when nearly every expert who has examined the matter has pronounced the "codes" perfectly natural and non-miraculous, we are ready to discuss the matter in more detail. But remember, you need not rely on any of the points that follow in order to see that, at best, claims of supernatural Bible codes are far from the sort of clear proof necessary to responsibly or justly attribute the Bible to God.

Let us, then, speak of the details.

---

something like the example cited earlier, of a fulfilled public prediction that, at a specified moment, all housecats will sprout wings, recite the 23rd psalm, and so on.

First, only one article in support of Bible codes has been published in a peer-reviewed scientific journal.[1] The authors of this paper made the remarkable claim that they found encoded in the biblical book of Genesis the names of many famous rabbis, who lived between the eighth and nineteenth centuries C.E.—and that encoded nearby their names were their dates of birth or death. Considering that Genesis was written at least two thousand years ago, this seemed to indicate that the Bible contained supernatural codes.

But even this one paper was never seen by the journal as legitimate scientific conclusion. The publisher of the journal, as well as its executive editor at the time the original codes paper was published, later stated in writing,[2] that the original publishing of the paper in support of Bible codes was not meant to give it the stamp of scientific approval, but was presented instead as a challenging puzzle—and that in light of a later paper published in the same journal[3] refuting the claims of the earlier pro-codes paper the puzzle is apparently solved.

Moreover, the nearly unanimous view of mathematicians and statisticians who have studied the issue is that claims of supernatural Bible codes are unsubstantiated, and that words seemingly encoded in the Bible represent a purely natural phenomenon. Numerous qualified mathematicians from across the world have signed a statement to that effect.[4]

Science, then, has rejected the claims of supernatural biblical codes. But, my son, I understand that you wish to hear the reasons for this rejection.

The first point to understand is that in any but the shortest of texts many words will be found seemingly encoded in equidistant letter sequences. This is not supernatural. There are only so many different letters in the alphabet; yet there are many thousands of words and phrases that could randomly be spelled

---

[1] "Equidistant Letter Sequences in the Book of Genesis," a paper by Witzum, Rips, and Rosenberg, published in the journal *Statistical Science*, 1994, Vol. 9, No. 3. An abridged version is available, at the time of this writing, on the Internet at the following site: www.torahcodes.co.il/wrr1/wrr1.htm

[2] See "Bible Code Mystery Explained," a press release by the Institute of Mathematical Statistics, quoting the introduction of Robert Kass to the 1999 paper refuting the claims of Bible codes, also published in *Statistical Science*. It is posted on the Internet, at the time of this writing, at: http://cs.anu.edu.au/~bdm/dilugim/StatSci/PressRelease.html

[3] "Solving The Bible Code Puzzle," a paper by Brendan McKay, Dror Bar-Natan, Maya Bar-Hillel, and Gil Kalai, published in *Statistical Science*, May 1999 issue. At the time of this writing, the paper and related information can be accessed on the Internet at: http://cs.anu.edu.au/~bdm/dilugim/StatSci/

[4] "The Mathematicians' Statement on the Bible Codes" is signed by several dozen qualified mathematicians who have reviewed the material and concluded that there is no good evidence for any supernatural Bible codes. At the time of this writing the statement can be accessed on the Internet at: http://www.math.caltech.edu/code/petition.html

out in such "codes." That messages were found seemingly encoded in the Bible is not surprising: Any text of similar length would also include apparently "encoded" messages. Indeed, it would be miraculous if we were *not* to find such messages seemingly encoded in the Bible.

To demonstrate that "codes" will be found in any text, scholars applying the same techniques employed to find coded messages in the Bible have identified comparable "codes"—in secular texts.

Constructing a similar list of rabbis to the list prepared by the authors of the peer-reviewed journal paper mentioned earlier, and using equally valid selection criteria, scientists found the names of these rabbis, along with relevant dates of birth and death, encoded in the Hebrew translation of Tolstoy's *War and Peace*—a text nobody claims to be supernatural.[1]

And to counter the Bible code enthusiasts and writers who claim to have found encoded in the Bible supernatural predictions of modern day political assassinations, mathematicians have found equally "miraculous" predictions in the text of Melville's nineteenth century novel, *Moby Dick*. Assassinations "foretold" in *Moby Dick* include those of John F. Kennedy, Abraham Lincoln, Martin Luther King, Leon Trotsky, Yitzchak Rabin, and others.[2]

And, in response to similarly non-credible claims of supernatural codes with the name Jesus encrypted in Isaiah and other sections of the Bible, researchers found the name of Jesus similarly "miraculously" encrypted in late twentieth-century Hebrew language books such as an Israeli novel and a school textbook.[3]

Thus, not only does mathematics tell us in theory that, by random occurrence, "codes" can be found in any long sequence of letters—this has actually been demonstrated in the real world. That such seemingly encoded messages are found in the Bible, too, is natural and unremarkable.

The second point to understand, my son, is that the same message can be written in many different ways. Numerous variations exist for expressing any idea—one can use words of related meaning, different versions of the same

---

[1] See "Equidistant Letter Sequences in Tolstoy's *War and Peace*," an article by Bar-Natan and McKay. In order to work with a text no longer than that of Genesis, and to thus keep the odds of finding the names encoded in this secular text no greater than the odds for finding the names encoded in Genesis, only the first 78,064 letters of *War and Peace* were used for the experiment. At the time of this writing, the article is available on the Internet at: http://cs.anu.edu.au/~bdm/dilugim/WNP/main.pdf

[2] See "Assassinations Foretold in Moby Dick" by Brendan Mckay. At the time of this writing, it is available on the Internet at: http://cs.anu.edu.au/~bdm/dilugim/moby.html

[3] See "The Rise and Fall of the Bible Code," a translation from Russian of an article by Mark Perakh, published in the journal *Kontinent*, No. 103, May 2000. It is on the Internet, at the time of this writing, at: http://www.talkreason.org/articles/Codpaper1.cfm

word, or different sequences of words in a phrase. Let us illustrate a multiplicity of choices using words of related meaning: If we were to search for the word "war" to be encoded in an English text, even if we did not find it we could significantly increase the odds of the code saying what we wanted it to say if we searched for the words "conflict," "combat," "battles," "invasion," "hostilities," "struggle," "explosions," "fire," "victory," "defeat," "casualties," and so on.

Additionally, when seeking supposed codes in the original Hebrew of the Old Testament, we can double or quadruple the number of available options, and have the findings seem more impressive, if we reserve the options of adding the Hebrew letter "Heh"—which means "the"—to the beginning of any word, and using the plural forms of words, which are often spelled quite differently from their singular forms. These are some of the alternatives employed, wittingly or unwittingly, by those who claim to have found miraculous codes in the Bible.

Even a phrase with essentially the same elements can be assembled in various ways, depending on word sequence. As an example, consider the date, June 7, 1824. It can be written in that way, but in many other ways, too—such as: 1824, June 7; 1824, 7 June; 7 June, 1824; 1824, 7th of June; 7th of June, 1824. And by adding the word "the" to the phrase, we can identify several more variations.

Moreover, in ancient Hebrew, the language in which the Hebrew Bible was written, and in which many of the supposed codes were found, there are in some respects even more available variations than in English, because it allows for different legitimate spellings of the same word. This holds true especially for words and names never mentioned in the Bible's text—for example: the names of rabbis living many centuries after the days of the Bible, the very names found "encoded" in the biblical book of Genesis.

Furthermore, in addition to the numerous variations in spelling, synonyms, and related words, a message could be "encoded" at any interval of letters: every twelfth letter, or every twenty-ninth letter, or every one hundred and seventy-second letter, to give three random examples. Furthermore, the message could be "encoded" going either direction in the text: forward or backward. Therefore, a seemingly impressive message is really only one of numerous ways such a message could have been written—and had it been written in any of the other ways, Bible code enthusiasts would have seen *that* message as miraculous. In short, because of all the available variations, there is so much to look for, and so many ways to look, that the odds of finding apparently meaningful messages by mere chance are far more likely than they may at first seem.

A third and related point: Those claiming to have discovered codes in the Bible have not gone about it in a way that establishes legitimacy. Crucial errors have been discovered in the methodology of their original experiment. There is no good evidence that they set up objective standards, *in advance*, for what results would prove their hypothesis—no good evidence that they specified which words would be found and how those words would be spelled. Mathematicians have argued that the evidence which is claimed to demonstrate the existence of supernatural codes in the Bible seems to have involved either intentional or unintentional "tuning" of the protocols and research formulae to fit the findings—and that this "tuning" relates to the "wiggle room" allowed by the many different words and spellings and other options that can be used to find what look like meaningful results.[1]

Thus, when Bible code enthusiasts claim that the odds of these codes occurring by mere chance are only one in many thousands, they are mistaken. This does not mean that the religious researchers were lying when they said they established clear criteria in advance—perhaps they did not realize how much "wiggle room" there was within their criteria, or perhaps they, subconsciously, so much wanted their research to prove the Bible supernatural that they rationalized why certain arbitrary tinkering with the criteria was scientifically warranted. In any case, fairness and intellectual rigor requires that we treat their findings as unremarkable, and their supernatural conclusions as invalid.

My son, to understand what a critical difference it makes that one specify in advance what will constitute meaningful findings, in determining the scientific validity of statistical claims, consider the following: If today, without benefit of advanced technology capable of such a feat, I predict precisely which days it will rain at this spot for the entire period of the next five years—and precisely how much it will rain on each of those days—and these predictions come true, I will have done something astonishing and, apparently, supernatural. Why? Because there are many millions of other possibilities—combinations of days and rain amounts—that could have occurred instead of the specifics of my prediction.

Now let us ask a question: If any combination of rain dates and amounts is only one of many millions of possibilities, should we then say that it is always astonishing that it rains when it does, and in the amounts that it does—even when the exact events were not predicted? Of course not: Only the prediction,

---

[1] See "Solving the Bible Code Puzzle" by Brendan McKay, Dror Bar-Natan, Maya Bar-Hillel, and Gil Kalai, published in *Statistical Science*, May 1999. At the time of this writing, the paper and related information can be accessed at the following Internet address: http://cs.anu.edu.au/~bdm/dilugim/StatSci/

Readers, especially those familiar with Orthodox Jewish terminology, may also be interested in seeing "The Case Against the Codes" by Barry Simon. It is available, at the time of this writing, on the Internet, at: http://www.wopr.com/biblecodes/TheCase.htm

Also see *Who Wrote the Bible Code?* by Randall Ingermanson, an intelligent book that most will find mostly accessible.

because it was done in advance, is remarkable. We have no reason to believe that whatever the rain pattern for the next five years ends up being is, in itself, supernatural. To the contrary, we know that over the next five years we are guaranteed to have some pattern of rain or no rain, even by unguided chance, and that whatever pattern we have will be only one possibility out of many millions.

So, too, with respect to words seemingly encoded in texts: Although any specific combination of words seems highly improbable, in that it is only one of many, many possibilities, there is nothing supernatural about this—by unguided chance, too, many words will appear to be encoded in equidistant letter sequences in the Bible, and in any other long book.

And not only, as mentioned, do we have no good reason to believe that the original research in support of Bible codes predicted in advance the exact words and spellings that would be found encoded in the Bible—more to the point, we have no good reason to believe that the words and spellings found encoded in the Bible follow any compelling rules as to why they should have been predicted or encoded instead of other similar words and spellings.

The fourth point to understand is that although all the findings of the supposed Bible code seem to be nothing more than those that would be expected by simple chance, there is another possible explanation for some of the words found—even if we were to assume that they were encoded intentionally. Humans—without sophisticated computers and with no great difficulty—could have encoded those words that do not involve predictions, but rather seem to encode the name of God or other meaningful words at equidistant letter sequences in the Bible. As scholars have pointed out[1] there are many simple devices, requiring no advanced technology, that make it easy to encode messages in a text. One such device is similar to a stencil or test-grading key, in that it involves a set of holes in a sheet of paper or parchment. The words of the code message are then written through selected holes in the sheet—every forty-ninth letter for example—and then the spaces between and around the code letters are filled in with letters and words not part of the coded message.

Fifth, another reason proponents of the Bible codes should at least pause and reflect is that scholars[2] have noted that the whole notion of a Bible code

---

[1] See, for one, "The Rise and Fall of the Bible Code," a translation from Russian of an article by Mark Perakh, published in the journal *Kontinent*, No. 103, May 2000. It is available for reading on the Internet, at the time of this writing, at the following address: http://www.talkreason.org/articles/Codpaper1.cfm

[2] See "The Bible Codes: A Textual Perspective," by Jeffrey Tigay. It is an intelligent and informed article, and at the time of this writing is archived on the Internet at the following address: http://www.sas.upenn.edu/~jtigay/codetext.html

requires the Bible's text to have remained uncorrupted and precise through the ages. Even a relatively few letters being changed would ruin the encoded words. Yet, they point out, there is much evidence that the Bible's text has not remained consistent over time—notwithstanding the great efforts of religious scribes to maintain the text's integrity.[1]

My son, you have asked for elaboration on these matters, and I have provided it to some degree. But if you wish to pursue it in greater depth and detail, I encourage you to avail yourself of the gifts many scholars have given us in their careful studies and writings on the subject. And the main point relating to Bible codes, as regards the search for religious truth, is that we cannot legitimately base our belief in God on supposedly complex mathematical evidence that only mathematicians would be able to verify and interpret—when the nearly unanimous conclusion of mathematicians is that the evidence is invalid.

The end of the matter, my son, is this: We shall not have the luxury of relying upon supernatural codes for deciding the questions of God and truth. Rather, in our quest to understand our responsibilities and destiny we are thrown back upon ourselves, and upon our own honest intelligence—our most unadorned yet excellent device. And though our spirits yearn for sorcery, and our minds for magic and mystery, these are but the reckless lustings after exotic harlots in the lonely, beguiling night. And you, my son, in the urgency of youth's blood, are sorely tempted. But turn, now, and behold unembellished Reason, the wholesome daughter of thy people, walking unashamed to greet you at brightest noon, a smile upon her loyal lips, and a joyful gaze in her honest eyes.

*****

Then the sage wiped a tear from his cheek and in a thick voice said: We who have loved the Bible; we who have been raised to kiss her pages and see her passages as sacred from on high; we who have exercised our greatest creativity in discovering her words to be incomparably wise; we who know the richness and pathos of her tales, and the justice and mercy in much of her law; we who feel the sharp or subtle emotions of her heroes, and we whose bones resonate to the ancient cadences of her songs and poems; we who recognize how false are the caricatures of the Bible as drawn by her bitterest foes; we who have found in her a shelter and a mission since the early days of youth…it pains us deeply to behold, let alone to hold forth on, her many flaws. But in the house of Truth, my brothers and sisters, even Love and Loyalty must speak—and tell all they know.

---

[1] For more detail on the integrity of, or changes to, the Hebrew Bible's text over time, see among others, sections 105-106, and 111-112.

VII. Dangers and Disadvantages of Religion

141. Is religion dangerous or damaging? Argument that people should be left alone to enjoy religion's benefits

Then a man said: You yourself have earlier explained many of the important functions religion plays in people's lives. So many are comforted or buttressed by faith and religious community. Why should we give up these good effects, especially since if you are right, religion's promises of heaven may be mistaken—and when we die there may be nothing more? In that case, let us at least feel oriented and reassured before our brief existence is forever extinguished. Is religion dangerous or damaging, that you would have us avoid it?

And the sage replied: My brother, religion does, indeed, offer much that is felt to be good; and in discussing the reasons we avoid challenging our beliefs,[1] as well as in discussing the reasons for the birth of religion,[2] I implied many of the benefits people gain from faith and religious community. And as you say, I have even directly enumerated some of religion's greatest gifts.[3]

And I have often asked your question of my own heart and agonized for years over whether it does more good or harm to awaken people to the possibility that their religious beliefs are in error.[4] Yet I have concluded that truth, for

---

[1] See Part III (section 15 and all its subsections).

[2] See section 67.

[3] See Part II (section 13 and all its subsections).

[4] Thomas Henry Huxley wrestled with this question, too, but both for the individual and for society he saw religion's dangers and damages as many. In his essay "Agnosticism" he writes: "I am very well aware, as I suppose most thoughtful people are in these times, that the process of breaking away from old beliefs is extremely unpleasant; and I am much disposed to think that the encouragement, the consolation, and the peace afforded to earnest believers in even the worst forms of Christianity are of great practical advantage to them. What deductions must be made from this gain on this score of the harm done to the citizen by the ascetic other-worldliness of logical Christianity; to the ruler, by the hatred, malice, and all uncharitableness of sectarian bigotry; to the legislator, by the spirit of exclusiveness and domination of those that count themselves pillars of orthodoxy; to the philosopher, by the restraints on the freedom of learning and teaching which every Church exercises, when it is strong enough; to the conscientious soul, by the introspective hunting after sins of the mint and cummin type, the fear of theological error, and the overpowering terror of possible damnation, which have accompanied the Churches like their shadow, I need not now consider; but they are assuredly not small. If agnostics lose heavily on the one side, they gain a good deal on the other. People who talk about the comforts of belief appear to forget its discomforts."

those who choose to learn and grow, is—even with its many pains—superior to the most pleasant complacencies of error.[1] And error, in any case, often bears its own suffering, as the bubble of its insularity cannot be counted upon to forever remain whole and unpunctured.

And, my brother, to address your question directly: Yes, many and deep are the dangers and damages of religion. She transgresses against us seven mortal sins, and afflicts us with numerous lesser betrayals, too.

First, religion drives us away from our deepest connection with the universe and with ourselves, in forbidding us to think honestly about the meaning of our lives and the puzzle of existence. Authenticity is impossible when we cannot truly encounter—free of the demands of faith and dogma—the great mysteries of life, death, spirit, and meaning. Like the captive eagle grounded from riding the wind in soaring flight; like the hobbled stallion constrained from thundering the plains at full gallop; and like the caged tiger barred from stalking the grasslands on the wild hunt, the religious human, with spirit reduced to imitation and mind imprisoned by doctrine, is but one more tragic, stunted figure, kept from embodying his authentic identity and achieving his mature destiny.

And religion not only deprives us as individuals, it robs humanity of our collective dignity and promise. For religion discourages profound honesty on the most important matters, often insisting—with seductive promise and fiery threat—that we must accept unproven beliefs about God and the universe, and reject or muffle the noble call of forthright reason. Yet reason is that gift which most distinguishes man from all other species; and to the extent reason is shackled, so too is shackled the human character and spirit.

Second, religion insults the dignity and decency of humankind when it insists that we need divine laws, and threats and promises of supernatural penalties and rewards, to behave well. Consider the libel upon our species in religion teaching that "Thou shalt not unjustifiably kill"[2] was necessary to be inscribed in the stone

---

And a bit earlier in the same essay he wrote: "I verily believe that the great good which has been effected in the world by Christianity has been largely counteracted by the pestilent doctrine on which all the Churches have insisted, that honest disbelief in their more or less astonishing creeds is a moral offence, indeed a sin of the deepest dye, deserving and involving the same future retribution as murder and robbery. If we could only see, in one view, the torrents of hypocrisy and cruelty, the lies, the slaughter, the violations of every obligation of humanity, which have flowed from this source along the course of the history of Christian nations, our worst imaginations of Hell would pale beside the vision."

[1] See the preface and section 14, among others, for elaboration.

[2] See text and footnote in section 118 where, in the context of discrediting certain alleged contradictions in the Bible, I discuss the matter of the appropriate translation of the passage in the Ten Commandments often translated as "Thou shalt not kill."

tablets of the Ten Commandments, and the implication that before this revelation from God to Moses, the Israelites, or any other people, considered murder,[1] or other behaviors such as stealing or bearing false witness, to be permissible.[2]

Not only does this view of humanity paint us as worse than various forms of communal insects and beasts, the ants and bees and wolves and lions and elephants, among others—who have the innate understanding that members of their own group are to be treated well and only punished for "crimes," and who generally behave as well as even religious societies—this religious view of humanity makes it more likely that some humans will, indeed, behave worse than beasts when their eyes see through the artificial pageantry of religion, and their ears detect the hollow ring of her teachings and prayers.

He who is taught that the only reason to behave well is to obey the commands of a supernatural God, is unavoidably being taught that the human being does not have it within his own breast to live in a civil and constructive manner, and that there is no natural or terrestrial reason to do so—and when the sun of understanding shines down and begins to melt the obscuring, hazardous ice of yesterday's ideas frozen, such a man will be terrified of his own and others' evil potential, and darkly tempted and demoralized, too—and, indeed, such potential may have been unnaturally enhanced. For he and others have been indoctrinated with the belief that good behavior can only stem from supernatural direction.[3]

The third disadvantage of religion is that it all too often engages in persecution, and foments division and hate—discord and passions not easily quelled, because those who indulge in such holy acrimony believe it to be the will of God. Religions have often persecuted, even killed, non-believers, and instigated hostilities and mayhem. And do we know of many generations in which wars have *not* been fought over religious differences? For, my brother, when people insist they know what God wishes, they are capable of taking any action—not to mention holding fast to any ideology—no matter how extreme, in the cause of what they see as sacred mission.

Religions, in teaching certainty about the most important matters, plant within us the seeds of enmity and strife. How can one not expect, for example, many who fervently believe that Jesus is God or the Son of God to, in difficult times, distrust, shun, even hate and scapegoat, those who do not believe Jesus to have been more than human? Or how can one not expect that many who are taught that Mohammad was God's greatest prophet will, in difficult times,

---

[1] The unjustified killing of members of one's own group—not to be confused with killing in war, or by the courts, or other forms of killing societies may allow.

[2] I have seen the irrepressible Christopher Hitchens make this point in debate—and make it rather more colorfully.

[3] Among others earlier and later, Freud makes this argument in his *Future of an Illusion.*

distrust, shun, hate or scapegoat those who do not believe in the divine origin of Mohammad's message? Or how can one not expect those who read in their Scriptures that they are the chosen nation and the apple of God's eye, to disrespect and mistreat other peoples when possessed of the power to do so?

And even in days of tolerance and coexistence, does there not lurk behind the religious man's neighborly wave to those of other creeds something less conducive to peace and goodwill? When others differ from his beliefs on the most important matters, and hold views he was taught will keep them from being valued by God as much as he will be—or especially if he was taught that their beliefs will cut them off from heaven and cast them into eternal hell—how can he not, on some level, see them as inferior? In one way or another, then, though he cannot prove the superiority or even the legitimacy of his own beliefs, the man of traditional religion looks down at his fellow man and thinks: I am noble and beloved of God in holding firm to my admirable faith; you, my neighbor, are sadly mistaken and eternally condemned for stubbornly clinging to your false beliefs; and that stranger, in not breaking free of his primitive superstitions, is barely human, nothing more than a thinly-disguised savage.

Moreover, let us not be overly complacent about the societal benefits of religious piety; for all too often has fervent devotion led to passive other-worldliness, even crossed over into lethal fanaticism. When believing in an all-powerful deity and an eternal heaven or hell, earthly life can seem insignificant, and terrestrial abuses and cruelties—not to mention mere neglect—can be easily justified, even applauded, when construed as leading to the greater glory of God.[1]

And this is one of the poisonous seeds at the core of religion. If we pretend to know what God said, and what God wants; and especially if our books of God include—interspersed amongst their good and uplifting passages—cruel commands and hateful sentiments, even teachings that denigrate earthly existence, as some Scriptures do; we should not be surprised if some in many generations, and many in some generations, actually take seriously these passages of sacred text, and attempt to implement or expand upon the less gentle, less ennobling messages in the books they consider holy.

And let not your heart be tempted to protest that your religion is currently peaceful and tolerant, even benevolent.[2] For the roots of persecution and war are pervasive—even if sometimes dormant—in our major religions. So long as a religion maintains the Bible to be the word of God—a Bible that, among other

---

[1] Blaise Pascal, famous for his Wager arguing in favor of religious belief, nevertheless said: "Men never do evil so completely and cheerfully as when they do it from religious conviction."

[2] See section 145 for more on this point.

things, condones slavery, commands genocide, teaches the persecution of other religions, or condemns the masses of humanity to eternal fiery hell—so long does it shelter within its complacent breast the sleeping menace that will, tomorrow or in a hundred years, awaken again to destructive malevolence.

My brother, most traditional religions[1] have been violent or repressive, and will likely be so again—if they attain great power, or when difficult days come. And so it is that religions have not, as a rule, given up the practices of persecution and violence of their own accord; instead, they have adopted tolerance only when weakened by the growing power of non-clerical government or the waning belief of a changing, less-insular populace.

The fourth disadvantage of religion is that it attempts to remove our focus, and our best energies, from the natural world, the only one of which we can be certain, and would have us instead focus on an afterlife or on a set of laws it claims originated with a supernatural God. What a terrible waste of human energy and life! How many real problems have not been solved—how many diseases remained unconquered, how many laws of nature remained undiscovered, how many hearts remained unhealed and minds unfreed—because sincere religious people devoted their energies to some hereafter or some imagined deity, instead of giving their all for the family of earth, in the only existence we can honestly know to be real and true.

And religion robs people of what might be their only chance at a deeply enjoyable existence. By teaching of an afterlife for which earthly life is but a preparation, religion often persuades people to forego happiness in this life and to await their rewards in the hereafter. But there may not be any hereafter—and religion is not honest about admitting this. How many tragic lives have been stoically endured, instead of being changed for the better? How many of our ancestors have prayed and worshiped daily, pleaded tearfully to God for deliverance from misery, and donated their last pittance to religion in the belief that they were earning heaven? And how many have killed and died in the hopes of meriting the blissful afterlife promised by religion? If people knew mortal life to be the only existence of which they could be certain, might they not be more likely to lead fuller lives, without regrets, without self-sacrificing illusions, and with fewer zealous missions to convert or persecute others?

Fifth, religion erodes the integrity of the family, and of society overall; for the fabric of trust in families is frayed when parents cannot be honest with their children about what they know and do not know—when they teach them beliefs nobody can responsibly be confident are true—on such important issues as God,

---

[1] Including Judaism by the accounts of its own Bible, and Christianity and Islam by numerous better-documented accounts of later history.

death, and life's meaning. And though parents and children may not consciously allow themselves to be aware of lying or being lied to on life's most important matters, at some level they cannot fool themselves. And foundations of larger society, too—its honesty and dignity—are compromised when religion demands of its adherents that they be false with themselves and their neighbors by participating in public displays of untruthful assembly and worship—where unproven dogmas and doctrines are insisted upon, dubious deities are dutifully praised and glorified, and innocent and open discussion is strongly discouraged.

Sixth, religion often fosters terrible guilt and fear on the part of those who cannot live up to its sometimes-lofty, sometimes-unrealistic, standards of belief or action. How many lives have been seared by the terrors of hell's blazing fires, and disfigured by threats of eternal torture?[1] How many young people have been plagued by guilt because of natural sexual thoughts? And how many well-meaning souls over the centuries have endured horrible self-hate because their minds could not shake religious doubts—doubts religion often insisted were intolerably evil? And have not numerous additional religious laws and beliefs caused untold painful guilt—all based on the dishonest claim of religion that it knew—and knows—the will of God?

---

[1] This has been for the majority of Christianity's history a mainstay of the faith—and innumerable critics of such religion protest this teaching. For one impassioned example, Robert Ingersoll in his lecture titled "The Liberty of Man, Woman and Child," says: "Where did that doctrine of eternal punishment for men and women and children come from?...I despise it with every drop of my blood. Tell me there is a God in the serene heavens that will damn his children for the expression of an honest belief! More men have died in their sins, judged by your orthodox creeds, than there are leaves on all the forests in the wide world ten thousand times over. Tell me these men are in hell; that these men are in torment; that these children are in eternal pain, and that they are to be punished forever and forever! I denounce this doctrine as the most infamous of lies."
Ingersoll continues: "When the great ship containing the hopes and aspirations of the world, when the great ship freighted with mankind goes down in the night of death, chaos and disaster, I am willing to go down with the ship. I will not be guilty of the ineffable meanness of paddling away in some orthodox canoe. I will go down with the ship, with those who love me, and with those whom I have loved. If there is a God who will damn his children forever, I would rather go to hell than to go to heaven and keep the society of an infamous tyrant. I make my choice now. I despise that doctrine. It has covered the cheeks of this world with tears. It has polluted the hearts of children, and poisoned the imaginations of men. It has been a constant pain, a perpetual terror...It has wrung the hearts of the tender, it has furrowed the cheeks of the good...What right have you, sir, Mr. clergyman, you, minister of the gospel, to stand at the portals of the tomb, at the vestibule of eternity, and fill the future with horror and with fear?...A man who believes that doctrine and does not go insane has the heart of a snake and the conscience of a hyena."

Seventh, traditional religion freezes in place notions on spirituality, preventing ongoing development of ideas in this realm—turning the flowering dance of ecstasy into, at best, a repetitive march. Yes, it allows innovation on the edges, but any challenge to its foundational premises is even today seen as heresy, and met with pity or censure, and for much of history was met with banishment or death. It insists it knows the one and only final spiritual truth, and thus discourages or forbids us from exploring or teaching new and different ideas on matters of spirit and meaning—ideas that may be more helpful to an individual or society, ideas that may be more accurate and honest. Thus, opportunities for new spiritual developments within a religion are, as a rule, few when compared to the opportunities offered by non-dogmatic spiritual exploration. And although religions may gradually evolve in their positions or beliefs, such change is usually slow, and strenuously resisted. For most of history only those intrepid souls with the passion or recklessness to risk persecution by the government, to brave being branded as heretics by the church, and to endure being rejected and humiliated by their own communities, even families—only those have dared challenge religion's authority or beliefs.

My brother, those are seven mortal sins of religion, failings that significantly damage humanity, as individuals and societies. Yet I will mention several additional damages, from a list that grows as one reflects upon the matter well.

Religion, in many of its traditional forms, teaches immaturity and dependence. Instead of encouraging each person to think carefully and with personal responsibility on the important issues in life, religions enjoin us to rely upon the guidance of religious leaders to tell us what is right and wrong, what we are to believe and how we are to live. Thus it teaches a form of childlike functioning; and in adults, dependent thinking is not only demeaning, but unhealthy for society. And the instruction to rely upon religious authorities is, of course, based on insufficient honesty—for it is a rare representative of traditional religion who candidly admits that he does not have a responsible basis upon which to claim he truly knows God or His will, and that his religious claims are built upon traditions or intuitions that may well be mistaken—just as he believes other religions mistaken.

Moreover, traditional religion tends to concentrate power in the hands of a few—the religious leaders who purport to speak with the authority and blessing of God. Such power can lead, and historically has led, to abuse. Church leaders can become wealthy, influential, and arrogant at the expense of their followers.

In addition, religion has often contributed to poverty and misery, in several ways: By banning birth control, religion has forced staggering burdens on countless families; historically, some religions have also disparaged wealth and profit, and many strands of religion have taught people to have faith that God would provide—instead of teaching the importance of earning subsistence, even building prosperity, by shouldering the responsibility for industry and innovation.

Furthermore, religion has slowed progress in medicine, science and other fields by frequently claiming that various scientific or intellectual explorations or even findings of fact were ungodly, unnatural, or contrary to the Bible. Some of the better-known cases are the persecution of Galileo and the excommunication of Spinoza. But the instances of religion attempting to muzzle science and honest thought are legion.[1] In a more general sense—less obvious, perhaps, but more pervasive and destructive—religions have often slowed progress by disparaging earthly existence, and teaching that the world to come, an afterlife they say follows death, is far more important than the life of this world.

My brother, you may correctly respond that religion has made significant contributions, too, to individual happiness, constructive community, and the advance of civilization. And, indeed, I have spoken of these.[2] But there is hardly any great loss without some attendant gain. Pointing to religion's benefits, therefore, is insufficient justification. As you would not exchange your heart and lungs for even the safest, warmest home filled with the most satisfying of foods and the most delightful of wines, neither should we barter our souls for even the most alluring of wares at the great bazaar of faith. For the price demanded by religion—the sacrifice of reason, honesty, and authenticity—is so terribly impoverishing, that all her possible offers are rendered but laughable, and all her eager buyers but pitiable and tragic.

142. Sub-argument that religion's atrocities were driven by political forces, were only used to rally the masses, were not authentic parts of religion, and without religion's involvement would have been committed anyway

And a devout man said: You speak unfairly of religion's bloodshed, for such terrible events are rooted not in the sacred, but in the political. Mass frustrations are manipulated by the powerful, toward political ends—and religion, misused, is the tool often employed. True, various mavericks and malcontents within the fold of religion may have used religion for bad ends; but this was never part of authoritative religion itself. Also, if religion were not the given justification, such atrocities would have been committed in any case—but for different stated reasons. Sadly, evil will always find its means, and at times it perverts even the

---

[1] Thomas H. Huxley is credited with saying, "The cradle of every science is surrounded by dead theologians as that of Hercules was with strangled serpents."

[2] See section 13 and all its subsections.

symbols and communities of faith. Real religion, however, is peaceful and loving, and advantageous to society.

And the sage replied: My brother, it is of course true that religions have not been exclusively bloody, and that much blood has been spilled for reasons other than religion. It is also true that some have perverted religion and the faith of the religious, to further their own selfish ends; and that religion has often done good.

But, my brother, let us be clear: When we speak of the persecution, even carnage, inflicted in the name of God, we are not speaking of fringe lunatics staining with their aberrant abuses the spotless robes of mainstream religion. The Bible commands genocide, and religious leaders of the highest order have advocated, even legislated, persecution and hate. If Moses and Joshua did not speak for Judaism, if Jesus and the popes and Luther did not speak for Christianity, and if the Old and New Testaments cannot be said to speak for these faiths, either, and if Mohammad and the Koran and the Hadith do not speak for Islam—are we not playing a poor game of semantics?[1]

---

[1] In several places (especially section 127) I document that although it offers many positive teachings, the Old Testament also includes some teachings we today can only see as morally abhorrent, among them the genocides and mass murders the Bible says were carried out at the direction of Moses and Joshua, by the word of God.

And on this point of the morality of the Old Testament and early biblical Judaism, even Walter Kaufmann, the usually sure-footed champion of intellectual honesty, seems to slip. In Part VII, section 52, of his *Faith of a Heretic*, in keeping with his very generous appraisal of the Old Testament in various of his writings, he speaks of genocide and mass murder being present in the Book of Joshua, but minimizes it by saying, among other things, "Many nations have their Joshuas..." But this great scholar quite familiar with the Bible does not there mention that Deuteronomy, too, in the Five Books of Moses, not only has God commanding Moses to commit genocide and mass murder, but has its verses record that Moses and the Israelites carried out these supposed commands of God. And in Exodus and elsewhere the Five Books of Moses commands or condones slavery. The Bible having God direct Moses and the Israelites—in the founding narrative of the Chosen People traveling toward and conquering the Promised Land—to commit genocide and mass murder and practice slavery cannot justifiably be brushed aside as aberrations, or as footnotes involving minor and regrettable figures in an otherwise virtuous account. Undeniably, the Old Testament—whether the product of the same men holding some admirable and some despicable values, or the cumulative work of different men, some virtuous and some villainous—contains, by today's lights, both high-minded ideals and degrading misguidance. The many important positive aspects of the Old Testament should indeed not be ignored, and Kaufmann makes a learned and impassioned case for celebrating these; and he is surely correct that the essence or genius of the Old Testament is no more to be justly seen in its massacres than is the essence or genius of the United States to be seen in those who slaughtered the Native Americans. And I understand, too, that he was trying to right the imbalance he saw in how favorably the New Testament was conventionally perceived in his generation of Christian America, and how negatively the Old Testament. But after acknowledging the good, let us confess, too, to the atrocities, to the behaviors we must in today's age brand morally unacceptable, yet which are commanded and condoned at the heart of the Old Testament, the document and narrative from which blossomed Judaism most directly, Christianity to an important degree, and to some extent even Islam.

As to Jesus and the New Testament, although they, too, offer various positive lessons, we have spoken (see sections 128 and 137) among other things of Jesus' teaching that sinners are to burn in fire for all eternity—a punishment reflecting a level of cruelty and vindictiveness far exceeding anything in the Old Testament—as well as his, and the New Testament's, tolerance of slavery, his degrading treatment of non-Jews, and the New Testament's inflammatory language and collective vilification of Jews.

As to the popes, there certainly were bright spots. Some forbade violence against those of other religions, or at least did not encourage it, in generations when they could have easily abused their power. Several popes even went out of their way to defend Jews against charges of using Christian children's blood in their rituals. Still—though this is painful for Catholics to confront—the leaders of the church, over well more than a millennia, all too often, though certainly not always, ignored, condoned, or even directed various forms of persecution and bigotry. Pope Innocent III, elected in 1198, led the Laterna Council in 1215 in its edict that Jews must wear identifying clothing clearly marking them as Jews. Pope Innocent IV ordered, in the mid 13th century, that the Jewish Talmud be burned; and, in the mid-16th century, Pope Julius II did the same.

For a particularly egregious example, Pope Paul IV, elected in 1555, wrote, in the papal bull *Cum nimis absurdum*, that the Jews were condemned by God to eternal slavery, that they should be subject to Christians and must wear distinctive clothing identifying them as Jews—males were forced to wear pointed yellow hats, and women forced to wear yellow kerchiefs; Jews were also forbidden to own real estate, to be physicians for Christians, or to hire Christian attendants, even to eat with or fraternize with Christians. Among other things, the papal bull also legislated that Jews must live in segregated areas separated from Christians, and for this purpose a ghetto was created in Rome. It also prohibited Jews from having more than one synagogue in any state or territory, and ordered that all but one synagogue in each area were to be destroyed.

Pius V, when elected in 1566—after a brief period of the more moderate Pius IV—reestablished these persecutory laws, and added to them. Among the new persecutions was the expulsion of Jews from many cities.

Pius VI, elected in 1775, renewed the persecutions of Jews, including requiring the wearing of yellow badges, ghettos, forcing them to attend Christian sermons, forbidding them to drive through Rome, and even to have gravestones in their cemeteries.

And those are only several examples of many. The long, shameful saga of oppression not only tolerated or condoned, but mandated, by popes—though punctuated by periods of relative tolerance—claimed countless victims, and for purposes of this book need not be spelled out in more detail. And the similarities are obvious between these papal laws, over many dark centuries across Europe, and Hitler's later laws enacted at Nuremberg.

And it should not surprise us that apologists for religion will do their best to justify or defend, or at least plead extenuating circumstances and "wider context," and do every-thing except acknowledge the gross moral oversights and abuses permitted and perpe-

461

trated in the name of religion. (Those interested in more detail can access this information in numerous sources; among them, Malcolm Hay's *Europe and the Jews*, and Stuart Rosenberg's *The Christian Problem*.)

As for Luther, after initially speaking well of the Jews and hoping to convert them to his new vision of Christianity, he later wrote and taught many abhorrent things including a long treatise entitled, *On The Jews and Their Lies* (1543) in which he not only speaks in his characteristically vulgar manner, using crude insults and referencing bodily functions, he also says that Jews are fully willing to poison wells, to hack Christian children to death, and to use their blood for ritual purposes. And Luther advocates, among other heinous measures, that all synagogues be set afire, that all Jews' houses be destroyed, that their money and valuables be taken from them, and that they be expelled from the country. Common sense, as well as prevailing scholarly opinion, sees Luther's influence—in addition to those of the popes—not only in the cultural anti-Jewish bias and the many smaller persecutions in Germany over the ensuing centuries, but in the infamous Nuremberg Laws of 1935, in the events of Kristallnacht in 1938, and in the atrocities of the Nazis in the Holocaust, overall.

As for Islam, with terrorists, at the time of this writing, wreaking indiscriminate carnage on civilians the world over, one is tempted to argue that no further inquiry is needed as to whether the religion teaches violence. And though these terrible and widespread actions do not by themselves prove that the foundational texts or historic leaders of Islam taught violence and hate—the telling silence, not to mention the not uncommon vocal support, of too many in the Islamic clergy, constitutes evidence that whatever its originator intended, many speaking for Islam approve of extreme intolerance and barbaric behavior. At a minimum, our own eyes and ears testify that far more anger and protest is generated from within Islam against any perceived slight or insult to their religion, such as an artist drawing an unflattering cartoon of Mohammad, than is generated by the innumerable atrocities—beheadings, bombings, streets strewn with body parts and pools of blood, and all manner of violence and hatred—committed and celebrated by their brothers and sisters claiming to be acting in the name of Islam.

And the authoritative texts of Islam—the Koran and the Hadith—which, like the texts of all religions, contain many good and noble passages—do speak, among other messages, of much that modern civilization must consider immoral, of making war on the unbeliever, of killing Muslims who leave the faith, and of legislating the unequal treatment of non-Muslims by subjecting them to additional taxes or fines. These authoritative Islamic texts—just as do the Old and New Testaments—also speak of non-believers in all manner of excoriating and insulting terms, and help incubate the devaluing and dehumanizing attitudes toward "infidels" that, given the right mix of stressors and influences, manifest in hatred and carnage. As the great majority of my readers are not Muslim, and as a significant portion of any Muslim readers this book may enjoy will have no great difficulty finding messages such as these in the Koran and Hadith, I will refrain from quoting specific offending passages. Many books, including the recent work, *The End of Faith*, by that man of courage and reason, Sam Harris, elaborate upon, and provide specific citations of, that aspect of Islam and its sacred writings.

In summary, religion, in the voices of its most authoritative leaders—Moses, Joshua, Jesus, the popes, Luther, and Mohammad, among many others—has, in addition to its

And cannot the apologetic defense you advance for religion be argued as well in the cause of absolving from guilt the most savage of criminals, the most heartless of tyrants, and the most inhuman of ideologies? Are there not always other causes, deeper roots, a bigger picture, to which we can point? And can we not postulate—and excuse any evil—that society must exercise some aggression, and that without these particular crimes, aggression would have manifested in other ways? Shall we justify the slaveholder because his cruelty in holding on to human chattel may stem from the fear of learning a new way of life not dependent upon the toil of others? Shall we minimize the horrors of genocide because it may have arisen from the humiliation of an ignominious defeat and the impoverishment of a harsh peace, amongst a people desperate for a taste of former glory—and a scapegoat for present distress?[1]

And are there not always deeper currents beneath the swift-coursing blood of the innocent, and have not pirates been powered by strong sea-winds to their barbaric, rapacious deeds? And shall we exonerate the murderer because his violence was stimulated by the ache of degrading poverty or the ever-echoing bellows of a father cruel with drink? And is not the cold sword of brutality often forged in the flaming furnace of passion and pain?

Moreover, if religion has been repeatedly exploited for evil—even if manipulated by underlying "real" causes—should we not investigate the source of this danger? Have you considered why it is that religion can be so easily turned to such oppressive ends? Is not her inherent and fatal flaw that she pretends to put the word of God in men's mouths and books, and thus confers upon them infallible authority and unlimited power to command the faithful, and to zealously disregard more cautious or compassionate second thoughts?

Most to the point, my brother, some have argued that without the binding cords of religion, society would begin to unravel. In response I say that religion itself, with its active and bloody hand, has repeatedly unraveled society. Whatever forces lay behind her consistent prejudice and periodic mayhem cannot change the historical record that religion has—too many times—undermined the civility of mankind. Thus, regardless of ultimate cause, these repeated crimes of the clergy and the faithful illustrate how deeply they imperil the welfare of us all.

---

valuable contributions, taught and practiced terrible things. Wars, atrocities, and persecutions are not departures from religion's "true" and "original" message. Religion, at its heart, even in its early teachings—because it claims to speak for God and claims for itself and its people divinely ordained superiority and the unhesitating confidence of Truth beyond all question or doubt—has, predictably, often descended into bigotry and worse.

[1] This refers, of course, to the set of circumstances many see as having led to the rise of German Nazism in the period preceding WWII.

Would not the loosening of the ancient grip of the gods, along with the loss of any salutary bonds, liberate us, too, from religion's considerable menace?

Not only might truth and integrity be well worth any price society may pay—even the loss of tradition's stability—the cost may not be so high when compared with religion's steep and terrible price our species has long been paying.

And remember, although violence and mayhem and all manner of divisiveness and oppression have been bitter fruits of religion through the ages, her most offensive produce were not these, but rather the trammeled minds and frightened spirits even within the many bodies she had not violated, the multitudes who lived and died strangers to their own best thoughts and wisdom, having submitted to religion's insistence that they sear into their hearts and into the hearts of their children dishonesty on matters deepest—that they dare not contemplate the meaning and orientation of their lives, but instead need surrender to the degrading, willful blindness of dogmatic faith.

But on your original point, my brother, it will not do to absolve religion of her misdeeds by blaming other "underlying" forces. Of earlier beginnings there is no end: Every cause has an earlier birth, and every birth an earlier mother. But even as we cultivate compassion and complexity, so too must we honor justice and truth. The hand that strikes the blow and the heart that turns away must bear the burden of innocent blood and be called to account for unheeded tears.

143. Sub-argument that tribalism and the instinct toward hero worship—and not religion—are the causes of religious wars and persecution

But another man said: Throughout history, and even recently amongst those with little religion, people have tended to identify strongly with their own group, and to revere powerful leaders and follow their direction. These tendencies, and not religion, combine to produce hatred and oppression of other groups.

And the sage said: My brother, you are correct in saying that humans have tendencies toward tribalism and hero worship, and that these can lead to hatred and oppression. I would ask you to consider, however, that merely because some causes of evil have been identified, does not mean that no causes of evil remain. Religion may play an important role in inciting division and discord, even if tribalism and hero worship play their parts. And surely those who care for the pragmatic welfare of our species—not to mention its dignity and its intellectual advancement—must not turn away from dealing with one important source of danger, merely because it is not the only source.

Indeed, religion often begins where other negative influences end: Religion takes the natural and earthbound tendencies of tribalism and hero worship and magnifies them to unlimited and eternal proportions by projecting onto the group's identity and the leadership's authority the halo of the supernatural. Thus, conflicts and divisions motivated by merely natural tendencies, which may have been resisted by those of wise or compassionate disposition, and which may have been healed by recourse to practical, diplomatic approaches are, when infused with the uncompromising intensity of supernatural directive, often rendered impervious to the moderating influence of natural considerations.

In short, my brother: Yes, there are various negative forces that give rise to evil. But not only has Religion, for lo these millennia, fought proudly as a stalwart member of those terrifying ranks, she has served, and continues to serve, a unique role in hardening the armor and intensifying the zeal of all her comrades. And, again, religion has done much good, too, but continues to pose a terrible threat in magnifying the human tendencies toward tribalism and intolerance. But most important—and even if religion never again were to be the cause of any oppression or hate—it degrades the basis and spirit of human life by insisting that we must claim to know what we do not know, and that we must teach our children that they know what they do not know, on the most meaningful matters of life, and on what awaits us after death.

144. Sub-argument that atheists have been guilty of mass killing and destruction too

And a religious man objected, saying: You speak of the harm and destruction caused by religion, and make it sound like all bloodshed was committed in the name of God. Why do you not speak of the harm and destruction and killing committed by atheists?

And the sage replied: My brother, you are correct that some atheists have undertaken terrible deeds, too. It has not been my intent to suggest that religion has caused all, or even most of the killing and persecution humans have inflicted and endured, or that non-believers have caused none. Indeed, the enemy of reason, the roadblock to progress, and the arch-adversary of peaceful civilization is not any particular ideology, but the surrender to unjustified certainty in any of its many forms: unjustified certainty in one's religious beliefs, unjustified certainty in one's political beliefs, unjustified certainty in one's intuitions, emotions, and any other source of counsel—the holding of dogmas to be above the proving grounds of debate, beyond the schoolhouse of dissent, and outside the realm of honest doubt—for even when the aim is to do good, and, at times, even by those who see themselves as correcting religion's errors, all these bow to the many false gods of irresponsible certitude, and offer as sacrifice not only their first-born, Reason, but also the brothers and sisters of us all, the victims and the vanquished in so many persecutions and so many wars, in so many ages and so many lands.

Indeed, my brother, dogmatic atheism—and by this I mean the belief that insists it knows for certain that there is no Creator, and no supernatural being with power over our lives—is similar to religion in an aspect most dangerous and degrading: Both forfeit knowledge and candor for the corrupt comforts of ill-gotten conviction.[1]

But why do I not hold forth more against dogmatic atheism? Because none can labor for all worthy causes or engage in battle with every dangerous foe—much less can one do so all at once. Shall we complain to one working to relieve famine that overeating causes difficulties, too? And shall we protest to one working on a cure for hallucination that blindness is a problem, too? And if one who does not advocate atheism is called to speak out on the errors and hazards of religion, is it a legitimate protest to point out that dogmatic atheism, too, can be destructive? Have not our fathers and mothers, or childhood companions, taught us early that two wrongs do not make a right? If some forms of atheism were as detrimental to society as is traditional religion, this would still not be a defense for traditional religion—but rather an indictment against both dogmatic atheism and traditional religion.

And, my brother, lest it be argued that pointing to the failures of dogmatic atheism is relevant because religion must be weighed against its alternative, I remind you that we are not limited to choosing between those two extreme options. They are opposite faces of the same counterfeit coin—the mistaking of conviction for truth, on life's most important matters. And while, for or against, both speak of God, they are animated by the all-too-human weakness to rush headlong into ideological certainty—to procure existential confidence at the cost of honesty. Instead, would it be so difficult, would it hurt too badly, for us to admit with simple humility that some things we do not know, and that among these are whether our universe in general, or the human race in particular, is the product—even if by indirect means—of conscious creation, and, if so, whether it is the will of the creating God or gods that we lead our lives by a particular set of laws? My brother, dogmatic atheism and traditional religion are but two poles, between which lies the vast, reasonable ground of those who do not pretend to know what they do not know.

Moreover, in one important sense, at least, even dogmatic atheism is less objectionable than religion: Religion most perverts truth and meaning. For religion—alone amongst ideologies—claims that her doctrines are supernaturally accurate and significant, transcending, and more essential than, all things human and natural. The atheist, even when vastly destructive, at worst insists with

---

[1] That extremists of seemingly opposite varieties often have more in common than might at first be apparent, is illustrated, in another context, by Eric Hoffer in his *True Believer* where he writes that in the days of building the Nazi movement Hitler said that he could successfully recruit from among the communists, but not from among the capitalists.

murderous arrogance that his philosophy of life is more correct than all others—but he cannot claim supernatural source or significance for his cause. In this way, his beliefs are not only less insulated from challenge and change, but his prescriptions are less a mockery of the human urge toward truth and meaning.

And, my brother, remember: The main arguments against religion are neither her bloodshed nor her other violations of the flesh, but rather the wounds she inflicts upon mankind's spirit, by teaching heaven, hell, authority, and faith—and thus seducing, threatening, directing, and deceiving us away from deep honesty about our fundamental beliefs, and from untrammeled inquiry about our ultimate destiny.

And though some atheists have blood on their hands, too, it may be argued—even on pragmatic grounds—that religion is the greater threat. For when people persuade themselves with ideological ferocity that their creed possesses correct certainties on life's greatest questions and that their deeds carry a mandate from the supernatural Creator, no earthly crime can feel weightier than the transcendent burden of their own convictions; no earthly logic or reason can be more compelling than their most sacred dogmas—and no earthly consequence, not even their own death or the death of all their people, need give them pause. For they believe they act on the unimpeachable authority of heaven, that all forms of hesitation and doubt are but different faces of the devil's ruse, and that immense rewards await them upon death—an afterlife of ecstasy unparalleled, and eternal, blissful communion with an all-powerful and ever-grateful God.

145. Sub-argument that today's religion is not extreme, therefore not dangerous

Then a priest spoke, saying: The extreme behavior of some religions, during some ages of history, and in some parts of the world, is regrettable, but it constitutes no reason to disapprove of religion in general. For today, in this land, my religion—Christianity—is not extreme, and does not advocate killing or persecution. To the contrary, it helps the poor, feeds the hungry, brings hope to the despairing, and inspiration to the devout. And it teaches kindness and tolerance, too. Why argue against such a benevolent and uplifting institution?

And the sage replied: I agree that many among the religious are good people, and apply their religion to doing kindness for others, and teaching tolerance and love. Still, my brother, such kindness and admirable intentions do not suffice to protect us from the damages and dangers of which I speak.

Even today, many variations of religion teach us not to think for ourselves, but to have faith in their texts and teachings, faith beyond reason—and even those that encourage reason in church, tend to end such encouragement if reason dares turn its impartial, critical eye toward foundational beliefs. Yet people taught to accept shackles on their mind and conscience, to let religious leaders and texts think for them instead, will, when dark days come, be far more readily persuaded to persecute and hate. And so it has been—grave danger come to terrible fruition—time after terror-filled time. So long as religion and her leaders claim to speak for God, yesterday's verses and today's sermons can inflame clergy and populace to any atrocity, no matter how barbaric—for they then believe such savagery to be the word and will of God, beyond the ken of human reason or the kinship of human compassion.

My brother, you would not engage in cruelty nor call it forth—but too many have. Even today, in varied regions of the world, religious leaders teach violence and hatred, and easily influence those who have been taught not to question but to believe. And in coming years and ages—so long as religion continues to teach faith beyond independent reason—its followers will remain stripped of the moral independence necessary to withstand incitement to malice and worse.

And think not that your religion will never stoop to this; for it has repeatedly done so in the past, and future conditions can readily bring about such depravity again. Within the sacred texts of major religions are stories or passages that can easily be interpreted as condoning violence or persecution—and popes and prophets have taught oppression, too. And we have discussed the Bible and its influence, and I have cited chapter and verse of such destructive lessons.[1]

And these biblical words—deemed sacred and inviolable—which spurred barbaric behavior in the past, can at any time be employed again to similar horrific ends. No major religion offers to reject its Bible, or even to repudiate its cruel or intolerant verses. Instead, even the broadminded among the faithful continue to call these harmful words holy—or insist they be retained within Scripture—while decorating them with apologetics and softer interpretations. But those with the simple, vigorous instincts to read and take to heart what their Bible actually says, are always in danger of resurrecting the dormant incitement inherent in such passages, and reenacting their terrible, traditional implications.

My brother: Do not lions and tigers prey upon humans only rarely? Yet their awful potential and the gruesome results of their episodic carnage teach us the wise fear of even seemingly gentle and sedate specimens of these large cats—so long as they yet possess their fangs and claws. So, too, with religion: Until she renounces the terrible weapon of claiming to know the will of God, or insisting she has in her possession His sacred books, we are wise to keep our distance from this beautiful but dangerous beast.

Vary the metaphor: Shall we build our homes atop a vast and powerful volcano—which has repeatedly erupted, displacing, maiming and killing untold

---

[1] See sections 127 and 128.

millions throughout history—merely because it hasn't spewed its liquid fire in several years? So long as destruction simmers within her, it is but naïve, even negligent, to be seduced into complacency by the blossoming flowers on her glorious peaks.

In short, my brother, it is far from harmless to inculcate unquestioning belief in, or obedience to, even compassionate and respectful teachings, by pretending we know them to be the word of God. How much more reckless it is to teach adherence to a book among whose passages are those that have repeatedly inspired hatred and violence, and may well do so again! For then we have taught the degrading vice of blind following—and bound our children's hearts to hold sacred a book not only capable of being turned to purposes of evil, but one with just such a repeated and tragic record.

And the principal point, my brother: Even if religion were never again to incite violence and persecution, even if its Bibles and faith were henceforth to be used only for charity and peace, it remains enormously destructive to the spirit of mankind, for it teaches us to lie to ourselves and to others about that which is most important. It insists that we pretend to know what we do not know—about God, the purpose of life, and our fate following death—and that we teach our children to be similarly untruthful. Such dishonesty about the most foundational issues hacks not only at the roots of trust between parents and children, but also at the stately limbs of profound self-acceptance, and at the sweet, sweet fruit of existential peace. For however cleverly we try to disguise these self-deceptions from our own souls; however energetically we commit to our dogmas in the attempt to banish doubt; however frenetically we distract ourselves with anxieties and responsibilities—deep down we know we are hiding from truth. And like Adam and Eve after sinning in the garden—cowering in dread of discovery and wrapped in the shame of self-knowledge—we know we are guilty, we know we are naked.

VIII. AGAINST THE SAGE

146. Pitying the sage

And a religious man said: I feel sorry for you. You are so misguided, so mistaken. You are missing the whole point of life, and the very meaning of existence. God is the answer, and I pity you because you clearly do not understand that.

And the sage replied: My brother, I thank you for your compassion. Pity can be an admirable emotion, and has brought about much loving-kindness in the world. Yet pity can also be, at times, fear in disguise—the fear of confronting the pitied one's arguments. Pity can choose to negate or diminish a person instead of dealing with his views or truly examining one's own views.

My brother, I do not say that you intentionally use pity to evade my arguments. But the powerful deeper regions of the mind seek to keep us from pain, and thus often prevent us from knowing our strongest motives—and blind us to those things the sight of which we would find profoundly troubling. It is not for me to say what moves in the mind and heart of another; but let each of us reflect upon our own loyalties, and attempt to discern our hidden motives.

Today, in discussing religion, I have given reasons for my conclusions, and answers to questions asked. To persuade me of your views—indeed, to truly persuade yourself—simply do the same; and speak directly to the questions raised and the answers advanced.

My brother: In our quest for truth, pity is unhelpful; for it is a tactic that can be employed against any opinion or position, including yours. If a believer in a different religion, or an atheist or agnostic, pitied you for what he claimed were *your* religious errors, would you be persuaded that his beliefs were correct? If not, I ask you gently, why should your pity persuade me—or you? And what have we gained if you pity me for what I do *not* believe, and others, in turn, pity you for what you *do* believe? Religion and truth will not have been addressed with courage, honesty, or dignity, and no light will have been brought to bear on the sacred or the real.

Indeed, my brother, allow your kind heart to feel pity for those who are misguided—but exert the humility and objectivity, too, to acknowledge that you do not know for certain who are the misguided, and that you yourself may be among them. Then join us in courageously examining beliefs and arguments, so that we may help determine whose views are mistaken, and attempt to educate them in all kindness and candor. And in thinking for yourself, though you bake but simple bread for your existential fare, will it not satisfy the soul far better than the breathless tales of others about an unseen world's elaborate feasts?

147. Expressing love for the sage

And an elderly religious teacher, his eyes filling with tears, stepped forward and said: I remember guiding you; come back to me. Come back to the path of truth. I love you, though you are mistaken and have rejected my teachings. And God loves you, too, with a love so strong you cannot even conceive of it—and He waits for you, desperately hoping you will return to Him.

And the sage said: My dear teacher, I remember you, too—and your intense spirit and kind heart. And I am grateful for your warm teachings in the past, and for your loving invitation today. And it has been too long since I have shared your earnest company.

Yet I say with respect, that love and reason have their separate areas of excellence. Just as reason cannot replace love in the fields of devotion—between man and woman, parent and child, friends of the heart, or even mentor and pupil—so too love cannot replace careful reason in the search for truth. For the walls of the house of truth are built with the hard bricks of knowledge and the thick mortar of reason, and will not stand if constructed with the soft cushions of love, and the watery intensity of tears.

And dear teacher, cannot love like pity be used by the hidden regions of the mind to avoid dealing with disconcerting views? For if you are moved by deep love for me, and by a yearning that I come back to you and your religion, might you not be too distracted by such emotion to notice that you have neither reasoned with me nor examined the specifics of my arguments, but have rather assumed, without sufficient investigation, that I am mistaken?

And would a believer in another religion, or an atheist or agnostic, in professing his intense love for you, persuade you to change your beliefs? Would you not thank him for his love but consider it irrelevant to the truth of your faith? Then, respectfully I ask: Why should you expect me, or any intelligent and honest person, to change beliefs based on your expressions of love?

And on your words about God's love: If a Creator is aware of me and loves me, can I have any doubt that He wants me to be straightforward with myself about what I know and what I do not know? Would a God who loves me insist that I lie to myself, crush my dignity and renounce my authenticity by forcing upon myself, in these most important of matters, beliefs that seem untrue?

My teacher, you are dear to me. I remember your depth, your enthusiasm, your devotion—and I love you for these. Yet let us not lead love to overstep her bounds into territory where reason must do his work. But if you will engage with me in reason, and persuade me of your beliefs, then I will gladly return to the God you love.

148. Praying for the sage and his blind and stubborn heart

And a religious woman said: I will pray for you, that God may open your blind and stubborn heart so that you might be saved from the prison of your darkness and be able to see the light of God's truth.

And the sage said: My sister, I understand that you believe strongly in your faith. I ask you to consider, however, that what is real or reasonable requires neither prayers nor miracles to make itself evident.

And would you find it persuasive, if someone of a different religion prayed for you, for what she considered to be *your* blind and stubborn heart, that *you* might see what she insisted was the light of God's truth?[1] No? Why, then, I ask you gently, should your praying persuade me?

And does it not disturb you that there are many different faiths, all with staunchly committed believers praying for what they consider the blind and mistaken of other faiths, yet no faith has sufficient evidence to persuade the others of its own truth?

Would it not be more helpful if we all sat down at the table of reason, and conducted a clear and honest discussion in the service of seeking truth? And if it happens that, when examined in the unapologetic light of objectivity, no religion can prove itself true, would it be so terrible to admit that we cannot be honestly confident of any religion's claims?

149. Mocking the sage

And a young man raised his voice and said: All day you have been going on about truth. You want the truth? The truth is that you are pompous and arrogant to think you know better than us. The truth is that your speeches are terrible, and your arguments worse; and all your words amount only to affected, delusional drivel. And the truth is that I have better things to do with my time than listen to your pretentious tirades. The truth seems so important to you. I have told you the truth. Are you happy now?

And a few in the crowd laughed, and the sage smiled and with twinkling eyes replied: My son, you may be right in some of what you say. No doubt, to the sensibilities of some, I seem insufficiently humble. And, in all likelihood, many

---

[1] Chivalry, it is said, was the practice of a knight seeking to release beautiful maidens from other men's castles so as to imprison them in his own. We might similarly say that the missionary seeks to release souls from the dark superstitions and dogmas of other men's religions, so as to chain these souls, instead, to the dark superstitions and dogmas of his own.

will find my words unappealing, and think me deeply mistaken. And laughter is important and enjoyable, and you seem intelligent and quick-witted. And, my son, I share with you this response of the ancients: If you knew me better, you would find far more to ridicule.[1]

I ask you, however, to remember what you already know, that wit and sarcasm, though at times entertaining, do not make one's intentions honorable, nor one's words accurate. And mocking is not always the confident expression it appears to be. Is not laughter, at times, a noisy disguise for fear—the fear of laying aside one's armor and opening one's heart or mind? And cannot mirth offer a tempting escape, by dismissing a person and his arguments without risking vulnerability by truly considering them? In searching for truth, then, should we not rather address, in a fair and direct manner, the points being made?

And, my son, cannot everybody, and every argument or position, be ridiculed and scorned? Cannot the religious leaders you follow be mocked—and cannot you, too, be mimicked on the very words you just spoke? Talented wit can make any of us an object of derision, but mocking is no argument in the search for truth, for it can be employed against no one fairly, and against everyone unfairly.

My son, grappling with views that conflict with our own can be unpleasant—especially when such views relate to foundational matters. Yet I welcome you to stay and take part in the discussion. Share with us your intensity—but through challenges and comments on the issues themselves. And from the ensuing dialogue we may all be enlightened. For beneath your dismissive words there are strong feelings, perhaps intelligent thoughts, on issues of religion and truth; why else would you have been so bothered by my message? And might not the deep relevance of these issues be the real reason your feet have walked you here today?

150. Argument that the sage is not objective, but biased

Then a man said: You pretend to be an objective and pure-hearted seeker of truth, but you are not. You have your own agenda, your own conclusions, and your own blind spots—just like everyone else. Why should we listen to you?

And the sage said: My brother, I agree with much of what you say. Like all humans, I cannot see everything, and am not completely objective, nor am I totally pure-hearted or free of bias—and I, too, have opinions and conclusions that would be painful for me to change.

Yet I do not ask you to follow me; I ask you only to consider my views. Indeed, it is precisely because we are all subjective that we must engage in dialogue

---

[1] Epictetus in his *Enchiridion* said: "If a…certain person speaks poorly of you, say, That man did not know all my faults, or he would not have mentioned only these…"

and expose ourselves to others' perspectives. Only then can we hope to glimpse an ever greater share of truth—and aspire to see somewhat beyond our inevitable individual and native limitations.

And, my brother, for many years I have agonized and toiled over such matters, with all the honesty I could muster. This does not remove all my blind spots and unrecognized allegiances, but sincere, sustained effort does help—and should be equated neither with the intellectual indolence of careless confidence nor with the moral corruption of conscious deceit.

But again, and most important, my brother, I do not ask you to have faith in me, nor to trust what I say without verifying it for yourself. I simply ask you to reflect with an open mind and heart upon the thoughts I lay before you. Then, with your own best efforts at honesty and learning, decide for yourself what seems reasonable and noble and what does not. And if you show me where and how I am mistaken, I will be grateful.

151. Argument that the sage turned against religion due to negative experiences

And a religious counselor said: A wise leader once explained that many people mistake psychology for theology. This is just an observation, but I have found that those raised in unhappy religious families, often shun religion as adults. I think perhaps they have experienced religion as oppressive and dogmatic, rather than liberating or loving. Perhaps you were raised by parents extreme in their religious beliefs and practices, and this turned you against religion. And I can understand that it may have felt too painful for you to remain in your community. But true religion is compassionate, and deeply worthwhile.

And the sage replied: Kind sister, you are correct in observing that some reject tradition after being exposed to oppressive or dogmatic religious training, or painful family experience. Yet related points are worth considering, too.

First, the majority of those raised in religiously dogmatic families and communities remain religious. This is most obviously true in traditional societies, but has also often been true in modern societies. Therefore, it is inaccurate to say that exposure to extreme religion causes one to reject religion. To the contrary, it can be argued that a childhood steeped in extreme religion is more likely, than is a religiously moderate or liberal upbringing, to create life-long loyalty to religion. And this applies to those raised in unhappy, as well as happy, families.

Second, even in the minority of cases where a religiously dogmatic upbringing stimulated one to examine, and ultimately reject, religious tradition, it is by no means clear that the results of such an examination are invalid. Simply because we know the psychological stimulus energizing a process that led to a set of choices, does not tell us whether the process or the ultimate choices were honest, accurate, and advisable.

If, for example, we knew that Einstein's father was a rigid, dogmatic, "all-or-nothing" thinker around whom young Albert felt miserable, and that this misery unconsciously stimulated him to search for relativity in the laws of nature—does this make his theory on relativity less true? No, my sister: We consider Einstein's theory true or untrue based on whether it remains consistent with objective observations of reality—irrespective of the psychological motives that may have stimulated the theory. Similarly, merely because discomfort may motivate one to question religion does not mean that the results of such an inquiry are mistaken. Only careful thinking, including exposing oneself with an open mind and heart to the opposition's best arguments, can legitimately decide such issues.

Third, many beliefs are mistaken, even when not based upon any discomfort or hidden psychological biases. For example, those who believed the earth to be flat generally had no childhood pain or unspoken motives spurring them on to this belief; they simply came to that conclusion based on what they saw as straightforward experience and thinking. Yet this lack of crude psychological motive did not make their flat-earth notions any less mistaken. Ideas, opinions, and convictions can be accurate or inaccurate, regardless of whether the formulation of such thoughts was stimulated by emotional discomfort.

Fourth, could not your argument be used against religion, too? If one's decision to leave religion is to be seen as tainted because one may have felt discomfort with religion or its adherents, what about the child raised comfortably, in a happy and warm religious environment, who remains religious, or returns to religion in adulthood? Are his motivations not suspect, too? Is he not psychologically biased in *favor* of religion, and seduced into *not* abandoning his inherited beliefs? Yet my sister, when a clergyman presents arguments in favor of your religion, do you challenge him by pointing out that he may be religious simply because he was raised in a warm, supportive religious family? And when the newly religious argue in favor of your beliefs, do you ask them whether they may be biased due to having been raised in an unhappy *non*-religious family?

Moreover, note how uncommon it is for one to choose another religion in place of the religion in which one was raised. The great majority of people raised within a particular religion either maintain that tradition throughout their lives, to a greater or lesser degree, in one variation or another, or put aside religion altogether. In part, this is because no faith can convince other faiths of its truth. And since all major religions contradict each other on essential matters, and no one of them encompasses a majority of the human race, all major religions consider most people's spiritual beliefs deeply mistaken. And even though it is plain to all that every religion considers the majority of humans religiously in error, most people blithely remain with the sacred beliefs they were taught as children, without being concerned that they may be part of the mistaken majority. This should tell us something about how deeply influenced we are by our parents' beliefs, and by our early education. It should also tell us that if we look for psychological biases on the matter of religious belief, we are wise to look skeptically at the great majority who cling to their inherited beliefs, in one form or another—and not only scrutinize those who break with those traditions.

Indeed, my sister, we are each tempted and chased by all manner of emotional or self-serving motivations, crude and subtle; none of us is perfectly just, unerringly objective, or completely self-aware. But this argues all the more for how necessary is careful, critical reasoning on such important matters.

Most to the point, my sister, I do not ask you to trust me, or to take my words on faith—or even to consider my motives pure or my mind whole. I only ask you to honestly reflect upon my arguments on God, religion, and life's meaning. If you have true and compelling cause, based upon reason, to conclude they are mistaken, reject them decisively—after telling me of your objections, so you may be confident that I have no persuasive response. But if my arguments are accurate, how does wondering about my experiences help?[1] Shall we not heed the morning-song of truth, even when truth is awakened by pain?

152. Argument that the sage is hypocritical, because he argues against people following religion, but he wants people to trust and follow him

And a man said: You tell me not to follow religion or believe her teachings, but you want me to follow and believe you. Is this not hypocritical?

And the sage said: My brother, I thank you for asking this because it allows me to again make clear a very important point—I truly would not wish you to suspend your own reason in favor of my authority. Do not revere me, or even believe me; instead, exert the courage and dignity to think for yourself.

Yes, I ask you to hear my arguments and to consider my evidence for the positions I take—but I would have you weigh them yourself upon the just scales of your own reason. I do not ask you to adopt my conclusions—unless your mind, after wide and careful investigation, is convinced of their truth.

---

[1] The same protest should not be raised against earlier sections of this book, which speak about some origins of religion and reasons for its perpetuation. Those passages were not attempting to dismiss religious belief by attacking its possible motives; rather, they were building the case for rigorously examining the accuracy of religion's claims, the more so because her popularity and endurance can be explained without recourse to the truly supernatural. And *my* arguments, decidedly natural, I quite agree should be subject to the same rigorous examination of their accuracy.

By contrast, traditional religion does not, as a rule, encourage independent thought on its central beliefs. Instead, adherents are taught to hobble their reason; to avoid any critical investigation of their faith's dogmas and doctrines; and to trust that church and tradition have the answers to life's deepest questions. This closing of the mind—this castrating and sterilizing of humankind's greatest fertility—has been, and remains, an insidious feature of most religion.

But if you were free, unimpeded and unmarred, who can say what your own uncovered eyes might see? Who can say what your own unstopped ears might hear? Who can say where your own unchained legs might take you? And who can say what gifts you might bring back for the family of the earth? And so, my brother, in your walk through life I would have you climb the mountain trails of your most challenging questions; I would have you peer over the precipice of your most terrifying doubts; and I would have you scale the peak of your own highest enlightenment—shrouded in mist though final answers may be.

153. Argument that the sage should have checked with religious leaders before reaching his conclusions

And a man said: If you truly believe you are right, you should have gone to religious leaders to discuss these issues, and not drawn your own conclusions. You walk your path of solitude, and then come to announce your views. But if you would consult with religious authorities you would see that they have answers for you—and you would not burden the people with your errors.

And the sage replied: My brother, you raise an interesting challenge—and I agree that a man should seek out points of view that differ from his own.

I ask you to remember, though, that there is only one way for you to learn whether religious leaders truly have compelling answers to my questions: Go you and investigate—and until you do, you live not by truth, but by indolent trust.

Yet, my brother, in the spirit of open discourse I will address the specifics of your challenge. I have done what you suggest I do. For many years I labored in religious schools, academies and seminaries, learning directly from religious scholars of this generation, and studying, too, Scripture and sacred writings of the near and ancient past. I have been steeped in the Bible and its commentaries, in works of religious law and lore, and in the ideas and arguments of religious philosophers and theologians. I have also, in younger days, devoted myself in all sincerity—even as part of religious educational organizations—to persuading non-believers of God's truth. And having been in the role of teacher and salesman, I became familiar with religion's most effective apologetics. In short, I have sat at the feet of religious leaders of today, I have studied well the sacred literature of yesteryear and the ages, and I have even, in my believing days, eagerly sought out the best arguments to help recruit others to religion's cause.

Moreover, while I do not, of course, claim to have spoken with all intelligent proponents of religion, I have, indeed, discussed many of my questions and challenges with religious scholars and leaders, and have sought, without success, responses from still others. Yet ultimately the important question for me became not whether there was a religious leader with whom I had not yet spoken, but rather—after all I had seen and heard and debated and learned—whether such a person was at all likely to offer anything helpful or new.

My brother, before speaking on such matters I asked myself this: Would it not be astonishing if there were a compelling argument for religion, that satisfactorily addressed the challenges of reason, but it is not found in the Bible; is not mentioned in any of the ancient or classic religious texts; is not spoken of in any of the many religious books or commentaries, ancient or modern, which I have read; was not discussed in any of the religious lectures I have attended; is not present in any of the religious literature produced by the best intellectually-oriented outreach and apologetic institutions; and was not offered by any of the religious scholars with whom I have conducted discussions and debates—but is known only to an obscure scholar whose thoughts I have not yet heard?

If answers to my questions exist, why would not a thousand religious leaders publish them in ten thousand books and pamphlets, and broadcast them in a hundred thousand speeches? For my questions are not mysterious nor my objections otherworldly; I have woven none of my words from secret knowledge, or by sorcery unfathomable. Instead, most of my difficulties with religious claims are straightforward, neither new nor rare, and if there were truly legitimate answers to them, many intelligent souls would be drawn to religion's ranks—and such answers would achieve for religion a decisive victory in the bitter war she has been waging with reason for lo these long, late centuries.

Yet I would not have anyone rely upon me in my claim that religion has no compelling answers for my questions. I would have each person investigate. And I encourage all to scrutinize my arguments and views, too. If I am mistaken in any significant way I welcome you to call this to my attention; for if I am brought closer to truth, my spirit will have grown. Losing a debate is no tragedy; losing one's integrity and authenticity—or remaining without them—is.

And, my brother, notice that I do not conceal my arguments, nor the reasons for my conclusions. I do not plead that I am too busy to document my thoughts on these matters; neither do I ask you to trust me. And I do not withhold the bases for my views and simply encourage you to read others' books—books which I condescend to assure you will vindicate my views. Instead, I risk detailing my thoughts on religion and philosophy for all to see; I tell you what I believe, and why. In this way I open myself to the prospect of being definitively refuted. Such transparency on the part of all would make dialogue far more fruitful.

And, my brother: Those who write and speak in support of your religion, do you ask of *them* that *they* first consult with every last scholar who holds agnostic, atheistic, or unfamiliar religious beliefs—views that differ from those of your religion? And if you do not ask this of them, but only ask this of me, and others whose positions you find disturbing, is this not a double standard?

Moreover, has anyone ever refrained from speaking or writing until approaching every possible objector—or *can* anyone? No, my brother: All we can do is try to think honestly and fairly, and educate ourselves on opposing arguments. But at some point, after long study has wrought what seems to be legitimate confidence, we must put forward our thoughts, and invite those who disagree to engage with our ideas. And one measure of our integrity is whether we take valid objections seriously—before and after we express our own views.

Most important for your life, my brother: If my thoughts seem reasonable to you, and you do not have ready answers for my challenges, are you not responsible to see whether any religious leader can truly address them persuasively—and not for me, but for you? Because now my questions are your questions, too. And if religious leaders truly have effective responses, these should not be difficult to elicit. But, as always, ask not merely whether you have received an answer; neither ask merely whether you have received an interesting or creative answer, for why religion may, after all, be true. Rather, ask yourself whether you have received an honest and compelling answer—that enables you, in good conscience and with authenticity uncompromised, to be certain of religion's accuracy.

Remember, my brother, Religion does not teach that *perhaps* her beliefs are accurate. She has enforced allegiance to her dogmas—sometimes with sword and stake, sometimes with but social or emotional penalties, and she has insisted at times with eternal threats and at times with mere condescension or earnest irrationality—that her dogmas are truth absolute, triumphant over every challenge, and ultimately impervious to any and all doubt.

154. Argument that the sage engages in faulty syllogisms—poor logic—and also does not match his responses exactly to the questions

And a man said: You may be misleading some others with your words, but you cannot deceive me. Many of your arguments use faulty syllogisms—so they may sound persuasive, but are actually illogical. And sometimes your answers do not match the questions perfectly, but speak also of other things.

And the sage replied: My brother, when you say that I use faulty logic you raise against me a serious charge. And any student of truth is grateful, even if uneasy, at being awakened to his errors. Show me, then—specifically—where I have erred, and I shall thank you. But anyone can accuse another of being illogical and of using poor arguments; such a critique only becomes credible when specific views or arguments are identified and shown to be faulty.

And I ask you respectfully, my brother, whether it may not be possible that you have too narrowly interpreted, or in other ways misunderstood, either my words or the specific laws of logic you cite—and therefore think me to have engaged in faulty thinking. Remember, too, that not holding to a particular pattern of logical argument is not the same as violating it—just as in mathematics, if a man is not taking the expected steps of addition, it does not follow that he violates the laws of addition, or of mathematics, overall: He may be doing multiplication, division, or any number of more advanced operations.

Yet even if it were demonstrated that I had occasionally violated a law of strict logic, remember, too, to distinguish between significant, telling inconsistencies—and inconsistencies that are minor and inconsequential. For unlike what religions have often taught about their scriptures and leaders, I make no claims to inerrancy or infallibility. And the seeker of truth asks himself not if the surface structure of all his opponent's arguments conform to an inflexible model, but rather whether his opponent has raised issues and challenges worth considering—even if, here and there, an academic rule of formal logic was not followed.

My brother, if a child runs to us bleeding and screams, "A dog bited off my finger," shall we, in that moment, focus upon grammar and tell the child, "The past tense of 'bite' is 'bit,' not 'bited'?" Or shall we, in realizing the critical import of the child's message—even if it was conveyed in a manner not perfectly consistent with every rule of grammar—instead attend to the far more important issue of the serious wound? And if someone points out that our souls are bleeding, that religion may have left us gravely wounded, that our deepest authenticity may be in great peril—shall we attempt to find minor faults in the way the message was formulated, or shall we sense the urgency of the problem and focus upon what really matters?

My brother: If we sift with a too-fine sieve not only can we mistakenly dismiss all but the most simple and mechanical of arguments, we will also, in our over-attentiveness to form, often miss the message's essential purpose and point.

And no simile, metaphor, or analogy is identical to the original scenario in all its details, or it would be nothing but a repetition. When the Bible compares God to an eagle caring for its young,[1] would it be valid to object that the eagle has a beak and talons, hunts for its food, and ultimately dies, while the God of the Bible shares none of those characteristics or behaviors—and that besides, God is not an eagle? Or should we not understand, rather, the overall point being

---

[1] Deuteronomy 32:11

made—that according to the Bible, God treats His people with powerful protection and tender care?

And if within a story the Bible teaches a few laws; or in the midst of a list of laws the Bible recounts a story; or if the Bible, at times, tells of earlier events after it related a tale of later events, do these departures from perfect form and organization in any way discredit the content of either the stories or the laws? No, because an open and seeking mind looks not for rules of form to disqualify a message, but rather for whatever truth, even painful truth, the message may hold.

And you are correct that my responses are not always limited to the parameters of the questions. Often I address the question and then expand on the issue, and address similar questions, too, or matters not directly raised, but which may, now or in the future, occur to some who are listening. For when I answer, I speak not only to the question—and certainly not only to the questioner.

But, again, my brother, I do not wish to minimize the importance of legitimate reason in discussion and debate. If you believe I have made substantive errors—that truly nullify the overall point my arguments were intended to convey—please bring specific instances to my attention, and I will be grateful. But the general accusation that my arguments employ faulty logic—such an unsupported charge can be leveled against all, and should therefore be considered effective against none.

155. Argument that the sage addresses only simplistic, outdated, "straw men" arguments for religion, and does not deal with more intelligent and subtle arguments

But the man persisted and said: You do not address religion's best arguments. Instead, you misrepresent what religion says so that you can easily refute traditional beliefs. Like one who dresses a straw scarecrow in men's clothing, knocks it down, and claims he knocked down a man, you make caricatures of religion's arguments, present their most simplistic and naïve forms, and then assail them with your best thoughts. And I will indeed give you an example: You argue against various passages in the Bible, but very few religious people in today's generation actually believe the Bible is meant to be taken literally; very few believe it to be the word of God; and very few believe it to be inerrant— either in its teachings or in its miracle stories. If you were honest, you would focus your arguments on what more modern ideas of religion explain.

And the sage replied: My brother, it is true that some who hold religion dear do not necessarily believe in every one of the traditional teachings of religion against which I have been arguing today—they may not believe in either the divine origin or inspiration of the Bible, or in what have historically been the foundational supernatural premises of their religion. And you are correct, too, that I do not limit myself to only addressing religious arguments that are brilliant and complex.

Yet I ask you: Have not the arguments I speak against been advanced by many religious men and women over these past decades and centuries—and do they not continue to be advanced today, too? Moreover, are most religious people philosophers and theologians who can spend their days in scholarly repose and debate—or are they not rather merchants and artisans, bakers and bankers, soldiers and seamen, and all manner of others who spend their days in action, in all varieties of labor and commerce, and in the effortful love of raising their young, and in the pleasures and pastimes of common life? And if I were to ignore all arguments save the most sophisticated and subtle, would I not be guilty of an elitist disregard for the vast hosts of our brothers and sisters, the teeming crush of earnest and dutiful worshipers who now and for ages have kneeled to numerous and varied gods, for uncomplicated reasons, and raised their children to do the same? Remember, my brother, I speak to people—not only to ideas.

But is it true that I address only religion's simplistic arguments? Have I not spoken of her better-crafted defenses, too? And if you believe I have neglected her superior arguments, those that would be more persuasive than the ones with which I have engaged, bring them to my attention, and I will be grateful. Religion has innumerable arguments made on her behalf by her myriads of adherents and defenders. One lifetime is not enough to directly respond to every variation of every argument. And anyone, on any issue, can accuse another of avoiding the best arguments; such a charge gains credibility only when those other arguments are presented, and shown to be superior.

And on the one example you did cite, my experience does not agree with your contentions regarding religious people's view of the Bible. Yes, there are some, especially those in liberal denominations, who do not see the Bible as inerrant, as the word of God, or as sacred writing to be understood literally. But many, many still do. Perhaps an age will dawn when addressing and arguing against traditional religious beliefs will be nothing but an academic exercise in contesting views long since abandoned by all—but that day has not yet come.

And most important, my brother, traditional religion has always claimed that it knew of the existence of a God or gods, and also knew what this God or gods wanted of men. This is either mistaken or dishonest, for we know no such things. And even the more moderate forms and denominations of religion today continue to teach about gods and their wishes, as if humans can responsibly claim such knowledge. If your religion does not pretend to know of a God and does not claim to know what this God wants of humans, then some of what I say today will not apply to you. But can we not agree that in that case, you, and not I, are misrepresenting what religion means to most?

482

156. Argument that the sage paints religion with a broad brush, treating all religious belief as though it were extreme, fundamentalist, or dangerous—and as though all religious people believe in the Bible as God's word, to be taken literally

And another man said: I agree with the one who spoke last. You attack the easy target of fundamentalist religion, of extreme and violent men, and of those who believe the Bible or sacred writings are the direct word of God. But in the real world, many religious people are kind and loving and responsible, the pillars of their communities—and they find in religion the inspiration to help others. Moreover, many, many religionists do not believe the Bible or other sacred writings are the direct word of God. Instead, they see Scripture as the record of man's struggle to understand the Divine, and many biblical passages as metaphorical, and they see religion as an evolving revelation from within the community of faith—a long and ongoing effort of mankind's conversation with God.[1]

And the sage said: My brother, indeed, many peaceful and charitable families and communities, even philosophically subtle thinkers, practice religion, and they or their admirers may wonder at how I can find fault in the form of religion they

---

[1] Over the years a number of religious people have read and commented upon pieces I've written. When I wrote an article critical of traditional religion's belief in miracles such as the resurrection, one woman, active in her church, accused me of attacking a "straw man," because, she said, Christians don't really believe that Jesus rose from the dead in a literal sense. Of course, this woman would have been hanged, burned, drawn and quartered, or at least excommunicated, in many previous ages by the Christian church for saying that, but now she not only considers those heretical notions to be reflective of true Christianity, she also insists that any representation of, and disagreement with, traditional Christian beliefs constitutes attacking a "straw man." Meanwhile, another religious person, having seen the same article, complained that I misrepresented Christianity in the other direction, as too watered down, when I said that religions tend to rely upon ancient legends and no longer claim direct divine revelation. With an earnest look on his face he said: "God talks to me all the time, and to a lot of people in my church, too."

Religions—and other ideologies and intense loyalties—are slippery and squirming octopi: If the rational questioner comes too close in the heated chase, multifarious inks are sprayed to effect obscurity and evasion; and if he should get a handhold on any one of the arms, he has not, at that moment, grabbed the other seven—and this is then raised as an objection. Yet as slippery and strong as are such appendages, he does well to maintain his hold, at any given time, even on one.

Words, concepts, and oral communication rarely prove up to the task of changing the minds of those who cannot bear to reconsider their beliefs. But these are the legitimate ways of attempting philosophical persuasion. If I could sing a melody so haunting and sweet that it melted all hearts, and drew along all minds to accept my views, I should probably not sing that song. Only the free man's loyalty is true loyalty, and—on the path of seeking—the reasoned change of mind is perhaps the only change worth having.

hold dear. To such people it may seem that I overestimate the danger of religion, and characterize it too negatively.

I have heard your objection, my brother; now I ask you to hear my response.

First, religion in the vast majority of its essential teachings—those teachings that made it a religion—was, in the old days, at best mistaken. Even today, with so much more knowledge readily available, traditional religion is dishonest with itself, with us, and with the tender minds of our children, on what it knows about some of the most important questions in life. Religion claims to know the will of a supernatural being who, it says, created the universe and demands that we behave in particular ways. Not only is religion dishonest on such fundamental matters—for it has no responsible way of knowing such things—it also alienates us from the authentic exercise of our unique faculty, developed reason.

Oh, religion does not always wage open war against reason, does not always burn books with which it disagrees, does not always kill or persecute infidels, does not always call reason the devil's whore—though at times that is exactly what it has done—but, because religion cannot withstand the scrutiny of untrammeled inquiry, in one form or another it has always devalued reason, and thus diminished the human spirit.

In more moderate forms of religion such devaluation of reason manifests as mere exhortations to tolerate "mystery" and "paradox" and "wonder" and "unfathomable grace" and to "live humbly with the questions" and to "walk in faith in spite of doubt which must be part of any faith worth its salt." In more traditional and less moderate forms of religion, one who uses reason to question religion's teachings is branded an apostate, an infidel, a doubting Thomas, a heretic, a traitor to his people, and an enemy of God, and is shunned by his community, and his family, too. In some parts of the world even today—and in most parts of the world a mere few centuries ago—he is subject to banishment, imprisonment, torture, or death.

Religion sees in reason an irreconcilable enemy, a dashing and daring commander it wishes it could call its own. Indeed, it often attempts to seduce this general to come over to the other side, and imposters dressed to look like the general are regularly paraded for the crowds. From the subtle debates in the Talmud to the confident theology of Aquinas, and in sermons and writings of the innumerable clerics and apologists through the ages, religion has always courted reason—provided that reason had the good sense and propriety not to stray beyond the arbitrary limits each religion placed on its freedom.

Yet in the end all such efforts at recruiting or emasculating reason fail, and it is again branded the rude and implacable foe, or at least the misguided and dangerous vigilante operating outside a legitimate structure of command. Notwithstanding this essential enmity between religion and reason, there are ages and locales where the wars have temporarily ceased, the border guards have grown fat and lazy in peace, and the only form of conflict is the smiling condescension with which the opposing sides view each other in passing.

From the field, then, to the drawing room, let us vary the metaphor. "Reason, Reason, on the wall," says each religion to the mirror, "you are the wisest judge of them all—so long as you proclaim me the fairest maiden of them all." Yet so soon as reason proclaims, or even wonders about, anything less flattering, every religion rejects the plain reflection that meets its eyes. Some forms of religion shatter the mirror with the tablets of Sinai stone, with the rock of Mecca, or with the rugged Cross of Calvary. Others cast the mirror aside and hang in its place kaleidoscopes and carnival mirrors, which create interesting, but obscure and dizzying images—and they say: "This grotesque and confusing collage is the true likeness of man, and only through my homilies and libraries of biblical commentary will you be able to discern yourself well." Still others leave the unaltered mirror in its place, but surround it with antiques and obsolete contrivances, and say with an amused and indulgent smile: "Yes, there was a day when some idealists believed that reason was the answer. Instead, not only was that belief simplistic and naive, it made human society far worse." "But," they add, "this old thing *does* make an interesting piece in one's collection, does it not?"

So, my brother, the great majority of religious movements—even in their more moderate forms—continue to be dishonest with us about what they know on the most important matters of our existence. I ask you then: For the sake of our dignity and that of our children, and to honor any God there may be, shall we not rise up and protest?

And, my brother, it is tender and evocative to conceive of the Bible, and of religious communities and movements through the ages, as a long and ongoing conversation of mankind with God. But if we are to be honest must we not concede that a conversation entails more than one speaker, and certainly more than one party? Yet throughout history religion has not acknowledged—and still today, even in its moderate forms, generally does not acknowledge—that not only do we not know the Bible or religious laws to either originate with God or meet with His approval, but that in this long exercise of fierce imagination and loyalty which some are pleased to call a conversation with the Divine—and which through the centuries has resulted in innumerable dead and tortured and almost universal lack of free and informed thinking on life's most important matters—humans may have been talking to no one but themselves.[1]

---

[1] Oliver Wendell Holmes, that man of generous spirit, balanced temperament, strong mind and articulate pen, criticized the negative tendencies of some manifestations of religion, but defended the institution itself. Writing in the 19th century, in his book *Pages*

from an Old Volume of Life, in the essay "The Pulpit and the Pew," and addressing the popular religion of his country and time, he said: "The real, vital division of the religious part of our Protestant communities is into Christian optimists and Christian pessimists. The Christian optimist in his fullest development is characterized by a cheerful countenance, a voice in the major key, an undisguised enjoyment of earthly comforts, and a short confession of faith. His theory of the universe is progress; his idea of God is that he is a Father with all the true paternal attributes, of man that he is destined to come into harmony with the key-note of divine order, of this earth that it is a training school for a better sphere of existence. The Christian pessimist in his most typical manifestation is apt to wear a solemn aspect, to speak, especially from the pulpit, in the minor key, to undervalue the lesser enjoyments of life, to insist on a more extended list of articles of belief. His theory of the universe recognizes this corner of it as a moral ruin; his idea of the Creator is that of a ruler whose pardoning power is subject to the veto of what is called 'justice'; his notion of man is that he is born a natural hater of God and goodness, and that his natural destiny is eternal misery. The line dividing these two great classes zigzags its way through the religious community, sometimes following denominational layers and cleavages, sometimes going, like a geological fracture, through many different strata. The natural antagonists of the religious pessimists are the men of science, especially the evolutionists, and the poets…It is not science alone that the old Christian pessimism has got to struggle with, but the instincts of childhood, the affections of maternity, the intuitions of poets, the contagious humanity of the philanthropist—in short, human nature and the advance of civilization."

And after setting up his model of pessimistic vs. optimistic religion, Holmes follows by strongly defending the latter, while urging the former—note, on pragmatic grounds—to mend its ways. He says: "The pulpit has long helped the world, and is still one of the chief defences against the dangers that threaten society, and it is worthy now, as it always has been in its best representation, of all love and honor. But many of its professed creeds imperatively demand revision, and the pews which call for it must be listened to, or the preacher will by and by find himself speaking to a congregation of bodiless echoes."

But as I say in this section of the book and elsewhere, the chief problem with religion is not her terrible propensity toward persecution—of the body by the fiery stake or the iron wheel or by calls for martyrdom or war, and of the emotions by fear of hell and by all manner of self-hate and guilt—no, the chief problem with religion is her fundamental dishonesty in claiming to know what she does not responsibly know, about the deepest, most important aspects of who we are and how we should orient our lives. And this is a problem that applies to Holmes's "optimistic" religion, too. And though I understand that nature zealously guards stability within a social species even as she slowly nudges it toward change, and there are therefore more born with the inclination to be traditionalists or pragmatists, open at most to moderate reforms, than those born to be idealists and purists, still I must be true to my calling, and speak my own values and voice, even though it is a minority opinion. So again I say that this corrupt practice of misleading our souls and deceiving us terribly on matters most meaningful and profound, though it is often well-intended and often, too, productive of some good, is not to be condoned, and certainly not to be accorded "all love and honor."

156.5 Argument that the sage is looking at the shallow and surface aspects of religion, and does not know about or address the deep secrets, the mystical truths

And a monk said: You have problems with religion because you seek only her shallow and surface aspects. You do not seem to know about, and you certainly do not speak about, the deep secrets, the mystical truths, the sublime levels of refinement leading to the loss of the crude self, and to union with the Divine. These are possible for one who is initiated into the deepest secrets of my tradition.

And the sage said: My brother, religions have indeed developed complex, intelligent, and often powerfully effective means of self-improvement, of using the mind and body in creative ways so as to transcend the mundane, refine one's character, and even imagine that one is joining with the Divine.

Yet many religions have achieved such effects, and each religion's beliefs contradict those of the others. The Jewish Cabbalist, the Buddhist monk, the Muslim Sufi master, the Christian mystic, and the Hindu sannyasi—among others—are all heirs to ancient traditions, which have over many centuries developed deep insights and often closely-guarded knowledge, and effective means for refining numerous aspects of man's character. Yet they each base their authority, in teaching this wise and helpful knowledge, on irresponsible beliefs about ultimate reality.

My brother, just as the legitimate mathematical knowledge developed by Pythagoras and his school does not prevent us from appropriate skepticism over some of their metaphysical beliefs about numbers; and just as the Samurais' sword-fighting prowess does not confer automatic legitimacy upon their philosophy and values; so, too, the character-refining techniques and systems of secret knowledge developed by various religions and groups do not speak to the legitimacy of their core teachings on things we have no reason to believe they know anything about—things such as deities and supernatural realms.

157. Argument that the sage feels a need for certainty, is limited to pure logic and simple rationality, and is unable to deal with mystery or complexity and jumps therefore to simplistic conclusions

But the man continued and said: You seem to have a need for certainty, and seem to be obsessed with logic and reason and rationality. And those can be helpful up to a point. But spiritual matters involve complexity and mystery and paradox and tantalizing apparent incongruities—and those who wish to deal maturely with matters of the spirit need to be able to tolerate such things. Indeed, it is the very tension between reason and religious belief that constitutes the mystery. But you seem unable to deal with that level of complexity and sophistication. Therefore, you draw simplistic conclusions.

And the sage replied: My brother, can we not all accuse each other of being simplistic—of being unable to tolerate complexity or sophistication, or any other worthy characteristic or ideal? It would be one thing if you supported your charges, if you showed me specifically which complexities I have avoided, which legitimate paradoxes or defensible incongruities I have rejected, which mysteries I have prematurely dismissed. Then I would be grateful. But when the finger of blame is pointed without evidence, has anything of value been offered?

And as I have earlier illustrated[1] the complexity of one's belief system or of one's arguments has no necessary correlation to their truth. Every major religion—and most minor ones, too—can boast of impressive and articulate advocates, philosophers and theologians who weave dazzling patterns of words and ideas in the service of their beliefs. Yet these religions contradict each other on foundational matters. Thus, by everyone's account, most religions are deeply mistaken, their complexity notwithstanding.

As to paradoxes and incongruities, my brother, I ask you this: How shall we determine which seemingly false statements or contradictory claims are to be rejected for what they seem to be—and which are to be elevated to the throne of adoration and adorned with such labels as "paradox" and "tantalizing incongruity"? If you ask me for direction to the east, and I instead point to the west, would you consider that a fine piece of mystery and paradox—or error or worse? And if I told you to use your reason and experience, and the best evidence from the most reliable sources of learning, for every arena of life except for the most important—and precisely there, in life's most significant arenas you are to chain and muzzle reason and her allies, and take direction instead from familiarity and tribal loyalty, from sentimentality and emotion, from ancient texts and modern clergy, from corrupted creativity and rank superstition—would this be "paradox" and "tantalizing incongruity"—or might it not be just what it seemed: a desperate and evocative, but no less mistaken or tragic, escape from reality?

And far from rejecting mystery, the true seeker who questions religion sings mystery's praises. I do not speak of the dogmatic atheist, who insists he knows that no Creator or supernatural force exists. I speak, instead, of one who exercises the humility and moderation to note that religions have insufficient basis for their claims about God, but that everyone else also has insufficient bases to draw confident conclusions on the source or earliest origins of all that exists, and on what or Who may transcend it or be its Cause.

---

[1] See sections 36-38.

My brother, is it not the dogmatic believer who insists on certainties? And do I not plead with believers to avoid the temptation of unwarranted conviction, and to instead accustom their spirits to the bittersweet flavors of existential mystery?

And it must be said, too, that religion has not taught, for lo these blind and bloody millennia, that spiritual matters touching on earthly responsibilities are mysterious and unknown. To the contrary, although allowing for some mystery about their favorite god's essence, organized religion has tended to insist it knows everything about what you must believe and of how God wants you to behave. Heretics question; churches answer. And when great power was theirs, religions' answer often came in the form of the sword, the flames, or the torture rack—or in more generous days, merely the stocks of humiliation, the social death of excommunication, or banishment's pious boot.

Finally, my brother, so strongly do I advocate for mystery that perhaps all my teaching today can be summarized in the following questions: Is it not far better, all the while we seek out knowledge with energetic wonder, to admit that we do not know, to concede that we do not have answers to the ultimate puzzles of existence? Is it not far nobler to embrace mystery, than to pretend, as religion often does, that we know with certainty the origin of the universe, the existence and name of its Creator, and His wisdom and will for how we should conduct our lives as we walk our few days on earth?[1]

---

[1] Religion has an aversion to honest doubt, yes, but so do many other ideologies, on matters of politics, medicine, education, metaphysics—and many other arenas. Indeed, religion's seeming antithesis, ardent atheism, often suffers from the same unjustified lurching into certitude. Much more honest, yet sadly uncommon, is the attitude of Thomas Henry Huxley, the man who originated the term agnostic, who said, in "Agnosticism" (found in his *Lectures and Essays*): "When I reached intellectual maturity and began to ask myself whether I was an atheist, a theist, or a pantheist; a materialist or an idealist; a Christian or a freethinker; I found that the more I learned and reflected, the less ready was the answer; until, at last, I came to the conclusion that I had neither art nor part with any of these denominations, except the last. The one thing in which most of these good people were agreed was the one thing in which I differed from them. They were quite sure they had attained a certain "gnosis,"—had, more or less successfully, solved the problem of existence; while I was quite sure I had not, and had a pretty strong conviction that the problem was insoluble."

157.5 Claim that the devil had thousands of years to practice his arguments, so he sounds convincing, but the faithful know he is wrong, and need not bother with his point of view

And a man said: Your words sound reasonable but we know better. The devil had thousands of years to practice his arguments, so he sounds convincing. But the faithful know he is wrong, and need not bother with his point of view.

And the sage said: My brother, such a justification to not think carefully, and to avoid confronting uncomfortable questions, is tempting for believers of all sorts, holding fast to all manner of ideologies they are unwilling to reconsider.

Not only can the Muslim say to the Christian, the Hindu, the Buddhist, the Jew, and others, "Satan has had many centuries to practice his deceptions, so I need not even think about your arguments against my belief in the Prophet and his book;" not only can the Jew say to the Christian, the Buddhist, the Muslim, the Hindu, and others, "Satan has been refining his seductive arguments to try to lead us astray throughout history—beginning with the serpent in our Bible's Garden of Eden—so even if his arguments, put in your mouth, seem impressive, we need not bother with them;" not only can the Christian say to the Muslim, the Hindu, the Buddhist, the Jew, and others, "The devil has always tried his arguments on us, and has refined them for many long years; even Jesus was tempted with all manner of arguments from the devil and his agents, so we need not bother with such things;" not only can every religion make such arguments to discount all doubters and questioners, even non-religious ideologies can do the same. The Soviet communist said to the outside world, "Oh, yes, you capitalist pigs seem persuasive, and make clever points, but that is because the wealthy oppressors of mankind have refined their arguments for thousands of years on how to justify stealing the labor of the common man, and the resources that rightfully belong to the collective," and the Nazi said to all others, "Your arguments against the policies of the Führer sound compelling, but everyone knows that the Bolsheviks and their subversive Jewish allies who control the world have conspired throughout history to refine their sickly intellectual arguments against the healthy and vigorous instincts and the rightful supremacy of the Aryan peoples, so we need not bother with your views." And, indeed, the atheist can say: "Religion is as old as the earliest human cultures. For untold millennia religions have been practicing their crafty arguments intended to mislead the earnest masses into falling to their knees and worshiping in the ways that benefit the priesthood or the ruling elite. With all this time to refine their approach, it is no wonder they can sound convincing. But we know they are liars, and we need not bother addressing their arguments."

My brother: An argument that can be advanced to shield every position, does not legitimately shield any.

And though the exercise of reason and the free exchange of ideas do not guarantee that truth will in every case prevail—at times in the complexity and urgency of life, confusion or worse carries the day—still, they are the best means we have. If we refuse to expose our position to others' arguments, we may, by a stroke of good luck, be in possession of truth; more likely, though, what we so anxiously and reflexively protect is not truth—but brittle error.

158. Argument that it is not worth speaking up, but that the sage's statements are mistaken or false

Then a scholar said: I, for one, have not avoided your perspective. I have considered your arguments, and have many objections and many answers, but I do not think it worth debating these issues with you. If you choose to be wrong, I cannot prevent that.

And the sage replied: My brother, although you are at liberty to retreat into the ever-echoing caves of self-satisfaction, doing so shall deprive us of what wisdom you may possess, and what knowledge your years may have gathered. And your own views, too, will suffer for your silence; it is all too easy to seem persuasive to oneself, in the protected confines of one's own mind. But in advancing your ideas to others of different viewpoints you will see far better how convincing or questionable your ideas truly are—even to yourself.

And be not tempted to confuse intelligence, even vast knowledge, with accuracy of belief. In the treacherous terrain of philosophical thought there lurk so many forms of camouflaged predators arrayed in the colors of the comforting familiar, and so many dark paths of unconscious blindness on which even a scholar's mind stumbles, that in searching for truth we dare not trust conclusions conceived in solitude, or those merely approved of by like-believing minds.

Furthermore, could not adherents of other religions say to you what you have just said to me? Would you be persuaded if they merely felt confident that they had legitimate answers to your questions, and compelling challenges to your answers—but they remained silent and did not offer them? Is *your* silence, then, any more credible?

My brother, you think me mistaken; perhaps you are right. Nevertheless, if you voice your objections, perhaps I can address them—and if you offer answers to my questions, perhaps I can explain why I think those answers unsatisfactory. Even if you should not consider me worthy of your efforts, speak out for the sake of the community. Come, let no one withhold ideas. Let us rather bring our thoughts joyfully to the feast of truth, that we, the spiritually famished family of earth, might feed each other our best delicacies. Perchance we shall find sustenance.

IX. RIGHT AND WRONG WITHOUT
SUPERNATURAL RELIGION

159. Is there no right and wrong?

And a father of young children stepped forward and said: If we cannot know that our religions are true, if we cannot even know that a God exists who asks of us specific behavior, then nothing is right or wrong—and families and societies cannot insist on a code of conduct. For then, "Everything is permitted,"[1] and life will be barbaric and out of control.[2] That is unacceptable. I must teach my children something solid, principles and practices to live by!

And the sage said: Yes, my brother, healthy families and societies must uphold values and insist upon codes of conduct. Let us examine more closely, however, whether such notions of right and wrong, in order to be effective, need originate with a supposed God.

When first a child goes off to school he may study diligently, and engage in all manner of good behavior, to earn a candy or a different prize, or to please others. Later he may treat his classmates well so as to gain his teachers' approval; he may refrain from spending all his money on trifles so as not to anger his parents; and he may engage in physical training in order to impress his friends.

When he attains adulthood, however, do we expect him to say, "I will no longer learn because nobody offers me a prize; I will treat others poorly because my teachers no longer control me; I will spend all my money on a whim because I no longer fear my parents' anger; I will not engage in activities of vigor because I no longer need to impress young friends"?

Certainly not: The primary rewards of engaging in constructive behavior are neither prizes from authority figures nor the approval or admiration of others. Rather, the natural, positive effects of beneficial acts are sufficient motive for a healthy adult. Learning bestows upon one knowledge and skill, makes of life a more interesting endeavor, and assists one on the path toward various forms of success. Treating others well not only creates a pleasant and productive society, it generally elicits favorable treatment in return. The wise use of money engenders

---

[1] A view of the implications of believing that there is no God and no afterlife, famously expressed in Dostoevsky's classic novel, *The Brothers Karamazov*.

[2] For additional discussion on these matters, see section 69.

financial peace; and physically vigorous activity improves health, and cultivates a sense of well-being.

The same pragmatic touchstone, my brother, applies to issues of right and wrong. That which brings good results for the individual and society is good; that which brings bad results is not. Natural morality is the art of arriving at refined judgments as to what leads to the best interests of individuals and society, and, where they conflict, balancing between them. Determining these things is far from easy, and different minds—and different cultures—will, on such matters, reach different conclusions. But no conceits of supernatural knowledge—and no dubious tales of divine revelation—are either necessary or sufficient for a parent or society to identify and teach guidelines for worthy behavior.

Consider taxes, rules for right-of-way on roads, and various other statutes and standards used to govern and regulate society. These do not, and need not, originate in the Bible or any religion; they are instead based on the straightforward understanding that society—the group—has the right to expect cooperative and constructive behavior from individuals. What is good for the collective, and not too heavy a burden on the individual, can be insisted upon with the ready assent of the great majority. Different societies may come to different conclusions about right and wrong, and therefore legislate different laws. And this is the case today, among both the secular and the religious.

In short, my brother: God is not needed to establish standards of right and wrong. Human experience and learning—as to what results in the pleasant and healthy, and what in the painful and unhealthy—constitute quite sufficient a foundation.[1] And this holds true not only for individuals and for families, but for cities and nations, too.

As to your father role: If your son asks you precisely how many stars twinkle in the heavens, do you pretend to know, and fabricate a sum? Or do you rather say with noble candor: "My son, though I marvel at the night sky with you, the number of stars is something no man knows"? So, too, if your daughter asks if there is a God in heaven, and if so how this God wants us to live, will you pretend to know? Or might you find the honesty and humility to say without shame: "My daughter, though I puzzle and ponder at life too, and though traditions teach varying claims about such matters, no man truly knows whether there is a God—or if there is, what if anything such a God may want of us"?

---

[1] Santayana, in his *Reason in Religion* says: "Man is still in his childhood; for he cannot respect an ideal which is not imposed on him against his will, nor can he find satisfaction in a good created by his own action. He is afraid of a universe that leaves him alone. Freedom appalls him; he can apprehend in it nothing but tedium and desolation, so immature is he and so barren does he think himself to be."

But teach your sons and daughters all the many things you *do* know, and which their eager hands and hungry hearts are waiting to learn from you. Teach them to plan and teach them to build; teach them to sow and teach them to harvest; teach them to work and teach them to play. Teach them the warm practice of love and the noble discipline of reason; teach them the healing bonds of friendship and of solitude's freedom and peace; teach them the mastery of self-restraint, and the freeborn exuberance of joy. Teach them the humility of an open mind and the confidence of fairness and justice; teach them the wisdom of compassion and concord, but also the courage for necessary battles. Teach them to live in community and contribution, but of authenticity, and of self-reliance, too. Teach them to use the powers flowing strong within them—to rejoice with full-throated laughter, and to grieve with free-flowing tears. And teach them, too, to celebrate the smile, yet see the teeth; to luxuriate in the warmth, yet respect the fire; to dance in the music of life, yet hear the silence of death.

My brother: Religion is a toxic stew that calms the pangs of existential hunger, but whose poison slowly takes the soul of all who were too quick to partake. When I warn you that the stew is poisoned I am not suggesting that you eat nothing; for that, in turn, will starve your soul. Repudiating religion and not replacing her with alternative, strongly-held values, and opportunities for inspiration and mission and brotherhood and beauty and legacy, taught at home and reinforced by community, will result not in an ideal society, but in one as corrupted as the worst of religious societies.

Make no mistake: Man harbors within his breast both angelic and diabolical tendencies; society must support and cultivate the former, and discourage and suppress the latter. But can we not do this with honesty? Are we reduced to being crooked with our children—in order that we may raise them up straight?

160. Argument that without a belief in God, we could not persuade someone to behave morally—if he disagreed with our ideas on morality

But another man said: It is all well and good to claim that you know without God what is right and what is wrong. And I concede that I once knew a man who was not religious, and yet was well-behaved. But most people cannot be good without religion.[1] In the absence of a belief in God revealing what is moral,

---

[1] David Hume, on his deathbed, being interviewed by Boswell, is reported to have said: "When I hear a man is religious, I conclude that he is a rascal, although I have known some instances of very good men being religious." For a man of kind and calm temperament as Hume is said to have been, these words may have been offered—even during his last hours—in the spirit of ironic humor, sporting with what was surely in his day, too, the grudging admission by some amongst the religious that they had known instances of non-religious men being good.

Yet even if Hume may have spoken with a twinkle in his eye, many other non-religious writers and thinkers have pressed the claim in all seriousness that religion is either a symptom or a cause—or both—of inferior functioning, character, and morals. And in horrific examples like the Old Testament's genocides and the New Testament's threats of eternal hell, and in religions' many wars and persecutions and acts of mayhem and destruction—but in many less dramatic examples, too—such criticisms are valid.

Yet in all fairness it must be said that those who argue against religion sometimes see only bad where they might have seen a more speckled view. For one illustration, let us skip over some of religion's better-known critics and highlight the less-remembered Elbert Hubbard, a courageous and prolific writer, popular in his own day, who said many pleasant and interesting things, but for whom even a dramatic death—going down, along with other notables and nearly 1,200 people, on May 7, 1915, aboard the Lusitania, the sinking of which by a German U-boat is generally seen as having played a role in the eventual entry of the United States into WWI—could not prevent a relatively quick fading of fame. Hubbard wrote in *Love, Life and Work*, "Wherever plottings, schemings and doubtful methods of life are employed, a ruler is necessary; and there, too, religion, with its idea of placating God has a firm hold. Men whose lives are doubtful feel the need of a strong government and a hot religion…" Hubbard continues, "Voltaire says, 'When woman no longer finds herself acceptable to man, she turns to God,' When man is no longer acceptable to himself he goes to church. If your life-work is doubtful, questionable or distasteful, you will hold the balance true by going outside your vocation for the gratification that is your due, but which your daily work denies, and you find it in religion, I do not say this is always so, but it is very often. Great sinners are apt to be very religious…" Hubbard continues (in a passage consistent with his involvement in the Arts and Crafts movement) "Why should you cease to express your holiest and highest on Sunday? Ah, I know why you don't work on Sunday! It is because you think that work is degrading, and because your sale and barter is founded on fraud, and your goods are shoddy. Your week-day dealings lie like a pall upon your conscience, and you need a day in which to throw off the weariness of that slavery under which you live. You are not free yourself, and you insist that others shall not be free…But the artist is free and he works in joy, and to him all things are good and all days are holy. The great inventors, thinkers, poets, musicians and artists have all been men of deep religious natures; but their religion has never been a formalized, restricted, ossified religion. They did not worship at set times and places. Their religion has been a natural and spontaneous blossoming of the intellect and emotions—they have worked in love, not only one day in the week, but all days, and to them the groves have always and ever been God's first temples."

Although Hubbard is at some of his best eloquence there, and is correct that various manifestations of religion in general, and of Sabbath in particular, are unhealthy, to me it seems that he overstates his case. True: Too often Sabbath observance has been reduced primarily to restrictions and punitive rules; but in essence it can be—and to many it has been and continues to be—a good and ennobling practice. To set aside one day a week for study and song, for rest and rejuvenation, for meditation and transcendence, does not mean that the other days were spent poorly; the sprinter tires and must regain his breath, though his heart sings as he runs. It also seems to me that Hubbard takes insufficient account of the value of ritual and consistent spiritual exercises tied to the calendar and

how will you persuade someone else to behave morally, if they disagree with your idea of morality?

And the sage said: My brother, let us bear in mind a few things. First, religion may provide a claimed authoritative basis for morality, but by the same authority it also provides an unimpeachable basis for all kinds of atrocities and barbarism. Bibles and religions have taught everything from genocide and slavery to religious intolerance and female subjugation. Religion, therefore, is no sure or safe basis for morality.

Second, the many different religions—even the multifarious authorities within each religion—provide competing and contradictory ideas of what is moral. Religion, therefore, does not solve the problem of disagreements on what is to be seen as moral. Observe a Christian attempting to persuade a Muslim, or a Muslim attempting to persuade a Hindu, on disagreements over what constitutes moral behavior—and you will see just how little a belief in God helps one persuade those holding different views.

Third, society needs no supernatural basis to support decent behavior in the great majority—those for whom it is in their bones to desire a peaceful and relatively stable life, wherein neither their neighbors nor the vengeful sheriffs of their conscience lie in wait. Indeed, other, non-human social species cooperate in groups, without bibles or gods, about as much as do religious humans—they

---

clock. Not all are by temperament spontaneous, and even those who are can often benefit by grounding themselves in some practices "at set times and places." Finally, even if expressing one's highest sentiments purely by impulse and "spontaneous blossoming" can work for certain individuals, it does not work well for communities. Just as if a man had the world to himself he would have little need for time-keeping, for the spoken word, or for a thousand other inventions and conveniences of society and culture, but the teeming world is greatly assisted by these things to facilitate effective interaction, so too does a spirituality that is purely self-referenced and unstructured serve communal living but poorly. The solitary man playing upon his flute or guitar need not follow any rhythm save that of his own impulse and whim; but let him attempt to make music with others without disciplining himself to a shared, uniform, beat, and sweet self-expression turns to jarring dissonance.

I do not argue against individual and spontaneous forms of spirituality and self-expression; I only point out that communal forms are not necessarily bad. And as humans are both individuals and members of communities, some mix of independent and cooperative forms of spirituality is likely most healthy and natural.

Moreover, and most to the point, the problem with religion's worship is not that it involves formal rituals "at set times and places," but that it involves dishonest belief at *all* times and places; and the problem with religion's Sabbath is not that it asks people to suspend labor, but that, in pretending to command this in God's name, it demands that we suspend honesty.

generally maintain civil behavior within their group, with episodic disquiet and revolution, and generally ignore, and occasionally attack, those of other groups.[1]

And as for the incorrigible minority—those who seem to be governed neither by a sufficiently strong conscience nor by an appreciation for stability and peace—they do not tend to be dissuaded from their impulses by religious teachings, either. All the centuries of crime and oppression during religious ages tell their story.

For these, society must resort to police power; it must enforce its standards upon those who refuse to respect the reasonable best interests of others. Fines, prison sentences, and other forms of penalty, backed by armed lawmen and soldiers has been, and will continue to be, the last defense of society from those who cannot or will not practice self-governance.

My brother, whatever rules are good and moral in religions have come not from some supernatural voice beyond, but from the just and compassionate voice within. Yes, religions have claimed to speak in the name of gods, but what they said—for good and for bad—came from sources far more close and familiar. It is degrading to the human spirit—traitorous to our species—to insist that without a God telling us how to behave, we cannot arrive at basic laws on constructive behavior.[2] Indeed, teaching the young that there is no other reason

---

[1] We humans, of course, unlike other species, have a pronounced capacity to learn from the errors and successes of our forebears, and also to expand our concept of the group to include ever greater numbers and ever more diverse populations—perhaps even all mankind, and more. In these ways we may hope to greatly reduce the frequency and extent of war and oppression. But religion has quite a mixed record on these matters, sometimes aiding, yet often hindering, such progress; for while she has taught charity and kindness, she has often also taught the superiority of her believers, and the inferiority—even the wickedness, culpability, or sub-humanity—of those who do not follow her practices or subscribe to her dogmas.

[2] William Kingdon Clifford, in his essay "Ethics of Religion," writes: "This union of men to work for common object has transformed them from wild animals into tame ones. Century by century the educating process of the social life has been working at human nature; it has built itself into our inmost soul. Such as we are—moral and rational beings...I say, Man has made us. By Man I mean men organized into a society...Conscience—the sense of right and wrong—springs out of the habit of judging things from the point of view of all and not of one. It is Ourself, not ourselves, that makes for righteousness. The codes of morality, then, which are adopted into various religions, and afterwards taught as parts of religious systems, are derived from secular sources. The most ancient version of the Ten Commandments, whatever the investigations of scholars may make it out to be, originates, not in the thunders of Sinai, but in the peaceful life of men on the plains of Chaldea. Conscience is the voice of Man ingrained into our hearts, commanding us to work for Man."

to be good aside from the commandments of a supernatural being corrupts the voice of conscience that, in line with its function as a guiding impulse for a social creature, can be best educated into morality not by rumors and speculations and dishonesties about gods, but by reasoned and compassionate appeals to the common interests of man. And this corrupting of man's natural capacity for compassion and justice can lead, and has led, to terrible things done in the supposed service of God—whose devotees sometimes seem ever more likely to use for Him appellations such as "All-Merciful" and "Compassionate" the more minds they terrorize by His word, and the more blood they spill in His name.[1]

And, my brother, whether or not you think religious belief makes men moral, surely, before teaching religion, we must first ask whether what religion teaches is true. For are you content to lie to yourself, your neighbors, and your children about the most important matters, simply because you think it may persuade some to adopt your standards of right and wrong? Do you not agree that such profound dishonesty is in itself a great wrong? And would you blur the lines separating fact from fantasy? Is not the real all we have, and do we not do violence to ourselves and the universe when we trifle with such distinctions?

161. Argument that we need absolute and unchanging standards of right and wrong

But the man persisted, saying: The picture you paint is of a society with arbitrary rules and laws. What a disturbing picture, indeed. Such a society would be

---

And though we can quibble with Clifford's choice of the Ten Commandments as an example of socially constructive ethics that originate in secular sources of Man, when the first several commandments speak of Yahweh's authority and outlaw all gods other than Yahweh, and speak of the evil of taking the Lord's name in vain, and of the necessity of keeping the Sabbath day holy, still, when applied to the later passages of the Ten Commandments, those outlawing stealing, murder and the like, his overall point is clear—that the foundational ethical principles which religions have long taught in the name of God, have been far more accessible all the while, as the pro-social instinct inherent and capable of being nurtured (along with other instincts pro-social and antisocial) in the common human breast.

[1] In the same essay just cited, Clifford writes: "When we love our brother for the sake of our brother, we help all men to grow in the right; but when we love our brother for the sake of somebody else, who is very likely to damn our brother, it very soon comes to burning him alive for his soul's health. When men respect human life for the sake of Man, tranquillity, order, and progress go hand in hand; but those who only respected human life because God had forbidden murder have set their mark upon Europe in fifteen centuries of blood and fire."

And we may add to these powerful words the obvious: that both earlier and later than the fifteen centuries of which Clifford spoke, and in regions far removed from Europe, too, men have been spreading fire and shedding blood in the name of a merciful God.

built upon nothing substantial—only the fickle judgment of men—and would result in but the unholy reign of chaos. We need, instead, standards of right and wrong that are absolute and unchanging!

And the sage replied: My brother, I know it can feel alarming to lose the confident orientation provided by what seems an unchanging code of right and wrong. Yet societies have for all of recorded history—and we may assume earlier than that, too—changed their laws, at times gradually, at times suddenly. And this did not, in the great majority of instances—judging by both historical accounts and contemporary experience—lead to upheaval. And many societies that have not changed their laws have, nevertheless, been torn asunder by turmoil and mayhem arising from within their own borders and ranks. Thus, by the lights of today and yesterday, you may wish to reconsider whether a change in laws and standards need result in chaos.

Moreover, religion in no way guarantees that codes of behavior and belief will not change. Observe that today's religions no longer follow much of what the Bible taught to previous ages. The Old Testament legislated death for working on the Sabbath[1] or practicing witchcraft[2] or committing adultery;[3] it also condoned slavery.[4] The New Testament preached a humble passivity in the face of violence; that we not resist evil, but rather when struck, turn the other cheek; that we love our enemies and bless those who curse us, and pray for those who use and persecute us.[5] It also warned against judging and punishing others,[6] and insisted that only those without sin should administer a penalty to the guilty.[7]

Yet the vast majority of Jews today do not attempt to administer the death penalty for desecration of the Sabbath or the practice of witchcraft or the commission of adultery, nor do they condone slavery. And Christian countries throughout history have engaged in violence with the blessings of clergy—especially in self-defense—by *not* turning the other cheek, and they continue to do so; and Christian societies have always judged and punished people, and still do so today. And popes and bishops and ministers and rabbis have, throughout history, changed small and large religious laws and doctrines innumerable times—from whether priests are permitted to marry and whether the death penalty is moral, to many larger and smaller issues—and such amendments have not pitched society into chaos.

---

[1] Exodus 31:14, 15

[2] Exodus 22:18

[3] Leviticus 20:10

[4] Leviticus 25:39-46

[5] Matthew 5:39-44

[6] Matthew 7:1

[7] John 8:7

For while it is true that, to thrive, society needs some measure of stability and continuity, it is also true that it can tolerate, indeed it requires, some measure of renewal and change. And no small part of wisdom lies in striking a healthy balance between these necessary poles of preserving what is good and worthy in the familiar, while seeking opportunity and growth in the unknown.

My brother, though the anxious heart sometimes longs to be free of the burdens and uncertainties of navigation, and venerates the anchor above the oars and the sails, the ever-moving ship of civilization affords but passages of greater adventure. For the voyages of peoples through history's waters have often landed them on shores more friendly and bountiful, securer by far, than those on which their fathers suffered. And the Promised Land ever beckons, and "vessels at anchor never advance." My brother, not wisdom and nobility demand unchanging standards—but habituation and fear.

162. Is morality completely subjective? And is every system of morality as good as any other?

And a philosophy student said: Right and wrong are words for simpletons; they are terms that the ruling elite use to keep the suffering masses in subjection, afraid to challenge the status quo. There really is no such thing as good and bad behavior. Everything is subjective, so every system of morality is as good as any other, and trying to determine better or worse ways of living is pointless.

And the sage said: My son, I can agree with some of your position. It is true that morality, unlike mathematical sums or chemical structures or bodily forms, does not lend itself to objective determinations and will continue to be open to debate, for it is based on values, which differ and cannot be conclusively decided, certainly not for all time. At best we may hope for a majority opinion approaching consensus—arrived at through free, effortful, and honest thought—as to what is right and what is wrong, and which right should be considered more important than which other right, and which wrong more grievous than which other wrong. But such democratic decisions would only be agreements, likely temporary, about right and wrong, and not an objective determination that this set of judgments is, in an essential sense, the only correct way to view morality.

Yet my son, we need not pin our hopes for constructive living on the quest for moral objectivity. Instead, we can advocate for why some values are best seen as more worthy than others, and thus a good basis for morality. Let us accept that humans will differ on such matters, but let this not dissuade us from making our best case for those values which—after careful deliberation—we consider most noble and wise. For as much as we humans vary in our inclinations and convictions, we are not impervious to each other's influence.

Moreover, simply because we have no precise and unassailable equations on morality does not mean that we can draw no conclusions whatever, nor does it mean that in any given age we are forced to value all behavior as equally good.

Societies must function by generally agreed upon standards of right and wrong within the group, and they will set laws and develop social rules based on what seems to them wise and appropriate—and individuals will be expected to abide by the agreed-upon morality of the group. One can attempt to persuade the group to change their code of morality—their laws and standards of right and wrong—but until such change comes, the group expectations remain what they are, and barring conventions that trample deep principle or crucial rights, the individual is wise and prudent to abide by the rules and standards of the group.

My son, right and wrong behavior is not a matter limited to notions of essential morality, it is also rooted in the pragmatic requirement that society agree on how its members are to effectively coexist and interact. Consider traffic conventions: Each specific rule—the side of the street on which vehicles are to travel, and what signals and signs are to indicate when vehicles are to move, stop, turn, and the like—is not essentially correct and all other options wrong. In a country where vehicles drive on the right side of the road, traffic will function about as well as in a country where vehicles drive on the left side. Still, whichever mode is followed by the entire populace is effective because it provides a common standard that enables the efficient flow of traffic and prevents much difficulty and discord. So, too, societies must arrive at laws that govern interactions between its members, not to legislate absolute and objective morality, but—informed by the lights of our best wisdom and fairness—to create and maintain stable common standards that allow for the smooth social, political, and commercial interactions that underpin a healthy society.

Yet even though societies must set common standards on certain matters whether or not any essential right and wrong can be argued for, there are some cases where essential right and wrong—within a human context—can indeed be argued for. A simple illustration: One cannot prove that life is better than death, and therefore that murder is wrong, but one can appeal to the values, the deepest instincts, and the straightforward best interests of all normal human beings, who share the innate and desperate desire to live—and therefore teach and legislate that murder is wrong. And while many other notions of right and wrong are less obvious, intelligent arguments and appeals to conscience can make the case for why certain moral standards are preferable to others.

And though on many issues intense disagreements will remain between those who value different ideals, such differences need not preclude dialogue and debate, and the attempt to teach and learn. In the halls of the legislature and in the meeting rooms of business and commerce, do not experts, advocates, and administrators debate with passion and eloquence on how best to regulate a lawful society or a profitable enterprise—even though they cannot prove that their ideas constitute the only constructive model, much less that they are supernaturally derived, or absolutely valid for every circumstance and for all time? Even so they do not despair of persuading each other of the helpfulness and justice of their ideas. Neither should we, in attempting to orient ourselves and our societies, for our day and age, on how best to live.

My son, try as we might, we cannot see the circumstances and values that might hold sway in future days. Yet in our contemplations of right and wrong we must still reach for the universal good, for the best interests of those alive today, and for what we think will be best for posterity, too. The members of each culture and era should accept the responsibility to base their morals on what seem to them foundational principles for the perennial best interests of man and mankind, and, where the interests of the individual and the collective conflict, for what seems to their eyes the best balance between the two. Still, no people or age should be so arrogant or rigid as to insist that their principles are the only reasonable or healthy ones for all time, or even that their specific laws and customs are the only effective ways those principles can be applied.

And, again, even if we have no precise and unassailable equations on morality, we must still make judgments about which values and ideals we will hold above which others, and unless we wish to bring down upon ourselves and our progeny barbarism and chaos, we dare not see all behavior as morally equivalent.

My son, morality is not merely a conceptual conundrum to be explored and argued by professors and philosophers; real people must interact with each other every day, and common standards and expectations must be in place, or the cloth of civilization covering the savage aspects of our nature quickly begins to fray. Humility and pragmatic wisdom ask of us not that we decide things with perfect clarity and unassailable logic on every matter for all possible time, but that we attempt to reduce at least a little, the confusion, the folly, and the injustice of our own unavoidable age.

163. On whether a society without religion will become permissive, and conservative views will be defeated on social and political issues

And a man said: I eagerly await the day society gives up on religion, because then everyone will see that liberal ideas are far superior to conservative ideas, and that on various policy issues—abortion rights, gun control, capital punishment, war, and many others—the stubborn old guard and the traditionalists were wrong, and liberals and progressives like me were correct.

And the sage said: My brother, religion has, indeed, taught many things that a society without religion would reject—things like dogmas about how many gods there are, what exactly are the correct beliefs about the nature of such gods, how exactly they must be worshiped, what have been their communications to mankind, and the many harsh threats and punishments for those who do not worship a particular deity in a particular way, or whose faith or actions are judged insufficiently devout.

But, at times, religion has also taught various positive lessons, such as charity, forgiveness, kindness and justice. Will you reject those, too, merely because some have taught these in the name of God and the church?

A little reflection makes clear that an honest and intelligent approach on political and social issues—issues such as those you mentioned—does more than simply accept or reject an entire set of positions based merely on whether they have historically been advocated for by religion.[1]

And to speak of the issues you mentioned, intelligent non-religious arguments can be made in many cases not only *for* abortion rights and gun control, but *against* those positions, too; and not only *against* capital punishment and war,

---

[1] Wise men of every age have noted the equally unhelpful extremes to which conservatives and reformers can tend. For one example, William Hazlitt, in *Table Talk,* speaks to this point at length. He says: "The greatest number of minds seem utterly incapable of fixing on any conclusion, except from the pressure of custom and authority; opposed to these there is another class less numerous but pretty formidable, who in all their opinions are equally under the influence of novelty and restless vanity...These swallow every antiquated absurdity; those catch at every new, unfledged project...These last turn away at the mention of all usages, creeds, institutions of more than a day's standing as a mass of bigotry, superstition, and barbarous ignorance, whose leaden touch would petrify and benumb their quick, mercurial, 'apprehensive, forgetive' faculties. The opinion of to-day supersedes that of yesterday: that of to-morrow supersedes, by anticipation, that of to-day. The wisdom of the ancients, the doctrines of the learned, the laws of nations, the common sentiments of morality, are to them like a bundle of old almanacs...With the one, the majority, 'the powers that be' have always been in the right in all ages and places, though they have been cutting one another's throats and turning the world upside down with their quarrels and disputes from the beginning of time: with the other, what any two people have ever agreed in is an error on the face of it. The credulous bigot shudders at the idea of altering anything in 'time-hallowed' institutions; and under this cant phrase can bring himself to tolerate any knavery or any folly, the Inquisition, Holy Oil, the Right Divine, etc.; the more refined sceptic will laugh in your face at the idea of retaining anything which has the damning stamp of custom upon it, and is for abating all former precedents, 'all trivial, fond records,' the whole frame and fabric of society as a nuisance in the lump. Is not this a pair of wiseacres well matched? The one stickles through thick and thin for his own religion and government: the other scouts all religions and all governments with a smile of ineffable disdain. The one will not move for any consideration out of the broad and beaten path: the other is continually turning off at right angles, and losing himself in the labyrinths of his own ignorance and presumption...The one is the slave of habit: the other is the sport of caprice."

but, in certain cases, *for* them. And it would be laziness, and an intellectual dishonesty similar to that which we criticize in religion, to simply assume that in rejecting religion's supernatural claims one can blithely reject all the values and positions many followers of traditional religion held, or hold, dear.

A person—religious or non-religious—need not choose between pre-assembled groups of opinions, but can, instead, with good intelligence and cause, maintain some opinions conventionally seen as conservative, and other opinions conventionally seen as liberal—and still others seen as neither. And many do.

My brother, the rebellious adolescent is certain that his parents' teachings are nothing but an authoritarian set of unnecessary restrictions, that his father's rules and warnings and his mother's lessons and pleadings are rigid, outdated, and irrelevant. And when he breaks free of his parents' control, he feels a sense of power, even euphoria, at stepping outside familiar boundaries and flouting the standards he was taught.

And this rebellious adolescent is not entirely wrong. He correctly senses that much of what his parents taught him was misguided—some rules were unhelpful or worse, while others were given dubious rationales, or no rationale at all and simply enforced on the parents' authority. And he feels that his parents did not treat him with sufficient dignity, but often degraded him by arbitrarily imposing upon him their naked will.

Yet the adolescent is generally unable, in his urge toward separation, to discern where some of his parents' teachings on behavior were correct. Instead—in the heady rush of burgeoning prowess—he notices the shortcomings and errors of his parents, and sees them and their lessons as entirely incompetent and wrong. Indeed, whatever is associated with his parents is for years, to his eyes, suspect and embarrassing. Only when he lives well into adulthood is he likely to appreciate some of their wisdom and ways.[1]

And so it is with religion and many who rise up against her. The rebel against religion correctly discerns that much of what she has taught was misguided—customs, values, and laws resulting in hardship, division, even hate. He also becomes aware that religion provided poor reasons for her teachings—dubious superstitions, poor science, or simple command by the claimed authority of God. And he sees, too, that religion has in some ways degraded her followers by imposing upon them various forms of control, censorship, and fear—and tried to prevent them from thinking their own best and honest thoughts. The rebel often

---

[1] Mark Twain is credited with saying: "When I was a boy of fourteen, my father was so ignorant I could hardly stand to have the old man around. But when I got to be twenty-one, I was astonished at how much he had learned in seven years." And we may add that in recent times when adolescence, in many, seems to have been extended to middle age, such recognition may not dawn until far later than twenty-one.

concludes, therefore, that everything religion taught, and every position associated with religious people, is incompetent and wrong.

What this rebel overlooks, however, is that rebellion is not a reflection of mature freedom, but, at best, of the attempt to break free; not a sign of independent initiative, but of influenced reaction. And the acts of rebellion constitute but a poor example for those already free.[1]

My brother, many teachings of religion are mistaken or destructive and I have spoken out against a number of them—indeed, it has been my main purpose in coming here today to speak out against them. Yet many other teachings of religion—when she stops speaking about gods and speaks instead of man—reflect the accumulated wisdom and experience of many generations. And even if religion teaches these, falsely, in the name of God, we need not play the adolescent and insist that because we found mistakes and worse in parts of her traditions, all of her lessons must be completely useless.

Do we not appreciate literature and music, architecture and art, even those works created by or for religion? Some of David's Psalms and Milton's devotions and Rumi's love-songs to the Divine; the religious compositions of Bach and Handel and the innumerable plaintive hymns of every people to their angels and gods; the Parthenon, Notre Dame, and the Blue Mosque, and uncounted houses of worship with arches and steeples, carvings and columns, mosaics and domes, and varied forms of splendor and grace; in these and other ways, religion has inspired works of excellence and beauty. And just as the intelligent man understands that we can appreciate the quality of such art though we may consider the devotional intent or otherworldly focus of the artists to be mistaken, so too can we appreciate the wisdom of many moral teachings advocated for by religion, even if we consider the supernatural claims or intents of such teachings to be misguided.

And so, in examining the legacy of religion, in thinking about her many lessons and attempting to distinguish between the perverse and the just, the wrong-headed and the wise, here as elsewhere we shall not be justified in taking the easy path of wholesale acceptance or wholesale rejection. Instead, we are called upon to exert the noble moderation of careful thought—asking, about one idea at a time, not "Whose idea is this?" or "Which group usually argues for this position?" but rather, "Does this idea hold a valuable lesson?" and "Why, beyond my emotions and impulses and loyalties, is this idea right or wrong?"

---

[1] Many years ago I came across, in a popular magazine, this lesson on human development: "You know you've finally become an adult when you do what's good for you, even if your mother told you to do it."

My brother, those who hold conservative values often have as much to teach us as those who hold progressive values. Mother's soft lullaby and father's stern rebuke can teach a child the love that is in strength and the strength that is in love; and when society veers too far to the masculine or too far to the feminine, everyone—men, women, and children—are poorly served. Cultures dominated by the traditional religions with which our people are most familiar have histori-cally tended to be pervaded with the masculine traits of rules, restrictions, harsh demands, self-reliance, and the frequent use of power; and some cultures that have slowly rebelled against traditional religion—indeed, even some religious denominations themselves—especially when such rebellion is sourced in the insular luxuries of plenty and some equally insular ideas of the academy, have come to embrace the feminine traits of pity, permissiveness, interdependence, and a reluctance to exercise power or pass judgment.[1] But though humans can change and choose much, we cannot escape the reality that in our bones—as individuals and as a species—we are made of both the masculine and the feminine,[2] and our spirits hear but poorly when listening with only one ear.

And while some societies slowly pushing away from religion may, at least temporarily, reject values and positions merely because these were once taught in the name of God and church, when we overreact and conduct ourselves immod-erately reality exacts its tuition fees soon or late. And though some of religion's teachings justly deserve to be consigned to the dung-heaps of history, the children and grandchildren of those who indiscriminately threw away all tradi-tional values merely because these were associated with religion will have paid a

---

[1] Of course, not all societies rejecting religion embrace the cluster of tendencies men-tioned in the text. The Soviet Union was one prominent example of an official and radical rejection of religion, yet it came along with militarism and authoritarianism, not an abundance of empathy and other soft traits. The text speaks, however, of a slow rebellion against traditional religion, and one significantly sourced in luxury and academia, of the kind the questioner in this section was speaking about, a circumstance current in the United States and Western Europe, wherein, for a complex set of reasons, those who do not subscribe to traditional religious beliefs are more likely to see the world through the above-mentioned "feminine" perspective than are their fellow citizens who hold traditional religious beliefs. (See following footnote for further clarification.)

[2] The perceptive reader will have observed through life experience that the easy and stereotypical division of humanity into "masculine" vs. "feminine" traits by actual sex is far from always accurate—that on matters such as justice vs. mercy some women are more "masculine" than most men, and some men more "feminine" than most women. It is also true, as I indicate in the text, that—even though it does seem that some innate, and some socialized, differences hold true between the sexes on average and in the aggregate—all healthy men and women harbor within them some mix of these and other opposing traits, and are not caricatures of either extreme.

dear price for their forebears' recklessness; and we may hope that even feeling the disillusionment of directionless enervation, or the danger, defeat or chaos that may be its fruit, they will exercise the wisdom and courage not to swing back to the other extreme and embrace authoritarianism or superstition—that in desperate yearning for safety and direction they do not again fall to their knees in submission to tyrants and strongmen who offer these things from below, or to phantom gods who seem to offer these things from above.

X. Meaning and Purpose

164. Without religion, what meaning is there to suffering?

And a gravely ill man spoke in a hoarse voice and said: O wise one, if religion is false, and I cannot be certain of God, what purpose remains for all my suffering? I have lived a cautious and virtuous life, and have been burdened with pain not of my own making. If I did not believe that God brought this upon me for a reason, I would long ago have succumbed.

And the sage replied softly and said: My brother, my heart grieves for your illness, and for all you have endured. Would that I could heal your afflictions, bind up your wounds, and bring blessed relief to all your distress. And how far from my aim it is to heap up emotional or spiritual sufferings atop the already heavy agony of disease. Yet you have listened to my words with courage, and asked a burning question—and I shall neither patronize you nor dishonor your inquiry by offering less than a candid response.

My brother, suffering, like the strangling weed-root in a garden's nightmare, eats down into the joy-soil of our souls; the gnarled, torturing tentacle encircles our life force squeezing and sucking, draining us deeply. Some of us, under such an attack—our appetites taken, our vanity devastated, our ambitions shattered—are reminded to let go of excess entanglements, to cling to our central stems and fiercely preserve that which we value deepest. Then, the most invasive of roots, even in their assault, may yet give nurture indirectly—stimulating authenticity, the queen of blossoms; and wisdom, the most noble of fruits.

Yet there are times, too many times, when suffering crushes all, and yields nothing but misery. Woe to the multitudes cut down by the sword, and the numberless wasted by famine, who were not given time to cultivate flower or fruit, and died clutching but bitter roots. Woe to the babes consumed by pestilence, who never tasted aught of life but the cruel pangs of disease and the choking fingers of death. Woe to the simpletons devoid of wisdom, and those with hearts too frightened to see, saddled with sufferings from which they cannot learn. And woe to the blameless beasts of the field, not given the intellect to bear truth or wisdom, yet gnawed at by hunger, afflicted by plague, and hunted and savaged by fang and claw. My dear brother, some suffering is transformed into beauty, character, and meaning; but if we are honest we must concede that much suffering cannot possibly be used for any good end.

Yet you who can ask this question about suffering may hope to cultivate grace and courage sufficient to wield its crushing power to focus your soul. Then your sighing may turn to consolation, and your wailing to sad-sweet song.

My brother, each of us, still an infant within, having learned the primal lesson that crying brings the warm breast of comfort, is tempted even now to whimper into silent skies. Your earnest question insists that agony must have meaning; yet the selfsame attempt to sweeten suffering with the candy cane of purpose, makes pain more biting by arming its source with the dagger of intent.

If pain is intentionally sent by God, it is bitter, indeed. Yet if pain is not dispatched by a Punishing Power, perhaps it need not be sweetened by transcendent meaning; for then, no guilt need be borne, no anger need be soothed, no injustice need be explained. When your toe bangs into a table leg, my brother, although you experience pain, you do not remain angry with the table—for it intended no harm; neither do you wonder about the justice of the table's motives. If, instead, your friend knowingly stomps on your toe, though the physical pain might be no greater, your anger *will* be greater—and you may be filled with a sense of resentment at the injustice—for you were attacked with intent. Similarly, my brother, if your pain was not deliberately caused by God but is rather the result of random occurrences triggered by the laws of nature, you need not be angry; neither must you feel guilty as one being punished for misdeeds. Perhaps your pain has no transcendent meaning; and though this may deny you confidence that a reward awaits you in heaven, it also leaves you far less burdened here on earth. Without guilt and anger to encumber its wings, cannot the soul lift off with far less fervor and fury?

My dear brother, be kind to yourself: Dwell not in the prison of pain, cowering between fear and anger, and holding fast to the bars of self-pity. Neither cast your joy into the debtor's prison of meaning, keeping her chained, until the Universe would repay your pain with coinage of deep significance. Neither look with envy upon those luxuriating in pleasure, for in a fleeting moment all flesh meets the same end. Walk, instead, toward the garden of equanimity surrounding the palace of contented abundance.

Know that we cannot say whether any Power collects our tears, gives ear to our groans, or even takes note of our passing. But know, too, that such divine attention is not needed to render most of our burdens bearable—or to give most of our brief days joy. Indeed, it is hope for the transcendent that makes the commonplace despised; reality pales beside poisonous paradigms of perfection. And in our jealous lusting for elusive eternity, the sacred, passing moments lose their light. Staring into the distant heavens blinds us, and keeps us from seeing delight near at hand on humble earth.

My brother, consider this, too: Only the man who hoards his treasure for the future, while living as a drawn-faced pauper all the while, is desperate for another sunrise, and yet another and another. But he who rejoices in his wealth, and expends his treasure enjoying each day's enchantments, feasting with pleasure, and loving with generous spirit—even while laying up provision for future years—such a man is not frantic for tomorrow to dawn, for he has never deprived himself in all his moments for the dubious sake of unseen days.

My dear brother, I charge you to gather peace without delay, the peace of those who do not depend on anything further. And I plead with you to reach for delight before tomorrow: the delight of those who take joy in the multitude of pleasures and passions and beauties; of intimacies, achievements, and contributions; of memories, imaginings, and inspirations; within terrestrial reach—without minimizing these gifts by dreaming of what might lie beyond. And may we all—all of us heir to blessings and doom—walk in peace the path of afflicted joy, and dance enchanted, undefeated, in the stark shadow of inevitable demise.

165. Argument that if God did not create the world, everything is an accident—and therefore by definition everything, including human life, has no purpose

And a religious man said: You make many pretty speeches, but you will be forced to admit that if God did not create the world, everything is an accident. And if everything is an accident, by definition there is no purpose to anything, including human life.[1]

And the sage said: I understand the hunger for purpose, and I assure you that nothing I say today need rob people of all sense of purpose.

In addressing your challenge, my brother, let us first note that even if what you said were true, that human life can only have purpose if God created the world, it would not prove the existence of a God. Either a God who created humans with a plan for them exists, or not. But if no such God exists, He will not magically come into existence merely because this might provide some with a greater sense of purpose.

---

[1] Many have argued this through the ages. One popular religious leader writes that if God did not exist, we would all be accidents, and "life would have no purpose or meaning or significance." And while I can sympathize with the inclinations and impulses that give rise to such a conclusion—indeed, as an adolescent and young adult that basic religious justification seemed to me so obviously true—I have come to see this proposition (that human life, to be of value, must have supernatural guidance or design—or for that matter, eternal existence) as not only false, but degrading. Over the next several sections I attempt to explain why.

But let us look more closely at whether it is, indeed, true that without a supernatural Creator human life would have no purpose.

My brother, if I collect stones lying about my field, and build with them a fence to protect my property from animals and men, does not that fence have a purpose? And must we insist that this purpose of my fence is dependent on the stones having been originally placed on the earth of my field by some greater power for the precise reason of me building a fence—and that unless that were the aim for which those stones were originally scattered about my field, the fence has no purpose?

No, my brother, we would never say this—because we understand the important distinction between *original* purpose and *current* purpose. We know that something may not have had purpose originally, but can be fashioned into an object or applied to a function that does, indeed, have purpose now.

And what of a child conceived by parents whose objective at the moment was rather more immediate and pleasure-bound, and who had no intention of creating another human? Shall we say that this child must consider her life purposeless because she was not at the very beginning the product of a purposeful plan? No, we would not be so cruel as to say this, or so irrational as to think it. We know that a person may create quite a purposeful life for herself irrespective of what were her parents' intentions at the moment of her conception.

The same is true for all of us as a species. If there is no Creator with detailed plans for us, and specific commandments for how we must conduct our lives—even if we came about by "accidental" processes—then we are like the stones of a field or the unplanned child. And even if we were to be certain there is no supernatural or original purpose for our lives, we are in no way prevented from creating of, and for, our existence natural, current purpose.

And not only can we create purpose out of an existence for which there was no original plan, such an enterprise—bringing forth what we will, and assigning what meaning we choose to our own lives—has us, arguably, acting with more power, more freedom, even more noble mission than ever we could by following a cosmic master. Indeed, some would say that wishing for meaning to be imposed from some god outside us, just as would be the wish to be a slave to another human, is a degrading evasion of existential responsibility.[1]

And how, you may ask, is one to create natural purpose and meaning? The answer, my brother, is that there as many ways as there are hearts and minds. No,

---

[1] Viktor Frankl, who wrote, among other books on the matter, the well-known *Man's Search for Meaning*, said: "Ultimately, man should not ask what the meaning of his life is, but rather must recognize that it is he who is asked." And one need not agree with all his thoughts on existential matters to appreciate these words.

there are many more ways—for every person has more talents to develop, more goals to achieve, more causes to fight for, more knowledge to pursue, more experiences to delight in, more gifts to bring to the family of earth than the brief span of years we are allotted will ever allow.

See this woman laughing with children, as she shines the sun of her love on the next generation; and see this man splashing in the water and running in the fields with his young. See the architect designing a building for people to live and work in greater comfort and beauty; and see the workers in stone and steel laboring to bring this vision into the realm of the real. See the musician writing a melody, or playing a song; see the dancer straining to speak beauty in language of motion; and see the audience rejoicing at such intense art. See the writer bleeding words joyfully, sentences and pages she hopes will touch the hearts of others, as they do her own; and see the reader's eyes hungrily collecting the thoughts and sentiments that render existence a little deeper, a little more informed, or at least more charming and entertaining. See the inventor working long hours designing or improving a machine, testing his practical imagination against materials and challenges; and see the merchant selling these machines to provide for his household and to make easier the lives of many. See the teacher patiently repeating the alphabet, the rules of mathematics, or the magic secrets of reading; and see the professor helping the minds of young men and women continue to grow. See the scientist investigating how to defeat dread diseases, how to bring sight to the blind and hearing to the deaf, or at least how to reduce the pain of the afflicted; and see the physician acting on such healing knowledge. See the lover dedicating his days to making music of the heart with another, transcending petty and primal barriers, and living two as one; and see, also, the individualist dedicating his life to autonomy and self-reliance. See the legislator helping to set the law, the judge helping to interpret and apply the law, and the policeman helping to enforce it; and see, too, those individuals fired by the passion to change the law, working to make it more just or wise. See the many bringing stability to work and home; see the many offering excitement and laughter to lighten our days; see the many studying and discovering all manner of knowledge and sharing with us their expertise; and see the many dedicating themselves to various devotions, and to causes and missions of altruism and love.

Indeed, my brother, see the man laboring to develop humility, to transcend the human animal's urge to be special and eternal and the universe's favorite son; see him exerting painful honesty, not pretending to know what he does not know on matters supernatural; and see him gathering his courage and taking accountability for creating the meaning of his own life.

And breathe in the scented breeze of a spring or autumn evening, then stare up at the darkening sky and the dazzling stars, hear the owl and the coyote, or the sounds of humans and their machines—or listen close to fleeting moments of pure silence—and know that you belong to, and are at home in, this terrible-wonderful web of life, with all its ambiguities and limitations and pain, but with all its glories and opportunities, all its delights and intensities, all its joys and pageantry, too.

166. Argument that for a religious person, losing belief in God would make life feel meaningless

But a young priest cried out and said: If I did not believe in God, my life would be meaningless! God is the entire focus of my existence; I have studied the Scriptures deep into the night, and awakened early for long prayers. All my effort takes its meaning from my conviction that I am doing the will of a transcendent Creator. Without God, all of who I am would seem pointless!

And the sage replied: My son, my heart aches for your distress; I, too, know the terror, the disorientation and the despair, of peering over the precipice of honesty and contemplating a fall into what seems a meaningless void.

Yet what else shall we do but pursue truth? Facts do not conform themselves to our desires nor amend themselves to prevent our pain. Reason allows for two possibilities: Either a God like the one in which you were taught to believe exists, or not. And if there is no such God, He will not come into being merely on account of desperate wishes. What is *is* and what is not *is not*. This is the iron law of reality, and if we make sudden impact with its unyielding strength, we may suffer agonizing wounds. But the unrelenting hardness of truth need not be resented as cruel; it can also be cherished as the most solid of materials, an immovable foundation upon which we can build the noblest of habitations—the grand castle of authentic living.

My son, life will not become less meaningful if you lose your religious belief; it will only—for a time—*feel* less meaningful. And your belief in God has not actually made your years of faith meaningful—they have only made them *feel* meaningful. Life's real and objective level of importance remains the same; for external reality does not change based on what we know, rather our thoughts and feelings change. And if we value truth, and real meaning—not merely comfort or the *feelings* of meaningfulness—we must be faithful to what is, and not confuse it with what we wish there was.

My son, I will tell you more. Although you may find this deeply disconcerting, I ask you to consider that even if God *does* exist it would still not necessarily make life very meaningful. If a superior being created you and wants you to follow his orders, does that constitute great meaning? Perhaps it is closer to undignified bondage. If a powerful dictator demanded obedience, and promised rewards or punishments based upon your level of compliance, would doing as you were told seem especially meaningful? And if you yourself created small creatures and commanded them to dedicate their lives to serving you, would you say they must see such lives as embodying deep meaning?

Furthermore, if you do not find your own existence sufficiently important, why would your existence become more meaningful if it was important to someone else—even a great and powerful God? After all, if in order to have a meaningful existence one needs an outside and greater force to consider one's life significant, and thus we need a deity to give our lives value—it would follow that God's existence—any form of monotheism's God—cannot be meaningful: for there is no greater force to consider *Him* significant. And if God is not Himself meaningful, why should His regard for us give our lives meaning?

This is perhaps the most frightening yet empowering realization: We must create our own sense of meaning. Even God cannot do this for us.[1] And if we accept this, we need not feel threatened by the possibility that there is no God, or by the prospect that any God there may be may not esteem us highly.

There is no essential, necessary, or objective meaning to the universe or anything it contains. Yes, there is objective truth to certain propositions: mathematical statements such as $2 + 2 = 4$ in base 10; or empirical statements such as "There is a lamp on my desk." We can determine through various means of investigation and proof whether such things are true. But there is no objective truth to be determined in the claim that something is or is not essentially meaningful. Because meaning is not an inherent and objective quality external to the observer; instead, it is an optional and subjective quality dependent on the observer—his values, his attitudes, his beliefs, his experience, and often his choice. Nothing in our lives, then, can be proved to have any meaning—but we can choose to impart meaning in our lives to anything. My son, we weave our lives with the stuff of mist; but if we choose, we can weave beautifully.

Furthermore, is it possible that your insistence on being meaningful and significant may be but a lack of realistic humility? According to some theories, the infant assumes he is the entire world. In any case, he is not conscious of much beside his immediate sensations and emotions. Later, recognizing the separate existence of others, he assumes that he constitutes a very significant part of the world. Gradually, he becomes aware of his smallness, and as life goes on he finally accepts that nearly all find him of little relevance, and that his parents—those who may have valued him most—will die. My son, each of us is a child of the universe, and, as a rule, never stops demanding to be the apple of our mother's eye—the celebrated center of all existence. But if we learn to be

---

[1] Valèry's words are devastating: "God made everything out of nothing, but the nothingness shows through."

humble, we can step free of our spiritual childhood—the smallness of insisting upon loving nurturance from Mother Universe.

Let us go deeper, still, my son, and ask: Is the instinct toward eternal meaning itself meaningful in any transcendent sense? Or is it merely one more instinct of an intelligent and social creature, which evolved, like other instincts, because it provided practical benefits? Allow me to explain: One thing upon which all life depends is the urge to survive; for many this can be strengthened by a sense of personal significance, even if only at the unconscious level: "I am important, and my life must go on" is a conviction that can see one through crisis and peril. Furthermore, as members of a social species, we are imbued with the beneficial instinct to want *others* to consider us important—for if others value us sufficiently, they will extend to us their aid and approval, enhancing our ability to survive, and to find a mate and reproduce.

Another way in which the instinct for meaning relates to survival is in the realm of resources. Consider early humans and their attitudes toward food: If one man was content having sufficient fare for this meal, while another had the urge to focus on what was more significant, on finding larger and superior stores of sustenance, or even understanding how to cultivate and shepherd farm and flock, would not the second man be more likely to survive better and longer, and thus reproduce more successfully and pass on his instincts to future generations—instincts driving his descendents to value the ever more meaningful?

And, as with all instincts, this urge to seek out the important would often be applied to arenas other than those for which it was originally useful. Once our basic needs are satisfied, the inclination to focus on the ever more important continues to drive many of us to demand ever greater levels of significance and meaning—thus, perhaps, the pining for supernatural meaning and communion.

Interestingly, this intense yearning for transcendent meaning or supernatural connection is more prevalent in some personality types and temperaments than in others.[1] This, too, suggests that the urge for spiritual or religious meaning is not especially meaningful in its own right, but merely an inclination with as little transcendent value as other temperaments' urges for excitement, impulse, and freedom; or for knowledge, autonomy, and achievement; or for stability, order, and communal belonging.

---

[1] Intuitive Feelers, also referred to by David Keirsey as "idealists" (or NF's) in his *Please Understand Me II* (a book on the Jungian-based temperament and personality type system) require, as one of their core needs, along with others such as authenticity and emotional intimacy, the cultivating of a sense of deep meaning or mission. The other three major temperaments—the SP artisans, the NT rationals, and the SJ guardians—generally feel more strongly pulled by other needs as alluded to, presently, in the text.

Thus, the need to feel important—to believe that we are essentially significant and perform acts of significance—can be seen as a natural extension of humans' individual and social instincts. And these instincts of the ancients, which would have led to survival and reproduction, would have therefore been passed on to us, their descendents. And so, my son, once we see that our yearning for meaning may be, at root, merely inclination designed for physical survival and propagation, can we not feel less intensely disappointed that such inclination cannot be fully satisfied—just as we inevitably accept that we are unable to satisfy our yearnings for unlimited pleasure, unlimited wealth, and unlimited love?

And yes, we grieve for the death of imagined powers or devotions, and for the loss of deepest values. Yet such pain need not preclude a sense of our own meaning—if we choose to create within our admittedly small lives a sense of passionate engagement with what our minds find compelling and our hearts find beautiful and dear. Paradoxically, inner peace and satisfaction with the level of meaning in our lives is easier to attain if we recall that even our yearning for meaning is, perhaps, not especially meaningful.

Honesty gives much, my son, but takes away all conviction of guaranteed, eternal, and transcendent meaning. And does this loss of imagined cosmic significance leave you disappointed, even disoriented? Of old it has been said that the truth shall set you free; but I remind you today that freedom, too, has its costs and limitations. When the blindfold of faith blackens a man's sight, he can invoke limitless visions: but when his eyes are uncovered by truth he may be disillusioned by how weak his real sight is, and how unimpressive the landscape. And when the prisoner's hands are held captive by dogma's ancient shackles, he can fancy himself powerful yet restrained; but when truth sets him free, he must face how little those hands can ever do.

Yet, my son, even so you are stronger than you think. In time, your tears of mourning will dry, you will cease to glance backward in fear, the bold spirit of integrity will settle within you in power and peace—and you will gladly choose palpable though humble reality over even the most extravagant fantasies. Not only can you survive this loss of religious meaning—you can prosper and thrive. And then, though bereft of your old meaning, you may find a deeper meaning still—that of dancing your own inimitable dance with the universe; and of daily poise and self-generated contentment, neither hounded by the ghosts of hallowed remorse, nor lured by the hauntings of desperate hope. And with bitter grief and sweetest relief will you finally make peace with the powerful irony, that in the days of kneeling to dubious gods and fanciful theologies you sold your soul for the meaningless, gaudy beads of self-serving illusion; and that by cleaving fiercely to the best of what you can know to be true and real, you hold within your spirit the warm gold of profound confidence and the dazzling gems of deep authenticity.

Vary the metaphor, my son: Losing religion is learning how babies are made. We stagger backward, certain there must be some mistake as we shrink from the horror of our crude origins, the shame of our long ignorance, and the shocking implications for our own fertility. And though we find ourselves cast out, disoriented, in the too-bright corridor of enlightenment, from which we can never return to the hollow cave of innocence, open lies the doorway to maturity, with all its perils and pleasures frighteningly, gloriously, at hand!

My son, vary the metaphor again: If one stands upon a false surface—a foundationless house, a wobbly ladder, a weak-legged table—and it gives way, it is not the world that has no solid ground, but one's chosen support. If you have stood for years upon religion—and thought it the "Ground of Being"—and now it does not hold, you may think the world is without stability. But happily it is merely the mistaken views that are unstable. Clear away the shaky platforms and feeble contrivances, and feel how truly solid is the earth beneath your feet.

And yes, my son, sadly, you may suffer greatly in the fall from on false high. But this does not mean the original elevation was either necessary or healthy— rather, that it hurts to fall. Neither will the pain persecute you indefinitely: Many wounds heal, and this one, in time, shall vanish too—save for the noble scars of wisdom, carved for a brief forever into the face of your deepening soul.

167. Argument that life is meaningless if there is no life after death

But another man said: If I cannot be certain there is a God, I cannot be certain there is any life after death, and then surely life is meaningless! This earthly existence is short, difficult, and leads to old age and death. Only the confidence that I will live on in heaven, forever, makes me feel that life is worthwhile.[1]

---

[1] Many have stated this through the centuries; some have stated it well. Let us pass over the innumerable sermons from the pulpit and the goodly number of well-remembered speakers on such matters and revivify for a moment the (translated) words of Victor Hugo who in addition to his many other talents and beyond his other achievements was an orator and a statesman. In a speech to a legislative body deliberating over the matter of state involvement in religious education he said: "...Let us not forget—let us everywhere teach it—There would be no dignity in life, it would not be worth the holding, if in death we wholly perish. All that lightens labor and sanctifies toil, all that renders man brave, good, wise, patient, benevolent, just, humble...great, worthy of intelligence, worthy of liberty, is to have perpetually before him the vision of a better world darting its rays of celestial splendor through the dark shadows of this present life. For myself...let me be permitted here to say, and to proclaim from the elevation of this Tribune, that I believe, that I most profoundly and reverently believe, in that better world. It is to me more real, more substantial...than this evanescence which we cling to

517

And the sage replied: My brother, those of us who have been taught as part of our belief in God to expect life after death can suffer doubly when discovering these promises of religion unreliable. Indeed, the pretension to transcendent significance—by being part of a divine plan—and the pretension to transcendent existence—by prevailing against death—are two of the most alluring illusions, and two of the most painful to surrender. And religion winks at us, and reassures us that for the price of but a little faith we need surrender neither—that an unbounded God loves us and plans the details of our lives, and that our souls will carry on in heaven for ever and all time.

Yet even so staggering a loss as eternity—and it is a terrible loss, and the prospect of death is so foreign to our sensibilities, so offensive to all we labor for and cherish, that even a philosopher, even a mortician, remembers his own ultimate death with a start and a shiver—need not always be felt as unbearable. The day may come when you will have lived and loved and mourned so well—perhaps after having partaken much at the table of existence, of bitter and sweet, of bland and tasty, of rancid and fresh, and seeing enough of what comes to pass under the sun—looked out at life with such unblinking, clear-sighted and well-sated eyes, that you will no longer be desperate to avoid death.

Moreover, only if eternal life were meaningless would temporary life be meaningless; only if temporary life can have meaning, can endless life have meaning. And if you argue that life builds for a future, why are future moments of an eternal life more meaningful than current moments of a mortal life? As ten thousand empty jugs contain no more wine than one empty jug, so too an eternal life of worthless moments holds no more meaning than a brief life of worthless moments; an endless supply of something meaningless is still meaningless.

Yet, my brother, you may argue that eternal life is not only quantitatively greater than finite life, it is qualitatively greater, and meaningful—that eternal life is not merely more life than temporary life, but a different kind of life entirely. Then ask yourself why a permanent life would be meaningful when a temporary life would not. How is it qualitatively more meaningful?

---

and call life. It is unceasingly before my eyes. I believe in it with all the strength of my convictions; and, after many struggles and much study and experience, it is the supreme certainty of my reason, as it is the supreme consolation of my soul."

Yet when Hugo juxtaposes the "supreme certainty" of his reason with the "supreme consolation" of his soul, we are reminded—if further reminders were needed—of how difficult it is to think clearly about matters that touch on our deepest longings. For while we may honestly hope for an afterlife, we cannot honestly state that we know one exists. With the heavy thumb of the lusting after immortality ever pressing down one side of the scale of reason on such deliberations, how easy and common it is to weigh the wares of existence and confidently state, "Yes; beyond this vale of tears we go to a better world!"

In order to explore this matter, let us clarify what you mean by saying that your life would be meaningless without life after death. Do you mean it would be, in some objective sense, meaningless? Or do you mean that it would feel, emotionally and *subjectively*, meaningless? If you refer to some objective or absolute meaning, I remind you that meaning is not a physical property such as size that can, for our purposes, be measured objectively. Instead, it is a psychological experience on the part of a conscious being. Nothing is essentially or objectively meaningful: All meaningfulness is in the subjective mind of a beholder. Thus, nothing can be meaningful to a rock, we suppose, because as far as we know a rock has no awareness. To a literate human, words on a road sign are meaningful, yet to a cat they are meaningless; conversely, the cat finds meaningful the subtle scents on the wind, scents the human may not even notice, much less consider meaningful.

As meaning is subjective, to whom must your life be important in order for you to consider it meaningful? If to you, it can always be meaningful—for while alive you are legitimately important to yourself,[1] and when no longer alive you cannot experience meaninglessness. And if you argue that knowing your mortality prevents you from feeling meaningful even while life pulses in your veins, I urge you to see that your pain is caused only by your insistence on thinking about what you will never experience. You have the choice to remember—without denying mortality—that you will never live meaninglessness, that for all the moments of your life you will be meaningful at least to yourself.

And, my brother, some find a type of meaning and immortality in influencing future generations—by having children of their own, or by helping, educating, or providing for others' children—or in other ways creating something or giving of themselves for the benefit of their community or of humanity—the family of earth that will endure beyond one's individual demise.

Still, for some this is not enough—for they protest that all life is transitory; that every individual life they birth or buttress will disintegrate to dust; and that all of life may well be destroyed by cosmic catastrophe—by a crashing meteor, a war of annihilation, or a dying sun—in the near or distant future. And thus they say: Of what benefit is it to build a family or contribute to community or teach the children—are we not all doomed, soon or late? My brother, if such an argument troubles your spirit you can fall back to the humble satisfactions of subjective, even if temporary, meaning. Humility has not been given her due:

---

[1] Miguel de Unamuno, who, in his warm and engaging manner, speaks sympathetically about certain aspects of religion and faith says, in his *Tragic Sense of Life*: "I, I, I, always I!" some reader will exclaim; "And who are you?" I might reply in the words of Obermann, that tremendous man Obermann: "For the universe, nothing—for myself, everything..."

Few speak of her transformative gifts; fewer still reach for her many faces of peace.

And, my brother, it may help to remember that Moses did not teach the Israelites of an afterlife—either an eternal heaven or an eternal hell—nor is there good evidence that, as a people, they believed in any such thing until many hundreds of years later, after being influenced by the beliefs of surrounding cultures. All the rewards and punishments and blessings and curses, all the promises and threats, in the Five Books of Moses speak only of earthly consequences—of peace and plenty and health, for oneself and one's people, or of invasion and scarcity and illness and death.

True: Because we will not live forever, we must make peace with a life of limited duration, and this tragedy calls forth an anguished cry from our very bones. We do not wish to die; we do not wish our loved ones to die; and we desperately rebel against the notion that all we are and all we shall ever be—even all we create—will, before long, meet with utter annihilation. This is the great wound and sadness of the human spirit—that if we live honestly we know of our inevitable demise and apparent futility.

Yet without minimizing that terrible burden, we can use our minds to soften the blow of mortality, to select how we shall think about such matters, still remaining honest, but guiding our thoughts and attitudes so that we are tortured rather less than more by our appointment with death. While we might prefer the option of a life that does not end, we need not adopt the extreme conclusion that a temporary life is devoid of meaning.

My brother, beware the trap of "all or nothing thinking." Merely because you cannot possess all the life you covet, does not mean the life you have been given is worth nothing. If you have but one small house, and long for a thousand mansions, is your one modest dwelling of no value? If you taste but one grape, and desire the entire vineyard, is the one fruit worthless and without sweet savor? If you hold but one woman, and lust after the hundreds of Solomon's harem, is the one companion of no blessing to you? And is this one mortal life, with all its limitations—but with all its magic and wonder, too—truly meaningless?

And is something that lasts long necessarily most meaningful? If a pebble endures one hundred thousand years, is it especially meaningful merely because it exists a long while? More meaningful than a flower that blossoms for but a few days? Or a dance whose magic sways for mere moments? Or the transitory flash of understanding in a child's eyes? Or the urgency of new love's stares and kisses—enchantment and ecstasy most fleeting?

My brother, we are unavoidably fated for the trail's end of doom; but the paths we walk in the interim have their landscapes of beauty, their challenging hills worth climbing, their trail stations worth arriving at, and their traveling companions worth communing with. And if each day of walking the trail is, by itself, meaningless, how would an eternity of walking be anything more than meaninglessness eternal? And what choice do we have? Would we have more meaning lying dead, early, at the side of the trail? It is a time-limited meaning we can attain; yet we can learn to appreciate temporary things, and also to bless the human family in ways that will outlive, at least for a time, our individual selves.

And it may help to consider that even if you lived forever you would have limitations, too. You would not be all-powerful, for example, or all-knowing. Yet you do not speak of this imagined form of eternal life as meaningless—though perhaps if you had it you would. Why, then, should limitations in time preclude you from experiencing at least some meaning?

My brother, it has been said that death, like the sun, cannot be stared at directly.[1] And though the sight of our mortality stings our eyes, and though creating meaning within its terrible glare asks of us profound humility, and demands of us, even as we pursue joy and love and all manner of ambition, that we befriend grief and loss and make peace with our impermanence; still, such maturity can be achieved. No, not all at once; and not without a thousand necessary forgettings of death, and a thousand painful rememberings. But it can be done—and it is the only deeply honest way to live.[2]

Moreover, my brother, at times a man feels lonely, or disheartened, or in pain, or wounded by departing love or dwindling fortune, and suddenly seems to be troubled by matters philosophical—yet in the days of friendship and confidence and pleasure and romance and wealth, the very same conditions of mortality applied, the very same facts pertained on the matter of religion and God, and the man did not then seem to be bothered. As many in the early throes of love speak poetry, but abandon it soon enough, and are not truly poets, so too do many in the throes of despair speak philosophy, seeming to earnestly be weighed down by the great tragedy and mystery of human existence—but it is not philosophy that is the source of their despair. If life would but again approach them with the wink of seduction and the spice of delight, or if they pursued their purposes with creativity's sparkling eye or ambition's jutting jaw, gone would be their despair, and with it their morbid philosophizing.[3]

---

[1] Some will recognize this as a variation on an aphorism by La Rochefoucauld.

[2] For a book some find helpful on this great existential challenge, see Irving Yalom's *Staring at the Sun: Overcoming the Terror of Death*. For most, though, no one book, no one approach, will definitively reconcile them to this primal loss. Instead, along with various other enterprises—more joyful and more mundane—the ongoing wrestling with mortality is one important thread woven into the rich tapestry of mature living.

[3] As a young adolescent I tried, for a while, to play the piano. In the piano bench at my parents' home were some old songbooks, one of which contained among its pages music

Let us not sweep away our existential concerns, my brother, for the wise man sees as much as he can bear to see. Yet let us also not persuade ourselves that upon honestly acknowledging that our supernatural religions cannot be trusted, we must be gripped forever by despair. Vigorous engagement with life, my brother, cures nine-tenths of all existential rumination.

And because we cannot honestly claim to know of an afterlife, it is a betrayal of human dignity, even identity, to belittle mortal existence—the only existence we can honestly know we shall ever have—and insist that it is worthless without something more in a great hereafter. And dishonesty about matters deepest— lying to ourselves about that which we consider most important—is too high a price to pay for extravagant comfort. Let us rather seek contentment in the gentle smile of humility; inspiration in the sparks of beauty and brilliance that light up the night-sky of mortality; and consolation of heart, strength of spirit, and peace of mind in the many gifts of nobility, wisdom, pleasure, achievement and love to which we can aspire. Let the idealist instinct in us create more intense, meaningful, and elevated experiences in the life we know to be real and true and ours, and not devalue ourselves and the universe by scorning these in favor of intemperate speculations and infatuations over what we cannot know to be more than empty fantasy. And if we live this life well, learn to love it for the finite endeavor it seems to be, we shall have respected ourselves and the exis- tence we have been given, even if "in death we wholly perish."[1] And if it should turn out that something greater does, indeed, lie in store for us on the other side, so much the better—and we shall enter with heads held high, honest men.

168. Paradox of finding meaning in refraining from false meaning

But the man persisted, and said: Are you telling me that in order to be honest I must accept a life of pointlessness, of no meaning? I would find such a life very difficult, indeed.

---

and lyrics about a Hassidic rabbi who responds with a song to a disciple's earnest question. The disciple asks, "How can God allow us to suffer so?" The rabbi answers with a melody, "Yanni yanni, yanni yanni, bim bum, bim bum. Yanni yanni, yanni yanni, bim bum, bim bum." The intent of the piece in the songbook, or of the folk tale it put to music, may have been laudatory, or may, conversely, have been to mock Hassidism or religion overall as shallow and offering nothing more substantive than the likes of a simple melody in response to an urgent philosophical concern. But we can choose to see in the piece, or in the Hassidic approach it reflects, an awareness of the point I make in the text—that most of us when we ask philosophical questions out of pain are not truly seeking philosophical answers, but comfort; and in such cases a song is a more effective response, a more relevant antidote to despair, than is a learned discourse.

[1] See the footnote earlier in this section on Victor Hugo's thoughts on an afterlife.

And the sage said: My brother, the loss of supernatural or religious meaning, far from condemning us to a life of degrading futility, allows us to build meaning most dignified. For instead of stifling our most honest questions, instead of rejecting what we know of ourselves and subordinating our deepest identity to others' rumors or intuitions of what God said we should be; instead of constructing and desperately clinging to grandiose or horrific illusions, and making of our very lives a mere exercise in theatre, playing a make-believe role in someone else's debasing drama; instead of these, we can adopt a deep authenticity, a growing awareness of who we are, and what is life, and a dignified insistence on conducting ourselves accordingly, with no pious pretending and no dogmatic denying of what we know, and with no allegiances that prevent us from being truthful on the most important matters. Is this not a life of superior meaning?

169. Pursuing earthly meaning and accepting that people differ in their need for transcendence

And the man responded: Yet what of higher forms of meaning? I feel the need to be inspired in my goals, in my work, in my dealings with others. Without religion, how shall I find such inspiration? Or do you insist that I give up such intensity and urges toward meaning, and see inspiration as illusion—and instead embrace a life of dullness and detachment? I refuse! And I refuse to allow other humans to live mired in meaningless mediocrity!

And the sage said: My son, not all feel the need for transcendent meaning, but your temperament seems to hear such a call. By all means, then, pursue meaning. That is what you must do, for that is who you are. A fish must seek water, and the honeybee the blossom—not because the water or the blossom is metaphysically or eternally meaningful, but because the fish is a fish, and the honeybee a honeybee. Be yourself, then: Seek purpose, significance, and meaning worthy of your energies—but do not make an enemy of honesty. Inspire yourself with the magic of love, with the gifts of teaching, with the grace of beauty, with the warmth of compassion, with the soul-shaping of parenting, or with a thousand forms of creative contribution. You need not limit yourself to what would be, for you, a gray and dreary existence of mere practical reason and passionless routine.

Yours is the spirit of the idealist, the crusader who feels he must lead a life suffused with larger meaning, with inspiring mission, and with emotional intensity and depth. Search out, then, those missions which make your heart beat faster, those goals which make your eyes shine, those people and dreams to which you can become deeply dedicated. Perhaps you can teach others to better understand themselves and each other; perhaps you can help motivate others to choose their best path and to walk it well; perhaps you can work towards peace within households or between nations; perhaps you can write stories or poems or songs that will touch many hearts. My son, the world awaits your gifts, and there are many ways you can engage with meaning and love.

But allow others to seek what they must seek, too. When considering your fellow man, my son, be humble, and do not demand that your instinct toward intense meaning and transcendence, a core need of your temperament, be a shared value of all humans—much less, the deepest value of the entire Universe. Does the dolphin insist we must all frolic in the sea? Does the spider demand that that the universe value above all, the weaving of webs? Does the oak argue that life, for all, must be centered upon acorns, a strong trunk, and a broad canopy of leaves? People are driven by different needs, too—some very unlike those that drive you. While you may be meaning-centered, another temperament feels the urge to act with excitement, to live in the moment, to honor impulse, and to make an impact upon themselves and others; another feels compelled to live with order and practical caution, with responsibility and structure, with respect for authority and rules, and with stability and communal belonging; still another is motivated to gather knowledge, to exercise autonomy and competitiveness, and to interact with the world employing an impersonal, analytic approach. All these are legitimate ways of being human, and many emerge from their mothers' wombs with just such natures and minds, though to you, my brother, a seeker of intense meaning—such inclinations may be foreign.

Therefore I counsel you: Live your deepest self but allow others the same privilege—for their authenticity is to be themselves, not to be you. And even in summoning your most fervent enthusiasms stoop not to imaginary, supernatural beliefs. For yes, meaning can be yours—but meaning of any value must not depart from honesty or it degenerates from the substance-filled valor of the real to illusion's shrinking cowardice. Inhabit the heroism, then, of your own true and glorious moments—for has ever a fantasy breathed, has ever a fable cried, and has ever a myth sung the melody of your own inimitable song?

170. Argument that if religion is wrong and there is no God, life is meaningless anyway, so why would it be important to show people that religion is mistaken?

And a man said: You have thought through these matters, but not far enough. If you are correct that religions are mistaken, and therefore that we know of no God, what are we but the meaningless products of a blind process of cosmic explosions and another blind process of evolution? And what will be our individual end but death and obliteration, and what will be our end as a species but some cataclysm of war or collision with a large object from space—or even if we somehow avoid these, at very long last the likely destruction of all life by the heating, the cooling, or the collapse of our solar system or the entire universe? In the face of such futility, with sure doom awaiting us, what do you have to offer better than religion? Why should people not at least indulge their vain hopes that what religion says is true—that there is a God who revealed Himself and spoke to us and who will shepherd our souls into a great beyond, and who will mete out goodness and mercy to us and our progeny?

And the sage said: My brother, you touch on the great wound of all flesh. We scurry about busily tending to our food and our clothing, and our gardens and our homes; to our communities and our schools and our governance and our wars; to our status and our fortunes and our knowledge and our skills; to our meanderings and our missions and our details and our dreams; to our delight and our despair and our pleasures and our pains; to our mates and our children and our enemies and our friends; to the hundred daily hurdles of our work and our love and our property and our health, and to the thousand daily flights of our restless hearts and minds. But back of all this inner and outer scurrying we know the shocking truth that all passes away, all our achievements and accumulations, all our creations and passionate commitments, all word of our virtuosity and heroism and renown—even all evidence that we ever lived—are but sand castles on the existential beach, destined for either gradual erosion by the tides licking away first their glory, then their shape, and finally their every trace, or the sudden unexpected wave crashing down and obliterating all in an instant. We know that soon or late nothing will be left of anything we have considered so meaningful in the days of our scurrying, of everything for which we have labored and worried, waited and hurried, hated and loved.

And about such an unthinkable fate the mind, generally, does not think. Instead, it gets busy with all the purposes, petty and grand, over which it hopes to have some influence, and in the face of which it does not feel so futile and small.

And some polite and pragmatic souls, having exerted the boldness to look beyond the noise and pageantry of life's tumult and parade, and having gazed upon existential futility longer than most, have concluded that—given the brevity of all our endeavors, and the speed with which their effects are likely to vanish— no ideals are worth striving for, beyond perhaps a reasonable degree of cooperation and comfort, and thus, that whatever illusions, including religion, people cling to in shielding themselves from confronting the horror of mortality, should not be challenged.

My brother, I have heard your thoughts; now, please, consider mine. If we would live as enlightened and accomplished men we must strive for higher values than mere avoidance of pain. And if we would truly inhabit this existence, and find a home in our own flesh and bones, and hear the best thoughts of our minds and feel the noblest movings of our souls, such clarity of being is found not by seeking refuge from reality, but by encountering it deeply. And so it is that life asks of us, along with its many burdens and delights, that we turn to face the challenge of mortality, and not deny our impermanence and approaching demise—that we not be overtaken by death with back turned.

And yes, our minds desperately wish to avoid such humbling, even humiliating truth, but we have no authentic alternative. We must integrate the fact of our fleeting lives and our ultimate ruin—and, having deeply accepted this, then build a life worth living, still.

And we do not, in fact, know that there is no Creator; and we do not, in fact, know that this possible Creator is uninterested in our deeds. And we do not, in fact, know that our scientific frame of reference—the physical laws of nature we can observe and measure—is the only reality acting upon us, nor do we know that the realm of existence we inhabit is the only one. The unexplained, the unobserved, and the unknown, are not necessarily the untrue.

But we *do* know that religion is dishonest when she claims knowledge of a Creator, presumes to teach us what it is He wants us to believe, and insists we follow her guidance on just how it is He wants us to live.

And the ultimate fate of the universe is a matter of speculation, even if informed by science's latest theories. Let us not draw despairing conclusions based on such conjecture. Perhaps the universe, or all human life, will perish at some point, but perhaps it will endure. Yet in any case—for those of our era and age— each of our individual lives will end, and with this we must learn to make peace.

My brother, you and I will die; the question is only how we will live. And we shall not help advance humanity—ourselves, our loved ones, and all the family of earth—in the direction of its best promise, by denying truth on the most important matters, even when such denial is pleasant. And if the day comes that humans will have uncovered the secrets of how to extend an individual's life indefinitely, and Adam's descendants will be free of the curse of death, we shall still have to determine what meaning we will give to life. Eternity can be endless barrenness, too; and mortal living a brief, beautiful blossoming.

In considering our mortality, my brother, let us ask this: Does a life of dignity and principle have value only if living lasts forever? Is a song beautiful only if it never ends? Is a meal delectable only if it sates the appetite for all time? Is a discussion or party or lecture or show only worthwhile if it continues eternally? And is a house habitable and warm only if we can be assured it will remain standing for a million, billion years, and, afterwards, for endless further eons?

Why, to have meaning, must something endure forever? And if something does endure forever, is it necessarily meaningful? If someone were to refuse to invest meaning in the concept or spectacle of an omnipotent, eternal deity, would this deity be inherently meaningful?[1]

To which outside observer must our life be meaningful that we will, ourselves, give it meaning? And who gives meaning to that observer's existence? And is externally provided meaning necessary? If I am hungry, is not bread meaningful to me? If I am lonely, is not the warm hand of friendship meaningful to me? And if I love my fellow man, is not helping him meaningful to me, irrespective of any other mortal or immortal opinion?

My brother, this is the greatest lesson of all: We create our own meaning; we pass judgment on existence, whether to make of it an absurd dream which we wile away in bitterness and distraction, or a deeply significant encounter, to which we bring our best energies and gifts. And though we are flowers who bloom for a day or a season and are no more, we need not say that our beauty is worthless. Indeed, we have the authority and dominion in our own hearts and souls to celebrate such beauty.

Ours is the burden and the freedom, the dignity and the terrible power, of creating our own meaning—of imposing our stamp of interpretation and value on that which we find, and like Adam of old, naming life what we will name it, and finding no help for that task.[2]

---

[1] The question is a good one, though if we place a healthy value on existence, we will not go so far as the French poet Jacques Bigaut, who said, "God is growing bitter; He envies man his mortality." Nor, of course, would we hasten to bring upon ourselves with our own hand our inevitable, and not necessarily enviable, end—as the author of that passage did, at the age of 30.

[2] The allusion here is to Genesis 2:19-20, which states: "And out of the ground the Lord God formed every beast of the field, and every fowl of the air; and brought them unto Adam to see what he would call them: and whatsoever Adam called every living creature, that was the name thereof. And Adam gave names to all cattle, and to the fowl of the air, and to every beast of the field; but for Adam there was not found an help meet for him."

The straightforward intent of this passage, as the surrounding verses make clear, is that Adam was naming animal species, and the help meet he did not yet have was woman. But to indulge in some humanistic Bible homiletics, we might see the story as saying that Adam, symbolizing the human species, found himself surrounded by life, the various manifestations of which had no pre-determined value, and whose meaning, even identity, depended on his own perception and pronouncement. In other words, man must make out of life what he will—and on this he has no outside source to consult. Indeed, in the biblical story no help can be expected from God—for it is God who brings the collection of life to Adam in the first place to see what names he would call them.

And a name, in biblical culture among others, was far more than a label; it was the meaning one attributed to something—its essence. Thus in various traditional cultures, a name is seen as sacred, as containing valuable information, and is to be withheld from those who may do one harm. Adam naming life, then, is Adam deciding what meaning to give to life.

And the powerful stories of Genesis can, indeed, be read on many levels—and it isn't unreasonable to speculate that many of these levels may have been crafted, with varying degrees of conscious intent—along with the unconscious speaking through symbol—by many generations of the devout, into what we now can legitimately read as multi-faceted gems. Who can say but that some of those who contributed to the shaping of this story, and the overall biblical saga, believed that deep truths must not be told directly to the masses, but must also be entrusted to them, hidden within a tradition they would transmit through the ages, and which only a select few would ever mine for its real treasures.

Such an approach would be consistent with the riddle form and the model of secret wisdom which we find in various ancient cultures, and in the Bible, too. Schopenhauer, in his *Religion: A Dialogue*, has Demopheles, the defender of religion, say: "All religions have their mysteries...a dogma which is plainly absurd, but which, nevertheless, conceals in itself a lofty truth, and one which by itself would be completely incomprehensible to the ordinary understanding of the raw multitude. The multitude accepts it in this disguise...and in this way it participates in the kernel of the matter...Naked truth is out of place before the eyes of the profane vulgar; it can only make its appearance thickly veiled. Hence, it is unreasonable to require of a religion that it shall be true in the proper sense of the word..." Later, Demopheles says: "If you want to form an opinion on religion, you should always bear in mind the character of the great multitude for which it is destined, and form a picture to yourself of its complete inferiority, moral and intellectual. It is incredible how far this inferiority goes, and how perseveringly a spark of truth will glimmer on even under the crudest covering of monstrous fable or grotesque ceremony, clinging indestructibly, like the odor of musk, to everything that has once come into contact with it. In illustration of this, consider the profound wisdom of the Upanishads, and then look at the mad idolatry in the India of to-day, with its pilgrimages, processions and festivities, or at the insane and ridiculous goings-on of the Saniassi. Still one can't deny that in all this insanity and nonsense there lies some obscure purpose which accords with, or is a reflection of the profound wisdom I mentioned. But for the brute multitude, it had to be dressed up in this form."

I quote Schopenhauer's character on the Upanishads to illustrate that although one sees glimmers of profound wisdom coming through certain passages in the Bible, one can find similar glimmerings in the ancient writings of other traditions, too. And this wisdom may, indeed, have been deliberately placed there—and may not be a mere figment of our overactive, over-clever imaginations projecting desired interpretations onto favored texts—but these glimmerings are no more evidence of the supernatural than are the profound creations of poets and philosophers and sages of more recent days. Indeed, if we—quite natural beings—can conceive of profound interpretations of a myth, is it not great hubris to insist that the writers of the myth, a myth which may have been refined over centuries, were, without supernatural aid, incapable of intending, too, just such interpretations?

Still, to be clear, I do not insist that the homily I have given was necessarily the intent or understanding—conscious or otherwise—of any possible contributors to the biblical story of Adam. We simply do not know what we do not know.

And this self-determined meaning is something we can indeed craft—with humility and courage and love—even from the stuff of temporary existence. And when we step into our uniquely human role, of deciding upon the meaning we will ascribe to life, I say to you, my brother, that if we are to maintain our dignity we cannot dispense with building our valuations upon solid reality, cannot avoid being honest with ourselves about what is and what is not, and cannot prevaricate with ourselves and others about what we can reasonably believe and what we cannot.

And in contemplating mortality, we must endure disappointment and sadness and grieving, all the cousins of despair—and shake off the numbness of denial and avoidance and rationalization, all the cousins of the lie. How intense these are and how long they last are a measure of the distance our spirits must travel to catch up to truth, and how willing we are to embark upon, and persist in, such a journey. And even once we accept the terrible truth of our mortality, our spirits are so constituted that every moment they take a few steps away from it, and if we do not force ourselves to run back consistently, we shall find that before long the feet of our spirits will have taken us so far, that the trip back is daunting and exhausting.

And if we have been falsely sheltered from this painful reckoning with mortality by the vain promises of religion, if our parents taught us religion's errors as their parents taught them, who were, in turn, taught these things by their parents, in a chain stretching back into the early mists of history—everyone a victimizer and a victim—it will indeed be painful to reorient ourselves to truth as it really is. Yet it can be done.

And again my brother, life without religion need not be meaningless—to the contrary, it is all the meaning we can ever count on having. Yes, one can choose to see only meaninglessness, but this would be degrading life from what it could be. And I ask you to consider that loving ourselves requires that we raise our lives toward the heights of which we are capable, and loving others requires that we wish this for them too, and work to make this possible. And spilling out into the gutter of self-deception our lifeblood, the deepest potential for honest meaning in our own lives, is committing suicide of the spirit—and doing so to another is committing murder of the spirit.

My brother, even aside from religion—in life development overall—different stages bring different challenges and different rewards. The child is not the adolescent, nor is the adolescent the adult. The child relies upon his parents for survival and direction: It is they who tell him how to live, it is they who give him sustenance so that he *can* live. Later, as an adolescent, he pushes away from his parents, he rejects their authority, and recoils from memories of his dependency upon them. He may be angry at them, he may labor to prove how different he is from them, yet still he reacts to them—and his very rebellion is one more form of dependence, a dependence of the spirit. As the years pass, however, if he grows into a healthy adult, he no longer rages at his parents, no longer compulsively separates from them, and no longer obsesses about how they cannot provide him with perfect shelter, guidance, and love. Instead, he begins to live his authentic life, to work toward goals that are truly his own, and into a peace that neither dependency nor rebellion knows.

And just so does the spirit develop. The spiritual child depends upon religion or notions of God, or upon family or society for orientation, for a sense of meaning, for guidance on what to value in life—and, indeed, for why to value life. Most remain spiritual children. But adolescence comes for some, and they rebel against religion and God, or against family or society. They realize with anger, fear, or bitter grief that religion's teachings are unreliable, that her God cannot save them, and that their tribe and kin hold values that are often arbitrary or worse. And many who get this far go no further; indeed, they do not know there is further to go. And so they remain tormented, at best stoic, or look back with longing at the days of their dependence and ignorance, wishing they could again believe, for now they dine daily on the hard bread of disillusion and on the bitter waters of fermenting despair.

My brother, your question asks: If shining the light of truth upon religion, if forcing such maturity will bring on this terrible state, why not allow people to remain with the dependency of childhood? Why open their eyes to the terrible landscape of unembellished truth? The answer, my brother, is that one need not remain in adolescence: One can grow into the relative peace and confidence of spiritual adulthood, wherein one leaves behind grievances over absent gods and resentments over stolen youth, and demands for eternal life and protection, and anger at imperfect justice and love—and one begins to inhabit a landscape wherein one crafts one's own life instead of continuing to rebel against the life one was taught in the days of innocent but ignorant belief. Such a path of spiritual adulthood asks of us a great deal, my brother, but it gives us a great deal, too—indeed, it gives us our very selves.

So each of us must fashion our own meaning—paint the portrait of our own soul, and write the story of our own spirit, living each day ever more into the hero's role. And as no one ever awakened from a dream and long felt proud of his imaginary exploits achieved in the realm of sleep, so too we cannot fashion dignified and durable meaning out of telling ourselves and our children sacred lies, and out of all the sacrifices and devotions built thereon.

Instead, my brother I implore you to open your eyes, and let the eyes of your children fly open, too, and as you gaze upon them, and they upon you, for the first time you will see each other, with love, as you really are.

XI. TO PREVENT MISUNDERSTANDING: WHAT THE SAGE IS *NOT* SAYING

171. Misunderstandings and clarifications

And some of the people began speaking against the sage, with all manner of objections. One said: The sage accuses all religion of being hateful and deliberately destructive!

Another said: The sage blames religion for all carnage and bloodshed, and believes religion has done no good. And he believes atheism is the answer, and he ignores all the killing for which atheists are responsible.

And a scholar said: The sage sees all religious people as simpletons and fools.

And a theologian said: The sage claims that atheism is more honest than religion, and he ignores dogmatic atheism's undue certainty about matters of God.

And a priest said: The sage is hypocritical because he tells us not to trust religious leaders, but he wants us to trust him!

And a judge said: The sage advises us to give up all standards of right and wrong. He wants to turn our society into chaos!

And a community elder said: The sage believes that all traditional and conservative values are wrong, and all liberal, permissive values are right.

And a religious teacher said: The sage thinks he knows everything, and that we know nothing!

And a moderate religionist said: The sage attacks all religion as though it believes the Bible has to be taken literally, and as though all people of faith insist that every person of another faith is condemned!

And another said: Why do we even stand here and listen to him, when he calls all our leaders liars?

These things and more some of the people protested against the sage, and looked at him with distrust and disdain.

And the sage called out above the clamor, saying: Brothers and sisters, brothers and sisters, I have heard your grievances; lend me your ears as I address your concerns. One who speaks of the new and the strange will meet with skepticism, and one who speaks poorly of the dear and the familiar will stir up the wrath even of the kind. So I have brought upon myself your bitter words and hard eyes.[1] Yet I ask you, husbands and wives, neighbors and friends: Do not

---

[1] Machiavelli, in Chapter VI of *The Prince*, states: "It ought to be remembered that there is nothing more difficult to take in hand, more perilous to conduct, or more uncertain in its success, then to take the lead in the introduction of a new order of things. Because the

suspicion and discontent often spring up within us not from what others do or say, but from the predispositions of our own minds and the shame and apprehension in our own hearts—which cause us to see in their deeds evil wishes, and hear in their words meanings they did not intend to convey?

Allow me, then, brothers and sisters, to make clear what I say and what I do not say. Then I shall have done my part in offering my words well—and you shall do yours in weighing them well.

I do not say that all religion is hateful and intentionally destructive; rather I say that most has been well intended, but that religion has, nevertheless, too often spilled innocent blood, and her capacity to do so in the future remains a grave threat—until such time as our species exerts the courage and humility to admit that we do not know the will of any possible God. And I also say that the greatest wounds religion inflicts upon society, albeit for the most part without ill intent, are neither the blood and bones of holy wars nor the fires and chains of sacred persecutions, but instead the cowed, inauthentic hearts and the closed and cloistered minds, in every complacent village on every peaceful day.

I do not say that all evil and bloodshed come from religion, or that religion has done no good; rather I say that evil comes from many sources, only one of which is religion; and that religion has brought many and varied gifts to the family of earth, too—but at a terrible cost. For her chief demands are neither money nor love, but that we blind our own eyes and send our best selves into existential exile; that we cleave our tongue to our palate, and silence our truest song; that we forget our right hand and forego careful thinking, our greatest strength. In sum, that we betray our highest birthright, reason, and the touchstone of our very authenticity—deep honesty.

I do not say that religious people are simpletons and fools; rather I say that intelligence, like all devices and capabilities, can be brought to bear in support of any allegiance, and used to fashion arguments in the service of any cause. Every religion has its scholars and geniuses, along with its lesser minds. And if I believe religionists mistaken, I do not believe them so because they are limited by poor thinking skills. Truth, integrity, and authenticity are matters not of intelligence, but of painful honesty. A fast dog does not catch its tail any better than a slow dog, for the tail runs as swiftly as the legs; so, too, an intelligent man does not see

---

innovator has for enemies all those who have done well under the old conditions, and lukewarm defenders in those who may do well under the new. This coolness arises partly from fear of the opponents, who have the laws on their side, and partly from the incredulity of men, who do not readily believe in new things until they have had a long experience of them."

his self-deceptions better than others see theirs. A deeply honest and courageous man does—whether brilliant or simple.

I do not say that all atheism is benign or incapable of evil; rather I well know that some with atheistic worldviews have been destructive, even murderous. I do not endorse the atheism that insists it knows there is no God, but rather I say that a worldview insisting it knows there is no God is mistaken or dishonest, as is religion—a collection of worldviews that insists it knows not only that God exists, but also what behaviors and beliefs He demands of humans.

I do not consider all religious leaders liars; rather I say that most religious leaders *and* followers, though I believe them in error, truly see themselves as doing God's will. Nevertheless, all of us harbor untruths—be they ever so deeply buried in the inaccessible regions of the mind—untruths we dare not challenge, and therefore do not see. And there is a great deal of difference between a liar— one who consistently and intentionally misleads—and one who is unable or unwilling to see clearly on select issues and is merely, even if deeply, mistaken. Indeed, I cringe at the humiliating spectacle of so many sincerely sacrificing so much for, and surrendering so completely to, creeds so dubious and unfounded.

I do not say that we should forego all standards of right and wrong; rather I say that all societies, families, and individuals need values and codes of behavior—or chaos replaces civilization. Yet I would have us base our standards of right and wrong upon what is shown to be good for man—to strike a balance between the needs of individual and society—and no longer deceive ourselves that we know how any God there may be wishes us to live.

I do not say that all traditional, conservative, or restrictive values are wrong, or that all permissive, liberal, or self-indulgent values are right; rather I say that Truth does not limit herself to one political ideology or social or economic worldview, and does not sit on any one side of a legislative aisle. Truth neither always agrees with extravagant compassion and the ideas of the empathic and modern, nor always with strict justice and the traditions of old—for each has much to learn from the other. And even if we think belief in God mistaken, some of the social norms religions have taught in the name of God we may yet see as best for man. Various active virtues and self-restraints have terrestrial benefits, for both man and mankind—and various traditional principles and standards, though taught by religion as the will of God, constitute cumulative lessons gleaned from the experience of many generations of wise humans. And some of the values and policies secularists have taught in the name of freedom and modernity, we may yet come to see—in light of further experience and wisdom—as the destructive counsel of naiveté: the mistaken idealism of unbalanced compassion and the untutored confidence of untested theory.

On each matter of importance, then, let all present their best arguments, and may we as societies weigh with just scales—and adapt our positions to the growing evidence—that we may guide ourselves and others well: neither from loyalty to ideology nor allegiance to tribe; neither from the will to power nor the seductions of bliss; neither leaning upon the walking stick of the old nor waving the rebel banners of the young; neither swinging the hammer of anger nor preening "the feather of pride"—rather deliberating in the warmth of compassion and advancing by the light of honest reason.

I do not say that I know everything, or that you know nothing; rather I say that in every arena of life there are things I do not know, and many of these things some of you *do* know. But I say, too, that on matters of religion and philosophy—for which I have given many of my days and nights, and much of my heritage and youth, too—on these matters I have seen more than most. Yet I do not insist that my conclusions are superior to yours. I simply would have you consider my thoughts and then ask yourself whether they may not be of some value in your quest for truth, too.

I do not say that all religion is fundamentalist or extreme, that all religionists take their scriptures literally, or that all who attend a church, a synagogue, or a mosque believe that anyone of another faith is inferior or condemned; rather I say that every religion has amongst its believers many women of kindness and many men of peace, who seek first the smiles of mortals, and only later the pleasures of the gods; many who would teach their own scriptures a thousand gentle new meanings rather than visit upon their neighbors one unfriendly word; many who see welcome diversity in the family of earth, and delightful variety in the multiplicity of its faiths. But I also say that when kind and tolerant believers continue to reverence a set of scriptures and commentaries whose plain words command genocide and religious intolerance, whose straightforward teachings condone slavery and female subjugation and encourage the killing or mistreatment of non-believers, or whose unambiguous passages hold infants guilty for the deeds of their distant forebears and whose repeated threats menace the dead with eternal torture in fire—and with all this, whose verses insist, too, with desperate irrationality, that the God in whose name these things are being taught is full of mercy and grace—I do say that kind and tolerant believers reverencing such a collection of scriptures, unwittingly desecrate the memory of the legions of its victims of the past, and provide unintended shelter and legitimacy for the many, many fundamentalists who do, indeed, even today see such scriptures as literal, and their own faith as the only true word of a transcendent God.

And though not wishing to cause harm, such moderate believers also cultivate the ground for future religious atrocities by continuing to tend the same treacherous garden that has repeatedly wrought within the family of earth so much suffering and hate, and they continue to protect the same ancestral plant swelled with poisonous seeds—the many passages still held as sacred, where injustice and persecution are unashamedly taught in the name of a perfect, compassionate, and all-powerful God.

But even if religious moderates are deaf to yesterday's screams, blind to tomorrow's horrid visions, and insensate to the jostlings of today's unpredictable mobs, even if they heed not the voice of blood, perhaps they might heed the voice of honor, which calls out to them to no longer maim their own minds and hearts, to no longer collaborate in the misleading of their neighbors and friends, to no longer disfigure the reason and conscience of their sweet, innocent children, by retreating behind vague and ever-changing propositions, twisting stories and words to mean what they never have meant, and reinterpreting eternal fire so that it does not denote what it plainly always has, and by refusing to condemn and excise those passages of their holy books that are unjust and cruel—but most important, by the unwillingness to be honest about what they know and do not know on the most foundational matters and, in rhapsodizing on faith, by blurring the line between honest knowing and irresponsible conjecture.

And, brothers and sisters, I do not ask you to trust me while advising you to distrust leaders of religion; rather I say that on matters of deepest meaning and highest value no man should entrust his destiny and authenticity to another. I would not have you place your faith in me any more than I would have you place your faith in tradition's clergy. Rather I hope that you might shoulder the burden and privilege of your own freedom, and while welcoming, indeed pursuing, the thoughts of others, that you become informed and then decide for yourself on ultimate issues. And as for my teachings, would that you bring me your severest challenges—and I shall welcome them with a smile, engage with them in sincerity, and return them to you with care; and I would have you pass judgment on this commerce, whether it has been of profit to your soul. And my blessing to each of you, brothers and sisters: May you—not I, not your leaders, not even your ancestors—direct your path in your walk on earth, and inscribe your story in the sands of time.

XII. Conclusions

172. Request for a "bottom line" so confident action can be taken

And a military commander stepped forward and said: I have listened to the many things you say. I have even heard you now tell us what you do *not* say. But what is your conclusion on the whole matter? After all your questions and arguments, what have you decided? Now that our old religions have been shown to be lacking, tell us: What should we believe, and how should we live? We must know the bottom line, so that we can plan and act with confidence!

And the sage replied: My brother, I will speak to you of my conclusions, but consider this: There are arenas in which confident action is critical, and deep reflection fatal. In the killing chaos of battle, for instance, slow deliberation can prove catastrophic. In seeking philosophical truth, however, the opposite applies: Quick, confident decisions are often mistaken; and deep, wide-ranging reflections nearly always fruitful. I readily concede that my orientation to careful contemplation does not lend itself to decisive military command. Yet just as military reality does not conform itself to my temperament and preferences, so too my martial brother, philosophical and existential truth does not change to accommodate those more comfortable with immediate, easily grasped conclusions. Even in the military realm, tactics are not strategies, and maneuvers effective on land may be ineffective at sea; and I remind you that decisiveness, which often works well in the arena of the practical, may not work well in the arena of ultimate truth—as frustrating as this may be to some.

And I know that nature does not allow much time for the pursuit of truth before we are called upon to be teachers of truth—in word or deed. It is not the aged, the wise and tempered by many decades of experience and learning and reflection, that bring forth the next generation, but the young, with impatient dreams and urgent flesh, those barely out of childhood themselves, to whom, for comfort and guidance, the toddling children look, as unto gods. Indeed, procreation aside, for each of us life speeds by, and few of us find sufficient time and focus to carefully investigate and teach even ourselves what to believe on matters of God, religion, and life's meaning.

Yet as much as a father and mother feel the heavy responsibility of leadership, and as much as even the childless scramble to stay ahead of time's ever-nearing footfalls, we must never let our yearning for quick decisions on existential matters fool us into prematurely believing we have arrived at conclusions that are accurate and noble.

The appetite for decision and clear direction is, like all natural cravings, healthy and constructive only in moderation. Beyond the point of moderation, though our appetites urge us on, it is in our best interests to refrain. The appetite for food can be overindulged to the point of obesity and illness; the appetite for achievement and status overindulged to the point of alienating family and friends; the appetite for harmony overindulged to the point of submissiveness and self-negation—and the appetite for certainty and decision overindulged to the point of premature conclusion, even self-deception, on life's most important matters.

My brother, as you would not seek a new bride on the day you lower your wife into her grave, so, too, be not overly eager to find new beliefs so soon upon the death of the old. For grief must sear itself into your heart, to do its work well. And if you demand a new love so soon, how will you know if your delight is truly for her charms, and your dislike truly for her flaws—or if delight and dislike are but different faces of your grieving lonesomeness, urging you on to desperate belonging or to stubborn comparisons?

Moreover, let us not confuse hearing a conclusion with having engaged in the process of thinking and understanding that leads to that conclusion. A destination offers neither the sights nor the lessons of the journey; and a mountaintop offers neither the perspectives nor the character of the climb. I would not have you trust my testimony; I would have you see for yourself what I have seen.

So I ask you all, brothers and sisters, to reflect on our discourses today, not with credulity seeking confidence nor with impatience seeking direction—but with honesty seeking truth. In that spirit I offer closing thoughts, not as a substitute for deeper study, not either as a final set of ironclad prescriptions, but rather as a reminder, and as a call to further learning and thought. And I speak to you neither as a prophet to awestruck masses, nor as a commander to dutiful legions, but as a fellow seeker to independent-minded men and women. Yes, I am honored that you entertain my arguments—but my conclusions, to be of authentic value to you, must satisfy your own questions, and pass the test of your own best efforts at reason.

And the sage addressed the gathered people in a loud voice, saying: Brothers and sisters, these things I would have you remember most:

I would have you remember that on the path of seeking, honesty is paramount and knowledge of reality irreplaceable; and that building a sense of deep meaning and purpose upon anything else—upon what we wish were true, upon what merely *may* be true, upon the dogmas of ancient faith and rumors of antique tradition, or upon the systems of charismatic teachers wielding modern words and dazzling concepts for a new age—is tragic and inauthentic.

I would have you remember that self-deception is everywhere; it belongs to our instinctive nature. The deeper region of the mind withholds from us truths it fears we will be unable to bear, and urges us to accept or maintain untruths that bring us comfort—or more bearable forms of discomfort.

I would have you remember that the confident teachings of religion on supernatural matters are but tales, conjectures, and suppositions—often contradicting the tales, conjectures, and suppositions of other religions—on matters about which humans cannot honestly and responsibly claim sure knowledge.

I would have you remember that important questions remain unanswered—perhaps unanswerable. We do not know if there was a Creator, or, if there was, whether He still exists, and if He does, whether such a Creator observes humans and wishes us to live by a particular code of conduct. And if He does wish us to live in a particular way, we do not know if ever He communicated His will to humans through a Bible or any other means—or if instead He wishes us to arrive at wisdom ourselves. Nor do we know whether any part of our awareness lives on in another realm following death. Thus, as painful as many find this, we cannot know with reliable confidence from where we come, to where we go, or whether any supernatural being takes heed of our lives, or asks anything of us while we walk the earth.

Yet I would have you remember that we can learn to live well, even in the shadows of such unquiet questions.

I would have you remember that honest ignorance is far superior to feigned expertise, for we and our loved ones, and the entire human family, are worthy of not being lied to, and not lying, on life's most important matters.

I would have you remember that religious faith is not anything so noble as trusting God. Rather, it is trusting one of the many contradictory *human* traditions, speculations, and intuitions *about* God—indeed, about a *rumored* God—and that if there is a God, He may be deeply disappointed, even offended, by those who shun distressing honesty and instead invoke faith, and perpetuate about Him irresponsible, even if popular and familiar, rumors. I would have you remember that clinging to religious faith, far from constituting commendable loyalty to God, is in fact accepting and passing along horrendous gossip concerning God—based upon the flimsiest of evidence, the likes of which we would never wish our friends or loved ones, even strangers, to rely upon in believing tales about us. And remember, accepting on faith the biblical account of God is choosing to accept as true that—among other sordid deeds—He repeatedly commanded genocide; He condoned slavery; He insisted that those who commit minor offenses such as working on the Sabbath be punished with death—and, according to the plain meaning and traditional understanding of the New Testament, that He tortures in fire for all eternity those who sin, for example, by neglecting to provide for the poor.[1] Believing in the plain meaning of all the New Testament also requires one to accept as true that salvation is available only to those who squelch reasonable skepticism and accept as unquestioned fact pagan-reminiscent tales of God impregnating a woman, and of the resulting son supernaturally rising from the dead and through his blood redeeming believers, all of whom are essentially sinful and doomed without such blood. Traditional Christian faith also demands that one reject the protest of reason and the cry of compassion, and see this set of beliefs as embodying a God of deepest love.

I would have you remember that rejecting basic standards for reliable evidence and stifling one's instinct for kindness and justice, by choosing to believe in the Bible, thus maintaining and propagating the notion of what by today's standards is a primitive, unjust, even cruel God, constitutes neither fidelity nor devotion to the Divine—but, instead, a profound betrayal of any good God there may be. And see this tragic irony: the most sincere, the most devoted among the faithful, will have to sacrifice and suffer most to loosen the many ties that bind them to these hoary beliefs. For only the most devout have given themselves over completely, heart, spirit, and soul, to religious ideals and commitments.

I would have you remember that gambling on religion is no safe bet. For perhaps a just and truth-loving God approves of the authentic, who admit what they do not know, and disapproves of wagering impostors, who debase themselves and degrade life's ultimate issues by treating them as a game of fortune—who lie to themselves, their children and their community, about what knowledge they possess on God and His will. If one believes in eternal rewards, perhaps God repays honesty more than pretense; and if one believes in a vengeful Almighty who condemns humans to everlasting hell, perhaps the most horrific sufferings and hottest-blazing fire pits await those over-clever, gambling souls who abuse His signal gift to our species—the uniquely human powers of refined reason—who emulate mere amusements of chance, and profess as truth what they truly do not know.

I would have you remember that great pain occasions the fall from religion—not the life without religion; that the losing of faith wounds, not the absence of faith. For the greatest part of the pain of truth is the pain of loss, not the pain of lack; and the pain of loss fades. After initial anguish and necessary grieving, life can again be joyous—indeed, more satisfying and real than ever were the days of self-negation in obedience to religion. And the next generation will be spared the mourning over ill-begotten gods—for if their parents pay the noble price of honest sacrifice, of foregoing time-honored idols and false, though

---

[1] See Matthew 25:41-46.

familiar ideologies, the tender hearts of their children will never have cherished—and will never suffer the agony of losing—such sacred illusions.

I would have you remember that the pain of truth is bearable, its sting but temporary. The anguish of truth is the sorrow of accommodating ourselves to reality, of giving up our complacent errors and bringing down upon ourselves the unpredictable terrors of honest thought. When we learn to let go of the illusions of knowledge about supernatural realms or beings, the question becomes not what to make of a possible God, but what to make of our actual selves. And though some will be crushed by the essential tragedy or at least impenetrable mystery of human life, and others by the cruelties of man and the indifferent blows of fate—those of us who yet stand, or can rouse ourselves to stand again, what else shall we do but take heart, and attempt to fashion from our days and our nights something kind or strong, delightful or joyous, beautiful or wise? And this we can do; for truth takes from us nothing we need—only unhealthy indulgences upon which we have come to depend. Truth is costly, yes—but worth its price. For though truth will half kill you, it will then, if you allow it, raise you up to a clarity, a nobility, an existential poise, that no dishonest dogma or pleasant fantasy can rival.

I would have you remember that one mortal life is all we can know is ours, but that if we live well, we can make it enough—and if we do not live well, even eternal life would be no great boon. And yes, the brevity of our days is tragic; but we can bear this heartbreak with an unashamed gaze, having turned away—with honor untainted—from the demeaning immoderation of groundless, fervent convictions on matters most vital.

I would have you remember that meaning is not dependent upon imagined supernatural realms, that deep engagement with life can be found without religion, by absorbing oneself in all manner of earthbound pursuits: in joy and nobility and sacrifice and love and parenting and friendship and beauty and wisdom and achievement and contribution and creative expression—even, ironically, by refusing to submit to seductions of irresponsible belief, and guarding with mature determination and open-eyed compassion one's integrity and intellectual honesty; and, overall, in choosing to value earthly existence even in all its humbling mortality and limitation.

I would have you remember that within the bounds of authenticity, and with no conclusions about the supernatural, we can create transcendence. We can elevate life beyond the pragmatic, to the inspired. We can transform walking into dance; sound into music; words into poetry; color into art; meals into feasts; vegetation into gardens; and all manner of mundane acts into resplendent—yet honest and honorable—ritual and celebration. And we can cultivate a spirit of enchantment, and gaze upon all the world with eyes of beauty and love.

I would have you remember that good behavior need not be dependent upon traditional religion. We groom and wear presentable clothing not to satisfy religious obligation; rather, we do these primarily to be presentable to humans—to elicit admiration, or to avoid feelings of shame. We arrive at our places of work and meeting not to please a deity, but to interact well with men. And we refrain from attacking the formidable not because of any biblical prohibition, but because we do not wish to suffer the pain of retribution. If most fear others' disapproval at wrinkled clothing or uncombed hair, and fulfill their social obligations and carefully avoid antagonizing the powerful, most will also, even without religion, avoid harming their fellow man—for fear of society's disapproval, and of the mighty, untiring hand of avenging law. Moreover, aside from shame and fear, another force would keep us in line: Most of us feel within our bones the urge for cooperation with our fellows. And even if some would not be restrained by such social inclinations, the majority would. And I ask you: Have societies *with* religion, and with teachings of supernatural punishment and reward, ever achieved anything more than merely a well-behaved majority?

I would have you remember that reason by itself is no panacea: Courage and effort, compassion and justice, and other noble constituents of good character, too, and the wisdom of balancing well between various forms of knowledge and values and virtues, are necessary for the family of earth to thrive in peace, and partake of honest fulfillment and meaning.

I would have you remember that none can do your most important thinking for you; none can arrive at truth in your place. Others can offer their best thoughts and arguments—but you must decide for yourself what you will accept as truth, and why.

I would have you remember the wisdom of being gentle and patient in pursuit of truth, and in teaching deep honesty to ourselves and others; for cherished beliefs on matters of the spirit have deep roots, cling to the earth of our souls with great tenacity, and when torn from their native soil cry a terrible cry.

Yet I would have you remember that it is not necessarily noble to remain religious for the sake of others. Not for parents, not for family, not for children, not for community, not even for ancestors. For must it be seen as best to allow others' degrading, even if well-intended, dependence on illusion tempt you into living a lie, into being inauthentic on life's most important matters and teaching others to do the same?

I would have you remember that the quest for truth is never fulfilled by one final vision, but is rather an ongoing and ever-refining way of seeing. The quest never ends just as the eye continues to see and does not go blind—and fix forever in its view one ultimate picture—even upon observing a breathtaking sight. Yes, we must make decisions so that we can live each day, but our minds should always remain open to learning on life's most important matters.

I would have you remember that the human tendency toward superstition and false religious beliefs cannot be uprooted once for all time; rather, like the innumerable weeds that spring up on cultivated land, seductive falsehood will sprout again and again, and we—as individuals and societies—must be prepared for continuous vigilance against those ideas that threaten humanity's garden.

I would have you remember that we can build and maintain communities upon foundations other than institutions propagating unwarranted claims about God. Let us raise our voices together in songs celebrating known blessings, not in hymns naming and worshiping unknown gods; let us deliver discourses and orations on living the good life now, not sermons and castigations on avoiding hellfire in the hereafter; let us perform acts of kindness and justice out of generosity and the kinship of man—not out of obligation, and the terror of gods.

I would have you remember that ingenuity and wisdom and love lead us into the palace of possibility, out of which we emerge armed with powers and adorned with graces—gifts we can share with each other and posterity, making of life an ever more grand endeavor. But as for supernatural knowledge—let us gaze about us with clear sight and conscience, avoiding our fathers' errors on sacred affairs, and resisting religion's pretensions and all her varied seductions.

I would have you remember that authority is not truth; Bible and belief are not truth; custom, cleverness, confidence, conviction, and complexity are not truth; dogma and devotion are not truth; emotion and eloquence are not truth; fervor and fellowship are not truth; generosity and gentleness are not truth; hope and happiness are not truth; intelligence, inspiration, and intensity are not truth; justice and justifying are not truth; kindness is not truth; love, loyalty, and learnedness are not truth; mystery, martyrdom, and mother's lullabies are not truth; passion, power, piety, popularity, performance, and perseverance are not truth; reverence and ritual are not truth; sacrifice, suffering, and success are not truth; tradition and transcendence are not truth; unity is not truth; virtue and virtuosity are not truth; will and wonder are not truth; excitement and excellence are not truth; yearning is not truth; zealotry is not truth. Truth, as mortals can responsibly make it out, is that which is accurate, consistent with reality, as best it can be determined through reason and experience; and living by truth means not claiming as true anything that falls short of such a standard.

Finally, my brothers and sisters, I would have you remember that humans have spent far too long pretending to prophesy in the name of God, and that it is long since time we learned to prophesy with honesty and hope—to speak a vision and labor to bring it to pass—in our own humble name.

XIII. PROPHECIES AND FAREWELL

173. Prophecies of man, and the sage's farewell

Then the sage looked off into the distance and said: *The day is coming, saith the spirit of man, that no longer will be heard, "On this rock of faith I build my church," or "On this mount of divine revelation I raise up my temple," or "On this stone of obedient piety I construct my mosque." Rather will all the peoples of the earth lift up their voices and together declare: "For this bedrock of reality we forego our churches; for this mountain of truth we transcend our temples; and for this massive stone of honesty we abandon our mosques." And the dark bandages of superstition shall have fallen away from the eyes of humanity as the black cloak of sleep falls away from the eyes of the awakened. And all nations shall walk together by the warm lights of benevolent reason, beside the living stream of truth's blessed waters, even to the Great House of all peoples. And there they shall sit at the grand table of unity; they shall break the bread of peace and pour the oil of harmony; they shall teach one another cunning and wisdom, and learn to sing each other's songs. And then they shall stand and embrace as brothers, and swear their allegiance to man; to share their plows in hunger and take up their swords at hate;[1] and all eyes shall see and all hearts shall know that only that which inflicts upon ourselves or our fellows earthly harm can we honestly call evil, and the only good of which we can be certain is happiness and wisdom on this humble earth.*

And the sage fell silent, and the people said: Yes, even if you have no prophecies from God, speak to us more of the prophecies of man.

And the sage spoke again and said:

Religion is the largest of the trees of superstition growing up against the house of man, its roots slowly eating into the foundation, its branches and twigs slapping and clawing against the walls with every breeze, the spread of its leaves blocking out the heavens. Because your fathers allowed this tree to grow, and did not pluck it when it was but a seedling or a sapling and easier to remove, now you stare up at a massive trunk and a towering canopy, and you cower in an unsound house, and you look down at the humble ax in your hand, and you shudder.

---

[1] It is wiser to turn swords to noble use than to recast them into ploughshares, for there will always be some aggressive leader at the vanguard of a troop or nation only too eager to take terrible advantage of others' idealistic defenselessness. Certain aspects of human nature are unlikely to change. Group aggression, like the often associated phenomenon of hero worship, is, in one form or another, here to stay. And applicable to the latter are the words of Stanislaw Lec: "When smashing monuments, save the pedestals—they always come in handy."

But I say unto you: Take courage, and be not despaired; hack away, though your blows merely glance off the tree as a hammer off a mountain, for your ax will at least take a few chips off the bark, and others will come along, with sharper axes and younger arms, and will hack away, too. And so also will their sons and grandsons, in turn, take up axes in their time. And one day, centuries after some thought it would fall, yet far earlier than others allowed themselves to hope, the great tree of religion will come crashing from its pretensions to heaven, down to the patient earth—which has been waiting lo these many ages for the old tree to fall and rot, that her rich nutrients might be turned to growing the fruit of reason and the flowers of love.

And yet it shall come to pass that even as one great tree of religion has at last fallen to earth, even on that day will another be growing taller on the other side of the house of man, and still another will first be sprouting under the careless gaze of many. Yea, even the great stump of the fallen tree shall send forth new shoots, and in its terrible state of decay attempt to reach for the heavens again. For the earth is ever fertile, and superstition always springs back vigorous; and there is no final victory against her, anymore than you can cut your hair but once, or eat one feast for all time, or sleep one long night to give you strength all your days on earth. For the wild will come forth, and hunger ever rises, and fatigue is always but a sunset away—and the spirit is tempted, too, and grows hungry and waxes weary, and steals a wistful glance at religion's tree of faith, and sees no harm in her sapling, and lusts after the fruit of her vigor, and feels pity and awe for the majesty of her age.

And you will say, But how shall I take up my ax against this tree of religion when my daughter has built her a play home amongst its branches, and my son is even now gathering its fruit? And how shall I disturb this great trunk when who can tell but that when she falls she may come down upon the house and many perish? And how shall I bring down the very thing that shades me from the summer's sun and holds back the worst of winter's blasts?

Verily I say unto you that many will indeed perish when the tree of religion falls, yea, many have already perished from the fall of some of her limbs; and many have suffered from an unmediated view of the heavens, and from standing to face alone the cold winds of the north which come in the end for us all. And this tree, even without the help of your ax, throws down sticks and clubs, great beams, too, when the mighty winds howl, and cuts down many who walk with innocence in her dangerous shade; and its roots, though often unseen, continue to crumble the foundation of the house of man, and it has been sending forth its poisonous fruit for lo these many ages, and we are all sick unto our souls for having eaten thereof.

Thus saith the spirit of man, Yet behold the day cometh when the house of man shall stand whole and strong, even in the fields of ravaging time, its foundation free of the terrible embrace of otherworldly roots, and its views of heaven and earth unimpeded by any too-near, too-dear canopy of shade. And lo, there in the garden grow the apples and wheat of sustenance, and there the grapes of diversion and delight. And the mighty oaks of reason and the grand maples of beauty can now be seen to slow the winds and provide moments of shelter, too.

Hark! From the house of man a vision and a song:

Come you morning, and come you sun, this day we rise to cultivate the earth; this night we rest in each other's arms. With the dawn we strive and bring forth our powers; bearing bittersweet blessings to a twilight longing; and with darkness we pause and cease our many labors, and stare up at the stars that make us small. Yea, and through the days and the months and the seasons and the years we shall plant and reap and learn wisdom and embrace and bring forth children, and build and rejoice and weep and be fierce too when such things must be, and we shall live in the house of man all our days. And when our last sun sets, and we lie down to join our fathers and mothers in the earth, it shall be with weeping, but without any lies. And we will know that the sons and daughters of our spirit or flesh shall continue the work and the dance of life until they too must lie down in the earth. And because we have not wrapped our eyes with tapestries of heaven and sack-cloths of hell, and because we have not flattered ourselves that gods lead our souls to a great beyond, we shall look out at the fading light—at the all that is so little and the little that is yet our all—and take our leave with nobility and peace, and we shall not profane our last moments by cowering or grasping at phantom hereafters. Instead, clasping the hands of our loved ones one last time, we will shed honest tears for dying and smile honest love for those we must abandon, those who will carry on in the house of man.

And when the sage finished speaking, he turned and stepped a few paces toward the path whence he had come. But the people said: You have succeeded in tearing down our old religions. Now there remains so much we do not know, so many questions we would ask of you. Stay a while longer, that we may understand: How, then, shall we live? How shall we engage with depth and beauty and meaning and joy in the shadow of death? And how shall we invite honest inspiration and ritual and grandeur into our days and seasons, into our communities, our families, and our private moments, too? Tell us these things, or at least speak to us more your words of terrible consolation.

And the sage turned back to the people and said: Brothers and sisters, I thank you for allowing me to speak with you on matters close and dear. Would that I might converse long hours with each of you, speaking words of reason unto your minds, and words of comfort unto your hearts. But see, the sun dips low, and darkness closes in. This night and more shall be for mourning the old; this season and more for grieving lost faith. Yet someday with the rising of another sun we shall meet again, and on that day we shall speak of many things.

In time you will fashion together—from the shards of yesterday and the molten, flowing glass of today—the beautiful, strong vase of tomorrow; you will see how best to guide yourselves, your children, and your communities—though not immediately, for you have lost much. Yet look about you at the raging forest: Does the maple, the sycamore, even the mighty oak, bring forth new leaves in the season it loses its old? Only the evergreen, incapable of the conflagrations and glories of radical change, never stands naked to face the winter.[1]

---

[1] On the matter of whether society and individuals can survive the loss of religion, see sections 69-71, and their extensive footnotes.

But one may argue that irrespective of whether it is theoretically possible, it is unrealistic to expect the bulk of humanity to make do without one form of religion or another—that the fields where grow the gods will not remain bare, that for one to be kept out another must be cultivated in its stead. Gibbon, in Chapter XV of his *Decline and Fall of the Roman Empire* writes: "A state of scepticism and suspense may amuse a few inquisitive minds. But the practice of superstition is so congenial to the multitude that, if they are forcibly awakened, they still regret the loss of their pleasing vision...So urgent on the vulgar is the necessity of believing, that the fall of any system of mythology will most probably be succeeded by the introduction of some other mode of superstition."

Santayana, in Chapter VIII of his *Reason in Religion*, speaking of the replacement, in certain lands, of paganism with Christianity, makes a similar point and rivals Gibbon's eloquence. He writes: "From the age of the Sophists to the final disappearance of paganism nearly a thousand years elapsed. A thousand years from the infliction of a mortal wound to the moment of extinction is a long agony. Religions do not disappear when they are discredited; it is requisite that they should be replaced. For a thousand years the augurs may have laughed, they were bound nevertheless to stand at their posts until the monks came to relieve them."

But perhaps we can be more charitable to man's spirit than were Gibbon and Santayana. If monks replaced the augurs, perhaps the monks in turn can be replaced with those who will not claim to know what they do not know about God, a supernatural purpose for life, and an afterlife of heaven or hell. For we may hope that just as great portions of humanity have, for several centuries now, transcended the long-standing, degrading intemperance of making for themselves kings and slaves, perhaps they shall at long last do without the intoxication of making for themselves gods, and not merely put away whiskey for brandy, or brandy for wine.

Yet even without supernatural religion, many will always seek to infuse and decorate mundane existence with some form of ennobling ritual, some collection of venerated traditions, some cycle of celebrations and feasts, some causes for altruistic and communal devotion, some sources of inspiration and meaning, some narratives of imaginative escape, and some systems of secret knowledge, even something or someone to worship or revere. And it is to this purpose—the envisioning, articulating, and implementing of deeply satisfying alternatives to supernatural-based creeds—that religion's critics would be well advised to direct their attention if they wish to do more than tell people why they are wrong, if they wish to hold up a vision of how they can live right. In coming years perhaps I can add my voice, in the form of a later book, to the many voices which have, especially of late, begun to speak of new and better ways to satisfy the hungers traditionally sated only by swallowing beliefs in supernatural gods.

And brothers and sisters, your mourning shall one day cease, your appetites and your vigor shall return, and again you will discover causes for engagement, and moments of joy and delight. Until then, walk with pride, though you weep as you walk, for nothing is beautiful like an open soul, and nothing is mighty like a spirit that fears no truth. And heed the counsel of ancient wisdom: Revel in the excellent things of pleasure, but scorn not the good things of pain. For often our greatest gifts lie on the other side of deep suffering, and our grandest enchantments on the far shore of powerful fears.

Brothers and sisters, I understand that you wish to know more. We look about us at a vast landscape teeming with complexity and order; and we look within and see the same. We remember the strains of mother's tender lullabies, and the fragile promise flickering in our own children's eyes. We shudder as one by one the heroes and loves of our youth—the once beautiful and strong—stoop, shrivel and perish; and every glance in the looking glass shows our own faces telling terrible time in lines and gray; and as the ambitions of younger days fade and die, we wonder from whence we came and to where we go, and we yearn to know the way to live while yet we walk the earth.

And though Religion steps forward attired in priestly vestments and confidently proclaims herself in possession of divinely ordained direction, her robes are but woven of vanity and her words of passionate illusion. For instead of honestly encountering the puzzle of existence in all its humbling opacity, she merely names the question God, pronounces it answered, and bows low in worship. Yet why not save the question the gilding, and our spirits the groveling? Let us rather rise up erect, shoulder the noble burdens of uncertainty and savor the bittersweet flavors of mystery, reflecting in open-minded eagerness upon the universe, being cautious in our conclusions, admitting what we do not know, valuing honesty above comfort, and truth above conviction. In this way, though we shall not have all the answers, we will at least remain loyal to the questions, to our magnificent souls, to the astonishing universe, and to any transcendent being who may have created all these.

GLOSSARY OF TERMS

agnostic I use this term to mean one who recognizes that he does not honestly know of the existence of gods or supernatural beings. (Some others use the term to denote one who believes it *impossible* to know anything about the existence of gods or supernatural beings.)

atheist As with many terms, there is some latitude and debate as to what the word "atheist" means or should mean. I generally use it to mean one who believes definitively that there are no gods—not one who merely has no definitive belief in any god.[1]

---

[1] It has been the chief point of this book to encourage people to be more honest about what they know and what they do not know on ultimate issues. For this reason, I consider critical the distinction between the position that insists there is no God, and the position that merely does not profess to know anything about, or to have sufficient evidence for, a God or gods, and therefore holds no religious beliefs. So I prefer not to muddle this distinction by using one word to denote both. I use the word "atheism," then, in one of its traditional meanings—the definitive belief that there are no gods.

I have seen some atheists insist that because they can read the word as a-theism, to mean "without belief in a god," therefore that must be the word's only legitimate meaning, and thus agnostics—having no definitive belief in God—are, by definition, atheists, too. But, of course, words mean what the language uses them to mean, and thus often have more than one legitimate meaning—not limited to what an analysis of their roots and components would have some think they *should* mean. And so it is that although a wit mused that if the term "vegetarian" denotes one who eats vegetables, the term "humanitarian" must denote one who eats humans, we may be confident that such wordplay never gave rise in any healthy mind to sleepless nights in fear of philanthropic cannibals.

Other atheists presume to insist that everyone, even the religious person, is an atheist—only that in the religious person's case, the atheism applies to all gods but his own. This is distastefully reminiscent of some religious apologists' insistence that all people, including atheists, are religious, only the objects of devotion and worship differ—and that atheists worship science or logic. To be fair, the religious person is a *non-believer* with respect to other religions, but he shudders at the idea of not believing in *any* God—that is, being an *atheist*. So, too, the atheist may *respect* and *rely upon* science and logic, but he shudders at the idea of these having supernatural authority—or of him being *religious*.

To me it seems that we should not torture labels into meaning what we wish them to mean, and especially we should not, by semantic games, presume to tell others which "team" they belong to, or what they believe. Let our thoughts and beliefs be sufficiently compelling that their legitimate persuasive power will truly recruit others to our cause; let us not pretend to have recruited them by merely redefining them into already holding such allegiances.

GLOSSARY

Bible Depending on context, this usually refers either to the Old Testament alone (in the case of the Jewish or Hebrew Bible) or to the combination of the Old Testament and the New Testament (in the case of the Christian Bible).

faith This could denote strictly natural trust—but when speaking of religious faith I usually mean commitment beyond reason to supernatural beliefs. Also, sometimes the word faith may be used as a synonym for religion, as in the (more optimistic than accurate) phrase "the common values and beliefs of all faiths."

God or gods When I use the terms God or gods I refer to one or more supernatural or supreme beings with awareness, who may have created, or may have supernatural influence over, part or all of our universe. Also, when the term "God" (with capital G) is used, I generally mean the Creator God of traditional monotheistic religions, while when using the plural and lower case "gods" I am usually referring to a wider group of conceptions of deity, though not necessarily excluding the monotheists' God.

Hebrew Bible This term is used interchangeably with "Old Testament."

inspired, inspiration Depending on context, this could mean a purely natural animated or emotionally exalted state, or, especially when speaking of the Bible, it can refer to the religious belief that the Bible's text was in one way or another supernaturally influenced by God, and is therefore the "inspired word of God."

Old Testament This term is used interchangeably with "Hebrew Bible"

reason When not being used to denote the common meaning of cause or rationale (as in "The reason I went to bed is that I was tired.") I use the word reason to refer to the practice and standard of seeking to learn, or to examine what we take to be true, by means of objective evidence and argument consistent with logic and the best available information—and which would therefore earn the assent of the informed, honest, and critical mind.

religion Unless otherwise specified, in this book the word religion refers to traditional forms of the major Western religions, especially Christianity and Judaism, and often Islam. Depending on context, however, religions such as Buddhism, Hinduism and others are sometimes intended, too.

soul I use the word soul in several related ways: to denote a person's authentic self; one's deeper, wiser inclinations; or even that within us which is aesthetically and emotionally deeply moved. No supernatural qualities are implied unless otherwise specified or obvious by the context.

spirit This word is used in this book in several ways, but never to denote a precise theological meaning. Instead, it is sometimes used in the sense of spirituality; at other times, in the sense of mood and attitude; or to denote the life force. It is even used interchangeably with the word "soul" to denote one's essence, or truest self. Still, I believe that clarity is not sacrificed by the flexible use of such a word, so long as context makes clear what the isolated word may not.

spiritual, spirituality That which touches on matters of meaning, transcendence, devotion, highest values, or deepest peace. Supernatural belief is not necessarily implied, but in the context of religious spirituality it often is.

truth, true Unless the context insists otherwise, by "true" or "truth" I generally mean that which is consistent with the facts of reality, as best this can be determined through reason and experience. As I explain in the text, other sources of information—intuition, epiphany, dream, "gut feeling," tradition, and more—may well be valid starting points, but cannot be responsibly used to definitively conclude that something is true; instead, they must be confirmed by reason, experience, or both, and contradicted by neither.

BIBLIOGRAPHY and SUGGESTED READING

Notes:
a) Not all works mentioned in the book are included in this list—most are found only in the footnotes. Nor, of course, are all works worth reading on such subjects included; on such inexhaustible matters, a complete list of worthwhile reading would be impractical, perhaps impossible. Instead, this list comprises a small handful of works, which are both mentioned in the book and which I think will be of further help and interest to a high percentage of seekers.
b) With the wide dissemination of computerized and Internet search capabilities, it no longer seems necessary to provide more than the author, the title, and the topic of a book, to ensure that the interested reader will be able to locate the desired material. Indeed, since some books have multiple printings and publishers, additional information can in some cases be more confusing than helpful.
c) As a general rule, it is best to check whether a specific title has an updated or revised edition.
d) There is likely no work mentioned here with which I agree on every point. The inclusion of a book or article on this list means not that I encourage readers to accept as true every last thing it contains, but rather—as in all good reading and learning—that they expose themselves to its information and opinions, but continue to think for themselves.

On philosophy and religion

Critique of Religion and Philosophy, by Walter A. Kaufmann
An incisive and wide-ranging examination of religion and philosophy from the perspective of a professor of philosophy writing in the middle of the 20th century and dedicated to intellectual honesty,. The text, though not quite as accessible as his *Faith of a Heretic* (see following entry), has a different emphasis and range, and many intelligent and literary laymen will appreciate both its message and its voice.

The Faith of a Heretic, by Walter A. Kaufmann
A wise, honest, and heartfelt work on ultimate issues of religion, and deepest values. The writing style is more personal than his earlier-mentioned *Critique of Religion and Philosophy*. Although unfortunately out of print at the time of this writing, if one can find a copy it is well worth reading.

The Future of an Illusion, by Sigmund Freud
A short, and surprisingly readable, classic on—and critical of—religion, by this pioneer of psychology.

BIBLIOGRAPHY

On the Gods, and *Some Mistakes of Moses* by **Robert Ingersoll**
These, along with many other writings, essays, and speeches of this 19th century warm-hearted American agnostic orator, are well worth reading—especially if one appreciates passionate and elevated, sometimes grandiloquent language and isn't put off by occasional polemics and hyperbole.

The True Believer by **Eric Hoffer**
An interesting study of mass movements, including, but not limited to, religion—worth reading both for its content and its aphoristic eloquence.

Interpreting the Sacred: Ways of Viewing Religion, by **William E. Paden**
An intelligent and accessible book on different ways of understanding religion, including the psychological, sociological, comparative, and experiential perspectives.

Eight Theories of Religion by **Daniel Pals**
This (and the earlier version, *Seven Theories of Religion*) is a helpful exploration of a number of major theories that have attempted over time to interpret the origins and functions of religion.

The Age of Reason, by **Thomas Paine**
Completed in 1796 by a significant figure in the American Revolution, this book vigorously attacks the Bible and religious superstition. Though it is sometimes harsh and immoderate, perhaps we can forgive its author if we remember that he wrote much of it while incarcerated in a French prison. It was a courageous work for its day; and it shows how tenacious and insular is religion, that centuries after this well-known man published it, the great majority of religious people not only have still not read it or grappled with its arguments, they do not even know it exists.

Reason in Religion, by **George Santayana**
Part of his *Life of Reason* series (originally published as five separate volumes, and later condensed into one) this book is, by turns, both admiring and critical of religion and, in addition to expressing many intelligent ideas, is gracefully written. It is not always fast reading for the layman, but effort expended on Santayana is amply repaid for those who enjoy intellectual stimulation and literary pleasure.

Why I Am Not a Christian and other essays on religion and related subjects, by **Bertrand Russell**
A combative, anti-religious collection of essays by this noted philosopher and mathematician.

BIBLIOGRAPHY

On the Bible

The Bible
Read the Bible, for yourself. It is remarkable that so many believe the Bible to be the word of God, yet so few truly read its entire text, without commentaries, to see for themselves what they make of it.

How to Read the Bible, by James L. Kugel
A long and interesting book that goes through the Bible examining various stories and passages by the lights of two very different perspectives—traditional religious commentaries and secular academic theories.

Who Wrote the Bible? by Richard E. Friedman
An informed, intelligent, and creative work by an expert in the field of biblical authorship. Within the context of arguing for the documentary hypotheses—the notion that several significant and independent texts were combined into what we now know as the Bible—the author illuminates many facets of history, politics, linguistics, and scholarship that relate to the mystery of the Bible's origins. The material is substantive and the writing accessible, even enjoyable.

The Documentary Hypothesis by Umberto Cassuto
A learned and intelligent critique of the documentary hypothesis, written over half a century ago. Whatever one concludes on the matter of biblical origins, it is both honest and intellectually stimulating to expose oneself to able advocates for different positions.

A Theologico-Political Treatise by Benedict de Spinoza
Among other things, this work of Spinoza constitutes one of the earliest systematic and critical examinations of the Bible's authorship, and many of its observations are still fresh and relevant today.

Textual Criticism of the Hebrew Bible, by Emanuel Tov
Contains a great deal of information, and many with a scholarly interest in the topic of the Old Testament's text will find the reading effort this book demands well rewarded.

The Text of the Old Testament, by Ernst Wurthwein
Not as comprehensive, or perhaps as uniformly updated, as Emanuel Tov's work mentioned above, but more accessible for the layman. A good introduction to textual criticism of the Old Testament.

Old Testament Parallels by V.H. Matthews and D.C. Benjamin

An anthology of texts from the ancient Near East—the cultures surrounding ancient Israel—which allows one to form a clearer perspective of the context within which the Bible was formulated and its people lived. With such points of comparison, one is better able to distinguish the Bible's innovations from those aspects of its form and content which it shares with other books and traditions.

The God of Old, by James L. Kugel

A relatively short book that explores, creatively and accessibly, early conceptions of God in the Old Testament, as they are reflected in many biblical passages.

Miscellaneous

Please Understand Me II, by David Keirsey

A book that illuminates a good deal of human nature, particularly the systematic differences between different types and temperaments. I have found this system—the most well-known instrument associated with it being the Myers-Briggs Type Indicator (MBTI)—to be helpful not only for understanding one's own nature and various arenas of human interaction, including mating, parenting, and vocation, but also for understanding religion and its texts and traditions, in their many manifestations and social and psychological nuances. Many good books have been written on this system, but Keirsey's (though it does not make religion a major focus) is, on matters of personality and temperament, a particularly intelligent primer.

Six Pillars of Self-Esteem, by Nathaniel Branden

An important work on self-esteem, by a man who has done a lifetime's work in teaching and writing on the topic. The book is helpful reading both in guiding individuals on how to enhance their quality of life and for illustrating how even a non-religious worldview can value principles such as personal accountability, vigorous self-reliance, and purposeful living, and need not degenerate into any form of apathy, dependence, or self-pity.

The Feeling Good Handbook and *Ten Days to Self-Esteem,* by David Burns

These books, though plain-spoken and unusually accessible, are based on solid research and teach cognitive-behavioral techniques for improving emotions based on making our thoughts more accurate, and taking constructive action. If one is tormented by the emotions unleashed when grappling with a loss of faith, Burns's books, as part of an overall plan of self-care, can be of some help.

INDEX

à-vis God's character 134; is there meaning to S. if religion is false? 164

Superstition: wonder and enchantment of reason vs. that of religion and S. 10; miracle stories originating in ages of S. 27; S. and ancestors visiting in dreams 33; pious fraud in the ages of S. 35; a possible God may wish us to rise above S. 44, 47; religion is ancient but so is barbarism and S. 64; rulers took advantage of the people's S. 67.10; S. interpretation of mental illness 67.24; argument that people need S. 70; faith often based on tales originating in ages of S. 86; science allowing us to escape S. 97; Bible comes to us from ages of S. 106, 112, 126, 138; skepticism of the supernatural in light of so much disproved S. 108; no S. has ever been proved 139; S. and the "Bible code" 139; perpetual sprouting of S. 172, 173; tree of superstition 173

Technology: and the Bible 99, 99n

Temperament: and the search for truth P; practical vs. conceptual minds in the search for truth 15.6, 15.6n; on meaning and T. 166n

Theology: T.'s beautiful and complex concepts 36; illustration of nonsense chicken theology 37; brilliant and obscure T. 38; intelligent and comprehensible T. 39

Thoreau, Henry David: on fashions 25n; on men being influenced by their generation 35n; on motives

and self-awareness 67n; on the masses and their manner of living 70n; on the morality of eating animals 133n

Tocqueville, Alexis de: on religion and hope 67.6n; on religion providing governmental power 67.10n; on similarity between a society's government and religion 67.10n; on society not caring whether its members' religions are true 69n; on a free society's need for religion 70n

Tolstoy, on the difficulty of accepting truth that contradicts ideas and loyalties one has aligned with and invested in 35n

Transcendence: need for feeling of T. as one reason some do not question religion 15.21

Truth: P, 2; importance of 2; definition of 3; price of 2; subjective vs. objective 4; T. and art or beauty 6; T. and intuition 5; art and beauty as T. 6; what religions mean by T. 7; postmodernism and T. 8, 8n; whether the word T. is meaningless 9; the value of T. vs. the value of denial 12; why the search for T. is avoided 15.1-15.31; T. vs. what kindness wishes were so 18-19; religious leaders' ability to discern T. 24, 35; authority and virtue, vs. T. 24; intelligence and T. 31; T. and interpretation 33; T. and our deepest longings 34; good intentions vs. T. 35; the unconscious mind prevents us from seeing certain T. P, 4, 15, 15.1, 15.2,

www.ingramcontent.com/pod-product-compliance
Lightning Source LLC
Chambersburg PA
CBHW052026090426
42739CB00010B/1802